A VIEW FROM THE FOOTHILLS

ALSO BY CHRIS MULLIN

Novels

A Very British Coup
The Last Man Out of Saigon
The Year of the Fire Monkey

Non-fiction

Error of Judgement: the truth about the Birmingham bombings

A VIEW FROM THE FOOTHILLS

The Diaries of Chris Mullin

edited by Ruth Winstone

PROFILE BOOKS

First published in Great Britain in 2009 by
PROFILE BOOKS LTD
3a Exmouth House
Pine Street
London EC1R 0JH
www.profilebooks.com

3 5 7 9 10 8 6 4 2

Text design by Sue Lamble
Typeset in Stone Serif by MacGuru Ltd
info@macguru.org.uk

Printed and bound in Great Britain by
Clays, Bungay, Suffolk

A CIP catalogue record for this book is available from the British Library.

ISBN 978 1 84668 223 0

FSC
Mixed Sources
Product group from well-managed
forests and other controlled sources
Cert no. SGS-COC-2061
www.fsc.org
© 1996 Forest Stewardship Council

The paper this book is printed on is certified by the © 1996 Forest Stewardship Council A.C. (FSC). It is ancient-forest friendly. The printer holds FSC chain of custody SGS-COC-2061

With love to Ngoc, Sarah and Emma;
in memory of Leslie and Teresa Mullin
and with gratitude to the people of Sunderland

CONTENTS

Illustration Credits // *page* viii

Preface // *page* ix

Acknowledgements // *page* xiii

Cast // *page* xv

CHAPTER ONE: 1999 // *page* 1

CHAPTER TWO: 2000 // *page* 64

CHAPTER THREE: 2001 // *page* 150

CHAPTER FOUR: 2002 // *page* 247

CHAPTER FIVE: 2003 // *page* 342

CHAPTER SIX: 2004 // *page* 437

CHAPTER SEVEN: 2005 // *page* 522

Index // *page* 559

Illustration credits

The author and publisher would like to extend their thanks for permission to reproduce the photographs in this book: BBC, 8: Getty, 15; Nunn Syndication Ltd. 19; Parliamentary Recording Unit, 20, 21; Press Association, 1, 2, 3, 4, 22; *Sunderland Echo*, 11, 13, 26. All other photos are the author's.

Preface

As the New Labour era draws to a close there will be no shortage of memoirs from those who have occupied the Olympian heights. This is a view from the foothills.

I have occupied three vantage points: as chairman of one of the main select committees, as a junior minister in three departments and (when not in government) as a member of the parliamentary committee. This obscure body, which rarely leaked, was the means by which the backbenches and the government kept in touch; serving as a safety valve when times were hard. When Parliament was in session it met each Wednesday, usually in the Prime Minister's room at the House of Commons and occasionally in the Cabinet Room at 10 Downing Street. Membership consisted of the Prime Minister, Deputy Prime Minister, Leader of the House, Chief Whip, two other members of the Cabinet (appointed by the Prime Minister) and six backbenchers elected at the beginning of each parliamentary session, of whom I was one. Membership of the parliamentary committee gave one a privilege denied to all but the most senior members of the government – regular access to the Prime Minister and a mandate to pursue with him whatever was exercising the minds of our colleagues, ourselves or our constituents.

I began keeping a diary in May 1994, on the day that John Smith died. I cannot now recall what prompted me. Probably a vague feeling that I was well placed to chart the rise – and perhaps the fall – of New Labour. The notes on which this diary are based are more or less contemporaneous, recorded in one of the red notebooks that I always carry in an inside pocket. Usually, I typed them up at home at the end of each week. I kept two manuscript copies. An uncorrected version stored in London and a master copy at home in Sunderland. For the first ten years or so no one but my wife, Ngoc, was aware of its existence. Later, I confided in my agent, the late Pat Kavanagh, and my friend of more than 30 years Ruth Winstone, who was in due course persuaded to edit them. Occasionally, I was on the receiving end of odd looks from colleagues who saw me furtively scribbling. My standard answer to frequent queries about whether or not I found time to write these days was, 'I keep the occasional note.'

This volume covers the period from July 1999 to May 2005. It includes both my visits to government and the period in between when I chaired the Home Affairs Select Committee for the second time. It begins and ends with a call from the Prime Minister – the first saying hello, the last saying goodbye – and amounts to nearly 200,000 words ruthlessly distilled from an original manuscript three times that length. Inevitably a great deal of worthwhile material has fallen on the cutting room floor. I hope one day to place a fuller version in the public domain for those with a more detailed interest. I also hope one day to publish an earlier volume, from 1994 to 1999, provisionally entitled *A Walk-On Part*, and perhaps a later one.

Inevitably a work of this sort entails the breaching of confidences. In my defence I can only say that, where they are political rather than personal, I have taken the view that any duty of confidentiality has been nullified by the elapse of time. To those who feel let down, I can only apologise. I apologise, too, to those who feel they have been unfairly treated by some of the snap judgements recorded here. I am well aware that first impressions are frequently wrong and it may be that some of the views expressed here are more a reflection of my own shortcomings rather than those of anyone else.

I cannot claim to have led a life as colourful as Alan Clark (how many of us can claim to have seduced three women from the same family?) or to be as well-connected as Chips Channon, Jock Colville, or Alastair Campbell. Nor were the events to which I bore witness as momentous as the Abdication or the Second World War. My only claim is to have provided a snapshot of political life in the last part of the twentieth century and the beginning of the twenty-first as the grim certainties of the Cold War have given way to the mayhem of the failed state. And as we struggle to come to terms with the inexorable rise of the global market and a growing realisation that we cannot go on using up the resources of the planet as if there were no tomorrow.

I have tried, too, to provide a flavour of life as a representative of a northern working-class city in the aftermath of the Thatcher decade which gave rise to the growth of a huge underclass of alienated people trapped in a benefit culture – ironically one of Mrs Thatcher's most enduring legacies.

Many colourful visitors flit across these pages. The great Mandela, the Dalai Lama of Tibet (whom I have known for more than 30 years), a clutch of African presidents, HM the Queen, George W. Bush. And some – successive heads of M15, for example – who rarely see the light of day. Not everyone is a politician or an apparatchik. True, there is a Sir Humphrey, or rather a Sir Humphry and he is no mandarin, but my friend Sir Humphry Wakefield, who rescued the magnificent castle at Chillingham from dereliction. Chillingham, in the north of Northumberland, is the most magical place in England. I had dreamed of spending my declining years there, presiding over the restoration of the walled garden, but alas it was not to be.

I have wasted no time on feuds or vendettas, never having been angry with anyone for more than about half an hour. I have always known there is a life outside politics and tried to reflect it in the good times my family and I have enjoyed in the wonderful countryside of Northumberland and the Borders. One of the great advantages of living in the north-east is that it is rarely necessary to go on holiday more than about two hours' drive from home.

Above all, I have never lost sight of my enormous good fortune, a sentiment reinforced with every visit to Africa. The Aids orphans encountered at a sugar plantation near Beira in Mozambique; the tiny blind beggar glimpsed in the centre of Addis from the comfort of the British Ambassador's land cruiser as we sped between engagements; Kathleen, a refugee girl about the same age as the older of my daughters, who lived with her family in the darkness of the derelict starch factory in Lira, northern Uganda – for all I know she is there still: these are the images that will live with me long after the encounters with the big men have faded.

What kind of politician am I? Had I been asked when I first went into Parliament, I might glibly have replied that I saw it as my mission 'to comfort the afflicted and to afflict the comfortable'. But over the years I have learned that there is more to politics than that. If you are to stand a chance of changing very much for the better, you have to be capable of forming a government and to do that you have to take with you a swathe of the comfortable. It follows, therefore, that in an age of majority affluence, any serious politician has to spend a fair amount of time attending to the needs of the comfortable. Today, if I were asked to define my politics, I would reply that I am 'a socialist with a small "s", a liberal with a small "1", a green with a small "g" and a Democrat with a capital "D"'. I hope that is apparent from these pages.

As Enoch Powell once said, all political lives end in failure. Mine is no exception. In May 2005, after 18 years in Parliament, I suddenly found myself ejected from all the little vantage points that made political life worthwhile. I can only hope that I did something useful along the way.

Anyway, here it is: my life and times as seen from the foothills. Whether it is of any lasting interest is for others to judge.

Chris Mullin
Spring 2009

Acknowledgements

My time in Parliament is drawing to a close. I would like to thank the many good friends I have made along the way – colleagues of all parties, officials great and small in the three government departments in which I have served, officers of the House (particularly those who serviced the Home Affairs Committee during my two periods as chairman), not forgetting Noeleen Delaney and her staff in the House of Commons Tea Room – the setting for many of the exchanges recorded here.

My thanks to the people of the Sunderland South constituency who have allowed me to represent them in Parliament these past 22 years. Sunderland, which took quite a battering during the Thatcher decade, has, I am pleased to record, undergone something of a renaissance in recent years. While I would not want to make any too large claims, I firmly believe that the fact that this revival was accompanied by a sustained period of Labour government is not entirely a coincidence. There are others in Sunderland to whom I owe particular thanks, notably Kevin Marquis, my agent in each of the five general elections between 1987 and 2005, and those who staffed my constituency office: Sharon Spurling, the late Jacky Breach, Pat Aston, Graham March, Michael Mordey and Karen Timlin.

My thanks, too, to Andrew Franklin and his colleagues at Profile for the faith they have placed in me, and to my literary agent Pat Kavanagh, who sadly did not live to see the finished work, for sticking with me through the long years of drought. Also, and above all, to my friend Ruth Winstone for her sensitive and skilful editing.

Last but not least, I pay tribute to my wife, Ngoc, who over these many years has laboured unsung to bring up our two children and minister to the needs of an all-too-often absent husband without always receiving the appreciation she deserves.

Cast

(In approximate order of appearance)

Listed according to responsibilities for the period of the diary, July 1999–May 2005

Number 10

Tony Blair MP, aka The Man, Prime Minister 1997–2007

Parliamentary Private Secretaries to the Prime Minister
Bruce Grocott MP
David Hanson MP

Officials and Advisers
Alastair Campbell
Kate Garvey
Brian Hackland
Robert Hill
Anji Hunter
Sally Morgan
Jonathan Powell

Department of Environment, Transport and the Regions, July 1999–2001
John Prescott MP, aka JP, Secretary of State and Deputy Prime Minister
Joe Irvin, Special Adviser

Ministers of State

Hilary Armstrong MP
Gus Macdonald (Lords)
Michael Meacher MP
Nick Raynsford MP

Parliamentary Under-Secretaries

Beverley Hughes MP
Keith Hill MP
Chris Mullin MP
Larry Whitty (Lords)

Officials

Richard Mottram, Permanent Secretary
Jessica Matthew and Chris Brain, Private Secretaries to CM

Department of International Development, February–May 2001

Clare Short MP, Secretary of State
Chris Mullin MP, Parliamentary Under-Secretary

Officials

Sir John Vereker, Permanent Secretary
Christine Atkinson, Private Secretary to CM
Sanjib Baisya, Assistant Private Secretary
David Mephan, Special Adviser to the Secretary of State

Parliamentary Committee, July 2001–June 2003
Backbench Members of Parliament

Ann Clwyd, Jean Corston (chairman), Helen Jackson, Tony Lloyd,
Andrew Mackinlay, Chris Mullin, Bridget Prentice, Gordon Prentice,
Doug Hoyle (representing the Lords)

Home Affairs Select Committee, 2001–3

David Cameron, Janet Dean, Humfrey Malins, Chris Mullin (chairman), Bridget Prentice, Gwyn Prosser, Bob Russell, Marsha Singh, Tom Watson, Angela Watkinson, David Winnick

Foreign and Commonwealth Office, 2003–5

Jack Straw MP, Secretary of State

Ministers

Denis MacShane MP (Europe)
Chris Mullin MP (Africa)
Mike O'Brien MP/Douglas Alexander MP (Trade)
Bill Rammell MP (United Nations/Latin America)
Liz Symons (Middle East) (Lords)

Officials

Sir Michael Jay, Permanent Secretary
Tom Fletcher, Bharat Joshi, Private Secretaries to CM; Kay Stokoe, Caron Rohsler, Assistant Private Secretaries
John Williams, Chief Press Officer

Sunderland Office

Pat Aston and Graham March

Significant others

Hilary Armstrong MP, Chief Whip
Tony Banks MP
David Blunkett MP, Home Secretary 2001–04
Tony Benn MP (retired 2001)
Hilary Benn MP, Secretary of State for International Development 2003–07
John Gilbert, a former defence minister, now in the Lords
Geoff Hoon MP, Secretary of State for Defence 1999–2005

Alan Howarth, Secretary of the Parliamentary Labour Party, now in the Lords (not to be confused with MP of the same name)

Gil Loescher, UK-based American academic seriously injured in the bombing of the UN HQ in Baghdad, August 2003

Clive Soley, Chairman of the Parliamentary Labour Party, 1997–2001, now in the Lords

Family

Nguyen Thi Ngoc, wife of CM

Nguyen Thi Hanh, sister-in-law of CM

Sarah (b. 1989) and Emma (b. 1995) Mullin, children of CM

Liz and Patricia Mullin, sisters

David Mullin, brother

Leslie and Teresa Mullin, parents

CHAPTER ONE

1999

Wednesday, 28 July 1999
St Bede's Terrace, Sunderland

A message from Kate Garvey at Number 10. I am to expect a call from
The Man within the next 15 minutes. In the event it was more than
an hour before the phone rang. 'I want you to go to Environment,' he
said. My heart sank. Of all the possibilities, I never anticipated being
on John Prescott's team.* I asked what my responsibilities would be
and he replied that he didn't yet know, but would be talking to JP
tomorrow. I asked what the options were and he replied vaguely that
it might involve 'something in the housing area'. Perhaps sensing my
lack of enthusiasm he said this was only a starting job. 'If you make a
success of it, you can work your way up.' He didn't ask whether or not
I wanted it and rang off saying, 'We may want you to come through
the door of Downing Street tomorrow.'

I rang Alan Meale in the hope of finding out what the job might
entail. His wife, Diana, answered the phone and said, 'He's been
bumped.'

'Who's got his job?'

'You have.'

Even so, she was friendly and gave me Alan's mobile number,
saying he was in a pub in Millbank. I decided to wait until tomorrow
before ringing. I then called Michael Meacher who was as upbeat and
cheerful as ever. He said that JP, contrary to what I had supposed, was

---

*The Department of Environment, Transport and the Regions (DETR).

a good man to work for and that there was a good spirit in the Department.

To bed, feeling miserable at the thought of the avalanche of tedium to come.

Thursday, 29 July

Awoke early wondering if I could pluck up the courage to say No. At 8.30 I rang Kate Garvey and asked to speak to The Man. She replied that he was in a meeting, but advised me to get on the earliest train 'since he will want to see you'.

She was burbling about how wonderful it was that I was to be a minister. I said very slowly, 'My – instinct – is – to – decline.'

It took a second or two for the penny to drop and then she sort of skidded to a halt. 'In that case he will want to talk to you in the next few minutes.'

Sixty seconds later the phone rang, an operator asked me to stand by ... I waited ... The operator said stand down. 'He will ring later this morning.' That's that, I thought.

A tremendous sense of relief. Ngoc came down. 'I'm no longer a minister,' I said cheerfully. Ngoc looked a bit dismayed. Secretly I suspect she likes the idea, although she has no concept of what it entails. I went upstairs to have a bath feeling relaxed. Life had returned to normal. I would continue to occupy the little niche I had carved for myself in Parliament. The holidays were safe. Weekends with the family would be uninterrupted.

The Man rang at 9.30. 'Why?' he asked.

'Because I will disappear without trace. Besides, I don't get on well enough with John to make a success of it.'

'I promise I won't lose sight of you. You are the one person on the backbenches who most obviously should be a minister.' He went on to explain that being a minister was very different from being a back-bench MP. 'You can't be a minister of state at once, but I have you in mind for something in home affairs, the Foreign Office or international development.' It might only be a matter of months, he added.

I thought he wouldn't much care, but he obviously did. 'We get on well, don't we?'

I assured him that we did.

'You have drive, energy. It would be a waste to stay on the back-benches being a wise man.'

'Are you saying that the job is still open?'

'I am.'

'Well since you put it like that...'

Suddenly I was a minister again.

To Number 10 to be anointed, walking as nonchalantly as possible past a battery of cameras.

The Man was on the terrace deep in discussion with JP so I sat outside the Cabinet Room chatting to Bruce Grocott, who quoted advice which Cabinet Secretary Richard Wilson had given recently in a symposium for junior ministers: First, be sure to demonstrate to the civil servants that you have a good relationship with the Secretary of State [difficult in my case], then they will be less inclined to go over your head. Second, remember, you are not going to be there for long so don't try to put the world to rights – have just two or three modest aims.

To which Bruce added a third which might come in handy in my case, 'If you have the ear of the Prime Minister, play it up.'

Bruce remarked that the present system of annual reshuffles was crazy. 'There is massive inbuilt insecurity. Ministers, who may not be there in a year, are on top of a civil service which is permanent and who have nothing more to worry about than who gets what gong. The chances of moving anything more than 0.1 per cent are slim.'

We were joined by Gisela Stuart and Beverley Hughes, who are also joining the government. They, needless to say, were overjoyed. While we were sitting there JP came out. He was about to walk past when, by way of an afterthought, it occurred to him that he ought to go through the motions of welcoming us, not least since two of us – Bev and I – are in his department.

I was then ushered in. The Man was in the small sitting room adjacent to the Cabinet Room. My audience lasted about ten minutes. He said how glad he was to have me on board, adding that Dennis

Skinner would have been a good minister, if only he'd been willing to take responsibility. I said I was apprehensive. 'People have been known to disappear without trace into Environment.'

'At the moment,' he said cheerfully, 'they are coming out rather fast.' (Four of the eight ministers have been sacked or reshuffled.) I said that I would miss the parliamentary committee. He asked who was likely to replace me and said it was important to get someone suitable. This is probably the last time our paths will cross until I'm sacked or reshuffled – most junior ministers do not have access to the Prime Minister. He shook my hand warmly. 'Don't forget me,' I said. He promised not to, but we shall see.

I stood around in the hall outside the Cabinet Room chatting to Bruce and Alastair Campbell, who said that yesterday, despite the fact that the hacks had been watching all exits, The Man had managed to slip out of Downing Street and over to his room at the House in order to spare The Dismissed the ordeal of having to walk past the cameras. Alastair said how unpleasant it was. A 'nightmare' was the word The Man used when he rang last night. Alastair told the story, which I heard before, of how after the election the Downing Street switchboard had confused Brian Donohoe with Bernard Donoughue and as a result Brian had been a minister for about four seconds. By now there were three other new ministers assembled: Gisela, Bev and David Hanson. We formed up into a line and went out and stood before the cameras and then walked out of Downing Street, chased by a young woman from the Press Association, who kept asking how happy we were. I couldn't bring myself to respond.

Bev and I shared a taxi up Victoria to Eland House. All the while her mobile phone kept ringing with people offering congratulations. For her this was a big moment. For me it is something of a humiliation. I have done what I always said I would never do, traded the little niche I had built for myself on the backbenches for the Department of Folding Deckchairs.

Our private secretaries were waiting for us at the Department. Mine is a pleasant young woman called Jessica, who exudes competence and good sense. She took me upstairs to my office on the sixth floor, previously occupied by Nick Raynsford, who has been promoted. The walls are hung with old prints of Woolwich and large photos of the Millennium Dome. I have a staff of four, all bright young people. David, the diary secretary, Shayne and Nicola, assistant private secretaries. They all refer to me as 'Minister'.

I am also entitled to a car and a driver. Entirely pointless since, as I pointed out, the 159 and 3 buses will continue to run past my door, even though I am a minister. Jessica, who cycles in from Brixton, was sympathetic, but explained that the situation is a little more complicated than I might suppose. For a start, red boxes cannot be transported by public transport. Secondly, there will be times when a vote is called without warning and we will need to get to the House quickly. Third, I might be glad of a lift home at 3 a.m. after an adjournment debate.

She also explained that the funding of the government car pool is geared to encourage maximum use of the car. The drivers are on a low basic wage and are heavily dependent on overtime. So, if I accept a driver, he will be hanging around all day doing nothing and hating me for not giving him enough to do. A trap I must avoid at all costs. (Later, I discussed this crazy situation with Keith Hill, who has the office next door. He is in charge of making sure the Department lives up to its green rhetoric. We agree that use of official cars is the obvious place to start. For the time being I intend to do without, although I shall make no public statements for fear of being accused by my colleagues of showing them up. And also because I may, eventually, be forced to retreat.)

Jessica explained that ministers must always be contactable. I will, therefore, need a mobile phone, a pager and a fax at home. I offered mild resistance, but I fear I shall have to give way on this before long. The first of what will no doubt be many little defeats at official hands.

While we were talking the door opened and in strolled JP. He made a little show of being pleased to see me. The word 'delighted' even escaped his lips, although his demeanour suggested otherwise.

'Thank you for having me,' I said as he walked towards the door.

'Glad you decided to join us,' he said dryly. The sarcasm remained in the air long after he had departed. Of course, he must know that I turned down the wretched job.

My induction over, I walked down Victoria Street to the House.

Outside Westminster Abbey I ran into Frank Field, who wished me well but said what a shambles the reshuffle had been. He claimed that seven members of the cabinet had been to see The Man and said they would not be moved and that, faced with this display of solidarity, he had simply backed down. Frank also confirmed that the government car service was a job creation scheme. He said that, when he was a minister, he had even been collected by car from Birkenhead, just to give the driver something to do.

Home on the 20.00, feeling very depressed. The hardest part of the next few days will be keeping a straight face as the congratulations come in.

Friday, 30 July
Sunderland

Jessica faxed through a draft list of my proposed responsibilities – aviation, housing, science, planning ... to crown all they include air traffic control. A few days ago I was sitting listening to Helen Liddell being pounded from all sides and thanking heavens that it was her rather than me. Now it is. It's like a bad dream.

Saturday, 31 July

Everyone, except me, seems happy about my appointment. Lily at the paper shop says it will be good for Sunderland. A man called out from a car, as I went to get the papers this morning. I notice that most of the congratulations seem to come from people who know nothing about politics. Those who do – including one or two of the more perceptive commentators (Michael White, Paul Linford) – are more cautious. They know I had a better job in my last incarnation.*

Glorious weather. We lunched in the garden and then our neighbour, Peter, and I picked up the litter in the street.

---

*As chairman of the Home Affairs Select Committee.

Sunday, 1 August

Awoke at 3 a.m., still worrying that I have traded my self-respect and the respect of others for the lowliest rung on the political ladder – and one which has not the slightest influence over anything that matters. If I was to get out now, I could still retain my place on the select committee and on the parliamentary committee. I lay awake until six compiling a resignation letter.

Monday, 2 August

London is bathed in a Bangkok-style haze of exhaust fumes, temperature approaching 30 degrees centigrade. Our first meeting of ministers. JP in benign mode, wearing a blue short-sleeved shirt, slumped in an armchair, one leg over the side. He did most of the talking, much of it stream of consciousness but there were occasional moments of lucidity. We had a problem with transport and, he said, everyone was under an obligation to help out. 'When Tony decided to make transport a priority, he didn't bring resources with it.' He added, 'And the one thing that might have raised some cash – a congestion tax – Tony isn't happy about.'

Michael Meacher remarked, 'We are challenging deeply held attitudes, but we have to stick to our guns.'

JP said modestly that he himself had to change. 'I just get angry.'

Keith Hill, an ex-whip, said the rebellion over air traffic control was building up steam. We had to head it off.

The unions were playing the 'safety card', but we were doing what everyone wanted us to do by separating safety from operations, said JP. Tony Benn, who made a hostile intervention the other day, had done something similar when he was in charge of North Sea oil. 'Benn's a hypocrite,' he added, pointing for some reason at me.

A stream of visitors. Among them Richard Mottram, the Permanent Secretary. A genial, easy-going grammar school boy in his mid-fifties. He assured me that, contrary to rumour, JP is a good man to work for and, if anything, too soft. I told him I'd turned the job down at first and he seemed surprised.

I also raised the car pool. Needless to say he has his own driver and car in which he travels in most days from Blackheath. I put it to him that we couldn't credibly hope to persuade the Great British Public to abandon the motor car if ministers and senior civil servants were being driven everywhere. He was decent enough to concede there is an issue, but I sensed he was in no hurry to resolve it.

We discussed my rag bag portfolio. 'What would make you happy?' he asked.

'How about giving me countryside?' In exchange, I offered to surrender anything. He suggested giving planning to Bev. I cheered up at once. Afterwards Jessica congratulated me on my first victory.

Back to Sunderland on the 20.00 from King's Cross.

Wednesday, 4 August

We packed up the car and set off for London, stopping on the way for a picnic at Chatsworth, where the children played in the maze. Emma fell in the pond. We drove to London in torrential rain, arriving in Brixton at the flat just before midnight only to discover that the living room was in an inch of water (caused by a blocked drain) which had been lying for four days, giving off a foul odour.

Thursday, 5 August
Brixton Road

An hour pressing newspaper onto the living room carpet. At 9.30 Jessica rang to ask when I was coming in. There was a definite tone of disapproval in her voice. I explained about the flood, but her tone suggested it was no excuse.

Much of the day was taken up with official briefings by groups on my various responsibilities – aviation, water, science. On the first two I surprised myself by managing to ask some reasonably intelligent questions, but by the time we got to the third my eyes glazed over. The news that I am in charge of science at Environment would be the cause of much hilarity among any surviving witnesses from my schooldays to my failure to come to grips with even the simplest scientific concept. Someone up there is playing a cruel joke.

Graham Allen, the Department's whip, came in to discuss how we are going to handle the proposed part-privatisation of air traffic control. He suggested an early meeting with Gwyneth Dunwoody and some of the other dissidents. He also suggested getting a Labour Party pager, which I am not so keen on. Perhaps, if it makes him happy, I could get one and leave it switched off in a drawer.

Graham offered one other piece of advice: 'Don't make jokes about air traffic control. Above all do nothing to imply to dissidents that you are sympathetic to their case.' Helen Liddell, he said, had kept her head down and ploughed on regardless. That was exactly the right approach. Which only goes to show how much I have to learn about being a minister. I thought her performance was perfectly disastrous and that a smile or two would have gone a long way to lighten her load. I discussed this afterwards with Nick Raynsford and was relieved to find that he agreed with me.

Today I took my first decisions. All very simple. Jessica places a pile of files in my in-tray. Each one comes with a summary sheet prepared by the relevant experts setting out the issue, any relevant considerations and any 'presentational' problems that might arise (i.e. will I get a bad press?). This is followed by a recommendation. All I have to do is signify agreement or disagreement by making my mark on the top of the page.

The first file concerned a proposal that KLM/UK Air be permitted landing rights for its service to Poland. Next, an application by Thames Water to discharge a small quantity of treated sewage into the Thames near Henley. The attached brief explained why the alternatives were impractical and assured me that no solids would be discharged. A small number of representations had been received, including an objection from the town council, but none from the local Member of Parliament (Michael Heseltine). I hesitated. This is exactly the issue that has caused so much trouble in Sunderland (although our sewage was untreated). Upon inquiry I was told that the Thames would dry up if it wasn't for the treated sewage discharged into it. What's more, too rigorous screening (ultra-violet, for example)

would kill the bacteria upon which fish thrive. After due consideration, I signed.

Next, I was asked to approve pay increases for the staff of the
Housing Corporation. That was easy. I signed. Then I was asked to
approve a Millennium fly-past across central London along the
Thames by Concorde at a height of a thousand feet. I asked for assurances about safety on that one. And so it went on. Jessica loaded the
files into one tray, usually with a little handwritten note attached,
boiling the issue down to a single sentence. I read, reflected and
usually signed, always remembering David Heathcoat-Amory's
remark: 'Government is about hundreds of little decisions about
which no one ever hears, unless something goes wrong.' Concorde
crashing into the Thames, for example?

Finally, there were letters. Hundreds. Almost all in response to
colleagues writing with queries from constituents. Each came in an
orange folder with the MP's letter plus supporting documents. One
foolish Tory had sent ten letters from constituents making the same
point about water meters and received ten identical replies. I left the
letters neatly piled on my desk for Jessica to take away in the morning.
I trust she will be impressed by my diligence.

Friday, 6 August

More briefings. The first, from officials of the Countryside division.
I asked about leylandii hedges (it is two years since I first took part
in a delegation to Angela Eagle on the matter) only to be told that
progress had been blocked by Downing Street. The boys and girls in
the policy unit have apparently persuaded The Man that to legislate
on so trivial a matter would spoil our image as deregulators. In my
previous incarnation, I would have bent The Man's ear on the
subject at the parliamentary committee, but now (having been 'promoted') I am powerless. (Jessica says that JP gets very upset if he
finds junior ministers going to Number 10 behind his back.) This
ought to be one of life's more easily resolvable problems. I intend to
persist.

Then a briefing on waste disposal. Not very sexy, but of vital importance for the future of the planet. Household waste is apparently growing at 3 per cent a year which is clearly unsustainable.

A call to Gwyneth Dunwoody, who threatened 'strenuous resistance' to the government's plans for the sale of a majority stake in air traffic control.

She wanted to know whether the Bill would be separate from the rest of the transport legislation. I replied that no decision had yet been made. 'Well, I strongly advise you to keep it separate. Otherwise it could drag down the whole of the government's transport programme.' We arranged to meet in September.

Two men came in to see me about security. Jessica was not allowed to sit in on the meeting or even to know what it was about. Apparently, I am one of five ministers in the Department whose responsibilities (in my case water and aviation) entitle me to see STRAP 2 (Top Secret) information. I had to sign a piece of paper promising to reveal nothing now and for ever more. One of the men was small, sturdy and grave. He was dressed in a grey suit and dark tie and had the demeanour of an undertaker, clearly relishing the titbits that came his way. The other was younger and more laid-back.

The Undertaker said, 'Some of the people we have to negotiate with are pretty uncivilised.' He added, 'Mind, we also deal with some very civilised people – and we spy on them, too.' The only people we don't spy on are the Americans, the New Zealanders, Australians and Canadians, who are all part of a little club that has agreed to share the products of their bugging, burgling and bribery. A pity about the Americans, since they seem to be the cause of most of our aviation problems.

When STRAP information needed to be drawn to my attention one of them would bring it to me, I would read it in his or her presence and they would then take it away. If I needed to discuss STRAP material over the telephone, I would be taken to a room with a secure telephone system. Every government department has one and so do most of our embassies. The Deputy Prime Minister was also in receipt of STRAP material on a wider range of issues which came from the Cabinet Office. The Undertaker remarked that JP was 'not averse to knowing the other side's cards'.

As I was leaving Jessica presented me with a mobile telephone and pager. Only the office, she assures me, will have the numbers. I managed to persuade her that, since I shall be on holiday for the next two weeks, I don't need them for the time being. As a result they remain lying in the in-tray.

Home to our ruined flat by 8.30 p.m.

Tuesday, 10 August
Gamekeeper's Cottage, Northchapel, West Sussex

Up early for a walk around the lake. En route I disturbed two deer, who went bounding off across a field and then stood nervously eyeing me from a distance.

Wednesday, 11 August

As the hour of the eclipse approached the sky clouded over, but when the moment came the cloud miraculously parted. We placed our bowls of water in the garden and stood poring over them. Old Bear was brought out to watch. The girls were under strict instructions not to look at the sun. An eerie twilight descended, accompanied by a chill. As we peered into our bowls the shadow of the moon passed across the sun until it was almost eclipsed and then gradually, but not before the elapse of some minutes, normal service resumed. Emma, oblivious, played in the rhododendron bush. She will be well into her nineties before such an event occurs again.

Monday, 23 August

Back to the Department, where a mountain of tedium awaits. I have set myself three modest targets for the (hopefully) short time I shall spend at Eland House: (1) to manage without an official car; (2) to do something about leylandii hedges; and (3) to play my part in the reorganisation of air traffic control with as little fall-out as possible.

I am besieged with invitations to address conferences organised by obscure but no doubt worthy organisations. Mostly they are the crumbs that fall from the tables of my many superiors and my first instinct is to reject the lot. However, they usually come with notes from officials advising acceptance and, reluctantly, I concede. Before long my whole life will be eaten up by pointless activity. One such invite, originally addressed to Nick Raynsford, came with a note from his Private Secretary still attached. It read: 'This is very low priority. I suggest we pass it to Chris Mullin.'

I wrote NO and waited to see what would happen. Sure enough, as I anticipated, someone was in my office within the hour, explaining why it was really of the highest importance …

Jessica has dug out a copy of the contract which this Department (and presumably every other) has with the government car service. It is truly incredible – designed to ensure maximum use of the car. Termination requires three months' notice and, if the car has to be sold, a payment for 'unrecovered depreciation' which would in my case amount to about £4,400. We are charged a basic £864 a week, not counting overtime, for a car and driver, regardless of how much use we make of it. The Department has ten cars – nine for ministers and one for the Permanent Secretary. For much of the time the cars and their drivers are idle. If – as in my case – a minister chooses not to have a driver, but to make occasional use of the pool facility, the Department is required to pay a penal £704.75 a week. During my four weeks as a minister I have not had sight of – let alone travelled in – an official car and yet we have paid out nearly £3,000. The time has come to put an end to this nonsense.

My private office is the one bright spot in what I have so far seen of life at the bottom of the ministerial pile. They are bright, young, efficient and anxious to please. David, the diary secretary, is spending part of his holiday working with underprivileged children in London's East End. Convention requires that they refer to me as 'Minister', but they are not over-deferential. Jessica exudes calm and competence. I must ensure that my general disenchantment does not rub off on them.

Tuesday, 24 August

The chief executive of the government car service came in to discuss the car. He was all charm and sweet reason. I invited him to justify the £700 a week we are being charged for a service of which we are making absolutely no use and he promised to come back to me with a lower price. He also agreed that there would be no difficulty about my using a pool car for the transport of boxes. He did remark in passing that the drivers were 'heavily unionised' and might not take kindly to a reduction in their numbers, but the matter was not pressed. He said that only one other minister – Charles Clarke at Education – had refused a car and since moving to the Home Office he has apparently been persuaded that a car was now necessary in the interests of security.

All in all, a successful outcome. Jessica was anxious to confirm the details in writing since, as she put it, 'the government car service is renowned throughout Whitehall for being slippery'.

Saturday, 28 August

To Newcastle in search of a new suit. Ngoc assures me that I cannot hope to be taken seriously as a minister who owns only one. In the event there was a sale at Fenwick's and we ended up buying three. My reincarnation as a clone is almost complete.

Wednesday, 1 September

A pleasant chat with Hilary Armstrong, who confirmed everything I already know about the JP regime. She says John is hopelessly insecure, ever afraid of being shown up by one of his underlings, constantly interfering in matters best left to junior ministers. His vast responsibilities mean that he is often tied up elsewhere. She says weeks go by without her seeing him to talk to. Personally, says Hilary, she gets on well with JP, but he has an image problem on account of his stream of consciousness approach to interviews and his partiality for colourful one-liners. 'John, have the courage to be boring' was Gus Macdonald's advice.

Thursday, 2 September

To Number 10 where Alastair Campbell was briefing new ministers in an airless basement room. He said that, contrary to popular belief, the Downing Street press office was not run by control freaks. His only anxiety was to impose some sort of overall strategy. 'We are not at all scared of ministers courting controversy or taking risks to get things up in lights.' His basic message was that ministers should raise their eyes to the big picture. 'We have a good story to tell and we must be confident enough to spell it out.' Alastair added, 'Political coverage in this country is a joke. Most of the national media treat politics as a soap opera.' He advised us to concentrate on the local media, who were generally far more receptive (did he mean docile?) and often had a wider audience.

Several people complained about the quality of departmental press offices. Peter Kilfoyle said there were 109 press officers in the MoD and it was hard to work out what they were all doing.

Alastair replied that one of the big difficulties was that the Whitehall press machine generally only worked weekdays, nine to five, which wasn't much use when the media operated round the clock. 'Whitehall is dormant at the time when the media is most active.' At Environment there were about 30 press officers, but when it had been suggested that they should provide weekend cover, some had resigned. 'Find good people of whatever rank, and then bust the system to bring them up' was Alastair's advice. Sally Morgan said we must be nice to MPs in general and select committee members in particular. She rather spoiled her point by adding that select committees were often run by bitter and disappointed people. Everyone looked at me and laughed.

Walked up Victoria with Charles Clarke, who recounted his battle to be rid of his official car. Apparently Blunkett wasn't keen, for fear that it would show up other people. Clare Short had raised the subject at the first Cabinet meeting and been jumped on by The Man for the same reason. Charles got away with it in the end by saying that he needed to walk for health reasons.

A talk with Gus Macdonald about aviation. He has an opinionated Private Secretary who, during a discussion of the air traffic control sale, remarked, 'Someone should take Gordon aside and ask whether it's worth all the shit we are going to get for a gain of £350 million.' My sentiments precisely, but I was amazed to hear it coming from a civil servant. For a moment I thought he was a political adviser. Gus said that JP was the only person who could do that and he would have to move quickly since time was running out. He added, 'The Treasury will only say that it's not just a matter of the revenue. It's about better management and attracting new investment that doesn't count towards the PSBR.' At this the discussion lapsed. I recounted it later to Larry Whitty, who said, 'Dropping it would save everyone a lot of trouble. Gordon doesn't need the money anyway. He's got money coming out of his ears.' I haven't yet met anyone who is keen on this so-called public–private partnership.

Friday, 3 September
Sunderland

To the roof of the new Debenham's store, where the mayor and I performed the topping-out ceremony. There are so many good things happening in Sunderland at the moment. A new shopping complex. A state of the art bus station. The metro on its way. A multiplex cinema in the pipeline. Mowbray Park being refurbished. The riverside reviving. I just pray that we have the economic base to sustain all this consumerism.

Monday, 6 September

Today I was allowed out on my own for the first time. To address the annual meeting of an organisation called Key Potential UK which has been set up to train housing managers. The Department had prepared a 20-minute speech full of impenetrable jargon. I managed to hone it down a little, but it was still excruciating. About five minutes in I realised – too late, of course – that I should have chucked it away and talked for five minutes off the cuff. That would have gone down far better and made me appear more than just a man in a suit. I was received politely, but without enthusiasm and hastily departed before anyone could ask questions. Humiliating.

I was walking down Whitehall this evening when an elderly estate car pulled alongside. I assumed it was someone wanting directions, but it turned out to be the former Tory Home Secretary, Ken Baker, offering congratulations on my supposed promotion. I replied, gloomily, that commiseration was more in order, but he would have none of it. 'You must be enjoying government. There's a tremendous buzz about it.' Early days yet, but so far the buzz has entirely escaped me.

He sped off without offering a lift. I suppose he assumed I had a ministerial car waiting.

Tuesday, 7 September

A meeting with Gus Macdonald and Keith Hill to discuss transport. Gus exudes competence and, unlike me, appears completely in command of his brief. Our difficulty, he said, is the long lead times. Money invested in transport now wouldn't produce results until our second or third term. We were already getting flak for road pricing which wouldn't come in for another five years. The difficulty with road pricing was that elsewhere it had been introduced to fund specific projects. No one has introduced it on existing roads as we are proposing.

As for the extra money we were supposed to be spending on rural bus services, 'I keep asking where these services are and no one can tell me.'

'Or whether anyone is using them,' added Keith.

We must avoid being seen as anti-car, said Gus. Why shouldn't poor people enjoy the same advantages as the car had brought to the middle classes? There was no inconsistency about favouring wider car ownership but less use.

'What about the humble bicycle?' I inquired. 'We will never succeed in persuading people to ride bikes in cities until there are dedicated cycle lanes in which bikes are separated from vehicles by a kerb, as they are in Holland and Denmark.'

Gus was very dismissive.

The discussion ended inconclusively. It's becoming clear that we are – rightly – terrified of taking on the car because we fear that, as with taxation, in the privacy of the ballot box the Great British Public will exact revenge on any party that tries to separate them from their beloved vehicles.

Thursday, 9 September
Sunderland

To the Hospital Trust for my annual general meeting with the chairman, David Graham, and chief executive, Andrew Gibson. Andrew is generally upbeat, but complains of being deluged by the Department of Health with circulars and guidance notes. 'They contain up to four pages of "Actions". It's becoming a serious problem. You end up not doing anything properly.' We are run by control freaks who, in the end, will finish up controlling nothing.

Friday, 10 September

Lunched with Jim Rafferty (the chief executive of Home Housing) at Picasso's. He mentioned a local housing estate which had always enjoyed a good reputation, where the social fabric is now beginning to crumble. As if to prove his point, a woman came to my surgery in the evening who had just handed in her keys and fled, after living there 13 years. She had three sons and had spent a lot of money making her home comfortable, so she can't have taken the decision lightly. The problem was a neighbour who was holding all-night parties and attracting ne'er-do-wells. Complaints to the housing manager had brought no action. She and her sons are now camped out in the living room of their brother's small house in Hendon. She wants me to help her get rehoused. Yet another case of evacuating the victims rather than the villains. I shall get on to Jim on Monday and make a fuss.

A Soviet defector has identified an 87-year-old woman living in Bexley as a spy. The security service has known about it for years, but neglected to inform ministers. The Prime Minister only found out yesterday as the newspapers went to press. An ideal moment to press my campaign for parliamentary scrutiny of the intelligence services.

Alas, however, I am sworn to silence – and impotence. I must concentrate on privatising air traffic control and keep my nose out of matters that no longer come within my remit.

Monday, 13 September

Paul Taylor, a local journalist, called in to see me with a recently retired regional crime squad detective. Their purpose was to convince me – which they succeeded in doing – that the police weren't trying hard enough to catch a villain who has defrauded a number of gullible (and in some cases villainous) local citizens out of several million pounds. The ex-policeman asked about the Birmingham Six case. I replied that I knew it was an article of faith among the police that they were all really guilty. 'I don't know about that,' he said. Adding, 'You've no idea what impact you've had on the way the police work.' In the seventies, he said, it was commonplace for policemen to write up their notebooks days after the event. No one ever checked. Since the Birmingham and Guildford cases, everything had changed.

Let's hope so.

To London on the 6.43 a.m. Jessica is back from her holiday. Things are looking up: she called me 'Chris' instead of 'Minister' when we talked on the phone this afternoon.

Bill Deedes has a story in today's *Telegraph* saying that Kosovo is littered with unexploded cluster bombs. A large number of people, many of them children, have been injured so far and many more casualties are expected. The problem could go on for years. Exactly as I predicted to The Man – and George Robertson and Robin Cook – at the start of the war. Were I still on the parliamentary committee, I could confront him with it, but of course such matters are now far outside my remit. I must be silent. What a useless specimen I have become.

Tuesday, 14 September

Lunch with the British Airports Authority top brass, which included Des Wilson, founder of the charity Shelter. It was preceded by a briefing which revealed that demand for air services is growing at an astonishing rate, especially in the south-east, which accounts for about 80 per cent of traffic (although no one wants an airport in their backyard, of course). By 2015, even assuming that terminal five is built at Heathrow, all the main airports will be choked to capacity with no prospect of further expansion. Until now it seems to have been a case of Predict and Provide. Exactly the mess we have got ourselves into with the motor car. Sooner or later politicians are going to have to pluck up the courage to call a halt. Needless to say the airport fraternity won't be satisfied until they have concreted over every blade of grass. Des Wilson (once a great radical, now a corporate fat cat) seemed to think that the right to cheap holidays took precedence over all other considerations. He bleated about all the business we would lose. So be it. One day we shall have to go back to being peasants. There are times when I think it can't come soon enough.

Among the papers which crossed my desk today a note from Jack Straw to the Prime Minister saying that the number of asylum seekers had reached 'unprecedented levels' (80,000 so far this year). He says there are hundreds more camped out at Calais waiting to cross and asks for emergency measures to tide him over until the Asylum Bill becomes law. He wants special detention centres run by prison staff, and a visa regime imposed on Croatia, the Czech Republic and (possibly) Poland. Also, transit visas for Colombians. The world outside Fortress Europe is disintegrating. If this goes on, we shall need a new Berlin wall to protect the fortunate from the depredations of the destitute. Will Europe be overwhelmed in the end? As Rome was by the barbarians.

JP has overruled my decision – one of the few I have so far been asked to make – to approve the line that officials were proposing to take in negotiation with Pakistan Airlines about slots at Manchester airport. He just wrote 'No' on the memorandum without explanation and attempts to discover his reasons have so far proved unsuccessful.

Which poses a problem because the official concerned is already in Pakistan trying to negotiate. Jessica says this is a fairly common occurrence. The odds are that by the time JP has been tracked down, he will have forgotten why he intervened in the first place. So, for the time being, officials are sticking to the line that I approved.

Wednesday, 15 September

Up at 6 a.m. and to Cheltenham to address 150 councillors on rural development. Then back to London for a meeting with Gwyneth Dunwoody about air traffic control. Keith Hill and a couple of officials were also present. Gwyneth was affable, but uncompromising. With magnificent aplomb she brushed aside our feeble attempts to justify the government's plans. Were any of us to appear before her committee in our present state of unreadiness, she would reduce us to mincemeat. A useful wake-up call for all concerned. There is much work to be done, if we are to emerge from this alive.

Jessica has heard back from the government car service. Magnanimously they have agreed to reduce their standing charge from £700 to £400 a week. Still an outrage. I favour cancelling forthwith, but Jessica says we must wait to see whether Michael Meacher will take on the Nissan car reserved for me so that they have no excuse for selling it and charging us depreciation, which they are itching to do.

Thursday, 16 September

To Lancaster House, where among the gold leaf and the painted cherubs Jack Cunningham had organised an induction course for new ministers.

Lots of sensible advice. 'Control the diary.' 'Don't take boxes home.' 'Big problems don't necessarily demand big solutions.' 'Keep your eye on the big picture.' Some of the advice bore no relation to my situation. This, for example, from Richard Wilson: 'Your relationship with the Secretary of State is the key. Your clout will depend on whether you have his confidence.' That let's me out, then. Apart from a team meeting three days after I was anointed, I've only seen my

Secretary of State on TV. Still, I look on the bright side. Jessica says Alan Meale was in and out of JP's office every five minutes – and a fat lot of good it did him.

Richard Wilson, who I first came across at the Home Office, is not at all the stereotypical mandarin. A tall, ungainly man with huge ears, a big nose and a mouth that doesn't seem to co-ordinate with the words coming out of it. He positively enthused about New Labour and its works. 'This government is focusing on delivery in a way that has never happened before.' He seemed genuinely committed to diversifying the upper levels of the civil service. Perhaps he was just chanting the slogans of the hour (Jessica says that civil servants are very good at changing their spots), but I don't think so.

Among the speakers in the afternoon, Michael Bichard (Permanent Secretary at the Department of Education and Employment). An extraordinary-looking man with tiny eyes, massive forearms, Mick Jagger lips and a scruff of beard on his chin. More like a Canadian lumberjack than a permanent secretary. He has just caused a stir by publicly criticising his colleagues. Apparently, he was brought in from the private sector and so the normal rules don't apply. He talked of 'putting pressure on officials to think outside their silos'. Civil servants, he said, were not sufficiently focused on outcomes. 'They tend to take it for granted that intellect equals creativity, which is often not the case.'

Finally, we heard from Sir John Kerr of the Foreign Office, the nearest we came to an archetypal mandarin, but even he could hardly suppress his enthusiasm for The Man and all his works. 'The PM is the big act in Europe. We need to capitalise on that.' Sir John has been representing our interests in Europe for most of the last decade. 'In Margaret Thatcher's day we lurked in the shadows. We won very few battles, except on the single market – I will give her credit for that,' he said. 'The trick,' he continued, 'was to break up the Franco-German alliance.' Our strategy had been to forget about the French and get in close to the Germans, knowing that the French would soon come running when they found the other two big players lining up against them. According to Sir John, it had worked a treat.

He was a total, unabashed Europhile. Goodness knows how he survived under Thatcher. He spoke only about Europe, nothing else, making no pretence of sticking to the official line. On the Euro: 'There is no point in asking, "Will it work?" The point is, it will happen. It's not going to fall apart. It's only going to be a problem for one or two peripheral countries like Finland. There is no point,' he added with a mischievous smirk, 'in holding a referendum until we were sure that we were going to win.'

'Don't believe the civil service has been Thatcherised,' whispered Jeff Rooker afterwards. All very interesting, but so much of what we heard today has little or no relevance to my situation. I am now a figure of absolutely no influence, reconciled to a period of total obscurity. I must sit tight, keep my head down and await rescue.

Friday, 17 September

Another day another speech. Today's was at the Institute of Electrical Engineers. Again, I read slowly with plenty of meaningful pauses. At the end I even felt confident enough to take a few questions. Gradually, I am mastering the art of reading out speeches that someone else has written.

Michael Meacher has said he doesn't want my Nissan Primera so it looks as if the government car service are going to try and sting us for £4,000 depreciation for disposing of it. If they dare, I shall threaten a select committee inquiry, which ought to do the trick. They must know as well as I that if ever this nonsense were exposed to the light of day they wouldn't have a leg to stand on. Jessica has written to cancel our contract, which means that they will demand several months' notice at £400 a week. After that we will be shot of them.

Home on the 18.30. This weekend I am the duty minister, which means I must be contactable at all times. As a result, the mobile phone and pager have reappeared. Jessica assures me that they are unlikely to be needed. I shall hand them back as soon as my stint is over.

Saturday, 18 September
Sunderland

With Sarah and Emma for our weekend stroll. As instructed, I carried my pager and mobile. Which was just as well. Just as we were admiring the view from a hill above a quarry the pager began to vibrate with a message saying that three people had been killed in an air crash at Luton and would I ring Jessica at home. A panic ensued while I attempted to work the mobile, and then because I didn't have Jessica's home number. Eventually I got through to a duty clerk at the Department and he got on to Jessica, who rang me back. It turned out there was nothing to worry about since the Department was just putting out the standard line saying that there would be an inquiry. I bet she only activated the pager to see if I was carrying it.

Monday, 20 September

To the office for an hour and then to London on the 10.45. These days I hardly notice the journey. Every minute is taken up with constituency correspondence.

A brief chat with Bev Hughes, the first since we were appointed. She shares my surprise (and Keith's) that we have been given so little responsibility. She had been talking to Jacqui Smith at Education, who has her own distinct policy areas. Bev used to be Hilary Armstrong's Parliamentary Private Secretary and so she is familiar with JP's way of working. Like me, she has only seen him on TV during the last six weeks. There is, she says, no sense of being part of a team. At the so-called team meetings, which she has been attending for the past year or so, JP just talks all the time. 'No one dares express a view for fear he will round on them.' We agreed that, if nothing else, we must keep talking to each other.

Tuesday, 21 September
Secretary of State's office, Eland House

JP, grim-faced in shirtsleeves, standing near the window. He beckons a minion who meekly follows him out onto the huge balcony where they briefly confer. It soon becomes clear that the reason for this morning's angst is yet more interference by Downing Street in the business of the Department. Speed limits are the subject of today's intervention. 'Every time Number 10 interferes, we're worse off,' JP mumbles as we take our seats. His black mood is compounded by the fact that he has come to work this morning wearing shoes that don't match. We are permitted a brief giggle at this. Towards the end of the meeting the said minion re-appears with a pink plastic bag containing an assortment of shoes, after which all is well.

JP has no concept of how to get the best out of people. His idea of conferring is to lie slumped in an armchair and deliver, at break-neck speed, a series of diatribes on whatever has hit him on the way into work in the morning. Occasionally he invites the briefest of contributions from one or other of his ministers, who are arranged around him on a circle of easy chairs. Now and then he solicits information from one of the advisors who sit behind us on upright chairs. There is barely time, however, for the interlocutor to complete a single sentence before JP races off again leaving the rest of us scrambling to keep up. Our main role is to laugh sycophantically at his jokes. This is how it must be at the court of Boris Yeltsin.

We discuss our plans for air traffic control. Or rather JP does. It appears that Downing Street is nervous. One hundred and sixty MPs have signed an early-day motion and the whips are predicting a substantial uprising. JP is anxious that, if there is to be any retreat, it should take place now and not – as he puts it – 'after we have entered the valley of death'. He and Gus are meeting Gordon Brown later today after which the picture might be clearer. Gordon is said to be gung-ho. JP himself says he has no difficulty with selling off half of air traffic control. The arguments are sound. We need the investment and the project management skills that the private sector will bring in. Plus it will relieve the pressure on the tax payer. He attacks the unions for playing the safety card. Something, he says, they always do when faced with demands for change.

A meeting of transport ministers in Gus Macdonald's office. Several people expressed concern about the fuel escalator on which Gordon is said to be very keen. On lorry tax, Larry Whitty said ours was ten times some continental levels 'and we have no explanation'.

Gus said we must stop setting targets for everything. As far as cars were concerned, the number was going to increase anyway and so we would only be shooting ourselves in the foot. Most targets were, as he put it, bollocks. He added, 'I sense a rising derision. We are getting a reputation as a party of busybodies.'

Keith Hill told me later that there has even been talk of setting targets for the number of people persuaded to walk to work. A later draft of our walking document had substituted 'benchmarks' for 'targets'. Later still, 'benchmarks' had given way to 'reference indicators'. Orwellian.

Keith and Joe Irvin agree that we are not doing enough for the humble bicycle. Indeed we are doing nothing. I may draft a little paper on the subject in the hope of persuading Gus to take cycling seriously.

Wednesday, 22 September

Gus Macdonald confided his surprise at the absence of team working in government. The Scottish Office (where he previously worked) was run by 'a bunch of affable freelances'. At Environment the problem is worse. 'We need a chairman at the top, not a charismatic.' He concedes, however, that JP will never change. We are stuck with a charismatic. Gus says he's been sent here to take the heat off John. If we can quieten things down for a while, the tabloids will find someone else to take it out on. 'Being attacked by the tabloids,' he says, 'is like being mugged by skinheads.'

Friday, 24 September
Sunderland

To Durham County Cricket Club's splendid new pavilion at Chester-le-Street to address a housing seminar. The speech that has been drafted for me is so dire that I dare not read it out. It comes accompanied by a thick yellow folder containing briefings covering just about every eventuality except the possibility that I might be talking to intelligent human beings who would prefer not to be addressed by an android. 'When you become a minister,' I say, 'you get given dull, impenetrable, triple-spaced speeches to read out. This is the one I have been given for today ...' Pause to display the fat yellow folder. 'I propose to ignore it.' Ostentatiously placing the folder on the table I proceeded to give a more or less on-message account of government strategy, illustrated with reference to my experience in Sunderland. It seemed to go down well. I had thought there were no officials present, but as I was leaving, a man from the Central Office of Information bore down upon me. 'Minister, I hope you won't take this the wrong way.'

I braced myself.

'That was very refreshing.'

'Thank you,' I said. 'By the way, who wrote the speech?'

'Ah, do you see that man over there ...?'

Monday, 27 September
Labour Party Conference, Bournemouth

This year's conference symbol, a rising sun. Increasingly the proceedings come to resemble those that take place in Beijing's Great Hall of the People. The speeches are for the most part bland, lacking passion or spontaneity. Nothing is left to chance. I even saw an arrow pointing to a room marked 'delegate training' – goodness knows what goes on there. And yet, just as one begins to despair that there is any life left in the poor old Labour Party, the comrades rise up and inflict a little pinprick on The Apparatus. This afternoon's defeat was prompted by the refusal of the chairman to allow a vote on two or three controversial paragraphs in an otherwise unexceptional document. All or nothing, he insisted. Conference took him at his word and voted the whole thing down. It won't make any difference, of course, but it did cheer everyone up.

Everyone keeps congratulating me on what they suppose is my good fortune at being made a minister. They then ask, 'How are you finding it?' Lacking the ability to lie or bluster, I tell them and end up sounding like an ungrateful old misery. Audrey Wise says I have sold myself too cheap. I am afraid she may be right.

Tuesday, 28 September

To Channel Four breakfast, where I sat next to Tony Benn, who amused himself filming the proceedings with his latest gadget, a small video recorder. Tony seems genuinely pleased by my elevation, although privately he must be contemptuous.

During the lunch break there was a large demonstration of fox-hunters baying 'Listen to us' and sounding horns and whistles. A mixture of tweedy toffs and ruddy-faced retainers. Many of the male toffs had caps perched on their heads and chins thrust arrogantly outward. I stood for half an hour watching them pass. By and large it was a good-natured affair, although there were some nasty posters depicting Tony Blair as Hitler. The more I watched, the more obvious it became that we have nothing whatever to fear from these people. They were by and large the blood sports wing of the Tory Party. To aid identification they held up placards saying where they came from. More or less a list of the safest Tory seats in the country. I came away greatly encouraged.

Decided not to stay for The Speech. I made my escape and watched on television. Typical Blair fare. Long on vision, short on specifics. Addressed to the nation, rather than the party (a lesson that poor Neil Kinnock never learned). He began with a reference to the demonstration. 'I know farming is in crisis. We are doing our best to help, but I don't believe that the future of the countryside depends on fox-hunting.' Hooray, he's decided to come out fighting.

Wednesday, 29 September

To the conference hall for JP's speech. As I was entering, two cars sped down the hill from the Highcliff Hotel to the conference centre and disgorged JP and Pauline. Alarm bells rang. Is it wise, when you are about to utter on prime-time telly lots of fine sentiments about reducing car usage, to travel 300 yards by car?

The speech went well. I sat next to JP's special adviser, Joe Irvin who had the text on his knee. It was laid out like a long poem. The sentences were short and each clause was on a separate line. Two new national parks – South Downs and New Forest – were announced. Air traffic control was tackled head on. A two-minute standing ovation followed. In contrast to yesterday's much longer one for The Man, this was the real thing. The Man is respected, JP is loved. He may be a curmudgeonly, impossible minister, but at the end of the day people know that he is on their side.

All would have been well had it ended there but, alas, it was not to be. Fresh from his triumph, JP went off to give a series of disastrous television interviews. Inevitably, he was asked about his 300-yard car ride to the conference centre. Equally inevitably, he lost his temper. The interview is running high up the television news bulletins. Tomorrow's tabloids are awaited with trepidation.

Thursday, 30 September

'HYPOCRITE' proclaims a headline in the *Mirror* this morning over the story of JP's short car ride. The *Sun* and the *Star* are just as bad. Poor old JP. I do feel sorry for him. So much effort went into that speech. There was a lot of good stuff in it and this is what he ends up with. And not only in the tabloids. Simon Hoggart has a wickedly funny piece in this morning's *Guardian* commenting on the angry tone in which all JP's pronouncements are delivered. Says Hoggart, 'He announced the creation of two new national parks in the way you might announce the annexation of the Sudetenland.'

To the Department, where several feet of paperwork awaited. Jessica produced a note from the press office headed 'Ministerial Travel':

> As a result of this week's press coverage from Bournemouth we are likely on Monday morning to have photographers outside Eland House looking at Ministers' modes of travel ... Private secretaries will want to give some thought to travel arrangements for ministers over the next few weeks. We will need to be whiter than white.

I, at least, have nothing to fear.

Monday, 11 October

Back to the Department after an absence of ten days. As I suspected, there is no truth in the *Guardian* story the other day alleging that the sale of air traffic control is to be abandoned. JP checked with Downing Street this morning and the line is that as long as he and Gordon are behind the sale, The Man will go along with it. I was told this by Richard Mottram, the Permanent Secretary, who I ran into in the lift. He added, 'Of course that doesn't mean they won't pull the rug from under us later. We've been shafted by Downing Street so many times.' Richard made no secret about his view of the proposed sale. There was, he said, no reason why Gordon couldn't come up with the money. 'The sums involved are trivial.' He added, 'The problem is, if we were to sell anything less than 46 per cent, the Central Statistical Office would classify air traffic control as being still in the public sector. A great system we've invented.'

We have managed to get the government car service off our backs at last. They had been demanding that we pay £4,000 depreciation on the grounds that they have no choice but to sell the car allocated for me. However, when Jessica informed them that I would like another meeting with the chief executive, he suddenly discovered that he was able to redeploy the car after all. Total victory.

The number of letters awaiting signature after my absence is so large that the overflow is housed in two large cardboard boxes on the floor of my office. According to Jessica, I sign more letters than any other minister in the Department. That's all I am really, a glorified correspondence clerk. Much of the recent upsurge has been caused by a postcard campaign organised by Friends of the Earth. About 500 MPs have written in, enclosing copies of the postcard, and they all have to be replied to individually. Some lazy sods have sent in up to ten postcards, each with a covering letter, and each has been replied to separately. I have sent word, via Jessica, that in future I will refuse to sign identical letters to the same MP.

Reshuffle. Peter Mandelson is back as Northern Ireland Secretary. Jack Cunningham is out, replaced by Mo Mowlam. Geoff Hoon becomes Defence Secretary, after just three months at the Foreign Office. Alan Milburn replaces Frank Dobson at Health. Frank, to everyone's amazement, has decided after all to run for Mayor of London. What on earth can have persuaded him? My guess is that The Man indicated that he would be leaving the Cabinet anyway and so Frank decided that he had nothing to lose. The most inexplicable appointment is Keith Vaz, who, after an undistinguished few months at the Lord Chancellor's department, goes to the Foreign Office as a minister of state. Keith is an utter lightweight. How on earth does he fit into the New Labour masterplan? As for Mandelson, it is now inevitable that he will become Foreign Secretary after the election.

Tuesday, 12 October

Buried deep in the pile of letters awaiting my signature was one addressed to Elliot Morley suggesting that I am opposed to the UK raising farm-animal welfare at the World Trade talks which are due to open in Seattle next month. This was accompanied by a copy of a letter from George Foulkes saying that to do so would be seen by the Third World as a ploy by Europe to erect new trade barriers. Elliot's letter, soliciting the comments of other departments, was dated 27 July and the deadline for responses had already expired. Since the views to which I was being asked to put my signature were the exact opposite of my own, I declined to sign and asked to see the officials concerned. In the meantime I rang Elliot, who urged me to stand firm. The officials duly appeared. I could get no sense from them as to why it had taken ten weeks to respond to Elliot. They then produced a new draft, which was a slightly watered-down version of the original. I refused to sign that, too. It then emerged that the matter had already gone to Cabinet committee last week and that our officials had pursued the line which I was being asked to endorse retrospectively. 'On whose authority?' They then claimed that in my absence the papers had gone to Gus Macdonald. I bet they did, buried in a big pile a few hours before the expiry of the deadline. We have been bounced.

Great excitement in the private office because we have received what they call 'a bid' for an interview from the Radio 4 *Today* programme. In my last incarnation, requests for interviews on *Today* were ten a penny, but in my present obscurity they have rarity value. It is no longer a case of a message left on an answerphone to which I may or may not respond. Nowadays all requests have to be channelled via the Department's vast press office. Nor are they any longer a question of turning up at the appointed place at the appointed time. First the bid has to be cleared with JP. Then appropriate officials have to be consulted as to the 'Line to Take'. This will eventually appear in the form of a note which has been copied halfway round the building. The subject of *Today*'s bid is air traffic control and safety, in advance of talks I am due to have with the unions tomorrow. I am not at all keen, since this is dangerous territory. Nevertheless, the wheels are in motion. A time and place agreed. A radio car is organised. Then comes word from on high that the interview is off. JP has vetoed it. No reason offered. I am forbidden. That is all. Perhaps he thinks I'll make a mess of it. Or worse still (but unlikely given the subject matter) I might prove an unexpected success. It is not as though JP's own appearances on *Today* have been such an unmitigated triumph.

Wednesday, 13 October

A meeting with Michael Meacher to discuss the dreaded leylandii. After two years of faffing, the Department has come up with a leaflet designed to advise on suitable hedging for suburban gardens. As officials proudly point out, it has been produced with the co-operation of the industry and will be distributed via garden centres. 'Where,' asks Michael, 'does it actually say that it is not a good idea to plant leylandii?'

'Ah, well, Minister, it doesn't quite put it as boldly as that. We have to be careful of upsetting the industry.' Pure *Yes, Minister*. In fact, as one of the officials cheerfully points out, the leaflet could be seen as encouraging the sale of fast-growing hedging – the exact opposite of what we are trying to achieve. To be fair, it is not entirely their fault. On the contrary, our officials are keen to act against the demon leylandii – about which we receive hundreds of letters each year. The problem lies elsewhere. Objections have been received from the Home Office, the Lord Chancellor and Downing Street. Incredibly, we are asked to believe that The Man himself has given thought to the matter and has personally vetoed legislation. So instead we are consulting.

Later, Brian Hackland – from Number 10 – comes to see me and I bend his ear on the subject of leylandii. Amazingly, it rapidly becomes clear that The Man has indeed given his personal attention to the matter. What's more, according to Brian, he is likely to veto even a consultation which might lead to legislation. Unbelievable. It's not as though we are upsetting anyone. We are in danger of exposing ourselves to ridicule if we can't cope with a problem as simple as this.

In the afternoon the air traffic unions came in to discuss safety with the regulator, the unfortunately named Mr Profitt. A heated meeting. They were an impressive bunch and put their case forcefully. Rightly they are angry about not having been consulted in advance. The more I think about this privatisation that we are not allowed to call privatisation, the more I wonder if it is worth the trouble.

A brief chat with Michael Meacher in the evening. He obviously enjoys his job. He is very good at it and JP lets him get on more or less unmolested. Michael, however, remains as far from being a paid-up New Labourite as ever. Geoff Hoon's promotion he called 'outrageous'. The private finance initiative, he says, will come back to haunt us. Our inability to come to grips with leylandii he described as 'risible'. I recounted this morning's conversation with Brian Hackland. Michael rang him there and then and argued for 20 minutes. By the end it had become clear that Hackland himself, pleasant and mild-mannered though he is, is part of the problem rather than the solution.

Thursday, 14 October
Liverpool

Our first call was the Housing Action Trust set up by the Tories to take over a huge slice of Liverpool's worst public housing which the city council was incapable of managing. Most of the Trust's 67 tower blocks are in the process of being demolished and replaced with good-quality low-rise. It was given a huge sum of money – £260 million – and told to get on with it. Needless to say there was a lot of squealing from Derek Hatton and friends, but from what I saw it's a great success.

I can't remember what Old Labour's line on Housing Action Trusts was, but I bet we were opposed. Something else the Tories were right about.

Liverpool city council, now run by Liberals, has seen the light and is getting out of housing management. We visited two other estates. One which had been handed over to a housing association and transformed and one which was just about to be. On one we witnessed two large black dogs attacking a villainous-looking youth while the owner, another obvious villain, was trying to get them under control. Afterwards the villain who had been attacked beat one of the dogs soundly with a belt. I was later told that the dogs were Neapolitans, which are said to be fiercer than Rottweilers. The villain apparently owned six. As one of my hosts remarked, 'You can't accuse us of stage-managing your visit.'

Friday, 15 October

Called Chief Whip, Ann Taylor, to put in a word for Jean Corston to be my successor as Home Affairs Committee chairman. Ann asked how I was getting on. I replied that it was every bit as dreadful as I had imagined. We discussed air traffic control. Ann is worried that it is going to cause us a lot of trouble. She said, 'JP has been asked directly' – by The Man, I assume – 'whether he still wants to go ahead and he insists on doing so.' She said it was a deal between JP and Gordon. 'Number 10 was not involved.' She added that it will hold up the Strategic Rail Authority, which JP is anxious to press ahead with. I asked if she had discussed this with JP. She said she had tried, but it was hard to get his attention. The sale has no friends apart from JP and Gordon. Number 10 is neutral. The Chief Whip is against. Parliament is hostile. So are the public. So is just about everyone in the Department, up to and including the Permanent Secretary.

Sunday, 17 October
Sunderland

Jack Straw returned my call, ringing from the back of his car on the way back to London from Oxfordshire with his family. We chatted for half an hour. We were cut off four times, although he assured me the line was secure. Halfway through he relayed a message from his daughter Charlotte: her friend Rosa had recently read *A Very British Coup* and cried at the end.

Leylandii was item one on the agenda. As I suspected, Jack is sound on the issue and was surprised to hear the Home Office were objecting. He promised to chase up the response to our consultation document and ensure it was friendly.

We discussed JP. Briefly, I described his disastrous management style. 'You can sack or reshuffle all the under-secretaries you like, but it doesn't address the real problem.' I added, 'I accept that politically nothing can be done.'

'Not any more,' replied Jack. 'That might have been true a year or two ago, but not now.' According to Jack, JP's star is waning. 'Floundering' was the word he used. He wasn't gleeful about it, just matter of fact, adding, 'I like the guy.'

Talk turned to air traffic control. Jack said, 'If you think it can't be delivered, let me know and I'll talk to Tony.' Suddenly it dawned on me that, were I to exert myself using my various back-channels to The Man (Jack, Ann Taylor, Bruce Grocott) I could probably get the whole thing called off. I hesitated, saying that I couldn't yet be sure, but I would come back to him if need be. The truth is that, unlike many, I have no principled objection to what is proposed. Much of the huffing and puffing on the subject comes from people who haven't got a clue what they are talking about. Many have disguised an ideological objection to the sale of any state asset with unfounded arguments about safety. So far as I can see there is no threat to safety. If anything, we are going to improve the safety arrangements. The problem is purely political, made worse by the rail disaster at Paddington.

Monday, 18 October

Another exchange about leylandii with Brian Hackland, the man from Number 10. 'The climate in Downing Street is not right,' he asserted.

'What climate? I bet the Prime Minister hasn't devoted more than 30 seconds of his time to the matter.'

He conceded that this was so. I pressed him on where the trouble lay and reluctantly he disgorged two names, Jonathan Powell and Anji Hunter.

'Anji Hunter? Where does she fit in?'

'The Prime Minister values her political antennae.'

So there we have it. Our entire effort is paralysed on the whim of someone officially described as the Prime Minister's Special Assistant. Come back Marcia Falkender.

Tuesday, 19 October

At my desk by 8.15, after a pleasant stroll through St James's Park, which was swarming with police awaiting the arrival at the Palace of the Chinese President, Jiang Ximin.

At 8.30 there was a meeting of ministers. It has now been decreed that these will be fortnightly (as opposed to monthly). JP, who was unusually subdued (although he still talked 75 per cent of the time), was slumped in his usual chair, tie undone. The royal standard on Buckingham Palace fluttered directly above his head. There was talk of Paddington. JP said it was nonsense to blame the accident on privatisation. Accidents had dropped by half since then. He added, however, that the number of trains passing red lights was up by a third.

Leylandii surfaced briefly. To much nervous mirth JP revealed that he had 16 at the bottom of his garden. He'd better get them cut before the media find out, otherwise we shall have another public relations disaster on our hands. Somebody mentioned the problem we had encountered at Number 10. 'As usual,' muttered JP.

To Birmingham, ostensibly to open the International Water Exhibition. I made a short speech to a handful of bemused visitors and cut a ribbon, but in fact the exhibition had been open a couple of hours by the time I arrived. 'I wondered if you'd notice,' remarked one of the organisers when I pointed this out. Of course I bloody noticed. Just as I noticed in Liverpool last week that the plaque I unveiled appeared to have been hastily erected in the middle of nowhere and no doubt removed soon after my departure. So much ministerial activity is entirely contrived and pointless. I spent an hour and a half touring stands, pressing flesh, and then sped back to London, where I rounded off the afternoon chairing a conference of prime ministers from the Overseas Dependent Territories, in the map room at the Foreign Office. Not as grand as it sounds since most of them represented populations no bigger than one or two local government wards. The Prime Minister of Anguilla (pop. 10,000) slept throughout, awaking briefly to demand that we build him a new international airport.

Tonight's *Standard* reports that the air traffic controllers are planning a strike. It's not JP who needs to be leaned on, but Gordon. He's the one pulling the strings and he will get off scot-free if the sell-off goes wrong. Just as he did over the single-parent benefit fiasco.

Wednesday, 20 October

I am savaged by Polly Toynbee in her column in today's *Guardian* for allegedly selling out the select committee system by joining the regime. She enumerates and then retracts all the good things she said about me when I took the chair of Home Affairs two years ago and then quotes me as saying, as I did, that I had no interest in being Minister of Folding Deckchairs. This she correctly observes is precisely what I have become. Some of it is unfair (it is not as though I just flitted through the select committee – I was on it for seven years), but she does have a point.

This evening was my debut at the Dispatch Box, replying to a Lib Dem motion on transport safety. Needless to say, I was completely out of my depth since, apart from air traffic control, none of it fell within my brief. It is much more difficult to wind up than to open a debate.

The opener can just read from a prepared text, but the winder-up is supposed to respond to points made during the debate. To make matters worse, no one except the handful who have attended throughout are interested in what is being said. The rest just chat among themselves while awaiting the division.

My worst fear was drying up halfway through. I am absolutely hopeless at ad-libbing on matters that I know little or nothing about. As a precaution, I came armed with a 15-minute speech which, if the worst came to the worst, I could just read out. It was a low-key debate. No one, apart from Shaun Woodward (who spoke for the Tories) wanted to score cheap points in the wake of the Paddington tragedy. Don Foster led for the Lib Dems with a very competent, sober speech. Keith Hill, for our side, made a similar response. The complicating factor was the large, brooding presence of JP. Transport, of course, is something he knows all about. As Shaun Woodward got into his stride, JP started muttering, cursing, heckling. Before long he was keeping up a continual barrage, winding up Woodward still further. 'You want the politics, I'll give you the politics,' he shouted. With that he started drafting notes for me to use in reply. There were references to dates (apparently plucked from the air), committees of inquiry headed by people of whom I had never heard, mysterious acronyms … All scribbled in barely legible black felt pen, accompanied by a continuous, high-speed, running commentary. On he went, long after Woodward had sat down. Confusion reigned. I began to panic. Visions of a breakdown at the Dispatch Box loomed. Notes were now pouring in from officials in the civil servants' box responding to points other speakers were making, but I could hardly absorb the contents, let alone hear what was being said, because of the overwhelming, disruptive presence of JP. Fortunately, with about an hour of debate to go, he finally shut up and I managed to sort the notes into some sort of order. At 9.15 a new crisis dawned. A whip, David Jamieson, appeared, to say that the debate was drying up and I might have to speak for more than half an hour instead of the expected 15 minutes. Oh terror. 'Impossible,' I replied. 'When I've said what I have to say, I will sit down regardless of the time.'

'You can't,' hissed Jamieson. JP, sitting next to me, overheard all this. I half expected him to come down on Jamieson's side and tell me not to be such a wimp. Not a bit of it. JP, God bless him, told Jamieson that it was unfair to expect me to busk. It was his job to keep the debate going. Jamieson slunk away. At this point I forgave JP every-thing. In the event John Heppell saved the day by getting up and speaking off the cuff for ten minutes. As it happened I probably could have filled the time. When my turn came I spoke very slowly and, using the notes that had come from the box, replied point by point to each of the speakers. Then I turned to my prepared script, but only managed a single sentence before time was called. It was a hesitant, nervous performance, but at least I scraped by.

Thursday, 21 October

I am in danger of falling out with Jessica who is getting fed up with my constant whingeing about the rising tide of pointless activity that my job seems to entail. 'Nick Raynsford worked much harder than you do,' she complained, blushing as she spoke. I could tell she was angry.

I pointed out that I was usually in the office by 8.30 a.m. and worked until 10 or 11 at night. I am frequently one of the last people to leave the building. 'When,' I asked, 'did Nick do all the work that I don't do?'

'At weekends,' she said. 'He saved his letters up until then.'

'Weekends,' I replied, 'are non-negotiable. I have a family.'

Whatever happens, I must avoid alienating Jessica.

Bob Ainsworth, from the whips' office, came in for a discussion with Keith Hill and myself about how to tackle the uprising over air traffic control. About half of backbench members have signed a motion objecting, although many will clearly fall by the wayside when the going gets tough. We agreed to divide them into groups of ten and invite them to the Department for a conversation.

Tuesday, 26 October

My first Question Time. A rising sense of terror. Answering is an entirely different art from asking. Gordon Prentice is first up. Needless to say he is asking about air traffic control and bound to attract supplementaries. In vain I try to memorise the brief. In truth, most of the answers are obvious, if only I could relax sufficiently to enable my brain to function. My greatest fear is being struck dumb.

The moment comes. Gordon rises and welcomes me. Then he asks his question. I can hear someone muttering about political suicide. To my right Dennis Skinner murmurs, 'He's drawn the short straw.' I affect nonchalance, leaning on the Dispatch Box, turning to face Gordon, beaming at him. I thank him, adding, 'I hope I continue to justify the honourable gentleman's confidence.' Everyone laughs. There is goodwill everywhere. Even on the Tory benches. Everyone knows that selling air traffic control wasn't my idea. The awful Shaun Woodward rises, his every word a sneer. By now my confidence has returned. I swat him easily. Cheers from our side. Even some of the Tories look pleased.

Next, an exchange with Ann Winterton, who has asked about drivers under the influence of drugs. I treat her respectfully. Then one of our colleagues rises and refers to 'spliffs'.

'The honourable gentleman is more conversant with the terminology than I,' I begin. Laughter all round. Congratulations flow in. Even JP is pleased. On my part, huge relief. It is over. I have survived – until next time.

Later, Gus Macdonald and I have a meeting with Sandra Osborne, whose marginal constituency is full of angry air traffic controllers. The poor woman has been attending meetings of up to 400 at a time. Before the election she was passing on assurances that we had no intention of privatising air traffic control. Now she is struggling to explain the difference between privatisation and a public-private partnership. She has been placed in an impossible position. She said that no one believes her assurances that Prestwick is safe.

Wednesday, 27 October

The more I talk to Gus Macdonald, the more I realise that he, too, is sceptical about selling air traffic control. He remarked today that he doesn't have a single ally in the Lords. He says he told the PM two weeks ago that selling this is going to be very damaging. It will eclipse all the good things in the Transport Bill. 'Up to you,' Gus told The Man, 'to decide if it's worth all the aggro.'

Congratulations continue to flow in for my little performance yesterday. Even JP went so far as to concede that it went alright. 'You've got the humour. They like that. And they sympathise. They're all saying, "That bastard Prescott's dumped you in it."' JP has strengths as well as weaknesses. Ann Clwyd, who worked with him in opposition, says he is loyal to colleagues. I must try harder to like him.

Friday, 29 October
Sunderland

A very heavy surgery. Three child abuse cases and a Somali whose children are trapped in a refugee camp in Kenya. His mother, who looks after them, is suffering from malaria and could die at any time, leaving them to fend for themselves. He is terrified of losing contact with them and desperately wants to bring them here. Rarely have I seen a man so depressed. His cheeks were sunken, his eyes downcast. Periodically, he burst into tears. 'Life is horrible,' he kept repeating, 'I will kill myself.' He is an illegal immigrant and seemed to think that I had it within my power to let him stay. If only I did. I promised to do what I can to hurry his case along and he shuffled miserably away.

Later, at home, I leafed through our photo album at the pictures of Sarah and Emma enjoying themselves in Cornwall, Sussex, Northumberland. What lucky little lives my children have.

Saturday, 30 October

'Just occasionally, even amid the waste of seaweed which character-ises Commons debate in our dreary one-party state, something spiny shows through,' writes Matthew Parris in yesterday's *Times*. He goes on,

> When this happens on the government benches a sensible chief whip makes sure to capture or destroy the creature.
>
> Chris Mullin is an example. A fearless interrogator and select committee truth seeker, he represented a small threat to the even flow of government in the subject he knew best: home affairs. So in the last reshuffle Tony Blair made him a junior minister – in the Department of Environment, Transport and the Regions. He has not been heard of since.

Right about the last point. Wrong to blame it on the Chief Whip. The fault is entirely mine.

Monday, 1 November

To London on the 10.45. Among my mail another piece of New Labour vulgarity: an invitation to have my photograph taken with Alistair Darling in the act of handing over a giant cheque to celebrate the fact that pensioners are about to start receiving their £100 winter fuel allowance. So far, so good, but the missive goes on: 'To make a real story for your local paper you are invited to bring along a pen-sioner ...' It gets worse; 'Speed is essential ... If you are bringing a pensioner, please warn them there is no time to talk to Alistair and no autographs ...' Yuk.

Tuesday, 2 November

Sarah's tenth birthday.

Walked up Victoria Street, self-consciously carrying my two, very heavy, red boxes. They are lead-lined so that in the event the unfor-tunate minister is blown up, the government's papers will survive. People stared. Half the pedestrians in Victoria at 8.30 a.m. are civil servants on their way to work and they aren't used to seeing ministers lugging red boxes through the mean streets of London. All part of the price I pay for refusing an official car. Sooner or later some trouble-maker, probably one of the drivers, will report me for breaching security.

Behind Eland House I came across Roy Hattersley and his dog, Buster. 'You're looking immensely ministerial,' he said. Kindly adding, 'I don't know if you are aware, but your right-hand box is about to burst open.' I looked down and, sure enough, he was right. Disaster narrowly averted.

Although she is not slow to point out (usually in a tone of exaspera-tion) my many shortcomings I begin to notice that Jessica is reluctant to consider the possibility that she may sometimes be mistaken – not that she is very often. On the contrary, she is extremely competent. This morning, however, I had a little triumph. She couldn't unlock one of my two boxes. A technician was summoned and about to force the lock when I appeared and offered to unlock it. 'But we didn't give you a key,' said Jessica in a tone that brooked no contradiction. Whereupon, in full view of the office juniors, I produced the very key with which she had indeed supplied me and triumphantly turned it in the lock. *Voi-là*. I threw it up, caught it and disappeared smugly back into my office leaving Jessica temporarily speechless. For at least the next half-hour I bathed in a warm, self-satisfied glow.

Wednesday, 3 November

Jean Corston reported that, at today's meeting of the parliamentary committee, The Man remarked, 'It does seem strange without Chris.'

Thursday, 4 November

To bed at 1.30 a.m., up at 5.45.

My existence is now almost entirely pointless. This week I have, among many other things, replied to two adjournment debates and made speeches to the British Geological Society, the Institute of Waste

Management and the Association of Residential Management Agents. In between I have worked my way through red boxes piled with letters to sign and papers, almost all of which are marked 'To See' rather than 'To Decide'. People keep asking if I am enjoying myself. 'Up to a point,' I reply, but how could one possibly derive enjoyment from so pointless an existence? With hand on heart, I can say that I have less influence now over government policy than at any time in the last eight years. The only possible excuse for doing this is the hope that it will lead to something better.

Friday, 5 November
Sunderland

The Somali who came to my surgery last week now haunts the office almost every day. My assistant, Graham, says he cries and bangs his head against the wall. We have been asking the Home Office to fast-track the case, but they refuse saying that there are hundreds of similar cases with equally tragic stories. I offered to contact the Red Cross to see if we can obtain some up-to-date information about his family, but for some reason he doesn't want me to. Goodness knows what will become of him. I wouldn't be surprised to hear he had been found floating under Wearmouth Bridge.

This evening, to the monthly meeting of my management committee. The local party is visibly disintegrating.

Monday, 8 November

To Leeds to see the chief executive of Yorkshire Water, Kevin Bond, a bright, pleasant man, not at all the stereotypical fat cat. He spent 18 years in the West Midlands police and, as a young PC, was on duty in Birmingham city centre on the night the bombs went off. He says he left the police because they were unwilling to change. 'There was a ray of hope with Sheehy, but they saw him off, too.' On water, he wanted (i) a stable and transparent system of regulation, (ii) to be allowed to take over smaller water companies – 'otherwise foreigners will take over the entire industry.' (The man from Thames Water, whom I saw the other day, made the same point.) Mr Bond added that the water industry had been given away (by the Tories). 'It was immoral.'

In the evening JP, Gus Macdonald and I had a meeting with a delegation of backbenchers led by Martin Salter. It went off well enough, but JP was f-ing and blinding up to the moment of their arrival. Throughout the first part of the meeting he maintained an unprecedented silence while the MPs stated their case, which they did calmly and moderately. Gus responded while JP, eyes down, sat scribbling furiously. Then when everyone had said their piece, he suddenly sprung to life. Words spouted like a huge geyser from which a temporary blockage had been removed. He was still talking when the division bell brought the meeting to a close.

Tuesday, 9 November

To Brighton, to address 250 housing wallahs. One of Nick Raynsford's hand-me-downs. Utterly pointless, since we have nothing to say. With as much enthusiasm as I could muster I read out the lacklustre speech that had been prepared. The applause was lukewarm. The announcement that the minister had to get back to London and would not, therefore, have time to answer questions was greeted with a cynical titter. Goodness knows why we do this sort of thing. It is so damaging.

Wednesday, 10 November

A talk with Richard Mottram about air traffic control and the Treasury. He referred to Gordon as 'PM in all but name'. The first time I have ever heard it suggested that The Man may not be wholly in charge. Richard went on, 'Gordon thinks his writ runs everywhere. To some extent we are protected by the Deputy Prime Minister, but some secretaries of state and permanent secretaries only find out about Treasury initiatives affecting their departments when they are announced.'

To the Department of Trade and Industry to take part in the launch of a report calling for bigger and better airports. The place was full of men in suits who, happily, had been infiltrated by someone from Friends of the Earth. It was left to me – and to be fair Lord Marshall (of British Airways) – gently to draw attention to the environmental consequences. I had to send back the original lily-livered draft of the speech I was given to read out. It came back much improved.

Our consultation document on leylandii has been given a very low-key launch. Downing Street is worried that, if we do anything about leylandii, we'll be accused of introducing a nanny state. I've never heard anything so pathetic. We've even got the *Daily Mail* on our side.

To Number 10 for the official photograph of last year's parliamentary committee. I am included. My first contact with The Man since my demotion. 'Hello, Minister,' he said. He seemed a little distant. I'm not sure he entirely approved of my being there. The picture was taken upstairs at one end of the state rooms. The walls were hung with bright new portraits of cultural glitterati – Naomi Mitchison, Dirk Bogarde, P. D. James, Kazuo Ishiguro and Darcey Bussell, to whom The Man referred as 'that Tory dancer'. I assumed that the paintings (which were much better than all that modern junk in Gordon's salon) were his choice, but he said they are changed without reference to him.

Two photos were taken. One of last year's committee and one of this year's. After the camera had flashed for the first one, I stood up and bowing slightly in the direction of The Man said, 'Positively my last appearance.' This triggered a touching little round of applause in which even Prescott joined. Afterwards JP took me aside and indicated that he'd prefer me not to write to Ian McCartney (who is conducting a review of the government car service) on the grounds that a letter could cause embarrassment if leaked. Instead he suggested I communicate orally with Ian. He was perfectly affable, even conceding that I had a point, but he doesn't want a letter sent.

Thursday, 11 November
Yvette Cooper, Ed Balls and their beautiful baby were on the train going home. A golden couple. He an intimate of one of the

most powerful men in the land and she, in her early thirties, already a minister. Yvette is bright and pleasant, but a swot rather than a natural talent. Lacks the magic to reach the top, but she will get close. Who knows, one day she and Ed may sit together in the Cabinet. I took the opportunity to bend his ear about air traffic control, 'We urgently need help.'

'We want to help, but first we have to be asked,' he replied.

'But you have been asked. I saw the letter.'

We talked obliquely to avoid being overheard.

'How many pages?'

'Three.'

'The one that arrived was less than a page. It didn't ask for anything. Just listed five principles.'

Would you believe it? JP, or someone, has backed down. We are still steaming full speed ahead towards the rocks.

Friday, 12 November
Sunderland

Rang Jessica and asked her to find a copy of JP's letter to Gordon. She faxed it back within the hour. Sure enough, it consists of just half a page. Pages two and three of the draft which was circulated have been deleted. All it asks for is 'an early discussion of the best way forward'. A fat lot of good that will do.

Jessica also reported that the unions have blabbed about our talks the other day and JP has blown a gasket. Word has come that I am not to organise the other meeting that we promised. Oh dear, whenever JP gets involved the misunderstandings multiply.

The sad Somali turned up at the surgery again. He simply won't accept that I don't have the power to legalise his entry. I offered to make inquiries about his family, but he won't have it, which makes me a little suspicious of the story he tells. I gave him a tenner to get himself something to eat, since he had missed supper time at Camrex House, the hostel for homeless where he is staying. Graham thought that was unwise.

Monday, 15 November

Another dreadful cold and another little homily from Jessica about my refusal to use a pager. As ever, I replied that I could think of no reason why I needed to be constantly in touch with HQ.

'We haven't been busy yet,' she says.

'What about last week – there was not an evening when I was in bed before 1 a.m. or up later than 6.30 a.m.'

'That was only medium busy.'

'Well, I am not proposing to manage on any less than five hours' sleep a night.'

Officials take no account of time spent at the House. So far as they are concerned, the day ends when they go home. The fact that the wretched minister's working day still has another eight hours to go is of little or no relevance. Well, I ain't standing for that.

A talk with Gus Macdonald about the letter to the Treasury that never arrived. It transpires that, although I am laughingly known as the Aviation Minister, there have been a number of developments of which I am unaware. In particular Gus has just had a meeting with Crédit Suisse at which there was discussion as to whether we could get away with selling only 20 per cent. The conclusion was that there were not likely to be any takers for so small a stake. Gus apologised for not inviting me, but I am not in the least concerned. Let events take their course, say I.

Tuesday, 16 November

JP was in subdued mode at the ministers' meeting this morning. His conduct was businesslike, going out of his way to solicit other opinions. He even made a couple of self-deprecating jokes. Has someone – Gus perhaps – given him a talking to? It won't last, of course. Indeed before the hour was up the strain was beginning to show, but it was interesting to behold.

A complicated little minuet is taking place over air traffic control. One possibility discussed this morning is for the State to retain the 5 per cent that was destined for the unions thereby giving the public sector a majority. But, as Joe Irvin remarked, the key question is whether – if we kept 51 per cent – any borrowing would count as part of the PSBR. JP wasn't all that concerned. He seems to have made up his mind to go with what was agreed. As we were leaving I remarked, 'It would be useful at least to see whatever options the Treasury has come up with. We wouldn't want to find out in two months' time that the Treasury had thought of an alternative, but hadn't told us because we didn't ask nicely.'

'Pah, it's fucking dancing on a pinhead,' snorted JP. And that seems to be the end of the matter.

Gus reported on the review of our press office. It appears it has a staff of 118 rather than the 40 or so that we originally supposed. Which makes it all the more inexplicable that we are unable to find anyone to turn out a decent speech. Many of them apparently concentrate on specialist magazines. Others are churning out pointless releases. Some are engaged in 'research' into goodness knows what. The consensus seems to be that we need to concentrate on putting out a few simple, common messages. The real difficulty, however, is that JP has a serious image problem. This 'Two Jags' business has taken hold and he just can't shake it off. Unfair, but the plain fact is that he just isn't taken seriously by the world at large and no press machine, however well-oiled, can cope with that.

To Number 10 for the reception on the eve of the Queen's Speech. The Man made only a brief appearance and told a lovely little story about the computer course he is taking. Students are apparently tested repeatedly to see how they are getting on and Tony kept failing. He noticed that the young man at the neighbouring terminal was getting extremely agitated.

'Am I making you nervous?' he asked.

'No,' the lad replied.

'What's the matter then?'

'It's because you keep failing these tests and I keep passing – and I've been unemployed for 18 months and you're the Prime Minister.'

Elliot Morley and I bent Home Office Minister Mike O'Brien's ear over fox-hunting. 'All this dithering is inflicting serious damage on the

Party,' said Elliot. Mike was unclear whether the inquiry recently announced by Jack is intended to kick the issue into the long grass or to resolve it.

Back to the office, where I worked until past midnight.

Thursday, 18 November

Environment was the theme of today's Queen's Speech debate so I spent most of the day at the House. We escaped lightly on air traffic control. Only Gavin Strang and Martin Salter made much of it. Gwyneth Dunwoody was particularly merciful. I remarked on this when I saw her afterwards in the taxi queue. 'It's going to get a lot rougher from now on,' she replied amiably.

The word is that we go ahead as planned. No more discussion of alternatives. A few concessions designed to offer reassurance on safety, but that's all. I am relaxed. The arguments about safety are tosh. There is no great principle at stake, unless you believe that state ownership is by definition safer than the private sector. In which case presumably you would prefer to travel Aeroflot than British Airways. The only issue is a practical one. And on that front, unless I am mistaken, things are calming down.

Friday, 19 November
Sunderland

A meeting with the Grove Cranes unions. The American owners have decided to close the plant with a loss of several hundred jobs 'We were better off under the Tories,' they whined. 'The government has done nothing for the north-east ...'

When we shook hands at the end only two of six could bring themselves to look me in the eye. I came away as depressed as they and the blackness stayed with me all day.

Monday, 22 November

To the Cabinet Office to see Ian McCartney. I put it to Ian that it is not credible for ministers to go around making speeches about reducing car use while being driven everywhere themselves. Junior ministers at least could do without cars and drivers – they could have access to the pool when necessary. Ian listened politely, but I had the impression that he was rather attached to his car.

We talked of the Great London Mayor Fiasco in which Ian has been closely involved. Ian said he thought The Man had been ill-advised to denounce Ken – because he may well end up having to work with him.

Swallow Hotels are to be taken over by Whitbread, which means Sunderland will lose the head office as well as the brewery. Exactly what everyone has been predicting since they got rid of Vaux. The directors have just taken the money and run. Derek Foster said that a businessman of his acquaintance had remarked to him that 'our entire manufacturing sector is up for sale'.

Thursday 25, November

To Swanwick to see the new state of the art Air Traffic Control Centre. An impressive space age concoction of glass and stone set tastefully among trees and lakes just outside Southampton. It is not yet up and running but the training has started. I was shown the computer screens which will track every incoming and outgoing flight, sector by sector. Terrifying.

Later, at Great Minster House in Horseferry Road, I sat in on a meeting between Michael Meacher and representatives of non-government organisations – ranging from Friends of the Earth to the National Farmers' Union. On Sunday Michael is off to Seattle for a big meeting of the World Trade Organisation and he wanted to sound them out before going. The NFU rep urged him to raise farm animal welfare. Now there's a sign of the times.

Afterwards I walked with Michael to Parliament. We talked of JP. I asked how he handled sophisticated negotiations like Kyoto.

According to Michael he can be formidable. 'I have seen him in a room full of people much cleverer than himself, drive things through by sheer, raw force.'

Jessica says she is having trouble persuading the drivers to carry me on the rare occasions when I need the use of the car, even when sharing with another minister. 'They see you as having done one of their colleagues out of a job.' The more I learn about it, the clearer it becomes that the government car service is run for the convenience of the drivers, not the government. They can be as pig-headed as they like, but I shall not give in to them. I heard today that another minister, Ross Cranston, has refused a car. The revolt is spreading.

Tuesday, 30 November

Ministers' meeting. The first 29 minutes – I timed him – were occupied by a monologue from JP. Mercifully, he was interrupted by a fire alarm about halfway through which brought some light relief, but he paused only to swear at the disembodied voice, and then ploughed on regardless. Gus Macdonald just stared blankly at the table. Keith Hill sat with his eyes raised to heaven, occasionally pulling a face to which I dared not respond since I was in JP's direct line of fire.

Question Time. The second of my short incumbency. Not a single one of the questions on the order paper related to my brief (I later discovered that this was because most of them had been planted by the parliamentary private secretaries and no one had thought to consult me). In the closing minutes, just when I appeared to have muddled through, Desmond Swayne, one of the Tory troublemakers, got up and asked, 'What about particulates?' That's all he said and then he sat down. I hadn't a clue what he was talking about. I opened my mouth, but no words came. The place suddenly went quiet. The Tories began poking fun. 'Help,' someone called. Then JP, whose interventions are not usually helpful, mumbled something about 'difficulties with Europe'. I duly repeated this with as much authority as I could muster, adding with a smile, 'The Hon. Member can rest assured that our finest minds are working on the problem.' A masterstroke. The House erupted. Betty Boothroyd beamed. Everyone was suddenly on my side. With one leap I was free. Once again disaster narrowly averted, but it is a dangerous way to live. The ice is very thin.

Despite his utter alienation from the regime, Tony Benn continues to be nice to me, poking only gentle fun whenever our paths cross. Today in the Tea Room he insisted on getting my cutlery, reciting as he did so, Gilbert and Sullivan:

> ... the privilege and pleasure
> That I treasure beyond measure
> Is to run on little errands for the Minister of State.

Wednesday, 1 December

To the weekly meeting of the parliamentary party to hear JP address the troops on the forthcoming Transport Bill. He spoke well, promising 'blood, sweat and tears' and giving a passionate defence of his – I should say 'our' – plans for air traffic. There was one hilarious moment when the following words escaped his lips, 'I've had more sex with Gordon ...'

'Success' was what he meant to say. However, he recovered well and was warmly applauded. Still no sign of this great rebellion we keep hearing about in the media – only one person, Mike Connarty, raised the subject.

Today I have addressed a conference of industrial water users in the City, spent an hour and a half in committee debating an Order on aircraft training regulations, addressed the all-party animal welfare group on the regulation of zoos and circuses and held a half-hour telephone discussion with EU Commissioner Neil Kinnock about how to defuse the row between Britain and the US over hush kits. None of these are subjects I know anything about. I live from hour to hour, never staying with any subject (except air traffic control) long enough to learn anything useful, praying that I can retain just sufficient information from the briefing to enable myself to bluff my way through without humiliation. As soon as it is no longer required, I press the mental delete button and the information is wiped from my mind, lost beyond recall. This is how it is every day. No wonder barristers flourish in this environment. I am beginning to lose my identity. Who am I?

Thursday, 2 December

'Prescott under siege', declares the front page headline in today's *Guardian* over a classic piece of synthetic journalism. 'Chaos', 'disarray', 'disaffection' – all the usual buzzwords so beloved of political journalists with nothing better to do. The report goes on to predict 'the biggest revolt of this parliament over air traffic control', although the only evidence for the proposition is quotes from Martin Salter and Gavin Strang, who are Usual Suspects. Poor JP, it is true he is sometimes his own worst enemy, but he does not deserve all the shit heaped upon him. First, because many of his so-called U-turns have been forced upon him by Number 10, which has had a failure of nerve when it comes to taking on the car lobby. Second, because he is up against problems for which there are no overnight solutions. To read the nonsense in the press anyone would think that traffic jams started in May 1997.

Friday, 3 December
Sunderland

Seventy mile an hour winds. The street is littered with debris. The big ash tree by our gate sways menacingly. One of the flower pots on the front steps was blown over and smashed.

I visited Camrex House, a doss house now taking asylum seekers. Men from disintegrated societies – Somalia, Togo, Afghanistan … Only about 60 so far, but under Jack Straw's plans for dispersal, Sunderland is due to receive a thousand by April. Little or nothing has been done to prepare for them. Many speak no English and they are very vulnerable. Disaster looms unless we get organised. I undertook to put pressure on both the local authority and the Refugee Council.

Saturday, 4 December

Ran into a boilermaker who was made redundant from the shipyards. To my pleasant surprise, he was upbeat. His daughter, he says, is £12 a week better off as a result of Gordon's tax credits and he cites a single mother who has gained more than £20.

Monday, 6 December
Brixton Road

The pear tree in our London garden has gone. It disappeared one day last week. It was 150 years old and 80 feet high and all that is left is a sawn off stump about six inches above the ground. True, it was dead and would have had to be removed anyway, but I had intended to cut it at a height of six feet and grow a clematis up the stump. I rang the neighbours. Jeremy knew nothing, but Katrina from the top flat said that men from Lambeth Council called last Monday and said they were going to cut it down. She did not object, assuming that Jeremy or I had made the arrangement. Why should Lambeth Council cut down our tree? I can only think that they believe they own our house. They don't, of course. Theirs is the one next door. Several years back they put up scaffolding and decorated our house. Twice I told the decorators that they had got the wrong house, but they wouldn't listen.

Tuesday, 7 December

The JP crisis is mounting. The Tories have called a debate for tomorrow. Effectively it is a motion of no confidence in JP, who is cutting short his trip to India and travelling back overnight to reply. The poor fellow will be exhausted. 'We have to save John from himself,' Hilary Armstrong whispered to me in the Tea Room. 'He must be persuaded to lie low in the New Year. No interviews, no speeches. He must leave all that to Gus Macdonald and concentrate instead on preparing for the next public spending round.'

Already there are signs that Downing Street is launching a 'Save JP' offensive. On 13 December he is to make a major speech at the ICA in the Mall, relaunching our transport strategy to focus on some clearly defined, achievable targets. A note has come round outlining tactics. It says that JP will walk the short distance from his apartment in Admiralty House to the ICA accompanied by a pool television camera. He will depart immediately after delivering his speech. Questions will be left for Gus to answer. JP will give no interviews. The unmistakable hand of Alastair Campbell. The question is, of course, will JP listen to anything anyone is telling him?

Wednesday, 8 December

The return of JP. He arrived in the early hours, taking care to travel from Heathrow by public transport, television cameras dogging his every step. Gus and I were upstairs, appearing before Gwyneth Dunwoody's select committee, so I missed the debate. By most accounts it was a triumph. Redwood, who had risen from his sickbed for the occasion, performed poorly. JP, by contrast, was on good form. The crisis is over for the time being. The hacks will have to find somebody else to hound.

To dinner at the Congress Club in Great Peter Street for a stimulating discussion about waste disposal. Most of the guests were businessmen involved with recycling. The gist of their message was that it cannot be left to the market. Unless we pull our finger out, we stand no chance of meeting the EC recycling targets to which we have signed up. They wanted more green taxes, laws to make producers take responsibility for their own waste, a tougher government procurement policy and state intervention to ensure a stable market for recycled goods. Overall, they want a regulator to drive progress. All very reasonable, but not a message the deregulators in Downing Street or the Department of Trade and Industry will want to hear. Perhaps this is an area where I can make a difference. We have to break out of the pointless cycle of consultation documents, task forces and working parties in which we are presently trapped.

Monday, 13 December

I set out from Sunderland to address the OFWAT Christmas knees-up in Birmingham. My fifth dispatch to Birmingham in a month. As ever, the omens were inauspicious. The sky was raining grey slush. Every horizon dominated by prefabricated concrete. My, how the Brummies love their concrete.

I had been given the usual 15-minute speech, typed triple-spaced, to read to the assembly. Had I been addressing a crowd of men in suits it would have been fine, but this was the office party. Everyone down to the typing pool and the cleaners was there and most were utterly uninterested in the minutiae of water regulation. They had come for the karaoke and the dancing, not for a ministerial speech. Not until I was about five paragraphs in, did it dawn on me that all that was required was to thank them for their hard work, wish them merry Christmas and sit down. On I ploughed, my morale sinking at their palpable indifference. Even my feeble attempts at humour fell on stony ground. Someone on the top table was whispering to his neighbour, no doubt about my inadequacy. Why on earth invite me – or rather Michael Meacher (for this was yet another of his hand-me-downs)? The only consolation was that Ian Byatt's speech received no better reception, and he was playing on home ground.

Departed for London feeling down. Seven hours of travelling only to show myself up in front of 200 people.

The papers are full of JP's alleged demotion and Gus Macdonald's alleged elevation. This latest round of hysteria has apparently been triggered by a piece in yesterday's *Sunday Times*. In truth, all that has changed is that the hacks have finally caught up with what happened in July. Gus has indeed been sent in to get a grip on transport – and by implication persuade JP to take a back seat, but that happened five months ago. The hacks are really falling over themselves to do down JP and, as ever, the *Guardian* is the worst. 'Rail fares shock for Prescott', shouts today's main headline over a story that ordinarily would have merited a few paragraphs on an inside page.

Tuesday, 14 December

Gus tells me that JP was, as ever, the author of his latest misfortune. Apparently he got wind that the *Sunday Times* was intending to run something on his son's property dealings and, no doubt without consulting anyone, rang to offer what he thought was a better story in the hope that the hacks would be deflected. Which, of course, they weren't. Result: the worst of both worlds. The story about the prodigal son duly appeared on page five and the front was dominated by the news that Gus is to take charge of transport. Once again, JP has set himself up. An exact repeat of Bournemouth three months ago. This time he has chosen the day of his big speech at the ICA which was supposed to relaunch our transport policy.

Somehow, says Gus, we have to persuade JP to stop interfering. Gus has talked to Richard Mottram who agrees that JP's office should cease monitoring every press release and details of every petty little decision that ought properly to be the job of us underlings. JP's job should be strategy, something woefully lacking in the Department. 'Look at Gordon Brown,' says Gus. 'He disappears for months at a time and only goes public when he has something important to announce.' Gus added that, contrary to rumour, neither Downing Street nor Gordon are fanning the flames. 'Alastair and Gordon have been brilliant.'

He said that JP is very down. 'I tried to cheer him up by saying it will all blow over, but he thinks his credibility is damaged beyond repair.'

So do I. The shadows are lengthening. Most people like John and want him to do well. Among those who know him, there is a general recognition that, under that volcanic exterior, there lurks a decent human being. At the same time there is a barely concealed contempt among both civil servants and ministers for his absolute lack of management skills, his inability to see wood for trees and his flat refusal to listen to anything anyone is telling him. Deep down I am sure he, too, realises that he is out of his depth. That accounts for the tantrums. It was the same with Neil Kinnock, who is much nicer now he is back in a job he can do.

Half an hour with Nick Raynsford. Again, the talk was of the latest JP crisis. For weeks Nick has been vainly seeking an audience to discuss the housing Green Paper and reducing VAT on brownfield developments – both matters which need urgent decisions. 'The man is immersed in trivia, blowing his top left, right and centre.' Nick went on to describe how at the weekend, at the Eastbourne policy forum, JP had needlessly alienated a roomful of people, all with goodwill towards him, by storming out of a transport workshop and retiring in a sulk to his hotel. Says Nick, who usually errs on the side of caution, 'As soon as the election is over, he'll be gone.'

Wednesday, 15 December

There has been a U-turn on the Christmas boat trip we were all supposed to be going on tomorrow. Some weeks ago a memo came round from JP ordering ministers to stump up £75 a head towards the cost of a party on board a Thames cruiser for the private office staff. The note made clear that we were all expected to attend. However, Hilary Armstrong has persuaded JP that in the current climate it would not be a good idea. He had apparently forgotten about 'The Ship of Shame', a similar enterprise which he organised in Opposition and which made the front page of the *Sun*. Tomorrow's trip had the smell of doom about it from the outset – the boat hired is a sister ship of the *Marchioness*. Anyway, thanks to Hilary, common sense has prevailed. The party will go ahead, but without ministers. Relief all round.

Friday, 17 December
Sunderland

Ngoc reports the following exchange with Sarah. 'Mum, I know all about Santa Claus.'

Her friend Rachel told her, although Sarah has been suspicious since last year when Santa Claus foolishly wrote her a note using a word processor with a typeface suspiciously like mine.

Ngoc neither confirmed nor denied. Sarah did not press the point since she is anxious not to jeopardise the prospect of this year's presents. She did, however, make Sarah promise not to share her suspicions with Emma.

Sunday, 19 December

Shaun Woodward has crossed the floor. I am astounded. He had his differences with the Tories – notably on tolerance of gays – but he never struck me, or anyone else, as terminally disaffected. On the occasions – the last being two weeks ago – that I have found myself debating with him, he was aggressive and unpleasant. There is speculation that he has done some kind of deal with our masters, but I don't believe that. The cynical view in the Tea Room is that he will soon be given a job, but that seems unlikely. The best he can hope for, and not until after the election, is a peerage. It's not as though we need him. In any case, the honourable course would have been to resign his seat. How anyone can justify being elected for one party and then simply switch to another without benefit of an election is beyond me. What's more it discredits the political process. Were I suddenly to wake one morning and decide I was a Tory, I wouldn't dare show my face in Sunderland again, let alone wish to go on representing it.

Monday, 20 December

Gus Macdonald was on the radio this morning enunciating our new line on the car, which is that we are not against cars, simply in favour of making more sensible use of them. He even went so far as to suggest, gratuitously, that increased car ownership was to be welcomed as an inevitable symptom of prosperity. On the same basis, everyone in China (where cars are killing an unbelievable 70,000 people a year) should have one. My own view remains that we would all be better off on bicycles.

Tuesday, 21 December

A meeting of transport ministers at which Gus reported that our 'repositioning' on cars was going well, although he had yet to discuss the subject with Michael Meacher, who might not share his enthusiasm since it was his job to cope with the pollution. In truth, I don't suppose it matters much what spin we put on our transport policy, as long as we continue to pump money into buses and light railways. All the signs are that there is some big money in the pipeline.

Keith Hill and I amused ourselves over lunch compiling a New Labour lexicon. We came up with the following: pathfinders, beacons, win-win, stakeholders, opportunities as well as challenges, joined-up government, partnership, best value. And, of course, 'new' as in New Partnership Company.

These words increasingly crop up in official submissions. I am forever deleting them from letters and draft speeches. Jessica says that in John Major's time official papers were full of cricketing analogies, but these have largely disappeared in favour of the new claptrap. One often hears it trotted out at Question Time. I am in awe of the facility with which it rolls off the tongues of some of our more flexible colleagues. Officials, of course, have a language of their own. 'Taking forward' is one of my favourites. It usually means doing nothing.

'I hope you are not writing a diary …' Jessica remarked this afternoon, watching me scribbling in one of the little red notebooks that I carry everywhere. I neither confirmed nor denied.

I was briefed by a group of men in suits about our plans for coping with environmental emergencies. The one who did most of the talking was the red-faced, puffed-up little fellow who came to see me about classified material soon after I was appointed. I asked what was the most likely cause of disaster and the answer, unsurprisingly, was nuclear power stations. I was shown a map of Europe on which they were all marked and several that are judged particularly unreliable were double-ringed. One was Chernobyl, one in Bulgaria and a third that was too far east to be included on the map, although there was a mark in the margin. However, an official added that it was the French who worried him most. Their nearest nuclear power station was only thirty miles away and they wouldn't necessarily tell us if they were in trouble.

Thursday, 23 December
Sunderland

A call first thing this morning to say that Uncle Brian is dead. I feel bad about not having gone to see him. No one from the family was present when he died, except of course that his 'family' were the nuns who looked after him so well and they were there. I hope when I die those who love me will come to say goodbye. Eerily, when I got to the office two hours later there was a Christmas card from Brian waiting. It must have been written even as he was dying. In a slightly shaky hand he had written, 'Very many thanks for the best card I have received. I have never seen the Crypt* and find it quite lovely ... I hope you will be able to come and see me again soon.'

The first batch of refugees to be dispersed to Sunderland under Jack's new asylum regime arrived yesterday. The council is arranging for them to be housed in empty private properties. A dozen Albanian Kosovars and Moldovans. Young, single males. One of the Albanians, the only English-speaker, said he came from the Serb-dominated town of Mitrovice and had fled to Macedonia at the start of the war. He arrived in England a few days ago, having paid 4,000 marks for a ride in a lorry. No one can blame these people for wanting to seek a new life in the West. In their place I would probably do the same, but it is hard to see how most of them can claim – now at any rate – to be fleeing a well-founded fear of persecution. I guess most are going to be sent back eventually. The sad thing is they have burned up their life savings to get here.

---

*Brian Foley, RC Bishop of Lancaster, 1962–85; the House of Commons Christmas card depicted the crypt chapel of the Palace of Westminster.

Friday, 31 December
Brixton Road

Spent an hour raking up sawdust and clearing twigs from the lawn where Lambeth Council mistakenly cut down my pear tree.

CHAPTER TWO

2000

Saturday, 1 January 2000
Brixton Road

A new century. My grandchildren, who I hope to survive long enough to meet, will live into the twenty-second century. What kind of world will they inherit? The planet is in a worse state now than at any time in my life. Beyond fortress Europe and North America much of the world is in meltdown. In Africa there are countries where all civilised life has collapsed. Afghanistan has returned to barbarism. The Balkans are in turmoil and even as I write the Russians are bombing Chechnya into the stone age. Already refugees from the chaos are placing strains on the political and social fabric of the developed world that may in due course become unbearable. We should not imagine as we sit smug behind our increasingly fortified frontiers that our civilisation can survive unscathed.

Our main problem, of course, is not other people's wars. It is that we have invented an economic system which is consuming the resources of the planet as if there were no tomorrow – and there well might not be unless we change our ways. In the United States, the home of the world's most voracious consumers, there is no sign at all that the political process is capable of persuading – or indeed has any desire to persuade – citizens to adopt a sustainable lifestyle. All over the democratic world, politicians increasingly follow rather than lead. And even were an ecological disaster to occur (perhaps it has already begun) the price will be paid by those least responsible and least capable of protecting themselves. Indeed the consumers of the developed world may not even notice. To crown all, the emerging economies of Asia are falling over themselves to emulate the mistakes that we have made. Indeed they insist that it is their right to do so.

Maybe, just maybe, this will be the century in which we learn to reduce, reuse and recycle our waste, develop benign sources of food and energy and stop burning up the ozone layer. Maybe Europe will lead the way and others will follow. Who knows, there ought to be money to be made out of going green, in which case capitalism will enjoy a new lease of life.

Or maybe it is too late. Maybe we have failed to heed the warning signs and a long, slow slide towards ruin beckons. By the end of my life the signals should be clearer.

As for me, I am entering a period of unprecedented obscurity. Hopefully my eclipse will be temporary. Not that I wish to be famous, only useful. At the moment I am no use whatever. I shall cling on in government until the election and, if nothing comes up, I shall return to the backbenches and try to pick up where I left off. One of my difficulties is that I am not very good at pretending. I have let far too many people know about my low opinion of my current office and, if I'm not careful, it could tell against me. Gradually, inevitably, perceptibly, the little store of goodwill and credibility that I have so painstakingly accumulated is eroding.

Tuesday, 4 January

Jessica rings to ask if I will stand by for an interview with the Radio Four programme *You and Yours* about the safety of Cuban airlines. They are really after Gus Macdonald, but he is indisposed. I agree. Briefing notes are faxed. Arrangements are made to open up the local BBC studio. Then comes word that the interview is off. Vetoed by JP apparently. So much for having turned over a new leaf. The JP of the new millennium is unchanged. Still interfering in every pettifogging little decision. Nothing too trivial to command his attention ... except, of course, the big picture.

Thursday, 6 January
Sunderland

With Joyce Quin for a walk in the Cleveland Hills. We drove to Nether Stilton and walked in bright sunshine along the old drove road, about ten miles in all. Joyce has been badly used by the regime. Every year a new department. In opposition she was our Europe spokesman, a job for which she was eminently qualified, whereupon as soon as we were elected she was made Minister of Prisons and the Europe job was given to Doug Henderson, who was equally unqualified. After a year, it became clear that this wasn't working out so Joyce was moved to the Foreign Office to do the job for which she was the obvious candidate all along. A year later, she was brushed aside to make room for Geoff Hoon. He stayed only three months to be replaced by Keith Vaz, who has no obvious qualifications. Now Joyce is at agriculture, about which she knows nothing. 'I feel totally demotivated,' she says.

Tuesday, 11 January

One of those days when I wish I could change jobs with the man collecting litter in St James's Park. Within the next 24 hours I have to reply to debates on Gatwick, sewage treatment in Thanet and the depredations of rent officers in Stockport. In addition, I have been allocated questions on acid rain in Wales, traffic congestion, empty housing in Burnley and stamp duty on houses in Torbay. Only the empty housing comes within my remit. Everything else is an adventure.

Keith Hill was the unexpected star of Question Time. Brazen, witty, he looked and sounded as though he was positively enjoying himself. With a flick of the wrist he brushed aside Tory spokesman John Redwood, labelling him – to general merriment – 'the *Il Duce* of the Home Counties'. As for me, I scraped by without incident. The relief when it was over was comparable only to that I used to feel as an insecure adolescent, emerging from the Church of the Immaculate Conception, having confessed 'impure thoughts' to Canon Wilson.

Wednesday, 12 January

Clare Short, resplendent in a handsome red jacket, addressed the parliamentary party. Now here is someone who has a job she patently enjoys. Indeed what better job has a Labour government to offer than redistributing the wealth of the middle classes to the poorest people in the world? She was passionate, committed, optimistic – and she has a good story to tell, especially on debt relief where we are leading the way. By 2020, she says, there will be nine billion people on the planet. After that there is a chance of stabilising the world population, but only if we can educate women so that they can take control of their lives. She was very critical of the EU, through which we are obliged to spend a third of our aid budget. 'A tragedy,' she said. 'Very inefficient. Even when committed the money can't be spent and much of what is spent goes on political gestures rather than to help the poorest.'

An American senator came to see me, accompanied by a blazered goon from the embassy with dead eyes and a square jaw. He came to talk about EU plans to insist on quieter planes, which has implications for the American aviation industry. 'Hey, Chris,' he greeted me as though we were old friends, but appearances can deceive. He was all business. I patiently explained that threatening to ban Concorde wouldn't cut much ice with the European Parliament since no one, apart from the Brits and the French, cares about Concorde. Undaunted, he kept referring to the need for 'leverage'. I just managed to restrain myself from the suggestion that they send B52s to take out Strasbourg.

Friday, 14 January

A call from Ian Dewhirst to say that he is shutting his clothes factory at Peterlee. Another 800 jobs down the pan. He explained that it was all down to the decision by Marks & Spencer to source offshore. He claimed that his three Sunderland factories, also heavily dependent on M&S, are safe for the foreseeable future, but he didn't sound very confident.

Saturday, 15 January
Sunderland

A government car arrived at St Bede's Terrace this morning with a red box. The first ever to cross the threshold. It contained a briefing for the committee stage of the Transport Bill, which starts on Tuesday. Jessica thought I ought to read it on the train down and, reluctantly, I conceded. I opened the box and sent it away immediately. It wasn't in the house for more than five minutes. Red boxes at weekends must not become a habit.

Monday, 17 January

To London on an early train in order to be on time for the first meeting on the Transport Bill, which looms like a vast black cloud over the next three months. The first 90 clauses, on which I am expected to bear the brunt, are on air traffic control. I can't bring myself to read more than a few clauses at a time and much of it seems gobbledegook.

Today I took a real decision. I agreed to place a 10 mile-per-hour speed limit on Lake Windermere, thereby outlawing power-boating. A tiny victory for civilisation over barbarism. Unbelievably it is seven and a half years since the matter was first referred to the Department. Even now the by-law which I have ratified won't come into force for another five years. The power boaters are such a mighty vested interest that they have everyone running scared. For months officials have been warning that I must not utter a word on the subject, for fear of inviting judicial review. Even now it will be another three weeks before the decision can be made public, to allow yet more time for lawyers to crawl through the small print. But one day – five years hence – I shall be able to look out over the tranquillity of Windermere, *sans* power boats, and say, 'I did that.'

Tuesday, 18 January

Alan Haselhurst, a very civilised Tory, came to see me about Stansted Airport. He says it's growing like Topsy and blighting the lives of his constituents. The noise is intolerable, roads jammed, commuter rail services disrupted. Estimates of the likely number of passengers are continually being revised upwards. Already there is talk of a second terminal and another runway. Alan wanted to know the government's attitude if the local authority tried to enforce the 15 million passenger limit which he expects to be breached before long. A good question. Sooner or later politicians are going to have to summon the courage to put an end to this madness (Ryanair are presently offering flights to Dublin for £4 return, plus taxes). Do we just accept exponential growth and the massive blight that comes with it? Or do we draw a line? And if so, where? Needless to say, the brief I was given was equivocal.

Wednesday, 19 January

To a posh hotel in Mayfair to address 300 deeply sceptical councillors and officials on the wonders of 'Best Value', the latest New Labour local government wheeze. The speech, one of Hilary Armstrong's hand-me-downs, was abysmal. The phrase 'Best Value' featured 43 times without any clear explanation of what it was about – I bet the hapless official who wrote it didn't know either. I was simply expected to stand and chant it like a Maoist slogan. I sent it back three times and by the last draft it was just about deliverable.

A briefing on the Transport Bill. Nick Raynsford, who is completely new to the subject, presided and I watched in awe as he picked his way with apparent ease through the maze of clauses and sub-clauses, showering officials with intelligent questions. I did my best to seem on top of it, but in truth it's all way above my head. My eyes glaze over when I look at the Bill whereas Nick's light up. Thus far I have survived mainly by bluff and good fortune, but it can't last. Any day now my cover will be blown. Afterwards, I remarked to Jessica how well-informed Nick seemed. 'He has been reading the Bill since before Christmas,' she said. Adding acidly, 'Any minister involved in the Bill would read it.' Jessica, of course, knows that until last Friday my copy of the Bill was lodged, untouched, in the middle drawer of my desk. My strategy is to keep just a few clauses ahead of the committee. I'm not capable of absorbing any more.

Friday, 21 January

Bad news. Jessica called to say that the Countryside Bill is now expected to be consecutive and not concurrent with the Transport Bill. Now they are clearing my diary for May and it could go on into June. How I wish I had never taken this loathsome job.

Monday, 24 January

Among the letters set before me for signature today were two declining lunch invitations from journalists on *The Times* and *Telegraph*. The invitations were dated 9 September and 26 October.

'Have I seen these before?'

'Er, no, Minister.'

'Why not?'

'There's a block on them. All invitations from journalists have to be cleared with the Deputy Prime Minister's office.'

So, I am not even allowed to decide who I have lunch with.

Tuesday, 25 January

An interesting little exchange about performance targets, at this morning's ministerial meeting, while JP was out of the room. Richard Mottram, the Permanent Secretary, complained of 'a naive, pseudo-management tendency' at the Treasury. 'All we are doing by setting unrealistic targets is setting ourselves up to fail. They take no account of politics.' Why set yourself up to be bashed? A particularly sore point in our department since 40 per cent of targets dreamed up elsewhere fall to us to deliver. Apparently, we are pleading with the Treasury not to set us any more but, according to Richard, 'It's a dialogue of the deaf.'

'In business,' said Gus Macdonald, 'targets are private and aspirational. You don't announce them to the world.'

A difficult morning on the Transport Bill. The Tories unleashed Portillo, who asked lots of difficult questions and stirred up confusion. Poor Keith Hill responded manfully, but was clearly struggling. I just sat there thanking heaven it was Keith rather than I who was in the firing line and dreading my turn. I tell myself that I am not intellectually inadequate, it's just that I can't be bothered to come to grips with things that don't interest me. Comforting though such thoughts are I fear they may not be the whole truth. What little repute I have accumulated over the years has been achieved by only opening my mouth when I know what I am talking about. Suddenly, I find myself required to open my mouth on subjects about which I know nothing and I am simply not up to it.

Wednesday, 26 January
3.40 a.m.

We are discussing a bizarre little piece of legislation designed to enable members of the Dáil to stand for the Northern Ireland Assembly and vice versa. No one seems to know where it came from or why it was so urgent. The general view is that it is another sop to Sinn Fein, and the Unionists, predictably, are up in arms. There is also some irritation on our side since patience with Sinn Fein is wearing thin. They are being given just about everything they asked for, but as yet there is no sign of the IRA handing over a single weapon.

The Unionists, along with a tiny band of backbench Tories, have mounted a filibuster. Our whips seem prepared to let it run on even if we lose tomorrow's business. At the last division we had a majority of 220 with only 13 in the opposition lobby. I go in search of the pairing whip, Tommy McAvoy, who as ever seems to be deriving sadistic pleasure from keeping us up all night. I find him, red braces stretched across his large belly, slumped in an armchair in front of a television. The programme, appropriately, is about Stalin. We had the following exchange.

'Tommy, do we really need to win every division by a majority of 200-plus?'

'Can you guarantee that the Tories won't suddenly turn up and vote?'

'They will if we keep this nonsense going until they return refreshed from a night's sleep.'

'This is class war, Chris.'

'In case you haven't noticed, Tommy, the other class is at home in bed.'

It cut no ice. We had to get the business through and that was that. No matter if half the government are too worn out to do any governing. We march until we drop. That is how things have always been done in this asylum and, if the likes of Tommy McAvoy continue to have their way, this is how it will be for ever.

4.30 a.m.

Keith Bradley, one of the more merciful whips, sends me home. Left a message with the office cancelling my first two appointments and caught a taxi back to the flat. It was 5 a.m. before I crawled into bed.

Thursday, 27 January
Brixton Road

Jessica rang. 'Bad news. The Department of Trade and Industry are insisting that we have a minister on the Utilities Bill. Michael Meacher has refused, so that means you.' Like hell it does. I am already on two Bills which will last into June. How can I possibly cope with a third? If necessary I shall appeal directly to JP.

Friday, 28 January
St Bede's Terrace, Sunderland

A car abandoned outside Millie Brodie's house was torched by yobs last night.

Customers at tonight's surgery included a deranged minor hoodlum who has been stalking me for eight years. Just when I think he has gone away, he reappears. 'You must sort out my problem,' he says, fixing me with his dead eyes, 'or I'll keep coming back. I'll never go away.' Home to find that the main item on the news is that Nigel Jones, the Liberal MP for Bath, has been attacked in his surgery by a madman with a machete. His agent, who intervened to save him, is dead.

Monday, 31 January

The news this morning is that Peter Kilfoyle has resigned from his lowly post at the Ministry of Defence on the grounds that the job is not the best use of his talents. I know exactly how he feels.

The papers are full of stories about revolting farmers. They are demanding another half-billion in subsidies on top of the three and a half billion they already get. Elliot Morley and Ian Cawsey were on the train this morning. Elliot says pig farmers are the only ones with a case for help, but the Treasury is unsympathetic. The Man is going to the conference of the National Farmers' Union this week and Elliot reckons they will boo him. 'It's time to start confronting the farmers, not appeasing them,' I said and Elliot agreed. Ian, who has a large rural constituency, says the only letters he has ever received suggesting that the farmers should be given more money come from farmers.

Tuesday, 1 February

I got off lightly at the Transport Bill today. Nick and Keith did most of the work and by the time my turn came the Tories had lost interest. Portillo disappeared halfway through the morning, saying he was off to Alan Clark's memorial service and later we heard that he had been appointed Shadow Chancellor. Seeing him at close quarters has been fascinating. It is hard to see why he arouses such fear and loathing. He is always calm, with a ready smile and a nice, easy debating style. Only when sitting scribbling and concentrating hard do his lips curl downwards and one gets the impression that he could be ruthless. During the morning I was called out to take a call from Michael Meacher. Would I go on the Utilities Bill?

'But I'm already on two Bills. Isn't there anyone else'?

'No.'

There is, of course. Michael could do it himself. Here is someone else whose charm belies a certain ruthlessness.

Wednesday, 2 February

To the parliamentary party meeting for a pep talk from The Man, who looked remarkably cheerful considering the slings and arrows raining down upon him these last few weeks. As ever, he was far-sighted, relaxed, confident. The message was upbeat. We are in a better position than any previous Labour government. The economy is strong. We are building up the public services. Everything will be okay, if only we keep our nerve. His best line was 'MPs must be ambassadors for the Labour Party, not shop stewards for every grievance.' He was well received. No one was openly hostile. A couple of calls for uprating the minimum wage. Dennis Skinner wanted more redistribution in the next budget, but even he was restrained. (Although he would never admit it, I suspect Dennis is an admirer of The Man.) Someone else called for a substantial pensions increase. The nearest anyone came to criticism was a mild expression of concern from David Winnick about control freakery.

At lunchtime, in the queue in the cafeteria, Don Brind took me aside and offered what he called a comradely warning. He had been present at a meeting with JP at which someone had remarked of me, 'He doesn't read his briefs.' JP had responded, 'We can't have that. I'll talk to him.' Needless to say he hasn't. Don was unable to identify the traitor, beyond saying that he wasn't a minister and that he didn't think he was a civil servant. The culprit was probably one of the legion of spinners who plague the regime.

Monday, 7 February

A 34-year-old Frenchman has been appointed to rescue the Millennium Dome. He is alleged to be the saviour of Disneyland Paris, but a story in today's *Times* says he was only one of 11 vice-presidents. In any case, do we want the dome Disneyfied? It is supposed to be a symbol of new, young Blairite Britain and ends up being run by a Frenchman. If it fails, I fear it will become a symbol of all that is alleged to be wrong with New Labour.

Tuesday, 8 February

A brief about Archie Norman's business interests was circulated for use at Questions this afternoon. JP demurred. 'I'm not in favour of all this mud-slinging. It demeans politics.' Yet more evidence that underneath that fearsome exterior there lurks a fundamentally decent human being.

Our little secret is out. Until now we have been assuring the world that the state will retain a 49 per cent stake in air traffic control. Now here we are on the Bill committee moving an amendment that allows the strategic partner to sell shares to the point where the state holding is diluted to a mere 25 per cent. There had been talk of omitting any reference to dilution for fear of muddying the waters, but the lawyers advised that it must be on the face of the Bill. The Tories seized on it immediately. Our lot, who had been forewarned, kept quiet – apart from Gavin Strang, who protested mildly. Happily it was left to Nick Raynsford to supply the justification, which he did with his customary panache. The line is that there is no intention to float the company. It's just a fall-back in case of emergencies. Nick did most of the work today. I wasn't called upon to utter a single word, which meant that the time passed slowly.

Jessica had an interesting little spat with the government car service. We occasionally hire a car to transport boxes from the Department to my room in the House. We pay by the hour for what is a journey of no more than 15 minutes, although the driver is also expected to deliver them to my room on Upper Corridor South. Today unusually, there were four boxes, which meant two trips from the Members' entrance to my room. The car service tried to insist that we hire two cars. Drivers, they said, could only handle two boxes at a time. Have you ever heard such nonsense? It's the London print unions all over again. Only when Jessica rang the chief executive did common sense prevail.

Thursday, 10 February

My sojourn on the Transport Bill is over. Suddenly, and unexpectedly, Nick Raynsford relented on his earlier insistence that I stay put until the bitter end. We were drifting towards a situation where, by some point in March, I was likely to be on three Bills simultaneously and until now none of my many superiors were willing to grasp the nettle. Bob Ainsworth, the Transport Bill whip, who has been sympathetic all along, said yesterday, 'The Tories will murder you if you only show up for the water clauses of the Utilities Bill' (which did wonders for my morale). Now the knot is cut. Next week I will put in an appearance at Utilities, although it will be some time before I have to open my mouth. From here on in, the Transport Bill is on congestion charging, local transport plans and a strategic rail authority. Keith Hill is much happier. '*Terra firma*,' he has written in red ink at the top of Part II. It isn't *terra firma* to me. Just another bog. Thank goodness I'm free of it.

Monday, 14 February

To committee room six in the Lords, for a meeting of ministers to discuss the Department's submission for the coming spending round. JP, beneath a huge picture of Mr Gladstone and his cabinet, presides. He takes each of the four ministers of state in turn and invites them to justify their bids. This is JP at his best. Acting for once like a chief executive, rather than just letting off steam. Short sensible questions, no waffle (at least not much), on top of his brief. I begin to see him in a different light.

'Have you noticed,' I whispered to our esteemed Permanent Secretary, Richard Mottram, 'that Gladstone managed to run the British empire with a Cabinet of just 14 members?' He had.

We were kept voting until after 1 a.m. To bed at 2 a.m. I have to be up again at 7.

Wednesday, 16 February

An hour discussing night flights with officials. This is an issue on which progress ought to be possible, given that only 16 flights are involved. The officials recited a long list of reasons why nothing could be done about anything. The more they went on, the more I realised how the aviation industry has had successive governments twisted around its little finger. The assumption seems to be that airports will carry on growing indefinitely, however unbearable life becomes for those who live under the flight paths. Sooner or later politicians are going to have to pluck up the courage to say no, although I see little sign of it so far. As regards night flights, it occurs to me that there may just be a small window of opportunity when the inspector gives the go-ahead (as I am sure he will) for a fifth terminal. At the very least, permission should be made conditional on ending night flights.

Thursday, 17 February

A rumour that the Countryside Bill could be held over or even abandoned. The Man is said to be anxious not to upset the landowners. 'Attitudes at the centre seem to be hardening,' said a note which crossed my desk the other day. Michael Meacher is fuming. This is his flagship. 'When will a decision be made?' I inquired of Ann Taylor.

'This weekend,' she replied.

Sunday, 20 February
Sunderland

Frank Dobson has narrowly beaten Ken Livingstone for the London mayoral nomination. A result that stinks. Frank owes his 'victory' entirely to the machine. He will be badly damaged by this. Come the poll many of our people will stay at home. You can fix the party, but you can't fix the electorate.

Monday, 21 February

A visit from Lord Sainsbury, the only billionaire of my acquaintance. A pleasant, down-to-earth man, completely without airs and utterly above the rat race. The purpose of his visit was to extract a commitment that we would use at least 2.5 per cent of our research budget to boost small and medium-sized companies. The official advice was 'resist' and I was given a long list of reasons why it wasn't a good idea. I could see the meeting ending badly, but when I pointed out that about 20 per cent of our research budget already goes to small companies, he simply came out with his hands up. There was some quibbling about definitions, but the meeting ended amicably and he appeared to go away happy.

The talk of the Tea Room is whether or not Ken Livingstone will stand as an independent. The *Standard,* under the heading 'Go For It Ken', is running a poll saying he would win by a mile.

Tuesday, 22 February

Lunch in the Millbank Room with Bruce Grocott. He asked about air traffic control. Would I have opposed it, if I were still on the backbenches (Jack Straw asked the same question the other day)? I gave my usual spiel. No ideological objection, safety arguments bogus. Adding, however, that it would save everyone a lot of trouble if Gordon simply wrote out a cheque. Bruce is a dissenter on air traffic control. I notice he drummed his fingers on the table as I attempted to justify our plans.

Friday, 25 February
Sunderland

To Pennywell, where Denise Barna gave me a tour of the shiny new community centre, complete with doctor's surgery, crèche and a little café. It also provides a base for successful parenting courses and much else besides. Great things are happening in Pennywell. No more refugees appear at my surgeries begging to be evacuated. For the first time I can recall there is an air of optimism. Just one little speck on the horizon, however: who is going to pay for all this in four years' time when the regeneration money runs out?

A call from Jessica (who is soon to leave me). 'Good news and bad news.' The good news is that the water clauses are being withdrawn from the Utilities Bill. The bad news is that I am under no circumstances to admit that it has anything to do with the government's grossly overloaded legislative programme. Oh dear, I am hopeless at dissembling.

Monday, 28 February

To Admiralty House, in the company of about 25 junior and middle-rank ministers for another of the informal lunches organised by the Cabinet Office. This one addressed by Jonathan Powell, a member of the magic circle. We sit in stiff-backed chairs in the music room. Above the mantelpiece a huge naval canvas depicting *The Attack on Martinique*. Elsewhere, oils of Australia in all its primeval glory, by John Webber, the draughtsman on Captain Cook's third expedition.

Powell, curly-haired, fluent, aloof (never quite looking us in the eye), offered what he called 'the view from Number 10'. He was unapologetic about the strengthening of the centre, saying that weakness had been one of the chief faults of John Major's government. He listed four main aims: on policy, to be proactive rather than reactive; better co-ordination; better integration between departments; efficient communication. The Number 10 apparatus has grown, he said, but it isn't going to get any bigger ('or else we will lose the ability to move fast'). He cited the German chancellery and the White House as examples of large, unwieldy bureaucracies that had grown up around the head of government.

Questions warmed up slowly. We treated him warily. This was, after all, a man who could make or break careers. Nick Raynsford talked of 'unhappiness at control freakery' to which Powell retorted that this government had given away more power than any other. 'Trying to be competent,' he added, 'was not control freakery.' Angela Eagle said that the recent upset over the London mayoral nomination had squandered a lot of good will. There was a lot of waffle about the need for better communication. When my turn came I asked, 'Have any lessons been learned from our recent difficulties in Scotland, Wales and now London* and, if so, what are they?' Lessons had indeed

---

*In Scotland the veteran Labour MP Dennis Canavan was excluded from the shortlist for his own seat in the Scottish Parliament. He stood as an Independent

been learned, asserted Jonathan, but when it came to saying what they were he was surprisingly reticent.

'You beast,' he said cheerfully as we were leaving.

'So what were the lessons that you couldn't talk about in there?'

'Well, for a start, we fucked up.'

'With you so far,' I said.

Then he spoiled it: 'But we couldn't allow a bozo like Livingstone to win.'

So there it is. The language of the Nixon White House. Bozo, indeed. Oh the arrogance of the unelected.

'A good question,' whispered the Cabinet Secretary, Richard Wilson, who had overheard the exchange. 'The truth is they haven't learned any lessons. They can't let go.' He added in an apparent reference to The Man, 'He's got teenage children. He's going to have to learn to let go sooner or later.'

There was a spring in my step as I walked back through St James's Park, sun shining on great drifts of crocuses and daffodils.

Wednesday, 1 March

Ran into Ken Livingstone in the corridor between the Library and the Members' Lobby.

'Don't,' I said.

He sighed. 'All my friends – I mean my *real* friends' (he touched my arm) 'say that.' He's obviously tempted to go it alone. 'I don't know what I'd say to all the people who stop me in the street if I didn't.' He said he was lying awake worrying about it. 'I'm going to have to take a decision before I'm ill.'

He is still hoping against hope that Frank will stand down. 'Frank's unelectable. Whoever gets into the final ballot with him – either Norris or the Liberal Democrats – will win. I think Millbank are just beginning to realise. That's why I have given them another week.' He

and ended up with the largest majority in the country. In Wales a disastrous attempt was made to exclude Rhodri Morgan from the leadership of the Welsh Assembly. In the London mayoral election Ken Livingstone was threatening to stand as an Independent.

added, 'I've been so reasonable. I've really bent over backwards. One day someone will publish the correspondence. When the left find out, I shall be denounced!'

'Don't rule out the possibility of staying here,' I said as he disappeared through the swing doors, coffee cup in hand. But he obviously has.

Jean gave me a report of tonight's meeting of the parliamentary committee. The Man went out of his way to say that there were lessons in this for him personally. He admitted he should never have interfered in Wales. On Ken, however, he remains unrepentant. He pointed out that not a single one of the 17 assembly candidates had voted for him (that says more about them than it does about Ken). Jean says no one spoke up for Ken. The Man did say he had given clear instructions that there were to be no personal attacks. 'Not only wrong, but counterproductive.' I fear there are still a few more lessons in the pipeline.

Thursday, 2 March

Waited more than half an hour for a bus this morning. The 159s all passed without stopping because they were full and there was no sign of any Number 3s. Then five came in convoy. They were still within a hundred yards of each other when I got off at Westminster.

General Pinochet went home today.* Jack made a low-key statement. There were cries of 'shame' from a few people on our side, but in truth most people are relieved to see the back of the old villain. The Tories were for the most part restrained (the more sensible of them have worked out that it would not be wise to appear too jubilant – he is after all a serial killer).

'Are you sure you are happy with the briefing for Questions today?' Jessica asked, seeing that I had just glanced at the file. She blushed as she always does when drawing attention to one of my many shortcomings.

---

*The former Chilean dictator was under house arrest following extradition requests from four countries seeking to try him for human rights abuses against their citizens, following the military coup in Chile in 1973. He was released on medical grounds.

'Why do you ask?'

'We've had feedback from the DPM's office.'

'Oh yes?'

'The word is that Chris Mullin is not off message, but that he doesn't know what the message is.'

I wonder where this is coming from? Is it really JP? Or the unidentified detractor who Don Brind warned me about several weeks ago?

Friday, 3 March
Sunderland

An hour with Dave Wilkinson, head teacher of Pennywell School. The poor man is in despair. Blunkett has just decreed that secondary schools achieving less than 25 per cent A to C grades may have to close. *The Times* has helpfully printed a list of the schools in question and one of them is Pennywell. Needless to say this was faithfully embellished by last night's *Echo*. 'PENNYWELL SCHOOL TO CLOSE?' shouted billboards all over town. Just at the moment when Dave and his staff are, with some success, in the process of recruiting students for next year. And how is he going to find new teachers or hang on to those he already has? Dave is an excellent headmaster. Tough, dedicated, battling against great odds in what is surely one of the toughest educational environments in the country. Under his stewardship results, although a long way short of official targets, have been steadily improving. He has had two good OFSTED reports. He could walk away and get a job in a leafier area any time he wanted and yet he chooses to stay. And all he gets for his trouble is a kick in the teeth from New Labour. Understandably he is incandescent. He is writing a letter which I promised to press into Blunkett's hand.

Saturday, 4 March

We are becoming unlucky. Not yet as unlucky as poor John Major, but the symptoms are unmistakable. Nothing goes right. The media, scenting blood, are becoming nastier. Every day brings news of more disasters, real and imagined. Some, of course, are self-inflicted, but that is not the whole story. Today's headlines are about a row between Clare Short and the Ministry of Defence over the cost of helicopters for Mozambique. Who, reading the headlines, would guess that the UK has provided more aid than anyone else? Worse still, one might be forgiven for thinking that New Labour was responsible for the floods to judge by some of the reporting. John Humphrys was practically hysterical on the *Today* programme yesterday. Things will get worse before they get better. Whether or not Ken runs, the London elections will be a disaster. Surprisingly, there is as yet no sign of a Tory recovery, but it can only be a question of time.

Monday, 6 March

The big story today is that Ken is running for Mayor of London as an Independent. He has chosen a lonely path. He has few real allies of any substance and, if elected, will end up with an assembly composed largely of members who are hostile, facing a government which will not give him the time of day. My instinct is that he will win, though not by the margin that many expect. Millbank will pile on the shit and some of it will stick. It's going to be a very nasty campaign – and deeply damaging to all of us.

In the Tea Room, Sylvia Heal and Estelle Morris were lamenting New Labour's tendency to overspin which nearly always backfires. Estelle cited the suggestion that the average nurse would be taking home £20,000 a year, which immediately resulted in a lot of nurses popping up saying that their earnings were nothing like that. They both said they were finding it impossible to justify the 75 pence up-rating to the old age pension. 'Does Gordon know the damage it's doing us? He must do.' I wouldn't count on it.

Tuesday, 7 March

A disturbing piece by Nick Davies in today's *Guardian* in which he alleges that Blunkett's much-trumpeted £19 billion extra for education over the life of this Parliament is really only about £6.7 billion

– and not that much more than the Tories were proposing to spend anyway. Most of the difference is accounted for by double and triple counting. Presumably a similar technique was used on the NHS and housing budgets. I have heard this alleged before, but never seen it spelled out so starkly. If true – and I hear no denials – it would help to explain why New Labour's lavish claims about spending on health and education don't seem to be reflected at the coalface. No wonder there is such a gap between expectation and delivery.

Ran into John Major on Upper Corridor South. We talked of The Great London Mayoral Fiasco. Blair, he said, should have made more effort to be nice to Ken, 'and then, if Ken had stood, he would have looked graceless'. He added, 'Heseltine only ran against Thatcher because he was told to put up or shut up.' Like everyone I meet he asked how I was finding life in government. I dipped into my little bag of stock responses and came up with 'I suppose it is one of those things that I will be glad to look back on.'

'You and me both,' he chuckled.

During the ten o'clock division I was sitting in the Aye Lobby with my head down, feet stretched out in front when someone play-fully kicked me. I looked up to find myself gazing into the eyes of our beloved Prime Minister. Our exchange included the following:

'How's it going?'

'Depends on which day you catch me. To be honest I have less influence now than I ever did as a select committee chairman.'

'For now,' he murmured. 'For now.'

Wednesday, 8 March

Incredibly, JP and Nick have talked the Treasury into allowing the most efficient 10 per cent of local authorities to fund social housing by raising capital from the markets. Angela Eagle remarked that JP is the only minister capable of persuading the hard hearts in the Treasury to let him get round the public sector borrowing rules. Thinking about it, she's right. He did it on air traffic control and on congestion charging. There's more to JP than meets the eye.

A meeting with Nick Raynsford, Angela Eagle and officials to discuss how we go about cutting the flow of housing benefit to rogue landlords. My little campaign is bearing fruit at last. Everyone is on board and the Green Paper – due next month – is positive. Nick says that, if legislation is required (and it almost certainly is), we can get something into the local government bill proposed for next session. There are complications, of course. Nothing in government is ever simple. If we were to impose the same conditions across the country, southern landlords would simply refuse to take housing benefit claimants so we would end up with a lot of homeless people. Further north, however, it's a different story. The landlords are dependent on public subsidy and would have no choice but to clean up their act if they wanted to stay in business.

Thursday, 9 March

Today I was Minister of Zoos. I went with Jessica to Bristol for the launch of yet another code of practice. We passed a pleasant two hours touring the local zoo and being photographed with penguins, seals and gorillas. I've never been keen on zoos, but this one appeared well-run – from the point of view of both animals and visitors. Then to the grim 1960s office block housing the Department's Countryside Division for a whistlestop tour. There are some attractive parts of Bristol, but I had forgotten how much damage the planners had inflicted during the 1960s and '70s. A drive around the ring road brought it all back.

Sunday, 12 March
Sunderland

Up into the wilderness above the Tyne valley to see Malcolm, Helen and family. Malcolm and I had a pleasant stroll along a section of the Roman wall that I have not previously visited. Malcolm recounted how the special school at which he used to work in Hartlepool had suffered two OFSTED reports which had come to absolutely opposite conclusions. The first, led by someone from Cheltenham, was very bad and led to the school being placed on special measures. The second, a year later, was extremely complimentary and led to the school being declared a beacon. The head was so disillusioned with the process that he has resigned from the Labour Party.

Monday, 13 March

At supper in the Tea Room the talk was of New Labour's tendency to double and triple count new public spending. We were joined by Jack Straw, who said the idea was Gordon's and he had been against it from the outset. He added, 'Fancy tactics never work. They always catch up with you in the end.'

Tuesday, 14 March

To lunch in the Millbank Room with the boys and girls from the private office in honour of Jessica, who is leaving us this week. I asked them all to stop calling me 'Minister' for a couple of hours, but Nicky was at it again within minutes. Sometimes, when I ring up, Nicky or Kerry will forget themselves (Jessica and Shayne never do) and say, 'Hello Chris,' but by the end of the conversation – and sometimes even by the end of their opening sentence – it's back again to 'Yes, Minister.'

Wednesday, 15 March

I have been drafted in to wind up tomorrow's opposition debate on planning policy – all those new houses for the Home Counties. As a result I spent an hour this morning being briefed on the housing crisis in the south, during the course of which one of the officials remarked that it was mainly down to the influx of asylum seekers. 'But for asylum seekers there would be empty property in London.' He added quickly, 'Actually, Minister, you'd be very unwise to say that.' He went on, 'We can't believe we have got through six debates without anyone mentioning asylum seekers. We have been waiting for it to happen, but it hasn't.'

To dinner at the Woollacotts. For most of the evening I sat next to Polly Toynbee, who I rather like, despite the clobbering she gave me last year. She reminds me a lot of Liz Forgan. Witty, refreshing, sensible and fundamentally decent. She said a number of people at the *Guardian* were getting worried by the constantly negative political reporting and were pressing the editor to get a grip on it. Many *Guardian* journalists – such as David Hencke (who someone recently described as a perpetual adolescent) – seem to regard bashing the government as a game, but the outcome could be serious. We will end up with another Tory government, not one that is more liberal. Polly was very hostile to the People's Ken. 'He's a liar,' she said. 'I heard him say in the presence of 40 journalists that Frank Dobson was clinically depressed. Later, he flatly denied having said it.' Polly says that when she rang Ken and challenged him he was shameless and simply said he had been speaking off the record. Ken, she says only half jokingly, is a monster. Charming, brilliant, infuriating, but a monster nevertheless whose mission is to destroy the Labour Party. A bit rich coming from a founder member of the SDP.

Thursday, 16 March

I don't have to wind up tonight's debate, after all. The Tories have dropped housing and decided instead to debate the collapse of Rover. It's not our fault if no one wants to buy Rover cars, but one way or another we will be blamed. John Humphrys was at it on *Today* this morning, asking Steve Byers if he was planning to resign. Why should he, for God's sake? He's done absolutely nothing wrong. Humphrys, like Hencke, is an opportunist liberal who has never had to take responsibility for anything in his life.

Monday, 20 March

To London on an early train since I had to wind up the second reading of the Countryside Bill, which, among other things, introduces a right of access to four million acres of hitherto closed areas of mountain, moor, heath and downland. Happily, it holds none of the terrors of the Transport or Utilities Bills. At last, I am being sent in to bat for a piece of legislation that I actually care about.

Earlier, I found Ken Livingstone sitting alone in the Tea Room. Everyone is giving him a wide berth and he looked a bit down, so I went up and had a few words but thought it wise not to sit at his table. I didn't realise, but he had come in to deliver his apology for the failure to declare his outside earnings. When the time came he picked a place in the shadows, at the furthest corner of the chamber, rattled off his short statement and was gone. It was all over in less than a minute. I doubt whether we shall see much more of him in this place. The regime seems entirely reconciled to a Ken victory. There is the smell of doom about Frank's campaign. Everything he does seems to rebound. Even the fuss over Ken's outside earnings backfired when it emerged that one of Frank's henchmen had been involved in setting Ken up. 'We could have done with a better candidate,' remarked Jack Straw, who joined me while I was eating my beans on toast during a break from the Countryside Bill. He added that he had favoured Tony Banks, but had been overruled.

Wednesday, 22 March

I showed a delegation of Vietnamese, including a vice-foreign minister, around the House. Afterwards, we took tea on the terrace in bright sunshine, one of them asked the question that I always dread. 'How much does a British MP earn?'

'About 75,000 US dollars,' I replied, taking care to explain that before he translated that enormous sum into dong he should bear in mind that about 30 per cent went in tax and national insurance and that there was a huge difference in the cost of living.

He thought about this for a moment and said, 'It is a pity you can't earn this in England and spend it in Vietnam.'

'I can think of at least one person who does,' I said. 'The British Ambassador in Hanoi.' Then I remembered the Vietnamese Ambassador, sitting next to me, whose salary is probably less than that of a London bus driver. 'Of course,' I added, 'it is not so good to earn your salary in Vietnam and spend it in England.' They all fell about laughing.

Friday, 24 March
Sunderland

To Southmoor School, for a conversation with the head, Mike Crook. A pleasant, cheerful man. Unlike most teachers I meet these days he wasn't angry or depressed (but then he is retiring in six months). He complained about OFSTED, bureaucracy and overwork. Literacy levels, he says, are still falling. He confirmed that one of the unforeseen consequences of the Working Families' Tax Credit was a huge fall in the numbers eligible for free school meals and most of those no longer eligible are now going without.

Sunday, 26 March

A bad night. Awoken at three by a dog which barked intermittently. It seemed to be coming from a household with which we had similar trouble ten years ago. After breakfast I penned the owner a polite note and posted it through his letter box as we set off for a picnic at Wallington. When we got back our neighbour, Peter, said an angry man had called and returned my note. On the bottom he had scribbled, 'My dog died five years ago, so I'd be surprised if you can still hear it.'

Friday, 31 March
Sunderland

How about this for a piece of New Labour claptrap?

> Dear Chris
> I am writing to give you advance notice that Sunderland is one of the local authority areas we have identified to be part of an enlarged Excellence in Cities (EIC) programme … I don't have to tell you what good news this is … In the next few weeks we shall be asking schools and authorities to form partnerships to develop EIC plans. These will create new patterns of provision – Beacon and Specialist schools; small Education Action Zones; school-based city learning centres; learning mentors and enriched opportunities for gifted and talented children.
>
> Best wishes
> David Blunkett

Goodness knows what all this means, although I am sure it is all terribly worthy. No wonder the teachers are so bewildered.

Sunday, 2 April

A video arrived from the Parliamentary Recording Unit which includes my first appearance at the Dispatch Box. Not very flattering. All the viewer sees when I'm bent over my script is an aerial view of my bald head. Emma watched it with me. 'Dad,' she asked, 'when you speak in Parliament why do you say "er"?'

Monday, 3 April
Brixton

Home at 1 a.m. to find a message on the answerphone from a *Daily Telegraph* journalist: the *Guardian* were running a front page story saying I had called for a boycott of Barclays Bank. Would I confirm the quotes? Fell into bed without returning the call. Some mistake, surely?

Tuesday, 4 April

The telephone started ringing at 7 a.m. Would I like to appear on the *Today* programme to discuss my call for a boycott of Barclays? I ignored several calls. Then Shayne from the private office rang. The press office at the Department were anxious to speak to me. The *Guardian* were running a front page lead saying I had called for a boycott of Barclays. The word 'boycott' was in the headline, 48pt bold. There was nothing in the story to indicate when or where I had made this great clarion call. It was apparently based on quotes from an adjournment debate a week ago. At no stage had I used the word 'boycott'. All I said was that exhortations from politicians were not likely to cut much ice with a hard-nosed commercial institution like Barclays, but there was nothing to stop customers voting with their feet. When I got to the House there was a message waiting from Alastair Campbell. I gave him my version of events and he didn't seem bothered. I guess he has to cope with nonsense of this sort every day. Later, I saw the transcript of his morning briefing with the lobby hacks at which my speech was the main item on the agenda. Alastair played a straight bat, sticking up for me throughout. Apparently William Hague was asked about it on *Today* this morning and, although he distanced himself from the idea of a boycott, he reserved most of his criticism for Barclays. It was left to a woman from the Institute of Directors to huff and puff and say how wicked I was. Needless to say, the entire discussion was based on the false premise that I had called for a boycott.

As the day wore on I began to realise that this little episode might, after all, be something less than a disaster. It has provided a temporary respite from the obscurity into which I have sunk and it seems to have made a lot of people happy. 'Stick with it,' said Jeff Rooker. 'Whatever you do, don't apologise. This will go down well with pensioners, the rural areas and in the party.' 'Don't worry, you spoke for all of us,' said Denis MacShane, brushing aside my attempt to explain that I hadn't actually called for a boycott. 'You've got the best of both worlds,' said Bob Marshall-Andrews. 'On the one hand, you can show that the speech is absolutely unobjectionable and on the other you get credit for something entirely different.' Even the former Tory Attorney General, Nicholas Lyell, who saw the speech on his monitor, was friendly. 'All you did was lend some encouragement to the working of the market. I can't see anything wrong with that.' The whole business is bizarre.

Chris Brain, my new Private Secretary, received a visit from JP's Private Secretary who said that JP was unhappy that I didn't have a pager.

'He hasn't mentioned that to me.'

'Ah, Minister, that's not how it works.'

'If he gives me a written instruction ...'

Pained expression. 'I hope it won't come to that ... It would be helpful, to the office.'

What nonsense. We've managed perfectly well up until now without a car, a mobile telephone or a pager. I promised to reflect, but in the end I expect I shall have to surrender.

Wednesday, 5 April

This morning's papers are full of the row over my supposed call for a boycott. There is a wonderful Steve Bell cartoon in the *Guardian* in which I am scruffily depicted as the mascot, clutching a red flag, on the front of a Rolls-Royce containing two very fat cats. One or two of the more serious journalists have taken the trouble to check what I actually said, but 'boycott' features prominently in most reports, including another front page story by Patrick Wintour, who still hasn't bothered to contact me. Presumably because he is too ashamed. I am roundly denounced in the *Sun* and the *Mail* (just like old times). The leader in the *Mail* is headed 'The louse and the flea'. Barclays is the louse. I am the flea. Gillian Shephard, who was present at the Barclays debate, was most amused. 'You didn't say any of that. What you said was about market forces. It was very reasonable.' I was afraid the subject might come up at Prime Minister's Questions and that The Man would be forced to dissociate himself, so I alerted Bruce, who didn't seem at all concerned. In the event, the subject didn't arise. I think the Tories have realised that this is a two-edged sword. Barclays, which is closing a lot of rural branches, is not very popular right now and no one wants to be seen taking its side. Pat says she spent most of yesterday answering calls from people ringing with congratulations. Many from the Home Counties.

This evening, just before five, I passed Nick Soames bending the ear of The Man in the corridor between the library and the Members' Lobby. The Prime Minister was pinned against the lockers, Soames's huge frame loomed menacingly, his face just an inch or two from The Man's. Suddenly, Soames slammed his fist into the locker a foot or so from Tony's head. The Man didn't flinch, his perma-smile remained intact. So far as I could tell the exchange was good-humoured. Exchanges with Soames usually are. 'What were you talking to the Prime Minister about?' I inquired when I saw him in the Tea Room later in the evening.

'I was telling him he must love the army. He does, but the Treasury doesn't.'

For the third night running we were kept here until after 1 a.m. There was a lot of hanging around. I spent 40 minutes in the Prime Minister's room with Bruce Grocott, on the sofa under the picture of Sir Walter Scott. According to Bruce, The Man is unduly impressed by people who are clever. '"Very clever" is the highest accolade he can award.' I said that I realised ten years ago, watching those Birmingham Six Appeal Court judges at close quarters, that it is possible to be very clever and stupid at the same time. Said Bruce, 'The cleverest person I've ever seen in this place was Enoch Powell, and he didn't do himself any good.'

'Have you said that to The Man?'

'Yes.'

On the way out Bruce proudly showed me the new basin installed last summer, at his insistence, in the PM's outer office. He said the staff were so pleased that they bought a bottle of champagne to celebrate. Unbelievably, they have until recently been reduced to carrying water upstairs in a bucket to make tea for the Prime Minister's guests. At first the House authorities argued that it was impossible to run water through to the outer office and only relented when Bruce threatened to bring in his son to do it for them.

Later, half an hour in the Tea Room with Archie Norman. He said it costs about £9 million a year to run the Tory party and about another £10 million to run an election. 'There won't be any more big poster campaigns because we can't afford them.' He added quietly, 'It is amazing what some people will do for a peerage. I know stories I could never tell.'

Thursday, 6 April

The 'boycott Barclays' nonsense has done wonders for my profile in Sunderland. 'MULLIN DEFIANT IN BANK BATTLE' was the splash in last night's *Echo*. And inside was one of the friendliest notices I have ever received. Sample:

> No matter what title may hang on his office door, Mr Mullin is not a parliamentary poodle … Chris Mullin does not appear to fit into the mould of the New Labour disciples who fawn to Tony Blair's mission. He is first and foremost a constituency MP whose intellect,

independence and single mindedness have elevated him to a higher stage on numerous occasions.

And so on. Perhaps I ought to send Patrick Wintour a thank you note.

Friday, 7 April
Sunderland

Rang Michael White about obtaining the Steve Bell cartoon. 'We owe you,' he said. Adding, 'You have been traduced in a good cause.'

Among the messages on our answerphone, one from Mildred Brodie, a dear old Tory neighbour. 'We're all behind you, Chris. Everyone I have spoken to agrees with you.'

Friday, 14 April

Ngoc and I were married in Ho Chi Minh City thirteen years ago today.

Saturday, 15 April

To the home of the great engraver Thomas Bewick in the Tyne Valley. We had the place to ourselves for most of the time. The National Trust custodian, a Yorkshireman, made us a cup of tea. He lived in an upstairs flat and said that he was one of 900 applicants for the job. Ten times as many as for a safe Labour seat.

Tuesday, 18 April

'Clare Short and I are the two happiest ministers in the government,' remarked Michael Meacher, as we loitered in JP's outer office this morning. 'Blair doesn't regard the environment or overseas development as important, so we are left to get on with it. JP isn't interested either so he keeps out, too.' I had noticed. When the music stops, either job would suit me fine.

Wednesday, 19 April

My new private secretary, Chris Brain, thinks I say No too much. It's true I turn down just about all invitations to socialise with vested interests, in keeping with my First Iron Law of Politics: avoid pointless activity. Specifically, Chris thinks I ought not to have declined an invitation to drinks with Richard Branson. It is not as if we have anything to discuss since he directs his angry missives – of which we receive about one a fortnight – to one of my many superiors. The latest – about the refusal to award Virgin a new route to South Africa – went to the Prime Minister, no less. To keep Chris happy I have agreed to show my face, unless something more pressing turns up. Iron Law of Politics Number Two: keep in with Private Secretary.

Thursday, 20 April

Lunch, in the Lords dining room, with John Gilbert. In fine form, despite having come off an overnight flight from Australia. For some reason he has taken a shine to me although we are as different as chalk and cheese. One thing we do have in common, however, is an interest in the big picture. He is full of shrewd insights and useful advice for a budding minister. 'Avoid publicity. If it's bad, it will only upset your superiors. If it's good, they will be jealous.' We discussed the difference between cleverness and intelligence. John cites David Marquand, John Roper and Dick Taverne (all of whom defected to the SDP) as examples of people who were too clever by half. 'You could spot them in the lobbies a mile off. They brayed.' David Owen, I ventured, was another. 'No. Owen is not clever. The sort of man who loses his temper with waiters, although he does have a certain charm. When he chooses to use it.' Nick Raynsford he cited as an example of a man who was intelligent as opposed to simply clever. 'My other favourite minister,' he said. 'He should be in the Cabinet.'

Thursday, 27 April

An article in today's *Guardian* about local election apathy, an area in which Sunderland leads the nation. The piece was illustrated by a brilliant photo of a lone canvasser in a deserted street, bending the ear of a householder propped insolently in his doorway in a pose that suggested complete indifference. My agent, Kevin Marquis is quoted: 'When I joined the local Labour Party, aged 19, I was one of the youngest members. I am now 41 and still one of the youngest.'

Friday, 28 April
Sunderland

As I was making my way into the hospital (for a meeting about saving the Cleft Palate Unit) I was waylaid by an angry old bigot who claimed once to have been a shop steward in the shipyard and is, therefore, one of our much-lamented core voters. His complaints were numerous. His language intemperate. He began with a genuine grievance: the government have done 'nothing' for pensioners like himself with small occupational pensions. 'This gentleman,' indicating the old boy with him, who remained silent throughout, 'pays £60 a week for his flat and the woman next door pays just £5.' In vain did I try to get a word in edgeways. He went on, 'The Labour Party is full of traitors and poofs.' The word 'scum' also featured. Then he was off on a rant about a footpath on some wasteland near his home and the alleged lack of action by his local councillors, although it was unclear whether he had seriously attempted to contact them. Then he turned to crime and the police. In between he found space to describe his various symptoms – suspected cancer which turned out to be a gall bladder. On and on he raved. What he really suffered from was Chronic Whinger Syndrome, a disease all too common in these parts. 'I blame the councillors,' he raved. 'And I blame you MPs. And I blame' – by now I'd had enough of him – 'Everybody but yourself,' I said. 'Goodbye.' And with that I walked away leaving him fuming. I felt much better afterwards. I'm going to do it more often.

Sunday, 30 April

The Vietnam War ended 25 years ago today. Ngoc and her family were crouched on the ground floor of their little house in Le Van Si while, outside, chaos reigned. Ngoc says she knew when the war was over because, by lying flat, she could see under the shutters that the boots of the southern army had been replaced by northern feet in sandals.

Tuesday, 2 May

There was a riot by anarchists last night. They defaced Churchill's statue and the Cenotaph, dug up Parliament Square and looted the McDonald's restaurant at the end of Whitehall. Nicholas Soames told me that his mother was in tears over the graffiti on her father's statue. I agreed that it was all very upsetting, but unwisely added, 'I think we can afford the loss of the odd McDonald's.' He smiled wickedly and said, 'Lucky I'm your friend.'

The Countryside Bill committee went on until 10 p.m. I gave a little tug at my strings today. David Heath, a Lib Dem, moved that the Ministry of Defence be required to report regularly to Parliament about what it's doing with the vast amount of land under its control. The advice was to resist, but I consulted Michael and he agreed that this was a perfectly reasonable suggestion so we agreed to consider. Officials warned afterwards that the Ministry of Defence would be upset. Sod them, I say. They can't always have everything their own way.

Wednesday, 3 May

On the way in this morning, I saw two homeless Sikhs sleeping rough on the seats on the traffic island opposite Kennington Park. I've never seen a homeless Sikh before. Where have they come from? Presumably off the back of a lorry.

At the meeting of the parliamentary party JP mounted a robust defence of our plans for air traffic control. Gus and I shared the platform with him. JP was on good form. He had prepared carefully. Notes written out in black felt tip, underlined at intervals in red. He began slowly and calmly. His language uncharacteristically moderate (expressing only 'disappointment' with the select committee report). The troops were attentive (scarcely anyone left during the entire hour and a half), but unenthusiastic. There was little laughter. Applause was lukewarm. Gwyneth Dunwoody sat at the back, a brooding, ominous presence who haunts all our deliberations.

Nick Raynsford tells me that he has received an inquiry from the Home Office as to whether we could see our way to granting accelerated planning permission for six detention camps for asylum seekers. He has said no. Nothing has been said publicly about this so far. I hope they are all located deep in the meanest part of middle England.

Thursday, 4 May
Sunderland

Local government election day. An hour with Stuart Porthouse (the Thornholme candidate) driving around deserted streets, urging people to come out and vote. The two polling stations we called on had attracted 32 and 42 voters respectively in their first four hours. I passed a woman emerging from the new housing in the east end of Hendon. 'Have you voted?' called Stuart. 'Nah,' she sneered, 'you've done nothing for us.' My blood boiled. Her little estate has been transformed in the last three years. It used to consist of prefabricated double maisonettes, vandalised and crime-ridden. Public money has been poured in. Now it's all neat houses with gardens. There's even a little police station in the base of one of the refurbished tower blocks. Yet most people see no connection between their transformed lives and politics.

In the afternoon I spent three hours with Gill Galbraith knocking on doors in the Hendon long streets. The first was opened by a man of about 65 who claimed he was Labour through and through, but he would not be voting by way of protest against the measly 75 pence pension increase. In vain I drew his attention to the £150 heating allowance and the changes in the tax threshold, but he wasn't having any of it. He was polite but firm. The 75 pence, he said, was an insult. It's hard not to disagree. For all our talk of helping the poorest, we just aren't getting through. There is real anger. There were the usual complaints about anti-social neighbours. The long streets used to consist of owner-occupied cottages, full of dignified working people with a good sense of community, but gradually the landlords are getting a grip, bringing with them a plague of criminal youths – every one of them on benefit. People complained of stolen cars being raced around the streets. Sooner or later someone, probably a child, will be killed. And in the midst of all this mayhem, decent people are trapped. Their homes unsaleable. And yet we seem powerless to help. It's no good chanting 'things can only get better'. These people's lives are getting worse.

Friday, 5 May

As predicted, we have taken a hammering in the local elections, losing about 600 seats. The People's Ken has been swept to power in London with Steve Norris the runner-up. It is almost exactly a year since I told The Man to his face that Ken would be elected under all circumstances. Still, I don't suppose he would thank me for reminding him.

Monday, 8 May

To London on the 09.00, stopping off at York for an hour and a half to open a new state-of-the-art (Lottery-funded) environmental community centre. I was conveyed the three miles from the city centre in a yellow cyclo (a most civilised form of transport) of which there are eight operating in York and several photographers turned out to bear witness. The return journey had to be made by car because, as luck would have it, JP was also in town. His minders (recalling previous disasters) had sent word that they did not want me upstaging my master by arriving at the station in a cyclo just as he tumbled out of his official Jag. In the event I missed him by about ten minutes and there were no embarrassments.

The whips are rushing hither and thither trying to contain tomorrow's rebellion on air traffic control. I have been given the names of Members thought to be persuadable and spent an hour or two bending ears. People keep nudging me and saying quietly, 'I bet you'd be in the other lobby if you were still on the backbenches.' I reply truthfully that I would vote with the government. My guess is that the rebellion will be large, but not disastrous.

Tuesday, 9 May

The air traffic control debate. JP (who never runs away from a fight) led for our side and Nick Raynsford brought up the rear so all that was required of me was to spend a couple of hours on the front bench, nodding in the right places. Our side were all grim-faced, but there was much merriment on the Tory side. One of the officials said to me afterwards that JP – who was not at his best – had been unnerved by an earlier point of order about the flat in Clapham which he rents on favourable terms from a trade union. Our majority was down to about 65 – 45 of our side voted against and goodness knows how many abstained. It could have been worse. The whips seemed remarkably cheerful. Several (Ann Taylor included) thanked me for my little effort, which they seemed to think had carried some weight with waiverers. JP seemed massively relieved. This has been a big test for him. He told me Gwyneth had sent a message saying that Blair and Brown were ditching him. 'I'm not doing it for Blair and Brown. I'm doing it because it's right. Mind you,' he added, 'I wouldn't have started down this road … I've used up enough credit. I'm not going to use up any more.'

Wednesday, 10 May

Came across JP, alone in the corridor behind the Speaker's chair. He had just fled the meeting of the parliamentary party, where some of the more strident sisters were demanding better facilities and more consideration from their male brethren. JP was in reflective mode. 'Is it just me who finds it hard being lectured by middle-class women about being too aggressive? I find some of *them* very aggressive.' He wasn't ranting or angry, just puzzled. 'It's not so much aggression, it's just that I feel passionately about things. And what would they know about how working-class women feel?' Someone had given him the book *The Women's Room* in an attempt to educate him. 'I was appalled to read how barren and empty they thought their lives were. Pauline says that the years when she was looking after the children were the happiest of her life.' This was not the usual angry, ranting JP. This was JP the Bemused. A side not often on display. Gradually, I warm to him.

Friday, 12 May

The two homeless Sikhs are still camped on the island opposite Kennington Park.

Monday, 15 May

To Admiralty House for an aviation 'summit'. The main issue is whether or not to break up the British Airports Authority on the grounds that it is a monopoly. We are due to hear presentations from the Civil Aviation Authority (in favour) and BAA (against, naturally). First, however, Gus Macdonald, the officials and I are ushered up to JP's comfortable pad on the top floor. JP is in informal mode. Carpet slippers, an open-necked short-sleeved shirt, a mug of coffee in hand. We assemble around the table in the dining room. Behind, on a smaller table, three magnificent displays of lilies (white, yellow and orange) which, upon inspection, turn out to be artificial. One or two photographs – Pauline and son, Pauline at the races. Through a half-open door, I glimpse an exercise bike. JP exercising? The mind boggles. From the moment JP speaks it is clear that we are just going through the motions. The suggestion came from the Treasury, not us. There are mocking references to Sir Stephen Robson, a Treasury mandarin, who will be present and who is apparently the Privatiser in Chief. 'The Devil himself,' says JP. 'The man who privatised the railways,' says one of the officials. 'And the rest,' adds another. Sir Stephen, allegedly, is on record as saying that his only hero is Keith Richards.

'Who is Keith Richards?' asks JP – to general incredulity.

We troop downstairs and arrange ourselves in a circle of armchairs and sofas in the grand drawing room. The decor is gold. The pictures of wild empty landscapes. JP, still in shirtsleeves, has a sofa to himself in the centre of the room. Mike Hodgkinson and the BAA team sit opposite, to his right. Sir Malcolm Field of the CAA and his guru, a bald Australian, are at the other end of the room. Everyone except me has removed their jackets. Sir Stephen, languid, urbane, thick black braces, has arranged himself on a sofa, well within JP's line of fire. He has a severe, pinched, long face – not unlike that of his only hero (except that he has weathered rather better). First question: is

BAA a monopoly? Undoubtedly, says Sir Stephen. 'IN CAPITAL LETTERS.' It has 90 per cent of the UK market. Ah yes, say the men from BAA, but our real competitors are not other British airports. They are the airports at Frankfurt, Paris, Amsterdam. Our charges are already very competitive. If you broke us up nothing would change. Sir Stephen says wearily, 'We heard all these arguments endlessly in relation to British Gas *et al*, only to be proved wrong by events.' JP piles in, peppering everyone with questions. He is supposed to be in the chair, but his views are appended to every question. His grasp of detail is impressive. JP really is very bright. It's just that his mind works faster than his mouth, which sometimes makes it difficult for those with slower brains to follow his train of thought. It must be obvious to everyone that we are just going through the motions. Sir Stephen, who has a mirthless smile, makes no great effort to press his case. The killer fact is supplied by an official. If we even so much as refer BAA to the Competition Commission, the chances are that the objectors will want to reopen the terminal five inquiry. And no one, but *no one*, wants to go through all that again. After two hours (at least half of which is occupied by JP) the parties are dismissed. I suspect we won't be hearing any more about breaking up BAA.

Over lunch a more general discussion. The official in charge of aviation talked with, I thought, a little too much enthusiasm about the likely growth of passenger movements from 160 million a year at present to 400 million in 20 years' time. At one point he used the word 'inevitable'. 'Not if we have the political will to slow it down,' I said (just about my only intervention in the entire proceedings). 'It means jobs,' said Gus (who firmly believes that Big is Beautiful). 'If it's sustainable, it's great,' said the official. The truth is, of course, it's not sustainable. It's madness and we ought to pluck up the courage to draw a line. It could be done by auctioning landing slots at the most congested airports (big money for the government there), which everyone agrees are seriously underpriced. JP complained that the airlines seem to think that they own the slots, but they don't.

One of the sad Sikhs is still camped at the junction of Brixton and Clapham Roads. This morning he was sitting apart from a derelict man and woman (who, unlike him, lack any sense of dignity), with his back to the fountain. Leaning forward, arms resting on his knees, contemplating his situation. One has the sense that his plight is only temporary. That he is waiting for something. What?

Wednesday, 17 May

To the Queen Elizabeth Centre for a 'Listening to Old People' event. A classic New Labour wheeze designed to create the illusion of consultation. A truly dire occasion. Thank goodness I was not participating (Keith Hill drew the short straw from our Department). I sat quietly at the back, praying no one would spot me (no one did). It should have been called 'Listening to Ministers'. The platform consisted of a long line of ministerial talking heads, each armed with long, leaden texts, full of talk of working parties and action plans, which they were expected to read out to an audience of sullen, whingey over-50s (yes, the lower age limit was 50). Most of whom looked as though they led prosperous, stress free lives. John Hutton (who does a passable imitation of Tony Blair) had the good sense to junk his text and speak off the cuff. When the sleek harridan compèring the proceedings announced that, regrettably, most of the ministers would have to flee before there was a chance to ask questions, rebellion broke out. At this point I slunk deeper into my chair, praying that I would not be called upon to plug the gap. No need to worry, however. The uprising was swiftly suppressed. The harridan conceded nothing. Ministers were busy people. We should all be grateful that they had found time to grace us with their presence. But the punters were not grateful. Not a bit. They felt they had been short-changed. And so they had. No doubt they all went home, saying what a waste of time it was. We probably even lost a few votes. Goodness knows what the cost was. I await the official note saying how useful and informative it was.

Monday, 22 May

To London on the 09.00. Whitehall was blocked by demonstrating Eritreans. The police had sealed it off completely and were herding the demonstrators into Richmond Terrace. Another crowd as being held at bay near the Treasury. Waiting at the pedestrian crossing on the corner of Parliament Square I encountered Madam Speaker, unaccompanied. 'Hello, Betty. Not often you're allowed out on your own.'

'I've come to see what's happening.'

It is the Speaker's job to make sure that Members have unimpeded access to the Palace of Westminster. The Home Secretary had telephoned to assure her that Whitehall was clear, but Betty had decided to see for herself. Suddenly I found myself co-opted as an unofficial escort. As it happened Whitehall was still blocked. We marched smartly across the road, Betty instantly recognisable in her smart black two-piece and luminous, grey-blue hair. Without glancing down, she stepped off the kerb, a gleaming shoe avoiding by millimetres two large deposits of police horse manure. Raising the ribbon in the manner of one born to command (although, it has to be said, Betty is utterly without airs), she marched up to the nearest policeman and gently interrogated him on the prospects for an early reopening. He was not well-informed.

'I'm just a small cog,' he pleaded.

'I know the feeling,' I whispered. With that, about turn and back to the pedestrian crossing, where we parted, still a few hundred yards outside her domain.

To Admiralty House to hear Hilary Armstrong discourse on the relationship between central and local government. Despite her background (north-east machine politics) Hilary is a moderniser. 'Best Value', 'Beacon Councils' – the New Labour watchwords trip effortlessly off her tongue. We are in danger, she said, of becoming hung up on structures rather than delivery. The discussion afterwards produced no great insights. The next Admiralty House seminar is on risk management. I will give it a miss. What do I need to know about the management of risk when even my lunch invitations are the subject of clearance by the Deputy Prime Minister?

To Trinity Hospice in Clapham to see Una Cooze, who is dying of cancer. I was feeling down when I set out, but Una (who has only weeks to live) was so infectiously cheerful that I felt ashamed. A wonderful woman. Not a trace of self-pity. We laughed and joked for an hour and even went for a little stroll around the garden. The eerie thing is that Una looks so well, apart from a huge inoperable swelling in her tummy. Dear, silly old Michael Foot, for whom she worked for years, has sent her a Get Well Soon card. She thought that was hilarious, too.

Una's husband John was there. His father was the coachman who drove the Queen to her coronation. John was brought up at Windsor and at Buckingham Palace. As a child he was even taken to pantomimes and picnics with the princesses. The experience turned him into a staunch republican. Sheila Williams recalled, during the 1959 election, driving into the Royal Mews to pick up John in a Rolls-Royce owned by the publisher Anthony Blond which was plastered with stickers saying 'Vote Labour for a fairer Britain'.

Wednesday, 24 May

Dinner with Elinor Goodman at the Atrium. One of the few political journalists I take seriously. She says that we're doing most of the right things on the issues that matter – literacy, youth unemployment, eroding the benefit culture, helping the deserving poor – but that it just isn't coming across because of New Labour's obsession with spin and control freakery. Even so, she thinks we'll win the election by 60 or 70 seats. She agrees about the lamentable state of political journalism. Even Channel Four News, she says, is no longer content to allow viewers to make up their own minds, but instead has appended its own spin.

Thursday, 25 May

My Private Secretary, Chris Brain, gently ticked me off for failing to show enough interest in the work of the Department. 'You need to raise your profile,' he said. 'Why don't you make more suggestions on the policy documents?' I replied that I am entirely reconciled to my current (temporary) obscurity. I am following Richard Mottram's advice on day one: 'Choose two or three issues on which you might make a difference and don't worry about the rest.' The issues I have selected are leylandii trees, night flights and making the payment of housing benefit direct to landlords discretionary. If a fourth one comes along, I will gladly consider it, but I resolutely refuse to waste time ploughing through piles of paperwork to no effect whatever.

When I die, I said, no one will ever remember that I was an under-secretary of state at the Department of Environment. One or two people may just recall that I once had some impact on the criminal justice system. They might remember *A Very British Coup* but no amount of activity in my present post will make the blindest bit of difference. On the contrary, favourable publicity would only upset my many superiors. So I propose to keep my head down and await rescue. If help doesn't arrive, I will return to the world of select committees.

Saturday, 27 May
Sunderland

A grey, drizzly day. We loaded up the car and, after lunch, set off for Melrose, where we are renting a cottage which is part of a little stable block on a small estate overlooking the beautiful River Tweed. It is entered through an elegant archway topped by a dovecote. On two sides, the garden is flanked by a huge field, the inhabitants of which include two donkeys, sheep, goats, pigs, eight geese, two turkeys and assorted breeds of chicken. A duck has recently given birth to a dozen tiny ducklings. In addition peacocks strut arrogantly around the estate, perching on fences and gates, sometimes right outside our window. The girls are over the moon. Within minutes of arrival they were leaning over the fence stroking the lambs and tearing up grass to feed the donkeys. Only two hours from home and yet we are on another planet.

Tuesday, 6 June

To the cramped offices of the Institute for Public Policy Research in Southampton Street to open a seminar on the future of aviation. The first time I have encountered representatives of the airlines around the same table as environmentalists. The word 'sustainable' was bandied around a lot, but there was no meeting of minds. An android from the London Chamber of Commerce spoke eagerly of a three-fold increase in demand for air travel in the south-east over the next 30 years and a five-fold increase in the regions which, he insisted, would have to be met if our economy was not to suffer. Someone from Transport 2000 pointed out that this meant three or four new airports the size of Heathrow would be needed by 2030. 'We can't afford to opt out of the "21st century",' said the android. 'At this rate the 21st century won't be worth living in,' I replied.

Wednesday, 7 June

Number 10 are saying they will not, after all, stand in the way of our attempt to legislate on high hedges, providing we don't seek a slot in the government's programme. The plan is to draw up a bill which we will offer to someone who comes high in the ballot for private members' bills. I have asked if I, rather than Michael Meacher, can make the announcement in the hope of being permitted a tiny footprint in the sand as a result of my otherwise fruitless year in office.

The Man was on excellent form at Questions today knocking Hague back into his little box, but, alas, the triumph was overshadowed by the news of A Great Disaster. This morning our leader had been addressing the massed ranks of the Women's Institute at Wembley. Middle England personified. It ought to have been his natural territory, but all went horribly wrong. He was heckled and slow-handclapped by these supposedly non-political ladies. True, those who misbehaved were only a tiny minority, but that is not how it will be portrayed. The Tories can't believe their luck.

Thursday, 8 June

Opinions about the fallout from yesterday's WI fiasco vary. Most of this morning's papers gleefully portray the affair as a turning point. However, there are those who believe it has provided the Lords of Spin with some welcome come-uppance.

'The end of Big Tent politics?' asked Gary Gibbon, a Channel Four journalist who took me to lunch in St James's. Gary thinks we will still win the election comfortably. I am not so sure. The Man is badly damaged and the regime has become so much of a one-man band that, if he goes down, we all will.

'You're a Blairite,' said Diane Abbott, who is always pulling my leg. 'Perhaps you can answer this: if the WI women don't believe all this guff about motherhood and apple pie (and we know it's not intended for us) what's the point of it?'

Friday, 9 June

'It will be interesting to see what lessons Number 10 learns from the WI fiasco,' remarked Yvette Cooper, who I had always taken to be ultra-loyal. 'Will they conclude that it's time to give up promoting the idea that Tony is friends with everyone and somehow floats above us? Or will they conclude that what is needed is even more effort to be nice to everyone?'

Which course does she favour?

'That he is a politician like the rest of us and should start acting accordingly.'

Wednesday, 14 June

This morning, the much-postponed meeting between the MPs for Putney and Windsor, Tony Colman and Michael Trend, and representatives of the airlines to discuss the night flights which plague the west of London. Officials have done all in their power to discourage action, but I persisted. We were given a long list of reasons why nothing could be done, of which the most ludicrous was high windspeeds over China.

Thursday, 15 June

Awoke this morning feeling positively light-headed. For the first time since mid-January I am not on a Bill committee.

To Number 10 for a meeting with The Man, one of a series he is doing with junior ministers. We sat around the Cabinet table for an hour. Just about everyone chipped in. When my turn came I said we were upsetting people on too many fronts and had to close some down. I mentioned postmasters, pensioners and teachers. 'We are pouring money into education and most teachers hate us. We must stop all this hectoring and naming and shaming.' At this The Man assumed a pained expression so I added, 'And I can see one or two people nodding just in case anyone thinks I'm entirely isolated.' At which point Mike O'Brien came in and backed me up. 'That's us finished,' he said to me afterwards, but I doubt it. Afterwards, as we walked up Downing Street, Bruce Grocott said cheerfully, 'There's no point in wasting time complaining about the ingratitude of the electorate. Every minister who has ever been must have said to himself, "Here I am working my bollocks off and all everyone does is complain."' He added, 'In politics it is useful to have an enemy. No good trying to appeal to everyone. About 60 per cent of the electorate will do.'

Monday, 19 June

A meeting with JP to discuss the huge bonuses awarded to the board of the Civil Aviation Authority on the basis of some not very exacting performance targets. JP was in belligerent mode. 'Do you agree with this?' he growled.

'No,' said I.

'Then where's your advice?'

In vain did I explain that, before I could consider the matter, word reached me that he wanted to discuss it so I had stayed my hand.

'So I saw it before you did?' The question hung in the air. A hint that I am not on top of my brief? He did not press the point.

'Well, what is your opinion then?'

'I don't like it any more than you do, but I don't see that there's anything we can do. It's in their contracts. That's the system we've signed up to.'

'I thought we were supposed to be in politics to change systems.'

At which JP turned his fire on the officials. What were the workers getting, he demanded. No one knew, but it was probably in the region of 3.5 per cent (as opposed to bonuses of between 28 and 32 per cent for the top brass). Gus Macdonald (who JP takes seriously) said that bonuses of 35 per cent were not uncommon in industry and that, in any case, the CAA salaries were not large by the standards of the private sector. The workforce was highly paid and the top brass earned only between two and three times the average salary. Suddenly JP mellowed. He even resisted a suggestion that we should trim. If that's what was in their contracts, so be it. For this year, he decreed, the bonuses should be paid in full. For the future, we would review the salary structure. The officials departed. The mood lightened. JP regaled us with an account of his recent trip to Nigeria. So far, he said, he had met 29 prime ministers and several heads of state, not to mention an Emir who had four wives and 40 children. Odd that he should be keeping count.

Tuesday, 20 June

Home after 2 a.m. I had to reply to the adjournment (one of three this week). After listening to a couple of messages on the answerphone, I let it play on while I got ready for bed. The tape played for about 20 minutes. Towards the end there was a long message from my old friend Joan Maynard. She's been gone more than two years now, but there she was as though it were yesterday making arrangements for us to meet, but of course we will never meet again – ever.

Wednesday, 21 June

Lunch with the Vietnamese Ambassador on the tenth floor of the Royal Garden Hotel, Kensington. He bent my ear at length on his disappointment that no senior member of the British government had visited Vietnam since Labour took office. Their senior politicians have all been here, but (as he put it) the traffic is all one way. Moreover, their prime minister was denied a meeting with The Man. Apparently Downing Street asked, when the request was conveyed, 'Does he have anything to announce?' The Vietnamese were deeply affronted.

This evening to Wellingborough (Labour majority 187) to speak for Paul Stinchcombe, one of the best and the brightest of the new intake. In a previous incarnation he was an overpaid barrister in Derry Irvine's chambers where on his first day he overheard one of his new colleagues ask another, 'How many crates of champagne can you fit into your Ferrari?' He used to work with Cherie and is, for this reason, privy to some of the early secrets of the New Labour court. Both Tony and Gordon blamed Smith's promised tax increases for the 1992 defeat. According to Paul, they were angry with Smith, who they reckoned had cynically calculated that he couldn't lose either way. If we'd won and he became Chancellor, he'd have money to spend. If we lost, he'd replace Kinnock as leader. Paul said that The Man originally wanted Gordon to run against John Smith for leader. Paul believes that he will stand aside for Gordon halfway through the next Parliament. The plan always had been that Gordon should be first. Cherie told Paul, 'Gordon's married to the Labour Party. He's got no other life.'

Thursday, 22 June

Dad's 80th birthday. Sarah has made him a beautiful card which I posted on Tuesday. When I rang home, he had not seen it. Mum had put it aside and forgotten about it.

Friday, 23 June
Sunderland

X, who has haunted me for eight years, was first in my surgery. He harangued me manically for 45 minutes before departing, calling me a gangster. He was followed by a fox-hunting obsessive and then by a couple who wanted me to get their grandchild into Farringdon school. Finally, a teacher from Sarah's infant school, whose daughter had been offered a place at medical school in Newcastle, but was unable to fund her studies. Did I have any suggestions? Of late we don't seem to have helped many constituents. In the old days we scored some big victories over the benefit agency and the housing department, but these days I increasingly find myself passing on letters explaining why nothing can be done. Our greatest victories usually involve helping people to move out of Sunderland, which doesn't enable them to express their gratitude to me at the ballot box.

Tuesday, 27 June

With Yvette Cooper, I appeared before the Lords' Science Select Committee which is investigating the effects of air travel on health. I mugged up carefully since I didn't want to be shown up by Yvette, who is fearfully bright, but it passed off without incident. We were interrupted by a division, but only four of the peers went off to vote. When I asked the others why they weren't voting, one replied, 'We only vote when we have heard the arguments.' How very civilised. I don't suppose it will catch on at our end of the building.

Wednesday, 5 July
Noi Bai Airport, Hanoi

A delicious little cameo. We had been told that the Vietnamese Prime Minister would be on the flight to Ho Chi Minh City, seated directly in front of me. In the event it turned out to be not the current Prime Minister, but his predecessor, Vo Van Kiet. Everyone was loaded onto the plane. The first two seats were conspicuously empty. From the porthole we could see a large black limo, with shaded windows, parked in front of the VIP lounge, but no sign of Mr Kiet. Suddenly the steps into the aircraft were driven away. Perhaps he wasn't coming after all? But no. A new set of steps was driven into place. This one had a red carpet. From the aircraft an ironic little cheer went up. Pure Monty Python. The door of the VIP lounge opened and the official party emerged, Mr Kiet (with his mop of white hair) clearly visible in the middle. Surely, this veteran revolutionary wasn't going to drive the 100 yards to the plane, à la JP. In Vietnam, however, anything is possible. Vietnamese politicians, of course, don't have to reckon with the tabloids. Mr Kiet, however, was made of tougher stuff. The car was waved aside and he strode manfully across the tarmac. But to everyone's surprise, the car followed and out got Mrs Vo Van Kiet, sporting a Pauline Prescott hairdo.

Friday, 7 July
Ho Chi Minh City

About 150 officials turned up for the water seminar. The news that I am a son-in-law of Vietnam prompted a spontaneous round of applause. After the opening speeches I escaped to the Christina Noble Foundation, which looks after abandoned babies. Lovely little people with shiny faces, rescued from hunger and despair. It was all I could do to keep from bursting into tears. Then on to the Saigon Children's Charity, run by a former teacher at Eton, which helps educate poor children and finds them work so they can support their families. I talked to Kieu, a little girl whose family lived in a shack on one of the stinking canals which the local authority is in the process of clearing. As a result they have been relocated to an area far away from the city centre. To carry on attending her classes, Kieu is cycling 20 km each way. Her mother, a cleaner, comes with her, at first sharing the same bike. Kieu has just had a giant stroke of luck. She has been offered a part-time job by the Hongkong and Shanghai Bank which will pay the stupendous sum of 50 dollars a month, for a four-hour day – more money than Kieu and her family have ever set eyes on.

Le Van Si

Suddenly I am out of the world of stratos dwellers and safe in the warm bosom of my extended family. Ngoc's mother, despite her crippled back, is radiant in silk pyjamas. Hong and Vuong now run a karaoke bar (they were into video rental last time). Tam, once a slim little fellow, is now unrecognisably plump. Duy and Nhan, children when Ngoc left Vietnam, are now handsome young adults. The scented bush I planted in the little square outside Hong's house during my last visit is flourishing. Brother-in-law Khanh's recycling business is going well, though heavily indebted. Bau, reflecting her family's improved fortunes, has put on weight since I last saw her. Dakla, who is Sarah's age, a little princess – bright, beautiful and with a smattering of English. All in all, the fragile fortunes of the family – like those of the country – are on the up.

Oh yes, one other piece of news. Mr Phuoc, whose family live five doors down from Hong and Vuong, was caught up in a huge financial scam – and shot by firing squad.

Saturday, 8 July

Ho Chi Minh City: a city of five, maybe six million people, almost entirely without public transport. The chaos is awesome. Much of the development is unregulated. Little metal-bashing factories have grown out of front or back rooms. Welding and banging is going on night and day alongside people trying to sleep and eat. This is how it must have been in England at the onset of the Industrial Revolution. The city is a huge construction site, everywhere little palaces are rising amid the shacks and shanties. Every fourth or fifth house, or so it seems, is a café emitting loud music.

On the outskirts the city is advancing remorselessly, gobbling up the little vegetable and fruit gardens; bypassing some, leaving them stranded. Islands of calm in the midst of the advancing chaos.

Khanh took me to see Le Qua and his family, who I have been supporting since he lost both arms in an accident on a building site. They live down a maze of alleyways. Only Khanh knows the way. For the first time that I can remember, Mrs LQ smiles, though goodness knows she has little enough to smile about. She has had major surgery – for cancer – since we last met. Given her exhaustion and malnutrition her survival is a miracle. The Vietnamese health service must be better than I supposed. Above the doorway leading to the dark interior of the house, a photograph of Ngoc's father has pride of place. He, after all, is their saviour. But for their chance meeting in the park Qua and his family would by now be destitute. As it is, their small economy is a miracle. He has managed to keep all his children in education, the oldest is now 21 and works part-time in a dentist's reception. Mrs LQ still works at her sewing machine, earning a dollar and a half a day turning out pillow cases. Also, they have let out half their tiny house. They must have been desperate to do that. Strangers lurk behind the curtain that divides the front and back rooms. We stay about 30 minutes. There is not a lot to say, so vast is the gulf that separates their small world from mine. Before we leave Khanh discreetly slides them the 600 US dollars I have brought. They do not know that in the UK they have a bank account containing more than 3,000 dollars. Were I to hand it over all in one go it would break their small economy. I have not told them how the money was raised. About my sponsored walk and the many people, including the Prime Minister and half the Cabinet, who contributed. This is information too great to absorb. It is enough for them to know that I will provide them with an income every year, until the children are old enough to support their parents.

Sunday, 9 July

A family outing to Dam Sen, a huge water park in what was once a Viet Cong-infested mangrove swamp. The entry fee is two and a half dollars a head, a price that only the prosperous can afford. Most of the small boys are overweight. A quote from V. S. Naipaul comes to mind: 'India is a very simple country. The poor are thin and the rich are fat.'

Monday, 10 July

To Tan Son Nhut airport, the scene of several tearful goodbyes in days past. Ngoc's family have been as generous and hospitable as ever and it is always good to see them, but Saigon no longer holds the romance that it once did. The dirt, the chaos, the skyscrapers do nothing for me. I long for the (relatively) fresh air and green fields of England. I am reading (as I do each time I come back) *The Quiet American*. A reminder of an age of innocence. A time when Saigon was a village of bicycles, cyclos and villas with red tiles and green shutters. Here and there the past can still be glimpsed, but it is fading rapidly and soon it will be gone for ever. There will be no one but a few naive and sentimental foreigners to mourn its passing.

Wednesday, 12 July

Among the messages awaiting my return, a stern e-mail from Bob Ainsworth, the Department whip. 'I need to talk to the Minister about repeated applications for absences on Thursdays …' The cheek of it. The implication is that I'm somehow skiving when in fact I'm worked out of my skull. I rang Bob, but he was in no mood for discussion. I have been ordered to cancel a visit I was due to make to Nottingham tomorrow and to stay down until late on Thursday. In vain did I protest that I was due to address a conference of industrial chaplains, on the New Deal, in Sunderland at 9.30 on Friday morning. Our flag-ship policy, no less, but I was ordered to cancel that, too. No skin off my back. In fact it saves me a good deal of work, but I do hate letting people down.

Betty Boothroyd announced that she is to retire at the end of the summer. She did it with great aplomb. 'Be happy for me,' she said when Members indicated disappointment.

Thursday, 13 July

Today sees the publication of the government's annual report. As last year, it has been received with general derision. Among the achieve-ments for which we congratulate ourselves, a national sports centre in Sheffield which doesn't exist. Another self-inflicted wound. Why do we do it? In the corridor behind the Speaker's chair I ran into The Man and took the opportunity to bend his ear about the importance of a high-level visit to Vietnam. 'I'll send JP,' he said. He looked washed out. A nerve was twitching in the side of his face, something I have never noticed before. I realised afterwards that he had just received a battering from Hague over this foolish annual report so I had caught him at a bad time. Saw Jim Cousins in the Library. 'We've talked ourselves into a crisis,' he said, 'and the truth is that there isn't one. It's the Blairistas who've done it. How on earth would they handle a real crisis?' Jim reckons that Gordon is planning a putsch soon after the election. Gordon's henchpersons, says Jim, are already putting out feelers. Jim has been approached. He named two of our colleagues, both disappointed seekers of office. One even suggested that Blair had a serious character defect (a bit rich coming from a fan of GB).

We were kept here until almost 1 a.m. in support of Jack Straw's Bill on football hooligans. In the event only six people voted against. By the end I was like a zombie. Since arriving back from Vietnam, I've only had one decent night's sleep.

Monday, 17 July

The Murdoch press has got hold of a memorandum, dated 29 April, written by The Man himself which is, to put it mildly, embarrassing. For a man whose greatest strength is his ability to think long term it is remarkably shallow and short term. There is an air of panic running through it. He focuses on five issues – the Martin case,* asylum, crime, defence and the family. 'These things add up to a sense that the government – and this even applies to me – are somehow out of touch with gut British instincts.' He goes on to call for 'eye-catching initiatives'. Example: 'Locking up street muggers … something tough with immediate bite.' (No doubt this is the origin of Jack Straw's nasty little Bill to mete out rough justice to football hooligans that is currently keeping us up half the night.) Needless to say the Tories and the media are having great fun. It is another spectacular own goal. Here is The Man saying in his own words that New Labour is out of touch.

1.40 a.m.

Bob Marshall-Andrews berated me in the Library corridor for not resigning over the Football Disorder Bill, which he regards as an affront to civilised values. In vain did I protest that it was only a minor piece of wickedness and probably wouldn't be much used. 'Oh, I see. You are supporting it because you think it won't be used. Is that it?' Actually, no. That isn't it. The truth is that you can only resign once and I don't consider this pathetic little Bill worth resigning over. 'Is there *anything* you would resign over?' he shouted. He was very po-faced. I've never seen Bob in such a mood before. Usually he is affable. I consoled myself with the thought that the hour was late.

Tuesday, 18 July

Gordon emerged from his Treasury bunker to announce his new three-year spending plans. Never has a Labour Chancellor had a better story to tell. Indeed, seldom has any Chancellor. This was Gordon the

---

*In April 2000 Tony Martin, a recluse, was convicted of manslaughter after shooting dead a teenage burglar: his case was taken up by the tabloids and he was released after three years.

Magnificent. He stood erect at the Dispatch Box, his notes laid out upon two thick copies of Hansard so that he scarcely had to bend his head. His finest hour. No ya-boo. No waffle. Just fact after remorseless fact. Beside him The Man, worn down from the battering of recent days, looked a pale shadow. Were the throne to become vacant now or at any time in the near future there is no doubt who would succeed.

Portillo made a lacklustre response. I've never seen him so bad. Not really his fault. What could he say? His only hope was to begin with a little self-deprecating humour, but instead he opted for phony indignation and was, as a result, doomed from the outset. The Tories looked pale. Not a spark of light from any of them. I guess they were reflecting that a government presiding over an economy so sound as ours could not possibly lose an election – no matter how hard we try.

Wednesday, 19 July

The Murdoch press have got hold of another damaging memo. This one from Philip Gould. It seems that the Tories have acquired a pile of internal memoranda and are controlling their release with a view to inflicting maximum damage. 'Our current situation is serious,' opines the King of Focus. '… For much of the time the government has been drifting … The New Labour brand has been badly contaminated. It is the object of constant criticism and, even worse, ridicule. Undermined by a combination of spin, lack of conviction and an apparent lack of integrity …'

Among his less remarkable insights: 'The Tories have outflanked us on patriotism …' On and on he drivels, digging the pit deeper with every paragraph. Panic seeping from every pore. New Labour is imploding. As Jim Cousins says, they are talking us into a crisis that doesn't exist. This man Gould is a complete disaster. This is the third of his doom-laden memoranda to be leaked. Any good he has ever done (and I'm not aware of any) has been far outweighed by the damage his leaks inflict. If we are not to self-destruct, The Man needs to get a grip. We must start leading and stop following. We must aim to please no more than 60, rather than 100, per cent of the electorate. Above all, we should dispose of the entire menagerie of spinners and focus-groupies – starting with Brother Gould.

'We need a step change,' I remarked to Clive Soley before he disappeared into the parliamentary committee this afternoon: 'Sack Philip Gould.'

'Oh, I don't know,' replied Clive airily. 'He tells the PM things he doesn't hear from MPs.' Maybe, but unfortunately he also tells the entire world.

Monday, 24 July

Awoke to the news that there is to be no reshuffle this summer. Damn. I had been counting on it.

To JP's room at Eland House for end-of-term drinks. He is looking happier and more relaxed than I have ever seen him. The bags under his eyes have receded. He has a ready smile and exudes goodwill to all men. The reason, of course, is not hard to divine. After years of toil and ridicule, JP has emerged triumphant. He has squeezed more money out of the Treasury than any environment secretary or transport minister in history.

Tony Benn has slipped me a copy of a spoof memorandum he has concocted on Downing Street headed notepaper. He says mischievously that he has only given a copy to Jean Corston and me and that, if it leaks, he will know where from.

TOP SECRET
To: PRIME MINISTER
Subject: NEW LABOUR: A MEDICAL REPORT

New Labour is suffering from BOGUS SPIN EXERCISES (BSE) and has brought about a condition known as CONTAMINATED JARGON DISORDER (CJD) which can prove fatal in political parties.

A further bulletin will be issued later.

I would be grateful if you would treat this report as being completely confidential.

Professor Philip Gould,
Medical Director,
The Millbank Clinic.

Wednesday, 26 July

We were due to announce our plans for dealing with leylandii today but, to my dismay, Michael Meacher cancelled the press conference at the last moment because he couldn't make it and flatly refuses to delegate even a matter so trivial as this. Instead he has rearranged the announcement for mid-August when I am on holiday and only he is available. I love Michael dearly and he is an excellent minister, but anything remotely interesting or likely to generate even a morsel of publicity, he greedily hoards. His idea of delegating is to let me sign the letters and do the adjournment debates. He is notorious for it. Angela Eagle once told him that he needed a secretary rather than a junior minister. I could have a row with him, but it's not worth the energy.

Friday, 28 July
Sunderland

To the University to make a speech about the environment at a little conference organised by the local authority. Its purpose is unclear. Principally, I suspect, so that the council's director of environment can tick a box showing that he has, in the best New Labour tradition, gone through the motions of consulting.

'How are you getting there?' asked my assistant, Pat, as ever solicitous for my welfare.

'I'm walking.'

'But it's on the other side of the river.'

'Yes, Pat, it is the best part of a mile ... but after all I am going to be talking about persuading people to leave their cars at home and there has to be some sort of connection between words and action.'

In the event it was a lovely walk. The sun was shining. Mowbray Park was blooming. Huge flower baskets are hanging from every lamp post in Fawcett Street. The scaffolding has been removed from the rear of the old Corn Exchange affording a fine view from across the river. How the city centre and the river front have been transformed from the low point we reached ten years ago after the loss of the shipyards and the mines. For all the complaining we must be doing something right.

We were supposed to be talking about sustainable living, but all anyone wanted to talk about was the depredations of the underclass and the failure of the council and the government to deal with the problem. On and on they whinged, unprepared to concede that anything, anywhere had changed for the better. Some of those who had come to talk about the bigger picture walked out. The chairman ruled some of the questions out of order, which only made matters worse. The underclass problem dominates everything. There are no quick fixes. Maybe there are no fixes at all. Will we ever put the genie back in the bottle?

Monday, 31 July

My attention was drawn to Andrew Rawnsley writing in yesterday's *Observer*. His theme is the alleged growing ineffectiveness of Parliament and includes the following:

> I always took Chris Mullin to be an MP of quality, intelligence and a man of independence. Unfortunately Tony Blair spotted that as well. The MP for Sunderland South was turning into an outstanding chairman of the home affairs committee. Then the Prime Minister tempted him with the greasy pole. Since he became a junior minister, Mr Mullin has been buried as effectively as if he had been fitted with concrete over-shoes and dropped into the Thames.

Tuesday, 8 August
Gamekeeper's Cottage, Northchapel, West Sussex

I saw the woodpecker this morning. For years I have sat in this garden listening to the tap tap tap in the trees around the cottage, but never actually seen him. Today, while I was reading, he appeared in the laurel tree near the front door, no more than three yards away. Green with a red head-dress. Sarah says she saw him on the lawn outside her window yesterday.

Monday, 14 August
Isle of Wight

Something dreadful has happened. A Russian nuclear submarine has gone down in the Barents Sea. There are 118 men on board and they have oxygen for seven days.

Tuesday, 15 August

With the children to the beach. The tide was high and it was crowded, unlike yesterday. The white cliffs make a magnificent backdrop. As I sit in the sunshine, watching the children play, I can't get those Russian boys out of my mind – the cold, the dark, the terror.

Wednesday, 16 August

A truly massive pile of correspondence awaits signature. My Private Secretary, Chris, estimates there are the best part of a thousand letters. It seems the signing system during recess has broken down because Michael Meacher, who was the duty minister before my stint, refused to sign any letters but his own. I am, therefore, left with everyone else's in addition to my own – and I already handle far more correspondence than any other minister in the Department, possibly in the entire government. Really this is too much. Much as I love Michael, he is not a team player.

Friday, 18 August

An interesting little insight into the mad world of nuclear warfare passed my desk today. I was asked to approve deletions, on grounds of national security or commercial secrecy, from reports by the Competition Commission into the pricing policy of two water companies. One related to a 1989 directive to water companies about what would be required of them in the aftermath of nuclear war. One of the requirements – which not surprisingly the Powers That Be do not want publicised – is that the companies must be capable of supplying water to 20 per cent of the population, presumably the optimum number of likely survivors.

Sunday, 20 August
Sunderland

Norwegian divers have entered the *Kursk* and found no sign of life. The question is might it have been different if they had been called in sooner? Probably not. All the same, many Russians must have noticed how foreigners were able to do in a few hours what their own navy had been unable to do in a week. It is time Russia's rulers stopped pretending to be global players and concentrated instead on looking after their people.

Wednesday, 23 August

Hardly a day passes when I don't compose my resignation letter. Version One goes something like this:

> Dear Tony,
> As you may recall from our discussion at the time I was appointed, I was reluctant to trade one of the main select committee chairmanships for one of the lowliest posts in the government. My only excuse for doing so was the hope that it might lead to something better. I now realise that this is unlikely. After much thought, I have concluded that my present incarnation is not a sensible use of my limited talents and I would therefore be grateful if you would accept my resignation.
>
> Please be assured of my continuing support.

A more robust version might omit the final sentence, remind The Man of his various assurances and suggest that my present job is more suited to an ambitious thirty-something. But that is liable to lead to charges of sour grapes, quite apart from which it would gratuitously upset all the ambitious thirty-somethings in the parliamentary party. A light touch is called for. Pomposity or the appearance of sulking to be avoided at all costs.

Friday, 1 September
Sunderland

Half a dozen girl guides came to ask questions. An interview with an elected representative being a requirement for a Baden Powell Award. They were bright, intelligent 14-year-olds, but one thing they said depressed me. 'When we receive our awards we don't want our picture in the *Echo*.'

'Why not?'

'Because the other kids at school would make fun of us.'

Their leader added, 'It's not cool.'

The alleged north–south divide came up at the monthly meeting of my local party this evening. I said there was a lot of claptrap talked about it. If you turn left at the end of my street you come, within a few hundred yards, to houses that are unsaleable. Turn right and you soon come to houses which change hands for £250,000 and more. The two communities live within a mile of each other, but they might as well be on different planets. They never meet – unless one burgles the other. The problem isn't a north–south divide. It's a class divide and it exists to a greater or lesser extent in every city in the country. What's more, anyone with a secure job on a national salary scale – teachers, nurses, doctors, MPs – is far better off in Sunderland than Surrey because the housing costs are so much lower. To my surprise, no one challenged this.

Wednesday, 7 September

A great new crisis over the Dome, triggered by the news that yet another huge wodge of lottery money has had to be thrown at it. The tabloids are baying for the head of poor Charlie Falconer. Most unfair considering that this great folly was well underway by the time he came on the scene. Peter Mandelson, the real culprit, is over in Northern Ireland keeping his head well below the parapet. This wretched Dome has become an albatross. A symbol of all that is wrong with New Labour: shallow, over-hyped, naff.

Friday, 8 September

The evening bulletins are leading with The Man's latest crusade – to persuade comprehensive schools to do more for brighter pupils. As with all previous education initiatives this one has been instantly denounced by teachers who say that, anyway, they are already doing most of what he is calling for. My goodness, how the teachers loathe us. Why can't we just leave them alone for a year or two? We are pouring billions into education and generating huge ill-will. Pray that we don't repeat the trick in the health service.

Monday, 11 September

A crisis brewing over fuel prices. Farmers and lorry drivers are blockading oil refineries, which has triggered a bout of panic buying. Queues at every petrol station and some have run dry. Are we catching the French disease? The *Echo* rang to ask my opinion and I said I had no sympathy whatever with the blockaders. The farmers, forsooth, are the most heavily subsidised people in the country. What's more, they can buy red diesel for a few pence a litre. Where do they imagine their subsidies come from, if not taxes? As for the lorry drivers, they are trying to pretend that recent increases in fuel prices are the fault of the government whereas they are almost entirely the result of increases in the world price of oil – from 10 dollars a barrel to over 30. To be sure, fuel is more heavily taxed here than on the Continent; overall however our taxes are far lower – and unlike France we have no road tolls.

Wednesday, 13 September

More to this than meets the eye. It's becoming clear that the main problem appears to be, not blockades, but a strike by tanker drivers in which the oil companies are conniving. The police are advising that access to the refineries is clear and yet very few tankers are emerging. Oil company bosses were summoned to Downing Street yesterday and given a bollocking, but they still appear to be sitting on their hands. They cite intimidation as the reason for dragging their heels, but incidents of intimidation appear to be few and far between. When pressed to provide examples, the best one spokesman could offer was 'Someone threw a traffic cone at one of our tankers on Friday.' A long talk with Richard Mottram, who has been involved in dealing with the crisis. He says that both ministers and officials were slow off the mark and that the machinery for coping with a crisis of this sort is very rusty. 'We had been lulled into complacency by the long period of calm since the miners' strike.' He added that part of the problem is that the oil companies mainly employ non-union drivers with the result that no one has much influence over them. JP, Joe Irvin and Gus Macdonald had been on to the unions who had been doing what they could to get the drivers moving, but their influence is limited.

According to Richard, 'there is no Plan B'. Talk of bringing in the army is bluff. There are only about 200 qualified tanker drivers in the military. Not enough was being done to apprise people of the consequences. We should be facilitating midwives, ambulance drivers and so on to get on the media and describe the havoc the blockade is causing. (A boy of 12 has been killed while dodging round cars queuing for petrol. His parents had made a very forthright statement laying the blame squarely on the blockade, but it has not been picked up. If these were striking miners, the story would have been all over the media by now.) There is a danger that millions of farm animals will start to die if fuel and food doesn't get through in a few days. Officials wanted to run with this, but Downing Street had vetoed it – at least for the time being. Two thousand petrol stations have been designated to provide supplies for emergency workers.

Richard was very critical of the police. There have been virtually no arrests. No trucks have been impounded. 'They keep advising us that no offences have been committed, but if you or I drove at five miles an hour down the A1, we'd get lifted pretty quickly. We are getting reports that the tankers delivering petrol are being followed. Surely they could stop that?' This afternoon the police have stopped a convoy of trucks who were proposing to blockade central London, so they can do it when they want to.

Even the *Mirror* has turned on us. 'EMPTY', says the front page of today's edition over mugshots of The Man, JP and Gordon superimposed on petrol pumps. A caption underneath reads: 'These three men run the country. Today, the country will run dry. None of them quite knows how to get it going again ... but they all agree it's not their fault.' Very damaging. Will we ever recover?

'Am I the only one to see similarities between the current petrol crisis and the power workers' strike in the film of Chris Mullin's book *A Very British Coup*?' writes A. J. Vaughan of Rochford, Essex, in a letter in this morning's *Guardian*.

Thursday, 14 September

To Preston for Audrey Wise's funeral. At Euston I ran into Ken Livingstone and we had a coffee together. How does he like his new job? 'I love it. Something to do at last instead of all that hanging around.' Assembly members, he said, were frustrated because the system devised by New Labour (with a no doubt tame candidate in mind) gave them no power. 'I can do what I like,' he chuckled. 'All they have to look forward to is a review of their pay by the Top Salaries Review Board.' I asked about his plans for congestion charges. Ken was, as ever, relaxed. 'They don't come in for another three years. And when they do, they'll be accompanied by large cuts in bus and tube fares.'

Audrey had a good send-off. One little-known fact: she was 68, not 65, having shaved three years off her age in order to improve her chances of selection at Coventry and never adding them back on.

Home by ten o'clock.

Friday, 15 September

Spent most of the day sunk in deep gloom. The media is full of vox pops with people saying they'll never vote Labour again. Some, of course, never voted Labour in the first place, but that's not the point. After years of creeping and crawling to Middle England, they've abandoned us at the first whiff of grapeshot. Come the election the Tories will run broadcasts of petrol queues and old clips of rubbish piling up in the streets in 1979 and say that this is what happens when you have a Labour government. How can we possibly counter that? This morning's *Sun* comes with an ultimatum: You have 60 days to deliver, or else.

Today came a call from Radio 4's Sunday morning breakfast show, *Broadcasting House*. My instinct was to do it. I rang Chris in the private office and asked if he could get clearance. To my surprise the answer came back, 'Yes.' There then followed a 30-page briefing from the Cabinet Office, most of it irrelevant. One amusing line, however: 'Don't use the word "crisis".'

Saturday, 16 September
Sunderland

Awoke to Gordon Brown on *Today* doing his Iron Chancellor act in response to the petrol tankers' blockade of the past week. He made all the right points but his style, involving constant, wooden repetition of the same on-message phrases, sends out bad vibes. In the afternoon I took the children to the beach and when I got back there were messages on the answerphone bidding me ring the BBC and the Cabinet Office. Sure enough, my many superiors have decided that I am far too lowly to undertake a national radio interview. Without consulting me, someone's minion has taken it upon himself to tell the BBC that Gus Macdonald will be doing the interview instead. This has led to a blazing row, of which I was blissfully unaware. In vain did the producer protest that she didn't want Gus, or anyone else parroting the government line. She wants me. It's either me or no one. Another triumph for the masters of spin. After a couple of fruitless calls to the special unit in the Cabinet Office which has been set up to handle the crisis that is not a crisis, I finally received a call from Alastair Campbell. As so often when you get to the top, I found him entirely relaxed about my doing the interview. 'You may be able to say some things that other ministers can't,' he said. He was scathing about the hacks and what he called 'the complete suspension of any serious analysis'. I asked why ministers had been so reluctant to come out fighting. He said, 'Because we were slow off the mark, we were on the back foot all week.' He added cheerfully, 'I have to curb my natural instinct to lay into the media. I think they are complete scum.'

Sunday, 17 September

Sure enough the Murdoch press is this morning running opinion polls showing that, for the first time in eight years, the Tories are moving into the lead. Hardly surprising, given the pounding we've had in the last five days.

Knowing that my many superiors would be listening, I prepared carefully for the Radio 4 interview. The other guests were Tariq Ali, Bruce Kent and Boris Johnson. I was taken aback to find that Tariq and Bruce made common cause with Johnson and the blockaders and laid into me as the nearest representative of the government to hand. I supposed I shouldn't be surprised about Tariq, who is, after all, a Trot, but I expected better of Bruce. Deeply depressing. If *he* can't see what's going on, what hope is there?

Monday, 18 September

Penned the following note to Bruce Kent:

> Dear Bruce, I was sorry to see that you have thrown in your lot with the blockaders. Be under no illusion, if they are allowed to win, what we will end up with is not a more left-wing government, but a Tory one. For heaven's sake, wake up.

Spent the morning with Nick Raynsford touring some of the tougher areas of Sunderland. Part of my campaign to persuade him to cut off the flow of housing benefit to rogue landlords. We visited Pennywell, Pallion and Hendon and met aggrieved citizens whose lives have been blighted by anti-social neighbours and villainous landlords. Finally we ended up at the Civic Centre for a conference with the movers and shakers. Nick was good. He promised licensing for landlords with three or more properties and was sympathetic to demands for an end to direct payment of housing benefit to rogue landlords. Whether any of it will come in time to save Hendon remains to be seen.

Thursday, 21 September

Barbara Castle, La Pensionoria as Polly Toynbee calls her, was on the radio this morning demanding the restoration of the link between pensions and earnings. As ever, she was brilliant, but goodness knows what it would cost. And the poorest would be far worse off if we had to divide our largesse by 11 million pensioners. Not that there's been a peep out of the poorest pensioners. Somewhere in Sunderland there are several thousand who are £10 or £11 a week better off as a result of Gordon's minimum income guarantee, but I have yet to meet even one who will admit to receiving it, let alone defend it.

Saturday, 23 September
Sunderland

A reply from Bruce Kent:

> Really, Chris, the question you ought to be asking yourself is this: How have you and yours managed to alienate so many thousands of traditional Labour supporters so quickly … like me? … The landmarks on my road to alienation are clear enough: student grants, Livingstone, pensions, arms sales, nuclear weapons and perhaps worst of all Kosovo.

He concludes, 'Sorry old chum. I do not forget the many good causes you have pursued and the many people in trouble you have helped. But at the moment our roads do not converge.'

Monday, 25 September

To Brighton for the conference. Too late to hear Gordon Brown's speech. He had flown back especially from an IMF meeting in Prague (shades of Denis Healey circa 1976?*) and returned there immediately. By all accounts he was well received (unlike Healey). He promised all

---

*During the 1976 Labour Party conference, the then Chancellor, Denis Healey, who had been on his way to an IMF meeting in Manila, had to be diverted from Heathrow to Blackpool to plead with the conference not to oppose his plans for an IMF rescue package.

sorts of goodies for pensioners, except the one thing they are all demanding – restoration of the link with earnings – but the details were obscure. As always with Gordon, you can't help feeling there's a catch which will only come to light the morning after. The problem with our policy on pensions is that it takes about 15 minutes to explain, whereas it takes a few seconds to shout, 'Restore the link.'

Tuesday, 26 September

To the conference centre for The Man's speech. Seldom has a leader's speech been more eagerly awaited. We are in a deep hole. Will he dig us deeper or lift us out? I sat in the rear of the side galley, beyond the reach of roving TV cameras, to avoid being implicated in the syco-phancy that is *de rigueur* on these occasions. As it turns out he was brilliant. On pensions and the Dome he began with a note of humil-ity: 'I get the message,' he said to loud applause (although he claimed that this was only with hindsight, overlooking the fact that many of us had been attempting to smuggle messages to him from the outset). Then some stuff about strong leadership – 'The test of leadership is not how eloquently you say yes, it is how you explain why you are saying no.' He rang all the right bells: no surrender to the blockaders, full employment, a second term more radical than the first, a bit of fun at Hague's expense, but not too much. Some naff stuff about the price of a pair of trainers, but no more nonsense about room for every-one inside the big tent. The bit that went down best seemed to have been inserted at the last moment (it wasn't in the official text). 'I am by instinct a unifier. I prefer compromise, but I have an irreducible core ...' By the end, shirt damp with sweat, he was our hero again, although of course the real test is how it plays outside. Early indica-tions are favourable, but it will take more than a good speech to dig us out.

Friday, 29 September
Sunderland

A letter from John Pilger enclosing a cheque, in response to my request for sponsorship to help the family of Le Qua, the Vietnamese man who has lost both arms. He upbraids me for failing to speak out about British involvement in 'containing' Iraq and the recent bombing of Serbia. He goes on, 'I saw the same in Vietnam, Chris – there is no difference, be assured. I'd very much like to hear from you and learn that your apparent silence has been broken. I know you won't send me one of Cook's or Hain's standard letters.'

Oh dear, first Bruce Kent, now John Pilger. On Serbia, I don't have a problem. We cannot allow the return of ethnic cleansing in Europe. Any doubts I had were clarified by the slaughter at Srebrenica. As for Iraq, Pilger may well be right, though whether a word from me would make any difference is another matter. There is also the tricky question of what would happen to the Kurds and the Shia if we took the pressure off Saddam.

Monday, 9 October

To the Hilton hotel in Blackpool to address yet another conference of housing professionals. Another of Nick Raynsford's hand-me-downs. Eight hours of travel, involving four trains, two taxis and a tube. The speech was 19 pages long. The text was faxed up last week. All I had to do was read it out. I couldn't bring myself even to glance at it until I was on the train. We had nothing new to announce and I departed with indecent haste (only two questions, both planted). I very much doubt I have made anyone happier. Why do we do it?

Wednesday, 18 October

To Manchester to address the annual conference of the Airport Operators' Association. Just one short paragraph of the speech is my own, but it is a significant one: a warning not to get too hung up on the prospect of indefinite growth. 'Predict and Provide did not work for roads. It has not worked for housing. And it will not work for airports.' I notice these words are beginning to find their way into most official pronouncements on the future of aviation. Perhaps, after all, I may leave a tiny footprint.

Thursday, 19 October

Another little homily from Chris, my Private Secretary, on my refusal to read most of the weighty documents marked 'To See' which cross my desk. The immediate cause was a tome on producer responsibility addressed to Michael Meacher on which Chris thinks I ought to comment. I pointed out (a) that my opinion was not being sought and (b) that I have never had the slightest involvement with the issue and that my opinion is, therefore, of no value. 'Other ministers would have read the document,' said Chris. To which I responded that I have better things to do with my time. I added that it is not laziness, but a realistic assessment of my situation. I have a clear strategy. Only to intervene when I might make a difference – and that is not often. In the meantime I sit tight and pray for rescue.

Friday, 20 October
Sunderland

With Ngoc to see *Billy Elliot* at the Boldon multiplex. It was shot mostly in Seaham and Easington against the background of the miners' strike. There must be hundreds of little Billy Elliots round here. Underclass children who, if they had had the same chances as my Sarah and Emma, might have been stars. Towards the end there is a scene where one of the little posh boys he meets when he goes for an audition at the Royal Ballet asks where he comes from. 'County Durham,' replies Billy. 'Durham,' says the posh boy. 'Isn't there a grand cathedral up there?' 'Dunno,' says Billy. I look at all the shiny, optimistic little faces waiting with their parents in the playground at Grangetown school for the doors to open. And then I look at their parents and I can see at a glance who will prosper and who is doomed. It is so sad.

Monday, 23 October

To London for the election of the Speaker. Voting was mainly along tribal lines, with most of our side supporting Michael Martin from the outset and most of the Tories falling in behind George Young. The Tories were upset because, by convention, it should have been their turn. Also, there is unease on our side as to whether Michael is up to it. 'The word from the clerks is that he isn't,' according to Donald Anderson. I should have voted for George, but faced with a choice between an Etonian baronet and a lad from the slums of Glasgow, my heart overruled my head. The outcome, of course, is that we have yet another Scotsman ruling England.

Wednesday, 25 October

A pep talk from The Man at this evening's meeting of the parliamentary party. We are no longer in awe of him as we used to be. The magic is fading. There are times when I think that he has become just another inadequate politician like the rest of us. Yet it was an impressive performance. With beautiful clarity he set out the dividing line between us and the Tories, on the economy, public services and Europe. By the end one was left realising that there is still no one else to match him.

Monday, 30 October

Awoke to reports of wind, rain, floods. Bognor Regis has been hit by a tornado. Drove to Durham only to be told there were no trains running south of York so I returned to Sunderland, spent the day in the office and flew down from Newcastle in the evening. Even the plane was two hours late. The transport infrastructure is breaking down and there is talk of hospitals being unable to cope. Also, the hauliers are said to be plotting another bout of mayhem.

Tuesday, 31 October

A meeting of ministers in JP's office. The first for three months. JP is to make a statement this afternoon. As usual, he was slumped in his armchair, huffing and puffing, but what he said made sense. 'We've got to start planning for windy and wet, rather than cold, weather. We can't continue calling this weather exceptional. It isn't. Two or three more of these and the insurance companies are going to say sod it.' He went on, 'Why is it that the power lines on our railways come down every time we get a bit of wind? It's because British Rail, at the insistence of the Treasury, went for the cheap option years ago. It isn't true to say that the current problems are all down to privatisation. Railtrack are investing more than British Rail ever did.'

Thursday, 2 November

With exquisite timing, given the floods and general pestilence, I have to give a speech on sustainable drainage at a conference in Newcastle tomorrow. The official draft was execrable so I spent two hours drafting my own, almost managing to render sustainable drainage interesting. I sent my draft back to officials and they came back with a couple of quibbles. I conceded the first, but not the second – my suggestion that we are addicted to the motor car. All day they kept trying to change my mind, but I held out. My, what sensitive flowers we are.

An extraordinary journey home. I went to King's Cross in good time for the 18.00 only to be told that the track was flooded and there were no trains north of York (on Monday there were none running south of York). I decided to chance it. To begin with all seemed well. We reached York in three hours, which wasn't bad considering the diversion around Hatfield. At York we were loaded onto a bus and set off for Darlington. It was raining heavily and in places water was running across the road. The further we went the more inundated the roads. The A1 was already closed so we headed up the A19, only to discover that was also blocked. We reached Northallerton to find the town centre was a lake (the roofs of cars just visible in the water). Three of the four roads out were impassable. Three times we had to make three-point turns in narrow roads. And the rain kept falling. We passed soldiers, firemen, abandoned cars. Backwards and forwards we went, splashing through floods that smaller vehicles dared not enter. 'I'm running out of options,' said the driver, 'if the Swale has over-flowed, you've had it.' And so we had.

Sometime after midnight the coach was brought to a halt by a dreadful scraping sound. A large piece of metal underseal had become detached. The driver, who remained in good humour throughout, clambered down into the mud and rain and set about extricating it. His radio sprang to life. A woman's voice inquiring anxiously where we were. None of us knew and the driver was busy under the bus. 'Don't worry,' said the voice, 'GNER will look after you.' At which a great cheer went up. Morale was high.

At about 1.30, having been driving round north Yorkshire for four hours, we were deposited back at York station and shepherded into an empty train. This was the low point. Despite assurances to the contrary, it looked as though we might spend the night there. But no. Within half an hour we were off again and before we knew it, booked into a four-star hotel. GNER, God bless it, was sparing no expense.

Friday, 3 November
Sunderland

Up at seven, after four hours' sleep. The television news is showing scenes of devastation in York city centre, less than half a mile away, where the river is said to be 17 feet above normal. But here all is tran-quillity. By breakfast, bright sunshine. From my table by the huge Georgian dining room window, a fine view of the twin towers of the Minster, set against a clear blue sky. Last night's mayhem is no more than a bad dream.

After breakfast we set off again, by bus. At 12.40 – almost 19 hours after leaving King's Cross – we are deposited at Durham Station. 'The frustrating thing is,' remarked a young man sitting beside me, 'there is no one to blame.'

As for my much-laboured-over speech on sustainable drainage ... I never got to make it.

Tuesday, 7 November

A chat with John Major in the gents' loo on Upper Corridor South (he asked to borrow my Listerine). John says he's not going to the House of Lords when he stands down next year. 'I wouldn't feel right in my skin,' he said. Adding mischievously, 'You right-wingers don't understand what working-class boys like me feel about the place.' I pointed out that (on our side at least) the Lords is full of working-class boys. He's working on two books: 'one about cricket and the other is a secret – except that it's not about politics'. I suspect he may be trying his hand at a novel.

For the second time this term, Sarah and Emma are off school because water is pouring through its roof and the heating has packed up.

To bed just after 1.00 a.m. According to the television Al Gore is likely to be the next US President.

Wednesday, 8 November

Awoke to find that George Bush is in the lead. Everything hangs on the outcome in Florida, which is on a knife edge.

Jack Straw at his most illiberal addressed the weekly party meeting. The Cambridge MP, Anne Campbell, referred to animal rights protesters against Huntingdon Life Sciences, in her constituency, as 'terrorists', a sentiment which Jack endorsed. 'It's time we stopped pandering to the anti-vivisectionists. No one wants to be gratuitously cruel to animals, but we do actually eat them.' (Speak for yourself, I thought.) Our scientists were too restricted, he went on. Medicines had to be tested on animals. It was time we faced up to this.

Then someone complained about travellers and that really got Jack going. 'If you think there are one or two liberals left among officials in the Home Office, you should try the DETR. Isn't that right, Chris?'

I indicated assent. At which point JP came to life, giving me one of his blackest looks. 'Do you agree?'

'Yes.'

'Then we must do something.' He scribbled furiously.

Actually, it's true. We are forever getting complaints about the huge quantities of litter and other detritus left by unauthorised campers: 10, 20, 30 tons of rubbish are not uncommon and yet the law appears to be virtually useless. Officials just make excuses. The latest is the Human Rights Act. 'Surely,' I say, 'the victims have human rights, too,' but they just giggle uneasily.

Much merriment at Prime Minister's Questions, at the discovery that Hague was a member of the Cabinet committee which gave the go-ahead to the Dome. He was even party to the wildly optimistic projections of visitor numbers which has haunted us ever since. As a result The Man effortlessly brushed aside poor William's attempts to stir up righteous indignation. An unexpected bonus. We shan't always be able to shelter behind the follies of the previous regime, but it's fun while it lasts.

Thursday, 9 November

Another meeting, against official advice, with Putney MP Tony Colman about night flights. After our previous meeting (which officials also advised against) it was agreed that the British Airports Authority would set up a meeting with the airlines to discuss channelling night flights into a narrower time frame, but needless to say nothing has happened. Our official who sat in on the meeting made no secret of his view that nothing can be done and deeply resents my meddling. He grew more surly as the meeting progressed and after it was over he had a long quiet chat with my Private Secretary, Chris, outside in the corridor. Later, Chris ticked me off for showing up the official, but I am unrepentant. The relationship between the airlines and the Department is far too cosy. The only hope of doing anything about night flights is to link them to the fate of terminal five. For that I must first get Gus and JP on board.

Tuesday, 14 November

Lunch with Bruce Grocott in the Millbank Room. Bruce is one of the most sensible people at court. An antidote to all those immature New Labour types who infest the higher reaches. As he says, 'Apart from Tony, I am the only person in Number 10 who is elected and who travels regularly beyond the M25.' Along with Alastair Campbell (of whom Bruce speaks highly) he is the only one who can be relied upon to tell The Man to his face what he might not want to hear. Bruce says he is regarded as an amiable eccentric by the courtiers. He is wholly opposed to the air traffic sell-off and has told The Man so. 'We had almost succeeded in making "privatisation" a dirty word and now we are making it respectable again.' I pointed out that with air traffic control, as with so many other things that get us into trouble (single-parent benefit, the 75 pence pension increase, the ridiculous over-spinning), the trail leads back to Gordon, who, when the shit hits the fan, is nowhere to be seen. Why doesn't The Man stand up to him? 'I think Tony is rather in awe of Gordon,' says Bruce. He adds that, since the fuel crisis, The Man has become more receptive to advice. 'Until then, New Labour had it too easy. They didn't have to listen, and they didn't.' Bruce went on, 'I don't believe New Labour has abolished the economic cycle either. Sooner or later there is going to be an economic crisis.'

Has he said this to The Man?

'Yes.'

Wednesday, 15 November

Cold, foggy, frosty. The Palace of Westminster invisible from Lambeth Bridge and in St James's Park the pelicans still have their heads under their wings. I spent the morning drafting a speech for a conference of local councillors I have been asked to address on Friday in place of Hilary Armstrong. The official draft was useless. Full of New Labour claptrap about strategies, visions, challenges and opportunities, which I was expected to stand and chant like a Mormon missionary. I rewrote it without reference to the official version and even included a couple of cautious paragraphs about proportional representation which upset the officials, but when I checked them with Hilary she was relaxed.

A breakthrough on night flights. To my pleasant surprise Gus has reacted sympathetically to my note and agreed that I should write something for inclusion in the aviation White Paper in December. The airlines won't be happy. Nor will officials. Incidentally, Keith Hill recalled lunching with Sir John Egan* four years ago and being told that the airlines would be willing to trade night flights in exchange for terminal five. He is the second person to tell me that (the other was Tony Colman). The trouble is that nothing is in writing and the airlines seem to have gone off the idea now they are confident of getting their new terminal anyway. I must find a way of smoking this out.

Friday, 17 November

A wicked piece by Simon Hoggart on the 'urban' White Paper which was launched in Manchester yesterday.

> This is a classic New Labour document, being printed on glossy paper and illustrated with colour pictures of the Elysium that is the new Britain. Happy people, many from ethnic minorities, gaze productively at computer screens. Pensioners get off a gleaming, streamlined tram which has just delivered them promptly and inexpensively to their grandchildren … The prose has the same unreal quality. Nothing actually happens. Nothing tangible is planned. But we are promised there will be 'innovative developments', 'local strategic partnerships' and 'urban policy units'. Town councils will have new powers to 'promote well-being' … and, just in case we think this will never happen, we are promised that 'visions for the future will be developed'. There will be a 'key focus' here and a 'co-ordinated effort' there. The government in its wisdom has 'established a framework'. The whole thing resembles those fantastical architect's drawings in which slim, well-dressed figures stroll across tree-festooned piazzas with no mention of empty burger boxes or gangs of glowering youths.

---

*Chief Executive, British Airports Authority, 1990–99.

Monday, 20 November

A meeting to discuss night flights. The memo from Gus has had the desired effect. This time the top official appeared. He was amiable and straightforward. He is wholly opposed to rescheduling and will resist every inch of the way. The airlines, who he described as 'bastards', will mount tough resistance. They may even, he suggested, use the Human Rights Act against us, 'corporations are people, too'. He considers it his job to see terminal five agreed with as few conditions and little fuss as possible. I asked him to provide me with a note setting out how a ban on night flights might be achieved. He reluctantly suggested that the idea might be floated at the aviation summit in February and that, if we decide to go ahead, it could be linked to the terminal five announcement next summer. The problem – as officials well know – is that I shall be gone from the Department by then and they will still be here.

Friday, 23 November
Sunderland

Lunch with Denise Barna, who runs the Neighbourhood Centre in Pennywell. During her time Pennywell has been transformed. Public money poured in and most of it was put to good use. All the same, she was pessimistic. Many residents, she says, are trapped in a huge benefit culture and determined to remain that way. Just about all the single mothers who registered with a child care provider (to qualify for Working Families' Tax Credit) withdrew their children as soon as they had qualified. Also, the first dozen women from an Into Work programme for single mothers found part-time work in order to qualify for the bonus on offer. Within weeks, however, all but one were back on benefit. The last followed soon afterwards. No doubt they all feature as successes in the figures reported back to Whitehall. She is worried about what will happen when the regeneration money dries up in three or four years. Says Denise, 'It will take at least a generation to make any permanent changes.'

Wednesday, 29 November

Mike O'Brien, a Home Office minister, whispered that he had come close to resigning today after a row with Jack over animal testing. There have been repeated complaints about Huntingdon Life Sciences and Mike wanted to set up an inquiry, but Jack overruled him. Jack also insisted that Mike sign a letter refusing an inquiry, which Mike was reluctant to do since he had more or less committed himself to one. Eventually, after considerable agonising and rewriting, he signed.

Thursday, 30 November

JP has sent Gus a note saying that he wishes to be kept informed about our plans for night flights. This in turn has triggered a note from Gus which, reading between the lines, appears to be backtracking on his earlier enthusiasm. Shayne, in my private office, has appended a note to the bottom: 'This looks ominous.'

This morning, in the absence of Gus, I was asked to sign a letter to the Foreign Office setting out the Department's view on continuing with the ban on air travel to Afghanistan. Naively, I suggested a minor amendment. 'Oh, that's not for you,' blurted my attentive Private Secretary.

'So why are you asking for my approval, if I am not allowed to change anything?'

A weary smile. He disappears. Five minutes later he is back. 'I've passed on your concern.'

'I don't want my concern passed on. I want to amend the letter.'

Off he trots to retrieve it. His demeanour leaving me in no doubt of his disapproval. The letter reappears. I duly add a sentence.

Some hours later: a call at the House. 'The option you suggested had already been considered by the Foreign Secretary and rejected so your final sentence has been deleted. I hope that's alright.'

'No, it's not alright. We were asked for our opinion. Why can't we give it?'

'Too late now. The letter has gone. I couldn't get hold of you.'

Of course he could. He knows precisely where I have been since the moment I left the Department. It is not the first time this ploy has been used. If I protest, I shall be told that I should have a pager. If I had a pager, some other excuse would be devised.

A sad little scene on the tube. A boy and a girl of East European appearance. He about ten. She perhaps 15, beautiful with her hair in a long plait. They are both well-dressed. The boy has an accordion which he shows no sign of being able to play. She, over her dress, is wearing a brand-new Father Christmas outfit. They are both wearing Father Christmas hats. They move along the carriage, the girl proferring a paper cup which she holds out to each passenger. Only one man drops in a few coins. 'What kind of parents do they have?' snorts the man next to me. 'They must be desperate,' I venture. The girl looks intelligent. Does she go to school? It must be humiliating. What is going on in her head as she pushes a cup under the noses of surly commuters?

Sunday, 3 December
Sunderland

Philip and Marjorie Deakin to lunch. The children acted out *The Very Hungry Caterpillar* for them. At the end Emma rolled up into a ball, disappeared under a coat and, after a bit of wriggling, emerged as a beautiful butterfly. Philip and Marjorie were most impressed.

Tuesday, 5 December

A quiet chat with John Major, who confirmed that he had contemplated banning foreign ownership of British media. He said he had been provoked by the continual attacks on him in the Murdoch press and in the *Telegraph*, which is owned by Conrad Black, a Canadian. I asked if he had commissioned any work on the subject and he said he had, but it was buried with the papers of the last government. He added, 'I'm not interested in any blow that isn't fatal.' Me neither.

Wednesday, 6 December

Nick Raynsford says that Alistair Darling is signed up to giving local authorities discretion to stop paying housing benefit direct to rogue landlords. Until now the Department of Social Security has been dragging its feet. Nick also says that it may even be possible to do something before the election since primary legislation is not needed. Perhaps, after all, I shall leave behind a small footprint. When I first raised the subject Nick was sceptical and so were officials, but now he's completely on board.

Later, ran into Alistair who was not so upbeat. He denied having reached any firm conclusion and said that primary legislation would almost certainly be necessary.

More pressure required.

To the House for the State Opening. Or rather not to the State Opening, for in 13 years I have never yet attended one. However, Her Majesty was still on the premises when I arrived so I tarried at St Stephen's entrance to watch her depart. Whatever one thinks of our ruling class, they do a good line in State occasions. Long lines of ramrod-straight Guards in blue coats and busbies; a resplendent herald in yellow and scarlet; four troops of Horse Guards in gleaming helmets (and moving incongruously among them, workmen in yellow jackets labelled Onyx, scooping up the droppings). Open-topped carriages manned by flunkies in tricorn hats parked by the Peers' Entrance. And in front of them, a rather-too-conspicuous ambulance, on stand-by in case of accidents – or worse. I had thought that the Queen would depart in one of the open carriages, but no. Hers was parked out of sight under the arch of the Victoria Tower. Much barking of orders and stamping of feet preceded its emergence, drawn by four large white horses and preceded by a magnificent ruling class specimen on an even larger white horse. What would the girls have given to see this?

Just as the Horse Guards were about to move off, a pallid John Redwood scuttled across in front of them, narrowly avoiding being pounded to strawberry jam. The Queen stared grimly ahead as she passed, at the last minute acknowledging a knot of people in the shadow of Cromwell's statue. And in the final carriage the unmistakable figure of Tommy McAvoy in top hat and tails, beaming from ear to ear. Apparently one of the whips (Graham Allen) is left at the Palace as a hostage against HM's safe return and Tommy has to go and collect him. If Tommy were the hostage, there would be more than a few votes for leaving him in the royal dungeons.

Thursday, 7 December

To Warren House, a Victorian mansion near Kingston upon Thames, for two days of bonding with colleagues. A damn nuisance since it means missing a day in the constituency. JP in benign mode. Gales of laughter coming from his table during dinner.

Friday, 8 December

And so to bonding. Each of the ministers of state gave short talks about their work. This was followed by presentations from senior officials on subjects such as 'communication' and 'integration'. I kept a low profile. My only contribution was to complain about the quality of the draft speeches we are given to deliver, about which there was general agreement. JP at his most genial presided, casual dress, shirt open at the collar. It is at times like this one realises there is another JP besides the exhausted, driven, angry, oafish one so often on parade. This JP is amusing, considerate, on the ball. A pity the outside world doesn't see more of him.

Tuesday, 12 December

Fifty-three today. Awoken by the phone – my beautiful daughters singing 'Happy Birthday'.

To a hotel at Euston to address 150 councillors on the merits of recycling. The speech contained the usual line about £1.1 billion extra resources 'for environmental, cultural and other services' over the next three years. As with so many New Labour figures this one does not bear close scrutiny. Inquiries have already established that 'other services' includes local authority pensions which are likely to swallow a large part of the promised increase and that nothing is likely to be available in the first year. Before we set out I asked how much the increase amounted to in real terms. Answer: 5.4 per cent. In other words, less than 2 per cent a year, under half of which will be available for recycling. So far no one has rumbled this, but it can only be a question of time.

Wednesday, 13 December

This evening, a call came from Gus Macdonald's office asking that I take his place tomorrow morning to assist with the 'roll-out' of the transport spending programme. Since this would have involved reneging on a delegation of Essex councillors who have already been put off once, I said no. (More important, it would also have meant cancelling the office Christmas lunch, a detail which I took care to conceal.) Whereupon a fascinating little power struggle broke out. Three times Gus's office rang back insisting that I go. Three times I refused. I even overheard someone in Gus's office threatening Shayne that they would get JP to intervene, if I didn't co-operate. Eventually Gus himself cornered me. For once, however, I stood firm. Then someone had the bright idea of sending Phil Woolas, Gus's upwardly mobile Parliamentary Private Secretary. Sure enough Phil was only too glad to oblige. Gus looked mightily relieved. As I was leaving he whispered, with just a hint of menace, 'Well, this has delayed your entry to the Cabinet by six months.' Shayne remarked afterwards that the official from Gus's office was impressed. Such defiance, by one so far down the pecking order as I, is unprecedented.

Thursday, 14 December

George W. Bush, an intellectually and morally deficient serial killer (he has spent years as Governor of Texas signing death warrants), is to be the next US President. Just what the human race needs.

Today I did something useful. I decided to alternate night flights so that the pain is shared more or less equally between the citizens of south-west London and those of the Royal Borough of Windsor. Until now, by a margin of four to one, they have descended over central London, which is by far the most heavily populated. I must not kid myself, however. It was only a question of going along with the official line. Anyone in my place (except perhaps the Member for Windsor) would have reached the same conclusion.

Tuesday, 19 December

Responded to an adjournment debate on the shortage of affordable housing in the south, which is beginning to cause serious problems. Jane Griffiths, who represents part of Reading, said she had actually campaigned against new jobs coming to her constituency because of the housing shortage. The first time I have heard a Labour MP admit to not wanting jobs. Martin Salter, the other Reading Member, whispered afterwards, 'I shall be going into the election with fewer nurses, teachers and policemen than we had when we were elected.'

These are problems not of poverty, but of prosperity. To some extent, of course, this is yet another of the bills coming in for the Thatcher Decade. If you flog off all the best public housing, encourage hospital trusts to sell off nurses' homes and abolish the police rent allowance, you can hardly be surprised if public servants can't afford to live among you any longer. We can get by on this argument for a while, but there will come a time in the not too distant future when the punters (especially those who voted most enthusiastically for Thatcher) will no longer buy it. There is another aspect of the problem which no one wants to talk about too loudly (although Fiona Mactaggart did touch on it): all the spare rental accommodation has been soaked up by asylum seekers.

Today's *Daily Mail* reports the latest above-inflation increase in nurses' pay as 'another Labour snub'. Most nurses will be 'only' £8 a week better off. The more one reads of this sort of nonsense, the more one realises that this country is in the grip of a terrible sickness. Materially most people are better off than ever and yet they are continually being told that everything is getting worse. The complaining grows louder and longer by the day. There is a progressive collapse of confidence in all our institutions. What used to be luxuries are now inalienable rights. Yesterday I received a letter from a pensioner who has just received her £200 winter fuel allowance (replacing a Christmas bonus that was a mere £10 three years ago). She wasn't writing to say thank you to that nice Gordon Brown. Instead she complained that an unmarried pensioner couple down the road had been treated as separate households and received £200 each. This caused her to conclude that she and her husband had somehow been cheated out of £200. What has caused this sickness? I am in no doubt that it began with our loathsome tabloids, although the virus has long since spread to most of the other media. But that's not the whole story. Obsessive consumerism has resulted in less, rather than greater, happiness. And it has coincided – indeed caused – a steady deterioration in the quality of life. Pollution, traffic congestion, crime are at record levels. How will it end? Badly, I fear.

As for me, with each day that passes I yearn for a simple life. One where we take pleasure from our immediate surroundings. Produce only what we need. Eat what we grow. Travel slowly. And value friendship. An impossible dream?

Thursday, 21 December

Today I saved the taxpayer £1.5 million. Officials came to me with a plan for yet more research into the effect of aircraft noise on sleep. 'What's the point?' I asked. 'Whatever the conclusions, you are still going to tell me that nothing can be done about night flights.' I refused to authorise any more research. They weren't at all happy and no doubt as soon as I am out of the door, they will put it under the nose of whoever succeeds me. Nevertheless, I felt for once that I had done something useful.

Also, I finally managed to wring out of officials in the aviation division details of the number of airline employees who have passes to the Department. I obviously touched a raw nerve because I had to ask half a dozen times over a period of several weeks. The answer is that, between them, British Airways, Virgin and British Midland have ten passes and the charter airlines have another four. I'm not sure there is anything very wicked about it, but the fact that merely asking the question proves so upsetting for officials makes me wonder.

Home on the 15.00. Ngoc and the children met me at Durham.

Saturday, 23 December
Sunderland

Emma proclaimed confidently that Santa was going to bring her a robot dog, which was news to us. It emerged that Emma believes that Santa is a mind-reader. Ngoc dashed into town only to discover that the said robot dogs cost a ludicrous £35. Instead, she came back with a little plastic made-in-China version costing a mere £4.50. Hopefully the tiny monster will be satisfied.

CHAPTER THREE

2001

Monday, 1 January 2001
Brixton Road

I passed much of the day cutting my own accursed leylandii hedge with our new hedge trimmer. All went well, until the blade went through the cable, fortunately without fatal consequences.

Wednesday, 3 January

The *Guardian* Diary is running a 'Turncoat of the Year' poll designed to identify the Labour minister who has most betrayed his roots. I am listed, 'more in sorrow than in anger', as a 60–1 outsider on account of my role in the part-privatisation of air traffic control. Happily there are others (Peter Hain, Clare Short) who rate far shorter odds than I. In any case my presence on the list is based on two false propositions. One: that I am in charge of the air traffic control sale. Two: that I once opposed it.

Monday, 8 January

Keith Bradley has been made a privy counsellor. We had a laugh about it during the division. In the run-up to the '87 election he and I featured in the *Sun's* list of 'Kinnock's Top Ten Loony Tunes'. Several of those on the list are now ministers.

Tuesday, 9 January

All quiet at the Department. JP is holidaying on the Nile. Although, true to form, he has been ringing in every day to harass the underlings. Yesterday he was only narrowly dissuaded from coming back early to deal with some wholly imaginary crisis which he assumed that no one but himself was capable of handling. The truth is that everything goes remarkably smoothly when he's away.

Our plans for air traffic control continue to attract an unremittingly hostile press. 'A devastating mid-air collision in our overcrowded skies is now inevitable, warn Britain's senior air traffic controllers,' says a report in today's *Express*. Ostensibly the story is about the huge explosion in low-cost air travel, which does indeed pose serious problems. Before long, however, it has turned into a diatribe against the sell-off. We are on a hiding to nothing. Sooner or later there is bound to be a disaster and, whatever the evidence, our critics will lay it at the door of the part-privatisation. We have taken a very big political risk. And for what? The money involved is peanuts. Once again the trail leads back to Gordon. Of course, if it all goes wrong Gordon will be nowhere to be seen.

Thursday, 11 January
Keswick

Today I am Minister for the Lake District. What better job has politics to offer? The sun is bright, the sky is blue. There is snow on the tops. Just the day for a stroll in the hills. Shayne, two officials and I are picked up from our guest house after breakfast and whisked away to a former TB sanatorium on the foothills of Blencathra, with stunning views towards Helvellyn. From there we are taken to see examples of footpaths eroded by four-wheel drives and overuse by walkers, muchneeded affordable housing and a cycle track through a spectacular gorge leading out of Keswick. I am treated royally. It is 'Minister' this and 'Minister' that. Photographers everywhere, flashing away. The ban on speedboats on Windermere has made me a hero with the Park Authority, although the acclaim is not universal. A mighty vested interest has been upset and there are still rumblings. Lunch at a hotel which has gardens leading down to Derwentwater. And all the while the sun shone. The traumas of air traffic control and the Homes Bill are but a distant memory. Being Under-Secretary of Nothing in Particular is not so terrible after all.

Saturday, 13 January
Sunderland

My annual Public Lending Right return – a paltry £107. The lowest ever. My books are gradually disappearing from public libraries. Soon they will be unobtainable and the waters will close for ever over my brief literary career.

Monday,15 January

To London in trepidation. This is going to be one of those weeks where I cling on by my fingertips. I spent the afternoon boning up on the four PQs I have been allocated for tomorrow – three on aviation, one on gypsies. All subjects within my remit, which makes a pleasant change. As ever, I live in terror of humiliation. Nick Raynsford, needless to say, knows it all inside out.

Also, this evening Gus and I were due to have our long-awaited audience with JP to discuss my suggestion that we make terminal five conditional on a ban on night flights. However, it was cancelled at the last minute on the advice of officials in the planning department who had even gone so far as to consult a QC. The whole place is in the grip of lawyers. The very mention of night flights or the proposed new terminal makes officials extremely jittery. Mentioning both in the same breath is enough to cause nervous breakdowns all round. A recent Appeal Court decision, questioning the right of ministers to be involved in planning decisions, has only made the situation more fraught. By evening another note had arrived countermanding the earlier one. By this time, of course, it was too late to reinstate our meeting so we have to start all over again.

Tuesday,16 January

Tea with Gwyneth Dunwoody who says that Gordon's acolytes have been putting it about that the sale of air traffic control was all JP's idea and nothing to do with Gordon, which is, of course, complete nonsense. All the same, it only confirms the general suspicion that, if it all goes pear-shaped, Gordon will be invisible.

Wednesday, 17 January

To Heathrow and then to West Drayton to visit the air traffic controllers. I spent 20 minutes in the control tower at Heathrow, which is between the two runways so, quite apart from their radar screens, the controllers have a bird's eye view of what's happening. The atmosphere seemed relaxed despite an interview on *Today* this morning with an anonymous controller who said she had recently resigned because she couldn't cope with the stress caused by the huge increase in traffic and by staff shortages. She sounded plausible, rejecting an attempt by the interviewer to suggest that safety was compromised, but the implication was that privatisation would make it all worse. I have to say I didn't recognise her description from what I saw, admittedly in the slack season. The safety regulator requires that no controller spends more than two hours at one time on a screen. In practice, however, no one spends more than 90 minutes and, at this time of the year, it can be as low as 45, which wouldn't be possible if there were serious staff shortages. They earn between £50,000 and £60,000 a year and work about 180 days a year. The responsibility, of course, is awesome, but they don't take their work home with them and the pensions are generous. It is hard not to feel that what's driving the opposition, from the union point of view, is that the new management might start questioning these comfortable arrangements.

I spent some time in the controllers' rest room, without officials, and detected none of the unremitting hostility that the unions and the media allege. No one suggested safety was imperilled or that stress was a serious factor.

The hunting vote. Predictably, another large majority for abolition.

Ominously David Blunkett, who is likely to be the next Home Secretary, was among the handful who voted for the so-called middle way, which is just a cover for the status quo. He also voted for a complete ban. Typical of David. On the national executive committee during the battles of the eighties he had a habit of being out of the room during crucial votes. Also, once again, The Man contrived to be absent, though he left behind a message saying that he would have voted for a ban had he been present. What is he playing at? We've got to get this out of the way once and for all. There is nothing to be gained by this endless shilly-shallying. We only end up upsetting everyone.

Thursday, 18 January

To Harrow to deliver my 'Why Politics Matters' speech to about 50 sixth-formers. Soft-skinned, rosy-cheeked youths whose lives are untouched by the harsh realities of the world beyond their doorstep. Several were already wearing pinstripes in preparation for their inevitable entry to the City. The young teacher who collected me from the station said that many of the boys were looking forward to the Countryside Alliance march in the spring. The applause was polite, but unenthusiastic. Most of the questions were depressingly predictable. (Sample: 'Why is New Labour so obsessed with gays and fox hunting?' Answer: 'We're not, but you seem to be.') Later, I dined with a group of boys and teachers at the magnificent tied 'cottage' of one of the housemasters. Interestingly, none of the three teachers present had voted Tory in 1997 and none seemed likely to this time. One said he thought we would get a bigger majority next time. 'We talk to the parents and they are not afraid of you any more.'

Before leaving for Harrow I put a copy of my speech in the post for The Man with a jokey little covering note saying that this was an attempt to extend New Labour's big tent ever outwards. I also sent copies to Alastair and Bruce. I'm not sure it was wise because it wasn't entirely on-message.

After Harrow, I caught a train to Redhill for another of these wretched ministerial away-days upon which JP insists. Arrived to find the company still at the dinner table, taking coffee. No sign of JP (his father has died). The venue is a splendid Victorian folly called Nuthill Priory which has recently been converted into a luxury hotel. No one seems to know why we are here. After all, it is an odd time to start bonding. Most of us will have been reshuffled in another four months. Gus Macdonald and his neighbour, the official in charge of the Department's software, were discussing computers. For want of something to say, I remarked that I had recently lost 15,000 words on Ngoc's new computer. At this Gus's ears pricked up. 'What were you writing? An account of life at the DETR?'

I laughed uneasily. 'Oh that's only worth a couple of paragraphs.' Gus didn't press the subject, but I could see he is suspicious. I must learn to keep my big mouth shut.

Friday, 19 January
Nuthill Priory

Breakfast in the cloisters. A great hall, complete with organ. An oak-panelled library and from the bedrooms at the back wonderful, almost unspoiled views across Surrey and into Sussex. The event itself is a complete waste of time. We could have held it in one of the conference rooms at the Department at no cost to the public (instead of the £210 charged for my presence). I kept a low profile throughout, resentful at having to throw away a Friday in the constituency for this. Gus, it has to be said, was on sparkling form. A fount of little insights and witticisms. At times he had everyone in stitches. I whispered to Keith Hill that I had never seen him on such good form. 'It's because JP's not here,' replied Keith. 'He's a free man.'

Monday, 22 January

The Tories are concentrating on Peter Mandelson, who is alleged to have been lobbying for a passport for an Asian billionaire called Hinduja who also put money into the Dome. On the facts so far published, I can't for the life of me see what all the fuss is about.

An interesting piece by Peter Preston in today's *Guardian* about the

New Labour obsession with targets. He argues they will lead to our downfall. A manifesto, he says, crammed with targets is in danger of becoming a long suicide note. New Labour, he goes on, is tolerated rather than loved. Blair is effectively a chief executive officer of the NHS, of Railtrack, of the Dome, of the Metropolitan Police. An impossible spin. I am sure he's right. We've got reviews, strategies, targets, action plans coming out of our ears. Our department even has targets for walking and cycling. As Preston says, it's suicide. In the dismal world of politics in Twenty-First Century Britain, one well-publicised failure (and we are not short of people wanting to publicise our failures) is equal to a dozen successes. He goes on: 'Governments are not giant corporations. They are, at best, the reconciler of hopes and reality. They can set a direction and, through prudent distancing, leave others to follow through.' I am sure he is right. Even at the hour of its greatest triumphs, New Labour has sowed the seeds of its destruction.

'I've got the most dangerous man in Britain in my cab,' remarked the taxi driver who took me back to the flat this evening.

'Who's that'?

'Aren't you Mr Chris Mullin, the one in charge of that committee?'

Evidence, if any were needed, that I have done nothing memorable since I gave up the select committee.

Wednesday, 24 January

Sensational news. Mandelson has fallen. Again. And this time it is likely to be for ever. No one saw it coming.

I first heard the news from Damian Green, a Tory, at about one o'clock. He said the Tories had been informed that Adam Ingram would be taking Northern Ireland questions today and that Peter had been summoned to Downing Street to discuss his involvement with the Hindujas. Then, soon after one thirty, word reached the Tea Room that he had resigned, but that he would be presiding at Northern Ireland Questions after all. As a result the chamber was packed. Peter took the first question. Flushed and miserable, but very calm. Hands resting on either side of the Dispatch Box. No sign of self-pity. Several people expressed regret at his passing, but the hear-hearing was muted. The truth is that most people on our side are delighted to see the back of him and are doing their best, with varying degrees of success, not to gloat. A tribute from Nick Palmer was heard in total silence. Dale Campbell Savours stirred things up a bit with a little homily about how vulnerable we all are. This provoked outcry from the Tories and, on our side, silence.

Then The Man arrived to take questions. In contrast to Peter's red face, his was pale but equally miserable. For him this isn't just a political disaster, it is bereavement. Hague tried to stir the pot (who can blame him?) by saying that it was all his fault for being so dependent on Peter and for reappointing him (after the Robinson loan), but The Man saw him off easily. He played it just right. No attempt at bluster. Just a dignified, low-key response. Hague's opportunism brought our benches back to life. There were cries of 'Hypocrite', 'what about Jeffrey Archer?' and, 'It's the economy, stupid.'

In truth, of course, Hague is right. Reappointing Mandelson was a huge error of judgement. Goodness knows how many people have warned The Man about Peter over the years. At least 50. And yet he chose to ignore them all.

Back at the Department, to Michael Meacher's office for a meeting. Michael loathes Peter, who, rightly or wrongly, he blames for all the anonymous bad-mouthing of him that used to appear in the press before every Shadow Cabinet election. As I went in Michael seized my hand, 'Isn't it WONDERFUL,' he almost shouted much to my embarrassment. I don't like kicking people when they are down and in any case the outer office was full of officials whose ears were no doubt flapping.

'Don't gloat,' I said later to Michael as we sat in the back of his car en route to the House.

'Oh, I wouldn't dream of saying anything in public ...'

'I don't mean in public. I mean in front of *anyone*.' He seemed a bit taken aback by that (what Michael doesn't seem to realise is that, in the current climate, he could be next: the row over his property portfolio has made him vulnerable, too).

This didn't stop him sounding off again, within the hearing of his driver. No doubt Michael's views on Peter will be all round the car pool by now.

Nick Soames is very full of himself. That is to say even fuller than usual. He's going around booming, 'A nation mourns.' On Monday night he was raising points of order about Peter and the Hindujas. Now he's after Keith Vaz. 'Leicester East is dead,' he roared as I passed him outside the Tea Room this evening. 'I've pressed the dead button on him.'

Thursday, 25 January

The press has gone bananas. 'Goodbye and good riddance' (*Sun*); 'You are the weakest link, goodbye' (*Mirror*); 'The end of the affair' (*Mail*) over a picture of Peter and The Man side by side on the front bench yesterday looking miserable. The news that the Nissan plant in Sunderland has been saved has been entirely eclipsed.

A long chat with Mike O'Brien, looking pale and shell-shocked at having been the catalyst of Peter's downfall. 'It's terribly, terribly sad,' he kept saying. He also fears that, although he is obviously blameless, some of Peter's bad karma will rub off on him – and he may be right. One intriguing little postscript: Mike's nine-year-old daughter said to him at breakfast this morning, 'But Dad, if he's your friend, why didn't you just keep quiet?'

I have been reshuffled. As I was getting ready to go for the train, my private office called to say that the Prime Minister was looking for me. I rang Kate Garvey at Number 10 and she said he was up north and would call when he got to Sedgefield. She was at pains to assure me that I wasn't in any kind of trouble. After I'd put the phone down, it dawned on me that I was about to be reshuffled, but I couldn't work out where the vacancy was. Maybe Keith Vaz had gone and I was going to be asked to replace him. But no. About half an hour later the phone rang again and, after a lot of clicking, The Man came on and asked if I would like to replace George Foulkes (who is going to the

Scottish Office in place of Brian Wilson) at International Development. I replied, 'Nothing would give me more pleasure than helping to redistribute the wealth of the middle classes to the poorest people in the world.'

A brief silence and then a chuckle. 'Ah, Chris, that's not quite how it works.'

'Don't worry, Tony, I'll be discreet.'

And that was that. My career as the lowest form of life in JP's empire is over. I am now the lowest form of life in a smaller, but more agreeable department.

Friday, 26 January
Sunderland

I am strangely unelated. After I received The Call I went down to the Tea Room and had my usual baked beans with an egg on top. I chatted to Keith Hill, but didn't mention that we were no longer colleagues.

Elliot Morley and several other colleagues were on the train. They knew that George had gone to Scotland and were speculating about who would replace him. I hinted that it was me, but they thought I was joking so I didn't press the point.

My first thought was this makes me well placed to succeed Clare should she be moved after the election, but then it dawned on me that she is unlikely to be moved because (a) she's doing a good job, (b) she is insufficiently on-message for any other Cabinet post, and (c) given the shortage of women in the Cabinet, she is unlikely to be dropped. All of which means I am destined to remain in the lower foothills for years to come. For how much longer can I stand this? Come the election I shall have to make up my mind whether or not to return to the backbenches and try and pick up where I left off.

A busy day in the constituency. I opened a community shop in Hendon, visited Sister Aelred, the head teacher at St Anthony's, and presided over the annual meeting of Pennywell Neighbourhood Centre. The surgery lasted the best part of three hours. A good 20 minutes was taken up by a bigot who ranted on interminably about the hospitality afforded to asylum seekers while pensioners like

himself were on the breadline. It was classic stuff: 'I'm not a racist but
...' and 'I didn't fight for my country to see it being taken over by
foreigners ...' I pointed out several times that he was fighting fascism,
but he was beyond irony.

Sunday, 28 January

The feeding frenzy over *l'affaire* Mandelson continues unabated. Even
the deaths of 20,000 people in an earthquake in India has not been
sufficient to staunch the unending flow of pettiness and trivia. More
and more people are being drawn in. Today Peter has struck back with
an article in the *Sunday Times*, saying he was persuaded to resign 'in a
moment of weakness' and, saints preserve us, even hinting darkly of
a comeback. The Tories are loving every minute of it. Goodness knows
the damage this is doing. Why won't he just go away and leave us
alone?

Monday, 29 January

Helen Jackson was on the London train. She was Peter's Parliamentary
Private Secretary until last week, but like others she found him remote.
'It was a one way relationship. He wasn't interested in me. He had no
real contact with the other Northern Ireland ministers, just with civil
servants, but he is very intelligent. Skilled at getting the various parties
to talk to each other.' Helen last spoke to him by phone on Tuesday
after a *Newsnight* interview in which he had referred to one of the
Hindujas as a friend. She told him that was unwise. She added, 'The
suggestion that Peter's done nothing wrong is missing the big picture.
It was his lifestyle. All the parties he went to.' Derek Draper, once a
friend of Peter's, put his finger on the problem. He has been quoted
as saying, 'Peter goes gaga in the presence of rich people.' Not only
Peter's problem. New Labour's, too.

To my new home, the Department for International Development,
otherwise known as DFID. A down-at-heel office block on Victoria
Street, opposite Westminster Cathedral. I had no idea where it was

until this morning. I have taken immediately to my new Private Secretary, Christine. A warm, friendly woman, exactly on my wavelength. As to whether there is a real job to be done, I am unclear. Clare is very hands-on and not many crumbs seem to fall from her table. The diary appears to consist mainly of running round in circles pretending to be busy. There are trips lined up to Georgia, Kyrgyzstan, Chile, the Caribbean, Albania. Mostly they start from Heathrow on Saturday mornings. That's out, for a start. My predecessor, George Foulkes, liked travelling, but I'm not so keen. I shall only go when I can see the point.

Clare seems glad to see me. I've always got on well with her. This is a much more intimate place than Eland House. Clare's office is just over the corridor. I'll see much more of her than I ever did of JP. This afternoon she had to make a statement on the Indian earthquake and I was pictured on all the news bulletins sitting beside her, which was useful, since the world can see that I'm now on her team.

Later, I tapped out a handover note for my successor, Bob Ainsworth. Item one: persuading JP to make terminal five conditional on a ban on night flights at Heathrow. The only thing I regret about leaving is not being able to see that through. The other thing I'm anxious for Bob to follow through is giving councils discretion to withhold direct payment of housing benefit to landlords who take no interest either in the condition of their property or in the behaviour of their tenants. After an uphill struggle Nick and I were just beginning to get somewhere on this. A pity if the momentum was lost.

What have I achieved during my 18 months at Environment? The only useful decision that was entirely mine was to ban speedboats on Windermere and that probably would have happened anyway. For the rest, I moved the High Hedges Bill on leylandii forward by a centimetre or two. The Countryside Act – and the right to roam in particular – were good things to have been associated with, but I can't pretend to have made the slightest difference to it (save perhaps for a concession to George Young about access over common land). As for my title as King of the Adjournment Debates, that I happily relinquish.

A call from the Foreign Office, asking if I would see Robin Cook in his room at the House at 10 p.m. I found him sitting with his sidekick Ken Purchase in his vast, gloomy cavern off the corridor behind the Speaker's chair. The only light came from a desk lamp on the far side of the room and from the TV monitor. He came straight to the point. 'Clare can be a bit temperamental. We might need a second opinion on one or two things.'

'Like what?'

'Oh, there have been many things.'

'Name one.'

'Montserrat.'* He did not elaborate, but Ken said there had been some terrible tantrums, culminating on more than one occasion in threats of resignation. I remained studiously non-committal. I am not going to be used to undermine Clare.

Talk then turned to the Peter Crisis. 'We've got to close it down,' said Robin. 'Otherwise it will become about our competence to govern.' The danger is that the inquiry Tony has set up will drag on. He mentioned Peter's article in yesterday's *Sunday Times*. 'It was all me, me, me. Not a word about the party.' He asked if I thought Keith Vaz was vulnerable. Robin clearly thinks he is. I think so, too. Not necessarily on the Hindujas, but there is a range of other possibilities. Keith's trouble is that he's a sleek wheeler-dealer. He has the attention span of a gnat and a tendency to fantasise.

Robin's parting words were 'DFID and the Foreign Office are not enemies. Keep in touch.'

Tuesday, 30 January

People keep congratulating me on my alleged promotion, but of course it's nothing of the sort. Merely a sideways move in the foot-hills. 'A little vote of confidence,' whispered Margaret Beckett in the division lobby last night, but I have my doubts. I fear I've been shunted into a cul de sac from which I may never emerge. My true friends are glad to see me escape from air traffic control and all those

---

*In the summer of 1997 Clare Short became embroiled in a row with leaders of the Caribbean island of Montserrat who were demanding more British aid following a devastating series of volcanic eruptions which rendered much of the island uninhabitable; she memorably remarked, 'They will be wanting golden elephants next.'

adjournment debates. Others are simply envious of the enormous potential for travel that this job entails. That's not how I see it. My travelling days are over. I'm a family man now. I want to go home at weekends. In any case my idea of travelling is to disappear for weeks at a time, using local public transport. This kind of travelling seems to involve air-conditioned four-wheel drives and many hours of Club Class flying. I propose to keep it to a minimum. Georgia has been excised. I am also proposing to pull out of trips to Chile, Honolulu, St Lucia and Spain which are mainly to attend conferences in luxury hotels. I have agreed to Albania and Kyrgyzstan on condition that they are reorganised to start on Monday morning, and not Saturday (as at present). Sanjib (in the private office) tried to make me compromise on Sunday instead, but I told him firmly that my weekends are ring-fenced. After a little research he discovered, evidently to his surprise, that there are direct flights from Newcastle to the destinations in Europe where we would have to change anyway so there is no need for me to come down to Heathrow after all.

I am under pressure to take a pager. Clare pressed me about it on my first day. If she mentions it again, I shall have to succumb. Mustn't get off on the wrong foot.

At lunchtime I made a farewell visit to Eland House. Chris, Shayne, Dan and Kerry were already hard at work on behalf of their new master. They presented me with a little parting gift, a pair of binoculars (to replace those that were stolen two years ago). I thanked them, handed in my pass and departed. On the way out I noticed that my photograph has already been removed from the gallery of ministers in the entrance lobby. The waters have closed over me. I was never there.

Back at DFID I begin to realise what a formidable politician Clare is. Everybody speaks well of her. There is a real sense of loyalty. In three years she has transformed overseas development from a backwater, firmly in the grip of the Foreign Office, to an independent department, with its own (expanding) budget, pursuing its own agenda firmly focused on the poorest people in the poorest countries. No wonder she is not popular at the Foreign Office. According to Christine, Clare had to fight hard to wrest international development from the clutches of the FO, not to mention the Department of Trade and Industry with its insistence on linking aid to trade. The recent White Paper on globalisation is written with beautiful clarity. Quite unlike any other I have seen. That's mainly down to Clare, too. Apparently the early drafts were risible.

Clare has one other strong card: she gets on well with Gordon. Only this afternoon she managed to wring £9 million out of the Treasury for the Indian earthquake.

Wednesday, 31 January

A succession of departmental directors have passed through my office in the last two days. This one in charge of Asia, this one Africa and so on. I find myself at ease with them. The world is now my oyster. We chat effortlessly about this country and that. Everyone seems happy. They are doing work in which they believe. Maybe I will like it here after all. The only fly in the ointment is Europe. About 30 per cent of our aid budget is dispensed via Brussels and, when it moves at all, goes mainly to middle-income countries around the Mediterranean, which we are not at all happy about.

Thursday, 1 February

The first public engagement of my new incarnation: a speech at the Royal Institute of Civil Engineers on the social and environmental consequences of dams. The first draft was undeliverable and I had to rewrite it from top to bottom (nothing has changed on that front). Before catching the train in the evening, I had to make a brief speech at the Royal Commonwealth Institute in Kensington. By and large my first week has passed smoothly. The workload is well down on my previous incarnation. It is 'Minister, will you be taking a box tonight?' rather than 'How many?' Clare seems to deal with almost all the paperwork. All I see is copies. I haven't yet signed a single letter. At Environment I signed at least 50 a night.

Friday, 2 February
Sunderland

A visit to Havelock Primary School in the most desolate part of my constituency – 83 per cent of the children are on free meals and 50 per cent on some form of special measures. I thought it would be a depressing experience, but on the contrary, it was truly uplifting. Everything bright and cheerful, in stark contrast to the mean streets outside. Pot plants on the window ledges, every square inch of wall covered in artwork, an atmosphere redolent with love and encouragement. Everyone I met was cheerful. The head, Jane Caldwell, a formidable woman, has been there nearly 30 years. She had organised breakfast clubs, evening clubs, Saturday morning clubs. There were computer classes for parents. And yet there was sadness, too. Looking closely at the children, you could see that many of them are destined to be claimed by the virulent yob culture which laps at the very gates of the school. Some arrive barely able to speak. Many of the little faces are blank and pasty. Mrs Caldwell says that, with a handful of exceptions, most parents are difficult to motivate and uninterested in the school or the progress of their children. To my surprise she said she had voted Tory most of her life (coming from a family of Unionists in Portadown). She added, however, that the Tories were now unelectable, which was encouraging.

I spent much of the day trying to persuade Keith Vaz to overrule the entry clearance officer in St Petersburg and grant a student visa to the Sri Lankan nephew of two local doctors. The matter was urgent since the boy's Russian visa expires next week The problem is this is the second time I have asked Keith to overrule this particular entry clearance officer and he is understandably cautious, given the pasting he is getting in the press (today's *Mail* has another three pages). He is also as slippery as an eel. No sooner had I caught up with him than he rang off, promising to ring back 'within two minutes'. Then I had to begin all over again. When I eventually cornered Keith he decided to refer the matter to John Battle for a second opinion and so I had to track down John and ensure that the papers were transferred to him. Then the officials attempted to throw a spanner in the works, by dragging in lawyers. John, who is very straight, was fuming. He says the

Foreign Office is not like other departments. The officials regard ministers as a temporary inconvenience and barely conceal their contempt. Especially, they don't like ministers who overrule them. I must have made more than 20 calls in all, but at the last moment John came up trumps. I immediately tapped out a letter bearing the good news and the boy's uncle came round right away to collect it. 'I knew common sense and justice would win in the end,' he said. I forebore to tell him that common sense had nothing to do with it.

Later, Councillors Dave Allen and Brian Dodds came round with two local policemen. They brought with them case studies of criminal youths against whom, despite all Jack's efforts, the law is completely ineffective. Time after time they are bailed when they should have been remanded in custody. They are literally walking out of the court and picking up where they left off. They had been arrested 70, 80 times and were causing mayhem. The police are tearing their hair out.

Monday, 5 February

Rain and sleet all weekend. The rivers are overflowing and south of Peterborough much of the landscape is under water.

Sat in on a meeting between Clare Short and the new head of UNESCO, a Japanese. Fascinating to watch Clare at work. She's very direct, warm, intimate, expressive – waving her arms around like an Italian, occasionally touching her interlocutor on the forearms. She talks a lot, but knows her stuff. In years gone by, when I sat next to her on the backbenches, I used to think of her as too noisy and temperamental, but she's also bright.

Dinner with Clive Soley in the Millbank Room. He's worried that Gordon is plotting a takeover, gradually sliding his men and women into place. He reckons Tony Lloyd is an agent of Gordon's and Clive wants to stop him succeeding as chairman of the parliamentary party after the election. Does any of this matter? I am sure that Gordon is plotting every hour of every day but there is not a lot we can do. In any case, it is difficult to shift a sitting prime minister who doesn't want to be shifted. Only the Tories are that ruthless. Clive thinks that Gordon's henchmen will start stirring as soon as the election is out of the way with a view to persuading Tony to stand down in mid-term. It is not desirable for Gordon to succeed to the throne. He may be clever, and not a bad chancellor, but he's also obsessive, doesn't listen, lacks hinterland and is the architect of many of our worst mistakes – the 75 pence pension increase, the cut in single-parent benefit, to say nothing of the air traffic control and London Underground privatisations.

I cautioned Clive to say nothing to The Man about this. There is nothing he can do about Gordon and there's no sense in making him paranoid. It is in everyone's interests that he remains above the fray.

Tuesday, 6 February

Clare and I were jointly briefed for Questions tomorrow. Clare in action is a sight to behold. A stream of officials flow through her office to be alternatively harangued and cajoled, all with great good humour. Every draft answer has to be rewritten. She doesn't believe in short, factual replies. Each must begin with a little homily, setting out the big picture. Myths must be punctured. We give out clear messages. She has some stunning statistics at her disposal. Watching her I feel so inadequate.

Later, a man from Afghanistan came to see me. He works for a Norwegian relief agency, one of the few Western agencies still functioning under the Taliban. He had a dark beard and was dressed immaculately in a tailored suit. Gentle, dignified, soft-spoken, his manner belied the brutal world in which he lives. Very quietly he spoke of catastrophe. Of half the country affected by drought; of 500 people in Herat recently dying of cold; of burying the entire family of his neighbour after their home had been hit by a shell; of being permanently at risk of being denounced as a spy. He spoke mainly in understatement – using words like 'disappointment' and 'negative consequences'.

He described himself as an intellectual, adding, 'There are not many intellectuals left in my country. You can only take so much.' His main message was that the sanctions on which the Americans have insisted (and with which we have lamely gone along) are hurting only the poor and making it difficult for foreign aid agencies to function. 'Sanctions are in no way linked to the human rights of the Afghans' was how he put it. He said warlords responsible for the slaughter of thousands of his countrymen were travelling the world with impunity. He claimed that the Taliban are disintegrating. Their commanders no longer obey orders from the centre. Mainly they are engaged in plunder, feeding themselves. However, he drew no comfort from the impending collapse of the Taliban. It merely means the return of the warlords.

He stayed an hour. It was very moving. Here was a man who had emerged briefly from the darkness to which, in two or three days, he will be returning and I could offer him not one crumb of comfort.

Dinner with Clare in the Millbank Room. Our first chance to bond since my arrival. Never have I come across a politician so in love with her job. She believes – and she is right – that she has the best job in government. What's more she has had it long enough to make her mark. Her enthusiasm is infectious. So much so that it is difficult to say no to her. She wants me to have a pager and (with a heavy heart) I found myself conceding. She says it may be necessary for me to attend some of the development bank meetings in foreign climes (the Permanent Secretary has already been complaining to her about my lack of enthusiasm for business travel) and I promised to look again at some of the propositions I have declined. As I suspected, I shan't be asked to take many decisions. With engaging frankness she describes herself as 'policy greedy'. I am welcome to be involved in whatever interests me, but decisions will always be hers.

Clare thinks that we will win the election by between 50 and 100 seats and that The Man will stand down halfway through the next Parliament having become the first Labour prime minister to have led us into two full Parliaments and having entrenched social democracy. Gordon, says Clare, will inevitably succeed. Blunkett, she says, has done us a lot of damage with his denigration of teachers and his endless initiatives. On Robin, with whom she has had a number of run-ins, Clare says that being Foreign Secretary has gone to his head. 'He's all puffed up.' She added that the Foreign Office deeply resents the size of our budget.

Sir Frederick Lawton has died. As usual with judges, the obits are full of sycophancy. Geoffrey Lane is quoted as saying, 'If Fred ever made a mistake, I have yet to discover what it is.' Well, for a start, in the 1930s, he was the British Union of Fascists' candidate for Hammersmith. Presumably even Lord Lane would agree that was a mistake? Oswald Mosley's newspaper reported Lawton's selection under the heading 'A fine, fighting fascist', words I once plastered across the front of *Tribune* over a picture of the old rogue looking gross in his wig. This resulted in a hurt letter saying it was only a youthful indiscretion and he had joined the Conservative Party soon afterwards. More seriously, he was also party to the disgraceful appeal judgement in the Guildford Four case – a fact that none of the obituaries are unkind enough to mention.

Wednesday, 7 February

I had an exchange with a bus conductor in Brixton who was berating passengers who got off at traffic lights. 'They're a lot of sheep,' he kept repeating, 'animals have got more sense.'

'You hate your passengers, don't you'?

'Yes,' he replied cheerfully.

'If you treated them with respect, they might treat you with more respect.'

But he would have none of it. 'I prefer animals to humans ...'

My fellow passengers just looked on expressionless. Maybe he was right.

My first Question Time. I prepared carefully, having been allocated questions on Brazil, the Balkans and St Helena, and it went off well enough. International Development questions are a good-natured affair. The Tories aren't really interested and so no one's trying to catch you out. Indeed most people aren't listening. They've come in early to make sure they have a seat at Prime Minister's Questions, which follow on immediately.

This evening, to the Travellers' Club in Pall Mall for dinner with the EC development commissioner, Poul Nielsen. The EC's aid programme is a disaster area. Most of it goes either to the undeserving or to the not very deserving and takes for ever to get there (average length of time between commitment and delivery, 3.7 years). Commissioner Neilsen, a decent but long-winded Dane, is doing his best to shake up the bureaucracy, but the struggle is an uphill one and victory by no means assured.

Friday, 9 February
Sunderland

The surgery this evening was a mix of immigration cases and neighbour disputes. One man had spent £40,000 on lawyers in a disagreement over a footpath and is now wanting to appeal. I did what I could to persuade him to cut his losses, but he is determined to go on. Eventually, the lawyers will take his house. The Sri Lankan student from St Petersburg – who I persuaded Keith Vaz to admit last week – came in with his aunt and uncle to say thank you and, despite my protestations, insisted on giving Graham, Pat and me each a box of inedible Russian chocolates. Some of my greatest triumphs are immigration cases. But I must keep absolutely quiet about them since the very mention of foreigners and immigration drives many of my constituents to apoplexy.

Monday, 12 February

No engagements, just piles of paper to leaf through, none of which require the slightest action on my part, reminiscent of my days as a copy-taster in the news room at Bush House. The truth is there is not a job for two ministers. Clare could easily manage without an under-secretary. For me the only issue is whether to own up and get out or lie back and pretend. I could while away the time travelling and inspecting. There is no shortage of tempting offers. Most colleagues envy my supposed good fortune. 'Why are you still in the country?' Gerald Kaufman inquired this afternoon. I shall soon have to decide whether or not I am a serious politician and, if so, pluck up the courage to return to the backbenches after the election. Ngoc says I should carry on and make the most of what I have. After all, not many people have a job they enjoy. The only issue is whether or not I am of any use. The irritating thing is that most people assume this is the ideal job for me. 'You said this was what you wanted,' Ann Taylor remarked the other day. Not quite, Ann. What I said was that, when the music stops, I would like to be the Secretary of State in this department, but that job is very definitely spoken for.

Thursday, 15 February

To a windowless room on the third floor of the Cabinet Office for a breakfast meeting about GM foods. I arrived early and it took 15 minutes to convince the man on the door that any such meeting was taking place. Mo Mowlam was in the chair. The basis for discussion was a paper from John Krebs, overlord of the Food Standards Agency. It triggered a rather esoteric discussion during the course of which it became clear that just about everyone present except Michael Meacher (who told me he had been outvoted seven–one at the previous meeting) is signed up to the advantages of GM and that the main issue is how to take the public with us. Michael's position is that the science is untested and we should await the outcome of the experiments. David Sainsbury said that millions of people in America and China had been eating GM foods for years without the slightest ill-effect. It reminded me of the enthusiasm for nuclear power in the early days. Let's hope this one has a happier ending.

Friday, 16 February

I am in trouble over my refusal to attend the annual meetings of the development banks. Officials are recommending that I attend all four, plus a special meeting of the Caribbean Bank in early March. I have refused the Inter-American and Asian bank meetings (in Chile and Honolulu respectively) on the grounds that they are not a justified use of public money or ministerial time. According to Christine, they are to a large extent social events. Some delegates bring their wives, and packets of money (which British delegates are instructed to refuse) are handed out by way of 'expenses'. I want as little as possible to do with all this. Why is it that the problems of the Third World have so often to be discussed in conditions of extreme luxury?

Sir John Vereker, our rather grand Permanent Secretary, has gone running to Clare to complain about what he regards as my failure to pull my weight and she has expressed her displeasure, so I am going to have to get organised if I am to outwit him. This evening I composed a memo to Clare putting my side of the story. I may also ring her at the weekend.

Saturday, 17 February
Sunderland

New Labour is hyperactive. Every day a new initiative. Sometimes two or three. One minute we are sorting out 'bog standard comprehensives'. Next the papers are full of Jack Straw's plans for courts to sit all night. He's also talking about recruiting an elite corps of police officers who will start as inspectors, missing out such humdrum tasks as pounding the beat. How very New Labour. A fast track to the stratosphere. Only the best and the brightest need apply. Not for them the tedium of the backbenches or boring old apprenticeships. Those are for losers. Every day we upset another vested interest. Sooner or later they will all gang up on us, although it has to be said there is no sign of it so far. Inexplicably, the polls still place us miles ahead.

Sunday, 18 February

American and British planes have bombed alleged missile systems on the outskirts of Baghdad; civilian casualties are reported. George W. Bush has wasted no time before getting down to some serious killing. Needless to say our spokesmen are on the airwaves within the hour, echoing the American line. It is so humiliating. We are the Bulgaria of Western Europe. Except that Bulgaria is now independent. No one else seems impressed. The legality is questionable and there is no evidence of an increased threat. We are in a pit and the only strategy seems to be to keep digging.

Monday, 19 February

Through Mowbray Park to the station at the usual hour, pulling my little wheelie-bag behind me. Only this time I am going not to London, but Kazakhstan and Kyrgyzstan. At Amsterdam I meet up with Sanjib and an official. We are flying, business class, to Alma Aty. The expense is unbelievable – £3,600 a head. How can this possibly be justified for what will be little more than a day and a half's activity? The futility of it all nags at me throughout the long flight. We land at 3 a.m. local time. A small reception committee from the embassy and the Kazakh foreign ministry awaits. VIPs we may be, but (as Ngoc used to say) there are procedures to proceed. Independent the Kazakhs may be, but the bureaucracy is Soviet. The customs form asks, among other things, if we are importing any 'poisonous, virulent or drastic substances'. Eventually, procedures proceeded, we are whisked away in the embassy Range Rover through wide, empty streets to the foreigners' palace.

Tuesday, 20 February
Regent Hotel, Alma Aty, Kazakhstan

Richard Lewington, the Ambassador, appears at breakfast. A pleasant, down-to-earth man in his mid-fifties with a classless accent which reminds me (if I close my eyes) of John Major. A Russian speaker, he started diplomatic life in Ulan Bator and has spent much of his career in the Soviet Union and central Asia. Kazakhstan is the size of Western Europe with a population of 15 million scattered around the limitless steppe. 'The question,' says the Ambassador, 'is which of the central Asian republics will turn outwards and which will turn in on themselves and implode.' Kazakhstan, still firmly a command economy, has oil and gas so it stands a better chance than most, at least until the fuel runs out.

Alma Aty has no centre. The public buildings are giant concrete monsters with no hint of concession to the local culture. The housing, a mixture of Soviet-style barrack blocks giving way eventually to more-traditional wooden cottages, each with its own vegetable patch surrounded by a crude stockade. The streets, a series of potholed, tree-lined, dual-carriageways, are wide enough to accommodate tanks two abreast (a requirement that no doubt featured in the original specifications). Not a bicycle in sight. We set off for Kyrgyzstan, a drive of 120 miles or so. There has been a light dusting of snow during the night but the road is passable.

The countryside is flat and mainly empty. Somewhere, invisible in the grey mist to our left, there are mountains, or so the Ambassador assures me. For the most part the landscape is featureless, barren, grey. At intervals we splash through mean, muddy villages. Once or twice we pass a horseman, now and then a flock of sheep or cattle, even a couple of shabby yurts, but mainly the land is empty and uncultivated. A few miles short of the frontier we halt for tea at a truck stop. We are the only customers. Our Russian drivers contemptuously remain outside in their vehicles. The inside is bare boards and a few plastic garden seats. A tap on a sink in the corner is running, unattended. A frumpish young Kazakh woman emerges. She is polite but does not seem overjoyed to see us, although the Ambassador assures us he is a regular customer. He hands over some photos he took on his last visit and she leafs through them without enthusiasm. Tea is served in bowls with a few bits of bread. We drink up and leave. The tap is still running.

At the frontier most vehicles pass through unmolested, but we are stopped. A soldier disappears with our passports. He is gone a long time. While waiting we are harassed by a ragged boy with a twisted, club hand, sore and cracked. One of the drivers gives him a few coins, but he persists. We have no money, or at any rate none that would be of use to him. Eventually Sanjib comes up with a plastic biro which seems to satisfy him. He disappears, clutching it to his chest with his bad hand. The soldier reappears with our passports and waves us on. We are now in Kyrgyzstan.

Bishkek, the capital, is a run-down version of Alma Aty. The main impression is of overwhelming greyness. Row upon row of crumbling barrack-like apartments, wide tree-lined avenues and bigger potholes. Unlike their neighbours, the Kyrgyzis lack oil and gas. All they have is water, agriculture and a goldmine run by Canadians. The country is 93 per cent mountains (not that we can see any today). Most of the industry collapsed when the Soviet Union disintegrated. Bishkek is a

1. Minister Mullin (left) and colleagues emerging from Number 10 on the day of their appointment. 'The others were over the moon. I was sunk in gloom. A woman from the Press Association chased us up Downing Street, asking how we felt. I couldn't bring myself to reply.'

2. Deputy prime minister, John Prescott: 'beneath that volcanic exterior, lurks a decent human being'.

3. September 1999: pro hunt supporters demonstrating outside the Labour Party conference: 'They carried placards naming the constituencies from which they came. More or less a list of the safest Tory seats in the country. I came away greatly encouraged.'

4. Autumn 2000: Lorry drivers, protesting at fuel prices, attempted to bring the country to a standstill. Strangely, there were no arrests for driving at 5mph down the A1.

5. The family Mullin, pictured in September 2003. CM, Ngoc, Sarah and Emma (in front).

6. With my two best friends – on the terrace of the House of Commons.

7. July 2002: The parliamentary committee, which met the prime minister weekly, in the garden at Number 10. *Front, l to r*: Paul Boateng, Hilary Armstrong, John Prescott, Tony Blair, Jean Corston, Chris Mullin, Liz Symons. *Back, l to r*, David Triesman, Andrew Mackinlay, Charles Clarke, Doug Hoyle, Helen Jackson, Ann Clwyd, Tony Lloyd, Gordon Prentice, Alan Howarth.

8. With David Dimbleby on *Question Time* in Torquay: 'A long way to go to be murdered in front of several million people.'

9. On the ministerial bicycle – in Hanoi.

10. With President Akiev of Kyrgyzstan in February 2001. 'I may be a small fish back home, but I am big in Bishkek.'

11. Addressing sixth formers at a St Aidan's school, Sunderland.

12. Assorted movers and shakers from the Sunderland South Labour Party.
My agent, Kevin Marquis, is at the back, fifth from left.

13. On the river Wear with the local canoe club, preparing to assert their right to paddle through Lord Lambton's estate.

14. I was showing a group of youngsters from Thornhill School around Parliament when we came across The Man and Jack Straw about to set off for Washington.

15. February 15, 2003: anti war protesters stage the biggest demonstration ever held in the UK: 'Let no one say that politics is dead or that New Labour has failed to mobilise the young and idealistic.'

16. Tony Benn comes to stay – and nearly sets fire to the house (see entry for May 29, 2002).

tired city. Maintenance, never a strong point in the Soviet empire, is a forgotten concept. The tiredness shows in the crumbling infrastructure, the half-finished buildings and in the pinched faces of the older folk, picking their way through the puddles and potholes, reminiscent of Hanoi in the early eighties, except that Hanoi with its French architecture, lakes and temples has an elegance that Bishkek lacks.

Wednesday, 21 February
Bishkek, Kyrgyzstan

Awoke to bright sunshine, illuminating a range of snowy mountains. A complete contrast with yesterday. Suddenly Bishkek is alive. At breakfast the Ambassador talks temptingly of an overland trip he is planning to Ulan Bator at the end of June, more than 2,000 miles across the great grassland. He is unsure whether the Russians will let him cross the 50-mile gap between the north-east corner of Kazakhstan and the western tip of Mongolia, but says he is sure to be admitted if accompanied by a member of Her Majesty's Government. Would I care to join him? You bet. Glen, the agricultural adviser, was talking last night about the 16-hour drive through the Tien Shan mountains to Osh, where he is based. Gradually my travel taste buds are being reawakened. For now, however, it is all a fantasy. There is work to be done. Today I have appointments with the Prime Minister, the Foreign Minister and the President – and various other engagements sandwiched in between. All day I will be racing back and forth across town in a car with diplomatic plates and the official flag flying. This is how it must be for The Man every day. At home I may be a small fish, but I am big in Bishkek.

We are driven to the White House, a monstrous, Soviet-era confection of glass, concrete and marble. By the entrance a gaggle of demonstrators with placards are protesting at the arrest and secret trial of an opposition leader, Mr Kulov. Should we be cheered by this evidence of nascent democracy or depressed that it was found necessary to put poor Kulov away during an election campaign? Everyone seems to agree that he is a rogue, but by treating him as they have, the Kyrgyzis have turned him into a martyr. Our line is that we have chosen to work with the Kyrgyzis because (a) they are poor and (b) in contrast to their neighbours they have chosen the path of democracy and economic liberalism. To be sure, there are some hopeful signs: they have abolished the death penalty; there are, so far as we know, no political prisoners apart from Kulov; they have drastically slimmed their top-heavy administration and are planning to decentralise power to the regions; and they are moving towards a market economy. But have we been taken for a ride? Have the cunning Kyrgyzis done just enough to entice Western aid while at the same time, just below the surface, business continues much as usual? Corruption is rife. The recent presidential election was rigged (although the incumbent would probably have won anyway). The media, while not exactly state-controlled, is not exactly free either. The jury, as they say, is still out. My job is to make clear that our goodwill is not unconditional. It requires clear evidence of progress.

After a wait of 20 minutes, we are ushered into a vast conference hall on an upper floor containing the largest table I have ever seen. By and by two or three men emerge from a door in the far corner. They move along our side of the table shaking hands. Mr Tanayev, the most senior, has the demeanour of an undertaker – grey and grim; his tie is black. Gradually, it emerges that the Prime Minister will not be coming. He has, it seems, been summoned at the last minute by Parliament to discuss the budget. Instead Mr Tanayev, his deputy, has been landed with the task of receiving us and he seems none too pleased about it. Apparatchik is written all over him in large letters. He relies on his brief, even for the standard pleasantries, and speaks for nearly 40 minutes before I am permitted to utter a word (shades of JP). As his speech wears on, the journalists and television cameras that attended the start of the meeting begin to drift away. When, at last, my turn comes, there are none left to record my message. (Perhaps this is a cunning ploy on his part? On second thoughts, no. There is no sign that Mr Tanayev's political skills extend so far.) After the usual pleasantries, I record my disappointment at the conduct of the recent elections. Mr Tanayev listens impassively, but makes no comment.

Lunch with the ministers of Foreign Affairs, Agriculture and Health is a complete contrast. These are jovial, self-confident men whose eyes sparkle, who make self-deprecating jokes and seem genuinely to enjoy themselves. They also seem to appreciate the interest that Britain is taking in their country. At the end I am presented with a magnificent cloak and high white hat, the Kyrgyzis' national dress (I know two small people who will enjoy dressing up in this).

The President, too, turns out to be a pleasant surprise. I am received this time not in the gargantuan conference room, but in a small audience chamber dominated by two huge canvases – one depicting an encampment of yurts by moonlight; the other, jagged mountains. The President and I, our interpreters behind, are seated side by side in two large armchairs. Our officials sit to each side and in front a battery of television cameras and photographers, flashing away. As I say, I am big in Bishkek (although back home I doubt this encounter will qualify for a single paragraph, even in the *Sunderland Echo*). After five minutes of banter the cameras disappear and we get down to business. President Akaev, a small, bald man with intense dark eyes and a ready smile, is an academic by profession. The only one of the Central Asian leaders not to have been a big communist. He speaks softly and without notes, exuding modesty and goodwill. He is also well briefed – referring even to our recent White Paper (Clare will be pleased). A man appears with a tray of drinks. I take mine. Before taking his, however, the President hands one to my interpreter and one for his. A nice touch. This man is no selfish tyrant. My turn comes. He fixes me with his brown eyes, apparently taking in every word. As lightly as possible, I repeat my points about our disappointment with the conduct of the election. He does not take offence, nodding appreciatively. Lessons will be learned, he says. Preparations are underway for the first ever local elections later this year (already people are voicing doubts about them). I make this point, too, and he repeats his assurance that lessons will be learned.

Our meeting lasts for more than an hour. 'He liked you,' the Ambassador said afterwards. I liked him, too. As we part, the President presents me with a signed copy of his book, *The Transition Economy through the Eyes of a Physicist*. Not a big seller, even in Bishkek, but better-written than the average DFID speech. I come away, as others have before me, charmed. Surely this decent man can't have been responsible for whatever unpleasantness occurred during the election? Outside a couple of journalists are loitering. I repeat my message about democracy, but I feel a bit of a cad. 'We have to justify this aid to our taxpayers,' I hear myself saying. I could be good at this.

Later, someone says, 'We've all been conned by Akaev's charm.' But is it as simple as that, I wonder? Perhaps it is beyond the wit of anyone to rescue so impoverished a state from the grip of the Stalin system.

We come back to earth with a bump. After seeing Akaev, I am taken to the local psychiatric hospital, which has seen many better days. In a land where even surgeons are lucky to earn US$20 a month, mental illness is not a high priority. We are harangued for an hour by the director, an exhausted man who does not attempt to conceal his despair and frustration. 'A revolution is an interesting thing,' he says, 'but I wish I had not lived to see it.'

Thursday, 22 February

Up at 5.30 a.m. in anticipation of a plane at eight, but word arrives that it has been delayed first by one and then by three hours. I take a walk into town, alone. We are at the crossroads of Asia and the streets are thronged with human beings of every conceivable size, shape, colour and nationality – from pale, round-eyed, sophisticated Europeans to ruddy, moon-faced, slit-eyed Mongols and everything in between. Many of the Europeans would not look out of place in the streets of London. I do not stand out from the crowd. No one gives me a second glance, not even when I penetrate the backstreets and the shabby, barrack-like housing where most people live. In the little playgrounds between the housing blocks, the seats are missing from the children's swings. I did not see one that was intact. Two or three streets inland I came across three or four luxurious villas in the process of construction, mocking the poverty and dereliction around them. Someone is making money. But how? The entire infrastructure is collapsing. Who is going to rebuild it when it falls, as inevitably it will? Already concrete cladding is falling from some of the monstrous public buildings on the main boulevard.

The Ambassador comes with us to the airport. He says, 'Although it is heresy to say this, most of these people were better off as part of the Soviet Union.' And, as if to underline his point, statues of Lenin can still be seen around the city, unmolested. 'I feel so sorry for them,' the Ambassador goes on. 'They have no heroes.' Gorbachev, he says, is detested. Will they succeed in establishing a market economy? 'I don't know,' he says. 'It is touch and go.'

At the airport there is more procedure to proceed. The old order are still very definitely in control here. Sanjib makes a minor error filling in his customs form. 'Twenty pounds, no problem,' beams the moon-faced customs man. To my fury Sanjib pays up before I can stop him. As we depart, the moon-faced customs officer is chatting up the Ambassador. He has a sister who wants a visa to London. 'Twenty pounds, no problem,' beams the Ambassador and the man falls about laughing. This is Mexico, not East Germany.

We fly west for two hours, over an empty, ochre wasteland, stopping briefly at Baku on the Caspian Sea. The sea, too, is empty save for a few rusting oil rigs. Then west again, over the barren, snowy mountains of Georgia and back across Europe. At Heathrow my Private Secretary, Christine, awaits with a bag of paperwork to keep me occupied on the plane to Newcastle.

Thursday, 1 March
London

Doom and gloom everywhere. Foot and mouth is spreading. The media is full of pictures of huge, smoking funeral pyres.

Friday, 2 March
Sunderland

Surprise, surprise. Chris Woodhead, the former chief inspector of schools, turned out to be a Tory after all. Just in time for the election, he has commenced a series of articles in the *Daily Telegraph* laying into New Labour in general and David Blunkett in particular in the wildest terms. In a nutshell we are accused of betrayal for failing to smash the comprehensive system. Grudgingly, he acknowledges the success of the numeracy and literacy strategy, but insolently attributes this mainly to the Tories. His most obvious omission is any mention of the Tory social policies which gave rise to growth of the huge underclass who have made teaching such a difficult job in the first place. There is a large grain of truth in what he has to say about New Labour's love of initiatives, and the resulting bureaucratic overload, but it is lost in the intemperance of his general assault.

This afternoon I visited Southmoor school, where Sarah will go in the autumn. It has a new and energetic head, Mrs Bowman. I spent half an hour chatting to some of the pupils and then she took me to see the teachers, about 60 assembled in the staff room. There were the usual complaints about deteriorating behaviour, on the part of both pupils and parents, and about the vast increase in bureaucracy. They all seemed to believe that they were underpaid and overworked. I just managed to restrain myself from pointing to all the new or nearly new vehicles in the staff car park, but I did gently point out that there was a connection between voting for parties that promised tax cuts and the amount of money available for spending on education. I asked whether the alleged improvement in numeracy and literacy at primary schools had yet filtered through and they all, as one, claimed that it hadn't (although as Mrs Bowman later pointed out this would only be apparent in the first year or second year intakes). I would have liked a longer and more robust discussion, but as soon as the final bell went most of them fled like a lot of schoolchildren.

Tuesday, 6 March

Six hours on the front bench, overseeing the International Development Bill. A bland little measure designed to stop a future Tory government re-linking aid to trade. 'No more Pergau dams' is our slogan.*
The Tories said they will go along with it, although not without a lot of shameless huffing and puffing.

---

*In 1991 Tory ministers were said to have authorised the use of overseas aid funds to help build a dam in Malaysia on the understanding that the Malaysian government would purchase arms from the UK.

Wednesday, 7 March

An amusing little crisis has arisen over the allocation of offices in the lavish new building that is being prepared for us next to Buckingham Palace. The ministerial floor consists of two vast suites overlooking the Royal Mews and a considerably smaller one on the corner. The grandest is obviously for the Secretary of State. The other, by some interesting alchemy, has been earmarked for our Permanent Secretary, Sir John Vereker (Sir Two Buzzes as I have taken to calling him).* I have been allocated the corner office and our political advisers have been exiled to a distant place. Fortunately, someone has shown the plans to Clare and she has ruled that I am to have the other suite and that the political advisers are to be moved nearer to her which leaves Sir Two Buzzes, who is a mite status-conscious, with the corner office. He is away on leave this week, but he will be apoplectic when he finds out.

Thursday, 8 March

This morning, donning a hard hat, I paid a visit to our new HQ at Palace Street. From higher up the building, there are fine views of Buckingham Palace gardens (before setting foot on the roof, it is first necessary to alert security at the palace in order to avoid being mistaken for a sniper).

A 'bilateral' with Clare. I warned that John Vereker would be upset. 'Don't worry,' she said, 'I have a good relationship with him.'

Lunch with my successor at Environment, Bob Ainsworth, who seems more at home in the job than I was. As I suspected, soon after I was out of the door, aviation officials came back to him with a modified version of the expensive and pointless research into night-flight sleep disturbance which I had refused to endorse. Bob hasn't decided what to do about it yet. I suggested he kick it into the long grass.

'I could never understand,' said Bob, 'why you accepted this job.

---

*Staff at reception in DFID have a buzzer to alert officials on the ministerial floor that one of the ministers or the Permanent Secretary is on the way up. One buzz denotes the Secretary of State; two the Permanent Secretary and three for the humble Under-Secretary.

It seemed to me you had an ideal niche with the Home Affairs Committee ...' He paused. 'It was curiosity, wasn't it?' Curiosity, yes that's what it was. It had never occurred to me to look at it that way before, but he's right. Not the only factor. But a big one. After being for so long on the outside, I wanted a glimpse of life on the inside.

This evening I was press-ganged into hosting a reception for the Commonwealth Parliamentary Association at 10 Downing Street. I refused the first two requests. 'Not even if the Prime Minister asks?' inquired the surprised official. 'But he hasn't, has he?' Sure enough, within the hour, Anji Hunter was on, sweet-talking (she kissed me on both cheeks when I saw her later). I was called upon to give a little speech of welcome. The Foreign Office sent over a suggested draft, pages long and full of pomposity. Not one word of it was usable. Where do they learn this nonsense? I thought the FO was supposed to be full of bright people. In the end I spoke for just 60 seconds, unwisely including a little jibe about the House of Lords which provoked displeased murmurs from Patrick Cormack and Geoffrey Howe. As I was leaving Number 10, I ran into Gordon Brown, who inquired politely about my new job and said we must have a talk. I can't think about what.

Monday, 12 March

To London on an early train. On platform 12 at Newcastle station there are trestle tables laden with flowers and tributes to those who died in the train crash at Selby two weeks ago, most of whom set out from Newcastle. The line is still closed between York and Doncaster and we have to travel between stations by bus.

Tuesday, 13 March

Up early to study the brief for the committee stage of the International Development Bill. This is the first committee stage of which I have been in sole charge and I don't want to make a mess. A great panic when I realised that officials don't have a clue. Unlike Environment officials, those at DFID have almost no experience of legislating.

Usually there are several hours of oral briefing and the minister is presented with a file of notes on every amendment, arranged in the order in which they are to be discussed, and all carefully tagged for ease of reference. In this case the oral briefing lasted barely 20 minutes. All I've been given is a wodge of notes on amendments, which arrived late last night, connected by a string and in the wrong order. Fortunately, this is a simple measure the details of which even my fuzzy brain has no great difficulty grasping.

The other piece of good fortune is Cheryl Gillan. Definitely not the A Team. She threw away the first half-hour with another diatribe against the iniquity of the timetable. She then tested the patience of the committee with a speech lasting the best part of an hour on the first group of amendments, several times having to be called to order by the chair. Once or twice I caught Tories on the benches behind her rolling their eyes; several times the Tory whip, Keith Simpson, winked at me. At one particularly low point, she succeeded in talking every one of her colleagues out of the room. By the end of the day we had covered just three clauses of a Bill which is entirely uncontroversial and uncomplicated.

Later, a chat with Tony Banks, who is having a whale of a time as chairman of the Works of Art Committee. He is proposing to hang portraits of Tony Benn and Dennis Skinner in the Strangers' Cafeteria, having persuaded the Speaker to waive the rule that no one shall have their likeness displayed in the main building until they have been dead ten years. Tony has commissioned portraits of Enoch Powell and Tam Dalyell and is talking about one of Diane Abbott, the first black woman to be elected. He's also taking soundings about installing a statue of Thatcher on the vacant plinth in the Members' Lobby. A number of people, myself included, have told him that this would be a bridge too far. Of course, it's inevitable that she will end up there, but not (I trust) in my lifetime and certainly not in hers.

Wednesday, 14 March

Unemployment has fallen below a million for the first time in a generation. Of course, the figures are a little phoney. A lot more work these days is low-paid and part-time, not to mention that most working class males over 55 seem to be on incapacity benefit. All the same it is a landmark and we must make the most of it. Even the *Telegraph* led with the news.

Gordon and Clare addressed a meeting in Portcullis House on Third World debt. Gordon was outshone by Clare. He spoke from notes. She from the heart. All the same they are a powerful duo. It's part of the secret of Clare's success that she gets on so well with Gordon. She said, 'Other development ministers are envious that I have a sympathetic finance minister.' Between them, they have succeeded in moving overseas aid up the political agenda. Some of Clare's public meetings are attracting upward of 500 people. For the first time that anyone can recall the boys and girls in Millbank have produced an election leaflet trumpeting our record on development. It has obviously dawned on them that there might even be votes in it.

Lunch with Tony Benn. Having been granted the Freedom of the Palace of Westminster, he's now written to the chairman, Clive Soley, asking if he can attend meetings of the parliamentary party after he retires. He asked my opinion. I think he's pushing his luck. Clive said later that, if he makes an exception for Tony, he'll come under pressure to admit anyone who has been in for 25 or 30 years. Where will it end? Besides, who wants to attend meetings of the parliamentary party for life?

Ten years ago today the Birmingham Six were released. The point at which my career peaked and the Establishment received me into its warm embrace. Since then it's been downhill all the way.

Thursday, 15 March

Sir Two Buzzes, back from a cruise on the Nile, is said to be fuming about the rearrangement of his plans for the new offices. The hapless official in charge of the refurbishment has been summoned for a bollocking. Now he's going to see Clare. I hear that he is even maintaining that ministers shouldn't be poking their noses in. Does he blame me? He was all smiles when our paths crossed briefly last night.

Another day listening to Cheryl Gillan. Today's session was

enlivened by a vicious little exchange between Cheryl and Jenny Tonge, who makes no secret of her exasperation with Cheryl's antics. Jenny, provoked beyond endurance, spat back that Cheryl was in need of HRT. Mercifully, the guillotine fell at five, leaving Cheryl complaining lamely that she hadn't had enough time.

Una Cooze has died. The third friend to die of cancer in the last year.

Tuesday, 20 March

Clare reported that last night she came across Charlie Falconer entertaining Peter Mandelson in the Pugin Room. After Peter had gone, Charlie said to Clare, 'Must keep him sweet.' Clare says she has the impression that Peter's finished, but that Downing Street is keeping him in tow until the election is out of the way. We discussed Sir Two Buzzes, who has quietly overriden Clare's instructions that the special advisers be moved closer to her office. Interestingly, he has said nothing about the suggestion that I should have the office that he had allocated to himself. No doubt he is playing for time in the hope that one or both of us will not be around after the election. He may also be relying on the fact that Clare is not much interested in office politics whereas he, I suspect, is a master. Clare promised to make her views clear, but will she?

To Misc 6 – the Ministerial Group on Biotechnology and Genetic Modification. Mo Mowlam in the chair. There was a paper by David Sainsbury (a GM enthusiast) on promoting competitiveness and one from Yvette Cooper on the human health applications (which are considerable). I confined myself to only one intervention: 'What are the implications for the number of live animal experiments? We were elected saying we would reduce them. I imagine this will lead to an increase.' David Sainsbury said, 'Yes, we must reduce the number and types of experiments, but greater numbers of animals will be used.'

'What are we saying in the manifesto?' asked Mo.

'I hope we will not say anything,' said Sainsbury. 'It gives us endless problems.'

George Howarth said something about animal rights fanatics to which I responded, 'You don't need to be a fanatic to be concerned about animal welfare.'

'I wasn't accusing you of being a fanatic, Chris.' He added with a smile, 'On this occasion.'

I suggested we commission a paper on the implications for animal experiments. Whether or not we will get one remains to be seen.

Wednesday, 21 March

This morning's meeting of the parliamentary party was given over to the general election manifesto. A ban on hunting with hounds was easily the most popular issue. There were lots of 'hear, hears' whenever the subject was mentioned. Several people said it was an issue of confidence. Alun Michael said, 'Let's get it out of the way, so we don't waste any more time.' Tony Banks said, 'It's not going to go away, even if we leave it out of the manifesto.' There were half a dozen calls for Railtrack to be renationalised ('Take Back the Track', as Harry Barnes put it) and four or five people mentioned reform of local government finance and the regulation of multi-occupied housing. Betty Williams wanted the pay-back threshold for student loans raised. David Chaytor and Malcolm Savidge said we should come out clearly against the proposed Missile Defence Shield. Jeremy Corbyn read out a little wish list which prompted Graham Allen to call out, to general amusement, 'What about the second week?'

At the end JP gave a characteristically tetchy response, pointing out that the days of wish lists were over. We should stick to themes. There must be no hostages to fortune. We shouldn't forget that everything had a price. In the case of Railtrack, the price of renationalising was about £5 billion. Did we really want to pay that? 'Don't forget, if the economy goes down, our reserves would disappear overnight.'

Thursday, 22 March

To Downing Street for a meeting of junior and middle-rank ministers. Naively, I thought we had been summoned to give The Boss the benefit of our views on the date of the election and the contents of the manifesto. Instead we were ushered upstairs to the Pillared Drawing Room for a series of pep talks from JP, Gordon Brown and a party pollster. Hard chairs had been set out in three rows along the centre of the room, exactly as they might be for a Mother's Day performance at a primary school. I concealed myself in the window seat overlooking the rose garden. At the end The Man, in shirtsleeves, appeared and gave us a little homily. 'This campaign will not be about a new gimmick every day. What will carry is that we have an agenda for the country.' We must exude confidence. In the eighties we had been on the back foot, now we must talk about the future. 'We have a better set of economic indicators than any other government. This is not accident or coincidence. It is the result of our sound policies. That's what we have to get across.'

No one said so, but the unspoken assumption throughout was that the election will take place on 3 May, regardless of foot and mouth. The wagons are rolling and they will not easily be stopped.

Monday, 26 March

All day I have been harassed by a journalist from the *Independent* who has discovered that I have written to the agriculture minister (on behalf of a constituent) asking for a copy of the report from the December inspection of the farm at Heddon-on-the-Wall, where the foot and mouth outbreak started. The journalist is anxious to pretend that the government knew, or should have known, about the disease several months before it became public. Such an assertion, if true, would be the holy grail for the Tories and the less scrupulous hacks are already dropping hints that this may be the case, even though there is absolutely no evidence. I am not responding to calls.

Tuesday, 27 March

Awoken by the phone at 7.15. Instinctively, I know what it's about. The *Today* programme is ringing about a story in the *Independent*. I lie still and let the answerphone collect the message. The phone rings again 20 minutes later. Again I leave it to the answerphone. As soon as I get to the Department someone from the press office draws my attention to the front page of the *Independent*, headed 'Slaughter, misery and now traces of a cover-up at the farm where it all began'. Amazing what can be done with a bland three-sentence letter requesting a copy of the inspection report. Sure enough, I feature prominently. 'Mr Mullin … redoubtable campaigner on freedom of information' etc, etc. Phooey. By 9 a.m. calls from *Today* have given way to calls from *The World at One*. I send word that I have nothing to say. Back comes the plaintive message 'Only a background talk …' Get stuffed. I lie low all day. Miraculously the calls dry up. And the story fails to take off.

A meeting with Clare to decide our line on Iraqi sanctions. The FCO, the MOD and the Cabinet Office have already been consulted but we were missed out of the loop until Clare sent a stiff letter to Downing Street. There is general agreement that existing sanctions have lost credibility. Saddam has been manipulating them for his own purposes. He is awash with money, but simply chooses not to spend most of it on his own people and we get the blame. After a bit of agonising we agree – or rather Clare does – to support a switch from positive to negative sanctions (which means letting in everything except military hardware or goods that can be used for military purposes). The no-fly zones and freeze on the assets and travel of leading members of the regime will remain. As for the Kurds, we shall have to watch carefully what happens to them. This, of course, is only our view. As with everything, the Americans will have the final say.

Clare told a chilling story about an Iraqi refugee, an ophthalmic surgeon, who recently came to her surgery. The woman had fled after a senior member of the regime had brought his son to her for a corneal graft. She told him that she couldn't do it because she had no facilities to store corneas. A few days later the man came back with a wretched-looking man in tow. 'Take his,' he commanded. She refused and from that moment on her life was in danger.

In the Tea Room, Dennis Skinner was arguing that we should postpone the election for a month as a nod in the direction of public opinion. No doubt he has said this to The Man, who listens to Dennis.

For the first time, I begin to think the election will be in June after all. Clare thinks so, too. Which is very inconvenient, since it involves cancelling our holiday in the Borders on which I have already paid a large deposit.

Friday, 30 March
Sunderland

Just before midnight. I am sitting in the study, reading. Suddenly I hear the unmistakable sound of car windows being stove in, followed by raucous laughter. One of the damaged cars belongs to the young couple at number 9, who only moved in last weekend.

Monday, 2 April

The election is off. It's official. A Bill is to be introduced moving the local elections to 7 June, which is effectively the same as saying that the general election will take place on that day. Incredibly, the *Sun* seems to have been tipped off as long ago as Friday, before the Queen and most of the Cabinet (Clare says The Man called her on Sunday evening).

Clare called a summit of officials and special advisers to resolve the dispute over office space at Palace Street. There was never any doubt that Sir Two Buzzes was going to emerge triumphant. The officials in charge of organising the move had obviously been primed in advance. They backed him all the way. Clare also seemed to have been softened up. The political advisers were disposed of first. They are aggrieved that their office is not adjacent to Clare's. 'It's on another floor,' David Mephan kept saying. Actually, it's only down five steps and round a corner. 'How many steps?' Sir Two Buzzes asked, as if he didn't know. 'Five,' the official dutifully replied. And that was that. The only other issue was whether he or I should occupy the other grand office. On this point Sir Two Buzzes kept very quiet, except for some guff about the impossibility of fitting his conference table into the smaller of the two offices and his need to hold large meetings. Someone asked why these meetings could not be held in any of the

42 meeting rooms dotted about the building, but for some reason this was out of the question. The matter was not pressed. My opinion was sought. I should have fought, but I hadn't the energy. All I said was, 'It's all about status and I don't care about status.' Unwisely I added, 'That's why I don't have a car.' The remark was aimed at Two Buzzes, but even as the words passed my lips I realised that they could equally apply to Clare. There was a stony silence. Two Buzzes said nothing. 'In that case,' said Clare, 'John can have the big room. Is everyone happy?' David moaned again about his office being on another floor. Two Buzzes allowed himself a little smile of triumph, directed at me as if we were on the same side.

Tuesday, 3 April

A message from Number 10: no minister is to take a foreign holiday over Easter. Imagine what the tabloids would say.

A meeting with Clare, the political advisers and Valerie Amos, the Department whip. Valerie is going to take on my Caribbean trip, as a result of the change of election date. Clare has plans to extend her empire. She intends to try and persuade The Man to give us a third minister, to look after our interests in the Lords. Also, she wants the Africa minister at the Foreign Office to report through her, since we do so much business in Africa. That must be a complete non-starter. I'd like to be a fly on the wall when Robin hears about that. As for a third minister, what would he or she do? Barely enough crumbs fall from Clare's table for one other, never mind a third.

An interesting little anecdote, from one of the political advisers, about the excellent leaflet that Millbank have produced on international development. On the outside a lovely picture of African schoolgirls. Inside, a series of messages illustrated by little photos – mugshots of Clare and Gordon and a good one of The Man with Nelson Mandela. When the proof was sent to Gordon's office they rang back to say that there were too many pictures of politicians. 'You want us to drop Gordon?'

'No, no, no ...'

So what did Gordon – or at the very least his acolytes – want?

Believe it or not, they wanted the picture of Tony Blair removed. Doesn't that say it all?

In the afternoon, a visit from Sir Two Buzzes. I had to ask him to come to the House since there was a three-line whip on and I couldn't leave. 'Sorry to drag you down here,' I said.

'No problem. After all,' he added cheerfully, 'I have a car.'

It was just about warm enough, so we sat on the terrace. He asked what I thought about Clare's plan for a third minister and I replied that there barely seemed enough work for two, let alone three. We'd all end up falling out with each other. He agreed and said he would speak to Clare. He asked how I was getting on and I said that I was having difficulty adjusting to the utter lack of influence. I made clear I wasn't complaining, that I admired Clare and that the present division of labour probably made sense, but that mine was a job for an ambitious thirty-something rather than a grown-up.

Wednesday, 4 April

The newspapers report tentative signs that the foot and mouth outbreak has peaked, but Michael Meacher, to whom I chatted briefly in the division lobby, is not so sure: 'It's into Shropshire and Kent. We've slaughtered a million animals, 97 per cent of them healthy. It's animal genocide. Just like the Somme. The Prime Minister won't opt for vaccination because the farmers object and he won't go against them.'

Thursday, 5 April

On the way up Victoria I came across Betty Boothroyd emerging from Sainsbury's, plastic shopping bag in hand, exuding good health and good will.

My former Private Secretary at Environment, Chris Brain, came in to discuss the annual report that he has to prepare on the other office staff. Afterwards, we chatted about the relative merits of ministers. 'You were good. You turned up on time, did your work and did as you were told.' Did as I was told? Excuse me. That, presumably, is the civil service definition of a good minister. I doubt whether it is the party's, or the public's. Who is regarded as a bad minister? Quick as a flash, he named Michael Meacher. Although I can see that Michael is infuriating to work for – he is miles behind with his letters and refuses to delegate – most people regard him as one of our more successful ministers. On top of his brief. Brilliant at explaining complicated issues. Unfailingly courteous. Chris added that JP was also difficult to work for because he was so grumpy. That I can sympathise with.

Friday, 6 April

There are reports that George Bush, having reneged on Kyoto, is about to do the same with the Anti-Ballistic Missile Treaty so he can go ahead with his lunatic missile shield. I wonder what those bone-headed Florida Greens, who threw away their votes on Ralph Nader on the grounds that there was no difference between Bush and Gore, have to say about that?

Sunday, 8 April
Sunderland

Sunshine. With the children to fly their kite and play football. Later, we spent a couple of hours on the beach at South Shields, which was fairly crowded. After we'd been there a while, two rough-looking women with seven young children, one a baby, in tow turned up and sat on the concrete slipway. One of them changed the baby's nappy which she handed to a small boy who simply tossed it into the sea. She then handed him the tissues with which she had been wiping the baby's bottom and he tossed these into the air scattering them over the slipway. Neither of the women batted an eyelid. What hope for the children?

Tuesday, 10 April

Our Bill went through without a hitch. Gary Streeter, who led for the other side, was on his best behaviour, even managing a generous tribute to Clare. Indeed there were tributes to Clare from all over.

There is no doubt she is an enormous success. It is a useful little Bill. As Clare whispered to me afterwards, 'It makes illegal many of the things the Foreign Office keeps pressing us to do.' It has also smoked out the Tories. Who, listening to the lofty sentiments emitted by Gary Streeter, would guess that his was the party of the Pergau Dam? He even committed a future Tory government to meeting the UN target for aid (0.7 per cent of GNP) and lambasting us for our slow progress. Who would guess the aid budget more or less halved during their tenure. I almost expected a thunderbolt to fall from heaven, but none did.

Angela Smith told me that the parliamentary committee had had two meetings at Number 10 with David Miliband and pressed for a commitment on hunting to be included in the manifesto, but no one believes it will be.

Wednesday, 11 April

Spent the day with Charles Frater at his editing suite, Silverglade, working on my interview with Uncle Brian. We boiled it down from over two hours to 30 minutes. Some nice lines: 'The Second World War was interesting in patches' (he watched the Battle of Britain from the beach at Shoeburyness). And the parish priest who, after hearing Brian's first sermon as his curate, asked, 'Have you got any more like that?'

Brian, thinking this was praise: 'Yes.'

'Then burn them.'

Thursday, 12 April
Sunderland

Mr Herring came to the house to take the photographs for my election literature. 'Have you seen what Quentin Letts has said about you in the *Mail*?'

I hadn't.

'It's terrible. I don't know whether I dare tell you.'

'Go on.'

'He says that you look like a deckchair that's been left out all winter.' Actually that's funny. Not bad for a toe rag like Letts. Mr Herring was surprised that I took it so lightly so I showed him my greatest insults – 'Loony MP backs bomb gang', 'Mr Odious', etc – framed on the wall of my study.

Letts has devoted most of his column to me. It reads (in part): 'Mr Mullin has the look of a deckchair left out over winter. His trousers flap emptily around his shins, his sparse hair is unkempt, his spectacles could do with a polish, and his manner of speaking is gentlemanly ...' He also says that one of my former colleagues at Environment, 'in the loyal way of politicians', recently took him aside at a drinks party and murmured that I was no good at detail. Who, I wonder, is the traitor?

Monday, 16 April
Easter Monday

To York to walk the walls and see the daffodils. Most of the footpath signs we passed en route had 'Keep out – Foot and Mouth' pinned to them. Everywhere in the countryside the plague hangs like a great dark cloud. The television is still showing huge smouldering pyres, herds of sheep and cattle in the line for death and interviews with depressed farmers.

Thursday, 19 April

A red box arrived full of paper to be leafed through in a leisurely fashion. For information rather than action. The only excitement is a handwritten note which Clare has appended, in response to my request to officials for a line on our activities in China. She writes: 'I am not keen on these queries being raised in writing with dept [sic] when I am personally involved in them. Could you consider raising with me in our regular meetings first? It is very odd for officials to defend my policy to you with me left out of the loop.' All I wanted was a line to take in case someone raised it with me, but she appears to have interpreted this as criticism of her policy. I penned a conciliatory little note, but it is bizarre. Taken literally, it means I can't ask about anything without going through Clare. She has no need of a deputy.

Tuesday, 24 April

Today's papers report that the Dome may be empty for three years, at a cost of a million pounds a month. A monument to New Labour folly. We are so lucky to have got away with it.

Wednesday, 25 April

Up early to cut the grass and clear the rubbish (among which I found two syringes) from the front garden at Brixton Road. And then to the meeting of the parliamentary party to hear Gordon Brown give a long-winded but upbeat assessment of the economy despite talk of recession in the US and thousands of redundancies at Motorola. At Questions I hardly got a look-in – most of the time was taken up by Clare responding on the EC and Aids. The most useful thing I did all day was cut the grass.

Thursday, 26 April

An hour with Clare and the special advisers. Like JP, Clare talks all the time, but unlike JP she has something to say, her passion is well-targeted and good-humoured. She was full of her recent trip to Sierra Leone and the uselessness of the UN military mission. She has had a sneak preview of the draft manifesto, which, she says, is far too long and contains no commitment to increase our share of the budget. She also reported that, at this morning's Cabinet, she had appealed for an end to all the anonymous briefing about who is going to get what after the election. 'It sets a bad tone,' she says. The Man gave one of his world-weary shrugs as if to say, 'I agree, but what can I do?'

'Not good enough,' said Clare.

Much of the briefing seems to be coming from Blunkett, who keeps being tipped as the next Home Secretary. He is clearly building himself to challenge Gordon when the time comes. Clare says that Blunkett is too illiberal to be Home Secretary. She also said that Gordon Brown had remarked to her, after the Cabinet, that Peter Mandelson may be behind the pro-Blunkett briefings. There is no evidence for this, but it does give a clue as to how Gordon's mind is working.

'Gordon's a megalomaniac,' said Clare.

'Wholly unsuited to be leader,' I chipped in.

To my surprise (I had always assumed that Clare was in his camp) she readily agreed. 'We'd be in deep trouble if Gordon's court took over Downing Street.' She added, 'What to do about Gordon will be the big drama of our second term.'

Friday, 27 April

A call from Clare's special adviser, David Mephan. Would I mind if Clare made both the opening and closing speeches in next week's development debate? Actually, I would. What's the point of having a deputy if she is not prepared to delegate the slightest responsibility? In what other Department would the Secretary of State insist on opening and closing? Not that it's any big deal. The Commons chamber will be more or less empty anyway. Having registered my dissatisfaction, I decided not to make a fuss. If I were to insist, she would only be sitting behind me, brooding. However, Christine rang back half an hour later to say that I would be winding up after all. Thinking she was protecting my interests, Christine had insisted and Clare had given in. I shall now have to rise to the occasion.

Wednesday, 2 May

Keith Vaz is back at work today after an absence of two weeks. Was he really ill or was it political? Whatever, it seems to have done the trick. The hacks are off his back and have gone in search of new prey (Geoffrey Robinson is back in their sights).

To the Foreign Office for a sandwich lunch with the governors of the British Overseas Territories, who are in town for their annual conference. Big fish in very small pools. Amiable, greying men in their fifties, coasting towards retirement. Once in post they tend to go native and make all sorts of unreasonable demands. The governor of St Helena (journey time three weeks by ship) bent my ear about his demand for an airport. He is also keen for a ministerial visit – no minister having set foot there in the 200 years we have been in charge. I am up for that, if I am still around after the election.

Thursday, 3 May

The development debate went off without incident. Gary Streeter and the few Tories in attendance were all sweetness and light. Everyone was full of praise for Clare. There is a surprising degree of consensus behind our new aid policy.

Friday, 4 May
Sunderland

Dressing-up day at school. Sarah went as Esmeralda and Emma as Red Riding Hood. They looked so beautiful.

Kevin Marquis called in with proofs of our election literature. Afterwards we went over to the local party's management committee where I tried to interest them in the coming election. It was the first management committee Kevin had attended for four years. He said afterwards that it was like passing through a time warp. Same old faces. Same old song. One of the councillors complained that a new member (God knows, we don't get many) had appeared at his branch without his being notified. There was a fuss about plans to hold a referendum on whether to have an elected mayor and an (entirely justified) suspicion that we are being rail-roaded by the New Labour high command into something that no one wants. Pat Smith said that only two members of the public turned up to the consultation meeting at Hall Farm and only three to the one in Silksworth. She said, 'The government keeps talking about public participation, but the public don't want to participate.' To which Charles Bate added, 'They just want us to get on with the job.'

Tuesday, 8 May

As expected, the election will be on 7 June. The Man went to the Palace this morning.

Mike O'Brien has been talking to John Bercow, who says that, if the Tories gain less than 40 seats Portillo will run against Hague for the leadership, although not until the second ballot (so that he can proclaim his undying loyalty in the first). Ann Widdecombe will also run and the Portillistas are desperate to stop her reaching the run-off because they fear that, if she does, she will win. She may not be popular with fellow MPs, but she has a lot of support in the Tory party and, under the new rules, the membership have the final say.

The threat of Widdecombe may be just what we need to awake the Labour heartlands from their torpor.

Friday, 11 May

Much speculation about which members of the New Labour elite will be parachuted into the safe seats vacated by MPs retiring at the last moment. Ed Balls and David Miliband are among the names being mentioned. Not for them the cutting of teeth in hopeless seats or the long, wearying slog around the selection circuit. A few high-level phone calls, a quiet word in the right ears and ... Bob's your uncle ... a safe seat for life. And who knows, within two or three years a foot on the ministerial ladder, first steps on the inevitable rise to the Cabinet. Most resentment, not to say anger, is reserved for Shaun Woodward, who is being touted for St Helens.

Monday, 14 May

Shaun Woodward has been selected in St Helens. Hearing him on the radio this morning promising to be a champion of the poor and downtrodden made my flesh creep. This is one of New Labour's vilest stitch-ups.

Tuesday, 15 May

A call from a young woman at Labour Party HQ in Millbank. 'Would you like to go to Calder Valley on Saturday?'

'Not particularly. Why?'

'They are having a two-hour electioneering blitz.'

'I am afraid I don't see the point of driving three hours each way to take part in two hours of activity which could just as easily be carried out by those who live there.'

'Oh, I hadn't realised it was so far away.'

'Do you know where Sunderland is?'

She giggled. 'No, not really.'

She rang off promising to find me a meeting to address in Carlisle or Tynemouth, where I am sure they have absolutely no desire to hear from me. Lord save us from the young master-strategists in Millbank, playing with imaginary armies.

Wednesday, 16 May

A bad day on the campaign trail. The launch of the manifesto was overshadowed by an angry woman who confronted The Man outside a hospital in Birmingham. Then Jack Straw was slow-handclapped by the Police Federation. Finally, this evening JP was filmed landing a punch on the jaw of a man who had just smashed an egg all over him. Poor JP, I sympathise, I really do, but he's a disaster waiting to happen. For how much longer can we afford him?

Thursday, 17 May

Everyone is talking about JP's altercation in north Wales yesterday. Far from having done us harm, it seems to have brought the campaign to life. I take it all back. JP is an asset, after all.

Monday, 21 May
Sunderland

This evening Kevin and I knocked on doors in Durham Road in the hope of getting up a few posters. In bygone years we have done well here. This time the reception was surly. Mainly complaining retired folk in their late fifties or early sixties. None was especially old or poor. One woman who had retired at 55, thought it was a scandal that she and her husband were having to pay tax on their joint income. 'We've worked hard all our lives,' she kept saying. All? She will probably live another 30 years. How does she imagine the state is going to look after her, if no one over 55 is paying tax. When challenged she simply changed the subject: 'And, of course, the health service is in a dreadful state.'

'Is it? I've had a couple of operations recently and it didn't seem too bad.'

Again, seamlessly, the goalposts moved. 'And there's crime. It's getting worse.'

'No,' I said. 'It's getting less.'

'I don't know if I'll bother voting,' she said.

'Oh well,' I replied cheerfully, 'let's hope not everyone feels as you do, otherwise we'll have another Tory government.'

'Oh no,' she said hastily, 'we don't want that.'

As I left, I noticed two nearly new cars parked on the drive. So much for not being able to afford taxes.

Wednesday, 23 May

I've seen my first Tory poster. Neville, four doors up, has one in his window, eclipsed by MULLIN/LABOUR posters which have gratifyingly and unprompted appeared in the windows of four of my neighbours.

Saturday, 26 May

To the town centre to harass shoppers. We arrived to find the Tories already there. Today they are posing as the 'Save the Pound' party. At first we mistook them for UKIP, until I spied their candidate, Jim Boyd. All very civilised. He came over and chatted for five minutes, even telling one voter what a good MP I was. They were inviting people to sign a 'Save the Pound' petition and seemed to be doing brisk business, mainly (it must be said) among the elderly. Of course, it relies on ignorance, of which there is no shortage. 'Save the Pound – Lose Nissan' would be a more honest slogan.

Wednesday, 30 May

Watched William Hague answering questions on television. Everyone keeps saying how awful he is, but I find him impressive. He is calm, cheerful, rational and exudes self-confidence. It is just that the tide of history is against him. Also, he has based his campaign on an appeal to the meanest instincts of the British people at a time when they – or most of them – want something better. Thank goodness.

Thursday, 31 May

To Doxford International, to visit One2One, a mobile telephone call centre, employing 1,200 people. Doxford is a big success. Altogether 7,500 people are employed there, mainly in jobs that didn't exist ten years ago, some in industries that didn't exist – mobile phones for example. Their fathers and grandfathers worked in shipyards and coal mines and they have graduated to computer screens. For all the sneers that call centres attract from metropolitan journalists, I doubt whether a single one of those employed there would trade his computer for the coalface.

I was shown around by a tall, Hispanic-looking man who appeared to come from another planet. His opening words were, 'What do you hope to get out of the next half-hour?' He spoke a language with which I am unfamiliar, using words like 'skill-sets' and 'functionality'; his workers were divided into 'communities'. Overhead a banner proclaimed that this or that community had won this month's award for 'A monopoly of Excellence'. Easy to see from where New Labour gets its claptrap.

Tuesday, 5 June

Eeerily quiet. Entire estates without a single poster. I wouldn't be surprised if our turnout falls to below 50 per cent.

Thursday, 7 June
Election day

Awoke to bright sunshine. Tony Benn rang before breakfast to wish me good luck, full of enthusiasm as ever, even though I must be a disappointment to him.

Our usual election day tour in an open-topped bus. A few elderly constituents gave us the thumbs-up, young children waved, but mainly we encountered cold-eyed indifference. The result was every bit as shocking as I feared. Our turnout down to 48 per cent. At first I was depressed, but as the night wore on it became clear that it was nothing personal. Indeed there were many falls bigger than mine, including The Man at Sedgefield. The good news is that our majority will be virtually unscathed, so the Tories are in much deeper trouble than we are. In truth, however, the entire political system is in trouble.

Friday, 8 June

The talking heads are asking how we politicians are going to reconnect with the people. Well, for a start, we could stop boring them silly. Elections these days consist of a tiny elite of political leaders racing around the country in battle buses pursued by an equally tiny elite of commentators, while the rest of us (candidates, party members and general public alike) are mere spectators, occasionally roped in as extras. Meanwhile politics as a participatory activity is dying. Membership is in freefall. Increasingly, the main parties are financially dependent on a handful of multimillionaires who are in many cases virtually interchangeable (indeed they do interchange with depressing frequency). How will it end? My guess is that the rot will continue until we are blasted out of our indolence by either (a) a world war, (b) an environmental catastrophe (but only one that affects us directly – someone else's catastrophe won't make any difference), or (c) another sustained period of Tory government. Of these the third is the most likely and most bearable, but even that is too awful to contemplate. It will be for another generation of politicians to sort out. My time is almost done.

Saturday, 9 June

Most of the new Cabinet posts have been announced. Jack Straw is the new Foreign Secretary. David Blunkett, as expected, gets the Home Office. Robin Cook becomes Leader of the House. Lots of women: Hilary Armstrong is the new Chief Whip, Margaret Beckett heads the new food, rural and environment ministry (Defra). Estelle Morris takes Education, a good choice. I've always liked Estelle, unflashy, down to earth. Hopefully she will reduce the flow of new initiatives to manageable proportions. No mention so far of Clare, but I am sure she will be reappointed.

On impulse, I rang Hilary Armstrong to indicate that I wish to move up or out. Two years as the lowest form of life in government was as much as I could bear and I wouldn't take offence were I to be returned to the backbenches. 'Tony values what you have done,' she replied (how many times have I heard that?). She asked what would interest me and I said minister of state at either the Home or Foreign Office. The Man is taking a day off so I am unlikely to hear from him until Monday.

Rain all day. I spent the afternoon delivering flowers to people who had helped in the election campaign.

Monday, 11 June

The Call came just after 12.30. After an exchange of pleasantries it was clear that there was nothing else on offer. 'I gather you'd like to go back to the backbenches.'

I replied that two years in the lower foothills of government was long enough.

He sighed. 'Ministerial life doesn't suit some people.'

I said that what didn't suit me was the utter lack of influence that came with low office. 'Every year since 1990 I could point to something that has changed for the better as a result of my intervention. All that stopped when I became a minister.'

He laughed. 'That's a great tribute to ministerial life.'

We agreed that we would exchange letters to avoid my having to spend the next three weeks explaining that I had not been sacked. He rang off saying that I should come and see him tomorrow to discuss what I would like to do next. 'We can go down the card' was how he put it.

The letter didn't take long to draft. I have been composing it in the bath every morning for weeks. It reads:

> Dear Tony,
> As I indicated when we spoke, after two years in the foothills of government I have concluded that I can be of more use to the party, the country and the human race in general, if I were to return to the world of select committees. I do not, therefore, wish to be reappointed. Thank you for giving me the opportunity to see the inside of government. Please be assured of my continued support.
>
> Yours ever,
>
> Chris

I faxed it to Sally Morgan and went home for lunch.

Naively, I assumed that I could rely on Number 10's assurance that they would publish my letter and The Man's reply. As the afternoon wore on, however, there was no response. I began to realize that I had better do my own spinning. I rang half a dozen lobby journalists and indicated that I was going of my own volition. Eventually, I faxed copies of my letter to Michael White at the *Guardian*, and the Press Association. It seemed to do the trick. The BBC added 'at his own request' to their little list of The Fallen. Later, I heard that Sally Morgan was now a minister in the Cabinet Office and is going to the Lords. No wonder she didn't ring back.

Rang Clare in the evening, thinking she would be a little miffed at my not tipping her off that I wasn't coming back, but she was affable and agreed that being her deputy wasn't a big enough job for a grown-up.

Ngoc has been very kind, considering that her husband has just slashed the annual household income by £27,000. Tony Benn rang to say that I'd done exactly the right thing (although since Hilary has stepped into my shoes, Tony has a foot in both camps).

As for me, I have an empty feeling. I know I have crossed a little bridge over which I can never go back.

Tuesday, 12 June

There has been a huge cull. More than 20 ministers out, including a lot of middle-aged, middle-rank workhorses, competent but unglamorous – John Battle, Mike O'Brien, Joyce Quin – who have been replaced by thirty-somethings. Chris Smith and Ann Taylor are the biggest casualties. There has been a big clearout in the whips' office. The only senior whip to survive is the only one who should have gone, Lance Corporal Tommy McAvoy. To everyone's astonishment Nigel Griffiths has been re-inserted into more or less the same job at the DTI from which he was sacked two years ago. The only possible explanation is that he was rescued by Gordon. Gisela Stuart and Kate Hoey have also gone. The irony is that I would have survived. I could have whiled away a pleasant two or three years visiting places that didn't need to be visited and meeting people who didn't need to be met.

My departure merits a couple of mentions in today's press. 'A bouquet is due to Chris Mullin,' writes Don Macintyre, 'who uniquely struck a blow for backbench careers by leaving his junior ministerial post with the aim of returning to select committee chairmanship.' A leader in today's *Guardian* says, 'Chris Mullin will probably be a better servant of the public interest as a select committee member than as a lowly factotum in the Department of Environment.' The author hadn't even noticed that I'd been at International Development for the last five months.

Thursday, 14 June

Everyone is going about congratulating or commiserating, according to who is up and who is down. The newly promoted boys and girls look upon me with incomprehension. How could anyone possibly prefer life on the backbenches to a world of official cars, red boxes and papers marked 'Restricted' – to say nothing of an extra £27,000 a year.

A talk with Mike O'Brien, whose services have been dispensed with after four years of dog's-bodying at the Home Office. He says Jack made heroic efforts to save him, but to no avail. No doubt Mike's role in the fall of Mandelson didn't help. Mike said that, until the late afternoon of 8 June, Jack had believed he was going to Environment. He had even been talking to officials there in preparation for moving in when the call came to say that he was going to the Foreign Office. Mike says Home Office officials take little notice of select committee reports. 'Robin Corbett's were barely read. Jack read yours because he took you seriously.' If I am to go back to the Home Affairs committee, I had better establish contact with Blunkett as soon as possible.

To King's Cross for the 20.00. The garden was swarming with snails, eagerly devouring the petunias we planted last weekend. I spent half an hour hunting them down and murdering them with a log of wood. From now on it's zero tolerance as far as snails are concerned.

Friday, 15 June
Sunderland

The *Echo* is excited about my return to the backbenches. Tuesday's paper ran a leader headed, 'Chris Mullin sets himself free'. Tonight, across the top of the front page, my weekly column is advertised under the strapline 'Chris Mullin is back'. I wish I could share their enthusiasm.

Monday, 18 June

To 12 Downing Street for a heart to heart with the new Chief Whip, Hilary Armstrong. From her window I can see baby Leo's toys, a red and yellow buggy, a red plastic box with large eyes, parked just below the terrace where The Man conducts most of his business in summer. Tea is served. Hilary, making occasional notes in a red foolscap notebook, claims to be interested in beefing up select committees and asks for suggestions. 'Create an alternative career structure,' I say. 'Pay the chairmen, encourage pre-legislative scrutiny and put on people other than fully paid-up New Labourites.' In an ideal world we wouldn't be having this conversation. Select committees should be a matter for the House, not for the whips, but the reality is that our world is not ideal. I also suggested that it was time we had a Labour chair of the Security and Intelligence Committee. Finally, I indicated that I would like to return to chair the Home Affairs Committee. She has already sounded out Blunkett on this and he seems agreeable.

To Clare's office at DFID for a farewell party. I had been dreading setting foot there. In the event it went off beautifully. Clare and George Foulkes made graceful, generous, cheerful speeches, as did my successor, Hilary Benn, who is a natural, and Valerie Amos, now a Foreign Office minister. I presented Christine (who is off to UNESCO in Paris) and Sanjib with signed copies of the new edition of *A Very British Coup*. On the way out, I put my head around the door of my old office. The only changes are a new chair and an upgraded computer. I picked up my few possessions and walked away down Victoria. I am sorry to be leaving. DFID is a happy, well-motivated department, full of good people who enjoy their work. Clare's job is the best in government and she does it brilliantly. It's just that she has no need of a deputy.

Tuesday, 19 June

Suddenly I am in demand. Requests for interviews are coming in thick and fast. I am free to have opinions again. In the first flush of enthusiasm for my new-found freedom, I have accepted every media invitation.

To the Home Office to see David Blunkett. His Private Secretary hummed and hawed about how busy he was when I rang, but a slot was soon found after I let slip that I was seeing the Prime Minister on Thursday.

The Home Secretary's office has changed a little since I last visited. A glass partition has been inserted, hiving off the conference area in the furthest quarter of the room. As a result it is less Soviet in scale. David insists on coming in through the main reception rather than being driven into the underground car park and whisked upstairs in the Home Secretary's private lift. Despite being blind, or perhaps because he is, David has immediately sensed the surly, unwelcoming air that pervades the main entrance lobby and has plans for change. It will be an early test of his authority. I would not be too optimistic about the outcome. There is something about the building that induces surliness and indifference.

We started with drugs. David knew all about the Nick Davies articles in the *Guardian* calling for legalisation, and to my surprise did not dismiss them out of hand. He is not keen on Nick Davies, who did him over when he was education secretary, 'but as a rational human being, I have to admit that he has a point'. Despite his reputation for illiberalism, David is keen to get cannabis downgraded and is even prepared to contemplate legalising and regulating the sale of heroin, 'although I don't accept that it's benign'.

The Home Office will have two big bills in the Queen's Speech tomorrow – on police and crime – although the details seem surprisingly sketchy (the special advisers didn't seem to have a clue about the contents when I chatted them up on the way in). The Police Bill will contain some of the measures on discipline and complaints recommended three years ago in the first select committee report of my chairmanship.

We chatted for about 40 minutes. 'This place is obsessed with legislation,' he said. He seemed to take it for granted that I would resume the chairmanship of the Home Affairs Select Committee.

In the Tea Room, John Hutton whispered that he had recently asked how many targets the Department of Health had set itself. Twenty? Fifty? 'Er, no, Minister.' How many? 'About 800.' John added, 'I don't think we want that publicised just yet.'

Thursday, 21 June

To Number 10 for an audience with The Man. A half an hour wait, listening to the ticking of the grandfather clock in the lobby outside the Cabinet Room. A party of schoolboys in red blazers were being shown round. Cherie sauntered through, humming. 'You're free,' she said, adding cheerfully, 'and poorer.'

I was shown through the Cabinet Room to the rattan armchairs on the garden terrace. The Man appeared after a couple of minutes. 'You must be disappointed in me,' I began.

'Not really, I knew you were the sort who might want to go a bit further than being in government will allow.'

'I wouldn't want you to think I was unhappy with being a minister. I am perfectly capable of taking responsibility. It's just that there wasn't any at my level of government. In four months at DFID, I never saw a piece of paper marked "For Decision". Not one.' He looked surprised. Of course, he has no experience of life at the bottom. In ten years he has probably never known a moment's tedium, save perhaps those awful negotiations with the Irish. 'Of course,' I continued, 'I could have whiled away a pleasant few years but I couldn't bear the thought. So I sent you a message via the Chief Whip that I wanted either to move on or out.' He again looked surprised. A penny was dropping. For me, too.

He said, 'The message I got was more "out" than "on"'.

Oh dear, oh dear. What precisely did Hilary Armstrong say? My fault, of course. I should never have entrusted her with so delicate a mission. And maybe I did lay on the 'wouldn't be upset' bit a mite too thickly. I should have rung my old friend Bruce Grocott ... Or just kept my big mouth shut and accepted the hand that I was dealt. My demise was not as glorious as everyone imagines. It was an accident.

'Never mind,' I said. 'What's done is done.'

We discussed prospects. I mentioned the chairmanship of the parliamentary party, saying that I wouldn't run against Jean Corston and that it would be nice to have a woman. He spoke well of Jean, saying he nearly made her a minister. Clearly he favours her.

On home affairs we discussed issues, starting with drugs. To my surprise he was relaxed about an inquiry into legalisation. 'I have no clear view,' he said. 'There are some issues a select committee can explore which I never could.'

On asylum, he confirmed that the voucher system was going, but only in exchange for some quid pro quo. On the Security and Intelligence Committee, I said it was time we plucked up the self-confidence to put in a Labour chairman. He replied that, although Michael Howard was lobbying hard for it, he had in mind someone from our side.

On party funding, I said that both the main parties were increasingly dependent on rich men. 'We no longer occupy the moral high ground. The public are becoming alienated.'

'I don't enjoy having to raise money from millionaires. They usually want something. I do it because it has to be done,' he said.

As he was showing me out through the Cabinet Room he paused by a window and said, 'There is sometimes a need for an outrider to float an idea. Maybe that's a role you could play.'

And as we parted, 'I'll come back to you on those two points.' It took me a moment to realise that he was referring to the chairmanships of the select committee and the parliamentary party. He clearly takes it for granted that they are in his gift. Maybe they are, but they shouldn't be.

Tuesday, 26 June

Tony Banks, who spends much of his time these days scouring the auction rooms for pictures of famous politicians past, says that only four or five of us from each century will be remembered. From the 19th century he nominated Charles James Fox, John Wilkes, William Wilberforce, Disraeli and Gladstone – the last two only because they were in office so long. From the 20th century – Churchill for his war leadership, Nye Bevan for the NHS. Of our contemporaries he nominated only Thatcher, 'because she was the first woman prime minister', Tony Benn ('maybe') for shaking off his peerage. Blair, of course, for having ended the Tory hegemony. After that he seemed to be struggling. Even if one allows that this assessment is unduly pessimistic, it doesn't bode well for the rest of us who strut these corridors.

Wednesday, 27 June

To the parliamentary party to hear The Man, who was on good form – passionate, witty, reasonable – but very definitely on the defensive. He was received well, but without elation. Indeed, considering that we were in the presence of the first ever Labour prime minister to lead us to two landslide victories, the mood was decidedly downbeat. Absolutely no forelock tugging. Instead the managing director was treated to some blunt warnings that this time around the boys and girls on the shop floor expect to be treated with more consideration. 'Take us into your confidence,' said Tony Lloyd. 'We must not allow ourselves to be portrayed as clones,' said Tony McWalter. He went on, 'We should not be as docile in this Parliament as we were in the last.' And then, the ultimate heresy: 'Ministers and the Prime Minister can make mistakes.' The chandeliers swayed gently, but remained in place. 'Fewer initiatives,' cried the usually ultra-loyal Caroline Flint, who was rewarded with applause. 'Remember,' said Dennis Skinner, 'responsibility is a two-way process. In all public institutions there is goodwill that you can't buy and sell in the City. Goodwill in the NHS is greater than anywhere else. Don't throw it away.'

The Man responded robustly. 'We need dialogue, not a shouting match. We must behave with intelligence and maturity, otherwise we shall go straight back into Opposition.' And then an historic admission: 'Of course I make mistakes. Of course, governments can.' Again the chandeliers swayed. He went on, 'Nobody's talking about privatising schools or the NHS. The press are trying to suggest that using the private sector equals privatisation. If we say that, we will fall into a trap. If we retreat on reform within the public service we will end up putting our arm into the swamp and lifting the Tories up onto dry land.'

At the Division I ran into Jack Straw for the first time since he became Foreign Secretary. He asked why I went. I said, 'I had to make up my mind whether or not I was a serious politician and I decided, on balance, that I was.'

'Tony should have made you a minister of state. I would have done.'

He asked what I was going to do and I said that I wouldn't mind the Security and Intelligence Committee, except that in my view it should report to Parliament rather than to the Prime Minister. He said, 'I agree.' The first time I have heard him concede that.

Friday, 29 June
Sunderland

I walked through the town centre. Sinister, truanting youths lurked in shop doorways. Pasty, vacant faces reflecting empty lives. It is hard not to feel sorry for them. As I passed the bus interchange two damaged youths latched onto me. 'You're Chris Mullin, aren't you. I've seen you on telly.' Oh dear, I was on telly yesterday calling for more criminal youths to be locked up. Fortunately, word had not reached them. 'You got the Birmingham Six out, didn't you?'

'Do you know Tony Blair? Do you have a big house and a body-guard like him?'

Tuesday, 3 July

A rare sighting of Gordon Brown in the Tea Room. He came and sat between Maria Eagle and myself and chatted affably for about 20 minutes. I guess we are destined to see more of Gordon pressing the flesh as this Parliament wears on.

Wednesday, 4 July

There is a motion on the order paper proposing to raise our salaries by an outrageous £4,000 over and above inflation over the next two years, in line with the recommendation of the Senior Salaries Review Body. I have tabled an amendment rejecting the increase and tying future ones to the average of those awarded to nurses, teachers, doctors and dentists. It won't make me the most popular boy in the House. Dennis Skinner thinks I should withdraw it. I was taken aback. Dennis was very definite. In his opinion I could only do myself damage and it wasn't worth it. I promised to reflect.

A minor triumph at Prime Minister's Questions. It marked my

re-entry to the earth's atmosphere. I had number three and went on Star Wars. It went down well with everyone on our side and with the Lib Dems. The Man responded at length and drew cheers only from the Tories. William Hague said, 'Any remaining puzzle as to why the Hon. Member for Sunderland South has left the government has now been resolved.' People were coming up all evening saying well done and wasn't it good being able to speak freely again. Ming Campbell said I looked three feet taller. I encountered The Man in the Library Corridor and he greeted me cheerfully enough.

Later, sitting on the terrace, I was joined by a member of the Blair inner circle. Conversation soon turned to Gordon. I mentioned that, following my departure from government, I had received a handwritten letter from Gordon saying how much he had enjoyed working with me. It seems that every ex-minister has received an identical letter. All the new Members have received letters, too. He must have been up half the night writing them. No stone is left unturned. Gordon's machine churns night and day. My friend was scathing. 'He's mad, quite mad.'

I was gobsmacked. 'What do you mean?'

'Gordon is obsessive, paranoid, secretive and lacking in personal skills. He's been responsible for two absolutely mad privatisations – air traffic control and the London Underground – and all this talk about privatising the NHS is coming out of the Treasury ... I'd probably pack in, if Gordon became leader.'

A chat with Ken Purchase, Robin Cook's former Parliamentary Private Secretary, about Robin's demise as Foreign Secretary. Was Robin surprised? 'Totally. He had a meeting with Tony on the Tuesday and there wasn't a hint. He didn't find out until Friday afternoon. He asked for an hour to think about it, but before the hour was up Jack had been told the job was his.' I said this only went to show how ruthless The Man could be. Ken exploded. 'Ruthless? He's hopeless. A fucking hopeless manager. He hasn't a clue about managing people. If he was in the private sector, they wouldn't spit on him ...' He added, 'I admire him for the way he has related to the public, but we could have had all that without the cronyism.'

Thursday, 5 July

We debated Members' salaries. Several people have added their names to my amendment, so there was no question of withdrawing it. Robin Cook spoke for the government. We must not undervalue ourselves, he said. Mendaciously, he suggested that my amendment would give us more not less. I made a self-deprecatory little speech which, I hope, limited the personal damage while conceding nothing. It was better received than I had expected, although according to Jean a lot of people are muttering behind my back. What they resent, of course, is being forced to vote. They'd much prefer that it went through on the nod so that we were all implicated. Well, I'm not going to oblige. In the event we did better than I expected, there were 66 votes for my amendment. Only about half were ours, the others a hotchpotch of Lib Dems, Scots Nats and even a Tory or two. Just to make quite sure, I forced a second vote on the main question and about a third of our number melted away. I guess they just wanted a token gesture for their local newspaper. A lot of people, including a number of great left-wingers, found urgent reasons to be absent.

It got worse. Not satisfied with having voted themselves an infla-tion-plus £4,000 pay rise, the boys and girls proceeded – against the recommendations of the government and the Senior Salaries Review Body – to up the Additional Costs Allowance by £4,000. Finally, as if that wasn't enough, they then voted to improve the rate of accrual for our already generous pensions from fiftieths to fortieths. Shameful.

Home on the 20.00. Ngoc told me firmly that we can't afford any more grand gestures.

Tuesday, 17 July

Standing beside Gwyneth Dunwoody at the Members' post office this morning, I noticed her opening a long letter, handwritten in black felt-tip, in an envelope marked 'Highgrove'. 'Charles has been very helpful to our committee and I've never betrayed his trust' was all she offered by way of explanation. Now there's an unlikely alliance.

Wednesday, 18 July

The first meeting of the Home Affairs Committee. David Winnick, as the senior member, took the chair and called for nominations. I was approved *nem con*. There then followed an extraordinary speech by Winnick in which he complained about what he alleged was my control freakery and rigidity. There was even a reference to my ego, which, beside his, is minuscule. If he feels so strongly, why didn't he run against me? I took it lightly and invited other comments. Several people made clear that they didn't share David's view of my steward-ship. The new members just looked at the table in embarrassment. Bob Russell said we ought to have a bit more fun. How about a foreign trip or two? Janet Dean pointed out that we were called the *Home Affairs Committee*. I said that it was sometimes necessary for a chair-man to tell committee members things that they didn't want to hear. I also spelled out my four rules for successful select committee mem-bership: turn up on time, remain seated throughout, read your papers in advance and ask concise, relevant questions. After that it was down to business. One of the new Tories, David Cameron, a former special adviser to Michael Howard, helpfully pointed out that short, focused inquiries were more likely to be taken seriously than long unfocused ones. We then agreed with surprising ease that our first inquiry would be on whether or not the government's drugs strategy was working. I suggested we might have sessions with the Home Secretary and the Lord Chancellor in September, but there was no enthusiasm for coming back during the recess, even for a day. Marsha Singh said he was against 'in principle'. Quite what this principle is was unclear.

To the parliamentary committee, to which I have been re-elected, around the big table in The Man's room, just like old times. He looked tired and tense. Andrew Mackinlay, who he can't abide, is back and Gordon Prentice, also a *bête noire*, has been added. In truth we are somewhat overloaded with critics. There is a danger that he won't take us seriously. At the outset there was an amusing little exchange. Tony Lloyd raised a query about biological warfare to which The Man replied, 'Robin knows all about that.'

'I did until four weeks ago,' replied Robin, who has yet to recover from his removal as Foreign Secretary.

The Man laughed but looked hurt. 'Thank you, Robin.' We all joined in the laughter. Robin was the only person present who kept a straight face.

Ann Clwyd asked whether missile defence would be on the agenda for his meeting with President Bush tomorrow. 'Very much so,' said The Man, 'but we should wait until we have a proposal.'

'Don't get steamed up about something that may never happen,' said Robin. 'The current debate is far ahead of anyone's capacity to implement. There will be no decisions until well into the next Parliament.' He added that the Americans may well go for a sea-launched system which targets missiles at the launch rather than re-entry phase, 'in which case Menwith Hill and Fylingdales early-warning systems would be irrelevant'. There was even a possibility that the Russians will go along with whatever is eventually proposed. Clearly they are hoping that the Americans and the Russians will cut a deal that gets us off the hook.

A call from Rachel Sylvester wanting an interview for Saturday's *Telegraph*. I declined on the grounds that many of her interviews with Labour politicians tend to become the subject of front page news stories based on a sentence twisted out of recognition.

'Not always,' she said.

'Often.'

Thursday, 19 July

Home on the 20.00. I sat with David Davis as far as Doncaster. We discussed the Tory leadership election. He thinks Iain Duncan Smith will win easily. Clarke, he says, would be absolutely untenable given his views on Europe. Portillo, he says, would have lost anyway. 'No one trusts him.'

He is confident that we will make a mess of reforming the NHS. What's needed, he says, is a mixed economy with some hospitals handed over completely to the private sector and we will never dare do that.

Monday, 23 July

With Ngoc and the girls to Newcastle Airport to see them onto a plane for Paris and then to Saigon. Every hour, for the rest of the day I plotted their movements in my mind. When I get up tomorrow morning, they will still be airborne.

Tuesday, 31 July

To North Ronaldsay to stay with Liz Forgan, who lives in a croft overlooking a small sandy bay. From Liz's kitchen sink there is a 180 degree view of sea and sand. To the right, a long spit of land jutting into the sea and, just visible, beyond that is the lighthouse on neighbouring Sanday. No trees. The land is flat. The skies huge and dramatic. The island (population 60) is presided over by a benign laird who visits for two months each summer. His house is just visible from Liz's window, the flag flying from the tower indicating that he is in residence. The island has a doctor (who also runs the bird observatory), two shops (one of which opens for an hour a day), and a bar. The plane from Kirkwall comes daily except on Sundays and the ferry (in summer) once a week. Liz has been coming here for nearly 30 years. She bought Neven 14 years ago and visits at New Year, at Easter to plant her vegetables and for five or six weeks in summer. She knows everyone on the island, their strengths, their weaknesses and every detail of the quarrels and tensions that lie beneath the tranquil surface.

Tuesday, 7 August
North Ronaldsay

Al fresco breakfast, watching the seals swimming in the bay. A final walk along the beach. Liz's partner, Rex, who arrived two days ago, is still sounding off about New Labour. Blair, he reckons, is the worst Labour prime minister ever. His comments are so unreasonable that I find myself retreating to the opposite trench. Liz, who has heard it all before, walks ahead smiling. And then we pile into the car and drive to the airfield. I am sad to be leaving. Even after only a week I feel at home here. Already I know about a third of the islanders.

Dead on time, the little plane appears out of a clear blue sky and bumps to a halt in front of us. As we take off there is a fine view of Neven and Linklett Bay along which we were strolling not 30 minutes before. One by one I tick off the islands as they pass below … Sanday, Stronsay, Shapinsay. By the time I reach Aberdeen the sky is grey. And by the time I am home in Sunderland it is raining heavily.

Saturday, 11 August
Sunderland

To the airport at Newcastle to collect Ngoc, Sarah and Emma – browner, thinner and relieved to be home; full of stories about the heat and the chaos. Ngoc says she couldn't bear to go back to live in Saigon, now she has grown accustomed to our green grass and fresh air.

Friday, 31 August
Sunderland

The guinea pig campaign continues. Ngoc is on the point of surrender. I had a quiet talk with Sarah and told her that I was far from persuaded.

Today's papers are full of New Labour's latest excess: McDonald's are to sponsor a reception at the Labour Party conference, to be attended by The Man, no less. That should guarantee us a riot at Brighton. Are there no depths of vulgarity that our masters will not plumb?

Friday, 7 September
Sunderland

I devoted my column in tonight's *Echo* to the subject of asylum; I was surprised to discover (upon inquiry) that we have 1,400 asylum seekers living here rather than the 300 I had supposed. But … they are doing us no harm. They occupy housing that would otherwise be empty or derelict, all the costs are paid for by central government and they are a darn sight more law-abiding than many of those who abuse them.

Even so, with numbers nationally growing at 5,000 a month, we have a serious problem and there's no point in denying it.

Tuesday, 11 September

An unbelievable catastrophe. At about four this afternoon, while I was sitting at my computer, Michael White of the *Guardian* rang. 'Have you seen what's happened?' My first thought was that The Man had been heckled to a standstill at the TUC, which he was due to address this afternoon. 'No,' he said, 'much, much worse; worse than the Cuban missile crisis. Turn on your TV.'

I turned on to see live pictures of smoke and flames bellowing from the twin towers of New York's World Trade Center. Madmen had hijacked passenger planes and flown them directly into the skyscrapers where thousands of people were at work. A third plane had crashed into the Pentagon and reports were coming in of a fourth and even a fifth hijacked plane the whereabouts of which were unknown. The White House and the State Department had been evacuated; all flights across America grounded.

As the afternoon wore on the full scale of the catastrophe became apparent: the dead number thousands, perhaps tens of thousands. Unreal. Like something from a Hollywood movie. Except that this is on a scale that even Hollywood has never envisaged. Reality intruded only gradually. Live interviews with hysterical, dust-covered people who had escaped the inferno; a glimpse of desperate people, a hundred floors up waving a curtain to attract attention. Then reports, and later pictures, of people jumping rather than waiting to be burned alive. Finally, before our eyes, the twin towers imploded in a massive heap of steel and concrete, fire and smoke, taking with them to eternity thousands of unseen people, including firemen who had gone inside to help with the rescue operation. A day we will remember for the rest of our lives. Who knows what horrors lie ahead?

Wednesday, 12 September

Awoke to a feeling that it was all a bad dream. But no, the fires in New York and Washington are still burning. Television footage of the second hijacked plane being flown at full speed into the World Trade building is being shown repeatedly. As the day wore on people came forward with amateur footage recording the impact from every conceivable angle. Now someone has produced a clip of the first plane hitting the tower and that, too, is being shown repeatedly. Eeerily, there are reports that people trapped in the ruins, who stand almost no chance of rescue, are calling on their mobiles for help. The dead are still alive. Death in America is a very public affair. Not like the countless thousands who disappear unnoticed in Third World catastrophes.

Page after page of today's papers are devoted to pictures with the barest minimum of caption material. Even the broadsheets are running single shots over an entire page. The most sickening show people in mid-air, leaping to their deaths from over a hundred storeys up.

Inevitably the calls for revenge are starting. Bush is talking war. So are many of his people. War to most Americans means bombing. They've plenty of experience at dishing it out, but rarely – until now – have they been on the receiving end and they are deeply, deeply traumatised. Not merely at the carnage, but at the sudden realisation that even the very citadels of American power, hitherto invincible, are no longer safe from attack. What use is Star Wars now, when a handful of terrorists armed, apparently, with nothing more than knives can strike at the heart of America? And who to bomb? No one knows who the enemy are, although the finger is pointing at Osama bin Laden, believed to be holed up in Afghanistan. Can he be extracted without levelling Afghanistan, which is, in any case, already a huge cemetery? And if we do level Afghanistan or for that matter Iraq or wherever else the perpetrators are thought to lurk, do we not risk creating a new generation of suicide bombers who will come back to haunt us? Might we not be sucked into an endless cycle of atrocity and reprisal which will eventually consume us all?

And what of us? Already The Man, in public at least, is writing

blank cheques placing us four square behind whatever degree of retribution that George Bush sees fit to organise. Anyone suggesting
caution, let alone that we should raise our eyes to the big picture, will
not be popular. Yet it has to be done. Parliament is to be recalled on
Friday. No doubt we shall have to sit through a good deal of impotent
huffing and puffing, but I shall go down anyway on the off-chance
that there is an opportunity to speak.

Thursday, 13 September

To London on the 18.47. David Miliband was on the train. He is in a
similar situation to the one I was in when I was first selected – enemies
occupy every office in his constituency party, although in his case it
is nothing personal. He says The Man – who was once in a similar situation in Sedgefield – advised him 'to go around smiling at everyone
and get other people to shoot them'. Advice which The Man seems to
have applied throughout his career.

The Man has, says David, extraordinary energy and equanimity.
His self-confidence is total. He does not need praise to bolster his ego
and neither is he good at dispensing it. He takes more interest in Parliament and the parliamentary party than most people realise and is a
good talent spotter. David believes he will fight a third election, but
not a fourth.

Friday, 14 September

Up early for a spot on the *Today* programme, saying that we shouldn't
give the Americans a blank cheque. I trod cautiously. It seems indecent, appearing to criticise while bodies are still being dug out of the
ruins, but it has to be done. Helpfully, Henry Kissinger was interviewed just before me saying that Americans do not always think
through the consequences of their actions. Also an aid worker, who
has just come out of Kabul, was interviewed and said that five million
Afghans are facing starvation this winter. I just quoted these two and,
hopefully, managed to avoid going over the top. Bruce Grocott, who
I ran into later, said he thought I'd got it about right.

The Man's statement was thoughtful and balanced. He pledged unswerving support for the Americans, but talked of the need for hard evidence and never losing sight of our values.

Saturday, 15 September
Sunderland

Martin Woollacott rang. We discussed the crisis. Martin said, 'It's a lesson to the Americans that it is not a good idea to have a cardboard cutout as president. You just can't get away with it. It's not a question of whether he's a conservative or not. You must have someone of substance because you never know when they will be needed.' What would he do? 'Nothing, until there is evidence that Osama bin Laden was responsible, and nothing against the Afghan government unless it's proven they are involved. Then you'd have to send in special ops troops to find him. Missiles won't work. Maybe nothing will.'

Wednesday, 19 September

Tonight's *Echo* carries a page of hate-filled letters about asylum seekers, triggered by my attempt two weeks ago to inject some sense of proportion into the debate. One claimed that the government has admitted that more than a million illegal immigrants are hiding in Britain. The government has admitted nothing of the sort. This particular falsehood is a straight replay of the *Sun* front page ten days ago. Much of the hate is aimed at me. One woman wrote, 'We won't forget this when the election comes.' A man who has been to my office for help wrote, 'I've had a bellyful of you people.' The editor told me that he has not received a single letter in my favour. Feeling very down.

Friday, 21 September

The tom toms are beating louder in Washington. Bush has made a speech to Congress which had them cheering in the aisles. Suddenly his ratings are soaring. Needless to say we are going along with everything. The Man, who was in the gallery at Congress when Bush made his speech, was rewarded with a standing ovation. All week he has been rushing hither and thither, delivering messages for Washington. I pray that he knows what he's doing. Hopefully, if we have any influence at all, we are using it to moderate the psychopathic tendencies never far below the surface in any US administration. All the signs are they are preparing for a massive attack on Afghanistan. There are also troop movements in the Gulf, which suggests they may have other targets in mind, but no one seems sure. Removing the Taliban would be no bad thing if it could be done quickly and cleanly, but then what? Are we going to leave the wretched Afghans to the mercy of the warlords?

Monday, 24 September

To Downing Street with the members of the relevant select committees to hear The Man outline his war aims. We assembled upstairs in the Pillared Drawing Room, seated on four rows of maroon ballroom chairs. Liz Symons and Adam Ingram were the only ministers in attendance. Alastair Campbell, Anji Hunter and Robert Hill were arranged along a sofa at the back. As we went in I was asked to stay behind afterwards, as The Man wanted a quiet word.

'With me and who else?'

'Just you.'

The Man, as ever in shirtsleeves, was relaxed, informal, occasionally humorous. He remained seated by the fireplace, sipping coffee. He spoke of 'scores' – he used the word repeatedly – of terrorist training camps in Afghanistan. The evidence against Osama bin Laden was clear, although they were still working out how much could be said publicly. All the major European nations and most Middle East countries were on board for action providing it was carefully targeted. 'If the net goes wider, there could be difficulties.' He foresaw three phases: (a) action against OBL and the Taliban, (b) a longer-term strategy – perhaps through the UN – aimed at closing down the finance networks, and (c) changes to our own extradition and asylum laws making it easier to flush out suspected terrorists. 'The attacks have brought home to us,' he said, 'that these people have the capability of striking again. If we don't act, we send a clear signal.' The discussion afterwards was random, disjointed and inadequate. Bruce George asked if we were taking civil emergency planning seriously and was assured that we were. There was a brief moment of hilarity when Donald Anderson asked a question about the panic buying of gas-masks which, he said, had been suggested to him by a Welsh journal-ist. Whereupon his mobile started ringing. 'Probably the journalist ringing to see if you've asked the question,' said The Man. (No doubt he was thinking, as I was, 'Is this the best the chairman of the Foreign Affairs Select Committee can manage?') Alan Beith warned against allowing the Home Office to take advantage of the crisis by dusting down measures such as ID cards that had languished on their shelves for years. A couple of Tories, Michael Mates was one, praised The Man for his handling of events so far. When my turn came I asked, 'Is it our intention to overthrow the Taliban and, if so, what thought have we given to what will come after?' I added that on no account must the wretched people of Afghanistan be left to the mercy of the warlords in the so-called Northern Alliance. Instead we should be looking for a UN mandate, as in Cambodia or East Timor, to govern the country until normality could be restored. 'The removal of the Taliban is not among our stated aims,' replied The Man, 'but if they get in the way they will be overthrown. As for the Northern Alliance, we want to make sure that they are a broad alliance.'

'A UN mandate?'

'We haven't really given enough thought to it.' He added some-thing about having talked to Kofi Annan last night, but it was clear that no serious thought has been given to what comes after the Taliban. At the moment they are clearly intending to depend on the squabbling warlords. One set of barbarians will replace another.

Someone asked about Iraq. There have been reports that the psy-chopathic wing of the US government is itching to take out Saddam. 'It is important that we proceed by way of evidence. We know Saddam has weapons of mass destruction, but we want to be sure that any action we take now is not dislocated.' He added mysteriously, 'I don't want to say more at this stage.' I take that to mean that a second front, against Iraq, is being considered although no one has so far produced any evidence of Iraqi involvement.

Afterwards, while awaiting The Man, I chatted to Anji Hunter, who was with him on last week's whirlwind visit to Washington. She claims the Americans are listening to Tony. 'He's been around for five years. He knows all the main players.' She added, 'Thank goodness for Colin Powell.'

Then a quiet chat with The Man. I repeated the point about not relying on the warlords. Also, I mentioned Israel. Tony said both he and Bush had sent a strong message to Sharon, but that Arafat was also to blame for the shambles in the Middle East. 'When I met him in Washington last year he claimed there was no difference between Barak and Sharon. I said, "Don't you believe it."'

I asked about reports that the World Food Programme had stopped distributing in Afghanistan and he said he thought they were untrue. Finally, I asked why he'd sought me out today and he said, 'You're important as far as the parliamentary party is concerned.' It would be nice to think so but I doubt it. I've been keeping my head well down of late, but at last I can see things that need to be said – inside and outside the tent – about the coming famine in Afghanistan and what kind of regime comes afterwards. Whatever happens I must avoid becoming co-opted into defending the indefensible. There is a tight-rope to be walked between retaining the ear of The Man and retaining my self-respect and credibility with the world outside.

A proposition instantly put to the test when I stepped outside the front door and found myself giving in to an impromptu press conference, bits of which went out on all bulletins. Later, I winced as I heard myself saying only that I was 'fairly confident' that The Man was a moderating influence on George Bush, but several people who heard it said that it sounded okay. Most comment was about the fact that I was wearing a green kagool and no tie, in anticipation of my walk across the Lake District which starts tomorrow.

Several of today's papers carry a picture of about twenty Westernised Arab youngsters, boys and girls, in front of a pink Cadillac. Everyone looks happy and relaxed. Ringed, in the middle row, is a thin young man in a green skinny-rib jumper and flared purple trousers. He is happy, too. This is Osama bin Laden and some of his many brothers and sisters, on holiday in Sweden, 30 years ago. In those far-off days, before the earth changed places with the sky. Before everything went so terribly, terribly wrong.

At five I went back to Downing Street for the parliamentary committee. We assembled around the Cabinet table: Ann Clwyd, Helen Jackson, Andrew Mackinlay, Gordon Prentice, Doug Hoyle and myself on our side. The Man, JP, Hilary Armstrong, Robin Cook on the other. Jean in the chair. The Man, a little wearier than when we last saw him, but still in good spirits. From time to time a nerve twitched in the left-hand side of his face. He listened carefully to each of our points, making notes and responding to each one. There was some light-hearted banter about whether Robin Cook's beard is long enough to meet with Taliban approval (the consensus was that it is not). Overall, however, the mood was sombre. The Man said, 'There is no doubt that these guys will try something else. They now know that they have carried out a spectacular coup. If they could have done something worse, they would have.'

I repeated some of the points I made this morning, adding, 'Don't row out too far on ID cards. As far as dealing with terrorists is concerned they are useless. They might be some use in coping with illegal immigrants, but the downside is that only people with different colour skins will be stopped and that will raise a whole new set of problems. Also, they will cost several billion and on reflection you might consider there are better uses for the money.'

The Man replied that it was damaging to good community relations to have an asylum system that was being abused.

On recalling Parliament we went round the table. Ann Clwyd, Andrew Mackinlay and Gordon Prentice were strongly in favour. Robin said there was no problem recalling as early as Friday and that it might be a good idea if we wanted to avoid flak.

Whatever anyone says about The Man he does give a good impression of listening. But how much difference any of us – he included – make, who knows? My feeling is that he still has no very clear idea about what happens next. No doubt the Americans will let us know in due course. And whatever happens, the realpolitik is that we will have to go along with it.

Overall, a good day. Two and a half hours in The Presence. Were I still Under-Secretary of Folding Deck Chairs, I wouldn't be allowed within a mile of him.

Tuesday, 2 October

I have decided not to go to Brighton for the conference since it has been reduced to little more than a rally. Instead I stayed home and watched The Man's speech on television. A minor masterpiece. His best ever. Sincere, idealistic, inspiring, wide-ranging – mercifully lacking in the usual, verbless New Labour claptrap. And when it was over there was none of the usual hanging around, prolonging the ovation. He left the stage, hand in hand with Cherie, looking serious and statesmanlike. No one else in British politics could rise to the occasion as he has. Even the cynics are temporarily silenced. 'He's lost that silly smirk,' Pat, who runs my office, said afterwards. 'It wasn't doing him much good.'

Wednesday, 3 October

To London for the recall of Parliament. Among the mail a letter from someone called Sebastian who lives at an address in a posh part of Camberwell complaining about my appearance outside Number 10 last week in a green kagool. 'One just had to look away,' he simpered. Get a life, Sebastian.

The main leader in today's *Telegraph* is headed 'Blair's finest hour'.

Thursday, 4 October

To Parliament for The Man's statement. The place is swarming with armed policemen and huge, unsightly slabs of reinforced concrete have been hastily placed around New Palace Yard with a view to warding off suicide bombers. This time round, there were fewer warlike noises and more about helping the wretched Afghans. I have the impression that the ground is shifting. It is beginning to dawn on the powers-that-be that simply sitting in the Arabian Sea or Indian Ocean firing cruise missiles won't work.

I asked Tony Benn what he thought of The Man's conference speech. 'A combination of Julius Caesar, Churchill and Mussolini,' he replied. He said he had recently asked Ted Heath what advice he would offer the Prime Minister in present circumstances. True to form, the old curmudgeon replied, 'Pipe down. You are upsetting the Europeans and upstaging Bush. They won't like it.'

Friday, 5 October
Sunderland

Far from piping down, The Man has his foot hard on the throttle. Last night he was in Moscow. Today Rawalpindi. And later, Delhi. A headline in the *Wall Street Journal* describes him as 'America's newest ambassador'.

Should we be pleased?

Graham in my office reports a visit from a constituent, clutching a plastic bag. The exchange that followed was pure Monty Python.

Constituent: 'Do you want to see what's in here?'

Graham (hesitating): 'What is it?'

'A pigeon.'

'Is it dead?'

'Yes.'

'No … just leave it there.'

'This global warming thing. I've come up with something big. This pigeon has been eating weeds. It's passing green stuff. I'll show you …'

'That's okay. I'll take your word for it.'

'If we could breed weed-eating pigeons, we could do without weed-killer.'

'That pigeon will be riddled with disease. Do you keep it in your flat?'

'It's fine, man.'

'It's dead.'

'It's fine. Look, I'll show you.'

'No, no, don't.'

He was eventually persuaded to leave after Graham suggested he contact a pigeon fanciers' club. The man is a neighbour. We can see him every day from our kitchen window, in his top floor bedsit in the terrace behind us. He sits there hour after hour, day after day, feeding pigeons and staring into space.

Sunday, 7 October

The attack on Afghanistan has started. It is a measure of our total lack of influence that we were not even able to persuade the Americans to delay for 12 hours until the British journalist, Yvonne Ridley, who is due to be released tomorrow, was out. Tonight's television news depicted The Man, looking pale and exhausted, in the Pillared Drawing Room at Number 10 reading a short statement. He was flanked by JP, Jack Straw and Geoff Hoon, silent and irrelevant. Although it is billed as some sort of great alliance, as usual it is just us and the Americans with other governments making vaguely support-ive noises from the sidelines. I suppose it has to be done, but there is something distasteful about the armed forces of two of the richest countries in the world sitting in the Arabian Sea firing Tomahawk missiles at £700,000 a shot at one of the poorest.

Wednesday, 10 October

A row has broken out over a leaked memo, dated 11 September, by an adviser to Steve Byers, suggesting it would be 'a good day to bury bad news'. What is particularly chilling is that the note was written within an hour of the planes hitting the World Trade Center, while the night-mare was still unfolding. In other words, at the very moment when thousands of people were in the process of being incinerated, while the rest of us were sitting transfixed in front of our television screens, this New Labour android had her mind firmly focused on the small picture. Unsurprisingly, she is a product of 1980s student politics which gave birth to the New Labour equivalent of the Taliban. I would have sacked her on the spot, but Steve, decent fellow that he is, is sticking up for her. I hope this doesn't do him too much damage.

Friday, 12 October
Sunderland

To the headquarters of the Employment Service, front line in the war against benefit culture, for a report on the New Deal. If we don't make progress here, we are destined for ever to go on manufacturing sullen, indifferent, useless youths; pouring into a bottomless pit money that should be spent on schools and hospitals. If we can't change this, we won't change anything. The news is good: a 40 per cent reduction in young unemployed in four years. 'You guys have got nothing to worry about,' says one of the managers. 'It's working.' Also, the gap between the world of work and the world of benefit is gradually widening. The Working Families' Tax Credit is, we are told, 'an outstanding success', enticing hundreds of lone parents back into the world of work. None of this is of much interest to the chattering classes or the cynics in the Lobby, but it matters up here.

There is still a mountain to climb, however. In addition to the 9,000 people in Sunderland (half of whom are lone parents) still signing on for Jobseekers' Allowance, a staggering 38,000 are claiming for sickness, incapacity or disability. None of these are even in the market for work, although many of them must be capable of doing something. Benefit culture is our greatest inheritance from the Thatcher Decade. It hangs around our neck like a huge albatross.

Saturday, 13 October

Reports from Kabul suggest that civilian casualties are mounting. A 2,000 pound bomb has hit a residential area and the Pentagon has grudgingly owned up to what it calls 'a targeting error'. Tonight's news showed a brief clip of desperate people scrabbling through the ruins of their homes, but because the cameraman was an Arab it isn't being taken seriously. The usual weasel words are being trotted out. What would be called a monstrous crime if it happened in New York or Omagh is merely an unfortunate targeting error in Afghanistan.

Monday, 15 October

The destruction of a village near Jalalabad has been confirmed. One man is said to have lost his wife and five children. We must be grateful that we do not have to look him in the eye and explain that, while the people who blew up the World Trade Center were evil terrorists, those who rained death upon his family were heroes engaged in a just war.

Tuesday, 16 October

Another debate on the war. Once again Jack was put up to hold the line. I was sandwiched uneasily between Tam Dalyell and Bob Marshall-Andrews. Tam was shouting 'gobbledegook' and 'tell that to the Macedonians' every time Jack defended the bombing by reference to Kosovo. By and large the dissidents were the Usual Suspects, although unease runs deeper. Our strategy is high-risk. If the Taliban implode, as the Milosovic regime did, we will get away with it. If they don't, and there is a huge famine, disaster beckons. Later some of us had a meeting upstairs with Jack. I told him that he should not imagine – contrary to what he asserted in the chamber – that only those who opposed the intervention in Kosovo were unhappy about the attack on Afghanistan. Also, it was nonsense to assert, as he had been doing, that all our bombs were carefully targeted. The Americans had always had a casual attitude towards civilian casualties. Jack didn't argue. In passing he even described the American airdrop of pasta and tomato sauce as 'gauche'. He said it was important to stick with the Americans to discourage isolationism. 'Because Tony has done the diplomacy, he has an enormous amount of influence in Washington. See the way the Americans have shifted on using the UN in the last few weeks.'

M came in this evening, hotfoot from Washington. 'Bush is a puppet,' he says. 'He doesn't know anything.' To begin with he was in hock to Carl Rove, a right-wing ideologue who occupies some obscure post in the White House. 'After September 11 they had to bring in the adults.'

Wednesday, 17 October

To a crowded meeting of the parliamentary party, to hear The Man. 'September 11,' he said, 'will define politics for the foreseeable future. Especially in terms of America's attitude to the outside world.' There is no alternative, he kept saying. No alternative. No alternative. (Where have we heard that before?)

As usual, Tam was first to stick his head above the parapet. 'Are you sure,' he asked, 'that by bombing you are not doing exactly what

Osama bin Laden wants?' Tam was heard quietly at first, but when –
for the third time – he added, 'And another thing …' people began to
groan audibly. Dear old Tam. Armed with the utter self-confidence
that he has carried with him since Eton, he just ploughs on like a
bulldozer. And, of course, he may well be right – it wouldn't be the
first time. At the end, The Man was applauded warmly. For the time
being he has nothing to worry about.

Afghanistan also dominated the parliamentary committee. Jean
went in first. 'Don't be fooled,' she told The Man, 'there is deep unease
below the surface. Everyone is hoping you are right.' Apparently,
David Hanson, his Parliamentary Private Secretary, has been telling
him this too.

Andrew Mackinlay raised Jo Moore, author of the 'good day to
bury bad news' memo. The consensus seemed to be that she should
have been sacked, but The Man was having none of it. 'Too harsh. The
end of her career – where would she find another job? She's got two
kids, she's the main breadwinner.' I warmed to him. It reveals an attractive side of his character. This is Tony the Merciful. Tony the Compassionate. He has only to raise his little finger to dispose of her and yet
he chooses not to. He added, 'In any case, once a minister has taken a
decision, I have a visceral reluctance to let the media decide.' Amen to
that. The trouble is it is doing terrible damage to poor Steve Byers.

Monday, 22 October

To an upper committee room to hear Geoff Hoon talking glibly about
the 'astonishing accuracy' of the bombing. Many Afghans, he asserted,
were surprised by the accuracy. As for Kumar, the hamlet west of Jalalabad where up to a hundred civilians are said to have been killed,
'that was not a village in any normal sense of the word'. I found this
too much to swallow. When my turn came I said, 'I have some difficulty with this concept of benign bombing and with the idea that the
Afghans were all that grateful to us for the pin-point accuracy with
which they are being bombed. If so, why were there so many desperate people at the border trying to escape?' I rounded off by asking if
we were dropping cluster bombs.

'There was one incident,' Geoff said hesitantly, 'but they were used against equipment rather than people ...'

About 40 members were present, but there was no real dissent apart from Tam. One or two people mildly expressed concern that there was no end in sight. Ann Clwyd asked what we were doing to persuade Pakistan to keep the borders open to refugees. My comments about the bombing attracted not even a murmur of support. What a tame, useless bunch we are. So far, apart from putting down the odd marker, I have kept quiet in public (a) out of loyalty, (b) in the hope that I am wrong and The Man is right, and (c) knowing that HMG has little or no influence anyway, but I'm not sure I can keep this up much longer.

Thursday, 25 October

The television news tonight showed a traumatised Afghan woman, in a Pakistan hospital, who is said to have lost five daughters, two sons and her husband in one of Geoff Hoon's 'astonishingly well-targeted' bombing raids.

Tuesday, 30 October

To the select committee for the opening session of our inquiry into drugs policy. The witnesses were various officials from the government's anti-drugs apparatus, including the 'Tsar', Keith Hellawell, who seemed depressed. We ambled along predictably for the first 90 minutes or so. It was only when I inquired why their written evidence had not addressed decriminalisation – half our terms of reference – that things livened up. The officials seemed to be in a state of denial. In the real world a huge debate is going on. Even senior police officers are arguing that the so-called war on drugs is lost and that the only way to defeat the criminals is to collapse the black market by ending prohibition. Round and round we went, but they seemed reluctant even to address the subject. It was clear they had given it no thought whatever, presumably on the assumption that this was territory on which politicians fear to tread. The poor woman from the Home

Office was distraught. When I suggested she go away and provide us, by Thursday, with a paper rebutting the arguments for decriminalisation her forehead actually touched the table.

Today I crossed the Rubicon. At Foreign Office Questions I went in hard over the bombing of Afghanistan. Alex Salmond followed on and backed me up. Then Field Marshal Winnick came in, talking of appeasement. I am on tricky ground now. On the one hand, I don't want to be bracketed with the handful who are opposed to all military action. That way lies impotence. On the other, I cannot sit quietly while the Americans spray bombs in every direction.

Wednesday, 31 October

To Thames House, headquarters of MI5, to discuss the proposed Anti-Terrorism Act with the Director, Stephen Lander. In appearance, though not in demeanour, he vaguely resembles Norman Lamont. Every time I see him I am struck by how down to earth he is – open, relaxed, frank, at ease with the democratic process, which could not be said of all his predecessors. At one point our committee clerk, Andrew Kennon, passed me a note: 'Did you ever dream you might hear a Director General of the Security Service bandying around articles of the European Charter of Human Rights with such fluency?' He gave every appearance of taking us seriously and not just going through the motions.

We sat around the table in the boardroom, with our backs to the fine view of the river and Lambeth Palace. Chocolate biscuits were offered with the coffee, though there were few takers. A couple of people – Winnick and Cameron – arrived late, which must give a bad impression. I asked if he had read Stella Rimington's book and he said he had seen about five different drafts. 'Was her description of the early days accurate?'

'Yes, there was a lot of drinking and laziness.'

The threat, he said, was threefold: (a) al-Qaida, made up of individuals who met during the Russian-Afghan war and who went on to fuel (b) individual nationalist struggles in Egypt, Algeria, Kashmir,

Chechnya; and (c) individuals radicalised by these events who choose to do something on their own. He added, 'There is a strong presumption that further events are planned.' He is seeking power to detain indefinitely (i) terrorist suspects who are denied entry and immediately trump a refusal by claiming asylum, and (ii) suspected terrorists, resident here, whose lives would be at risk were they to be deported to their country of origin.

Afterwards, we had a briefing from Ben Gunn, of the Association of Chief Police Officers (also Chief Constable of Cambridgeshire), who detailed the extra powers the police are seeking to interfere with bank accounts of suspected terrorists. 'We recognise this doesn't sit easily with the Human Rights, Freedom of Information and the Regulation of Investigatory Powers Acts,' he said. Surprisingly, the police have no legal power to collect intelligence. 'Previously, we could do what we liked, but now we need specific authority.' He said that as the law stands the police can't photocopy a passport or examine baggage at ports. So far the law is untested. 'Until challenged, we do it.' He added that it was time to look at a new offence of conspiracy to commit terrorism.

Briefing over, we waited for someone to show us out, but no one came. We put our heads outside the door. No one was around so, strictly against the rules, we made our own way to the lifts and down to the ground floor. We passed no one on the way. The most striking thing about Thames House is how eerily empty it seems.

In the Tea Room, George Howarth tells an hilarious story. Out shopping last weekend he was flagged down by a constituent: 'Hey, George. I want to talk to you about this Osman Bin Liner' (sic). The man's wife was three paces behind, weighed down with carrier bags full of groceries. He, by contrast, was unencumbered.

The man proceeded, at some length, to offer George his analysis of events since 11 September. 'Terrible,' he said, 'the way these Arabs treat their women.'

Meanwhile the man's wife, standing a little distance away, surrounded by her shopping bags, was urging him to get a move on. Whereupon this magnificent product of Western civilisation responded, 'Shut up you soft bitch. Can't you see I'm talking to my MP?'

Thursday, 1 November

At lunchtime I went over to Millbank for an interview with Tyne Tees and when I got back to the House there were two urgent messages from Jack Straw at the Foreign Office. Unfortunately, an hour having passed, he wasn't there when I rang back. In due course a letter from Jack appeared on the letterboard correcting the answer he had given me about accidental bombings during our exchange on Tuesday. He had said, 'I understand that, across more than 3,000 targets, there have been misses in respect of five.' The new version read, 'The coalition has fired around 7,000 weapons at 118 targets of which six show no damage on target.' A somewhat different picture: 7,000 bombs, any number of which could have gone astray, aimed at a relative handful of targets, most of which must have been destroyed in the first few days. What have they been bombing since?

Friday, 2 November
Sunderland

My ambiguous stance on the war prompted a bit of flak at the management committee this evening. In vain did I protest that bombing civilians wasn't going to help us find Osama bin Laden. Several people took my side, but we were a minority. There was a bit of talk about supporting our boys (not one of whom has yet set foot on Afghan soil). Someone proposed that any British Muslims found fighting for the Taliban should be tried for treason. 'They should be shot,' said another. At times it was like a *Sun* readers' convention.

Wednesday, 7 November

The Man was at this morning's meeting of the parliamentary party, cheerful but tired. I caught him yawning once or twice, but he was on good form. He had a fairly easy ride. Criticism was directed mainly at the Americans. 'Many people in Britain are revolted by what's going on,' said Jeremy Corbyn, referring to cluster bombs and depleted uranium. On a point by David Winnick about Israel, he said, 'The Americans want to take the initiative, but a minimum level of calm is needed first. The timing must be right.' On the big picture, he spelled out the realpolitik: 'No one has 6,000' (he keeps using that figure, even though the true figure seems to be about half that number) 'of their citizens wiped out and says they'll do nothing.' It was important that they didn't act alone. That, of course, is the bottom line. We are all but irrelevant. The only choice for us was whether to go along in the hope of exerting some influence or to sit quietly on the sidelines and let them get on with it.

The Man's schedule is awesome. After questions this afternoon he's off to Washington on Concorde for dinner with Bush, returning overnight in time for the Cabinet at 10 a.m. tomorrow. Is all this rushing about strictly necessary?

Thursday, 8 November

Anji Hunter has resigned. She's off to BP for an absurd sum of money. It's only four months since the party had to stump up an extra £60,000 in order to persuade her to stay. We've also lost Henry McLeish, our First Minister in Scotland, after a row about alleged misuse of the office costs allowance. The hacks have tasted blood. They will now increase pressure on Steve Byers.

Bev Hughes told me that Blunkett wanted to use the forthcoming anti-terrorist package (which includes an offence of inciting religious hatred) to abolish blasphemy, but the Archbishop of Canterbury produced a long list of conditions in return for his approval and so the idea had to be abandoned.

Monday, 12 November
Manchester

A city awash with drugs. Doomed youths begging in every other doorway, shootouts between dealers in Moss Side. The epidemic has also spawned a vast industry of publicly-funded agencies full of well-meaning people who are trying to cope with it. The further they are from the coal face, the vaguer their prescriptions. They all seem to use phrases like 'issues around'. We (members of the select committee) had a pleasant dinner with several of them. The most impressive was a man from Transform with plenty of front-line experience who argued for the legalisation of everything with the possible exception of crack cocaine (which produces violence, as opposed to most other drugs, which lead to indolence).

Tuesday, 13 November
Manchester

A morning visiting drugs projects. Everywhere we asked people what they would do and most, but by no means all, replied that they would move towards decriminalising, starting with heroin. One of the most vehement was a police superintendent, another a Methodist minister. Decriminalisation, of course, would bring its own problems. One woman said, 'I worry that we shall become as complacent towards drugs as we are towards alchohol.' GPs will not be keen to have addicts shooting up in their surgeries. There would also be a problem with leakage – prescribed drugs finding their way into the black market. We talked to a couple of addicts, one of whom had just come back from Germany, where he said they have 'shooting galleries'. Safe houses where heroin can be injected in private and needles properly disposed of, instead of being left around in streets.

Wednesday, 14 November

Kabul has fallen, along with Jalalabad and Herat. Our new friends in the Northern Alliance are rolling up the map with hardly a shot being fired. The Man made a statement. He did it very well. There was no triumphalism although he must be mightily relieved. No one expected this. A week ago there was talk on all sides that the war would last all winter and now it could be over in a matter of days. Victory, of course, brings a new set of problems. From Mazar there are reports that the Northern Alliance have massacred several hundred Arab volunteers. Some of today's papers carry gruesome pictures of a wounded prisoner being dragged around and summarily executed. Our new friends are not nice people. Television screens are full of pictures of wild Alliance gunmen swaggering around Kabul. Of the UN there is no sign. It was never meant to be like this.

The Man appeared only briefly at the parliamentary committee. Someone mentioned King Zahir. 'The king will play a part in a transitional government,' he said. Adding that Taliban members were ringing up the BBC's Pashtun service saying they wanted to surrender to the king.

'Nothing like 30 years' exile in Rome for improving your poll ratings,' I interjected.

'I hope I never have to find out,' he responded to general hilarity.

The Man said there must be three stages. First, the US, the UK, France and a few others would establish secure bases, Bagram airport for example. Second, there needed to be a UN force, involving Islamic countries. Third, the creation of a proper Afghan force. As regards al-Qaida he said, 'There is a risk that these people have pre-cooked something before September 11. We can't be sure there aren't more out there.'

While all this was going on The Man was, as always, autographing photographs, cartoons and bottles of House of Commons whisky which he has been asked to sign. With Christmas approaching there were more than usual. I counted over 30 whiskies and a couple of champagnes lined up in three rows like a regiment of toy soldiers. There was a sort of conveyor belt. JP and Robin Cook were passing them to The Man, JP indicating those that required particular dedications. It was, as someone remarked, a practical demonstration of joined-up government. By the end the Prime Minister and his deputy were visible only above a sea of whisky bottles. A great *Private Eye* cover.

Thursday, 15 November

A meeting of the select committee to finalise our report on the Anti-Terrorism Bill. It all has to be done in a great rush, because the Bill is due its second reading on Monday. In truth we have been rather timid and we are likely to be criticised. 'Reluctantly' we have accepted that there is a case for interning people who can't be deported, and confined ourselves to calling for a sunset clause so that the government has to legislate again if it wants the measure to continue after five years.

We have an impressive new Tory on the committee – David Cameron, a young, bright libertarian who can be relied upon to follow his own instincts rather than the party line.

Tuesday, 20 November

We had the police to our drugs inquiry. Francis Wilkinson, a former Chief Constable of Gwent, argued for heroin legalisation and Brian Paddick, who commands the Lambeth Division, rocked the boat a bit saying that he wouldn't regard chasing 'weekend drugs-users' as a sensible use of his officers' time.

Steve Byers gave the go-ahead to Heathrow terminal five this afternoon. His only nod in the direction of banning the 16 night flights was a promise of more research. I'm afraid I got quite shirty with him. We've got research coming out of our ears. What's needed is a decision. This was a golden opportunity to put some limits on the endless demands of the aviation industry and he's funked it.

Wednesday, 21 November

Lunch with Ann Taylor in the Millbank Room. She is still smarting after losing her place in the Cabinet. It came as a total surprise and was contrary to assurances she claimed to have been given personally, by The Highest Level, shortly before the election. So, Ann is one of the growing band – Derek Foster is another – to whom promises were made and not kept. The Man's word is not his bond. He says whatever is required to meet the needs of the hour, relying on his undoubted charm to get him through when rumbled.

According to Ann, I made a mistake opting out of government. 'If you had hung on for another year, Jack might have taken you at the Foreign Office.'

She also revealed that The Man offered JP a chance to drop the air traffic privatisation just before the Transport Bill was tabled. JP had turned it down, unwilling to renege on his deal with Gordon. Now there's a man whose word *is* his bond.

Later, we had the first day of the committee stage of the Anti-Terrorism Bill. The speed with which it is being rushed through is disgraceful and everyone was up in arms. One of the most controversial clauses, enabling the government to implement, on an affirmative order, anything – whether or not it has to do with terrorism – agreed by the Justice and Home Affairs council of the EC was voted through without debate.

Everything went according to plan with my amendments, although there was very nearly a disaster. I was at the parliamentary committee in the Prime Minister's room when I saw Blunkett's name come up on the screen. I rushed into the chamber and just made it in time to hear David announcing that he was accepting changes along the lines of the amendments. Nice to be relevant again.

Thursday, 22 November

Yesterday the *Telegraph* carried a report from a village in northern Afghanistan which has been bombed three times since the Taliban fled, killing 11 people, mainly women and children. On the roof of the school, terrified villagers have written in English in letters ten feet high, 'THIS IS A SCHOOL'. 'Please tell the Americans they are bombing their allies,' pleaded the local mullah.

Yet another example of Geoff Hoon's 'astonishingly well-targeted bombing'. I sent him the cutting with a handwritten note asking for an explanation. Pointless really. He has no more influence over the Americans than I do, but at least he could have the decency to stop boasting about the accuracy of the bombing.

Friday, 23 November

Brian Paddick is in trouble for his remarks about drugs in evidence to the select committee on Tuesday. His bosses at Scotland Yard have issued a rebuke which has been plastered all over the media. I rang to ask if I could be of any help. We agreed that I should send the Commissioner, John Stevens, a letter pointing out that Paddick had made clear that the views expressed were his own, that he had been responding to our questions and saying that we don't expect our witnesses to be leaned upon.

Wednesday, 28 November

Gordon Brown addressed the parliamentary party in the wake of yesterday's pre-Budget statement. It was Gordon at his best. Ringing all the right bells. Credible, radical, staking out a little piece of territory to the left of centre against the day when the throne is vacant. Beneath it all, however, lurks the same old Gordon who still bites his nails; the same mirthless smile, switching on and off like a neon sign.

Sunday, 2 December
Sunderland

A cold, damp, clear day. To Wallington, where we picnicked on a fallen beech tree by the China Pond. Walked along the path by the river Wansbeck and back through the woods to the west lakes. A world entirely free of litter, dog shit or junk architecture. Paradise.

Wednesday, 5 December

Robin Cook addressed the parliamentary party on his plans for reform or, as he put it, making Parliament look as though it belongs to the same century as the one in which our constituents live. Most of the neanderthals were either absent or keeping their heads below the parapet so he was received with enthusiasm. Later, at the parliamentary committee, as Robin had requested of me, I raised his plans for a shake-up, saying there had been a lot of support for it at this morning's meeting. The Man merely smiled benignly, as if to say 'Did Robin put you up to that?'

'You take a lot of notes,' Gordon Prentice remarked afterwards.

Tuesday, 11 December

Ran into Tony Benn who said, 'I was looking for you earlier – I had Saffron Burrows to lunch and I wanted to introduce you.' Damn.

Wednesday, 12 December

Parliamentary committee: Ann Clwyd kicked off calling for an inquiry into the treatment of prisoners captured at Kunduz by our friends in the Northern Alliance, at least 40 of whom are reported to have suffocated after being locked in containers for three days. I added that these were war crimes and we risked discrediting the whole enterprise. The Man replied that there was little chance of an inquiry, but that some very strong messages had been sent and we were 'putting in people alongside the Northern Alliance'.

'What's our bottom line?' I asked, apropos suggestions that the Americans were about to turn their attention to Iraq or Somalia. 'What is it that we will not sign up to?' The Man, calm as ever, replied that we wouldn't sign up to anything with which we disagreed. 'I can honestly say that there is not a single issue in Afghanistan that we have not been consulted about.' As far as Iraq and Somalia are concerned, no decisions had yet been taken.

Thursday, 13 December

An amusing little cameo at Business Questions in the House when Eric Forth invited us to celebrate Margaret Thatcher's golden wedding anniversary. At once the po-faced, pinstriped men on the Tory benches started hear-hearing and waving their order papers. Even now, ten years on, the very mention of her name drives them wild. They genuinely regard her reign as a golden age. As long as the illusion persists, we are safe. Kevin Hughes brought us all down to earth saying that his sympathies were with Denis on the grounds that 'anyone married to Lady Thatcher for 50 years deserves a medal as big as a dustbin lid'. Whereupon the Tory benches again erupted, this time with howls of outrage. All save a handful of traitors, discreetly covering smiles with their hands.

Monday, 17 December

To Committee Room 8 to hear Home Secretary Blunkett outline his priorities for this Parliament. Lots of warm, New Labourish words – enabling, citizenship, cohesion, building communities. Quite what it all means remains to be seen. On the Home Office, he was outspoken: 'It is one of the least efficient, least competent, least connected-to-the world-outside organisations that I've ever seen. What we have achieved so far has been in spite, rather than because of ...'

Later, a chat with Jean Corston, who says she has been pressing The Man to deal with hunting once and for all. When she last raised the subject, he started going on about the problem in the Lords, to which Jean responded by asking why hunting was the only issue on which we were not able to take on the Lords. If that's true, she said, we'd better get the Leader of the Lords and our Chief Whip to come and explain to the parliamentary party why nothing can be done. Whereupon The Man changed tack and said that a ban would be unenforceable. In which case, said Jean, he had better come and explain that. One way or another, the issue had to be confronted.

Tuesday, 18 December

A call from the Home Secretary to say that the first arrests under Part IV of the Anti-Terrorism Act will take place tomorrow. He says the security service offered him more than 20 names and he whittled it down to 14 ('because the others didn't stand up'). Of those one has already left the country and several others could be charged with other offences, so that left ten. David added that he didn't expect many more. 'Maybe four or five in the New Year. I'm so tired I can hardly stand up,' he said.

To a Christmas party at DFID's swish new offices opposite Bucking-ham Palace. Hilary Benn gave me a tour of the ministerial floor, including his office, which would have been mine had I stayed. I felt a twinge of regret, but it lasted no more than a second or two. Sir Two Buzzes is off to be Governor of Bermuda in February. We had a pleas-ant chat and he invited me to look him up should I ever find myself fact-finding in the Caribbean, which is not very likely.

Wednesday, 19 December

To Committee Room 14 for the meeting of the parliamentary party. The Leader of the Lords, Gareth Williams, was the only other person there when I arrived so I took the opportunity to put in a bad word for Derry Irvine's proposed reforms: 'Electing only 20 per cent is not saleable.'

'Derry's going to explain it all,' replied Gareth cheerfully. Gareth is always cheerful. He went on, 'An all-elected chamber would be a disaster. There are 700 of us. If they were all elected, they'd want increased power.'

'Can't we phase them out?'

'The trouble is they don't die fast enough – only 17 or 18 a year.'

'How about a retirement age?'

'I wanted 75, which some said was too young. The difficulty, which can't be spoken aloud, is that many peers depend on the allowances to survive. They've given up jobs and pensions. The allowances are their only income.'

'So it's true then, the Lords is just sheltered accommodation for the elderly.'

At which the familiar twinkle appeared in Gareth's eye: 'I just put this to you neutrally – which House performed better over the Terrorism Bill?'

As ever, The Man was sitting surrounded by whisky bottles when we filed into his room. As fast as he was signing, staff were taking them away. Someone, probably Jean, has whispered to him that we prefer to have his full attention and so he was trying to get them out of the way before we started. (Helen said that one was auctioned for £200 in Sheffield last week, so all this signing obviously spreads happiness.) He was wearing specs and saying that it is only a question of time before he had to use them in the House. 'I can't see a thing,' he said. 'Did you see the struggle I had today reading that quote?' Jean offered hers, he tried them on and looked around. 'I see you all in an entirely different light,' he said to much merriment.

We started with Afghanistan. Someone asked about our contribution to the peace-keeping force. The Man replied that it was nonsense to talk about overstretch. We would be sending about a thousand troops for a maximum of three or four months and then someone else would take over. 'We were told by the so-called experts that only Muslim troops would do, but the truth is that most Afghans don't care. We could never get the Pashtuns into government without a multinational force. They are terrified of the Northern Alliance.'

Gordon Prentice raised faith schools. 'I haven't met anyone who is signed up to our policy.'

'We are between a rock and a hard place,' said The Man. 'Better to have Muslim schools which are properly inspected and regulated than leaving education to the imams and the mosques.'

Someone asked about the plan to sell an expensive, overly sophisticated air traffic control system to the Tanzanians to which The Man replied lamely that there were rules that must be followed. He added, 'We must be careful about getting into a position where we are telling the Tanzanians what's good for them.'

Someone mentioned by name one of our recently appointed peers. 'How did he get into the Lords?'

The Man came over all innocent, as if to say, 'Don't look at me.'

Helen Jackson said, 'Everyone knows he's a crook.'

The Man affected shock, raising his eyes to the ceiling, making a little joke about concealed microphones and the subject was swiftly dropped.

CHAPTER FOUR

2002

Monday, 7 January 2002

Sarah and Gordon Brown's baby has died. The Man was visibly moved when the news reached him. He was pictured on the evening bulletins at Bagram airport, Afghanistan, apparently close to tears, making a lengthy statement of condolence. The new Afghan leader, Hamid Karzai, was hovering alongside looking bemused. Meanwhile US bombing is becoming increasingly casual. Another huge disaster is reported from Qalaye Niazi in eastern Afghanistan in which up to 100 people, mainly women and children, have been blown to pieces. Such mistakes are becoming so commonplace that they are barely reported. I wonder if The Man, so moved by the death of one small child, has even raised the subject in his many talks with his friend George Bush. He sent me a letter the other day after I broached the subject at the parliamentary committee, full of the usual platitudes – 'every care taken' etc. It's all crap. The only casualties that interest the Americans are their own.

Wednesday, 9 January

To the meeting of the parliamentary party to hear Derry Irvine bravely attempt to sell his master plan for House of Lords reform. It was, he said, a compromise for today not a solution for all time. There is, he asserted, no scope for electing more than 120 peers. 'It would be an historic mistake if we allowed a largely elected Lords to take pre-eminence over the Commons.' To begin with he was heard respectfully, but it rapidly became clear that there was scarcely a person present who agreed with the official line – including Robin Cook, whose job it is to sell it in the Commons. (I noticed Robin screwing up his face as Derry listed him as one of those on his Cabinet subcommittee who were signed up to the official line.) There then followed a good-natured debate in which just about every one of the 20 or so contributors favoured a different solution.

By the time Derry rose to reply, the natives were restless. He attempted to curry favour with a little joke, 'Well, I certainly enjoyed that – the best morning I've had for a long time …'

'You should come more often,' someone called.

'The alternative to doing something is to do nothing,' blurted Derry.

'No it isn't.'

'Be serious,' heckled someone else. By now there was general merriment at Derry's obvious discomfort.

In the end Gareth Williams saved the day. Without conceding anything he treated us all to a calm, reasoned, brilliant little homily which was heard in respectful silence, save for laughter at his dry asides. 'This is,' he concluded, 'a necessary compromise. The great prize which we are trying to deliver is that the remaining 92 hereditaries will go and 120 elected members will take their place.'

He sat down to prolonged applause, even though his message was essentially the same as Derry's. The contrast between their performances couldn't have been more marked. No prizes for guessing the identity of the next Lord Chancellor.

Thursday, 10 January

Geoff Hoon made a statement about our contribution to the Afghan task force. He was at pains to emphasise that our soldiers would be confined to Kabul and its environs and that after three months another country (probably Turkey) would take the lead, which is not very reassuring. Where are the Germans, the French, the Australians? Let alone the Americans, who seem to be losing interest by the day except that they are still randomly bombing anyone who looks like a

Taliban. In the north and east of the country mayhem reigns and in the interior people are said to be eating grass. I asked if our troops would be lending a hand with the distribution of aid, but Geoff said blandly that they wouldn't. Meanwhile all the second-rate army officers on the Tory benches were bobbing up and down complaining about overstretch and demanding assurances that we will abandon the Afghans to their fate at the earliest opportunity.

Tuesday, 15 January

To the Wilson Room in Portcullis House to hear Jack Straw, who had just come from talking to Colin Powell about America's treatment of the Taliban prisoners. 'I told Powell, "This isn't doing America any good." He understands.'

Afterwards I remarked to Jack that, although political realities dictated that we had to be nice to him we should never lose sight of the fact that George Bush and the Republican Party represented – I was going to say, 'some of the meanest, greediest, most selfish people on the planet,' but Jack finished the sentence for me: '... a bunch of bastards.' He added, 'Colin Powell is a decent man. He could just as easily have been a Democrat.'

Wednesday, 16 January

To the meeting of the parliamentary party to hear The Man give his start of term address. Confident, lucid, not a note in sight and no sign that he is flagging. On the contrary, he appears to know exactly where he is going even if many of the rest of us have doubts. He ended with a reference to 'an historic third term'. There can be no doubt that he intends to take us there.

Dennis Skinner brought us all back down to earth. 'It would be wonderful, Tony, if a few words from you could resolve everything. But out there in the party these fine words are not going down too well.' Some crises, said Dennis, are too big to handle. The party had got lost along the way. One would have thought that with all these good things happening, we'd have no problem signing up new members, but in fact we were hardly recruiting at all. 'The party needs revitalising. We need reassurance from the Secretary of State for Health as to which way we are travelling. You need to send out ministers, not to meet managers but to get out and meet the party.'

The Man was unapologetic. 'I want to issue a warning, too. Believe me, the problem we face at the election will not be that we have reformed too much, but too little. If we don't reform, then the dismantlers will take over. I promise you we are right. Reform is always opposed. Our changes on literacy and numeracy were opposed.' ('By the same people,' murmured John Reid.) 'The whole purpose of our NHS reforms is to push power down. Those who are doing well will have a less heavy hand from the centre.' He concluded with three points: First, we are employing more people in the public sector than ever before. Second, we are the only government in recent years to have increased education and health spending. Third, public sector pay increases had recently exceeded those in the private sector.

He sat down to much clapping and desk thumping, but it can't conceal the deep unease. There is a feeling that we are losing our way. Outside I ran into Ken Purchase, who had steam coming out of his ears. 'He's wrong,' said Ken. 'He doesn't believe in a National Health Service or a national anything else. He believes in atomised services … Look at the mess we're in with the railways. There's no magic about private sector management.'

Thursday, 17 January

To Eland House with Lynne Jones and Dale Campbell Savours, to bend the ear of Charlie Falconer about the High Hedges Bill, which has run aground. An odd feeling, to be issued with a visitors' pass, escorted up to the ministerial floor and told to sit in the ministerial waiting room to await the ministerial pleasure, in a building where I once came and went as I pleased and where delegations awaited *my* pleasure. A handful of familiar faces – the tea ladies, the receptionists and Frank the cheerful Indian who so efficiently processes the ministerial mail. My old office, *sans* pictures and pot plants, is now just another meeting room. The private office where my industrious officials – Chris, Shayne, Nicky and Kerry – once laboured is now dark and empty. Desks once piled with orange case files are clear. Not a scrap of paper in sight. Not the slightest sign that I ever set foot there. As for Keith Hill, his office has been physically eliminated. That is to say the walls have been unbolted and taken away. The space he once occupied is now part of what is known as the Corporate Management Section.

Some things, though, never change. Here we are again, sitting around a table in what was once Hilary Armstrong's office, discussing how to temper the remorseless advance into suburbia of the dreaded *Cupressocyparis leylandii*. Naively, when I came to the Department in July 1999, I believed that this was one of the few issues in which I might make a difference. Yet here we are, nearly three years on, and precisely nothing has changed. Charlie was affable and constructive, but pessimistic about persuading our lords and masters, whose minds are relentlessly focused on The Big Picture, to make room for a measure so trifling. Nevertheless, he promised to do what he could. I am not hopeful.

Jim Sensenbrenner – a big, pallid, jet-lagged US Congressman who looks as if he has spent too long on aeroplanes and in smoke-filled rooms – came in to discuss terrorism. He is chairman of the House Judiciary Committee that played a part in constructing the draconian American anti-terror laws which provide for secret military tribunals and firing squads. The purpose, he said, was to avoid a replay of the OJ Simpson trial, where proceedings were televised and dragged out endlessly by publicity-seeking lawyers. I asked whether the United States, having invested so much in destroying Afghanistan, would be playing a big part in the reconstruction. 'It could be argued,' he said, 'that we've done our share.' He said Bush would have to pull out all the stops to get a big aid package through Congress and, with mid-term elections approaching, he might not want to do that. 'It's hard to justify to your constituents in Wisconsin the need to build a bridge in Kabul when they want one at home.'

Which only goes to show that one can never be too cynical.

Sunday, 20 January
Sunderland

With Sarah and two of her friends to see *Lord of the Rings* at the Boldon multiplex. A sign on the wall said, 'Born to shop? Visit the store.' Which they did, of course, immediately on arrival. How can I convince my children that spending money does not bring happiness when everything and everyone around them seems intent on proving the opposite?

Monday, 28 January

The Man is quoted in today's papers as saying that if we haven't sorted out the NHS by the election we must suffer the consequences. Unwise words that will come back to haunt us since, in the current climate, however great an effort we make, no one is ever going to acknowledge the slightest improvement. Steve Byers recently said something similar in relation to the railways and at various times in the past Prescott and Blunkett have made similar statements. Is it wise to create such hostages to fortune?

A brief chat with Steve Byers in the Tea Room. I remarked how calm he seems, however rough the going gets. 'The trouble is,' he smiled, 'I don't take it very seriously.' Even as he spoke, however, a nerve in his cheek twitched and his hands fidgeted, which I haven't noticed before.

Wednesday, 30 January

David Blunkett addressed the parliamentary party. Once again, he was very rude about the Home Office: 'A nineteenth-century department with enormous status and self-importance, but not really engaged.'

Afterwards, there was a brief discussion on immigration, prompted by the Keighley MP, Ann Cryer, who said that arranged marriages were increasingly being used as a way around the immigration laws. She was backed up by Alice Mahon, who said she was having to deal with women fleeing forced marriages at the rate of about one a month. Some imported spouses were walking out within days of arrival. She added, 'People shouldn't be allowed to hide behind religion or culture any more. This is about human rights.' Gordon Prentice talked about the near invisibility of Asian women. Ashok Kumar said, 'I support equal rights against cultural values.' Interesting that people on the left are slowly waking up to the gross abuses perpetuated in the name of multiculturalism. Until now we've turned a blind eye, for fear of being labelled racists.

Mike O'Brien asked me up to his room. 'I'm going to tell you the biggest secret in Whitehall,' he said. 'The Prime Minister has reopened the Hinduja inquiry. The press would have a field day if they found out.' Mike is worried that some way will be found of getting Peter Mandelson off the hook and dumping on him. He wanted my advice.

My guess is that Peter has been badgering The Man to reinstate him on the basis of new 'evidence' and that, rather than say no straight out, The Man has agreed to sound out Sir Anthony Hammond, even though he knows it doesn't amount to more than a row of beans. My advice was do nothing and await events.

Thursday, 31 January

Bad news. Federal Mogul, which makes piston rings for petrol engines, is to close its Sunderland factory with a loss of 400 jobs. It is merely the latest episode in the progressive collapse of our manufacturing base which has continued unabated under Labour. The sad truth is that neither MPs, local authorities nor government have the slightest influence on decisions taken thousands of miles away. We are all at the mercy of forces beyond our control.

Ann Clwyd and several colleagues had a meeting with the new Afghan leader, Hamid Karzai, this afternoon. She said everyone was very polite and respectful until the end when she said to him, 'I wouldn't want you to leave here thinking that everyone agrees with you about the status of the prisoners. It's not for you or George Bush to decide. It's a matter for an independent tribunal.' She says that in the corridor outside he gripped her arm hard and whispered, 'You're quite right.

Keep it up.' The poor man is totally a prisoner of the Americans. One word out of place and they will lose interest in him.

At lunch in the cafeteria I asked David Davis what the Tories are planning for the health service. 'A mixed economy,' he replied. The State would continue to fund medical treatment, but the customer would be given a choice of where to obtain it. He added that the present monolithic, bureaucratic health service was hopelessly inefficient – 'Our hospitals are killing 60,000 people a year,' he said cheerfully. Where does he get that extraordinary figure? From the Public Accounts Committee, he says.

Monday, 4 February

A big row is brewing over The Man's speech in Cardiff yesterday in which he appeared to accuse those of not supporting his public services reforms of being 'wreckers'.

'Does Our Great Leader's use of the word "wreckers" help or hinder your argument with health service workers?' I asked Alan Milburn in the Tea Room this evening. He replied, 'The strategy is to isolate John Edmonds "who has been a complete bastard". Unfortunately, this has pushed all the unions into the same camp. But,' he added, 'we'll get them out.' Let's hope Alan is right.

Wednesday, 6 February

To the meeting of the parliamentary party to hear Jack Straw. 'The end of the Cold War has enabled us to adopt a distinctive foreign policy,' he asserted. By way of example, he mentioned Sierra Leone and Kosovo although, as several people pointed out, our long tradition of humiliating subservience to the United States remains undiminished. Alice Mahon asked about Star Wars (an early test of our alleged distinctiveness) to which Jack replied, 'I'm happy to have a debate, Alice, as long as your mind is not made up beforehand.' It sounds, however, as though Jack's is. On Afghanistan, Jack said we are 'actively considering' Hamid Karzai's request to extend the peacekeeping force to other cities. Good news, if true. Until now we have been dead against mission creep.

Thursday, 7 February

An historic day: without help from anyone, I managed to e-mail my column to the *Echo*. Until now I have had to throw myself upon the mercy of one of the Commons Library staff.

The Home Secretary launched his asylum and immigration White Paper, signalling the start of a crackdown. Asylum seekers will no longer be imprisoned, but new arrivals will be required to reside in holding centres if they want to receive benefit or other assistance. For new citizens there will be oaths of allegiance, English lessons and a clear indication that with rights come responsibilities. Mostly, it was received with cheers on the Tory side and in silence on ours, although it seemed reasonable to me. Oliver Letwin's response was civilised and thoughtful, in line with all his recent pronouncements. The more I see of him, the more I like.

Friday, 8 February
Sunderland

To Federal Mogul to discuss the impending closure. As if that wasn't depressing enough I returned to the office to find a message from Ian Dewhirst to say that he is to close his ladies' wear factory in Leechmere Road. Another 350 jobs down the swanny. At this rate there won't be a single manufacturing job left in Sunderland by the time we leave office. I rang Mr Dewhirst. Needless to say he is as powerless as I am. Wages in Turkey and North Africa, he says, are a fifth of those in England. Marks & Spencer, his main customer, is increasingly sourcing from abroad. What else can he do? He adds, 'The sad thing is that these skills, once lost, will never come back.'

I opened tonight's *Echo* to find, emblazoned across an inside page, the headline: 'MULLIN: PAY REJECT ASYLUM SEEKERS'. Oh Christ, that's all I need. The *Echo*'s eager young Lobby correspondent has managed to make a huge mountain out of my modest suggestion to

David Blunkett yesterday that asylum seekers with children, who would otherwise be destitute, be given a small resettlement allowance to help them re-establish themselves in their country of origin.

The following letter appears in the same edition:

> I wonder if, like myself, your readers are bemused as to why Chris Mullin ever chose to become an MP for Sunderland. His column never misses an opportunity to berate some section of our community. In June it was the voters of Pennywell for exercising their democratic right not to vote. In September he upset some members of the Jewish community for his wholly inaccurate analysis of the events that led to the September 11 tragedy. This week it is the parents and children of Sunderland for lacking educational ambition, compared to their Afghani counterparts. He seems blissfully unaware that the average debt of a medical student in the UK is £13,000 – wasn't it his sanctimonious attitude in the last Parliament that voted to introduce tuition fees? If this rate of attrition against his traditional support continues, there won't be a Labour voter left in Sunderland South at the next election. No doubt he will then carpet bag a seat somewhere else at the next election, preferably Kandahar Central.

It is signed by a Mr Gordon Hill of the School House in Pennywell. I once saved his daughter's job. At the time he professed himself grateful, but there is no gratitude in politics.

Among the customers at the surgery this evening a family of asylum seekers from the Ukraine, evangelical Christians who claim to have been persecuted for their beliefs. I believe them although it is clear that a large part of their motivation must be a desire to escape the poverty and hopelessness of their homeland. And who can blame them? The problem is that their first port of call was Spain and so, under the terms of the Dublin Convention, they are the responsibility of the Spaniards. There is no argument I can make. Their son, a bright little chap a year younger than Sarah, sat between them translating. The mother sobbed as I explained that I can do nothing beyond asking for a few weeks' delay to allow for a dignified exit.

How I wish our bored, spoiled, disaffected youth could see this little scene. These people would have given anything, *anything*, to change places with any one of us. For a chance of school, work, hope. And yet they are the doomed and I can do nothing to save them. I lay awake worrying. What is to become of them?

Tuesday, 12 February

Alastair Campbell came to the Northern Group of MPs this evening, attracting a better turnout than most Cabinet ministers. Despite the shells exploding all around, he was as cheerful, relaxed and uncompromising as usual. 'We can afford to relax about the daily feeding frenzies,' he said. 'You've got to believe in what you are doing and take the crap. Eventually the dots will join up and make a picture.' The big lesson of our first term, according to Alastair, is that the media don't speak for public opinion. 'If we stick to our basic argument, we can get it out.'

Wednesday, 13 February

An entertaining lunch with John Gilbert in the Lords' dining room. John says that Europe's dependence on the Americans to carry out any meaningful operation is an embarrassment – they flew 85 per cent of the missions over Kosovo. Star Wars, says John, is 'madness – a complete waste of money, but if the Americans want to waste their money, let them'.

On the events of 11 September: 'We must all be grateful to those guys who brought down the fourth plane. If it had hit the White House, with or without Mrs Bush inside, the Americans wouldn't have asked questions, they'd have nuked someone.'

On Iraq, John sounded alarm bells. The other night he attended a dinner in honour of Senator Sam Nunn. Of the dozen people around the table, everyone believed that the Americans are preparing for a land invasion of Iraq. 'Insanity,' says John. 'We won't back them, will we? Blair couldn't get it through the parliamentary party.' (I wouldn't count on that). 'My approach to Iraq,' he said cheerfully, 'would be to say to Saddam, "By all means waste your money on missiles, but use one and we'll take 18 inches of topsoil off your country."'

'Before opening a new front in Iraq,' I said, 'perhaps the Americans should spend a little more time helping us to clear up in Afghanistan.'

'Haven't you heard what they say?'

'No.'

'"Great powers don't do the dishes."'

To Committee Room 11 to hear The Man report on his Africa trip. 'Africa,' he said, 'is the only continent going backwards.' He talked of a new Marshall Plan. Africans must take action on corruption and conflict resolution. We have to move on aid and trade. Most of the peacekeeping could be done by regional (mainly African) forces, trained, funded and equipped by developed nations under a UN mandate. Listening, you realise that he's serious. He's thought it through. He is treading where other leaders fear to tread. There are no votes in it, or at least very few. He's doing it because it is right. Maybe something will come of it, maybe it won't, but he's determined to try. Believe it or not, we are led by an idealist. Moments like this enable one to look the cynics in the eye and say that New Labour is not just a collection of control freaks and spin doctors. Idealism is not dead.

At the parliamentary committee Gordon Prentice triggered a discussion about hunting, pointing out that the Scots had just voted for a ban. 'Our problem is the Lords,' said John Prescott. At which point the spotlight turned on the Lords' whip, Denis Carter, who said that, if the Parliament Act was to be used, it would have to be done this year. There was not enough time.

'Why not bring the Lords back in mid-September?' I suggested. Denis hummed and hawed. It was soon apparent that he didn't want to disturb their holiday.

'Fine,' I said. 'Let's have all that on the table. If the Lords is the problem, let's expose that, so the public won't think we are hiding behind them.'

'If we are to have a constitutional crisis, I can't think of a better time or a better issue,' said Tony Lloyd.

I asked Denis if there was any way we could get a hunting ban through the Lords.

'In my view, no.'

At which point JP suddenly sprung to life. 'At the heart of this is political credibility. If we don't use the Parliament Act now, when can we? This is a small issue, but it's gnawing away at our credibility. It's a gut issue. We've got to get it cleared out of the system. If we get beat, fine, but we've got to try.' He said he would raise it at Cabinet tomorrow.

Finally, to Wimbledon for dinner with my old friends James and Margaret Curran, Liz Forgan and Rex Cowan. Also there were Jean Seaton and Ben Pimlott. James and Margaret said they were no longer Labour Party members. New Labour's handling of the London mayoral selection was the final straw. Liz told the story, which she had heard from Laurie Taylor, of John Birt's walking holiday in France with a group of friends. It all had to be scientifically organised. No detail unattended. Laurie had been deputed to put together a brief containing everything there was to know about the terrain through which they would be passing. In the end he had funked and paid someone to do it for him. They arrived at the top of a mountain, John opened his rucksack and produced a mini-washing line, complete with clothes pegs, on which he hung his shirt to dry. Clearly, a man who leaves nothing to chance.

Thursday, 14 February

Jo Moore, Steve Byers's spin doctor, has resigned. The hacks have been determined to get her ever since she survived last September's folly. My guess is that they won't let up. They'll be after Steve next.

My goodness, it's coming down hard. Every day a new feeding frenzy. No sooner is one falsehood knocked on the head than a new one appears. The Lobby are growing increasingly shameless, no longer bothering even to check with their victim before publishing and when caught out they simply move, unblushingly, on to their next target. A favourite tactic is to wilfully misrepresent a statement by a minister and then ring around looking for someone to denounce on the basis of that misrepresentation. Increasingly, even the BBC takes its cue from the tabloids. This must be what's known as 'news with attitude'. Each day begins with John Humphrys waxing indignant (he no longer makes much effort to conceal his own views) on *Today,* and ends with Jeremy Vine, a cynical smart arse if ever there was, on *Newsnight.* The subtext is generally the same: all our politicians are corrupt/incompetent/dishonest. To be fair it isn't just politics, it's everything. All our institutions – the health service, the railways, the monarchy – are under daily assault. The media have given up on the Tory party and increasingly manufacture their own news. It's nothing personal. For the most part it is not political either. To some extent, of course, it's our own fault. In opposition we played all the same cards and now we are reaping the whirlwind.

Saturday, 16 February
Sunderland

To South Hylton to attend a public meeting about a mobile-phone mast that is about to be erected, with a minimum of consultation, in the centre of the village. I usually avoid weekend engagements, but Ngoc advises that I have to be seen taking more interest in the issues that concern my constituents, and she's right. I must overcome the notion that I am some kind of obsessive do-gooder interested only in helping asylum seekers and terrorists. The meeting was full of elderly folk who fear that they – or their grandchildren – are all about to be irradiated. Understandably, they don't believe official assurances that the technology is harmless. As one of them said, 'That's what they used to say about asbestos 30 years ago.' I promised to do what I could, taking care not to arouse false hopes, and to my amazement they all applauded when I left.

Tuesday, 19 February

In the company of management I toured the Dewhirst Menswear factories at Hendon and Pennywell. Row after row of women in yellow smocks sitting at machines which ingeniously cut, stitch, press and iron in accordance with instructions from a computer. The end result of which is six thousand Marks & Spencer suits a week. The problem, which no amount of scientifc organisation can avert, is that the same skills are available in Morocco for a fifth of the price and in China for, who knows – a tenth? 'We are staring at a black hole,' said John Haley, the managing director. He is desperately trying to diversify. The only practical option is America, where there is a market for volume menswear. The problem is that the home of free trade imposes a 23 per cent tariff on textile imports from the UK. So much for the special relationship.

Friday, 22 February
Sunderland

To lunch with *Echo* editor Andrew Smith. I proposed – and Andrew agreed – that we reduce my column to once a fortnight. It's become a chore and I am upsetting too many people. I sense I am beginning to get up the nose of *Echo* readers. They need to see less of me.

Monday, 25 February

A new feeding frenzy has developed around Steve Byers over his attempt to get rid of Martin Sixsmith, the chief press officer at his department. It had been announced that Sixsmith had resigned at the same time as Jo Moore, but now it appears he hasn't. Yesterday Sixsmith went public with his version of events, which included a memorable quote from the Department's Permanent Secretary, Richard Mottram, on discovering that his resignation had been announced prematurely: 'We're all fucked. You're fucked. The whole Department is fucked.' It's certainly a mess. Gordon Prentice was on the radio this morning talking about 'a spreading stain'. True, but unhelpful. This is a moment that calls for a little basic solidarity.

Tuesday, 26 February

Steve made a statement in the House this afternoon. It was make or break for him. Just about all the papers are screaming for him to go. He acquitted himself well, remaining calm throughout, conceding just enough to earn himself a little credit, but not so much as to dig the pit any deeper. Most of the Cabinet turned out for him, although not The Man. 'Where's Blair?' the Tories were calling.

Theresa May, for the opposition, made the same mistake as Neil Kinnock over Westland. Instead of homing in on two or three key issues, she asked a long string of who-said-what-to-who questions which let Steve off the hook. The Tories, realising she had blown it, began to look glum. Our benches laid on a magnificent display of solidarity. One after another we rose to put in a good word for Steve. Tam was the only dissident, but even he didn't lay it on too hard. The outcome was a minor triumph, although the hacks are mightily upset at not getting their way. No one is under any illusions. They will be back.

Wednesday, 27 February

Sure enough this morning's papers are full of indignation about Steve's miraculous escape. They are not going to forgive him. It can only be a question of time before a new crisis is organised.

The parliamentary committee met in the Lower Ministerial Conference Room. The Man, flanked by Hilary Armstrong and Charles Clarke, sat on one side of the huge table (or rather a dozen tables pushed together) and the rest of us on the other. The mood was upbeat. 'And now Mr Blair, why do you think we should give you the job?' joked Jean as we faced him across the vast table. The Man opened, saying he was grateful for the way everyone had rallied round yesterday. 'Much of what appears in the press is complete and total lies. I don't bother reading it any more, although it outrages me when I think about it.' He added, 'British politics is turning into a game of "Gotcha".'

Ann Clwyd pressed him to concede to the prior parliamentary scrutiny of arms sales. 'It's asking very little. A few crumbs in the direction of the party, that's all. It would be done by a committee of MPs that you would choose. I would have thought ministers would welcome that.'

The Man gave nothing away. 'We must be careful not to get into a situation where we regard all arms sales as bad. There are some huge contracts ...'

At which point Tony Lloyd spoke up, saying that as a Foreign Office minister he had vetted arms contracts.

'And are you in favour?'

'Yes.'

The Man said he'd think about it, but his demeanour suggested that he wasn't planning to think very hard.

I asked about the proposed shake-up of the Post Office. 'Is it true that the Regulator has pushed out the boat further than the EC requires?'

'Yes. We are working on it. We have to be careful about interfering with the Regulator.'

Hilary Armstrong reported that there had been eight applicants for the two vacancies on the Public Accounts Committee. However, they were all men. She asked for a further week in the hope that a suitable woman could be persuaded to put her name forward. This was greeted with scepticism by those of us who believe that Hilary is looking for an excuse to exclude Frank Field. Andrew Mackinlay asked the killer question: 'How many women applied when the committee was formed in July and how many did you put on?'

Answer: five applied and none were put on, although three were found places on other committees.

'So why the sudden interest in finding a woman?'

Hilary protested innocence, but no one believed her. In the end we reluctantly conceded that she could have another week although Jean Corston made clear to her afterwards that there would be a fuss if Frank was excluded. I regard this as the first test of whether or not anything has changed since the election. 'Hilary has got the message,' Jean said afterwards. We shall see.

Tuesday, 5 March

Supper with Alan Milburn and Mike O'Brien. Alan regaled us with the latest NHS crisis (there is one every day): an official has been found sitting on 1,000 unanswered parliamentary questions and he was coming in at weekends to falsify the figures, making it appear as if they had been answered. He was scathing about the civil service.

'Everyone thinks they are white knights and that we are the villains whereas the truth, which we all know, is that many officials are useless.' Alan says he favours a cabinet system such as they have in France where a minister brings in his own team to run a department. I reminded him that Tony Benn suggested something similar 25 years ago. 'Better keep quiet about that,' he said.

Mike talked about the chaos he discovered at the Immigration and Nationality Department when he was at the Home Office. Once, on a visit to IND, he opened a cupboard and found it full of unanswered mail, having just been assured there were no more outstanding letters. A hapless junior official was summoned. His explanation? 'We put them there so that the Minister wouldn't see them.'

Wednesday, 6 March

To the meeting of the parliamentary party, to hear Gordon Brown outline his anti-poverty strategy. 'For the first time in 50 years,' he proclaimed, 'we have unemployment lower than Japan or the US. We are now in a position to convince people that we can create a stable economy so we can now borrow to invest.' This was Gordon the Great Redistributor. He talked of integrating tax and benefits, investing in public services. Tax credits, he said, were the central building block of our strategy to eliminate child poverty and low pay. He spoke with passion. A man with a plan, operating on a plane far above the petty wrangling that consumes lesser mortals. He was impressive. If there was a leadership election now, he would certainly win.

Afterwards Hilary Armstrong invited me to her office for a quiet chat. I knew at once what it was about: stopping Frank Field from getting onto the Public Accounts Committee. 'I'm concerned about all the lobbying for Frank' was her opening gambit. 'He has his own agenda … He'll go in with the Tories … It's difficult to find places on select committees for younger members.' And so on. I listened patiently and then told her firmly to close her eyes, grit her teeth and get on with it. Blackballing Frank would cause more trouble than it's worth. She seemed resigned to the inevitable, but as I was leaving she said, 'Some of my Cabinet colleagues think I will lose us the election.'

Which only goes to show how utterly some of our masters have lost touch with reality. We are only talking about one place on a committee for goodness sake. Not even the chairmanship. Despite all the trouble it gets them into, they just can't stop fixing.

Rumours of an impending attack on Iraq dominated our session with The Man this afternoon. He looks washed out having spent a long weekend at the Commonwealth conference in Australia, touching down at six this morning. I assumed he must have slept, but no. He says he finds sleep difficult on planes, 'but I got through a lot of work'. So here he is, back among us after two 24-hour flights in five days and a great deal of activity in between. A little off colour, but otherwise on good form. He recounted an exchange with the King of Swaziland, who had advised him that the second coming was due any moment.

On Iraq, The Man said nothing was planned in the immediate future. He would be seeing Bush in April. 'We have to tread carefully. It depends on what's proposed. Weapons of mass destruction is the real issue. The latest intelligence is very strong.' He added ominously that North Korea survives only by selling missile technology.

'The key question is with what are we going to replace Saddam's regime?' I asked. 'Another tyrant? Our tyrant rather than a maverick. Who is going to clear up afterwards? Will it be us again? As in Afghanistan.' I quoted John Gilbert: 'Great Powers don't do the dishes.'

'They did in Vietnam,' growled Prescott unhelpfully.

The Man didn't dispute any of this. 'I say to you very privately,' he replied, 'that my strategy is to get alongside the Americans and try to shape what is to be done and that won't be done by grandstanding.' He added that this strategy had worked in Afghanistan. 'Things were done differently as a result of our involvement.'

After he had gone, there was a row about Frank Field. Hilary announced that a woman – Vera Baird – had been found to fill one of the places and that she would prefer George Howarth for the other, but it had been put to her that there would be a fuss if it didn't go to Frank …

'Frank is obviously the best. His name leaps out of the page,' I blurted. 'We are only talking about one place out of sixteen. Surely the whips could live with that. Do we want a repeat of what happened last time over Gwyneth?'

At which point they started getting indignant. 'I think Chris owes us some kind of explanation for his last remark,' said Charles Clarke, but before I could respond someone else was demanding a vote, which has never happened before. There was a discussion about who was entitled to vote.

'If we are to have a vote,' I said, 'I hope we will take into account the opinion of those who are absent.'

'Only those who are here have a vote,' said Prescott. 'If you don't attend, you can't vote.'

I pointed out that Andrew and Ann had both forcefully expressed their opinions last week and apologised in advance for their absence. Ann had even written to Jean indicating her support for Frank. Jean, who had been keeping her head well down, confirmed that this was so.

'You're on your own,' someone said.

'I'm not,' I said. 'The chairman agrees with me.' I shouldn't have said it, but I was furious. It was obvious we had been tricked. Jean reddened, wobbled and then said that she wasn't necessarily in favour of Frank. A chasm opened.

In the end Robin Cook saved the day proposing that we should put forward Vera's name and then invite colleagues to choose on a show of hands between George and Frank. There was nothing for it but to agree even though the whips will certainly make sure that George wins. Hilary could hardly believe her luck.

Thursday, 7 March

Rang Frank to tell him what went on yesterday. It's up to him if he wants to organise a fuss. If truth be told, there is a case against Frank. Brilliant, interesting, principled he may be, but he is not a team player; in fact he is seriously disloyal and a maverick.

Monday, 11 March

Much concern that The Man is going to sign us up to a war against Iraq. Rumours of discontent in Cabinet. Alice Mahon tried to persuade me to sign her early day motion, but I declined since the other signatories were mainly Usual Suspects, but there is no doubt that unease spreads well beyond. 'The Prime Minister should pay more attention to the Labour Party and less to the Republican Party,' remarked Malcolm Savidge.

An unexpected piece of good news. George Howarth says he does not want to be considered for the Public Accounts Committee. His letter to Jean, announcing his withdrawal, begins, 'I put my name forward at the request of the Chief Whip,' which blows the gaff on Hilary's little games. Later in the evening Frank Field came up to my room with a letter saying that he was withdrawing, too. The ball is now firmly back with the parliamentary committee.

Tuesday, 12 March

I pointed out to Vera Baird that she would have to come off the Human Rights Committee if she wanted to go on Public Accounts. She said she had already received an e-mail to this effect from Jean Corston and she will withdraw her name from Public Accounts, too. Very satisfactory. Hilary is now in a deep little pit of her own making. The question is, will she have the sense to stop digging?

Wednesday, 13 March

To the Gay Hussar for lunch with Andy McSmith, the token socialist on the *Daily Telegraph*, a grudging recognition by the crazed ideologues who run the paper that they need to maintain some sort of link with the ruling party. Andy recounts introducing himself to Conrad Black at an office party. The Tyrant was raving that Britain should leave the EC and join the North American Trade Association and Andy made some mildly sarcastic remark. At first Black thought Andy was agreeing with him and then the penny dropped and he skidded to a halt.

'Where did you work before?'

'The *Observer*.'

'Well don't you bring any *Observer* attitudes here. I shall be reading your copy very carefully and if I detect any, I shall ring up Charles Moore at 2 a.m. – I do you know.' I bet he does.

Five thousand angry, white (almost entirely) male police officers descended on Westminster to lobby against Blunkett's reform plans. An awesome, slightly scary spectacle. Many were overweight, fit only for light duties. No wonder they are so upset at the prospect of going back to the beat. The organisation was scientific. Just about every committee room in the building was put at their disposal and each force lobbied us in relays. About 120 from Northumbria crowded into the Jubilee Room to meet their MPs. The mood was uncompromising and occasionally ugly. 'You're arrogant,' 'You don't understand us,' they kept saying. One detective of seven years' experience claimed improbably that he took home the same as a 'pasty stacker' in Gregg's, the baker's. Faced with this, one or two of our colleagues opted for appeasement. David Miliband made a brave attempt to hold the line. Ronnie Campbell provided light relief and John McWilliam made a disastrous intervention, haranguing the assembly for five minutes while the rest of us just looked at the floor. For my part, I confined myself to asking a few questions and avoided expressing an opinion on the righteousness of their cause. If anything, the experience hardened my resolve and I'm not the only one. One colleague, emerging from a meeting with Manchester's finest, remarked on how rude they had been. 'If they talk to us like this, imagine how they treat a 16-year-old black youth.'

I arrived ten minutes late at the parliamentary committee, just in time to catch the tail end of an exchange between Gordon Prentice and The Man on the Post Office. 'Why are we opening up the market so fast? That's what I can't understand.'

'Other post offices in Europe have changed and we haven't. We can't bury our heads in the sand.'

Talk then turned to Iraq. 'Listen to the folks on The Hill,' pleaded Andrew Mackinlay. 'It isn't obvious that September 11 has changed anything in relation to Iraq,' said Tony Lloyd. 'I'm not under any illusions, but I can't see what's changed.'

'The only way in which September 11 is relevant,' said The Man, 'is that we can't leave these problems to fester. How to deal with them is the issue.' He repeated that no decisions had been taken. Reports that we had been requested to supply 25,000 troops were 'nonsense'. He was, he implied, a moderating influence on George Bush. 'I wouldn't underestimate the importance of giving the Americans another way of dealing with this. I don't intend to do anything I don't believe in.'

Beware of phoney intelligence, I cautioned, mentioning 'yellow rain'. He clearly hadn't heard of it, but Robin Cook nodded sagely.*

We turned to the police. 'We are fighting on too many fronts,' I said. We need to look for one we can close down quickly. My candidate would be the Post Office.

After The Man had departed there was an extraordinary row over the proposed Hunting Bill. Gordon insisted on tabling a resolution for next Wednesday's meeting of the parliamentary party which would bind the government to re-adopt the previous Hunting Bill rather than a new watered-down version which might come too late for the Parliament Act to be used. 'We don't vote on policy at party meetings,' objected Charles Clarke.

'Why not?' said Gordon.

'This has been going on for a long time,' said Andrew Mackinlay. 'Every once in a while we are getting out of our pram.'

Several people objected on the grounds that there was already a full programme for next week's meeting and that anyway Alun Michael was due to give a statement to Parliament the next day setting out the government's intentions. Gordon persisted: 'We've been round this course so many times before. We are in danger of ridicule.'

Debate grew heated. Gordon then insisted on a vote as to whether his motion should be put to the parliamentary party. We voted.

---

*In the late 1970s the Americans, anxious to justify a hugely expanded chemical warfare programme, tried to convince allies that the communists were spraying the hilltribes in northern Laos with a new and deadly form of chemical weapon, which they dubbed yellow rain. Great effort was put into convincing sceptics, but no hard evidence was ever produced. Once the programme was agreed, however, no more was ever heard of yellow rain. See Grant Evans, *The Yellow Rainmakers*, Verso (1983).

Gordon lost. 'I want the minutes to record that my motion was rejected.'

Andrew Mackinlay said, 'Last week we were duped', a reference to the row over Frank Field and the Public Accounts Committee. (Oh dear, I thought, we've still got all that to come.)

Once again, Robin came to the rescue. 'I suggest we all put down our revolvers.' He proposed by way of compromise that Alun Michael be invited to next week's meeting. Gordon wasn't having that either. He forced another vote. Again he was outvoted. By now he had rubbed just about everyone up the wrong way. There is a suspicion that he is anxious to portray himself in a heroic light and the rest of us as shoddy compromisers. The irritating thing is that we are all agreed about the necessity to resolve the hunting issue once and for all. All Gordon has succeeded in doing is portraying us as divided.

To everyone's pleasant surprise the filling of the vacancies on the Public Accounts Committee went through easily. Hilary had finally got the message that she wasn't doing herself any good and simply caved in, pausing only to profess her innocence of any jiggery pokery. No one believed her, but no one rose to the provocation. Jean Corston said afterwards that she had remarked to Gordon Brown that everyone believed he was behind the attempt to blackball Frank. Far from denying it, he had smirked and said, 'Fancy that.'

Thursday, 14 March

The place is like a morgue. Odd, we fight so hard to get here and yet so many of us seem so reluctant to remain on the premises for a moment longer than we are obliged. The more we vote ourselves extra facilities, the less use we make of them.

Sunday, 17 March
Sunderland

We have acquired a cat. A hairy, black and white cat called Bruce, despite being female. She used to belong to the family who lived next door but one. They moved and took Bruce with them, but she kept coming back and camping in our garden. She used to camp out all night in the top of the leylandii tree next to our back door. Eventually we took pity and started feeding her. We made a little house out of a cardboard box, covered with plastic and left it on the back doorstep, but Bruce refused to use it and now – much to Ngoc's annoyance – she has inveigled her way into the house. Ngoc has relented on the strict understanding that she remains confined to the storeroom at the back. Bruce, however, is not satisfied. She lurks behind the door and every time it opens makes a dash for the interior of the house only to be rounded up and deposited back in her box, but it's only a question of time. The small people, needless to say, are delighted. Meantime the pressure to buy a guinea pig has abated.

Monday, 18 March

Steve Byers boarded the train at Doncaster and sat behind me. He says that, since the election, the Cabinet has found its voice. There was a good discussion on Iraq the other day, lasting the best part of an hour.

A meeting (at his request) with Alun Michael. He's had two meetings with The Man and there is 'no enthusiasm' for using the Parliament Act to push through the existing Bill, but he believes he has found a formula which will satisfy most people. Instead of an outright ban, he is proposing two tests – cruelty and utility. The result, he believes, will be an end to stag-hunting, hare coursing, and lowland foxhunting. I am sceptical. I foresee years of litigation, during the course of which the judges will drive a coach and horses through Alun's Bill, triggering off demands for yet more legislation.

Later, we voted by another huge majority for a complete ban on hunting with dogs. For the first time The Man voted with us. According to Jean Corston, he was adamantly opposed, as recently as November, to doing anything so there has obviously been some movement. Who says the parliamentary party is powerless?

Tuesday, 19 March

There is a whiff of treason in the air. Tam Dalyell suggested at the weekend that the time may be coming for a leadership election and Mo Mowlam had a piece in Sunday's *Mirror* suggesting – outrageously – that New Labour is sleazier than the Tories. Mo, of course, is a loose cannon, but Tam is a rather more serious matter. Who does he have in mind as a stalking horse? Himself perhaps. It's early days yet, but one can foresee a scenario where, if The Man ignored all warnings and fell in behind Bush over Iraq, a challenge from Tam could inflict considerable damage. It is not as though there is no alternative. The brooding, ever-present figure of Gordon is waiting in the wings.

Friday, 22 March
Sunderland

Another parent with a daughter on heroin at the surgery this evening. The third in the last couple of months. Before that I'd never had any. He was a hard-working, decent man of about my age. He had two daughters, one of whom was successful and the other in the process of self-destruction. Although he had spent much of his savings repaying debts she had run up he was completely without bitterness. 'I love both my daughters,' he said, 'unconditionally.' His complaint was about the loan sharks who, without the merest inquiry, had doled out loans to his daughter at rates of up to 40 per cent.

Monday, 25 March

A bad day. First, a statement from Patricia Hewitt presaging redundancies in the Post Office. She provoked much merriment on the Tory benches by referring to the 'sea air at Harrogate', where they have been holding their spring conference. After that it was downhill all the way. Steve Byers followed with a statement that, contrary to all his previous pronouncements, he would be offering £300 million to buy off the Railtrack shareholders. This provoked derision on the Tory side and bewilderment on ours. At a stroke Steve has shot away the basis for much of the support he was given in his recent difficulties. I assume, although no one said so, that he has done it because he has been advised that the shareholders would have a case if they took him to court and that, even if they lost, it would drag on for years. That, however, calls into question the wisdom of putting Railtrack into administration in the first place. Steve was on his own this time. Hardly anyone on our side rose to defend him. Reminders that we wouldn't be in this mess in the first place if the Tories hadn't privatised the railways only provoked further derision. The Tories are growing increasingly shameless. 'Five years,' they kept chanting. It's true, we can't go on blaming them for ever. Our alibi is wearing increasingly thin.

Thursday, 28 March

A call from an immigration official to say that he was about to issue an order for the Ukrainian refugee family to be deported to Spain (their first port of entry to the EU). It will take effect within 15 days, unless I get on to Jeff Rooker. All I can do is plead for a few weeks more to enable the boy to complete his year at the Grindon Christian School, where the poor little chap is doing well. This is the only stability he has ever known. Now he must be uprooted and sent to Spain, where he will have to start all over again and the odds are that this, too, will end in failure and that one day a year or two from now he and his family will be unceremoniously dumped back in the Ukraine, where a life of impoverishment awaits them. It haunts me that I am powerless to help.

At midnight I turned on the radio and heard that the Queen Mother is dead.

Sunday, 31 March
Sunderland

Easter Sunday. The airwaves are thick with tributes to the Queen Mother although, to be fair, the BBC has not gone completely doolally, as was once threatened. Parliament is to be recalled next week, which is a bit daft. What is there to say? Most politicians are already struggling. Joan Maynard and I once encountered her at Fountains Abbey. Not wishing to tug our forelocks, but not wanting to seem churlish either, we hid behind a clump of shrubs until she had passed.

Wednesday, 3 April

In the afternoon I called on the local drugs action team. They are swamped – five years ago they had 46 referrals for heroin addiction; last year there were 574. In addition, they had another 843 for alcohol, amphetamines and prescribed drugs. Alcohol is still the biggest problem, but heroin is rapidly gaining.

Sunday, 17 April
Sunderland

The Man is in Texas, where he appears to have signed us up to the overthrow of Saddam Hussein – unless the tyrant comes out with his hands up, which is not very likely. Is this sensible? The Middle East is ablaze, we are by no means out of the woods in Afghanistan and yet we appear to be organising – or at least conniving at – a new war in Iraq. A provocation too far. It could mark the beginning of the end of the Blair ascendancy. If he's not careful, sooner or later he will face a challenge. Indeed, in my darker moments, I fantasise about throwing down the gauntlet myself, but do I want to be the man who puts the skids under arguably the most successful Labour administration ever? Of course I don't.

Monday, 8 April

To London on an evening train and straight to Parliament, where I couldn't resist a peek at the Queen Mother lying in state in Westminster Hall. Beefeaters in red tunics, pikes inverted, heads bowed, guarded the catafalque. Overseeing the proceedings, from the top of a flight of steps, a magnificent figure in a plumed helmet. And on either side an unending stream of silent pilgrims, flowing down the steps from St Stephen's entrance, through the Great Hall and out into

New Palace Yard. It was like stumbling onto a vast film set and so sudden. Not for us representatives of the people a six-hour wait. One moment I am hanging my coat in the cloakroom and next, wham, I am facing the flag-draped coffin topped with the crown and its wreath of white lilies. I lingered for about 15 minutes, soaking up atmosphere (hoping that Dennis Skinner wasn't standing at the back taking notes). A marked absence of deference. A few people bowed their heads as they came alongside; a woman genuflected and made the sign of the cross, but for the rest the prevailing sentiment was curiosity rather than a desire to pay homage. There were exceptions, of course. Nick Soames, looking sombre in his great coat. I bet he's been round at least half a dozen times, like a Tibetan making circuits of the Barkor, storing up merit for the next life. Especially poignant for him since, quite apart from the fact that he's an unreconstructed royalist, his grandfather was the last person to be given this treatment.

When I went home on the bus, at about 11.30 p.m., the queue still stretched through Victoria Tower Gardens, over Lambeth Bridge and back along the South Bank as far as the London Eye.

Tuesday, 9 April

To New Palace Yard to see the Queen Mother's coffin taken away to the Abbey, escorted by the princes and the exquisite sound of 126 Scots pipers. The shadow cabinet, no doubt anxious to demonstrate that they are more loyal than us, marched into Westminster Hall in morning dress. This is a Tory occasion *par excellence* and yet only Iain Duncan Smith had an invitation to the service, whereas from our side the entire Cabinet was present in the Abbey. It must have been very galling. From my room on Upper Corridor South I could hear the choir and the Archbishop of Canterbury's tribute relayed to the crowds outside. When the service was over, I came down and stood by the main gate, watching the captains and the kings depart.

In the afternoon the select committee met to consider our drugs report. Ours was the only meeting in the entire building. Everything else having been cancelled out of deference to the Great Event. Progress was slow. There was an argument over reclassifying cannabis.

Angela Watkinson was flatly opposed. David Winnick wanted us to go all the way and legalise. Humfrey Malins, who I hope to take with us, wobbled about all over the place. It was the same when we came to Ecstasy, which most of us think should be downgraded from A to B. Again Angela objected. Again Humfrey wobbled. 'I know it's right,' he kept saying, 'but I just can't go that far – yet.' More than once, when we reached an impasse, David Cameron came to the rescue. The more I see of him, the more I like. He's bright, personable and refreshingly open-minded. No doubt he'll soon be whisked away to the Tory front bench.

Wednesday, 10 April

To the meeting of the parliamentary party to hear The Man. The press has been building this up as a confrontation over Iraq and so there was a big turnout, larger than at any time since the election. Dennis Skinner was the warm-up man. He did not mince words: 'In the Labour Party generally, as well as in the higher echelons, most people can't stand the sight of George W. Bush. Some of us don't think he was elected – he had a worse result than Mugabe. And some of us think he's not far short of being a bastard.' He added to laughter, 'I'm not saying what *I* think.'

The Man, as ever, addressed the big picture. 'Progressive', 'moderate', 'centre left' were the watchwords. Next week's budget, he said, will set out the case for increased tax. This, not Iraq, will be the principal battle of this Parliament. 'It will be a huge test of whether or not this country is a progressive democracy.' As for George Bush, 'With all due respect to Dennis, I don't choose the President of the United States or any other country, but I will work with the leader of any country to represent the interests of this country.' On Iraq: 'Saddam is developing weapons of mass destruction. Allowing him to carry on is not an option. Whatever we do, we will do in the same calm way as we did in Afghanistan.'

Not all the complaints came from Usual Suspects. Joan Ruddock said there was no basis in international law for an attack on Iraq; nor was there evidence that it posed a threat. All neighbouring states were against an attack. Clive Soley said we must act on Palestine first. Alice Mahon wanted a commitment that any action on Iraq would be through the UN. Michael Connarty accused The Man of sending out two different messages – gung ho in the United States, reasonable here. We must solve Israeli aggression against Palestinians first, he said. This attracted a few 'hear, hear's, but there was no sign of the promised uprising.

In response, he flatly denied putting out different messages on either side of the Atlantic, adding, 'However, when the British media go to Texas, they are not interested in a nuanced, balanced message. They say, "He's got a problem with his backbenchers; how can we make it worse?" You have to understand the degree of frustration there is on the right. They think they should be in government. We're supposed to be principled people – but in Opposition. The thing they get down on their knees and pray for is that the Labour Party will tear itself apart. It's a game. So far we've been intelligent enough to avoid that. If we are to govern, we have to weather short-term unpopularity so that we are still celebrating in ten years' time.' He sat down to thunderous applause. With one leap he was free – for now at least.

A sandwich lunch with Martin Narey, head of the Prison Service. Decent, humane, level-headed. We couldn't hope to find a better man to put in charge of the nation's jails. His main message was that the rapid growth of the prison population was putting at risk all recent progress on overcrowding, purposeful activity and education. 'I have 12,000 inmates having to defecate in front of one another. Sooner or later I am going to lose a human rights case.' About 65 per cent of the prison population are either illiterate or semi-literate, many are school drop-outs. The huge rise in school exclusions is making matters worse. Some head teachers, he said, are promoting their schools on the basis of a tough exclusion policy. Many of the excluded were destined to end up in prison: 'You might just as well book them a place now.' As if all this wasn't difficult enough, he was expected to return 1 per cent of his budget to the Treasury every year as part of Gordon's so-called efficiency savings.

A brief moment of merriment at the parliamentary committee this afternoon. Robin Cook came in carrying a hot drink. The Man peered at it. 'Is that cocoa?'

'No, Tony, it's cappuccino. I'm very New Labour. Cocoa's Old Labour.'

'Robin does sail close to the wind,' Jean said to me afterwards. 'He did a lot of lobbying against Derry's Lords reform plans.'

Doug Hoyle again raised Iraq. 'What has changed? What evidence is there that Saddam poses a greater threat now than he did a year ago?'

'We know,' replied The Man, 'that he is continuing to develop chemical and biological weapons and there's no doubt that he's developing ballistic missile capability. What has changed in America is that they think they were negligent over al-Qaida and they are not going to be caught out again.'

'Afghanistan was not an unalloyed triumph,' I said. 'We've unleashed the warlords and they are causing mayhem. We should concentrate on sorting that out before opening a new front.'

'We're not even at the stage of options yet,' said The Man. 'Iraq is just on the agenda for discussion.'

There was a brief discussion on the Middle East. Robin said, 'At some point the penny is going to drop that the Israelis are creating another generation of suicide bombers.'

Somewhere – not necessarily in relation to Iraq, but to life in general – The Man remarked, 'I am basically an interventionist. If you've got the power, use it.'

Friday, 12 April
Sunderland

Customers at this evening's surgery included a plump young woman with a ten-month-old baby desperate to be evacuated from her home on a local housing estate. She has come under attack from local youths, one of whom threatened her with a knife. And a young couple with six children (all boys aged under 12) who are under siege in their home. Their property has been repeatedly vandalised. They are spat at and abused in the street. Their offence? They are comers-in. He's a southerner, a former soldier. So much for any idea of a kinder, gentler north.

It is intolerable that people should have to live like this. Once again we shall end up evacuating victims, rather than evicting villains. Why are we so powerless? The police – lately at least – are doing their best, but the courts are either unwilling to deal with this plague of criminal youths or they are incapable of doing so. As a result they are laughing at us. In four years only three anti-social behaviour orders have been granted in the whole of Wearside. Why, for heaven's sake? It's not as though we are short of candidates.

Tuesday, 16 April

A letter from Jeff Rooker refusing my plea for the Savchenkos to be allowed to stay so the boy can stay in school until the summer. I went immediately to find him. He was on his feet in the Lords, guiding through the Police Reform Bill. I waited until the dinner adjournment and then pounced. 'A couple of months, that's all I'm looking for,' I said. 'This is the only stability this little lad has ever known and I just want him to be able to depart with dignity.'

Jeff didn't hesitate. 'Have you got that?' he said to a Private Secretary who was loitering. 'Fix it.' And that was that.

Wednesday, 17 April

Gordon's Budget has made everyone happy. Our side because we've finally decided to bite the bullet. The Tories because they can accuse us of a return to tax and spend, just like the good old days. No one is quite sure how it will play with the punters. Although the polls have been saying for some time that most people would be willing to pay more tax to fund decent public services, no one can be sure that, when the chips are down, they will not all turn back into Tories. Certainly, Gordon has hit the prosperous fairly hard – the family Mullin, for example, will have to shell out another £600 a year.

We discussed the latest funding row – the Department of Health have awarded a contract for smallpox vaccine to a company run by a

Labour donor. 'It has all the hallmarks of a cock-up,' said Andrew Mackinlay at this afternoon's meeting of the parliamentary committee. Not so, said The Man. The correct procedures had been followed to the letter. The contract was awarded on the basis of advice from officials. He added, 'I don't know what to do; whatever we do to make the process transparent only makes it worse.'

After The Man had gone there was an amusing little discussion about the unseemly jockeying for seats, within range of television cameras, that preceded the Budget. Jean said she had witnessed some ugly scenes which had taken place within sight of the hacks. The parliamentary private secretaries to senior ministers had been unable to sit behind their masters because the places were already occupied and the occupants refused to budge, even at the request of the whips. Someone was overheard to say, 'You are sitting in the seat I inherited from Barry Jones,' as if the hereditary system applies in the Lower House.

We arrived at no particular conclusion, except that Alan Howarth was instructed not to minute the discussion for fear of inviting ridicule.

Thursday, 18 April

To the Chamber to hear Alan Milburn explain how he is proposing to spend Gordon's largesse. The Man and Gordon came in and sat beside him to mark the significance of the occasion. To begin with Alan seemed flustered. His statement contained a bizarre reference to 'the sound of bed-pans being dropped in Tredegar' which caused much merriment on the Tory side and bemusement on ours. At the mention of plans to set up a health service commission, they shouted 'More bureaucrats.' Alan was on better form when he challenged the Tories to say what they would do. The truth, which they daren't face up to, is that an insurance-based system would cost even more then we are proposing to spend. All the same, the Tories seemed in remarkably high spirits. They clearly think we have dealt them a winning card. Our side, by contrast, were subdued. Can it be that, deep down, we suspect the Tories may be right?

A fax from Jeff Rooker's office, saying he had changed his mind about the Savchenkos. Under the terms of the Dublin Convention (by which asylum seekers can be returned to their first port of call) they had to be sent back to Spain within a month of all procedures being exhausted. I rang Jeff's private office to ask on what date the clock started ticking and eventually I received a call from a man who explained that they should have been removed in November 2000. In which case, said I, what difference would another couple of months make? Alas, he explained, he was honour-bound. It was such a civilised dialogue that, in an attempt to inject a note of reality, I said that this was a small tragedy. 'Most of these cases are,' he said blithely. So that's it then. I have failed. Any day now the little fellow will be taken away from his school and his playmates and the only stability he has ever known and, with his distraught parents, bundled onto a plane bound for Spain with no idea of what awaits them.

At my suggestion, the good Christian lady who has been helping the family is arranging for the Savchenkos' papers, giving evidence of the persecution they suffered in the Ukraine, to be translated into Spanish. I have also written a covering letter, 'To Whom It May Concern', setting out their case. That, too, is being translated. Finally, I wrote out a cheque for £50 so that at least they will have some money in their pockets when they arrive.

Saturday, 20 April
Sunderland

To the County Hotel at Durham to address the annual dinner of the Crimewriters Association. Giles and Lisanne Radice were there. Lisanne told me that when the Treasury Select Committee, which Giles used to chair, published a report that was anything less than a perfect replica of the official position, Gordon Brown used to ring up Giles at midnight, incandescent with rage, f-ing and blinding, demanding retractions, slamming the phone down. At times, she said, it was so bad that Giles stopped answering the phone when it rang after midnight because he knew it would be Gordon. Giles said, 'He had no concept of the proprieties that should exist between a secretary of state and a select committee.'

Tuesday, 23 April

Ngoc reports that Emma, observing that Bruce spends most of the day sleeping and eating, has declared that she wishes she were a cat.

'But cats don't have nice clothes and good fun like you do.'

'No, and they don't have homework either.'

Wednesday, 24 April

To Buckingham Gate to see the law officers, Harriet Harman and Peter Goldsmith. For Harriet this must be like having died and gone to heaven. Plush offices overlooking the tradesmen's entrance of the Palace. Highly paid, not too strenuous, somewhat removed from the cut and thrust of day-to-day politics (which I sense she misses). I am not sure what the law officers do, beyond vaguely floating around offering advice to the government. Harriet's predecessor, Ross Cranston, told me that he had visited all 42 regional offices of the Crown Prosecution Service, which suggests that he was having trouble filling his time. I suspect Harriet is, too. Today's meeting – to discuss deaths in custody – was at her suggestion. Attorney Generals are usually grand figures like Patrick Mayhew, but Peter Goldsmith seems refreshingly normal (although I am told he was until his preferment a million-a-year QC and has just bought a house in Queen Anne's Gate). He is from the same stable as Charlie Falconer. Bright, rich, decent – and A Friend of The Man.

I walked back across the park. In front of Buckingham Palace a team of gardeners were uprooting the magnificent, and still blooming, display of red tulips set in beds of yellow antirrhinums. Sheer vandalism. 'Why?' I asked a young woman standing atop a huge pile of uprooted tulips in the back of a truck, treading them as though they were grapes.

'They will all die soon,' she said pleasantly.

'And what will happen to the bulbs?'

'Compost,' she said and resumed trampling.

On the way home in the evening, I ran into Bernard Jenkin, who has just returned from a 36-hour trip to Afghanistan. Needless to say, he is not happy. We will be stuck there for a minimum of two years, he says, and many of the Europeans there are already talking about ten. 'We need to make clear to the Afghans that we can't go on holding their hands for ever.' Bernard, of course, wouldn't have gone there in the first place. Or into the Balkans. We should only intervene, he says, when our national interest is at stake and his definition of the national interest is narrow.

Monday, 29 April

To the Treasury with Bill Etherington for a cup of tea with Gordon Brown, ostensibly to discuss the fate of Federal Mogul, although in reality there is nothing to discuss since that is all over bar the shouting. I mentioned Dewhirst's complaint about the tariff imposed by the Americans on menswear imports and Gordon promised to make inquiries. He also undertook to inquire which government departments were in the process of relocating work out of London in the hope that something might be pushed in the direction of Sunderland. If anything comes of that, it will have been time well spent.

Rang Sally Morgan at Number 10 in the hope of persuading The Man to open a new school in Sunderland. 'What do you think of this child benefit story?' she asked. (The papers are reporting that The Man was considering docking the child benefit of the parents of out-of-control youths who refused to co-operate with efforts to tame their offspring.) She said that far from being a local election gimmick, as some unkind people are suggesting, it had leaked out by accident. 'We are very depressed about it. It is still being worked up, but no one is suggesting it should be applied widely. It is only intended to put a kick in the system for parents who are colluding with their children's misbehaviour.'

I said that if we wanted to make an impact on anti-social behaviour, we should cut off the supply of housing benefit to rogue landlords who take no interest in either the condition of their property or the behaviour of their tenants. 'Why don't you send Tony a note and I'll put it in his box,' she said. I will indeed. Just as well I'm not a junior minister, otherwise I could never hope for such access.

Tuesday, 30 April

Mrs Rogers, a friend of the Savchenkos, rang to say that they were taken away on Sunday. Although we were expecting five days' notice, police and immigration officers turned up at 8 a.m. and gave them an hour to pack. They were put in a cold, windowless van. No one knew they had gone until next day when a man from Immigration came to return the keys to their flat. Later, Mrs Rogers had a phone call from Mr Savchenko to say that they were being detained near London and would be deported to Spain in ten days. When she went last night with the pastor from the local church to clear up the Savchenkos' flat they found a note on Sasha's bed bequeathing his few possessions to the pastor's children: 'I leave my Lego to Mary and Samuel ... Pokemon to Samuel ...' As though he were about to die. The pastor broke down and wept when he read the note. So did I.

The Savchenkos were/are (I keep thinking of them as though they are dead) such dignified, decent people. They would have made model citizens and the little chap was doing so well at school ... I can't get them out of my mind. If only I could have saved them. I keep going over the arguments I might have made.

I tapped out a note on housing benefit and rogue landlords for The Man and sent it over to Sally Morgan. For good measure, I added a paragraph about air weapons.

Don Touhig, who dined recently with Neil and Glenys Kinnock, says Neil recounted an occasion at a state banquet at Windsor where, after dinner, he and Glenys found themselves sitting either side of the Queen Mother. 'Mr Kinnock,' she said, 'may I say something in absolute confidence?' And then, *sotto voce*: 'Don't trust the Germans.'

Wednesday, 1 May

Andrew Mackinlay dropped a little bombshell at this afternoon's meeting of the parliamentary committee. Apparently, under the Freedom of Information Act, by January 2005 MPs' expenses will be subject to public scrutiny, retrospectively. Goodness knows what mayhem that will cause. 'We are in a jam,' said Robin Cook. 'Few members have yet tumbled to the juggernaut heading their way.' He said he had been advised that we could probably get away with publishing headline figures and it would be desirable to start publishing a year before the deadline so that any fuss would have died down come the general election. It was agreed not to minute the discussion.

Later, in the division lobby, David Hanson (Parliamentary Private Secretary to the Prime Minister) whispered that The Man was interested in my suggestion for sorting out rogue landlords. 'I think he's bitten,' he said.

Thursday, 2 May
Sunderland

Local elections. I spent a couple of hours with a loudspeaker being driven around Hendon by Lennie Lamb, urging people to vote. A few unpleasant yoblets shouted 'BNP' after us, but indifference was the overwhelming sentiment. It is the same all over the country. No serious hostility. Only indifference. I fear we shall be massacred.

Friday, 3 May

The feared massacre never came, although we lost Hull and Norwich to the Liberals and the Tories gained about 300 seats, but it could have been a lot worse. In Hartlepool a monkey was elected as mayor, which is very satisfactory. Another of New Labour's foolish wheezes – elected mayors – bites the dust.

Saturday, 4 May

Sarah has spent £16 of her own money on a luxurious basket for Bruce in place of the old cardboard box she has been sleeping in, but Bruce will have nothing to do with it, preferring to spend last night outside on the bird table. 'I am very cross with that cat,' declared Sarah. 'She is very ignorant.'

Tuesday, 7 May

A handwritten note from The Man in response to my memorandum on housing benefit and on air weapons. It reads: 'I agree strongly with what you say and thank you for the sensible and constructive terms in which you say it. I am looking into both issues urgently and will report back.'

Wednesday, 8 May

Mrs Rogers left a message on the office answerphone to say that the Savchenkos had been deported on Monday and that, contrary to what we had been assured, no one in Spain was expecting them. Instead they were simply waved through and spent Monday night camped at Madrid airport. No one knows where they are now. I was livid when I heard this and immediately rang Immigration to demand an explanation. However the official who had insisted both to Jeff Rooker and I that they had to leave immediately on account of the Dublin Convention was away at a conference in Brussels. 'I am sure he has a mobile,' I said. 'Call him.' But no, he could not be rung. 'Then call his opposite number in Spain.' But she was in Brussels, too. 'Then ring someone else in Spain.' That wasn't possible either, 'because our only Spanish speaker is away, too'. And so it went on. The woman was courteous, but it was hard work generating a sense of urgency. The Savchenkos were just names on a closed file as far as she was concerned, but then of course she has never had to look them in the eye.

Thursday, 9 May

Steve Byers is in trouble again. The Tories are making a huge hullaballoo about the fact that in February he was claiming that Martin Six-smith had resigned whereas it now turns out that he is still, nominally at least, employed by the Department and that the terms of his departure have only just been agreed. Pretty small beer really. It's perfectly obvious to anyone of average common sense that Steve's error was inadvertent and based, although he cannot say so, on misinformation from officials. However, an enormous palaver was organised. Steve was summoned to make another statement. The Tories were shouting and bawling, working themselves up into a huge, entirely synthetic, frenzy. Our side weren't much better. To be fair, Steve's statement was a little naff and would have benefited from a note of humility. When my turn came, I just poked fun at the Tories and suddenly the bubble burst. Our side were very chuffed. 'You changed the mood,' Mike O'Brien said afterwards. 'The *coup de grâce*,' said Keith Hill. The truth is that Steve is by no means out of the woods yet. Three years ago I considered him a potential leader, but now he's a busted flush. In politics you never can tell.

Most of the day was spent in the select committee, completing our drugs report. Angela Watkinson had tabled 47 amendments, which took up most of the time. Fortunately, David Cameron has signed up to the reform agenda and so there is no danger of our splitting along party lines, which I had feared. In the end even Humfrey Malins, who was wobbling at one stage, voted with us so all is well. We are on course to make a difference.

The Savchenkos have been located. They are in a Red Cross hostel in Madrid where they are safe for the next two months or so. Goodness knows what will become of them after that.

Friday, 10 May
Sunderland

Customers at the surgery this evening included a young man called Rambo, an asylum seeker from Goma in the eastern Congo. He is half Tutsi, which, he reckons, puts his life at risk were he to be returned to Kinshasa. He made his way to Germany, where his asylum claim was rejected and then to England, where he has been since December 1999. Immigration attempted to bundle him onto a plane back to Germany dressed only in nightclothes and handcuffed, but the pilot refused to carry him after objections from passengers. He then spent four months in detention before being dispersed to Sunderland. The man is terrified and absolutely desperate. He was with me for nearly an hour. 'Please help me,' he kept saying, but what can I do? I have run out of ideas. In the end I gave him a tenner and sent him away promising vaguely to make further inquiries, but where and of whom? These cases haunt me. We've grown used to watching horrors on television and then, after a couple of minutes' ritual sympathy, getting on with our own lives. But now the victims are no longer thousands of miles away. They do not go away when we push the 'off' button. They are here, wandering our streets, popping up in our lives. They can talk to us in our own language. They bleed, as we would, were we to change places. One day, who knows, we might.

Saturday, 11 May

There has been another serious train crash, at Potters Bar, only a few miles downline from Hatfield, which was the scene of one of the last big ones. How long, I wonder, before the Tories try to pin the blame on Steve Byers?

Tuesday, 21 May

Unless I am very much mistaken, Peter Mandelson isn't talking to me. He cuts me dead whenever our paths cross (which is not often). The other day I was sitting with Sue Nye and Sally Dobson in the atrium of Portcullis House when Peter came up and chatted amiably for several minutes without the slightest acknowledgement of my existence. Obviously it is a skill he has perfected over many years. I can guess my offence: that letter I wrote to Sir Anthony Hammond confirming that Mike O'Brien had recounted to me his version of the telephone call that led to Peter's downfall. There are a lot of people Peter no longer talks to so I am in illustrious company. It must be very wearing having to remember with whom you are on speaking terms and who you are ignoring. I couldn't keep it up for more than a few days.

Wednesday, 22 May

Our much-leaked, long-awaited drugs report is published this morning and has attracted widespread attention. The BBC and several newspapers are leading with it. I was up bright and early and gave about twenty interviews, starting with *Today*. The reviews are generally favourable. 'The MPs … have done the nation a service as the first substantial group of elected politicians to join an adult debate,' says the *Standard*. Not everyone was up for an adult debate: 'Soft MPs want junkies to get safe houses,' screams the ludicrous *Daily Record* under a front page headed 'Smack in the face'. Unfortunately, Blunkett has muddied the waters by issuing a statement refusing to contemplate recategorising Ecstasy and saying there are no plans for safe injecting houses. Silly man, having called for 'an adult debate on drugs', he promptly closes it down.

Tony Banks says he is being pressed by Charles Clarke to run against Ken for Mayor. He has set various conditions, one of which is that he be allowed to renegotiate the deal on the London Underground – he is seeing Gordon about that shortly. Also, he doesn't want to be forgotten if he loses. He plans to stand down at the next election and wants to go to the Lords, which will be a first for a founder member of the Campaign Group. Should he run? How badly does he want the job? Dislike of Ken and his monstrous ego seemed to be Tony's principal motivation. Not, by itself, a good enough reason. My advice was 'Don't' on the grounds (a) that Tony is likely to lose (although he is undoubtedly a credible candidate) and (b) that I am not convinced he really wants to be mayor.

Tuesday, 28 May

Steve Byers has resigned. The bastards have got him at last. I guess it was inevitable. He wouldn't have made it past the next reshuffle. 'Don't budge,' I said to The Man at the parliamentary committee two weeks ago, but he didn't react. He knew we were approaching the point of no return. A new piece of nonsense was appearing every day. To be fair, Steve has made mistakes. None by itself a resigning matter but in the end it was sheer attrition. As he said himself, he was becoming a distraction. We shall all have to grit our teeth while nationwide rejoicing is organised by the junk journalists, egged on by the awful Theresa May. Who will they go for next?

Wednesday, 29 May
Sunderland

To the County Hotel, Durham, to collect Tony Benn, who is performing to packed houses the length and breadth of the country – last night Middlesbrough, tonight South Shields. I gave him a whistlestop tour of Sunderland, highlights and lowlights, from the mansions of Ashbrooke to the boarded, vandalised houses in the darker part of Pennywell. Then home to a delicious vegetarian lunch prepared by Ngoc at which we were joined by Kevin, Pam Wortley and the office staff. There was a brief excitement when, after he failed to extinguish his pipe, it burned a hole in his jacket pocket, filling the house with fumes. He took it out onto the front step and I poured water over it. Ten minutes later, when we were out, he might have burned the house down.

Saturday, 1 June
Whitsun, St Boswells, Roxburghshire

Our host, Mrs Dale, says that a week ago a monster cat – of the sort occasionally sighted in the West Country – climbed into her walled garden and murdered most of her ducks. One of her guests, who witnessed the slaughter, said it was the size of a labrador and that it played with the ducks as a cat plays with mice before killing them. I found a rotting duck's head, presumably one of the casualties, in a saucepan. The survivors are now locked up at night.

Monday, 3 June

Awoke to dark skies and torrential rain. By afternoon, however, the weather had miraculously cleared and we spent the afternoon at Sir Walter Scott's house, Abbotsford, where the little people paddled in the river for an hour and attempted unsuccessfully to divert the course of the Tweed by building a dam. This evening on television we watched the pop concert in Buckingham Palace gardens, the highlight of which was Barry Humphries introducing the Queen as 'the Jubilee girl'. Charles made a crass little speech about the wealth of British talent without referring to the foreigners who had flown halfway round the world to take part. The Beach Boys looked very pissed off. I would have been, too.

'Who's that man who follows the Queen everywhere?' asked Emma pointing at Prince Philip.

Tuesday, 4 June

A fascinating little ritual takes place outside our front window at breakfast time each morning. Griselda, a huge, greedy, chestnut mare, waits by the fence for Mrs Dale to appear with her daily ration of oats. Behind, at a respectful distance, the other, smaller horse lingers and behind her a sad old donkey who never really gets a look in. As soon as Mrs Dale appears, Griselda starts pushing and shoving, trying to get her nose in the bucket, watched enviously by the donkey who brays quietly. At this point the goats and Jasper, the big black pig, come running, closely followed by the little pink cluny pig whose round belly almost touches the ground. Meanwhile Mrs Dale has released the turkeys and a bunch of vicious, arrogant geese who come running to join the melee. Finally, when the horses have had their fill and moved off, a flock of crows who have been watching from nearby beech trees, swoop and search out the few undiscovered grains, chased at intervals by the geese. All this takes about 20 minutes and by the time it is over not a single morsel is unaccounted for.

Saturday, 8 June

On the way home we called at Bemersyde, home of the Haigs, where we were the only visitors apart from a couple of fishermen. On the way up from the river we encountered the laird, a pleasant, erect old fellow who told us that the family had been in residence since 1150.

Monday, 10 June
Sunderland

This morning's post brought a postcard from Lord Haig. 'If you are coming this way again,' he writes, 'please let me know. I would be happy to show you and your family the house – and without the £2!' He must have gone back to the house, looked me up and got his card in the post even before we were off the premises. I shall certainly take up his offer.

Westminster

Everyone is congratulating or commiserating in the wake of the Byers reshuffle. Mike O'Brien, who has been given a job at the Foreign Office, is looking happier than he has done for ages. Angela Eagle is looking very down. There she was working hard, doing (or so she thought) a reasonable job and with no inkling of what was to come. The Man told her she had had a good run and that was that. At the lower end of the pecking order, reshuffles are an entirely random process. No one had anything against her. Her name just fell off the end of the page because, once the new faces had been accommodated, there was no one to speak up for her. Unlike Michael Wills, whose miraculous resurrection is the subject of much derision in the Tea Room. He obviously has someone very important (no prizes for guessing *who*) to speak for him. No sooner had he been sacked than he was reinstated, *sans* salary, in the Home Office. It couldn't have been more blatant.

Tuesday, 11 June

We are debating another Asylum Bill, the fourth in the last decade. 'Unless we are worried about the gene pool, what's the problem?' asks Brian Sedgemore, in the privacy of the Tea Room. 'Most asylum seekers are dynamic, hard-working, educated people of the sort we badly need to refresh our ageing, lethargic population.' Not a view that would command widespread support in Sunderland. Neil Gerrard, who I ran into on the way in this morning, is sceptical that Blunkett's Bill will be any more effective than the previous three. Says Neil, 'A chap from Nigeria turned up at my surgery the other day. I made representations on his behalf five years ago. He was turned down and yet he's still here. What's the point? Why did I bother? I should just have told him to keep his head down.'

Wednesday, 12 June

A quiet talk with The Man's man, Robert Hill, who wanted my views on the reshuffle ('because the Prime Minister values your opinion' - how many times have I heard that?). I said there was some dissatisfaction at Angela Eagle's treatment and derision at Michael Wills's reappearance (Robert had the grace to concede that there was embarrassment in Number 10 at this) and that, while there was no problem with the promotion of David Miliband or David Lammy, there should be a limit to the number of clever young men and women on the inside track. 'There is also merit in hanging on to a few fifty-somethings who can remember what happened last time around.' I also said I hoped that there might be a way back for Steve Byers. Robert said this was possible, but not until our third term. He added that Steve's Permanent Secretary, Richard Mottram, was very lucky to survive.

How, I inquired, does The Man assess the performance of ministers? According to Robert, Hilary Armstrong prepares a report, the permanent secretaries feed in via the Cabinet Secretary and David Hanson, Sally Morgan and himself also offer their opinions. Then, seizing the moment, I revealed that I still entertained hopes of returning to government, though not as an under-secretary. I said I wanted a job that required a mixture of competence and idealism such as Environment or International Development. I was careful to emphasise that this was without prejudice to the present incumbents, both of whom were doing excellent work. Robert said they had considered moving one – he didn't say which (Michael, I suspect) – this time round, but decided to leave it another year. He added, 'I need to get you together with Tony.' We shall see. I am not holding my breath.

To the Chelsea Arts Club for lunch with my old friends Brian Eads and Claes Bratt. Claes says that for the first time the Swedes are beginning to discuss the great unmentionable: immigration. Gothenburg, his home town, was now 25 per cent recent migrants and some, especially the Muslims, were starting to demand that the Swedes adapt to their culture rather than the other way round. The Swedes had already conceded that immigrant children had a right to be taught in their own language. Now there were demands for Muslim public holidays to be observed, there had been an outbreak of so-called honour killings and an increase in crime, attributed to an influx of Kosovar Albanians. According to Claes, Sweden's liberal ethos was being stretched to the limit.

Thursday, 13 June

To Torquay to appear on *Question Time*, in the company of Menzies Campbell, Teresa Gorman, John Maples and a pleasant but vacuous young woman called Emma Jones, who has a column in the *Sun*. A long way to go to be murdered in front of several million people. The audience was almost wholly hostile. I was isolated, inept and failed to land a single punch. Nothing I said attracted more than the merest ripple of applause.

Tuesday, 18 June

The Harmsworth Lie Machine has gone into overdrive. 'And now: the great hospital blunders cover up,' screeches this morning's *Mail*. 'Even more NHS blunders,' rages the early edition of the *Standard* (which has reverted to type since Max Hastings departed). By mid-afternoon, however, the *Standard* had found another outlet for its boundless indignation: an unexceptional remark by Cherie Blair at a Medical Aid for Palestine event which unfortunately coincided with a horrendous new suicide bomb in Israel. However, the nonsense over the Queen Mother's funeral, which raged all weekend, has all but disappeared.* Yesterday the Tories were calling for Alastair's head and demanding a statement. Today they've dropped the subject. So have

---

* A wholly synthetic row sparked by the spurious allegation that Tony Blair had lobbied for a more prominent seat.

their friends in the media. Almost as if someone has flicked a switch. Which may be exactly what has happened. My guess is that the Palace has sent word, probably via Nicholas Soames, that Her Majesty is none too pleased to see the memory of her mother's funeral dragged through the mud. Soames told me that he had been on to the Tory Chief Whip demanding that the dogs be called off.

Robert Harris has a piece in today's *Telegraph* suggesting that Gordon will be leader by this time next year. The boldest prediction I have yet seen.

Monday, 24 June

To Number 10, with the parliamentary committee, to see The Man. Security has been stepped up since our last visit. All visitors now have to pass through a metal detector after which there is a policeman cradling a sub-machine gun. According to Hilary Armstrong, the security services recently picked up word of a threat to his life – from a Chechen – which they are taking seriously. He now has a motor cycle escort everywhere he goes and the children are driven to school by armed detectives.

The Man was looking tired, yawning and rubbing his eyes. As we were leaving he said, 'You made a big impression on Euan on *Question Time* the other night.' Amazing. I thought I'd made a hash of it. Good old Euan. What a perceptive fellow he must be. The Man added, 'I didn't think Euan was interested in politics, but he's even talking about canvassing.'

A chat with Treasury Minister Dawn Primarolo in the Tea Room. She says that Gordon has changed since the death of baby Jennifer. 'He recognises there are other things in life.' Does he, indeed?

Wednesday, 26 June

George Foulkes, who has just been made a privy counsellor, tells the following tale. Some time ago Clare Short and Mo Mowlam were attending upon the Queen when Clare's pager started vibrating. Clare surreptitiously checked the message. Whereupon Her Majesty looked up and inquired, 'Someone important?'

Monday, 1 July

The Americans have bombed a wedding party in Afghanistan, killing goodness knows how many people. Entire families have been wiped out. They have reacted with the usual arrogance. First, they said they came under anti-aircraft fire, which is obviously nonsense. Even now they are refusing to apologise, implying that it was somehow the fault of the victims. We've seen it all before. In Cambodia, Iraq, Kosovo and they always behave in the same way. As if the only lives that matter are American. No wonder they are hated.

Tuesday, 2 July

Ngoc recounts the following exchange with Emma last night:
'Is Daddy here?'
'Daddy's in London. You know he goes to London every Monday.'
'Oh yes, I forgot.'
'Would you like Dad to work in Sunderland so he comes home every night?'
'No. I like to tell people that my Dad's in Parliament.'
'Why?'
'Because Daddy is famous.'
'Is he?'
'A bit.'

Wednesday, 3 July

At the parliamentary committee, the main topic was the growing list of disagreements with the Americans. The latest is that they are threatening to collapse various peacekeeping operations, starting in Bosnia, if they are not granted immunity from the proposed international criminal court. As regards the tariffs on steel and textiles, The Man said it was straightforward protectionism, pork barrel politics. 'The

Democrats are as bad as the Republicans – I lost count of the number of weird conversations I had with Bill Clinton about cashmere sweaters and bananas.' However, he warned, we should beware of the Tory agenda which was to suggest that we had to make a choice between Europe and America and that a Labour government couldn't do business with a Republican President. It wasn't true. In Canada recently, at the G8 summit, relations between himself and George Bush had been as warm as ever. He added that, on the Middle East, he had made clear to Bush that we would only make progress if everyone was genuine about a Palestinian state and that we would work with whoever the Palestinians elected.

I raised the latest atrocity in Afghanistan. Couldn't we at least persuade the Americans to compensate the victims? 'There's a long history of these accidents,' I said. 'The Americans are becoming increasingly gung-ho and their lack of contrition only makes matters worse.'

The Man said quietly, 'I don't disagree with that.'

Monday, 8 July

To Brussels in the company of half a dozen members of the select committee. Our purpose, to unravel the mysteries of the European Union's Justice and Home Affairs 'pillar' in which we are supposed to take an interest. The clerks have supplied us with a blue file containing everything we need to know, but my eyes glaze over at the very mention of the Article 36 committee and words like 'communitarisation'. Until now I have managed to avoid Brussels. I last passed this way in the summer of 1969 when Sue H and I set off on our ill-fated trip to Greece in my old Ford van. All I can recall is a series of underpasses. Dinner with Nigel Sheinwald (Harrow Grammar School, Balliol; three sons at Eton) at the residence on the Rue Ducale. A rising star. Charming, confident, brilliant – reminded me of Portillo. He gave every appearance of taking us seriously even though we must have seemed an unimpressive bunch, given our hazy grasp of matters European.

Tuesday, 9 July
Brussels

Wall-to-wall meetings – with the head of the Justice and Home Affairs secretariat for the Council of Ministers, a sleek Belgian whose name apparently translates as 'grave-digger'; the Danish permanent representative, who amused us with mimicry of his Italian colleagues; the president of Euro-Just, once a public prosecutor in Sussex; and finally with Commissioner Vitorino, a balding, diminutive, rotund bundle of energy from Portugal who cheered us all up. 'A sense of humour,' he says, 'is essential for survival in this place.' I bet it is.

In between we were entertained to lunch at the European Parliament by a couple of our Euro colleagues. The Parliament building is a gargantuan, soulless, monument to powerlessness. Gaining admission involved lengthy rigmarole (passports confiscated and returned on departure). 'How,' I asked one of our hosts, 'does a citizen who wishes to see European democracy at work gain entry?' He scratched his head. In his eight years as a Euro MP no constituent has ever contacted him with such a request. And as for turning up unannounced, that is out of the question.

Nothing unpremeditated takes place in this building. In the chamber every speech is strictly timed, typed out triple-spaced, read into the record and simultaneously translated into goodness knows how many languages before being lost in the ether. Has a single memorable speech ever been made in this building?

The Justice and Home Affairs committee consists of 40 members with another 40 in reserve. How does the chair cope. 'Don't worry,' I am assured, 'rarely more than half turn up at any one time.' And every few weeks the entire circus decamps from Brussels to another gargantuan, soulless, powerless monstrosity in Strasbourg. This is William Cobbett's 'tax-eating' on an awesome scale. And to what end? Nothing, nothing, nothing would tempt me to be a Euro MP.

Wednesday, 10 July

To Queen Anne's Gate to see the Home Secretary about this afternoon's statement in response to our drugs report. He is proposing to reclassify cannabis, thereby reducing the penalties for use, but to double those for dealing. He is willing to look at managed prescribing though not – 'for the moment' – safe injecting houses. Unfortunately the waters have been muddied by the so-called 'Drugs Tsar', Keith Hellawell, announcing, on the *Today* programme, his resignation in protest against the cannabis decision. In fact he was on his way out anyway – his two-day-a-week contract was due to expire in three weeks. The statement itself was not well received. People fired off in all directions. Some wanted more. Some less. Letwin, unusually, was hopeless. He made no mention of heroin or crack, which are the real problem, and concentrated instead on playing to the tabloids over cannabis – contrary, I suspect, to his instincts, which are usually sound. To listen to the nonsense one would have thought Blunkett was proposing to make cannabis a sacrament. Kate Hoey kept on about 'sending out the wrong message to our young'. If people like her would stop peddling the wrong message, there wouldn't be any confusion. Peter Lilley scored a bull's-eye: what we are doing, he said, is leaving cannabis in the hands of the same people who deal in heroin and crack. He's surely right. The more I think about it, we should legalise and regulate. Though goodness knows what hysteria that would trigger.

At the parliamentary committee this afternoon I pushed again on compensation for the survivors of the bombings in Afghanistan. Couldn't he at least raise the matter privately with George W.? Apparently not. 'We must wait for a report' was all The Man said. For all this talk of a special relationship, The Man comes over all coy at any suggestion of tackling our bosom buddies on difficult issues. Not because he's cowardly, but because he knows it's hopeless, but daren't say so. In an attempt to engage his attention I said, 'All these mistakes are undermining support for Karzai.' He looked pained, but said nothing. The truth is, as he knows all too well, that when the chips are down we have little or no influence with the psychopaths now in charge in Washington.

Thursday, 11 July

'BLUNKETT GAMBLES WITH OUR CHILDREN,' screams the front page of this morning's *Sun* on the decision to downgrade cannabis and there is more of the same in several other papers. So much for the mature debate that he was hoping for. Is it possible to have a mature discussion about any difficult issue in this country? Instead of wobbling around in the middle of the road, attracting flak from all sides, wouldn't it be nice just to do the right thing for once and tell Rupert Murdoch, Paul Dacre, Conrad Black et al to fuck off?

Our committee clerk Andrew Kennon is upbeat. He says, 'I've seen some mealy-mouthed, weasel-worded responses to select committees in my time, but my impression is that the government really have made an effort to engage with us this time.'

Saturday, 13 July
Sunderland

To the Durham miners' gala. Tony Benn and Jeremy Corbyn were on the balcony of the County Hotel along with dear old Michael Foot, who looks more than ever like a will'-o'-the-wisp, swaying uncertainly in the sunshine. I feared the effort would kill him, but he seems to have survived. We marched down Old Elvet, behind the Wearmouth Banner, in glorious sunshine, past the prison. Somewhere up there behind the bars is Rose West, who will never be released. It must be an eerie feeling to hear the sounds of people enjoying themselves a few yards away and know that you can never take part. I once asked Judith Ward, who spent 14 years in Durham jail, if she knew she was in the most beautiful city in England. 'Yes,' she said, 'my mother gave me some tourist leaflets.'

Sunday, 14 July

Three derelict cars have been abandoned in our back lane. One by our back gate, which makes it difficult to get our car in and out.

Wednesday, 17 July

To a well-attended meeting of the parliamentary party for a debate on the Euro. Gordon was not best pleased. He wanted to discuss his spending review, but Jean insisted in sticking with the advertised programme. He gave an impressive performance. Gordon is master of all he surveys. In total command of his brief. If anyone can lead us to the promised land, it is he. Our future – even The Man's – is in his hands (and which of us is better equipped than Gordon, armed with his five tests?) but Make-Your-Mind-Up-Time is drawing nigh. He promised a conclusion by June. If he gets it right, his rise will be unstoppable. If he screws up, he is doomed – as are we all.

'Isn't Gordon a commanding figure?' remarked the Leader of the Lords, Gareth Williams, as we walked out together. 'One has an impression of strength and confidence.'

I replied that, as regards the Euro, I wasn't clear which side he was on, but Gareth was. 'He'll come down in favour.'

Dmitri Kozak, the Russian deputy head of the Administration of the President, came to see me. He has been given the onerous task of reforming his country's system of criminal justice. Ostensibly he was here to learn about ours, but he didn't ask a single question. The main problem with ours, I remarked, was that too many criminals were getting off. 'We have the opposite problem,' he replied. 'In Russia the acquittal rate is 0.4 of 1 per cent.'

To Number 10 for the annual photograph of the parliamentary committee, which, this year, was in the garden. What greater privilege than a walled garden in the centre of London? Evidence of the children is everywhere. A trampoline, a climbing frame, a football in the pond and a miniature goal for little Leo. Later, while we were having our meeting in the Cabinet Room, came the sound of girlish laughter. It was so loud that eventually the doors to the garden had to be closed. 'I am afraid that's my daughter,' said The Man.

We discussed Iraq. Ann Clwyd quoted Scott Ritter: 'Bush needs a war and he'll drag everyone else in.'

The Man said that the Republican right were not necessarily in favour of intervention and neither were we. It depended on the context. There was no doubt that Saddam will, over time, build weapons of mass destruction. 'The question is, will he let the inspectors back in?'

'What's your opinion?' asked Doug Hoyle.

'He might, if the heat's turned up enough.'

'There are a number of questions we should be thinking about,' I said. 'What would Saddam do if cornered? How much collateral damage – the last time we encouraged the Kurds and the Shia to rise up the result was not merely disastrous, but catastrophic. And how much help would we get from the Americans when it came to clearing up afterwards?'

'Those questions have to be answered,' said The Man, 'and, if we can't answer them, we won't do it.' He added that, contrary to what most people seemed to believe, the Americans had stayed engaged both in Kosovo and in Afghanistan. After the Taliban, Iraq was the world's most repressive regime. There was torture and murder on an unbelievable scale. If we had an opportunity to get rid of it, we should.

'That argument could have been made any time since the 1980s,' I said.

'I've had two wars – Kosovo and Afghanistan – and I think I can claim that we got it right.'

'The jury is still out on Afghanistan,' I said. 'The situation is still very bad in some parts.'

The Man looked hurt. 'We had a report from our ambassador the other day. Kandahar is thriving. If you took a poll ...'

'What's your alternative, Chris?' sneered Prescott.

'I think I can say we haven't done anything rash so far.' The Man grinned sheepishly.

'Is that the best you can offer?' I said.

'We can indict the Iraqis now,' said Ann. This seemed to come as news to The Man, although Ann has been pressing the point for ages.

'Why don't I look into it and come back to you?'

Thursday, 18 July

I asked George Young whether everyone in the Tory Party was signed up to a war with Iraq. He replied that he had a lot of military people in his constituency and they were all opposed: 'I imagine the American military are offering the same advice to George Bush.' He added, 'We are trying to disengage Iain Duncan Smith from the Americans.'

To the Banqueting House to hear the parliamentary choir sing Mozart's *Coronation Mass* which they did brilliantly. As we were going downstairs, someone tapped me on the shoulder. I turned to find Cherie Blair. 'You weren't too unkind to my husband on Tuesday,' she said referring to his appearance before the Liaison Committee.

'He and I have an understanding,' I replied.

'I think you do.'

Monday, 22 July

Several angry letters from NHS consultants upset at my description in the *Echo* of them as 'a profession notorious for their self-importance and their pursuit of self-interest'. I've been feeling guilty ever since, thinking of the dedicated consultants of my acquaintance – Mr Mellon who removed my kidney stone and Mike Laurence who is among the most generous and least self-important men I know. I must try to avoid gratuitously offending entire professions.

Tuesday, 23 July

A frustrating hour and a half trying, and failing, to be called during Alistair Darling's aviation statement. I put in a note reminding the Speaker that I was a former aviation minister, but it didn't make any difference. Alistair's statement was couched in the form of a consultation – the word 'sustainable' featured a lot – but the underlying message was that, like it or not, the south east of England is going to get more runways, more terminals and even a new airport or two – and sod the environment. Where aviation is concerned, Predict and Provide is alive and well. There was not even a nod in the direction of demand management. Cheap air travel has been elevated to a fundamental human right. Alistair kept saying that there is no alternative. But of course there is: when in doubt, DON'T. I am glad I live in the north. Life in the south-east is becoming unbearable.

Wednesday, 24 July

The stock market has been plunging all day. 'Spare a thought for those of us who were told we had to sell our house and put the proceeds into equities,' remarked The Man as we assembled for the parliamentary committee this afternoon. He said it with feeling. As well he might. He has been well and truly shafted. Equities have plummeted, house prices have soared. That one disastrous piece of professional advice has probably lost him more in five years than he's earned as prime minister.

My views on new airports sparked a spirited exchange. I said, 'During my 18 undistinguished months as aviation minister I learned two things about the aviation industry. One, that its demands are insatiable. Two, that successive governments have always given way.' I continued, 'There is nothing wrong with expanding regional airports, providing we insist that they are accessible by public transport, but as far as London and the south east is concerned, isn't it time we made a stand?'

There were no takers. The Man said something about bigger and better airports being essential for the health of the economy. Doug Hoyle said that the second runway had made a big difference in Manchester. Tony Lloyd said that airports in the regions benefited from investment in the south-east.

'You helped write the White Paper, Chris,' offered JP, vigilant as ever for evidence of backsliding.

'I only managed to insert one phrase,' I said. 'It was: "Predict and Provide didn't work for cars. It didn't work for housing and it won't work for airports."'

Liz Symons said, 'As Minister for Trade, I'm quite worried about what Chris has said.'

Someone asserted that, if we failed to expand the south-east airports, fares might have to rise by £100 to which I responded, 'So what? Cheap air travel is not a fundamental human right.' At this The Man's face assumed a pained expression. No doubt he was thinking of all those Middle Englanders who would never forgive us if they had to pay more for their fortnight in the Canaries.

'Have you been on the cannabis again, Chris?' inquired JP to general hilarity.

'I can see I won't be allowed anywhere near the transport department again,' I said.

The Man laughed. 'You have rather talked yourself out of that one,' he said, adding quietly, 'Don't worry, there's plenty of other things.' My ears pricked up at that. There may, after all, be a second coming.

It was a good-natured discussion, but there is a serious point: New Labour believes that Big is Beautiful.

Friday, 26 July
Sunderland

A brief telephone chat with Steve Byers. Our first contact since The Fall. He and Jan have spent a couple of weeks in Crete. He sounds calm, but subdued. Steve reckons that The Man's enthusiasm for an attack on Iraq has cooled since Christmas. 'I have the impression that he's trying to talk Bush out of it.' If only ...

Tonight's *Echo* billboard reads: '621 perverts living in Sunderland'. Part of the tabloid campaign to persuade everyone that they have a paedophile living next door. For some reason the *Echo* is obsessed with perverts.

Tuesday, 27 August
North Ronaldsay

We are staying with Liz Forgan in her croft, having spent four days meandering up through the Western Highlands and the Orkney mainland. The Orkneys, in contrast to the rest of Britain, have enjoyed a good summer. For the first time in years the cattle fodder is being harvested in August. This evening on the beach the girls and I commenced building a Stone Age house like those at Skara Brae.

Wednesday, 28 August

Work on our Stone Age house proceeds apace. The two small Stone-Agers are hard at work. We have laid a double-width foundation of flat stones collected from the beach, Sarah has filled the gap with bucket-fuls of pebbles and the result is a solid wall about two feet wide, slowly rising. At one end we have built a two-storey table topped with two great slabs of stone which I rolled along the beach. Ngoc is building a cupboard into one of the walls, Emma finding shells to decorate our table.

A day of simple pleasures. One of the happiest of my life.

Thursday, 29 August

Our house is complete. In the centre we have made a little stone hearth. On one side, by the wall, we have inserted stone slabs, side-ways up to make a bed and the children have collected reeds and seaweed for bedding. And in one corner we have dug a little pond where Stone Age man would have stored his live fish and crabs until he was ready to eat them. Here we have cheated slightly. It should be lined with clay to make it waterproof. There is clay on the island, but Liz isn't sure where. So, to save time, Ngoc adapted a plastic milk container washed up on the beach which she has cunningly con-cealed under a layer of stone to make it appear authentic.

Tuesday, 3 September
Sunderland

Sarah's first day at St Anthony's. I delivered the little nugget to Sister Aelred's office, looking beautiful in her new uniform. I was more nervous than she was.

The Man, hotfoot from Johannesburg, has declared that we will be backing the Americans over Iraq, come what may. So much for Steve Byers's suggestion that he's trying to talk Bush out of it.

Thursday, 5 September

A call from M in Washington who describes the Iraq enterprise as 'crazy to the point of being demented. I'm surprised that Blair is encouraging it.' He says the intelligence agencies, the military and the State Department are all opposed. The CIA, he says, 'are almost openly pissing on the whole thing'.

'If you ask the two key questions – has Saddam got nuclear weapons and has he ever given weapons of mass destruction to terrorists? – they say there is no evidence whatever. On chemical and biological weapons, they say he has got them, but there is no evidence that he has a means of delivery.

'If you talk to the right-wing loonies, they reply that those opposed are all wimps who need to be beaten into shape and that, in any case, the CIA failed to predict September 11 so why should we listen to them now.'

Has it got to do with oil (as Mo Mowlam asserts in today's *Guardian*)? 'No, it has more to do with Israel – most of the people pushing it are close to Sharon.'

I have been reading Margaret Thatcher's memoirs: page 331 offers an interesting little insight into the state of the much-vaunted special relationship, even in her day. She woke up one morning to discover that (in the teeth of her strong objections) her bosom buddy Ronald Reagan had invaded Grenada. She writes:

> I felt dismayed and let down by what had happened. At best the British government had been made to look impotent; at worst we looked deceitful … only the previous afternoon Geoffrey [Howe] had told the House of Commons that he had no knowledge of any American intention to intervene in Grenada. Now he and I would have to explain how it had happened that a member of the Commonwealth had been invaded by our closest ally, and more than that, we would also have to defend the United States' reputation in the face of world-wide condemnation.

I guess we'll have to wait until The Man produces his memoirs to find out what he really thinks of George W. Bush and friends.

Friday, 6 September

Nick Brown addressed my local party this evening. Afterwards he came home and we talked for a couple of hours. He says relations between Gordon and The Man are 'poisonous' and that Cherie in particular loathes Gordon. He says there have been some big rows, one or two of which he has witnessed. So the rumours are true. This is the first time I have heard it confirmed by someone so close to one of the parties. He says the differences are part personal, part political. In particular Gordon resents the obsession with presentation (a bit rich coming from the man who employed Charlie Whelan). He says Gordon is against an attack on Iraq and that he - Nick – would have to consider his position if we become involved in a war. Gordon, he says, is not likely to run against Tony. It would be self-indulgent and disastrous for the party. Nick also said, as others do, that despite his image as a dour obsessive, Gordon in private is good company.

Monday, 9 September

Lunch with Peter Candler, a local developer. Unemployment is at its lowest for 30 years and house prices have risen to the point where it has at last become worthwhile to do up some of our magnificent Victorian terraces which have been sliding towards dereliction for years.

Can it last? Is it all built on sand? To be sure our manufacturing base is remorselessly eroding. One after another, all along the river the old industries are closing – Vaux, Grove Cranes, Federal Mogul ... The major exception is Nissan and, according to Peter, it's only a matter of time before that goes, too. He reckons that the death of manufacturing is inevitable, part of an historic cycle which politicians are powerless to reverse. He also believes – as many do – that our ubiquitous call centres are only a passing phase. If so, we are going to be in trouble again, ten or twenty years down the line. Peter, dynamic, far-sighted businessman that he is, is optimistic that something will turn up. And indeed who, ten years ago, could have predicted that we would be where we are today? I, being one of nature's pessimists, am not so confident. I fear it is only a matter of time until the bubble bursts.

Thursday, 12 September

The war drums are beating ever louder. This afternoon George W. Bush gave an uncompromising address to the United Nations General Assembly. It was billed as an ultimatum to Iraq, but it was really an ultimatum to the UN: get behind us or else.

Friday, 13 September

This evening three hours in the company of PC Les Jordan, patrolling his beat, Doxford Park and Farringdon. PC Jordan is that rare phenomenon: a policeman on a bicycle. Everywhere, loitering teenagers, many known to Les by name and they seem to respect him. We came across a girl who was the worse for wear with drink and he phoned her parents to come and take her home. Outside Morrison's was a crowd of underage youths clutching a slab of lager. He ordered them to pour it down the drain. Incredibly, they obeyed. We came upon another group of youths bouncing a football off the roof of a shopping parade and he threatened to confiscate the ball if they didn't go elsewhere, which they did. He managed it all without rubbing anyone up the wrong way, always treating them with respect, which was generally reciprocated. Most of them weren't bad kids, they just lead empty lives.

Saturday, 14 September

David and Louise Miliband came to dinner. An attractive, engaging couple. He, awesomely bright, but so far as I could see without arrogance or conceit. Despite having been parachuted into the shark-infested political waters of South Tyneside, he appears to have won over the natives and is destined for a glittering career in government. By the election or soon after he will be in the Cabinet. He claimed not to have given any thought to becoming an MP until he allowed himself to be persuaded by The Man days before he was chosen in South Shields. If ever anyone was on an inside track, it is he. Not for him the long, unglamorous, humiliating slog around the selection circuit or the years of unrecognised toil on the Opposition front bench that was the lot of so many of our number. With one wave of The Man's magic wand he finds himself in one of the safest seats in the country. With another wave he is in government. It would be easy for us lesser mortals to be resentful, were he not so obviously talented and infectiously likeable.

Tuesday, 17 September

To Portcullis House for a meeting of the Home Affairs Select Committee. Part of my plan to acclimatise the boys and girls to September sittings. The great thing about conducting hearings when Parliament is not sitting is that we have everyone's full attention. There is none of the constant nipping in and out to deal with supposedly urgent telephone messages. Also, the media tend to take more interest.

This morning we dipped our toe in the murky waters of asylum policy. Among our witnesses Sir Andrew Green from an outfit called Migrationwatch which publishes statistics suggesting that inward migration is much higher than the official figures and that anyone who gets in illegally has a nine out of ten chance of remaining. Various people have raised their eyebrows at our giving a platform to Migrationwatch, but I refuse to accept that it is not possible to have a rational discussion about immigration and asylum without being labelled racist. There is a growing political problem which we ignore at our peril and we can't simply leave the floor to those well-meaning (and usually publicly funded) organisations who see it as their duty to poke holes in whatever measures the government comes up with without suggesting any realistic alternatives – some, indeed, do not even concede that there is a problem. As it turned out, Sir Andrew (a former ambassador with impeccable credentials) was a decent, if slightly long-winded, old cove whose presence helped offer a little balance to what might otherwise have been a one-sided discussion. Having got some facts and figures on the table my aim is to focus on how we can make the removal process (a) more efficient and (b) more humane.

Wednesday, 18 September

The session with David Blunkett went well. He looked a little pale. Not quite his usual, chipper self, but then he has been getting rather a battering of late, partly because of some of the silly things he's been saying. He was accompanied by Bev Hughes, who exudes quiet competence. She is not given to grandstanding and retains a streak of decency essential for anyone in charge of immigration. I pressed David hard on the need to humanise the removals process – perhaps by way of a small resettlement grant. He promised to think about it, but I am not optimistic. We also pressed him on air weapons. Some signs of movement there. Is the Home Office waking up at last?

Tuesday, 24 September

To the House to hear The Man explain why we need a war with Iraq. The chamber was packed and so was the upper gallery. I was squeezed between Anne Campbell (who is deluged with anti-war letters from all those intellectuals in Cambridge) and Jean Corston. Betty Boothroyd, resplendent in scarlet, was in pole position in the peers' gallery and somewhere in the background, wearing his CND tie, lurked Tony Benn. The Man's performance was flawless. He made his case calmly, without exaggeration or hyperbole. He met every argument hard, head on, and treated his critics with respect. Mostly he was heard in silence. The first rumble of discontent came about 20 minutes in when he referred to Saddam's war with Iran in which a million people died. There were cries of 'And we supported him.' To which Angela Eagle, sitting in front of me, added, 'Not only that, we sold him arms.' The Tories looked uncomfortable as well they might for it was not 'we' who supported Saddam, but 'they'. Duncan Smith kept his contribution mercifully short, well aware no doubt that too much indignation about the wickedness of Saddam in the eighties could easily backfire. Later, during questions on the statement, there was a tricky moment when The Man proclaimed that partnership with America was 'an article of faith with me'. The Tories cheered wildly. From our side there was a stony silence. A sign of just how far out on a limb he has gone. If he's not careful, he'll fall over the edge.

Elfyn Llwyd, an affable Welsh Nationalist, asked the key question: will we still support the Americans if they go it alone? The Man said something which implied that we might 'in the event of the UN's will not being complied with', which prompted further rumbling from our side. 'Oh dear,' said Jean.

Immediately after the statement we trooped into his room for a meeting of the parliamentary committee. 'One of your biggest problems,' I said, 'is that, outside of Texas, no one has the slightest confidence in George W. Bush or in those who surround him.' I added, 'No doubt, we shall have to wait for your memoirs to find out what you really think of him.'

'No need to wait,' he replied cheerfully. 'I'll tell you now. George Bush is intelligent, open and easy to deal with.'

'You must see a different George Bush to us,' interjected Doug Hoyle.

'There is a problem,' The Man conceded, 'with the rhetoric coming out of the Administration. The American mindset has been changed profoundly since September 11 and that explains a lot of it.' He went on, 'I personally have no objection to taking out Saddam and I don't see why the left has this problem. I'm an interventionist. I can understand where the right are coming from, but I can't understand the left.'

'Let me stop you there,' I said. 'It isn't just the left. No one has the slightest enthusiasm for a war with Iraq.'

He went on, 'I am bewildered by the reaction of some parts of the international community. It was always obvious that Saddam was going to offer to let the inspectors back in. The intelligence we have – and I have this from right inside the regime – is that Saddam believes he can play around with the inspectors again. Europe has to face up to some of these issues. We often call for American help and then accuse them of unilateralism. My role in relation to America is not to say, "Yes but …", but to say, "Yes and …"' In passing, he remarked that, unlike Afghanistan, the Americans did understand that they would have to help with rebuilding Iraq. An interesting admission. When challenged on that point in the past, he has always claimed that the Americans were helping with reconstruction in Afghanistan.

Again I pressed the point about whether we would go in without UN backing and again The Man dodged, saying only that he was hopeful that we would get it.

Gordon Prentice remarked that he had not met anyone who agreed with our position on Iraq and that in any case there wasn't the slightest chance of replacing Saddam with a democracy. To which The Man replied that just because we couldn't introduce democracy wasn't an excuse for doing nothing. He added that the British public were open to persuasion. They were not saying no, but simply asking legitimate questions such as whether there was a *casus belli*. 'I wanted the moment to come a bit later, but if the international community backs down, Saddam will take that as a green light.'

Andrew Mackinlay said that he thought The Man's stewardship of events so far had been absolutely correct. He added to laughter, 'That will be one life peerage, if you don't mind.'

Later, I received a message asking me to go and see Robin Cook, who wanted to talk about Iraq. Robin said, 'My star is not high at the moment because of my lack of enthusiasm for bombing Iraq.' At yesterday's Cabinet only Clare and he spoke against a war. 'Estelle asked some serious questions. Everyone else was keen on demonstrating their loyalty to Tony.' However, he detects some tension between Number 10 and the Foreign Office. Jack's speech this afternoon had, said Robin, been the greatest encomium to the United Nations that he had ever heard. When he remarked on this afterwards Jack had replied, 'I'm glad you noticed.'

Robin is not entirely gloomy. 'The regime may implode. There are signs. And Tony is right when he says that the Americans will take more interest in rebuilding Iraq than they did Afghanistan, if only because Iraq has oil.'

Will we support the Americans if they go it alone? 'I don't know. It will depend on public opinion, not opinion in the party. He might not, if he can't get away with it. Tony is a shrewd politician.'

As I was leaving Robin said, 'We'll just have to hope that there isn't a war because there isn't the money to pay for it. Our spending plans may have to be trimmed.'

Monday, 30 September
Party Conference

To Blackpool arriving in time for the debate on the public finance initiative. For a while I found myself sitting behind Peter Mandelson, who spent much of the time talking into his mobile. While he was speaking a nervous young woman appeared with a note which she slid into his hand. Without addressing so much as a glance in her direction he waved her imperiously to one side and continued with his conversation, eventually deigning to acknowledge her existence, but only after the poor girl had been left in no doubt of her insignificance, at least so far as this great panjandrum is concerned. And Peter wonders why no one loves him …

Tuesday, 1 October

On my way to a lunchtime fringe meeting I came across Clare Short, full of good cheer, sitting in sunshine outside a café. She thought yesterday's Iraq debate had gone well. 'I was proud of the Labour Party,' she said. 'We need to tie the government to the UN. I trust Jack, but not Tony.' On Afghanistan she thinks we need to create a united Afghan army and secure the whole country – which The Man is in favour of anyway. We talked about asylum policy. 'It's in a mess,' she said. She then went on to outline her own plan for dealing with it: genuine asylum seekers should be allowed to work instead of being left to fester for years; economic migrants should be sent home as soon as possible, preferably within a week. I said that wouldn't be possible under the UN conventions. 'If necessary, I would resile from them,' she said. She added that Blunkett was about to start repatriating Zimbabweans at a time when half the country was facing famine. The Foreign Office had given the go-ahead, but she had warned against.

I didn't go in for The Speech. Instead I went back to the hotel and watched on television. As ever it was full of stirring stuff (lots of talk about the need for boldness). The delivery was brilliant, but I am afraid I dozed off.

The Tribune rally was held in a tacky nightclub which it took me half an hour to locate. Given the location, they did well to fill it although the audiences are half what they used to be 20 years ago. The speeches were lacklustre with one notable exception: Christopher Hitchens, who argued the case for military intervention in Iraq. He appealed to those present 'as internationalists, as people who can think for yourselves'. It was not a war on Iraq that was proposed, he argued, but a war on Saddam. He urged the left to be a little self-critical. 'Why do we spend our time urging our prime minister to give Saddam yet another chance?' He went on, 'If the left had its way, General Galtieri would still be President of Argentina; Milosevic would still be in power in Belgrade; Kosovo would be an empty wilderness; Mullah Omar would still be in Kabul.' It was a courageous speech, cleverly delivered. He managed to challenge all the received wisdoms without rubbing anyone's nose in it. Most people had the sense to see that he might have a point, even if they didn't agree. He was heard in silence and applauded politely.

Afterwards I went for a drink with Christopher. He was surprisingly upbeat about George Bush. 'He's not conceited. He knows his limitations. The people around him know what they are doing. The long-term plan is to reduce dependence on Saudi oil.' I put to him the counter arguments: chaos, civilian casualties, the danger that Saddam if cornered will resort to chemical weapons. Christopher dismissed them all. He reckons the regime is crumbling and that the odds are it will implode without the need for an invasion. Fingers crossed that he is right.

Wednesday, 2 October

Passing up the chance to commune with Bill Clinton, I went with the Ramblers' Association for their annual conference walk. About 20 people turned out, including Jeff Rooker and Andrew Bennett. We were taken by minibus about an hour north. From there we followed a four-mile circular route and had a pub lunch. The views were stunning. Over lunch I remarked to Andrew Bennett, apropos of Iraq, that The Man had gone out too far ahead of the party. 'Yes,' replied Andrew, 'almost as far as Ramsay MacDonald.'

Tuesday, 15 October

Passed Robert Hill in the corridor behind the Speaker's chair. 'Tony's rowed out a long way ahead of the public, never mind the party, on Iraq,' I said.

'He's aware of that,' said Robert. 'And working day and night to keep George Bush onside with the UN. There are phone calls nearly every day.'

'We have hitched our wagon to the least credible US President since Nixon,' I said. 'Tony may think Bush is intelligent and easy to deal with, but the public doesn't see it that way.'

Wednesday, 16 October

At the parliamentary committee I passed The Man a cutting from the *Guardian* about an Afghani woman who had lost her husband and six of her eleven children in one of America's 'mistakes' and who was still living in the rubble of her ruined home, not having received a penny by way of help. 'I want to know what we are doing to help such people in general and this woman in particular,' I said. He glanced at the cutting and passed it to an aide. I said I was serious about this. We had to take responsibility for our actions. Later, I told David Hanson that I wanted a serious response, not a lot of Foreign Office blather. I don't intend to let the subject drop.

Thursday, 17 October

Everyone is talking about the dire state of the Conservative Party. Apparently (I wasn't present) Iain Duncan Smith was slaughtered at Questions yesterday. Both Portillo and Ken Clarke have been putting themselves about this week and they were much in evidence at the recent Tory conference. It is inconceivable that they would elect Portillo. Clarke (who looks fat and unhealthy) might be a possibility if the government decided not to hold a referendum on the Euro. According to Andy McSmith, the real problem is the Tory party. 'The membership is elderly and most of them would like Winston to lead them. If they can't have Winston, they'd like Thatcher.' Could it be that the Tories are in terminal decline? Phil Willis and David Miliband, with whom I travelled home, think it a possibility although Tory roots are strong and they have vast resources to call upon. Plus, as someone said the other day a lot of people want to vote for a nasty party. They will come back.

Monday, 21 October

Tea with M, who called in en route to Washington. He says The Man is doing okay on Iraq. Bush listens to him. He added, 'I get the distinct impression that, whatever they say in public, HMG thinks an attack on Iraq would be insane. They are backing Bush into a corner, tying him down with lots of little ropes.' M says the Americans have lost interest in Afghanistan. All they are doing is handing out dollars to warlords. 'Exactly the conditions that led to the rise of the Taliban in the first place.'

Tuesday, 22 October

JP made a statement on the looming dispute with the firefighters. He went out of his way to avoid offending them (in contrast to recent noises from Downing Street which speak of 'Scargillites'). David Davis responded for the Tories. He did his best not to sound too gleeful, but couldn't resist a bit of hyperbole about a return to the dark days of the seventies – and who can blame him? The Tories demanded to know why the soldiers who will be standing in for the firefighters in the event of a strike will only be allowed to use the ancient Green Goddesses when there is modern equipment available. A good question. After all, the equipment belongs to the public, not the firefighters. Why should it be confined to barracks when lives are at risk? JP responded by accusing them of wanting to inflame the situation. An answer he may be able to get away with this week, while there is still a possibility that a strike can be avoided, but it won't wash once the strike starts. It worries me that JP has been put in charge. I fear he will opt for a fudge when what is needed is an exemplary defeat.

To an upper committee room to listen to Jack Straw. What

benefits do we get out of our relationship with America, Peter Temple Morris wanted to know? Jack bravely insisted that, despite the odd hiccup, America was a force for good reflecting, he asserted, European values. It was also the only superpower. 'The reason I bite my tongue,' he added, 'is because I want to support all those Americans who want to keep America within the international system.'

'I find it hard to accept that Americans are a force for good,' said Julia Drown. 'They are selfish and imperialist.'

'I know what you are saying,' replied Jack. 'I wouldn't have voted Republican either. There are some complete raving nutcases in Washington who want a holy war.' Hastily he added that the raving nutcases weren't in the Administration. 'I know for a fact that Bush doesn't want a war.'

Wednesday, 23 October

A briefing with JP and Nick Raynsford on our problem with the firefighters. Several people wanted to know why we were still relying on Green Goddesses. 'What happens to the newer engines when they are finished with?' 'That's what we asked,' said JP. Apparently they are sold off to other countries rather than being kept in reserve.

An incredible state of affairs. Apparently it had not occurred to anyone that we might need to provide our armed forces with something better than 50-year-old Green Goddesses in the event of another strike. JP seemed to think there was still an outside chance that a strike could be averted. 'But something will have to move by the weekend. Either we move together or we move unilaterally.'

Ann Clwyd, who has just returned from Afghanistan, reported to the parliamentary committee that the situation was desperate – 'a bullet away from civil war', she had been told. Karzai was referred to contemptuously as 'the mayor of Kabul'. Everyone was asking for an expansion of the intervention force. The Man replied, as he did last week, that he remained hopeful that the force could be expanded once the Germans took over. He added that he had followed up Ann's suggestion that Saddam and his cronies be indicted for war crimes. The police weren't keen, but they had been asked to take another look. JP reported that the Afghan vice-president and his fearsome defence minister had paid him a visit. There was some merriment when The Man suggested a job swap – JP would make a good warlord.

On the victims of the bombings, which I raised last week, The Man said the Americans were willing to pay compensation; it was just a question of receiving and processing claims. I don't believe that for a minute, but we must hold them to it. He promised to put it in writing.

Someone mentioned elected mayors – in the wake of another crop of bad results last week. 'I don't think there will be any more,' said JP merrily (he has been opposed from the outset). 'It's been an interesting little experiment.' He added that we had quietly stopped forcing local authorities to hold referendums on the subject.

At about 11 p.m. I heard that Estelle Morris has resigned.

Thursday, 24 October

Everyone is talking about Estelle. Her resignation came as a bolt from the blue, given that she seemed to have weathered the storms of the summer. A big blow. She is modest, unassuming, down to earth, and knows education inside out. A perfect antidote to some of the slick New Labour types who inhabit the upper reaches. Just the sort of politician we needed more of. Some people are saying she was hounded out of office by the Harmsworth Lie Machine, but actually she was a victim of New Labour's love affair with targets. Blunkett planted the bomb several years ago by saying he would resign if his education targets were not met. Later, Estelle was asked at a select committee hearing if she, too, would go and – not wanting to contradict her superior – agreed that she would. The years passed and her words came back to haunt her. Blunkett meanwhile was long gone. It's what the Americans call 'blow back'.

To Chelmsford to see Mum who is in Broomfield Hospital with pneumonia. Her fourth or fifth fall. She and Dad could easily afford help, but they won't hear of it. They are so stubborn.

Mum was lying in bed with a drip in her arm. Frail and shaky but in good spirits. I insisted she wear an alarm and for the first time she accepted that it might be necessary.

Tuesday, 29 October

Oh dear, I am in trouble. My speech opposing Robin Cook's modernisation plans to finish business three hours earlier went badly wrong. I have ended up offending not just The Sisters, but a number of my friends. I had put down an amendment forcing a separate vote on Wednesday sittings which Robin – fearing he might lose – was anxious to avoid. He was not best pleased and circulated a crib sheet describing mine as 'a wrecking amendment'. The modernisers were well-organised and when I got up to speak they were all around me heckling and trying to intervene. 'Get a life,' shouted that ambitious pipsqueak from the Rhondda. I was doing all right until about halfway when I chanced a little joke. ('If I was a spouse living at the other end of the country, I would want to be assured that my other half was snug in the warm bosom of the Mother of Parliaments and not wandering the streets with too much time on his hands and too much money in his pockets.') From this point onwards they all went bananas. The harassment became so bad that the Deputy Speaker had to intervene in order that I be heard. I sat down to some hear-hearing from the Tories, but with just about everyone else I had blown it. Jean Corston was furious with me for not giving way to her in the debate. She thought I'd deliberately ignored her, but in truth I hadn't seen her (I eventually managed to convince her of this). Dawn Primarolo, a friend for over 20 years, told me that she thought my speech was 'despicable'. Even so, the vote when it came was close. There was some tension since no one had a clue how it would go. In the event it was carried 274 to 267. So they only just got away with it. We have once again voted for our own convenience over the public interest. (Diane Abbott told me she had voted for the reduction in hours 'out of naked self-interest'.) The quality of scrutiny will not be improved one iota. On the contrary, it will be diminished. How on earth are we going to cram all the activity that goes on in this place – select committees, standing committees, backbench committees – into a day that is three hours shorter? And what are the 450 of us who can't return to our families on weekday evenings supposed to do after seven o'clock? Wander around the building in twilight?

By a stroke of bad luck elections for the parliamentary committee are due next week. I will be lucky to survive.

Wednesday, 30 October

A rescue operation is underway. Jean and I plotted over lunch at the Dispatch Box café how to organise a comeback. 'Lucky your amendment was defeated,' she said, 'otherwise you would certainly be off the committee' (a price worth paying, I thought, but I didn't want to upset her again). Jean says that two people had remarked to her that they used to regard me as a role model, but never again. All sorts of unlikely people have chosen to interpret my remarks as a personal slur ('I've been married for 42 years and I don't need this shit,' Ken Purchase raged at me in the Tea Room). Oh dear, oh dear. Why are they so damn precious? Don't they recognise a joke when they see one. Joke. J.O.K.E. Never mind, dear Jean is beavering away on my behalf. We agreed that I should write a bland little note soliciting the votes of the hundred or so Labour members in my lobby last night. Jean meanwhile will try to mend fences with some of my erstwhile supporters. By late this afternoon she reported that she had spoken to Hilary Armstrong who agreed that it was in the general interest that I should be preserved. Jean also reported a conversation with Robin in which she had suggested that revenge ought to be avoided. Robin, she said, was cool. However, twice during the day he went out of his way to strike up a conversation, which suggests that he is anxious to limit the fallout. The other good news is that I have made up with Dawn.

To the parliamentary committee, possibly my last. There was no mention of the events of last night. Instead we jumped ineffectually from one issue to another – Afghanistan, Chechnya, regional assemblies, the row over Andrew Adonis, the Downing Street adviser who is alleged to be urging politically disastrous university top-up fees upon us. John Reid making his first appearance as party chairman

urged us not to play what he called the media game over special advisers. 'There are half a million civil servants and 70 or 80 special advisers. The fact is these are our people. *Our people*,' he repeated. That, of
course, is precisely the problem. There are those who suspect that
Andrew Adonis is not one of our people.

I asked about top-up fees, saying that they would get us into big
trouble with the middle classes. The Man agreed but said that something had to be done. 'A lecturer at a top university was earning less
than a solicitor's clerk in the City. This is one of those things that you
won't notice if you do nothing for five years, but you will in 15 or 20
years.' He added we were starting to slip down the world league. Universities such as Bangalore in southern India were now as good as any
in the First World.

Monday, 4 November

To London clutching letters addressed to the 93 heroic Labour backbenchers who voted for my amendment last week, asking for their
support in the annual election for the parliamentary committee. By
no means all my natural constituents, but I hope to pick up enough
to make up for any losses I have incurred as a result of my little mishap
the other day. I have never before lifted a finger to campaign, but one
can't be too lofty in these difficult times.

To Buckingham Palace – one of the few Establishment citadels I
have never previously penetrated – where the Queen laid on a reception for backbench MPs. I strolled in darkness through St James's Park,
showed my ticket (number 1300) to the policeman on the gate and
crunched across the gravel forecourt glancing smugly at the tourists
peering through the railings. Under the arch, across the courtyard and
through the vast portico which leads up to the state apartments,
where we were corralled by footmen into various drawing rooms
(green, blue, red) to await Her Majesty's pleasure. Eventually our
drinks were confiscated and we were marshalled into line to shake
hands with the Queen and the Duke. They received us in the yellow
drawing room, under a portrait of Queen Alexandra (in Sunderland
we have a bridge named after her). As we came into The Presence a

flunkey called our names. She was wearing elbow-length black gloves. Afterwards we lingered for an hour in the Royal Picture Gallery while footmen plied us with drinks and canapés and various members of the Household moved among us. Kevan Jones recounted an exchange with Sir Robert Fellowes about the recent difficulty with Diana's butler.

Sir Robert: 'Has it damaged the Queen?'

'Yes.'

'What do ordinary people think?'

Kevan then proceeded to regale Sir Robert with his mother's analysis of the situation whereupon the unflappable courtier assumed a pained expression and melted into the crowd.

Twice I came across Prince Philip. First, we had a conversation about our proposed new sitting hours and then about satellite television ('What's wrong with satellite TV, apart from the fact that it is owned by Mr Murdoch?') I didn't catch sight of the Queen until chucking out time. She waved an arm. 'Time for you to go and vote the right way,' she said, adding hastily, 'whichever way that is.' (It was the vote on allowing unmarried couples and gays to adopt – no prizes for guessing which lobby she'd be in.) Then she strode away down the length of the picture gallery, which was by now almost empty, a vision in blue, stouter than I had imagined, swinging her handbag and flanked by two elegant young men. As she reached the end, the huge mirror-doors swung open and she disappeared into that part of the palace beyond the reach of ordinary mortals.

Tuesday, 5 November

The Tories are imploding. Instead of (as we did) allowing a free vote on whether to allow gays and unmarried people to adopt, IDS foolishly turned it into a vote of confidence in his leadership with the result that a number of people – including Clarke and Portillo – defied their whip, prompting a crisis. This morning IDS compounded his folly by summoning a press conference at which he demanded, to general derision, that the party either unite or die. Ken Clarke replied contemptuously that he wasn't going to take lectures in loyalty from someone who built his career undermining John Major's administration. It is wonderful to behold. Tories are gathered in the corridors and lobbies in earnest little groups which go quiet whenever someone from another party approaches. Clarke and Portillo, who are usually nowhere to be seen, are suddenly everywhere. One can't turn a corner without bumping into one or the other. Meanwhile the Tories have practically abandoned the chamber. This evening, on the Immigration and Asylum Bill their front bench spokesman, Humfrey Malins, was alone for much of the time. There wasn't even a Tory whip in sight, let alone a backbencher. I have never seen anything like it. We keep telling ourselves that it won't last. They will recover one day and in my heart I still believe that, but one does begin to wonder.

Wednesday, 6 November

Raked up leaves in the garden for an hour before going in to hear the result of the election to the parliamentary committee. To my pleasant surprise there was a large swing in my favour – I moved up from fifth to second place. Andrew Mackinlay was the only casualty, replaced by Bridget Prentice.

At the committee, I again pressed The Man on top-up fees and he again repeated that there was a problem that had to be addressed – 'The alternative is genteel decline.'

On Iraq, The Man said he was reasonably optimistic that war could be avoided. 'I spoke to George Bush earlier today and he was down the line. If Saddam Hussein opens up to the inspectors there will be no war.'

We briefly discussed the Queen's Speech. There is to be an anti-social behaviour Bill dealing with, among other things, air weapons, graffiti, car dumping. The Man said, 'Reform of public services and crime and anti-social behaviour have to be buttoned down before the election.'

Friday, 8 November
Sunderland

The half-yearly returns on our ethically sound investments are tumbling. Disaster. The entire proceeds of my two years in government have been wiped out. The market nose-dived the moment our money came into contact with it. Dreams of retirement to a walled garden in Northumberland are fading by the week. At this rate I shall have to work until I'm 70.

Tuesday, 12 November

The firefighters began a two-day strike this evening. Next week there will be an eight-day one. This is going to be a long, bitter dispute. Whatever happens we must not give in. A fudge will only lead to years of nonsense from every part of the public sector. Last night's *Echo* contained a hint of things to come unless we nip this in the bud. Under the headline 'Ambulance staff's pay fury grows' was a story which began, 'An ambulance strike is looming in the North East as pressure mounts to match the firefighters' wage claim ...' Before we know where we are every little Unison Trotskyite will be on the march. Fortunately, the firefighters have played into our hands by digging in behind a demand so outrageous that it can't possibly be conceded.

Wednesday, 13 November

To the Parliamentary Labour Party's office above St Stephen's Entrance for a little party organised by the staff to mark the State Opening. From the windows there were grandstand views of the comings and goings below. The third carriage behind the Queen's contained Messrs Tommy McAvoy and Keith Hill, resplendent in morning coats and top hats. As it passed beneath our window Keith leaned out and gave us a cheery wave. Dave Triesman recounted an illuminating little exchange that he had recently with the editor of the *Sunday Times*, John Witherow. David had been complaining about that paper's unrelentingly hostile coverage of the government and all its works. 'It's nothing personal,' Witherow replied. 'We treated the Tories the same way.'

'What are your values?' asked Dave. 'What do you stand for?'
To which Witherow shamelessly replied, 'The bottom line.'

Monday, 18 November

To the Foreign Office to see Mike O'Brien. Getting through reception
is a tremendous palaver. 'Which company are you from?' asks a pleasant but vacant young woman behind the desk. I flash my MP's pass.
It rings no bells. 'What's that?' I explain, but it is not sufficient. 'You
will need a pass. Please look at the camera.' She taps into the computer in front of her and within seconds a sullen photo-pass emerges.
'Who have you come to see?'

'Mike O'Brien.' She flicks through the internal directory, running
her finger down the 'O' column. 'We don't have anyone of that name.'

'He's a minister.'

She is unimpressed. 'Well, he doesn't seem to be here ...'

She consults the young woman sitting next to her, who helpfully
points out that O'Brien is spelled with an 'e'. 'Ah ...' She rings a
number. It is engaged. 'Please take a seat ...'

Eventually I am shown up to Mike's grand apartment in what was
once the India Office. An oval room where Lord Curzon himself is
reputed to have held sway. Two identical doorways open inward from
the corridor, designed so that two maharajas might be received simultaneously without one having to give way to the other.

This meeting arises from my exchange with The Man three weeks
ago, about compensation for innocent Afghani victims of American
bombing. The official line, Mike explains, is that the Americans don't
compensate for collateral damage. Unofficially, they might put some
aid the way of villages that were accidentally bombed – 'but you can't
say that'. Shameful, I say. But that's how it is, says Mike. He is friendly,
but matter of fact. I draw his attention to the article in the *Guardian*
about the woman who lost her husband and six of her eleven children
and who is still living in the ruins of her home. 'Surely, we can do
something for her?' Mike replies he is having lunch with the minister
at the American embassy tomorrow. He will raise the matter and
report back.

This evening, in the Tea Room, I mentioned to Alan Milburn my interest in returning to government – but only in a serious job. Alan seemed delighted. 'I thought you'd lost interest,' he said. He is seeing The Man tomorrow and promised to mention the matter.

Wednesday, 20 November

To the weekly meeting of the parliamentary party to hear Jack Straw on Iraq. He took us through the UN resolution. 'So far, so good,' he said. 'There are many opportunities for a peaceful outcome.' He went on, 'We have set the bar high. If military action is required, we will be asking our sons and daughters to put their lives on the line and we're not going to do that for trivial reasons. If we do, we deserve to be driven out of office. I can guarantee that any action we take will be justified in international law.' What he could not guarantee, however, was a further UN resolution before resorting to war. 'A second resolution is not required, but the UN does have to meet and there has to be an assessment.'

How confident was he, asked Des Turner, that the US will accept a report from the inspectors that Iraq has complied?

'At what point would we say to the Americans that we can't support them?' inquired Tony Lloyd.

Paul Flynn asked, 'Is following the Bush agenda going to make another Bali massacre more or less likely?'

'We are not Bush's poodles,' Jack protested indignantly, 'and anyone who had been listening in on the endless telephone calls with Bush, Powell and Condoleezza Rice would know that. We are working hard to keep the US onside. You shouldn't take the more extreme statements coming out of Washington as holy writ.' He became quite passionate: 'If Blix says, "We've found this and we've dealt with it" or that there is no problem, what possible reasoned argument [for war] would I have if I came before you ...?'

'It's not you, it's the Americans,' interjected Alice Mahon.

'The Americans know what the score is.' He sat down to warm applause. Everyone knows Jack is walking a tightrope and he did it brilliantly. He was by turns humorous, passionate, robust. A far cry from his early days in the job when he was long-winded and diffident.

Dinner with Charlie Falconer in the Barry Room in the Lords. The ostensible purpose was to discuss the Crime Bill, but we talked mostly of the Birmingham and Guildford cases. Charlie said that in 1987, shortly before the Birmingham Six appeal, he came across Igor Judge* brandishing a copy of my book. 'Do you know of this man?'

'Yes,' said Charlie.

'He's a communist engaged in an assault on the criminal justice system.'

'But supposing he is right?' asked Charlie. To which there was no clear answer.

Charlie also confirmed what I had heard from other sources, that the trial judge, Lord Bridge, is still going around saying that the Birmingham Six were guilty, which only goes to show that it is possible to be very clever and stupid at the same time.

Mike O'Brien reported, during tonight's division, that the Americans are prepared to consider compensating the woman who lost half her family to one of their bombs. I said I would be checking, to which he replied, 'I told them you would.'

Thursday, 21 November

To the Liaison Committee, where there was an amusing discussion of a suggestion from David Curry that members of select committees be allowed to use laptops and other electronic aids during committee hearings. Gerald Kaufman, Gwyneth Dunwoody and several of the other veterans were resolutely opposed. Gerald said, 'I was going to be agnostic until I heard someone say that we must move with the times.' There was a vote on whether to allow David's committee to experiment. I hesitated and then put up my hand in favour on the grounds that we couldn't stop others from experimenting, but laptops will never be allowed into the Home Affairs Committee as long as I'm in charge. Gerald snorted and walked out.

---

* Appointed Lord Chief Justice in July 2008.

Monday, 25 November

To the House to hear The Man respond to an urgent question about the firefighters' strike. He has been away at the NATO summit in Prague and in his absence things have drifted. But no more. He set out the position with beautiful clarity: any wage increase over 4 per cent must be paid for by the proceeds of modernisation and, in case there was any doubt, he listed the issues that need addressing. From our side there were only a couple of dissenters. From the Tories came a large dose of shameless opportunism, but they were knocked firmly into their box. The Man is back. Long live The Man.

Tuesday, 26 November

The firefighters' strike has taken a turn for the worse. For some inexplicable reason (presumably it was his way of demonstrating that he was still in charge after The Man's bravura performance yesterday) JP made a statement to the House implying that modernisation of the service might cost 10,000 jobs and suddenly confusion reigns where, yesterday there was clarity. Overnight the dispute has been transformed from a fight about an outrageous pay demand into one about jobs. Exactly the territory we don't want to fight on.

Wednesday, 27 November

To the weekly meeting of the parliamentary party to hear David Blunkett speak of what he called 'my struggle' to convince the *liberati* of this country that, unless people feel secure, then all the progressive politics in the world come to nothing. On asylum he said that, despite our best efforts, this year's figures were 20 per cent higher than last, 'We are at breaking point.' He spoke of 'administrative chaos' in some parts of the Immigration and Nationality Directorate. On the judges he said, 'It is proving difficult to bring them from the medieval to the Tudor.'

Gordon made his pre-Budget statement, bullish and upbeat as ever, but behind the barrage of bluster there is no disguising that we are in trouble. Savings and investment are falling, trade deficit mushrooming, stock market sinking with all that that implies for pensions. Last year's growth predictions proved wildly over-optimistic. Kevin Hughes said, 'Gordon's speeches always sound alright until you unpack the case and come across the smelly socks hidden between the clean shirts.'

At the parliamentary committee, a long discussion about the fire strike. Tony Lloyd kicked off, saying he had seen the draft agreement from last week and it was difficult to see what was wrong with it.

The Man begged to differ: 'It contained no guarantees; the government was going to have to pay the difference and the firefighters' idea of modernisation is more men and machines.' He went on, 'We are at a critical stage. We either make the mistake that every previous Labour government has made or we avoid it. If the union walk away with a victory, we've had it. It would be the end.' He added that the firefighters would never have dared take such a stand against a Tory government. 'I feel quite aggrieved about that.'

Gordon Prentice said it had been a terrible blunder to say that modernisation could cost 10,000 jobs. Bridget Prentice added that there was a perception that the dispute had changed from being about pay to jobs. The Man defended JP, who he said had been the victim of a tawdry spin operation by the firefighters' union.

Helen Jackson said that we were letting local government off the hook. In South Yorkshire until recently the same man had been in charge of the Fire Authority for 30 years and he wasn't even capable of modernising his own kitchen let alone the fire service.

I said, 'We have to win and be seen to win, otherwise we'll have years of this nonsense. We need to be looking for a deal that will take us past the next election, maybe even a no-strike deal – that would be worth paying a few bob for.' We were fighting on too many fronts, I added. 'We need to close one down. My candidate would be top-up fees.' At the mention of top-up fees The Man assumed a pained expression and shook his head. As he was leaving, however, he paused at the door and called over to me, 'I've heard what you say about not fighting on too many fronts.'

Friday, 29 November
Sunderland

To the graduation lunch at the university where the Chancellor, David Puttnam, bent my ear briefly about the iniquity of top-up fees. The Man, says David, seems to be hooked on them, although they have no support from anyone beyond the vice-chancellors of a handful of top universities. According to David, Estelle Morris was opposed (and that may have been one of the factors that led to her departure). Margaret Hodge is a problem. 'I have always regarded her as the cuckoo in the nest.' On the Broadcasting Bill, which comes up for a second reading on Tuesday, he said he had recently managed to wring a couple of concessions out of Number 10, but there was still nothing in the Bill to prevent ITV being sold to the Americans even though no foreign media corporation could buy up an American one. David said he could get no sense out of anyone in Number 10 on the subject and could only assume that it was the product of a fireside chat between the Two Most Important People on the Planet.

In the evening, to the function suite at the Leisure Centre, for the Sunderland South Labour Party dinner, the first evidence for years that Sunderland South Labour Party is capable of organising anything. Steve Byers, the guest speaker, remarked during the course of the evening that The Man once told him that he would like to stay in power for longer than Margaret Thatcher, which means another six years. The first clue I have ever unearthed as to The Man's long-term plans.

Monday, 2 December

To London on an early train. A horrendous week lies ahead. Among many other things, I have to draft a speech on the Criminal Justice Bill for Wednesday, open and close the debate on our drugs report on Thursday and prepare for the Extradition Bill next Monday. Scientific planning is required. For the last couple of weeks I have been getting in before 8 a.m. and working through until 11 p.m.

Tuesday, 3 December

I intervened on Tessa Jowell as she was introducing the Communications Bill and she confirmed that there will be nothing to stop the Americans buying up our media even though we can't buy into theirs. 'But we're going to negotiate …' she added pathetically. An odd way to negotiate, giving away your trump card before you start. 'That's not the worst bit,' said the former Culture Secretary, Chris Smith, who was sitting next to me. He went on, 'The worst bit is allowing Murdoch to buy Channel Five, which he will use to undermine ITV and Channel 4.'

'Are you going to make that point?'

'Er, no, I've only got ten minutes and there are other points I want to make.'

'But you just said that was the worst.'

He blushed and said awkwardly, 'It's for others to make.' Really? I can't think of anyone better qualified than the former Secretary of State.

Chris confirmed that Downing Street had been taking a close interest in the Bill. 'Tony felt he had to give something to Murdoch.' He then got to his feet and made a speech describing the Bill as 'a good one which could be even better'.

'Rather generous, in view of the conversation we have just been having,' I said when he sat down.

Chris just smiled. I guess that's why he was in the Cabinet and I never will be.

Wednesday, 3 December

Gordon outlined his plans for tax credits at the meeting of the parliamentary party. They are fairly dramatic. I had a chat with Dawn Primarolo, who is in her fifth year at the Treasury. Tax credits, she says, present us with a challenge. 'The top 10 per cent of earners are going to take a big hit. Not only are we removing the cap on National Insurance payments – everyone earning over the current limit (£32,000) will pay an additional one per cent – but they won't benefit from the child credits either. And even those who do benefit may not be entirely grateful, because it will be paid to their wives.'

At this point a little cloud began to cross a clear blue sky. If the principal beneficiaries of child tax credits are predominantly the non-voting classes and those who take the hit are predominantly the voting classes, will we necessarily be rewarded at the ballot box? Worse, supposing that those who benefit believe that their good fortune is a gift from heaven rather than New Labour? That, says, Dawn is the challenge. A considerable one in these cynical times.

At the parliamentary committee Hilary Armstrong announced that, as a result of the new hours, standing committees would start sitting at 08.55. Helen Jackson seemed surprised by this until one or two of us pointed out that this was what she had voted for. Jean Corston said afterwards that she hardly had time for the chamber, what with all her other commitments and I gently remarked that this was the very point I had, in my cack-handed way, been trying to make when I upset all the modernisers three weeks ago: it is impossible to fit all our activities into a day which is three hours shorter.

Later, in the Tea Room, Tommy McAvoy whispered to me that my amendment on the shorter hours motion had provoked 'hysteria' from otherwise rational colleagues.

'Robin seems to have staked his life on it,' I remarked.

To which Tommy intriguingly replied, 'Chris, sometime when we've got ten minutes for a quiet chat, I'll tell you what went on.'

Thursday, 5 December

I opened and closed the debate on the select committee's drugs report and was for once exempted from the time limit on backbench speeches. Nick Hawkins, who spoke for the Tory front bench, didn't quite rise to the occasion, but apart from him (and that dreadful man from Romford) there were some excellent contributions from all sides. As far as users are concerned, there has been a real shift of policy in favour of harm reduction and away from retribution. I do believe we have made a difference.

Sunday, 8 December
Sunderland

A feeding frenzy is developing over Cherie Blair's use of a convicted conman – the boyfriend of her 'lifestyle guru' Carol Caplin – to help her buy two flats in a posh part of Bristol. Number 10 then dug the pit deeper by understating the boyfriend's role in the affair, since when a set of e-mails have appeared suggesting his involvement in the transaction was rather greater than has so far been acknowledged. So far as anyone can see Cherie hasn't actually done anything wrong, but she has been foolish.

Monday, 9 December

I came across Hilary Armstrong in the Tea Room, looking glum. No prizes for guessing why – the Cherie debacle. 'It's awful,' she said. 'Absolutely awful. They won't let go.'   Having poured on the poison for several days the Harmsworth Lie Machine is now commissioning opinion polls to gauge the effect. A poll in yesterday's *Mail on Sunday* reported that only 51 per cent of those asked believe that Tony Blair is honest – the lowest rating of any of the big three party leaders.

Tuesday, 10 December

Today's instalment in the 'Cheriegate' saga alleges that she telephoned Peter Foster's solicitors on 22 November which, if true, suggests she took a greater degree of interest in his deportation case than had hitherto been admitted. 'The truth, the whole truth and anything but the truth,' screeches today's *Daily Mail*. 'It stinks, Cherie,' rages the *Mirror*. 'If Cherie was a minister, she'd have been fired,' proclaims the *Sun*. 'I was quite sympathetic to Cherie until I heard about that call,' remarked Clive Efford in the Tea Room. 'We are all being damaged by the action of someone who isn't accountable to us. Tony needs to understand the resentment this causes.' He wanted me to pass on the message at the parliamentary committee tomorrow.

To the Attlee Room in Portcullis House to hear Noam Chomsky. He spoke softly, without notes, for 45 minutes, in a relaxed conversational style, dressed casually in a grey sweater and an open-necked shirt. In the main his message was predictable, but with some dry asides. The present Republican regime was 'as hardline as you can get, within the realms of sanity'. They needed to keep the American people in a permanent state of fear in order to take their minds off the domestic agenda. War with Iraq was only a first step. The longer-term aim was to restore Anglo-US power across Iran and Saudi Arabia. There was no question of democracy being permitted in post-Saddam Iraq since two-thirds of the population were Shia and the US would not want to extend Shia influence – and by implication Iran's. Also, any moderately democratic Iraqi government would want to control its resources and that would never be permitted. In the past, American policy makers had talked of the need for 'an iron-fisted junta' to control Iraq and this was a strong possibility. US culture, he said, was more fundamentalist than that in Iran. 'The strength of Christian fundamentalism is such that anyone who wants to be president has to pretend to be a born-again Christian.' Someone asked about the extent of Tony Blair's influence on Bush and his court. 'I don't want to be offensive,' replied Chomsky, 'but it's zero.'

This evening Cherie came out fighting. She used an appearance at a charity function in the Atrium at Millbank to try and draw a line under the events of the past week. She struck just the right tone: dignified, apologetic, with just a hint of defiance. With any luck this will put an end to the nonsense.

Wednesday, 11 December

This morning's media is dominated by Cherie's speech last night. Most of the coverage is mildly sympathetic with the notable exceptions of the *Mail* and the *Mirror*. If anything, the *Mirror* is nastier than the *Mail*, devoting nine hate-filled pages to the subject. Cherie has obviously done something to upset the odious Piers Morgan. At questions, Duncan Smith made a feeble attempt to climb on the Cherie bandwagon, but was easily seen off. 'Typical of the Right Honourable Gentleman to dive into the swimming pool after the water has run out' was The Man's magnificent parting shot. I detect the magic hand of Alastair.

Thursday, 12 December

My 55th birthday. The girls rang at 8 a.m. to wish me many happy returns. Emma sang while Sarah played the piano in the background.

Three US Congressmen, all Republicans, came to see me about drugs. The man from Georgia did all the talking. The tone of his questioning suggested he wanted nothing to do with any namby-pamby European nonsense about harm minimisation – controlled prescription, needle exchange and the like. 'They tried needle exchange in Baltimore with the result that the problem was worse than ever. It was the same in Vancouver ...' I gently pointed out that collapsing the banana economies in the Caribbean in the name of free trade was only going to make the problem worse and that, if they wanted to stem the flow of heroin from Afghanistan, it would be an idea to engage in a little nation-building, but I am not sure that any of it registered. I walked out with them to St Stephen's Entrance. Someone pointed out his car and the man from Georgia just walked away in mid-sentence without so much as a goodbye and got into the car without looking back.

A cup of tea with Tony Benn who I came across in the corridor outside the Library. Needless to say, he is supporting the firemen's ludicrous wage claim. When I pressed him, he came out with all sorts of irrelevant, Socialist Worker-type guff about boardroom greed. 'You would never have supported a claim 20 times the rate of inflation during any of the 11 years you were in the Cabinet,' I said. He didn't deny it. It was all very good-humoured. I love him dearly but he's getting worse.

Friday, 13 December
Sunderland

I am becoming forgetful. This morning, going out of the front gate, I mistook a neighbour for the man who repaired our heating some time ago. He looked bemused when I asked about his back and whether his daughter had got a place at Oxford and then I realised my mistake. Later, walking back from the town, I passed the time of day with a woman I feel I should know well, but I can't for the life of me put a name to her. Nothing serious, I hope. Grandma Mullin had Alzheimer's.

Saturday, 14 December

We drove to Whitburn to buy a Christmas tree and Sarah and Emma spent the afternoon decorating it. In the evening Ngoc and I went to see *The Quiet American.* Wonderful. Gripping, realistic, faithful to the original. Michael Caine was excellent. Fifties Saigon brilliantly re-created. Apparently the American distributors had delayed its release for more than a year. And no wonder. It portrays the American government up to its neck in terrorism. Very inconvenient.

Monday, 16 December

To London for the second reading of Alun Michael's hunting Bill. Arrived at Westminster to find the House surrounded by several thousand baying huntspersons, blowing whistles, firing rockets and being generally obnoxious. At the underground entrance our way was blocked by an oaf in a check cap, wearing a lapel badge which said 'Bollocks to Blair'. He stood in the revolving door and refused to let us pass until we had told him which way we were intending to vote. It wasn't until Andrew Bennett came along and physically removed him that we were able to get in. Later, we heard that the entrance from Parliament Square had been closed as a result of 'a serious incident'. All in all, the police seemed to be treating the demonstrators lightly – although there were one or two arrests later. Goodness knows what would have happened if the miners had behaved like that.

During the division I had a chat with Michael Meacher, who says that the Environment department has had virtually no input into the recent announcement about spending more on roads and that Margaret has sent Alistair Darling a strong letter. He also says they had not been seriously consulted about the proposed changes to the planning regulations or on airport expansion. To cap it all, he says, there is even a debate about building more nuclear power stations even though nuclear power is more expensive than wave energy; it has generated 10,000 tons of waste (rising to 500,000 by the end of the century) that no one knows what to do with; not to mention that nuclear power stations are vulnerable to terrorist attack. 'To be fair to Margaret, she has taken a stand.'

Tuesday, 17 December

A meeting with Frank Dobson and someone from *Searchlight* about the rise of the British National Party. They do best in places where the Tory vote has collapsed. They've started winning seats in Blackburn and Burnley and in the recent mayoral election in Stoke the BNP polled more votes than the Tories and Lib Dems combined. If things continue as they are, it can only be a question of time before Sunderland elects its first fascist. A Tory revival will put a stop to them and there is no sign of that.

Alan Milburn addressed the Northern Group of MPs. The polls, he said, showed absolute scepticism about the ability of the government to translate tax rises into improvements in services. As regards the NHS there was a discrepancy between the opinions of those who had recently used the service, 70 per cent of whom expressed satisfaction, and those who had no recent experience of the NHS, less than 50 per cent of whom thought the NHS was working. He ascribed the difference to the tabloid effect, especially the *Mail*, which, unhappily, was the paper most read by nurses. Alan concluded, 'By the time we get to the election, the improvements have got to be so obvious that the public can see through the crap.' Not a small ambition.

Wednesday, 18 December

A chat with Alan, who is decorating the hall and stairwell at Brixton Road. He lives on the 17th floor of a tower block on the Mile End Road which, he says, is plagued by drug addicts shooting up in the corridors and in the rubbish chutes. One of the flats was set on fire and people are scared to go out. He said millions had been spent regenerating a local park, but most people dared not walk there because it was plagued by addicts and dealers; so was the tube station. He was trying to get out of the block, but there was nowhere to go. Listening to Alan, a decent, hard-working man, it's easy to see why people in traditional Labour strongholds are so disenchanted. The mayhem going around them dominates their lives. If we can't make the streets safer, no amount of tax credits or minimum income guarantees are going to make any difference.

At the parliamentary committee there was a brief discussion about Iraq. Helen Jackson said that military action would destabilise the region. The Man said it was up to Saddam to decide. If Saddam ends up being found with material that he says he hasn't got, then he's miscalculated. 'I honestly can't tell if there will be a war, but we are more likely to avoid it if we take a firm stand.'

Doug Hoyle said we were making too many enemies at once. He listed the various fronts – Iraq, Star Wars, top-up fees, trade unions ...

'The next six months will be tough,' The Man replied lightly.

Gordon Prentice said, in that laidback way of his – which always contains a sting in the tail – 'Tony, I'm hugely impressed that you can let it all wash over you. You just seem permanently relaxed.'

'I'm a good actor.'

Gordon then asked whether we would go back to the Security Council before declaring war. The Man replied, 'I think the Security Council will act, if it is plain that there has been a breach.'

'We should scrutinise any US claims very carefully,' I said, reminding him about yellow rain and the Gulf of Tonkin incident.* I added, 'It isn't just the Labour Party that's sceptical. It's the public.'

He nodded, but said nothing. The truth, as we all know, is that in the end we will sign up to whatever George W. Bush and his cronies come out with.

Thursday, 19 December

I asked a question of Margaret Beckett about the impact of the aviation industry's plans for indefinite expansion on the environment. It's

---

*In 1964 the US invented an attack by Vietnamese gunboats on a US warship in order to justify the bombing of North Vietnam.

the third time I have raised the subject in the chamber in the last couple of weeks. I feel a little campaign coming on. I spent the afternoon drafting an article on the subject which I will offer either to the *Evening Standard* or to the *Guardian*.

Sunday, 22 December
Sunderland

With Sarah and Emma to distribute Christmas cards to neighbours. As usual we called on Violet and Andy Bigham, a brother and sister who have lived in the same house in The Oaks since 1918, having taken it over from an uncle who had been there since the 1890s; much of the furniture and fittings are unchanged. If you stand in the hall and close your eyes, all you can hear is the sound of ticking grandfather clocks.

Tuesday, 24 December

This evening we put out refreshment for Santa (an apple, a satsuma, a few crumbly bits of shortbread and a small glass of rum) on a table by the fireplace.

Wednesday, 25 December

Sure enough Santa turned up on schedule. The apple, satsuma and the shortbread were eaten, only the peel and crumbs remaining. Emma thought she detected Santa's footprint in the ashes by the fireplace.

We opened our presents by the Christmas tree. Emma grudgingly kept a list of who had sent what. I did my best to look cheerful, but I find it a deeply depressing experience watching children who have everything piling up new possessions. Such a relief when it was over.

Sunday, 29 December
Chelmsford

Mum has recovered from her pneumonia and, though frail, is back to normal stubbornness. She is already talking of dispensing with the emergency alarm that, with some difficulty, we persuaded her to take after the most recent crisis.

In the afternoon, while Dad snored loudly on the sofa and Ngoc chatted to Mum, Emma played with the toy soldiers that survived my childhood. Some of the medieval knights are quite sophisticated, with detachable swords, spears, visors and so on. It must be forty years or more since I last handled them.

CHAPTER FIVE

2003

Wednesday, 1 January 2003
Brixton Road

I cut the accursed leylandii hedge in the back garden, cleared the drains and put out the three weeks' rubbish that had accumulated in my absence (apart from Keith on the third floor, who has been ill recently, I am the only one who puts out the bins). Then to Streatham for dinner with a friend of Ngoc's, an interpreter, who had spent most of the day at Heathrow helping immigration officials interview asylum seekers. She says the whole thing is a scam. Agents or facilitators travel to Vietnam with passports borrowed from Vietnamese who already have British citizenship, which are used to smuggle illegal immigrants onto planes bound for Europe; once on the plane the facilitator collects up the passports and when they arrive at Heathrow they simply pronounce the magic word 'asylum'. When asked why they want to come to England they always reply, as they have been taught to, 'because Britain respects human rights'. Today's arrivals, coffee farmers from the central highlands, had been charged US$12,000 a head. They, or their relatives, won't have to pay until they are safely in the UK. The 'agency' concerned guarantees a safe passage to the European country of choice within twenty days. She is amazed that we tolerate it. Why don't we just send them back? And, if we must let them in, why don't we allow them to work, so that at least we will reduce the burden on the state. Most, she points out, are going to work illegally anyway.

Saturday, 4 January
Sunderland

Awoke late, to a light dusting of snow. Making my way into town through the park I found the little bridge across the old railway cutting taped off although there was no apparent obstacle and people were stepping under the tape and carrying on anyway. Eventually a short, stout, middle-aged man, wearing shaded glasses, a peaked cap and a Securicor uniform emerged from the cabin by the bowling green, bawling and shouting. I asked what the problem was and he said he had fenced off the bridge because people might slip and sue the Council. 'With all due respect,' I said, 'this is daft. Why not just put down some salt?'

'Not my job,' he said. 'In any case I haven't got any.'

'Tell you what,' I said, 'why don't I buy some in town and give it to you on the way back and then you can spread it.'

'Not my job,' he repeated. He added almost pleasantly, 'Someone will probably tear down that tape in the next ten minutes, then I'll have to close the whole park.'

In town I came across Dennis McDonald and good old Sam Glatt, soliciting signatures on a petition against war with Iraq. 'Sign here if you oppose Blair's war,' Denis was shouting. A trickle of people, mainly middle class, obliged but as with all other forms of political activity in Sunderland the prevailing sentiment was indifference. I declined to sign, but told Sam that I won't support any war which is not endorsed by the UN Security Council.

Wednesday, 8 January

To the House in a snow storm. Brixton Road looked almost beautiful under a carpet of virgin snow.

A long talk in the Tea Room with Jack Cunningham, who has been charged with sorting through the various possibilities for Lords reform. His committee has just reported, coming up with a list of eight options ranging from wholly appointed to wholly elected, from which we will shortly be invited to choose. Jack said that, in his opinion, the Upper House should have strictly limited powers and be wholly appointed; an independent appointments commission should be set up whose remit would include ensuring that membership reflected gender, ethnicity, age, regionality. In addition, as is already more or less the case, certain public office holders – ex-Cabinet ministers, senior judges, churchmen, the chiefs of staff and the like – would automatically qualify for a place. Finally, a percentage of appointments would be reserved for the prime minister of the day to ensure that he had enough qualified ministers. Membership would not be for life, but for a set period – one or two terms of seven years? The more I think about it, the more sense it makes. After all, it is not as though the public are demanding any more elected politicians. On the contrary, most people think we have far too many already – and they may not be wrong about that.

Much of the discussion at the parliamentary committee was taken up with Iraq. 'What happens after the inspectors report on January 27th?' asked Gordon Prentice. The Man was at pains to assure us that there was no immediate threat of war. 'The inspectors have only just begun their work. They are only just up to their full complement. A lot of attention is being paid to the 27th, as though it is a red letter day. It isn't.'

'I have written you a letter,' Helen Jackson said.

'You and Prince Charles,' smiled The Man.

'What's our strategy in the event of the UN not endorsing action?' she asked.

'If the inspectors don't make a breakthrough, then we've just got to go on. It's not impossible that Arab leaders will put pressure on Saddam to go.'

'I don't think Bush will go it alone,' said Robin Cook. 'He is not going to ignore public opinion in the US and, surprisingly, it is showing that most Americans are against unilateral action.'

'A lot of people believe that Bush has made his mind up. They don't trust him,' said Doug Hoyle.

'My position,' said The Man, 'is that there is no doubt that we have to take a stand against weapons of mass destruction and that it has got to be done through the international community. It's got to be done the right way.'

'Supposing the inspectors find nothing?' I asked.

'For us to justify action, there has to be a breach of a UN resolution. The UN route means there is a process. Things have to be found to demonstrate a material breach.'

'How long do the inspectors have?'

'I don't know, but they think there are massive gaps in the December 8 declaration and they are reasonably confident that they will find something. The question is, will Saddam have a change of mind first?'

'If Saddam did level with us, is it conceivable that there will be no war?'

'Yes, though I think Saddam will miscalculate.' He added that the Egyptian leaders, to whom he had talked over the New Year, were in no doubt that Saddam was hiding something and that the outcome over Iraq would have an impact on the situation in Korea, which he described as 'absolutely terrifying'.

The House packed up after the votes at seven. By eight there was hardly anyone to be seen. The Tea Room, which would normally be full at this time on a Wednesday evening, was empty save for a handful of Scotsmen. The oxygen is being sucked out of the place, thanks to Robin's reform of the sitting hours. The entire evening economy is collapsing.

Thursday, 9 January

The lead story in the *Guardian* is that 100 Labour MPs are threatening rebellion over Iraq and that there would be resignations, at least among junior ministers, in the event of a unilateral attack. An unnamed Cabinet minister is quoted as saying that not one of the Cabinet is in favour of going to war at this moment. The report also says that 'concern was conveyed to Tony Blair yesterday by members of the parliamentary committee'. The Deputy Chief Whip, Keith Hill, whispered that Hilary Armstrong believes Robin Cook to be the source and that he is out to show her up because of her lack of enthusiasm for some of his reforms. Keith agrees with the *Guardian*'s estimate of the potential rebellion (I told him to include me in that) and says it is potentially the party's biggest crisis in living memory. He added, however, that he believes the chances of a war have receded for the time being at least.

David Blunkett has at last announced that he is raising from 14 to 17 the age at which air weapons can be used without supervision; also, there will be a presumption against carrying either air weapons or replicas in public. A little victory for civilisation over barbarism in which I can claim to have played a part. Until I sent my memo to The Man, we were getting nowhere with the Home Office.

Monday, 13 January

Dinner with David Blunkett in the Members' Dining Room. On Iraq, David thinks there will be a war and that Tony will back the Americans come what may. I asked if he thought that Gordon and Clare were preparing to take over if it all went wrong and he said he was sure they are.

Tuesday, 14 January

With the Home Affairs Committee to the immigration detention centre at Harmondsworth, near Heathrow, the last stop for asylum seekers who have reached the end of the line; it is also the last stop for criminals and other undesirables awaiting deportation – 19,000 people passed through last year. The staff were at pains to assure us that the centre is well-run – and it is. Everything was provided for, except freedom. We were shown a little room where children plucked from classrooms around the country spend their last few days on British soil before being dispatched to goodness-knows-where. On the wall outside were little notes tapped out on computers by children who had passed through. 'Oh look, there's one from Sunderland,' someone said and, sure enough, there was. It was Sasha, the little chap whose family I failed to rescue last year. It read (in part):

> My name is Sasha Savchenko. I am twelve years old. I come from the Ukraine.
> I live at 12 Gray Road, Sunderland. I speak four languages.
> My favourite toy is Pokemon cards.

When last heard of he and his parents were in a hostel in southern Spain.

The *Evening Standard* has published my article on the need to stand up to the demands of the aviation industry. It has also prompted a friendly leading article. It won't be popular with the regime, but I've been dying to get that off my chest.

Wednesday, 15 January

To a jam-packed meeting of the parliamentary party, which the media has been billing as a showdown between The Man and his critics on Iraq. He looked tired and strained, as well he might – under the new arrangements Prime Minister's Questions follow on almost directly from the party meeting. A lot to expect that he does both in one morning. In the event, he hardly mentioned Iraq in his opening remarks saying only, 'I hope the UN process works and I believe that it will do so.' For the rest he talked of the domestic agenda – the economy, public services, asylum, law and order. Even so, most of the points from the floor were about Iraq. There were a couple of loyalists – Stuart Bell and George Mudie. 'The Prime Minister knows best. Trust him. Full stop. That's what we should be saying,' said George. If only life were that simple. 'I applaud the way you have led us so far,' said Joan Ruddock, 'but we must side with the UN.' Anne Campbell, who represents Cambridge, said she was finding it difficult to hold her local party together: 'What will happen if the inspectors find nothing?' she asked. 'Do not join a unilateral attack,' said Glenda Jackson. The Man responded robustly. 'The question is, do weapons of mass destruction matter? I believe they do. If George Bush wasn't raising the issue, I would be. There is a link between weapons of mass destruction and terrorism. At some point terrorists are going to get hold of them. The issue has to be faced. We have had 11 years of UN resolution on Iraq. Of course, the best way is through the UN, but the inspectors wouldn't be in Iraq if pressure hadn't been put on. If we take away the pressure, there will never be a peaceful resolution. The only circumstances in which Saddam will co-operate is if he thinks we are serious.'

He went on, 'If the inspectors say Saddam is not co-operating, I hope there is no one who will not accept that the UN has to enforce its will. The consequences of not enforcing are horrendous. I believe there will be a second resolution, but I do not want to give anyone the impression that our will is lacking.' He sat down to thunderous applause. With one leap he was free – for the time being at least.

Later I spoke to Michael White of the *Guardian* who has been talking to some of The Man's American friends. Michael says he has more influence in Washington than any other non-American. 'The fact that he was willing to go that extra mile after September 11 and that his advice that Bush should go to the UN won plaudits is money in the bank. The fact is, however, that no British prime minister can afford to fall out with the President. The last one who did was Anthony Eden and look what happened to him.'

Iraq surfaced again at the parliamentary committee. The Man said, 'The message we are getting from inside Iraq is that we should concentrate on regime change. The one advantage of the hard rhetoric that George Bush is using is that it is fracturing the Iraqi leadership.'

Someone remarked that an invasion would set the Arab world against us. Not so, said The Man. 'The Arabs aren't saying don't do it. They are saying, do it quickly.'

Supposing a second UN resolution was vetoed, someone asked. The Man replied, 'If you say that you will accept a veto, you increase the possibility that someone – Russia perhaps – will use it irresponsibly. They've got to believe we're serious.' He added, 'We've got a process. Given a chance I believe it will work properly. If it doesn't, there will be some very tricky decisions to take.'

Gordon Prentice asked what we were going to do about North Korea. 'Iraq is the first test of whether the world is serious or not,' The Man responded. 'If we pass, North Korea will be easier to deal with.'

There was a discussion about asylum. I inquired about the suggestion, being peddled assiduously in the Murdoch and Harmsworth press, that EU enlargement would lead to a huge new wave of migration. Robin Cook said the same argument had been made when Spain and Portugal joined, but it had come to nothing. Anyway, he added, there were transition arrangements to deal with eastern Europe. The Man said he was very worried. The asylum issue was bubbling away beneath the surface. It was not true that we were taking more asylum seekers than anyone else in Europe. Numbers in Germany were rising again and there were no reliable figures for France and Italy. John Reid said that the English language and the fact that we had a relatively strong economy were the two major attractions.

'Might there come a day' I inquired, 'when we might have to consider resiling from the UN Conventions?'

'I don't want to say that,' said The Man, 'but the situation is very difficult.'

Monday, 20 January

The tabloids are working themselves up into a frenzy. 'Widow, 88, told by GP: make way for asylum seekers,' rages yesterday's *Mail on Sunday*. 'Asylum hotels revolt,' proclaims today's *Express*. It goes on: 'Fury mounts over plans for refugees to enjoy life of luxury in country hotels.' Meanwhile the *Sun*, under its evil new editor Rebekah Wade, is running a series of shit-stirring reports subheaded 'Asylum Meltdown'. 'Read this and get angry' is the headline over today's dose of poison, as if *Sun* readers need yet another reason to be angry. Before long we shall have mobs of shaven-headed *Sun* and *Express* vigilantes laying siege to the homes of terrified asylum seekers, just as we did with alleged paedophiles a few months ago. What are we going to do about this tabloid virus?

To a dinner hosted by the journalists and broadcasting unions, to discuss what can be done about the Communications Bill which is threatening to deliver ITN into the hands of the Americans and Channel Five into the hands of Murdoch. Those present included David Puttnam, Duke Hussey and Tom McNally from the Lords, and John Grogan, Nick Harvey, Austin Mitchell and Terry Rooney from the Commons. 'A step towards the Berlusconisation of the British media,' said Puttnam. Number 10, he said, was desperately naive. If Murdoch got his hands on Channel Five he would use his other interests to cross-promote it and destroy Channel Four. 'The Tories invented Channel Four. Does Labour really want on its gravestone that they destroyed it?' He added that, in contrast to the Press Complaints Commission, the Advertising Standards Agency was so good that the standard of the advertisements in most newspapers was better than the editorial content.

Tom McNally said, 'If giving Murdoch 40 per cent of our print media, our only satellite broadcaster and a major foothold in terrestrial TV isn't against the public interest, what is?'

Someone described Murdoch as an elephant. 'He's not an elephant,' said Duke Hussey. 'He's an alligator. I know Rupert very well. I like him. He is a genius, a very dangerous genius. He should not be given Channel Five.'

There was some discussion about possible amendments in the Lords. The problem is that the Tories are backing the government. I was seated next to an elderly Tory peer who intervened every five minutes to say that whatever we did we should keep it simple and that, in any case, it was all hopeless.

Tuesday, 21 January

To Portcullis House for the Liaison Committee's biennial joust with The Man. He, alone at one end of the horseshoe, *sans* jacket, *sans* officials, elbows on desk, fingers touching lightly below his chin. This is a formula at which he excels. His only props, a single blank sheet of paper, a bottle of water and a glass. The paper was still blank when he left two and a half hours later. The entire session was devoted to Iraq. We each took turns. Mostly it was a ritual. He has thought it all through. There is nothing he hasn't been asked ten times already. Several people – John Horam, Edward Leigh, Tony Wright – got briefly under the wire, but mostly he was unruffled. 'You tell me what we have got out of this?' whispered Gerald Kaufman (who is cynical about the whole exercise).

'He's put his case across ...'

'Brilliantly, but it's not our role to be his patsy.'

No sooner had Gerald spoken than he intervened with a soft-ball question which The Man effortlessly hit towards the boundary.

I was lacklustre, devoting my eight or nine minutes to the so-called special relationship. The Man replied to each point at length. I should have interrupted, but didn't. We share the same values as

America, he said, tolerance, democracy ... Nonsense, I should have replied – the Republican Party is a front for some of the greediest, meanest, most selfish people on the planet. We have nothing in common with them. I should have said that, but I didn't. I like the guy and I don't want to fall out with him.

'How does he manage to come across as so reasonable?' Edward Leigh remarked afterwards. Both he and John Horam reiterated that they are against the war and that Tory voters are as divided as ours. Sure enough a poll in today's *Guardian* suggests that public opinion is 43/30 against. If the Americans go ahead without UN backing and if we were to back them – as I'm sure we will – then the Man will be in deep trouble.

Wednesday, 22 January

Geoff Hoon, fluent, emollient, disingenuous, addressed the parliamentary party. The meeting was thinly attended at first, but people drifted in. He didn't endear himself to the doubters by affecting not to understand the arguments against our participation in a missile defence system. He had a similar problem on Iraq: 'I find it difficult to understand the attitude of our opponents to the role of the UN,' he said. Several people tried to enlighten him. Malcolm Savidge pointed out that, as regards missile defence, there were doubts about the existence of a threat, about the technical feasibility, the cost and the long-term diplomatic consequences. 'You know perfectly well what the arguments are,' Diane Abbott told him, listing proliferation as the main one. She then started on, at some length, about Iraq. 'Spaceship New Labour has lost touch with planet earth,' she said, provoking groans from loyalists.

'You're on your own,' Dari Taylor sitting behind me called out.

'No she's not,' I hissed. '43 per cent of the public agree with her.' Afterwards I was berated by Dari, who can be a bit of a pain.

Geoff replied that missile defence was a 'modest proposal intended to deal with the threat posed by countries, such as North Korea or Iraq, which have small numbers of missiles and no regard for the welfare of their own people and which would not, therefore, be deterred by the prospect of retaliation'. On Iraq, he claimed that there was no inevitability about war. 'You all know the argument. Unless we are prepared to demonstrate our resolve Saddam won't take us seriously.'

'I thought he was facile,' Jonathan Shaw remarked afterwards. Jean Corston, who chaired the meeting, said much the same.

Who should I come across beavering away in the otherwise deserted Library at ten o'clock this evening? None other than that ultra-moderniser Oona King who a few weeks ago was arguing passionately for knocking off at seven thirty on the grounds that her husband would divorce her if she kept coming home late. She was still there when I went home at 11.

Thursday, 23 January

Yet more evidence of dissatisfaction on the Tory benches with their leader's slavish support for George W. Bush over Iraq. Jonathan Sayeed, my neighbour on Upper Corridor South, drew my attention to his speech – in yesterday's defence debate – dissenting from the official line. No one seems to have noticed that he is a front bench spokesman. 'I expected to be sacked, but nothing has happened,' he said scarcely able to hide his disappointment. 'Do me a favour,' he said. 'Ring around some of your left-wing friends in the lobby and mention my speech.'

'Why?'

'Because as long as we are behind the government, it's easy for Blair to get away with support for the Americans. There's quite a lot of dissent below the surface on our side and I want to stir things up a bit.'

So I rang Ann Perkins and Andy McSmith and did the necessary. We shall see what happens. Nothing, I suspect. No one is interested in the Tories.

Once again today's tabloids are full of poison about asylum. 'Asylum is going to bring us down,' Ross Cranston remarked this evening.

'Whatever the issue, it comes back to asylum.' Bob Ainsworth said he was being stopped in the street by irate constituents.

Meanwhile today's *Mail* is telling its readers that students could be leaving university with debts of up to £50,000. On Monday they were saying £21,000. And if we were to suggest paying for students out of general taxation the *Mail* would be the first to scream blue murder. What are we going to do about these loathsome tabloids? Must we lie back and take it or can we find some way of striking back?

Friday, 24 January

Rang M in Washington. 'Only about five people are enthusiastic about this war,' he said, 'and I can name all of them.'

Monday, 27 January

At supper in the Tea Room, I was joined by Jack Straw, who is looking remarkably well all things considered. He spent today in Brussels, last week he visited America twice, the week before he was in the Far East. The secret, he says, is no booze, exercise and the ability to fall sleep any time, any place. According to Jack, there is a better than 50/50 chance of getting a second resolution through the Security Council. He seemed confident that the French ('who are entirely without scruple') will come round in the end 'because they want a slice of the action'. He thinks there is a slim chance that the Iraqis will blink at the last minute and that Saddam will go into exile – 'that's why we are ratcheting up the pressure'. I wonder if Jack is entirely signed up to this enterprise? I may be wrong, but I thought I understood him to say that he wished we weren't where we were.

Tuesday, 28 January

Jack used a similar phrase ('people may have different views about whether we should be here') when he addressed the Foreign Affairs Committee in an upper committee room this evening. That apart, however, he was entirely on message. The Blix report, he asserted, contains the clearest possible evidence that Saddam has weapons of mass destruction, including anthrax, VX nerve gas. Also, several thousand chemical rockets are unaccounted for. 'Some people have been in denial,' he added.

'Who was the chief salesman? Donald Rumsfeld, I think,' growled Tam Dalyell.

'With all due respect, Tam, I have watched you on four separate occasions – the Falklands, Kosovo, the Gulf and now Iraq – oppose war and on each occasion you have been wrong.' Jack added, 'My father was a pacifist. He went to jail for refusing to fight in the Second World War. I understand why. I respect that, but he was wrong. George Lansbury was wrong over Abyssinia; he nearly wrecked the party ...'

Later, at the Channel Four political awards, I ran into Tony Benn, who is off to see Saddam on Friday. 'Don't let him use you,' I said. His son Stephen and Jean Corston, among others, have been saying the same.

'I'm too old to care what anyone thinks,' he said angrily. 'I shall see children who in a few weeks time may be dead.'

'Saddam has killed a lot of children,' I said.

'That is already done. This is the future.'

I asked what he was going to say to Saddam and he started spouting about the wickedness of Israel. 'If you want to stop the war,' I said, 'you should advise him to give up his anthrax and his nerve gas.'

Actually, you have to hand it to him. He may be a stubborn, self-indulgent old grandstander, but there are not many people of 77 who would get it into their heads to fly to Baghdad in the hope of talking Saddam Hussein out of a war. It is not for those of us who are doing nothing to criticise.

Wednesday, 29 January

'SURRENDER TO ASYLUM', screams today's *Express*. The strapline read, 'We're all set to take on Saddam, but we can't even stop the refugee invasion of our land.' The *Sun* now claims to have received 385,000 responses in support of its 'campaign against asylum madness'. A headline on page 2 says, 'HIV, TB, Hepatitis C. We're not racists Mr Blunkett, just terrified for our children's health.' Not to be outdone, the Tories are now demanding that asylum seekers be incarcerated in prison ships. So much for that nice Mr Letwin. I toyed with the idea of summoning the tabloid editors to the select committee and giving them a going over, but have decided against on the grounds that it could easily backfire.

At Questions Alice Mahon asked The Man what next, after we had sorted out Iraq, and he blurted out that we would have to 'confront' North Korea. Oh Lord, a vista of endless war unfolds. Some on our side were openly heckling and the Tories were cheering. Diane Abbott claimed that Alastair Campbell's face was a picture.

Keith Hill, our ever cheerful Deputy Chief Whip, joined me at lunch in the cafeteria. 'We are fighting on so many fronts that I've lost count,' he said. He describes his troublesome charges as 'the three disses – dissidents, the dismissed and the disappointed'.

'Also,' he added, 'I detect a new tendency, the parliamentarist who believes he was elected *sine* Labour and is, therefore, free to exercise his judgement as he sees fit.'

At the parliamentary committee Ann Clwyd kicked off, saying that we should not allow Iraq to overshadow Afghanistan. The Karzai government was fragile and he was facing elections in 18 months. The Man agreed: 'We'd be crazy to throw it away.' He went on, 'Some of the countries that aren't with us on Iraq could help us in Afghanistan. That's one of the things I'm going to say to Bush on Friday. The struggle can take many forms' (a quote from Gramsci as Alan Howarth pointed out afterwards).

We had a long discussion about asylum, which is rising to the top of his agenda. The Man said he had spent six and a half hours on the subject on Monday. Big changes are on the way. 'We are looking at whether we need to withdraw the whole system for certain specified countries and in certain specified circumstances. We need to make it a seven-to-ten-day process.' He talked of the need for safe havens in places like northern Iraq or Somalia in which applicants could be held while their claim was processed. There was, he said, no question of resiling from Article Three of the Human Rights Convention, which is absolute. Neither, contrary to recent speculation, did we want to resile from the Geneva Convention, which, in any case, was very general in its approach. It was our courts which had interpreted it as requiring a Rolls-Royce system of appeals and it was up to Parliament to regain control of the issue. He went on, 'I've no illusions. Unless we deal with the asylum problem we will kibosh ourselves. It is poisoning community relations. We cannot say it is not a problem and look as if we are in the real world.'

There was a brief discussion about taming the tabloids. Jean drew attention to a paper from Clive Soley containing half a dozen suggestions for taking them on, including removing editors from sitting on the Press Complaints Commission and challenging the *Standard*'s near monopoly position in London. The Man said he wanted to open up the media to competition. 'That's why I'm not bothered about letting in big foreign corporations. They can't be any worse than Conrad Black.'

After The Man had departed there was a discussion about the Electoral Commission which was set up by us in 2000 and according to the party's general secretary, Dave Triesman, is becoming increasingly arrogant, stupid and aggressive. 'I told them we can't lift ourselves over the hurdles they have created and they threatened me with imprisonment and swingeing fines. They are threatening to investigate all 13,000 candidates in the local elections. I can't see why anyone would want to be a party treasurer. I told them they should be putting their effort into increasing public participation. We need to take them on.'

'They cannot carry on as if every party treasurer is a qualified accountant,' said Robin Cook. 'We need to get them into the real world.'

John Reid said, 'We have created a monster.'

I spent ten minutes chatting to Estelle Morris, who said she had been against top-up fees from the outset, but The Man was dead set on them. I asked how much it would have cost to pay all fees out of taxation and she said about £400 million a year, rising to £1,000 million once the top-ups came into effect.

So, as with so much else, the will of The Man prevailed in the teeth of opposition from his Secretary of State. 'He's a great man,' said Estelle, 'but great men sometimes make great mistakes.'

Friday, 31 January

The Man is off to Washington for a pow-wow with his friend George W. Bush. No longer talking if, but when. As Alan Howarth remarked the other day, the mood has changed. We are drifting inexorably, inevitably into war. It could be very bloody. A leaked UN report talks of millions displaced and casualties in the tens or even hundreds of thousands. What do I think? So far I have kept my head down. The question opponents of the current strategy must answer is 'What would you do about Saddam's anthrax and nerve gas?' Those who say that there is no evidence he has any are deluding themselves. To those who say, 'He'd never dare use it', the answer is 'He has, twice.' To those who say, 'Containment has worked well until now, what has changed?' the short answer is '9/11'. Sooner or later this stuff is going to fall into the hands of terrorists and the results could be devastating. That, in a nutshell, is the official line. Do I buy it? Not entirely. Containment was working. There isn't any evidence of leakage. Saddam is getting on in years, not short of enemies and won't last for ever. On the other hand, we are in too deep. Were we to back down now Saddam would declare an enormous triumph and the credibility of the UN would be in tatters. Perhaps, however, there is another reason why my head is so far below the parapet. Am I too close to The Man? Too dazzled by his undoubted brilliance? It is not as though I am dependent on his patronage. Or am I? Do I secretly, improbably, foolishly nurture hopes of a return to office? Has ambition finally triumphed over principle? Or is it just that I think that he may, just possibly, be right?

Polly Toynbee has a brilliant piece about the tabloids and asylum in today's *Guardian* in which I am quoted and described as 'a good and humane man'. I hope she's right. The phone rings. It is Simon Walters of the *Mail on Sunday*. His editor has seen the piece in the *Guardian* and wants to know if I would write a piece for his loathsome rag about asylum seekers in Sunderland. He must be joking.

Monday, 3 February

Peter Hain (quoting Sally Morgan, who was present at the meeting with Bush) says The Man had a hard time in Washington. George and the boys aren't making any secret of their contempt for the UN and they are reluctant to make even a nod in that direction, despite The Man's pleading.

Tuesday, 4 February

The long-awaited vote on the Lords. We didn't exactly cover ourselves in glory, voting down all seven options. The Man, hotfoot from a summit with Chirac at Le Touquet, made a rare appearance in support of an all-appointed chamber. Jack Straw, also just back from Le Touquet, said he doesn't think the French will veto a UN resolution on Iraq. 'They need a way out,' he said. Then, grabbing my arm and falling about with laughter, he added, 'So do we.'

Most of this evening's Channel Four news was devoted to Tony Benn's interview with Saddam Hussein. It wasn't very rigorous. Just a series of statements, mainly interesting because it was the first time in years that anyone from the West has come face to face with the tyrant. For a man facing oblivion Saddam seemed remarkably relaxed. He spoke slowly, calmly, without notes, occasionally fidgeting with a pen. Perhaps he has no idea of the trouble he is in. The problem with shooting people who give you disagreeable advice is that people tend to stop telling you things you don't want to hear.

Wednesday, 5 February

For the first time in ages, my name came up at Prime Minister's Questions. I decided it was time to get something on the record about Iraq. Nothing sensational. Short and to the point. I would not support a war, I said, without a second resolution. I tried to lighten it with a self-deprecating reference to not being a Blair Babe, but I could tell he was exasperated. 'I have set out my position for my honourable friend on many previous occasions ...' he began. As soon as I left the chamber, I was pounced upon by a couple of New Labour women, both ministers. It wasn't my point about Iraq that upset them, but my reference to Blair Babes. 'A sense of humour is very dangerous in politics,' remarked David Taylor, to whom I recounted the exchange afterwards. 'In the last Parliament there were only three ministers who displayed a sense of humour at the Dispatch Box. Keith Hill, yourself and Denis MacShane. Keith has been kicked upstairs, you've gone and I daily await the demise of Denis.'

At the parliamentary committee, Gordon Prentice asserted that the party was losing members faster than at any time he could remember. Before The Man could respond John Reid cut in, insisting that there had been no recent rise in resignations as a result of Iraq. Dave Triesman backed him up, saying that numbers hadn't dipped as a result of the Afghan war either. The trend was down, but the main problem was lapses.

'No one in my constituency has protested about our stand on Iraq,' said John Prescott. 'The working class don't write. It's only if you've got a university that you get a lot of letters.'

'There is no university in Pendle,' replied Gordon.

I said, 'Perhaps we should stop encouraging the working classes to go to university. Otherwise they'll all start writing.'

Thursday, 6 February

Geoff Hoon announced the deployment to the Gulf of lots more warplanes, helicopters and airforce personnel, prompting a rumble of dissent on our side when he suggested, contrary to what others have been saying, that there might not be a vote (in Parliament) until after the commencement of hostilities 'in order to retain the element of surprise'. When Diane Abbott pointed out that Congress in America had already been permitted a vote he retreated into bluster about 'different constitutional arrangements', prompting more rumbling. 'He hasn't got a clue,' someone muttered. Geoff took a hard pounding. The only covering fire from our side came from Field Marshal Winnick. Meanwhile Geoff sailed on regardless. It's not that he's incompetent. On the contrary. It's just that his body language is all wrong. He gives the impression of being gung-ho and uncaring. Also, everyone knows that, like all clever lawyers, he could make the opposite case with equal dexterity.

Saturday, 8 February
Sunderland

It transpires that parts of the latest Downing Street dossier on Iraq, cited with approval by Colin Powell at the UN the other day, have been lifted without attribution from the PhD thesis of a student in California. Unbelievable. One begins to wonder whether there is any serious recent evidence that Saddam is still producing chemical or biological weapons. Many of the earlier claims have turned out to be either hogwash or years out of date. The inspectors have found little or nothing. One hears whispers that the intelligence services, on both sides of the Atlantic, are not best pleased with the way in which politicians are twisting their evidence. The case for war is slender.

Sunday, 9 February

Awoke to find our front gate had disappeared. I later discovered it, in undergrowth further down the street. Two other gates had also been pulled off and Richard at number 12 had his car window smashed. Really it is too much.

Monday, 10 February

Frank Dobson, who has been tasked with organising resistance to the British National Party, addressed a meeting in Sunderland's council chamber. About 60 people, mostly councillors, attended at short notice. There's no doubt we have a problem. The BNP have correctly calculated that there are rich pickings to be had in Sunderland (anyone in doubt need only glance at the letters page in the *Echo*). They are circulating a poisonous (but well-produced) flyer, The *Sunderland Patriot*, which pushes all the buttons – asylum, drugs, crime – and is cynically designed to stir up fear and loathing among the righteous. Goodness knows how we are going to breathe life into the complacent, indolent, moribund local party, but somehow we must. If we can't even persuade our members to fight the fascists, what's the point?

There is a story in today's *Guardian* about a British citizen of Pakistani origin (his father is a bank manager in Manchester) who was kidnapped in Pakistan by American special forces, stuffed into the boot of a car and driven across the border into Afghanistan, where he has been detained at Bagram airbase. Apparently, he has not seen daylight for a year. Repeated Foreign Office requests for consular access have been refused. Which shows precisely how much influence we have with our beloved American allies – none, zero, zilch.

The headline in tonight's *Standard* reads: 'NATO FACING COLLAPSE ON IRAQ'.

Tuesday, 11 February

Robin's new hours are a disaster. Everyone is moaning about them, including several of those unwise enough to vote for the change. I was the only member of the select committee present at 08.45 this morning. For a while it looked as if we were going to be inquorate, but several others eventually dribbled in.

A poll in today's *Times* says our lead over the Tories has shrunk to one per cent. 'What a mess,' I remarked to David Hanson, The Man's man.

'He knows he's in serious difficulty,' said David, 'but he still thinks it will be alright. He thinks Blix will come up with a clear report, that there will be a second resolution and that the French won't use their veto.' He added, 'That's why I'm hanging in there.'

'A worst case scenario,' I said, 'would be an equivocal report from Blix which the Americans ignore and they go ahead anyway.'

'In that case,' said David, 'we're in deep shit.'

Wednesday, 12 February

The Man took a battering at Question Time. The Tories, prompted no doubt by the recent decline in our fortunes, seem to have perked up. Iain Duncan Smith was unusually buoyant, shamelessly playing the

asylum card. The Man repeated his foolish pledge to cut asylum applications by half by September; goodness knows what unpleasant contortions we will have to go through to achieve that. Most of the
questions from our side were, unhelpfully, about Iraq and Glenda
Jackson followed up with a devastating point of order on the same
subject ('I am not ashamed of my party, I am ashamed of my
government').

The Man wasn't at the parliamentary committee – he was on his
way to Ireland for a bit of light relief. JP stood in for him. Gordon
Prentice opened, saying that at yesterday's private briefing with BBC
correspondents, it was asserted that the decision to invade Iraq had
already been taken and that the war would begin in the first week of
March. Hilary Armstrong switched on that fixed, mirthless smile that
she always displays at moments of difficulty. 'I don't know why you're
laughing, Hilary,' snapped Gordon, 'this is war and peace.'

Hilary denied that she was laughing. Gordon went on, 'There
should be a vote in Parliament. People are fed up with all the fancy
footwork.'

'I'll pass that on,' JP said tersely. Unable to leave it at that he
added, 'I'm surprised you haven't got a resolution' – a reference to
Gordon's enthusiasm for votes at meetings of the parliamentary party.

'That's unworthy of you,' replied Gordon, who (unlike JP) never
loses his cool.

Robin Cook stepped into the breach. 'There is no wish to side-
step a vote. It is just that the precise timing depends upon events. It
is inconceivable that British troops could be committed to a war
without a vote in Parliament.'

'Pick a date, any date,' challenged Gordon.

Hilary quoted Jack Straw as saying that no date for war had been
agreed. 'Do you believe a BBC journalist more than you believe Jack?'
she asked incredulously.

'That's clear,' sneered Prescott.

'I assure you,' said Hilary, 'that the question [of a vote] is considered daily.'

Helen Jackson said naively, 'If there is no second resolution, there
may have to be a split between the US and the UK. That's what the
party would expect.'

No one had the heart to tell her that she was barking up a gum tree.

Bev Hughes, the immigration minister, told me something extraordinary this evening. She said that The Man's promise to halve the number of new asylum cases – first made in an interview with Jeremy Paxman last week and repeated at Questions today – was a mistake. 'He's got the year wrong. We were planning for September 2004. When we contacted Downing Street they claimed that Tony had intended to say what he said because he wasn't satisfied with progress. That was the first we had heard about it.' As Dennis Skinner says, The Man is becoming increasingly reckless.

Thursday, 13 February

Lunch with John Gilbert, who grows grander by the day, calling me 'Dear Boy' and 'Old Thing', but I like him. Always a twinkle in his eye. A charming, wise, unashamed *bon viveur*, with a fundamental streak of decency ('in any conversation with an American, I always try to get in a mention of the death penalty'). John reckons that, in the event of war, the Americans will reach Baghdad in two or three days and that after that it will depend whether Saddam's republican guard are capable of drawing them into street fighting, which could be very bloody. Blair's fate, he says, will depend on (a) a second resolution and (b) a quick, clean end. He doesn't think the Americans will necessarily embark on another adventure after this one. When we parted he said, 'By the time we meet again – unless we convene an emergency session – Tony Blair may no longer be Prime Minister.'

'Are you that Labour MP?' a taxi driver asked as I waited for Ngoc at Durham station at 11 p.m. this evening.

I agreed that I probably was.

'Well you tell that Mr Blair that I've voted Labour all my life and I am never voting Labour again.'

'Why?'

It was asylum of course. 'You've got shoot-outs between Turkish gangs in London, killings in Manchester …'

I pointed out mildly that asylum seekers had been coming since well before Tony Blair was elected.

'Well he should be getting rid of them.' By now the man was raving. 'I'm from a mining family. They've all voted Labour. Never again. There are asylum seekers here, in this station. I've seen them hiding so they don't have to pay the train fare. I've seen them. Here, HERE.' He gesticulated wildly at an empty parking lot. I wanted to ask him what newspaper he read, but he climbed into his car and drove away, still raving.

Friday, 14 February

My mood grows increasingly black. War looms, the party is imploding and I have nothing useful to say, hopelessly compromised by being inside the tent. Every day the *Today* programme leaves messages on my answerphone, but I don't respond. What is there to say? Until now my silence (or near silence – I did fire a little shot at Prime Minister's Questions the other day) has been possible to justify on the grounds that events are still unfolding, but make-your-mind-up time is fast approaching. I have drawn question four at PMQs for the first week back after the recess. That's twice in three weeks that my number has come up (after nothing for more than a year). Someone up there is trying to tell me something.

Saturday, 15 February
Sunderland

In London a huge demonstration, allegedly the largest ever, against war with Iraq. Let no one say that politics is dead or that New Labour has failed to mobilise the young and the idealistic. Not even Thatcher provoked opposition on this scale. Unfortunately it sends the wrong message to Saddam – the odds are he will continue to prevaricate, increasing the likelihood of war.

Meanwhile in Glasgow, The Man has come out fighting – Baghdad or bust.

Saturday, 21 February
Sunderland

Another promising row is brewing in the Tory Party over Duncan Smith's decision to abandon all that phoney nonsense about helping the vulnerable and revert to the old formula which has failed them at the last two elections – fear and loathing about crime and asylum seekers and tax cuts for the prosperous. Portillo has helpfully waded in today. Who will be first to swing from a lamppost – IDS or Saddam? It's going to be a close call.

The Man, meanwhile, is in Rome, explaining his war-plans to the Pope.

Monday, 24 February

Rang Mike O'Brien at the Foreign Office to say that I have Question 4 to The Man on Wednesday and I am thinking of raising the failure of the Americans to respond to our query about compensating the Afghan woman who lost her husband and six of her eleven children to an American bomb as an illustration of how little influence we have. Far from being dismayed, Mike was delighted and promised to alert the Minister at the embassy in the hope that it might prompt him finally to get his finger out.

An extraordinary piece in tonight's *Evening Standard* saying that, despite all recent embarrassments, Cherie and that Carole Caplin woman have been spotted shopping together in Chelsea. It is reported that they visited an emporium and expressed an interest in six pairs of £300-a-time shoes and that – so it is alleged – La Caplin rang back and tried to bargain for a lower price. She is quoted as saying, 'Well they're very expensive, you realise. Don't you know Cherie has four children?' Dear Lord, hasn't the woman got any sense? No sooner has the Bristol flats fiasco blown over than she's at it again. I showed it to Jean Corston, who shared my amazement.

Tuesday, 25 February

To Thames House, Millbank, with half a dozen members of the Home Affairs Committee, for our first meeting with the fearsome-sounding head of MI5, Eliza Manningham-Buller. Actually she was charming. A stoutish woman in her mid-to-late fifties, sporting eye shadow and two large pearl earrings; a small, downward-curving mouth, implying severity, but in fact she smiled readily, reminding me slightly of Liz Forgan. I suspect she could be good fun. She hinted, but didn't quite say, that she might favour legalising and regulating drugs, but wouldn't be drawn when I pressed her, except to say that a lot of chief constables were privately sympathetic to legalising. She knocked firmly on the head Ann Widdecombe's ludicrous scheme for locking up and vetting all new asylum seekers, saying it would be a waste of resources and that, in any case, most terrorists didn't enter the country in the backs of lorries, they tended to travel first class and had multiple identities. Finally, and most interestingly, I asked whether an attack on Iraq would make us more *or* less vulnerable to terrorism. She replied without hesitation, 'More – it will radicalise a new generation of young Arabs.' I wonder if she's told The Man.

A call from Elizabeth, a political officer at the US embassy about the poor Afghan woman. Her every word reeked of insincerity. 'Oh hi Chris, great to hear from you. I've put together some stuff about what we are doing to help the people of Afghanistan …'

Not interested, I said. 'What I want to know is what you are doing to help the woman and her family whose case Mike O'Brien drew to your minister's attention four months ago.'

She started to explain that the great, good, merciful United States did not compensate individuals on whom it dropped bombs by accident, presumably on the grounds that there were so many of them that the coffers would soon run dry. 'If it was up to me, I would compensate them all, but then I'm a softie …' she prattled. I began to feel physically sick.

'If we want to occupy the moral high ground in Iraq, we'd better try seizing it in Afghanistan,' I said through gritted teeth, hoping that the mention of Iraq might cause a little light to come on, but there was no sign that it did. Gradually, it transpired that she had lost the newspaper cutting: 'I guess it got lost in the minister's briefcase.'

Five months since the subject was first raised, by the Prime Minister himself, and they have done nothing, absolutely nothing. I said tersely that I would fax her another copy and put the phone down, seething.

Wednesday, 26 February

The day of the big Iraq debate.

At this morning's meeting of the parliamentary party Ann Clwyd reported back on her visit to northern Iraq. It seems that despite Saddam, the Turks and sanctions the Kurds have set up a more or less functioning statelet; nobody is starving, the children are in school, there is a rudimentary health service, infant mortality is lower than in Iraq proper, the Kurds even have their own little parliament. As Ann says, it gives the lie to those who argue that the piteous condition of Iraq's people is all down to sanctions. According to Ann, the Kurds are terrified that, in the event of war, they will be occupied by the Turks, who they fear as much as the Iraqis.

The subject came up at the parliamentary committee this afternoon. The Man's response was forthright: 'I can assure you that will not happen. We have reached a very clear set of understandings with Turkey. The territorial integrity of Iraq is sacrosanct.'

'Why,' asked Gordon Prentice, 'if the case [for war] is so compelling, can't public opinion be won round?'

The Man responded calmly, 'Public opinion is not so fixed. It will come round if there is a second resolution.' He added, 'I still believe that we will get one. I can't be certain, but I don't think there will be a veto.' In response to another shot from Gordon he said, 'It's not a question of giving the Americans what they want. If it had been up to them, significant parts of the Administration would have gone in six or eight months ago.'

Someone mentioned the Lib Dems. 'Their behaviour is contemptible,' he snorted.

Ann said, 'I couldn't look the Kurds in the face again if I didn't support the Prime Minister tonight.' She added, 'Even though he sacked me in 1995.'

'Did I?' The Man's jaw fell. He had clearly forgotten.

'Yes, over a visit to the Kurds, actually.'

There was much merriment around the table. Ann didn't rub it in. Her only point was that she was no poodle, which nobody needed convincing about anyway.

I briefly changed the subject – to asylum. 'Did you really mean to promise that asylum applications would be halved by September this year?'

The Man said he did.

'Because Home Office ministers seemed to be under the impression that September next year was the target date.'

No cock crowed. The Man repeated that he had been of sound mind, adding that applications were falling steeply since the Act came into force in November.

Considering the pressure, he is in remarkable shape. True, his face has shrunk slightly. The lines are sharper, cheeks indented but, contrary to what one sometimes hears, his hair-line is not receding rapidly. Pictures from ten years ago show the same isolated tuft at the front; there *has* been a retreat, but nothing remarkable. Sometimes his face is shrouded in a haze of exhaustion; very occasionally he suppresses a yawn, but always he remains focused. The eyes never wander. He never glances at the clock. And next day, after a good night's sleep, he is as right as rain. If we can get through the current crisis, he should be with us for a long time.

Snippets:

First: Steve Byers reports that he has had several long conversations with The Man about our current predicament. Steve says he has told him frankly how damaged he is by getting too close to Bush and The Man privately acknowledges that this may have been a mistake, but claims that it was necessary if the Americans were to be headed down the UN route. According to Steve, a search is underway for something to give the French in order to provide them with cover for a U-turn; the hope is that they will not want to wreck the UN.

Second: Alex Salmond says that, two years ago, he and Sean

Connery spent an hour and a half at the White House in the company of George W. Bush. Bush arrived an hour late, having been held up in a meeting with Congressmen over the stalemate with China after an American spy-plane was forced to make an emergency landing on Chinese territory. 'Idiots,' he said.

'Idiots, Mr President?'

'My party. They want to attack China when all we need to do is find a form of words that will make the old guys in Peking happy.'

According to Alex, Bush was endearingly frank about his alcoholic past. He had been to Scotland eight times, but claimed he only remembered about 10 per cent of the last trip because he had been on the booze. Says Alex, 'I was impressed. We've all been misled about Bush. He's calm in a crisis, self-deprecating, humorous.' He added hastily, 'Of course that doesn't make him right about Iraq.'

Third: Jean Corston tells me she drew The Man's attention yesterday to the *Evening Standard* report of Cherie's recent outing with Carole Caplin, warning him that the association was damaging both to Cherie and to himself. All he said was that he hoped she hadn't spent all that money on shoes.

The Iraq vote: a huge uprising, possibly the largest ever. Chris Smith's 'not proven' amendment attracted 199 votes of which 121 were from our side. The roll call of rebels includes just about every backbencher for whom I have any respect. As for me, I trooped pathetically into the government lobby, which was peopled almost exclusively by payrollers, Tories and ultra-loyalists. With a handful of exceptions such as Ann Clwyd, almost all those capable of exercising independent thought were in the other lobby. I have made up my mind that I will stick with the government for as long as there is a chance of a second resolution, but in the absence of one I shall cross over.

As I was emerging from the Aye Lobby, after the second vote, I felt a tap on the shoulder. It was Himself. 'Hi, Chris.'

'Fancy seeing you here,' said I.

'Good to see that you are.'

'All the best people,' I responded, adding *sotto voce*, 'and some of the worst.'

He laughed and marched off through the Members' Lobby. There was no one in attendance. The first time in years I can recall seeing him striding the corridors *sans* flunkies. Outside the Tea Room he paused to exchange some banter with the ever youthful David Miliband about their respective heights, remarking that David seemed to be getting taller. 'Are you still growing?' Then he strode away alone up the Library Corridor in the direction of his room. He didn't seem at all downhearted though he must know that he's in deep trouble.

Alan Milburn was on the train home. 'Tony knows he's in a tight corner,' he said. Alan thinks all will be well if we keep our nerve. The odds are, says Alan – though he concedes it is by no means certain – there will be a second resolution, that Saddam will fall, the politics will change and The Man will emerge immeasurably strengthened. In which case the moment will have come to take on Gordon. 'Everything you hear about the relationship between The Man and Gordon is true,' says Alan (exactly what Nick Brown, who is in the other camp, says). 'In fact,' beams Alan, 'it's worse.' At one point, shortly after the 2001 election, Tony was becoming worn down by Gordon repeatedly demanding to know when he would be going – in fulfilment of that famous promise, real or imagined. Gordon, according to Alan, is the source of all sorts of problems – briefing against the Public Finance Initiative, top-up fees and goodness knows what else. Alan adds that Gordon was also the cause of our problems over the London Underground and air traffic control. He says all that nonsense over air traffic control saved the taxpayer a mere £8.5 million, not the £1.2 billion we were all led to believe. 'I was Chief Secretary at the time. I went into it in detail.'

So what was it all about then? 'Goodness knows, but Gordon never does anything for ideological reasons. Tony must have a sortout with Gordon. Not sack him, but he must make clear who is boss. He can't allow this situation to continue.'

As we parted Alan said, 'We may be having a very different conversation if we meet on the train in a month's time.'

Friday, 28 February
Sunderland

M e-mailed from Washington with details of recently released official papers detailing America's relationship with Saddam in the mid-eighties. It appears that the Adminstration knew all about the chemical weapons but agreed to eliminate any references from public pronouncements in order to concentrate on the greater good of smashing Iran.

This morning, on the radio, it was reported that Saddam's son-in-law, the source of most of what we know about the chemical and biological weapons, told his interrogators that stocks had been destroyed in the mid-nineties, but that this part of his testimony had been carefully excised from the published version.

Saturday, 1 March

The Man's pronouncements grow increasingly apocalyptic. 'History will judge me,' he says in an interview with Jackie Ashley in today's *Guardian*. The trouble is, if he goes down, he will take us all with him. What's more, he has another life to go to and most of us don't. Nor do most of those who depend on us.

On the other hand, if he is vindicated and there is a quick clean end to it – a prospect that looks increasingly unlikely – then the politics of Iraq may look entirely different in a month's time. Whichever way it crumbles, The Man has taken a reckless, foolish gamble. He's bet the whole shop, not just his future, but that of the Labour Party and everything we have achieved in government, on a single throw of the dice.

I walked the children to their art class. Backhouse Park is a carpet of purple crocuses and white snowdrops, lifting the spirits in these terrible times.

Monday, 3 March

Awoke to hear the French Foreign Minister ruling out his country's support for a second resolution in language which seemed to me unequivocal. He didn't actually say they would use the veto, but that was the implication.

Alan Beith, a member of the Security and Intelligence Committee, was on the train. He says the spooks were livid about that sixth-form essay on Saddam's chemical arsenal cooked up several weeks ago by Number 10. What particularly infuriated them was the implication that they had contributed, which, of course, they hadn't. Needless to say, they weren't even consulted.

Later, I remarked to Hilary Armstrong that the French aren't sounding very helpful. She replied, 'The Boss is still hopeful.' But she didn't sound optimistic either.

Tuesday, 4 March

Bev Hughes came before the select committee to discuss asylum. The Tories, Ann Widdecombe especially, pressed her to say whose bright idea was the ludicrous and now abandoned target of 30,000 removals a year. No prizes for guessing, but Bev managed to stonewall. She was asked about the origin of the latest target – halving applications by September – and managed to bluster her way out of that, too. I kept my mouth firmly shut.

We have finished the Communications Bill. I had tabled an amendment limiting national newspaper owners to one Sunday and one daily per proprietor. In the event, it wasn't reached until half an hour before the end (which allowed me eight minutes of Murdoch-bashing). Not that it mattered. The government had made clear from the outset that there would be no upsetting the newspaper barons so we were only playing. For the serious stuff – on ITV and Channel 5 – we shall have to rely on David Puttnam in the Lords. So humiliating.

Ray Fitzwalter has sent me a paper by an American professor, Michael Tracey, which describes our plans to permit the sale of ITV to the Americans as 'about as wrong-headed as it is possible to be without being totally insane'. At least I managed to get that on the record, in an intervention on Patricia Hewitt.

Wednesday, 5 March

At Questions The Man was still exuding confidence that there will be a second resolution. He is in remarkably good shape despite his awesome schedule. Two hours later, when we filed into his room for the parliamentary committee, he was in his usual good humour. A little tired perhaps but no sign of depression, irritability or distraction. He has just returned from two days in Ireland where, as he puts it, the parties are reasonable in inverse proportion to their influence. He admires Adams and McGuinness ('top-quality politicians') but says they are 'chisellers' – 'just when you think you have reached the bottom line, they start chiselling again.' Trimble, he seems less keen on, describing how partway through the discussions he went AWOL. 'I was on the phone to the Swedish prime minister when Trimble put his head round the door and said, "Bye."'

On Iraq, I said that the French didn't seem to be leaving themselves much room for manoeuvre. Was he still optimistic about a second resolution?

'No, but we might get it.'

'What happens if Blix says the Iraqis are co-operating?'

'If Blix says that, I am with him. I keep asking Blix to explain why no Iraqi scientists are giving him interviews. Why not take them out of the country? Blix says, "I don't want the fate of their families on my conscience." Why not say that? I ask.' He added, 'I think there is some movement. People want to avoid conflict and I do, too, to be honest, but the French position of playing around until July simply isn't on. The French are in a very deep hole, but it will be a big thing if they veto something that has a majority.'

I asked about the Middle East peace process, saying there seemed to be no evidence of any political will in America to move it on.

'I believe there is.'

'What's the evidence?'

'Conversations I've had with George Bush ...' he hesitated, '... promises to me, undertakings given. Not just to me, but to others as well.'

The discussion on the Middle East continued after The Man had departed. Robin Cook said that child malnutrition in the Occupied

Territories was now on a par with Zimbabwe. He added that he was sceptical about the bona fides of Cheney and Rumsfeld where Israel was concerned.

Later, in an upper committee room, I came across David Puttnam, who said, 'I'm willing to bet £5,000 that Murdoch will go for Channel Five before the end of next year.'

Friday, 7 March
Sunderland

At my party management committee this evening Dave Allen turned up with a resolution opposing the war and demanding that I support tomorrow's demonstration. Fortunately we were rescued by the Silksworth ladies, who amended it to a demand for a second UN resolution, the position to which I desperately cling.

Sunday, 9 March

The big story is that Clare has said she will resign if there is no second resolution. What's more, she is reported as describing The Man as 'reckless', which must surely be fatal?

I spoke to Mum this evening. Her little church, the Holy Hut as she calls it, is to be closed and the congregation merged with a bigger one two miles away where she knows no one. Poor Mum, she has had to give up driving, which means that she is almost housebound and the quacks (who after months of testing still can't find out what's wrong with her) have advised against using public transport. So she is trapped at home with Dad, who is increasingly deaf and irascible. She said sadly, 'Everything is coming to an end.'

Monday, 10 March

Alistair Darling was on the train. In contrast to poor Steve Byers, when he held the same job, Alistair smoothly glides above the fray. A stranger to controversy. His path to the top effortless. The burden of office lightly worn. Or so it seems. For much of the journey he was reading a William Boyd novel. 'Too early to panic,' he said. 'The Labour Party always likes to get its panic in early.' Clare, he says, gave no hint of her reservations at Cabinet last Thursday. He adds, 'To be in favour of a second resolution is one thing, but calling the Boss reckless is not very clever.'

'The problem,' said I, 'is that The Man genuinely believes that his friends in Washington share our values, but they don't. Has there ever been a discussion in Cabinet about that?'

'Not in such terms, no. The trouble is we have just bounced along from one stage to another.'

Jack Straw looking, as ever, relaxed and self-assured (despite commuting almost weekly across the Atlantic) was in the Tea Room. 'When this is over,' I said, 'what are we going to do when the Americans come to us with their next demand?'

'They won't,' he asserted confidently. Unfortunately there wasn't time to cross-examine him as to the basis for his certainty.

Later Jack gave a little briefing in an upper committee room. He made no attempt to hide his disdain for the French. Their foreign policy is founded on cynicism, he said. ('Question: what do you call a group of Frenchmen advancing on Baghdad? Answer: arms salesmen.') He is still predicting a vote in the House before hostilities. 'It's going to be bad for a while,' he said. 'I can't say how long it will last, but in my view there will be a benign outcome.'

As I was going home I came across Kevan Jones, who, like me, has been telling everyone that he will only support a war if there is a second resolution and whose bluff, like mine, is about to be called. He reckons the rebellion next time will be a lot bigger – maybe 150. He said, 'If I vote to go ahead without a resolution, my lot will never trust me again.'

Tuesday, 11 March

A call from Ed Richards at Number 10. Would I mind asking the Lib Dems to drop their amendment allowing the sale of ITN? 'There is a danger that it could go through and we could end up with Berlusconi buying it.' I rang Tom McNally and asked, 'What's to stop Berlusconi buying ITN, if your amendment goes through?'

'I can't answer that,' he replied. I'll take advice and come back to you.'

The more I learn about this Communications Bill, the less I like.

I came across David Hanson, The Man's representative on earth, in the corridor behind the Chair. 'For deep background,' I said, 'if you ever find yourself discussing a vacancy for international development, please put my name on the table.' He promised he would, but even as he said the words I knew it was hopeless for, unbeknown to David, The Man and I are about to part company. 'Tony is hopeful of getting nine or ten countries, plus two vetoes,' he said, as though that was somehow sufficient, but it won't do at all. I simply don't buy all this nonsense about an unreasonable veto. A resolution is either vetoed or it isn't.

I hung around until ten o'clock. The House ought to be buzzing at a time like this but, thanks to Robin's new hours, it is deserted. I chatted to Kevan Jones again, who confirmed that he is not budging without a second resolution. Nick Brown popped in briefly to an otherwise empty Tea Room. Remembering what he told my management committee last year, I asked if he knew of any other minister considering his or her position. He said he didn't, adding that he has considerable sympathy for Clare. I felt he wanted to say more, but just managed to stop himself. 'What do you advise?' he asked. 'Sit tight and await events,' I said.

The Man, who looks washed out, was slow-hand-clapped by an audience of women this evening during one of the televised question and answer sessions which is supposed to reassure the nation. There is a rumour that Peter Goldsmith, the Attorney General is about to resign.

Wednesday, 12 March

To a packed meeting of the parliamentary party. It had been due to be addressed by Goldsmith, but he has pulled out saying he was needed in court. Which court? At what time? – were my immediate thoughts but, upon checking, I found that his alibi stood up. It appears he is not resigning after all, but there is much speculation about the advice he has offered on the legality of war.

Instead we were addressed by Jack, who gets better every time I hear him. He was confident, witty and one had the feeling (as one always does with Jack) that he was levelling with us. He sat down to huge applause, carefully orchestrated by Keith Hill and a clutch of whips. Diane Organ received the loudest cheer for denouncing those (Alice Mahon, Tam Dalyell, John McDonnell et al) who are calling for The Man's head. Most contributions from the floor were sympathetic to the regime. One or two appeared to be job applications – Huw Irranca-Davies talked of 'surprising solidarity' in his local party. Such dissent as there was came from some Usual Suspects – Harold Best, Tam Dalyell, Diane Abbott. There was some mild sneering from junior loyalists like Phil Woolas and Lorna Fitzsimons, but nothing too unpleasant. Kevin Barron was applauded for saying that we must at all costs avoid self-indulgent personal attacks à la the 1980s. By and large it was a good-natured meeting. At times one could have been forgiven for believing that everyone present thought an invasion of Iraq was an excellent idea.

I lunched with Keith Hill, who says that the whips are advising that on a worst case scenario (a Tory abstention) the government may not have a majority. 'If you add all the people who have been calling for a second resolution to those who voted for Chris Smith's amendment the other day then we are in trouble.' Of course, it is in the whips' interests to turn this into a vote of confidence in the hope of frightening waverers. I don't for a moment believe the Tories will abstain.

The Man was signing whisky bottles when we filed in for the parliamentary committee. 'My daily intake,' he joked.

'And it shows,' said Gordon Prentice, ever tactless.

'Thank you, Gordon,' The Man replied sounding ever-so-slightly hurt, but he laughed all the same. 'I was feeling fine until I read what I looked like.' Actually, he is not looking too bad considering the pressure. Nothing that a few good nights' sleep won't cure. A little tense perhaps, cheeks a millimetre or two hollower than they were last week and once or twice I thought I saw a nerve twitching in the side of his face. For much of the time he sat, hands clasped in front of him, only drawing a hand across his mouth to conceal his expression, as he often does when someone starts wittering. At the mention of the French he came alive. 'It can't be right for France to say it will veto under all circumstances. It is a wrecking tactic, done with absolute calculation. Until a couple of days ago I thought I had a majority ...'

He went on, 'I do feel these countries [France and the 'no' voters] have let us down. Four months on and what have we got to show – a few missiles dismantled, a few interviews in bugged hotel rooms. If they weren't prepared to do anything, they shouldn't have voted for 1441.'

I asked him to take us through the likely sequence of events over the next few days. 'We'll carry on negotiating. Kofi Annan is anxious not to have a vetoed resolution but, subject to that, there will be a vote.'

'What happens if there is no vote?'

'We decide what we are going to do.'

'How quickly will war start?'

'I don't know. We need to give Saddam time to get out. That's what the Arabs want.'

'What is the basis for your confidence that the Turks and Iranians won't pile in?'

'Our military and the Americans have had discussions with the Turks.'

'And the Iranians?'

'We have sent strong messages to the Iranians. I think we'll be able to protect ourselves on that.'

'Will there be war by this time next week?'

'Don't press me on that.'

why?

Thursday, 13 March

The Man no longer looks such a dazzling figure ('fatally damaged' is how Angela Eagle put it, although I take Angela with a pinch of salt since she is one of The Disappointed). Relations with the French are at an all-time low. The UN is seriously damaged. What once looked like a brilliant strategy of persuading the Americans to follow the UN route no longer seems such a good idea. I don't imagine his American friends are best pleased with him either for embroiling them in this mess. Of course, it could all look different in a week or two. Saddam might succumb to a well-placed bullet or slip away to the safety of Syria, our television screens may be full of happy Iraqis chanting the name of our own dear leader. Who knows, a year from now Clare Short may be an unknown backbencher and no one may be able to recall that they were ever against the enterprise. But it's not very likely. So far everything that could go wrong has gone wrong. There is a widespread feeling that, whether he survives or not, the Blair ascendancy is at an end. The magic is fading. When the immediate crisis has passed we shall have to have a serious conversation with The Man about his style of government. Ideally, it should take place around the Cabinet table. Failing that, it will fall to those of us on the parliamentary committee.

Kevan Jones is wriggling. He has spent the day ringing the movers and shakers in his party and, blow me down, they are all saying they won't be too upset if he votes with the regime, which, by a complete coincidence, is exactly what he wants to hear. I suspect we shall see more of this as the evil day approaches. It wouldn't surprise me if a few of those who rebelled last time have, with a little cajoling from the whips, talked themselves back into the fold by next week. For me, alas, there is no such escape. For weeks I have been assuring all inquirers that a second resolution was my bottom line. I even said it at PM's Questions so it's there, on the record, in Hansard. At the time it seemed like a cop-out since (until the last few days) we have been repeatedly assured, on the highest authority, that a second resolution was assured. Now, suddenly, it is about to become an heroic posture.

Jean Corston spent three-quarters of an hour with The Man this afternoon and found him in good humour, all things considered. He even spent 15 minutes asking questions about her life until she reminded him that they had more important business to discuss. He thinks, depending on what the Tories do, that the government could fall. Jean, bless her, touched briefly on the question of who will succeed Clare telling him that, so far as she was concerned, I was the only candidate. And how did he react? 'He just smiled.' The trouble is, as I pointed out, I am about to disqualify myself. Might he be big enough to give it to me anyway? I think not. That is expecting too much. For him this is a matter of life or death. Is there a loophole through which I can crawl, principles and job prospects intact? Jean suggests that we might both abstain and we agreed to sleep on it.

Friday, 14 March
Sunderland

Awoke to hear Andrew Marr speculating that there are likely to be two resignations from the Cabinet – Clare and Robin Cook.

Sam Glatt and John Hargrave turned up at the surgery in the evening to find out how I was proposing to vote. I told them that, in the absence of a resolution, I would vote against. So that's it then. No turning back.

Monday, 17 March

To London idly dreaming of the trouble I could cause, were I so minded (Question: 'My Right Honourable Friend is a practising Christian; what makes him think he is better qualified than the Pope and the Archbishop of Canterbury to distinguish right from wrong in relation to Iraq?' Pause for laughter to die down before adding, 'And might I suggest to my Right Honourable Friend that he considers applying for the Throne of St Peter when a vacancy arises as I am sure it will in the not too distant future.') But, of course, I don't want to cause trouble. On the contrary, I want The Man to be right. In the long run that is what is best for all of us.

3 p.m.

The Tea Room is buzzing with rumours that Robin Cook is about to resign. The Cabinet are to meet at four and an announcement is expected shortly afterwards. Clare Short's future is also in doubt although there appears to have been some rowing back since her outburst last week. I came across Steve Byers, looking flushed and biting his nails. He could be back in the Cabinet by nightfall. Steve fears that

Robin's departure could be the beginning of the end for The Man. On the backbenches Robin could be a formidable enemy. 'If he's sensible,' says Steve, 'he'll blame George Bush and the Americans.' According to Steve, relations between Gordon and The Man are bad ('as bad as I have ever known them'), which only confirms what Nick Brown and Alan Milburn have been saying. What are the issues? I asked. 'Public sector reform, Foundation hospitals, top-up fees, you name it. Tony is worried about the Budget, too. Also, I don't imagine that Gordon is keen on the war.'

Another call from the woman at the US embassy, prompted no doubt by the fact that I have tabled a question to Mike O'Brien asking what had been done about the poor bombed-out Afghan woman and her family. 'Good news,' she said breathlessly.

'Oh?'

'I have had an e-mail from our embassy in Kabul saying that USAID has helped 800 people in her area.'

'Yes, but what about the woman who lost her husband and six children?'

'I thought I might not even get a reply,' she said, evidently disappointed that I did not share her joy.

'If we're going to drop bombs on people,' I said coldly, 'the least we can do is clear up afterwards. Especially, if we are about to do it again.'

5 p.m.

To an upper committee room for a meeting which Ann Clwyd has organised with Dr Barham Saleh, 'prime minister' of northern Iraq. A soft-spoken, civilised man, with a large, round, cheerful face and circular spectacles, who exuded warmth and charm. He knew he was speaking to an audience of sceptics, but did not attempt to hector or bombard us. He just said quietly, 'If it is inconvenient for you to find yourselves on the same side as the United States, it is an intellectual inconvenience. For us it is a matter of life or death.'

We emerged to find that Robin Cook had resigned and would be making a personal statement later. Clare, incredibly, is staying.

The chamber was packed for Robin. But first there was a

statement from Jack Straw who reported that the government had reluctantly concluded that a second resolution would not after all be possible. Mostly he was heard in glum silence, but there was sporadic heckling, first from our side and then from the Lib Dem and national- ist benches. When, referring to France, Jack said, 'One country has ensured ...' he was interrupted with cries of, 'More than one country.' When in response to an intervention, Jack said, 'We are not intending to rely on the Liberals,' he was greeted with shouts of 'No, you are relying on the Tories.' There was some angry skirmishing on the benches behind. David Winnick got into a spat with Alice Mahon ('If you heckle us, we'll heckle you ...'). The Man was conspicuously (and wisely) absent, provoking shouts of 'Where is he?' from the Opposi- tion benches.

Robin was seated in the fourth row between those two other refu- gees from the Cabinet, Frank Dobson and Chris Smith. Uncomforta- bly close to the seat from which Geoffrey Howe delivered his deathblow to the Iron Lady. Is history about to repeat itself? Robin was at pains to assure us of his admiration for The Man. Then, in the space of 15 riveting minutes, he proceeded scientifically to demolish the version of events which Jack had just spent the previous hour painstakingly constructing. Robin sat down to applause which gradu- ally turned into a standing ovation. It began on the rebel benches behind him and spread across to the Liberal Democrats and the nationalists while the Tories, the payroll and the loyalists sat in stunned, grim silence. The ovation continued for several minutes while the Speaker called impotently for order. An astonishing scene. Unprecedented except for when Eric Heffer, who was dying, came to make his last speech. I was seated directly in front of Robin and, tempting though it was, I did not join in. On impulse, however, I turned and shook his hand; he grasped mine warmly, looking as though he were about to burst into tears. 'An Exocet,' I remarked to Diane Abbott as we left the chamber. Unfortunately I was overheard by Hilary Armstrong. 'No, it's not,' she said angrily. 'It's not good enough to sit in Cabinet for six years, accept the Queen's shilling and then call on people to vote against the government. He repeated myths that he knows are myths and that he has agreed with me are myths.'

Is this a Heseltine moment or a Geoffrey Howe moment? A temporary blip, albeit a large one, or the beginning of the end of New Labour? That is the question on everyone's lips. For all his undoubted brilliance, Robin doesn't have a big following. He is perceived by many as arrogant and has relied on intellect rather than charisma for his mastery of the House. No one knows how big tomorrow's rebellion will be. If the Tories were to devise a last-minute excuse for abstention (as we unscrupulously did over the Maastricht Treaty) it could be fatal. Much to my surprise Jean Corston remarked, 'I've never expected Tony Blair to lead us into the next election.'

Tuesday, 18 March

To a hastily convened, jam-packed meeting of the parliamentary party at which The Man sought to persuade us of the righteousness of his cause. Actually, he didn't have to do a lot of persuading since, to judge by the thunderous applause which greeted him, the whips have been busy and most of those present were onside. A number of people conspicuously failed to applaud, but the dissidents were all but invisible. If one didn't know better, one might conclude that all this talk of crisis is put about by an excitable media. But it is a crisis. A big one. Whatever happens tonight, nothing will be the same again.

And yet on the surface all seemed calm. Gerald Kaufman read out a suspiciously word-perfect e-mail, urging loyalty, which he claimed had come to him this very morning from an unknown constituent. (I quizzed him afterwards, but he was adamant that it was genuine.) There were a handful of sceptical questions, but no one really got stuck in. At times it was like a revivalist meeting. Several people (Hugh Bayley was one) who until now had been demanding a second resolution rose to announce their conversion.

'I don't seek to persuade you out of loyalty,' said The Man, 'I want you to be convinced by the arguments.' But there's the rub. I am not in the least convinced by the arguments, but I might, out of loyalty, be persuaded to support The Man if I thought his survival was at stake.

We have lost a couple more ministers – Philip Hunt in the Lords (who John Prescott shamelessly abused on the radio this morning) and John Denham, whose departure was a bolt out of the blue. Clare has decided to stay and is now a deeply discredited figure, which is a pity because she has been such a good minister.

I lunched alone in the cafeteria. JP passed by, pausing at my table to reach for a piece of paper from inside his jacket. He ran an eye down it and returned it to his pocket. 'You're not on my list,' he said cheerfully and walked on. Upstairs there was a message from Number 10. Would I care to call on the Prime Minister in his room at 4.30? 'How many are there in my group?' I asked the Downing Street woman. 'Just you,' she said.

Mike O'Brien spent ten minutes in the Tea Room trying to convince me to vote with the government. His arguments were the standard ones – the wickedness of Saddam, the perfidy of the French and, more persuasively, that if we failed to act against Iraq all the little tyrannies would want their own dirty weapons. My difficulty is that for weeks I have been telling anyone who asked, on the basis of repeated assurances from the highest levels, that a second resolution was my bottom line. I cannot suddenly switch just because it is inconvenient. A cannier politician would have kept his head down and his mouth closed, but I am not made that way. Which is no doubt why my political career peaked at Under-Secretary of Folding Deck Chairs. I asked Mike if there was any message I should give The Man when I see him. He dropped his voice. 'Tell him not to make any more promises to George Bush. Somewhere along the line he's promised Bush that we would be there with him and now he can't back down because his integrity is at stake.' Well, my integrity is at stake, too, and I'm staying put.

3 p.m.

Jean Corston came to my room. She has been quietly agonising for days and has more or less decided to vote against the government. The whips, not to mention The Man, don't yet know that Jean is not with them and they are going to be mightily upset when they find out, which they will shortly (she has an appointment with Hilary Armstrong at 4.45 p.m.). It is a big thing for the chair of the parliamentary party to vote against the government. Jean, like me, has been telling everyone that her bottom line is a second resolution and she feels she can't talk her way out of it. 'The words just don't come out,' she said. She added, 'I've been very loyal up to now, but once in a while I want to be myself.' She is intending to vote for the amendment and then abstain on the main resolution and I will do likewise. We agreed that if either of us changes our mind, we will report back. There is much to be said for sticking together at this hour of need.

4.30 p.m.

To the Prime Minister's room for my audience with The Man. He has been seeing people at ten-minute intervals since he left the chamber two hours ago and still has some way to go. Keith Bradley went in ahead of me and emerged looking unhappy.

The Man didn't beat about the bush. 'Chris, I need your help.' Oh dear, that is the one argument I find hardest to counter. I want him to survive. I really do. He looks worn down. Bleary-eyed with exhaustion. 'It's tight,' he said. 'Very tight.' He glanced across to Dave Hanson, who confirmed that it was.

Should I believe him?

'If it wasn't, I wouldn't be doing all this.' A fair point.

I explained that, like others, I had been banking on a second resolution.

'So was I,' he said.

'My difficulty,' I said, 'is that I have been telling all inquirers for months that my support was conditional upon a second resolution. Only ten days ago I persuaded my constituency party to amend a resolution demanding total opposition to the war to one making it conditional on a second resolution. I don't feel I can renege. It's a matter of personal integrity. My problem, not yours.'

He explained for the umpteenth time that he had been totally derailed by the French.

I added, 'I don't share your faith in George Bush and his cronies. I don't believe they share our values. I believe they are the political wing of the military-industrial complex. Guns, gas and oil. That's what they stand for.'

He mounted a brief defence of George Bush, saying that the recent publication of a Palestine peace plan – the 'road map' – was a significant step forward.

'What would you do differently,' I asked, 'if you were starting this again?'

I had hoped he would say that he wished he had never got started, but perhaps that would be asking too much just at this moment. All he said was, 'I'd tie the French down earlier.' He added, 'And the Russians.'

I departed saying I would reflect carefully, but making clear I could make no promises. To cheer him up I recounted Nguyen Co Thach's* devastating reply when I asked why the Vietnamese hadn't gone to the UN instead of invading Cambodia ('Because during the last 40 years we have been invaded by four of the five permanent members of the Security Council').

'I suppose we were the only ones who didn't,' he said.

'No, we occupied the south under General Gracey in 1946. The Russians were the only non-invaders, but they in their way were colonisers, too.'

Outside in the corridor I ran into Alan Milburn talking to Maria Eagle, both looking grave. Alan said, 'People aren't budging.' As if to prove the point one of the newer members passed by and Alan asked if he would be voting with the government. 'No,' he replied coldly and went on his way without looking back. Alan said, 'Tony will go if he has to rely on the Tories.' Maria pointed out that The Man had dropped a hint to this effect at the end of his speech.

A little further on I came across Sally Morgan, who was more upbeat. They were 'fairly confident', she said, of a majority among Labour Members. I asked if she thought The Man would resign on impulse if the result was bad and Sally said she thought not. She said he had been gobsmacked when, after he had lined up a majority on the Security Council, the French had announced that they would veto under all circumstances. She added that The Man had been instrumental in persuading Bush to sign up to the Palestinian road map. She had listened in on the telephone call and seemed to think he was

---

*Foreign Minister of Vietnam, 1980–91.

sincere. Apparently Bush had remarked, 'I've only got 15 per cent of the Jewish vote and I've already lost most of them so I might as well do what is right.' She said that we (and the Spaniards) had insisted that any post-war humanitarian operation be carried out by the UN and not by the American military.

'This must never happen again,' I said.

'Tell him that. I'll arrange for you to come in and see him when all this is over.'

Steve Byers was in the Tea Room. 'It's serious,' he said. He reckoned that we are looking at a rebellion of 160-plus. 'Tony knows he's damaged and that he's tested loyalty too far. I've said to Sally Morgan if he looks like throwing in the towel, call me at once.' Steve added that he was in the Strangers' Bar last night and it was full of Gordon's people, Charlie Whelan included. 'They scent blood,' he said.

Out in the Library Corridor I came across Jean who is beginning to wobble. She had just seen Hilary, who was mightily upset. Until now they had been taking Jean for granted. Hilary told her that The Man would be devastated to find Jean in the wrong lobby. An audience has been arranged for 7.30 p.m. We arranged to reconvene at eight and compare notes.

7.00 p.m.

I decided the time had come to try and dig myself out of the hole I've got myself into. Armed with a list of telephone numbers for the movers and shakers in the constituency I repaired to a phone booth (my office walls are paper thin) and began to work the phones, starting with Paul Watson, Charles Bate and John Donnelly. I explained that this had become an issue of confidence and there was a danger of regime change here, never mind in Iraq, whereupon they all said they would back me if I were to change my mind. I then called Sam Glatt and John Hargrave to whom I had categorically asserted, as recently as last Friday, that in the absence of a second resolution I would not be supporting the government. They were unimpressed by my assertion that The Man could fall if this went wrong. 'He's not indispensable,' said Sam. Sue Lane said likewise.

8 p.m., Strangers' Cafeteria

Jean says that The Man had pleaded with her to stay on board and that was what she had now decided to do.

8.45 p.m., Upper Corridor South

A message to ring Fraser Kemp, who said the whips were anticipating that the rebellion could be within four or five votes of a majority of Labour backbenchers, with 25–30 Members who aren't saying what they proposed to do. He had been asked by Keith Hill to request that I think again. I tracked down Tommy Wright and Dave Allan, expecting them to be pragmatists, but they weren't. 'A lot of people in Sunderland respect you,' said Tommy urging me not to throw it away. Dave Allan was blunter: 'It's not just Blair's integrity that's at stake, it's yours too.' That did it. I telephoned Fraser saying I was sticking to my guns. Within minutes I received a call inviting me to an immediate meeting with the Chief Whip.

9.15 p.m., Chief Whip's office

Hilary was affable, but left me in no doubt that my intransigence would do me no good with The Man. 'He'll be very hurt,' she said. 'He has a high regard for you.' Roughly translated this means that I can forget any aspiration I may have (does she know?) to return to government if I set foot in the wrong lobby tonight. I explained that I had telephoned as many of the movers and shakers in my party as I could find and most of them were urging me to stand firm. Hilary, who knows Sunderland well, responded that my *constituents* would be in favour of the government's stand by a margin of two to one. My neighbour, Bill Etherington, was already in the rebel lobby, so it was only fair that those in favour of war should be represented, too. Finally, she deployed her most devastating weapon: 'If Tony goes, he'll take the entire Cabinet with him and there will be a general election.' I said I didn't think that was very likely, but she seemed to think it was a possibility. On my way back to my room I came across Clare Short in the Library Corridor, looking miserable and much the worse for wear, propped up by Dennis Turner.

10.00 p.m., the Aye Lobby

As I made my way through the throng to vote for the amendment and against the government, who should I come face to face with but The Man, who was, of course, heading resolutely in the other direction. He affected not to notice, but I am sure he did. The Lib Dems and the Nationalists were there in force but, despite promises to the contrary, there were only a handful of Tories. No sign of Roger Gale, who only days ago assured me that there would be many more Tory rebels next time around. It is clear that the rebellion is not as large as the whips had been predicting (a lot of people have been talked out of it in the final hours), but it is still enormous – 139 Labour Members have defied the whip. Nothing will ever be the same again.

Wednesday, 19 March

To the meeting of the parliamentary party, where The Man, looking mightily relieved, put in a brief appearance to offer thanks for his deliverance. He also thanked Hilary for the brilliance of the whipping operation, which, as Jean remarked afterwards, was somewhat rubbing people's noses in it.

Geoff Hoon addressed the gathering. As with the Afghan war, he was at pains to assure us that the utmost care would be taken over targets, although this time round he managed to avoid any glib talk about 'astonishingly accurate bombing'. He did, however, assure us that the brilliance of the technology would ensure that the missiles were accurate to within a few metres. Afterwards, I reminded him that, during the Balkan war, several missiles had landed in the wrong country, never mind hitting the wrong target. 'Ah yes,' he said, 'but they didn't explode.' (Small consolation if ten tons of cruise missile intended for the country next door come crashing through your roof.) There were questions about depleted uranium, cluster bombs, land-mines and historic sites, to each of which Geoff offered soothing replies. Nothing ever seems to ruffle him. Later, in the queue for tea, I asked if he was concerned about a downward spiral of revenge and chaos, if (as many anticipate) the Iraqi regime collapses too quickly. Yes indeed, he said cheerfully. The Americans had devised a name for exactly that scenario – 'catastrophic success'.

I asked Dave Hanson if The Man would really have gone if a majority of Labour Members had voted against him. 'No,' he said. 'Only if he had lost the motion.' As I suspected, Hilary was over-egging the pudding. Thank goodness I didn't fall for it.

What a difference a day can make. The Man, who obviously enjoyed his first good night's sleep for weeks, is transformed. Gone is that dehydrated, haunted look of yesterday. Instead, at the parliamentary committee this afternoon, he was positively light-headed. Ann Clwyd remarked upon a rumour that Tariq Aziz had defected which somehow got twisted into a joke about Robin Cook's defection.

'Robin's not going to Baghdad,' said The Man.

'Is Robin going to Baghdad?' JP, whose mind had obviously been elsewhere, suddenly sprang to life. Whereupon everyone fell about.

Tony Lloyd brought us all back to order: 'Is this the healing process?'

'Sorry,' said The Man. 'My fault. I apologise,' but he was still laughing.

We discussed the momentous events of the past two days. At least it wasn't like the 1980s, said The Man; he had always believed that it ought to be possible to disagree without reaching for the old betrayal thesis. The party was more mature these days. Most people were reasonable once they understood there was another side to the argument. Even as he spoke, outside in Parliament Square, we could hear the baying crowds laying siege to Carriage Gates.

Thursday, 20 March

Awoke to news that the attack on Iraq has begun with a hit on a 'leadership target' in the south of Baghdad. Also, there was an interview with Hans Blix, who made it clear that he wasn't at all happy with the course of events. He was, he said, curious to know whether Iraq actually has anthrax and nerve gas (aren't we all?). If they do, he asked, why didn't they own up? It would have resulted in a loss of face, but it would have saved the regime. He said that much of the intelligence material with which his inspectors had been supplied turned out to be inaccurate and, in the case of the supposed attempt to obtain uranium from Niger, documents had been falsified (who by, he didn't say). Blix maintained the inspectors were making progress and that the Iraqis, latterly at least, had been co-operating.

To the Boothroyd Room in Portcullis House for a meeting of the Liaison Committee, where a wonderful, hilarious, shameless discussion took place about the extent to which select committees should travel club class. It was triggered by Alan Williams's very sensible proposal that all short-haul flights to Europe and the east coast of the USA should be by premium economy. Whereupon a forest of objections were raised. Gwyneth Dunwoody said there were sound medical reasons why she had to travel club on any flight longer than two hours. She illustrated her argument with reference to some recent fact-finding she had undertaken in China, adding that the Chinese had not been particularly helpful when it came to catering for her demands. 'Even the Chinese want her dead,' chuckled Michael Mates wickedly.

Nicholas Winterton expressed concern that to travel by economy would diminish our status. Status is something with which Sir Nicholas is frequently preoccupied. He went on, 'It's not the food, it's the sort of people ...'

'He doesn't want to meet his constituents,' remarked Michael Mates to general merriment.

'You're totally missing my point,' huffed Sir Nicholas.

Someone pointed out, as if it were some sort of clinching argument, that Sir Patrick Cormack, who is even grander than Sir Nicholas, refused to fly anywhere by anything less than club.

On and on the discussion went. There were learned interventions on wind speeds, civil service comparators, seat sizes. At times one might have been forgiven for thinking that the very fate of parliamentary democracy itself was in the balance. Goodness knows what our constituents would have made of it all.

It was brought to an end by Edward Leigh. We weren't doing ourselves any good spending 30 minutes on this subject, he said. We should bear in mind that we were spending a million pounds of public money. He added that Nick Winterton's comments were pompous and ridiculous – those were his very words. One could almost hear the expulsion of wind as Sir Nicholas visibly deflated.

The Carriage Gates have been sealed for much of the day as relays of school children, protesting against the war, blocked the traffic in Parliament Square, hurling themselves against the police lines. All week long the sound of their chanting, occasionally drowned by the racket from a police helicopter, has been audible throughout the building. The gates were still sealed at seven o'clock as I made my way, via the tunnel under Westminster Bridge Road, to the tube station. On the way I passed Robert Jackson. 'Nice to feel relevant again,' he said cheerfully gesturing towards the chanting protesters.

Joyce Quin was on the train. She complained that a post office in her constituency was threatened with closure as a result of government insistence that pensions and benefits are to be paid directly into bank accounts. The postmistress was telling everyone it was the fault of the government. 'We've done a lot of good things,' she said, 'but the bad is beginning to outweigh the good.'

Sunday, 23 March
Sunderland

To Mount Grace Priory where we picnicked in the sunshine. Emma asked Ngoc, 'Mum, what does "sue" mean?' Ngoc explained that a person who considered themselves to have been sinned against – as many in Sunderland do – could take their case to a lawyer and that, if successful, they would receive compensation. 'What does compensation mean?'

'Money.'

Later, Ngoc remarked to Emma that she was lucky to have an older sister to play with. Yes, replied Emma, except that Sarah has a lot of homework and so there is not enough time to play.

'You will have to talk to Sarah's school about that,' said Ngoc.

To which, quick as a flash, the Nugget replied, 'Don't worry, Mum, I will sue them.'

American prisoners have been put on show on Iraqi television, which has led to a big bout of hypocrisy about war crimes and breaches of the Geneva Convention. Never mind that for the past week our media have been displaying hooded Iraqi prisoners of war with hands behind their backs and guns to their head – to say nothing of what has been going on at Guantanamo Bay and Bagram Airbase for the last year or more. Somehow it's different when they do it to us.

Monday, 24 March

Among this morning's mail, two letters of resignation from the party. One from Mac McCarthy, a long-standing member of St Michael's branch, and the other from Dick and Gwen Ellison, stalwarts from Hendon. I have replied gently reminding them that, as they demanded, I voted against the war and that it makes my position more difficult if I am promptly abandoned by those whose position on the war is the same as mine.

It is becoming clear that the war isn't going to plan. Resistance is unexpectedly stiff and the Iraqis do not seem to be as keen to be liberated as we had been led to expect. The Man gave a sober, factual statement this afternoon, full of words like 'difficulties', 'tragedies', 'accidents'. He was heard mainly in silence apart from sporadic sniping from the likes of Harry Cohen, calling 'What about civilians?' and muttering about Guantanamo Bay every time Iraqi mistreatment of our prisoners was mentioned.

Wednesday, 26 March

Andy McSmith, a lobby journalist, told an amusing tale about a head teacher in Islington who went chasing after pupils who had walked out of school in protest against the war. 'Do your parents know what you are doing?' she demanded of the child leading the uprising. Of course they did. She was talking to the daughter of Tariq Ali.

A party of children from Thornhill School visited. Pat, by some extraordinary alchemy, managed to conjure them up gallery tickets for Prime Minister's Questions and I showed them the terrace and Westminster Hall. On our way through Speaker's Court who should we run into but The Man? On his way to Washington with Jack Straw. The bombproof Jaguar was waiting, engine running, door open. A police outrider had already gone ahead to stop the traffic. Special Branch men hovered, whispering into invisible microphones. Alastair Campbell, loitering in the background, relaxed and cheerful as ever, winked. The Man couldn't have been nicer. He shook hands with each of the kids, chatted for a minute, posed for a photo and went on his way. As for the kids, it made their day. So much goodwill for such little effort.

Later, in the Central Lobby, I came across Anji Hunter, The Man's former PA. She is now a big shot at BP. Relations with Gordon have much improved during the last nine months, she said. Gordon had been particularly supportive during the recent difficulty. (Why might that be? Has he been given reason to believe that he will shortly inherit?) Anji confirmed that Alastair keeps a diary. 'In tiny writing on foolscap sheets, three or four a day.' At last, an eyewitness.

Friday, 28 March

The Americans – or was it us? – have bombed another market in Baghdad, this time killing at least 50 people and maiming hundreds of others. The evening television news is full of weeping, screaming, angry Iraqis. As usual official spokesmen are lying or obfuscating. Cambodia, Iraq (last time around), Kosovo, Afghanistan, it's always the same. They never own up. I am so glad I voted against this lousy, rotten war.

Monday, 31 March

Today's *Mirror* carries a large picture of a little, curly-haired, Iraqi girl called Sarah, in Disney pyjamas, looking for all the world as if she is asleep, lying on her back in a Baghdad mortuary. According to the report, she was one of four children from the same family, two died and the other two have yet to regain consciousness. More victims of Geoff Hoon's 'astonishingly accurate bombing'?

I went along to a little briefing that Geoff was giving in an upper committee room. He is so laidback it isn't true. No matter what he is asked about – cluster bombs, dead children, friendly fire – he always responds in the same complacent drawl. I suppose it's a talent up to a point, but Geoff carries it too far. One has the impression he could sell anything to anyone. 'How come one of our "astonishingly accurate missiles" seems to have hit a bus in Syria?' I asked.

'I don't know,' chortled Geoff as though it were a source of amusement (five people are reported to have died). 'I'm still trying to get to the bottom of that. Maybe the CIA know something which cannot be vouchsafed.' Surely the CIA could be persuaded to confide in the British defence secretary. Or am I being naive?

Tuesday, 1 April

This morning there are reports that American soldiers in Iraq have killed at least seven (it turned out to be 11) women and children after raking a minibus with gunfire. The official line is that it failed to stop after repeated warnings, but fortunately there was a journalist present who says no warning was given.

'What did you think of Geoff Hoon last night?' asked Betty Williams, in the Tea Room. She went on, 'I was upset at how relaxed he was. At least Tony Blair looks as though he feels the weight of the responsibility he is carrying, but Geoff doesn't.'

So it isn't just my imagination.

I rang Dad. There is always a great kerfuffle while he finds his hearing aid, but he seems to be managing okay. Goodness knows how they are going to cope when Mum comes back from hospital. 'Maybe we'll have to go into a home,' he said. I tried to assure him that wouldn't be necessary, if only they would accept help, but whether they will or not remains to be seen. Liz, who I spoke to later, said that Dad kissed Mum's hand when he visited her in hospital today. He must know that the end is in sight.

Wednesday, 2 April

A photo on the front of today's *Guardian* shows a distraught Iraqi, grieving over the body of his mother. He is said to have lost 15 relatives, including six children. So far there is no sign that the Iraqis are all that grateful to their liberators. Is it any wonder?

I whiled away the afternoon trying to amend the Criminal Justice Bill and as a result missed the parliamentary committee. Jean reported The Man as saying there were four tests of the success of our policy in Iraq: (1) that Iraqis must be better off; (2) that they must be in charge; (3) that there must be a role for the UN; and (4) that we must make progress on peace in the Middle East.

'By this time next year?' asked Helen Jackson.

'Sooner,' he replied.

According to Jean, The Man seems supremely untroubled. 'He doesn't seem beset by any of the doubts that give the rest of us sleepless nights.'

Thursday, 3 April

Signs that the Iraqi regime may be crumbling. There are reports this evening that 60 coachloads of soldiers and civilians, waving white flags, crossed the American lines south of Baghdad. The interesting point is that no one seems to have tried to stop them. There has been no sign of Saddam Hussein for more than a week and our side are putting it about that he may be dead, but I don't believe that for a moment. If he was, the regime would already have imploded. Ann Clwyd has just spoken to Barham Saleh, who is back home in northern Iraq. He told her that an ominous message was read out on Iraqi television yesterday warning the Kurds not to advance a step nearer Baghdad. Ann interprets that as a threat to use chemical weapons. If the regime has them, this is the moment when they will be used.

Wednesday, 9 April

As we filed into The Man's room for the parliamentary committee, the television in the outer office was showing crowds in Baghdad toppling a giant statue of Saddam Hussein. The regime, it seems, has fallen.

'I hope there will be no triumphalism,' said Helen, 'thousands have died.'

The Man displayed not a glimmer of triumphalism (although the same could not be said of John Reid and Hilary Armstrong, who are already dreaming of clothing George Galloway and Tam Dalyell in orange jump suits and dispatching them, bound hand and foot, to Guantanamo). The Man merely remarked that he expected public opinion to swing solidly behind the government 'as the nature of the regime becomes apparent'.

Someone mentioned our two most wanted men. 'Tam can say what he likes about me, I don't care', replied The Man, 'but George,' he said ominously, 'is another matter.'

'What happens if Saddam fetches up in Syria?' I asked innocently, immediately triggering a great explosion from JP about the irresponsibility of even raising so delicate a matter in public.

'I only asked a little question, just six or seven words,' I said.

'We don't want to open another front,' huffed JP.

'I have no plans to open another front.'

The Man, much amused, said, 'Nobody I've ever talked to has talked about invading Syria.'

Doug Hoyle mentioned that the Communications Bill was going to run into trouble in the Lords over the possibility that it would open up Channel Five to Murdoch.

'It's a competition issue,' said The Man. 'I've dealt with them all and I don't believe that some [proprietors] are better than others. I've yet to find a cuddly one.'

'Murdoch is a competition issue,' I said. 'He has four national newspapers, a satellite channel which can reach 40 per cent of homes, and, if he gets his hands on Channel Five – and David Puttnam believes he will – he will ruthlessly cross-promote and before long Channel Five could overtake Channel Four and even ITV.'

The Man's eyes showed signs of glazing over. He thinks we are all obsessed with Murdoch. 'I'll look at it,' he said quietly, but it was obvious that he won't – unless the Lords force him to.

Later, while I was scouring the Lords in search of David Puttnam, I ran into Bernard Donoughue, who invited me to tea. 'I enjoy our little talks,' he said. In truth, he does most of the talking, which is fine by me since I find him an engaging companion. Despite appearances, Bernard's origins are impeccably working class. 'All the instincts of the working class are Tory,' he says. 'On race, patriotism, you name it.

It's just that they happen to vote Labour. Murdoch understands that, which is why the *Sun* has been so successful.' He added, 'And that is also why, unless we get a grip on asylum, it will do us a lot of damage.'

Thursday, 10 April

Grim news from Iraq. Mayhem has broken out in Baghdad. Even the hospitals and the museums are being looted and the Americans are just standing on the sidelines pretending it has nothing to do with them. Jack made a statement, but there was no euphoria. He was heard mainly in silence; such hear-hearing as there was came mainly from the military wing of the Tory Party. Michael Ancram received a big cheer from his own side when he bashed the French and Jack, as ever, reserved his harshest words for the Lib Dems rather than the Ba'ath party.

I had a cup of tea with Mike O'Brien, who is being sent to Syria and Iran at the weekend. 'Syria has got some hard decisions to make very fast,' he said.

Monday, 14 April

A stern letter from Keith Hill pointing out that I had failed to support the government in the votes on the Criminal Justice Bill about bad character evidence and demanding to know why I had not given written notice of my intention to rebel, to the Chief Whip – as the standing orders of the parliamentary party apparently require. I sought out Keith in the Tea Room and pointed out that I had gone one better than writing to Hilary. I had announced in the Second Reading debate, as long ago as 4 December, that I would not be supporting the Bill if the clauses on the admission of previous convictions were not amended – and the select committee had unanimously backed me. Moreover, I had proposed half a dozen alternative modifications to Charlie Falconer, all of which he had rejected. For good measure I added that, if the Bill were to be returned from the Lords without the bad character clauses deleted or amended, I would be voting against the government again. Keith agreed that, in the

17. Minister Mullin, staff and family – on the steps of his grand apartment in the Foreign Office

18. Our Man in Africa: *above*, in Ghana; *below*, with Aids orphans in Mozambique.

19. Attending upon the Queen in Nigeria.

20. Alongside The Man on the government front bench. At the time it looked as though I was riding high. Looking back, however, it may have been the moment my fortunes peaked. 'What's the answer to that?' he whispered. I was so busy soaking up atmosphere that I hadn't even heard the question.

21. My last appearance at the Dispatch Box, 5 April 2005.

22. With the Dalai Lama who I have known for more than thirty years. 'Tibetans need to have more children,' I said. 'Yes,' he chuckled, 'and less monks.'

23. One blurred photograph. The only souvenir of my meeting with the great Mandela (see entry for November 4, 2003).

24. On the road again: *above*, addressing refugees from the Lord's Resistance Army in northern Uganda; *below*, Liberia, a glimpse of Armageddon.

25. *Above*, arriving in Somaliland, the first minister to visit in almost fifty years. I received the full treatment; a hundred metres of red carpet, a police band and almost the entire government lined up to shake hands. Crowds lined the street from the airport into the city. *Below*, in the Nuba mountains, Sudan. We were accompanied by a British army officer called Nigel who talked incessantly about fox hunting and school fees.

26. Re-elected in a record forty-two minutes – for more than half an hour the only MP in the country. I could have formed my own government... Given what happened four days later that might have been a good idea.

circumstances, a formal meeting would not after all be necessary. I agreed to drop Hilary a note, the first sentence of which would contain the word 'apology' for failing to notify her in writing and the rest of which would be an unrepentant résumé of my exchange with Keith. It was only after I had posted my note to Hilary that it occurred to me to check standing orders and, sure enough, they say nothing about notice of a rebellion having to be in writing.

Wednesday, 23 April

The newspapers are full of allegations that money from the Iraqi regime had found its way into the pockets of George Galloway. All based on documents which the *Daily Telegraph*'s man in Baghdad claims to have unearthed in the ruins of the foreign ministry. Needless to say, George is denying all and threatening the Mother of All Libel Suits.

Friday, 25 April
Sunderland

A call from Ludo Kennedy. He and Moira, recognising that they are growing frail, have moved out of their lovely house in Avebury into a sheltered apartment near Oxford, where they continue to live independently in beautiful surroundings without the responsibility of maintaining their own property and where help is on hand as and when they need it. The move went smoothly because the children had booked them into a hotel for the duration. They moved into their new home to find everything in place. Brilliant. If only Dad and Mum would let us do the same for them.

Customers at the surgery this evening included a mother of two who complained that there was no sign of Gordon's promised tax credit and as a result she was struggling to feed her children and pay her rent. She had spent hours on the phone trying to access the helpline, but it had proved impenetrable. Graham says he has received several such complaints in the last few days. So far it is only a trickle but he fears an avalanche. Oh dear, this is not how it was supposed to be. Once again New Labour is in the process of alienating the very people it boasts of helping.

She was followed by a hospital porter, upset because he and his colleagues believe that (contrary to the official line) they will be financially worse off because of Alan Milburn's much vaunted 'Agenda for Change'. He had worked at the hospital for 23 years and claimed that morale was lower than at any time he could recall. What was the cause of all this gloom, I inquired. 'Targets,' he said. Interestingly, he placed the blame firmly on the government, not on the hospital management. Everywhere the story seems to be the same – teachers, students, doctors all up in arms against reform. All – or just about all – claiming to be worse off. All complaining that they are stressed out of their minds by New Labour and its obsession with targets. Surely we must have made someone, somewhere happy?

Monday, 28 April

Dawn Primarolo made a statement about the new Child Tax Credit and was assailed from all sides. She seemed to be describing a parallel, New Labour universe full of happy, contented citizens. The chink in her armour was the admission that two million people had tried to phone the hotline. If everything was so rosy, why would two million people need to ring for help?

Tuesday, 29 April

To the annual meeting of the all-party Saudi group. Not my normal territory, but I wanted to hear what the Saudi ambassador, Prince Turki Al Faisal, had to say about recent events in Iraq. An intelligent, civilised, sophisticated man whose modest, unpompous manner belies the fact that he comes from the Saudi top drawer (he was formerly the head of the Saudi intelligence service) and represents one of the world's most absolute tyrannies. The Saudis are taking their relations with Europe more seriously now that they have fallen out with Washington. 'The view of the Arab world is that this is an exercise in empire building,' he said. Al-Qaida posed a bigger threat than

Iraq, 'because it is a small group that can be imitated'. Like Mrs Manningham-Buller, he was firmly of the view that the war had made the threat from terrorism worse, not better. To be credible, a new regime in Iraq would have to be seen to have power; there must be no under-the-table deals and above all the military must not make deals with Iraqi factions on the basis of ethnicity. 'Are you optimistic or pessimistic about the long-term outcome?' I asked.

'Pessimistic,' he replied.

Friday, 2 May
Sunderland

Lunch with Peter Candler, who says that 65 per cent of the new apartments on the Newcastle quayside have been purchased by investors and many of them are empty. 'A house of cards which could come tumbling down at any moment,' he says.

Sunday, 4 May

Bright sunshine. Sarah and I cycled from the seafront at South Shields along the Tyne to Newcastle. We arrived home to find a message from Jeremy, our upstairs neighbour at Brixton Road, to say that our flat has been burgled. A woman broke in through the kitchen window in broad daylight, triggering the alarm; once in she found she couldn't get out and the police found her under my bed.

Wednesday, 7 May

'Where does the idea of Foundation hospitals come from?' Malcolm Savidge asked as we waited for a lift. 'It wasn't in the manifesto.'

'Like top-up fees,' I replied.

'No, they were in the manifesto. We said we wouldn't have them.' These days, he said, policy was announced from on high and we are bullied into line. The Man, he said, despite being a practising Christian, doesn't even listen to God. Witness the war in Iraq, which was opposed by both the Pope and the Archbishop of Canterbury.

At seven we voted on Foundation hospitals. The rebels, about 65 in number, were fewer than predicted, but the unhappiness is widespread. Alan Milburn was not happy either. 'Gordon's friends have done their best to stop this,' he said when I saw him in the lobby. 'They've used the media to run it down and they've succeeded in emasculating it. People are saying, "You can't have a party within a party."' By 'people' I presume Alan means himself. What can this mean? A purge of Gordon and friends? A high-risk strategy, if ever there was. The tension at the top is greater than I'd imagined. It can only be a question of time before the poison in the body politic spills out into the open, to the disadvantage of us all.

Thursday, 8 May

The Home Affairs Committee's report on asylum removals, published this morning, has stirred a hornets' nest. The tabloids have seized on a sentence in the first paragraph – warning of social unrest if the flow of illegal migrants isn't checked – as a vindication of the poisonous campaign they have been running. The *Express* is raging about 'Asylum chaos', although there is nothing in the report to justify such a headline. Interview requests poured in and I spent much of the day trying to douse the flames.

The Chief Whip, Hilary Armstrong, was on the train going home. She confirmed that The Friends of Gordon had behaved badly over Foundation hospitals. Could it be that Gordon didn't know? Inconceivable, she thought. She even quoted one of our colleagues as having been encouraged to rebel by Gordon's agents on the promise that they would be looked after in due course. Gordon, she said (as if we didn't know), was paranoid about losing the succession and ruthless about disposing of rivals. 'He is convinced that Alan is being set up to succeed Tony and once said to me, "I've sorted David [Blunkett] and I'll sort Alan." However,' said Hilary, 'he has been "brilliant" during the war.' Apparently, she put it to Gordon that The Man was more likely to anoint him if he co-operated than if he didn't and once that point had been grasped Gordon played his part to perfection.

I floated the idea of a comeback, remarking that DFID would be my ideal job, but she offered no encouragement, saying only that 'a lot of people are after that'. Who, I wonder? On the other hand she didn't rule out a return.

Friday, 9 May

Charlie Falconer rang to say that he is going to propose that suspected terrorists can be detained for up to 14 days, instead of the present seven. Really, there seems to be no end to the repressive measures pouring out of the Home Office, all without time for proper scrutiny. On Wednesday David Blunkett announced that he is proposing a 30-year minimum for the murder of policemen, prison officers and that life should mean life for most child murderers. Charlie also mentioned there is a leader in today's *Independent* comparing our asylum report to Enoch Powell's 'rivers of blood' speech. For goodness' sake.

Monday, 12 May

To London on the 10.42. Just after Doncaster, the Scarborough MP, Lawrie Quinn, passed by and said he had heard on the radio that Clare Short had resigned. Damn, I thought, it's happened before I could buttonhole Jack. Later, I heard that Valerie Amos had been appointed and that the announcement had been made within half an hour of Clare making the call, so it was obviously all sorted well in advance. Jack and the Foreign Office have staged a coup. Valerie was only a Lords whip when I was at DFID and, until today, one of Jack's junior ministers. The contrast with Clare couldn't be more blatant and having a secretary of state who is beyond the reach of scrutiny by the elected House is not at all satisfactory. As soon as I arrived at the Commons I rang Jack's Parliamentary Private Secretary, Colin Pickthall, and arranged to see Jack immediately after Clare's statement.

Clare rose as soon as Jack had finished his statement on Iraq. She was seated a couple of rows back from the Speaker, between Tom Clarke and Dennis Turner, who, after the twists and turns of the last few weeks, are just about her only friends in this place. I was standing a couple of yards away, waiting to pounce as Jack left the chamber. Clare was heard, for the most part, in dead silence. Only when she broadened her attack, away from Iraq and on to The Man personally, was there a certain amount of mumbling and when she sat down there was no hear-hearing, not even from those who share her view on the handling of the war. She has alienated everybody. A sad end. Until two months ago, Clare was arguably one of our most successful ministers. It is down to her, and the battles she fought in the early days, that aid policy has been prised free of trade and foreign policy and no one can take that away from her. If she'd gone, alongside Robin (and with his dignity), she would have retained the respect of everyone and would probably have had a future running a UN agency or even the IMF or World Bank. As it is she has blown every bridge.

Jack emerged looking sombre. I remarked, unwisely perhaps, that although Clare was difficult to work with, the Department for International Development had been a success. He replied ominously, 'We could have achieved all the good we have done without setting up a separate department.'

I said that, given that Valerie was in the Lords, there was an urgent need for a credible figure at this end of the building and I was available, if called. Jack, who is off to South Africa this evening, said, 'I'll pass that on tout de suite' and off he went.

Later, at about eight o'clock, I was sitting with Gil Loescher (an American academic with whom I travelled in China in 1971) in the atrium at Portcullis House when Jean Corston appeared and said the Prime Minister was looking for me. She had come straight from an audience with The Man at Number 10. He had apologised for not discussing in advance his plan to replace Clare with Valerie and asked what she would do about the job in the Commons. Jean had seized the moment. 'I'd give it to Chris Mullin,' she said. 'Right,' he replied, 'I will.' I kissed her and went straight to the telephone. Sure enough, there were two pink slips on the message board: the first, timed 19.23, said ring the Prime Minister's office; the second, timed 20.00, was from the whips and said the same. They had 'Urgent' stamped all over them. For the first time in my life I could have done with a pager.

I rang Number 10. The woman on the switchboard said my call was expected and asked me to hang on. Several clicks and then silence.

She came back to say that The Man was tied up. Would I call back in ten minutes? I rang again. More clicks, more silence. While I was holding on, Hilary Armstrong and John Reid came by, beaming all over their faces and giving me the thumbs up, confirmation, if any were needed, that the job was mine. More clicks, more silence and then, 'The Prime Minister isn't available this evening. He will call you tomorrow morning.'

There was no reason at this stage to suppose anything was wrong. After all, the Chief Whip herself had indicated to me that my hour had come. Or had she?

At about nine o'clock, a message from the *Evening Standard*. Would I write an overnight op-ed piece denouncing today's demand by the British Airports Authority for lots more runways? The devil had offered me a chance to self-destruct in exchange for £600. Needless to say, I resisted temptation and began to make plans for tomorrow. I was due to chair the Home Affairs Committee at 09.30 and, in my absence, the task would fall to the senior opposition member, Ann Widdecombe. Given that asylum was the subject of our inquiry, this did not seem a good idea. I decided to seek advice from Hilary. It was then that it became clear that all was not as it seemed.

'The Prime Minister hadn't realised that you voted the wrong way on Iraq,' she said slyly.

'Nonsense,' I replied. 'He and I had a 15-minute conversation on the subject, on the day.'

'Well, he had forgotten.' It soon became clear that, as soon as word reached her of my impending appointment, Hilary had rushed over to Number 10 to put the boot in and that this was the reason why he had suddenly become unavailable. She must have been with him at the very moment of my first call. No doubt she was saying that rewarding a dissident would send the wrong message to the boys and girls. I can't really blame her for that. It is the job of the Chief Whip to draw The Main Person's attention to any downside, but why the smile and the thumbs-up when she passed me in Portcullis House? (I realise now that she must have been on the way back from the very conversation.) That, surely, is over and above the call of duty, even for a Chief Whip.

There was, she indicated, a sliver of hope, but I should not get too excited. The Man had decided to sleep on it. 'Your name is still in the frame, but there are one or two others, too.' In the meantime, she added, I should take nothing for granted.

I could kick myself. Had I returned The Man's call immediately, I'd have been anointed before Hilary could have got to him.

Tuesday, 13 May

I slept well, all things considered. By eight I was back in my office on Upper Corridor South. At 8.30 I placed a call, via the Number 10 switchboard, to Sally Morgan and received a message that she was just going into a meeting and would ring back in half an hour, but she never did. Then I rang Jean at her flat, who said she would get on to Pat McFadden immediately. She rang back a few minutes later to report that the omens were not auspicious. Pat had confirmed that The Man hadn't realised I voted 'the wrong way' on Iraq. To Jean's argument that appointing me would send a good signal, building bridges and all that, Pat had responded ('in that Scottish way of his') 'Ah no, Jean, this is Iraq.' He went on to explain that a great deal of the international development work concerned Iraq and the Tories were bound to make trouble if a dissident were appointed, especially as Clare, in her resignation speech, had made such a big deal about what was going on at the UN. I don't agree, but I can see his point. That's half my trouble, I can usually see the other side's point.

My fate sealed, I settled down miserably to read the papers for the select committee. The Call came at 09.17. It went as follows:

CM: 'Tony.'

The Man: 'Chris, I am sorry not to have come back to you earlier. As you probably realised there was a problem.'

'I had heard there was some to-ing and fro-ing.'

'I would have liked to put you into DFID, but the timing is not quite right. However, I have something in mind for you, at the level you want, development-type things, in the reshuffle.'

So, all is not quite lost, but what can he possibly be thinking of? And what did he mean 'at the level you want'? Obviously word has reached him that I am reluctant (for the second time) to trade a select committee chairmanship for the lowest form of life in government. There wasn't much time to reflect. As soon as I put down the phone, I reported back to Jean and toddled off to chair the committee. Later, I heard that Hilary Benn had been appointed. Lucky old Hilary. That's the second time he has stepped into my shoes, but I can't complain. He's a good choice, brilliant and everyone likes him. Later, David Hanson whispered to me that the reshuffle would be at the end of June. I remarked that the entire episode had been about the Foreign Office regaining control of foreign policy, to which he replied, 'You are very astute, Chris.'

Wednesday, 14 May

To the weekly meeting of the parliamentary party to hear Charles Clarke rattling off facts and figures designed to prove that all is for the best – at one point he recited a little table which included the percentage of youngsters in higher education in Iceland. Even Charles, however, with his bulldozer delivery and utter self-confidence, cannot disguise the fact that education is in a mess. Students and teachers loathe us and local authorities are apoplectic about our attempt to blame them for the latest funding fiasco.

Top-up fees and the Tory attempt to outflank us came up again at the parliamentary committee in the afternoon. The Man replied that the Tories' sums didn't add up and predicted confidently that they would unravel. Gordon Prentice brought the meeting to life. 'Policy-making,' he asserted, 'is like the dance of the seven veils. Policy seems to be made by the few for the many.' He went down the card – Foundation hospitals, top-up fees, the Euro. 'Who is consulted?' he demanded, adding mischievously, 'Just an observation.'

That really set The Man off. I haven't seen him so passionate in a long while. As for the Euro, he said, the Cabinet will take the final decision. Tuition fees were not dreamed up by some boffin in Number 10. They were first suggested by Ron Dearing. The idea for Foundation hospitals came from the hospitals themselves, not Number 10. By now he was as worked up as he ever gets, using his hands like an Italian. 'Tuition fees may be right or they may be wrong, but they have nothing to do with arrogance or a presidential style. In the end we have to decide.'

He went on for about five minutes with Gordon lobbing in the occasional hand grenade. Above all, The Man said, we must avoid having the sort of debate that the Tories and the media wanted – about spin doctors and aides in Number 10. 'That will be the death of this government.'

Jean, who earlier had her regular private audience, reported later that he had apologised over what happened to me and confirmed that I would receive an offer come the reshuffle.

Thursday, 15 May

Mike O'Brien took me aside after the division in the afternoon and whispered that he was thinking of resigning.

'When?'

'Tonight.'

'Why?'

'Because I don't believe what I am being asked to say about the existence of weapons of mass destruction. The security service is still saying they will be found, but I don't believe them. Even if they are, I no longer believe that they were ever a threat – although I did at the time.' He added that Clare was right about what's going on over the latest UN resolution. 'It's a mess. The Americans aren't making the slightest effort. Jack is not happy, but he tends to believe what Colin Powell tells him.'

'Have you spoken to Jack?'

'I've been trying for three weeks, but he won't see me. He knows what I want to say.'

Mike wanted my advice. 'Stay put,' I said. The war is over. There is no longer any great issue of principle at stake that requires another act of self-immolation.

Later, Jack – just back from South Africa (and looking as though he had been no further than a day trip to Blackburn) – strolled into the near-deserted Tea Room. 'What happened?' he asked, adding that as promised he had passed word to The Man immediately after our exchange on Monday. I told him, taking care to mention that I had voted against the war (I didn't want him hearing that from Hilary Armstrong); he didn't bat an eyelid. I mentioned The Man's promise of a development-type job. 'That'll be the Africa job at the Foreign Office,' he said, 'the one that Valerie Amos has vacated.' Of course, it is. I went immediately to the Library and looked it up in the list of ministerial responsibilities. It is only a lowly under-secretaryship and – despite what The Man said – I very much doubt whether it will turn into a minister of state's job. Never mind. If it is offered, I will take it. This is my last chance to do anything useful in government.

Tuesday, 20 May

Another afternoon on the Criminal Justice Bill. Today we nodded through Blunkett's plans for ratcheting up life sentences and doubling (from 7 to 14 days) the length of time that terrorist suspects can be held without trial. Both of these measures have only appeared in the last ten days, so there had been no previous opportunity for discussion (apart from a little informal session that I and half a dozen members of the committee had with him last week).

Wednesday, 21 May

Mandelson is up to his tricks again. In a supposedly off the record speech to women lobby correspondents (who always seem to leak) he remarked, apropos the Euro, that The Man had been 'outmanoeuvred by an obsessive Chancellor'. Suddenly all hell has broken loose. Why can't Peter keep his trap shut? He can't bear not being the centre of attention. The only reason anybody listens to him is because they assume he is speaking for The Man, which, these days at least, is not very likely. Number 10 were quick to distance themselves, but the damage is done. 'Some of us spent 18 years in Opposition and we don't want to go down that road again,' said Clive Soley to a lot of 'hear-hearing' at the meeting of the parliamentary party this morning. At the committee in the afternoon, The Man said that, contrary to rumour, 'Gordon and I have had very good discussions'; he was confident that a reasonable solution will emerge. Jean said there was dismay in the way that personal discussions appeared to leak into the press. I said that I hoped Peter's friends would make clear to him that his contribution had been unhelpful. 'It astonishes me that someone whose judgement is normally so good, could make such a misjudgement.'

'Maybe it wasn't a misjudgement,' muttered JP.

The Man gave us one of his helpless shrugs that he reserves for occasions like this. At some point the phone rang. The Man ignored it. JP leaned across, lifted the receiver and then replaced it, prompting a sudden flurry of activity among the bag-carriers. David Hanson appeared at The Man's side and whispered, 'You've *got* to take that call.'

Someone said, to general merriment, 'It's George Bush again', whereupon JP suddenly sprang to life. 'Have I just put down the phone on George Bush?' he beamed. 'That's made my day.' Then, while everyone was giggling, 'I don't want that appearing in the diaries ...'

'Why ever not?' I said. 'It'll do wonders for your street cred.'

Later, I checked: it wasn't George Bush, after all. Damn.

Thursday, 22 May

While waiting for a bus to the Commons this morning, I noticed a villainous-looking male disappear into a neighbour's garden. I followed and found him peering into the basement window. When challenged he claimed to be looking for a friend in Camberwell New Road, half a mile away, but instead of heading in that direction he disappeared around the corner into Lorn Road. I found him in the back lane, apparently casing the rear of our terrace. A white male, in his late thirties, of south European appearance but with a London accent. A can of lager in one hand (at 9 a.m.), 'criminal' written all over him in large letters. On seeing me, he turned nasty. 'Are you calling me a burglar,' he snarled putting his face menacingly close to mine. 'I don't know what you are up to,' I replied angrily, 'I've been done three times already this year and I'm fed up with it.' I thought he was going to hit me at first, but he dawdled brazenly away up Lorn Road, still peering in windows.When I got to the House 15 minutes later, I rang Brixton police station, but the phone didn't answer. I rang Kennington, but that didn't answer either. I rang the direct line of DC Adams, the officer who has been dealing with my latest burglary. One of his colleagues answered, but wasn't interested; instead he diverted me to the switchboard, but it still wasn't answering. I gave up. No wonder the criminals are so brazen.

Sunday, 25 May
The Holmes, St Boswells

We are back with Mrs Dale again. A handsome young white horse gallops around the field trailed by the usual quota of donkeys, pigs, goats, geese and various exotic species of chicken. We spent the afternoon in the Duke of Sutherland's glorious garden at Mertoun and once again had the place almost to ourselves.

Tuesday, 27 May

I am sitting by the Tweed reading Roy Jenkins's biography of Gladstone. In most respects a masterpiece, except that Roy is almost as pompous and long-winded as his hero. Palmerston said of Gladstone, 'He had the ability to persuade himself of the rightness of any view which he chose to hold.' Of whom does that remind one?

Saturday, 31 May

We packed our chattels, bade our farewells and departed, meandering home via the Wallace Monument, Scott's View, the Hirsel (for lunch), the beach at Bamburgh and finally tea with Charles and Barbara Baker-Cresswell. We reached Sunderland at nine to find our back entrance blocked by a dumped car, which fortunately we managed to shift with the help of a passing youth.

Sunday, 1 June

The Man is in trouble over his failure to come up with evidence of weapons of mass destruction. Clare is in the papers this morning saying we were duped and the Americans have been saying for some days that they were never really all that important anyway. The Man, who is floating between a knees-up in St Petersburg and the G8 summit at Evian, is still insisting that evidence will be discovered (and even hinting that it has been) but his protestations are beginning to look a little thin. The vultures are circling. This could end badly. Just my luck, were I to rejoin the regime as it slides beneath the waves. Should I stick with the select committee after all?

Tuesday, 3 June

The row over Iraq is growing. It is being suggested that The Man, or at least someone in Number 10, 'improved' the intelligence on weapons of mass destruction in order to justify the war. One or two of our more excitable colleagues, ever ready to believe the worst, are using words like 'Watergate'. Demand for an inquiry is growing and I can't see how it can be resisted. Jean went to see Sally Morgan this afternoon to say that there has to be an inquiry and that the report must be published and debatable in Parliament. According to Jean, Sally says that, far from exaggerating the intelligence, Number 10 toned it down. Jean thinks The Man will survive. I am not so sure. Iraq is beginning to boomerang.

To the Lords to listen to the debate on the Communications Bill, now on its sixth day. The prospects for an uprising over Channel Five look promising. Only the two front benches seem determined to plough on regardless.

Wednesday, 4 June

A rousing speech from JP at this morning's meeting of the parliamentary party. A *tour de force*. JP at his most lucid; positively fluent, indeed. The integrity of the government is at stake, he warned. If we lose that we lose everything. At one point he proclaimed, 'Tony Blair is not a liar.' The very fact that he needed to make such an assertion is a measure of the trouble we are in. He also made the very reasonable point that most of those on our side who are self-indulgently going on television demanding inquiries and signing motions occupy safe seats and all they are doing is jeopardising the survival of colleagues in the marginals. He sat down to warm applause.

As if we haven't got enough trouble, John Reid was plastered all over the front page of today's *Times* alleging that a rogue element – 'or elements' – in the security services are briefing against the government. This morning he had one of his memorable head to heads with John Humphrys on the *Today* programme on the subject. All very amusing, but do we really need this?

Everyone was holding their breath at Questions, but they needn't have worried. As always when in a corner, The Man was on top form. He knocked IDS, who kept coming back for more, all around the chamber. Easy wins in the chamber, however, are not enough this time. The feeling that we were misled over Iraq is widespread and it is beginning to infect everything. In the debate that followed, Clare again accused The Man of deceit. There is no doubt she is trying to bring him down. We are walking on egg-shells. One little push from Gordon and the entire edifice could crumble. My guess is that Gordon will wait for the inquiries – one by the Foreign Affairs committee and one by the Intelligence and Security Committee – to report and, if they are damaging enough, he will make his move then. We badly need to find a stash of nerve gas.

Fresh from his rout of IDS, The Man was upbeat at the parliamentary committee. 'Have no doubt,' he said. 'It is more than my life's worth to start mucking around with stuff from the Joint Intelligence Committee.' He was also confident that incriminating evidence would be uncovered. The BBC source – alleging that nothing has been found – had got it wrong. 'We have turned up stuff that is still in the process of being verified. It will come out in due course. Let's not give a running commentary.' He was sure that the Iraqi scientists would eventually cough up. 'Obviously the scientists aren't going to co-operate, if they think they are going to end up in front of a war crimes tribunal.' We must beware, he said, of falling into the trap that the Tories and the media were setting for us. 'If they can't destroy the policy, they will destroy trust in the government and me in particular. There is a tendency for our folk to fall for right-wing propaganda. The centre-left's capacity for committing hara-kiri is legendary. There is a tendency to say that because the Tories are so hopeless we can do what we like, but we can't.'

After The Man had gone talk turned to the latest demands from the Electoral Commission, which brought Paul Boateng, who doesn't usually say much, briefly to life. 'We've created a monster and it's all our fault. None of them have any political experience. These are people who have spent all their lives being Great and Good. They have never sullied their hands with the things to which we have devoted our lives.' It was agreed that Sam Younger be invited to address the parliamentary party and that the other parties be encouraged to do likewise in the hope that exposure to the political realities will cause the commissioners to mitigate their demands.

Later, in the corridor behind the Speaker's chair, I came across Alan Milburn and we had a little *sotto voce* conversation about the current state of play. He shares my view that the situation is dangerous. 'Some of our colleagues have decided they want regime change here.' He thinks Clare could run as a stalking horse for Gordon. 'We need to have a grown-up conversation with the unions. Tony must tread carefully and not just say, as he has in the past, fuck them.' He added, 'We'd be mad to get rid of the most successful prime minister for years.' He went away saying he was going discreetly to check the party's standing orders to see how many MPs would be needed to endorse a challenge.

Thursday, 5 June

A quiet chat with Robin Cook, behind the screens at the far end of the Tea Room. 'I think we're in trouble,' he said. 'The news over the next month or so will be dominated by the American congressional hearings. The problem is that the Americans never wanted to use WMD as the reason for going to war. They only went along with it to keep us happy and now that the war is over, they no longer see the need to keep up the pretence.' The Man, says Robin, will 'probably be acquitted of lying, but he will be very damaged'. He will want to talk about anything but Iraq, but it won't go away. The one thing he will not face up to is that to focus on WMD was a mistake. 'All he keeps saying is, "This is what the intelligence said at the time."' Robin said that this side of an election Gordon was the only possible successor. After the election, it would be a different story.

Home as usual on the 20.00. JP was on board and stopped by for a brief chat. He was robust: 'No one can touch Blair. There isn't going to be an election this year. Clare, he said, is very bitter. He reckons Robin is, too (over losing the Foreign Office) – 'but he's not making the same mistakes as Clare'. He went on, apparently referring to The Man and Gordon, 'I've got to live with the two of them. One's concerned with his legacy. The other with his inheritance.' He added with a laugh, 'It's nice to be normal.'

Friday, 6 June
Sunderland

At the monthly meeting of the management committee in the evening people were openly saying that The Man should go and that the talk in the clubs is that no one trusts him any more. Oh dear, oh dear.

Monday, 9 June

A reshuffle is expected this week and I am among the expectant. The Call could come at any time and I can't make up my mind how to respond. First, because there is a fair chance that The Man will be gone by the end of the year in which case, were I to accept his offer, I shall be left high and dry, having sacrificed my select committee chairmanship, my place on the parliamentary committee and a certain amount of self-respect. Second because, despite my messages, the odds are it will be a humble under-secretaryship. Dare I *again* trade one of the main select committee chairmanships for the lowest form of life in government? If I am cast aside after six months, there will be no shortage of people muttering, 'Serves him right.'

Thursday, 12 June

The House is eerily deserted. 'Here's a man who won't be waiting by his telephone,' remarked one of the Tory whips as we passed in an otherwise empty corridor. Little does he know.

Friday, 13 June
Sunderland

I was visiting Havelock Primary School when Pat rang to say that Hilary Armstrong wanted to talk. Why Hilary, I thought. This can only be bad news. In the event it wasn't. Not quite. She was calling to sound me out on whether I'd be willing to take an under-secretaryship since (as I anticipated) there are no suitable vacancies at minister of state level. I had been considered for Michael Meacher's job at Environment, but Margaret Beckett felt strongly – and who could argue – that it should go to Elliot Morley. Would I be interested in either Elliot's job at Environment or the Africa job at the Foreign Office? I closed my eyes and plumped for Africa. Then I drove to Durham Cathedral for the funeral of poor John Williams.* When I got back there was a message to ring The Man. The conversation lasted less than a minute. He said he was delighted and I said I was, too, though in truth I am riven with doubt. I may have booked a third-class berth on the *Titanic*.

Saturday, 14 June

Jack Straw rang, just as I was departing for my quarterly haircut. 'One condition,' he said. 'You must get a pager and a mobile phone.'

'Okay,' I said, 'but no official car.'

'Up to you, but there will be a lot of highly classified stuff which can't be taken by public transport.'

He went on, 'A lot of very bright people work in the Foreign Office, but they do need watching otherwise they go off and do their own thing.'

---

*A former director of education at Sunderland City Council.

Monday, 16 June

Everywhere I go I am showered with congratulations (we do spend a lot of time congratulating each other in this place), but among the more discerning there is bewilderment. 'You have sold yourself cheap,' a not unfriendly Tory whip remarked. George Young said much the same. Perhaps, but I do have one strong card. I am the only member of the government to have voted against the Iraq adventure. No one can accuse me of having sold my soul for a job.

Tuesday, 17 June

A barely legible handwritten note from Gordon Brown offering congratulations on my new incarnation. If the past is anything to go by, every new minister will have received an identical missive. 'A great challenge,' he said. Actually, my principal challenge will be to survive if Gordon becomes leader.

Wednesday, 18 June
The Foreign Office

Day Three. I still take wrong turnings on the way to and from my luxurious apartment (I even have my own bathroom). Everything is larger than life. Ceilings so high as to be in the clouds, huge double doors which can only be opened with effort, miles of polished corridors, marble statues, pillars, vast (politically incorrect) murals. One half expects to see Sir Edward Grey or Lord Halifax sweeping down the grand staircase. Today I returned from lunch to find the Princess Royal on the steps outside my French windows, addressing a reception in the Durbar Court.

I sit alone in my vast room, behind my oh-so-large desk, the half-dozen boys and girls in the private office commute back and forth attending to my every need. When I close the door there is no sound but the ticking of the clocks on my two mantelpieces. I feel as though I am trapped in the penthouse suite of a five-star hotel, far removed from life in the streets of London, never mind Africa. At any moment I could be asked to pay the bill and leave.

The news from Africa is unremittingly, mind-numbingly awful. Mayhem in Liberia, barbarism in the Congo, looming famine in Ethiopia and Zimbabwe, entire peoples laid low by Aids. Almost everywhere power is in the hands of corrupt elites, stuffing their pockets with little concern for the welfare of their people. The countries with the greatest natural wealth are in the worst condition because they have assets worth plundering.

Here and there a ray of light. Mozambique, after years of chaos, is said to be doing reasonably; Uganda, too (although President Museveni is showing signs of the disease that eventually afflicts most African leaders, good and bad – a reluctance to contemplate retirement). In Kenya, after 24 years of corrupt dictatorship, there has been (to everyone's surprise) a peaceful transfer of power. In Angola the 30-year civil war is over, although the problems of reconstruction are awesome. How, from my luxurious boudoir in Whitehall, can I hope to make the slightest impact on all this?

Monday, 23 June

A quiet word from Jack. 'Just so you are aware, there is a bit of chatter about the fact that you voted against the government on Iraq ...' Bob Ainsworth, the Deputy Chief Whip, said something similar.

Tuesday, 24 June

Jean Corston whispered that The Man had told her that the Chief Whip, Hilary Armstrong, is reporting 'unhappiness' at my elevation. Jean responded that no one had complained to her. Quite so. It's all coming from Hilary and the whips.

Wednesday, 25 June

Mike O'Brien has also heard bleating from the whips about my appointment. Odd that the small minds in the whips' office can't grasp that, in these difficult times, The Man needs to be building bridges rather than dynamiting them.

Wednesday, 2 July

Among the issues which crossed my desk today the tricky question of what to do about the Liberian warlord, Charles Taylor. Everyone agrees that he is a very bad man and that it is in Liberia's best interests that he be persuaded to leave the country as soon as possible. The difficulty is that the Special Prosecutor in Sierra Leone has, without consulting anyone, issued a warrant for Taylor's arrest, thereby derailing peace talks that were underway in Ghana and causing Taylor to scuttle back to his bunker in the capital, Monrovia, triggering a new wave of mayhem in which hundreds have died and thousands are facing starvation. The only way out is for Taylor to be offered a safe passage out of the country; indeed the Nigerians have generously offered to take him. Before doing so, however, they very reasonably wish to be assured that they will not be criticised for harbouring an indicted war criminal. The dilemma for us is that, having helped to set up and fund the war crimes tribunal in Sierra Leone, we can't be seen to undermine it. The recommendation is that some weasel words (or as the official note puts it 'a more nuanced line') be found in the hope of squaring the circle. Needless to say I concur. There is no room for the pure of heart in the Foreign Office.

Thursday, 3 July

Among my visitors today the UN Secretary General's Special Representative for Africa, Ibrahim Gambari, a former Foreign Minister of Nigeria. Intelligent, decent, wise. Makes one realise that there are many good men in Africa. It's just a question of giving them a helping hand.

Monday, 7 July

In at the deep end. Today, at short notice, I was called upon to respond to an emergency question from Douglas Hogg on the news that the Americans are planning to bring before military tribunals two of our citizens held in Guantanamo Bay. Maximum indignation all round. The questions come thick and fast. How dare they? By what right? What's the government doing? Why aren't we making a bigger fuss? And so on for half an hour. After initial hesitation, I just about held the line. By the end I was even ticking off the Tories for indulging in megaphone diplomacy. The line is that we are making the strongest representations, but are we? Certainly Jack is sending a tough letter to Colin Powell, but the trouble is we are up against Rumsfeld and the Pentagon and strong messages to the State Department won't make the blindest difference. If we are to get anywhere, The Man will have to tackle George Bush and there is no evidence so far that he has done so.

Tuesday, 8 July

An amusing little memorandum crossed my desk today on the subject of national day messages. Apparently the world is divided into A, B and C countries, according to the extent of our approval for their governments. A countries receive national day messages as a matter of course. B countries 'we need to consider carefully, but with a presumption to send perhaps a toned-down message'. For C countries there is a presumption against sending any kind of message. I am asked to approve the elevation of Gambia from B to A, the downgrading of the Central African Republic from B to C, and the promotion of Eritrea and the Congo from C to B. Anxious to demonstrate how seriously I take my responsibilities, I vetoed the proposal for the promotion of Eritrea.

Wednesday, 9 July

'Congratulations on your performance the other day,' remarked Michael Howard as we passed on the Upper Committee Corridor, 'a masterpiece of semi-detachment.' Oh dear, was it really? The trouble with compliments from Michael Howard is that one can never be sure whether they are intended to cheer up or demoralise.

A visit from the Secret Intelligence Service. The 'Two Michaels' as they are known in the office. Smooth, affable, apparently anxious to please. The extent to which they level with ministers, particularly junior ones, is impossible to gauge. As Tom, my Private Secretary, pointed out afterwards, most of their sentences contain tiny qualifying clauses. They also appear to have their own direct links to some African heads of state. They invited me to visit them at Vauxhall, an offer I accepted with alacrity.

Thursday, 10 July

My pager has arrived. From now on (assuming I can work the damn thing) I shall be entirely on-message.

Tuesday, 15 July

Ministerial life is full of surprises. This afternoon I returned from lunch to find preparations underway in the Durbar Court for some grand event.

'What's going on?' I innocently inquired.

'A reception. For Chevening scholars. About 500 people. You're speaking.'

The moment came. The scholars and their sponsors were assembled. The French windows leading from my room into the Durbar Court swung open. A man with a gavel banged on a table. I stepped grandly up to the microphone and made my little speech. Then I mingled. A man from Prudential Insurance bore down on me. 'I'm having lunch with the Vietnamese Ambassador tomorrow,' he said.

'Oh,' said I, 'he's a friend of mine. Please give him my regards.'

The Man from the Pru was momentarily nonplussed. 'But you're hosting the lunch!'

Monday, 21 July
Ghana

This is going to be one of those weeks when I get to play at being The Man. From the moment my foot touches the soil of Africa I shall not be permitted to carry my own bag, to open a door or to walk unaided for more than a few paces. There will be servants, bodyguards, sojourns in VIP lounges and throughout I shall be addressed as 'Excellency' (there are many Excellencies in Africa and most of them are not all that excellent).

High Commissioner's Residence, Accra

I had visions of an old colonial mansion, yellow stucco and green wooden shutters, á la Dalat or Hanoi. Alas, however, the residence is a 1960s job, all glass and concrete. A whiff of damp pervades the guest suite. Previous occupants of my bed include the Princess Royal and Clare Short.

Tuesday, 22 July

Terrible things going on in Liberia, just up the road. Everyone is waiting for the Americans, but Bush is dithering. The State Department are saying openly that Rumsfeld is the problem. Word is that he would prefer to close the embassy in Liberia and make a run for it, leaving the wretched Liberians to their fate. I sent word to Jack suggesting I say something tough about the American position (perhaps including the word 'shameful') on the basis that the only hope of engaging the attention of the Americans is to upset them and I am better placed than he to express such sentiments. According to my Private Secretary, Tom, there were several sharp intakes of breath as he relayed my message to HQ.

Thursday, 24 July
Freetown, Sierra Leone

A message from Jack, delivered via his Private Secretary: 'Tell Chris that, if he criticises the Americans, he's on his own.'

Tuesday, 29 July
London

To Lancaster House for a pow-wow with President Obasanjo of Nigeria. Purpose of exercise: to impress upon the old rogue that if – and it is a big if – he is serious about improving the lot of his much put-upon people, we are willing to pull out all the stops to assist.

Facing us across the table His Magnificence the President, resplendent in flowing Yoruba robes, his bloated features topped by a purple and gold head-dress. On the wall behind, only marginally more colourful, a life-size portrait of debauched-looking Charles II in full regalia. On the President's right, in deep-blue national dress, his impressive new Minister of Finance, a woman in her forties who long ago fled her homeland for the warm bosom of the World Bank and who, as she later made clear, has only with the greatest reluctance been persuaded to forsake the comforts of Washington to take charge of the black hole that is Nigeria's economy. Other members of the President's considerable entourage include the Foreign Minister, the governor of the State Bank and an assortment of experts, advisers and heavies airlifted into London on the President's plane, which is, according to Tom who has travelled in it, the last word in vulgar luxury.

To the President's left, World Bank chief Jim Wolfensohn, who has jetted in this morning from Kenya and who departs this evening for Iraq. Wolfensohn, hunched shoulders, mane of white hair – a wise old snowy owl, the only person in the room older than the President and, therefore, the only one who stands a chance of being taken seriously. Age counts in Nigeria.

Our side of the table is considerably lighter. Valerie Amos, in a luminous orange two-piece, flanked by myself and Suma Chakrabarti, the Permanent Secretary at DFID, and last, but by no means least, Philip Thomas, our excellent High Commissioner with whom I dined in Lagos last week.

Valerie invites the President to open. He does so with a rambling, barely audible, deeply uninspiring speech which eventually (but not before some time) grinds to a halt in the middle of nowhere. Then the bright new finance minister delivers, in stark contrast to her master, a brisk, competent analysis of Nigeria's plight and what must be done to haul the country out of the deep, deep pit into which it has sunk. Her recipe: stabilise, reform, privatise, cleanse. Although she has the attention of everyone else it is soon apparent that the President's concentration is wandering, eyes constantly on the move, gazing at the ceiling, then at the floor, right, left and so on. Before long his fingers are drumming audibly on the table.

A flunky appears with a pot of coffee and, lo, the huge man seated immediately behind – The Bearer of the President's Sweeteners? – produces a pack of saccharine tablets which he discreetly places on the table in front of his master. Music from the Guards' band in the Mall, drifts in through open windows. From somewhere within his voluminous robes His Magnificence produces a large nut which he proceeds noisily to bite.

Jim Wolfensohn speaks. His tone is friendly, but firm. He calls for 'clear, unambiguous steps' without which, he says, there is absolutely no point in Nigeria approaching the Club of Paris for debt relief. 'To do so risks rebuff.' At this point it is apparent that, for the first time in the proceedings, he has the President's full attention. Obasanjo's fingers have ceased drumming; he has pulled himself out of slouch-mode; he is sitting bolt-upright, half facing Wolfensohn. And to be fair, he appears to be taking the message in good heart.

The discussion wanders on. Various other Nigerians contribute from time to time, amiably interrupted by their leader. Then it is our turn. Valerie first, then Chakrabarti and finally myself. The buzzwords from all sides are the same; transparency, benchmarks, quick wins. How easily these New Labour slogans trip from Nigerian tongues. Even the President seems familiar with them. The issue: how to translate words into action.

Tuesday, 2 September
Sunderland

Among the items in the box that came from London, a questionnaire from Government Hospitality about my entertainment preferences.

> Do you prefer pre-theatre or post-theatre suppers?
> Do you have a preference for either champagne or sweet wine with dessert?
> Are you content for port to be served at dinner for Toasts?

To most questions I answered 'pass' and at the end scribbled, 'I prefer simplicity and lack of extravagance to pomp.'

Monday, 6 October

An afternoon with the SIS at Vauxhall Cross. As with MI5 at Thames House, the building seems eerily empty and yet about a thousand people work there. SIS have managed to avoid many of the controversies that have engulfed their brethren over the river and still seem to indulge in many of the Cold War wheezes – the top man likes to be known as C even though everyone knows his name is Richard Dearlove – with which MI5 long ago dispensed.

I asked what had changed in the last 30 years and they were at pains to assure me that these days they were more ethnically diverse and employed more women (even though just about everyone I met was a white man in a suit). I was told there is also a degree of internal democracy. They hold 'town hall meetings' at which any employee can attend and speak; those on Iraq apparently attracted up to 500 people. On Iraq, they remained surprisingly robust, saying they were still hopeful that something would turn up once the Iraqi scientists had been offered immunity from prosecution.

Tuesday, 7 October

M from Washington called in. He says that, contrary to what I was told yesterday at Vauxhall Cross, many of the Iraqi scientists are talking, they are all singing the same tune and believed to be telling the truth. Namely that Saddam disposed of his remaining chemical and biological weapons after his sons-in-law defected and has had nothing for the last seven years.

Wednesday, 8 October

A day of meetings, ten altogether, including two with Jack. Through my office come a constant flow of officials, ambassadors, high commissioners, ministers from countries great and small. Many of the Africans are impressive, sophisticated people, fluent in several languages, soft-spoken, modest, wise – in short, hard to reconcile with the corruption and violence laying waste to their continent.

We talk of good governance, democracy, transparency and they make all the right noises. Only on one subject – Zimbabwe – do they have their heads firmly in the sand. Despite Mugabe's evident wickedness, despite the ruin he has inflicted on his country (which in private they usually acknowledge), no African, or virtually none, will say a word against him in public.

The South Africans (who are playing host to a million Zimbabwean refugees) talk of quiet diplomacy, although their efforts are so quiet as to be inaudible. There are mutterings about African solidarity, plenty of foot-shuffling and suggestions that it is all our fault for failing to come up with the cash to buy out the white farmers. When pressed, even the good guys like President Kuofor of Ghana come out with that line. Mugabe may not be much good at feeding his people, but he has certainly done a good job of persuading his neighbours that his country's troubles are all someone else's fault.

Friday, 31 October
Kisumu, Kenya

My first taste of Big Man politics. The Big Man in question is Raila Odinga, overlord of the Luo tribe and son of the late nationalist hero Oginga Odinga. All day we raced around in a convoy of gleaming Land Cruisers, mobbed by cheering crowds. At every stop a visitors' book was produced. At first, I duly filled in my name and details across a single line. The Honourable Raila was unimpressed. 'That's not how you do it,' he snorts, 'you must fill the whole page.' I flicked back through the book. Everyone else seemed to have made do with a single line, but that apparently is not how Big Men sign their names.

Honourable Raila takes the book and scrawls his signature across a full page. 'There.' He holds it out for me to admire. Try as I may, I cannot rise to the occasion. By the end of the day I am managing a mere three lines.

Tuesday, 4 November
Johannesburg, South Africa

An audience with the great Mandela. 'Make sure to organise a photographer,' I kept saying to the High Commissioner. I said it so often that I was becoming tedious. 'Don't worry, it's all in hand,' she kept assuring me. Barry the High Commission fixer has been charged with this important mission.

We spent 40 minutes with the great man, chatting away in an entirely relaxed fashion about Aids, the Queen, Mugabe, until a young woman came to remind him that he had to catch a flight to Cape Town, where he is being deployed to persuade a delegation from FIFA to let South Africa host the football World Cup. The High Commissioner and I helped him to his feet. One of us on each arm, he walked to the door and out into the waiting area, where the wretched Barry was loitering, but even as he clicked away I could see that he was making a mess of it. He kept his distance and after two or three shots stood aside. Mandela hovered for a full five minutes, arm around my shoulder, but Barry just stood gawping, camera at his side. I could cheerfully have strangled him.

Sure enough, we returned to the High Commission only to discover that Barry's pictures were all out of focus and no amount of digital jiggery pokery could make any difference. To be fair, it wasn't Barry's fault. Unknown to us he had been told not to use flash because of the old man's eyes.

So that was that. The photo opportunity of a lifetime, squandered.

Thursday, 20 November
London

To the office amid insane levels of security. Helicopters, armed response units, you name it. My bag was searched twice on the way in. Bush and Blair were due to give their press conference in the Locarno Room at noon. I went out onto the steps at the King Charles Street end of the building and found myself alone except for one security man with an earpiece who ordered me back inside. I pulled rank shamelessly ('I'm a minister, I can go where I like'), regretting the words as soon as they were out of my mouth. The poor fellow was only obeying orders which seemed to be coming from a goon on the roof.

Several minutes elapsed. The vast courtyard was empty apart from security men and a small group of journalists wearing special passes penned up against the north wall. By now I had been joined by Tom, my Private Secretary. The hapless security man made several more attempts to persuade us to go inside, each of which I firmly rebuffed. Eventually George Bush and The Man appeared through the arch that leads from Downing Street, striding purposefully towards the Ambassadors' Entrance. As they turned, much to my amazement and quite unprompted, Bush waved in my direction. I assumed he was waving at someone else. I glanced at the windows behind, but there was no one.

Prime Minister's Room, House of Commons, early evening

With other junior ministers, a meeting with The Man. Amazing that he has time, given everything else that's going on. He looked washed out. Taut, tense, dehydrated. When holding forth he's as lively and engaging as ever and he's still a good listener, but increasingly I notice that when others are speaking he fidgets. The purpose was to brief us on New Labour's latest wheeze – an alleged consultation on the contents of our next manifesto. From beyond the hallowed confines we could hear the distant chants of anti-Bush demonstrators.

As we were leaving he called me back. 'I saw you at the Foreign Office this morning,' he said. 'I told George you were one of his greatest fans.'

Thursday, 27 November

A hilarious incident. I was due to see the Sudanese Ambassador this afternoon and we duly received a call from reception to say that he was on his way up. Kay opened the big door to my office which opens directly out onto the corridor and a man was ushered in together with the young woman from the Sudan desk who was there to take notes.

We sat him down, offered him a cup of tea. I asked if he had enjoyed his two years in England and he replied that in fact he had only been here six months. 'Oh dear,' I said, 'I have been given the wrong information.' At this point a pained expression appeared on the face of the young woman from the Sudan desk.

Unfazed, I asked how the peace talks were going.

He looked puzzled. 'Er, which peace talks?'

'You know, between North and South.'

At this point, out of the corner of my eye, I saw the young woman from the Sudan desk making a dash for the door.

'You are the Sudanese Ambassador?' I inquired.

'No, I am the Ambassador of Brazil. Who are you?'

He took it well. It turned out that he had been passing when the door of my office opened and he found himself ushered inside. Meanwhile the real Sudanese Ambassador had arrived and was waiting outside. We had a good laugh, shook hands and the Brazilian went on his way.

Friday, 5 December
Commonwealth Conference, Abuja, Nigeria

Jack has gone home so I am 'attending upon' the Queen, who is officially opening the new British Council offices. We are on the roof terrace. Her Majesty, the Duke, a fresh-faced equerry, an immaculate lady-in-waiting and myself. David Green, the Council's top man, has just read out a little speech with the Queen standing impassively beside him. I am next to the Duke, alongside a group of English women. When Green has finished the Duke remarks loudly, 'Huh, that speech contained more jargon per square inch than any I've heard for a long time.' Then he turned to the women. 'You're teachers, aren't you? Can you tell me what all that meant?'

One of the women, a bit right-on, replies, 'No, sir. We're not actually teachers ...'

'Not teachers? What are you then?'

'Well, sir, we empower people.'

That set him off. 'EMPOWER? Doesn't sound like English to me ...'

By now the Queen, noticing that trouble is brewing, has turned and is pointing vaguely over the balcony. 'Look …'

The Duke, stopping mid-sentence, retreats instantly to her side, somewhat bemused.

'… at the pottery.'

When they have gone, I go and look. I see no pottery.

Sunday, 7 December
Abuja

This morning I called in quick succession on three presidents: Mogae of Botswana, Museveni of Uganda and Muluzi of Malawi. Inevitably much of the talk was about Zimbabwe. The Botswanans, who have had decades of hassle from their Zimbabwean neighbours, were fine. Museveni, an intelligent, engaging man, who I had expected to be sound, was wobbly; clearly he is beginning to suffer delusions of grandeur (he is presently trying to change the constitution in order to wangle himself a third term – in reality his fifth since he had already served two terms before the constitution came into existence); he talked a lot about vision. Muluzi (who I expected to be the dodgiest) turned out to be the most robust. He spoke with passion about the damage Mugabe was doing to his people and claimed to have said as much both to Mugabe himself and to Mbeki, who has been lobbying furiously for Mugabe to be readmitted to the Commonwealth. He agreed that the only way out was a dignified retirement for Mugabe and I said that it was important for African leaders to be seen to be speaking up so that Mugabe couldn't pretend that it was a blacks versus whites issue.

The row over Zimbabwe was due to come to a head this afternoon when the leaders went into their Retreat in the presidential compound. Tom and I drove to the Residence to await the outcome. It was as though I had stumbled onto a film set: Cherie, in a swimsuit, sunbathing in the garden; the entourage lounging around the pool; officials at the table in the dining room drafting a statement for The Man to make in the House on Tuesday. Our plan was to hitch a ride home with the Prime Minister rather than hang on for another two days.

While Tom drafted reports of this morning's meetings, I spent a pleasant hour chatting to Cherie. 'What do you think of student fees, Chris?' she inquired archly (there is apparently a report in this morning's *Daily Express* suggesting falsely that I am threatening to resign in protest). I replied that, while accepting the principle that students should contribute, I remained to be convinced that universities should be allowed to charge variable fees. She argued strongly in favour of the whole package and seemed confident that, when the middle classes discovered that they would no longer have to pay their children's fees upfront, they would be in favour too. 'I hope Tony's not going to put his life on the line over this,' I said.

'Oh I think he will,' she replied. 'And he thinks he will win.'

7 p.m.

Still no sign of The Man. Such slivers of information as have drifted down to us from the Big House indicate that a fierce struggle is in progress. Much to my embarrassment (since none of the officials are offered food) Cherie invites me to supper on the verandah with the newly-knighted High Commissioner Sir Philip Thomas (surely our only senior diplomat sporting a number one haircut). We dine on elephant fish, rice and green beans washed down by champagne, and talk of Cherie's ambition to become a judge. She thinks it will never happen because (a) she will be too old by the time she is eligible (i.e. when Tony is no longer prime minister) and (b) she will also be vulnerable to the allegation that she is too close to government to be impartial.

Just before 8 p.m. The Man returns. We can hear the sirens from his convoy long before he arrives. He is in good humour considering he has just emerged from five and a half hours of tedious haggling. The outcome is good: Zimbabwe will remain suspended. The South Africans are mightily upset. Thabo Mbeki and Chissano of Mozambique made most of the running on Mugabe's behalf. As ever, it was left to the leaders of the white Commonwealth to insist that Mugabe remained suspended although the presidents of Ghana and Kenya made some mildly helpful points. Museveni was unhelpful. Most other African leaders, including Muluzi of Malawi (despite what he said to me a few hours earlier), kept their heads down. Improbably the hero of the hour was Obasanjo who, according to The Man, chaired the meeting with great dexterity.

By now officials are beginning to flap. The window of opportunity for take-off is rapidly closing. Kate Garvey practically orders the Prime Minister – 'and you too, Minister Mullin' – into the car.

Then 30 miles to the airport in a convoy of seven or eight vehicles; sirens, flashing lights, two carloads of (British) protection flanking The Man's car on either side. Little knots of curious Nigerians gathered by the roadside to watch us pass. Sir Philip and I mid-convoy in his bombproof, bulletproof white Range Rover which two days ago was used to ferry the Queen. At the airport we are ushered straight to the plane. Tony and Cherie stand aside to let us pass, as if they are waving us off. Protocol dictates that they must be the last to board – along a red carpet that leads from the terminal to the steps up to the front of the plane upon which only they can tread.

No sooner have the doors closed, than the plane started to move. This is not like ordinary travel. The plane goes when we arrive.

The Prime Minister's plane, somewhere over the Sahara

For the next few hours I am an honorary member of The Court. Cast, in order of appearance, is as follows:

Window seats, left: The Man, Liz Lloyd (a bright, earnest young woman who, with the departure of Anji and Alastair, has served The Man for longer than any other courtier), Tom Kelly (the Prime Minister's official spokesman) and Gavin the Unflappable (in charge of logistics).

Centre: The First Lady; behind her Nigel Sheinwald, the PM's principal foreign affairs adviser, formerly Our Man at the EU (low boredom threshold, very upwardly mobile, not much interested in Africa); David Hallam, the pleasant young Number 10 official who stood in for Liz Lloyd during her maternity leave from which she has just returned (he will be departing shortly); Minister Mullin and Private Secretary, Mr Tom Fletcher.

Window seats, right: Andre, who attends to The First Lady's hair and make-up (very camp, frock coat, dressed from head to toe in black and never far from her side); the tabloids have yet to find out about Andre and when they do they will have fun; Sue Reeves, personal assistant to The First Lady; Kate Garvey, personal assistant to The Man.

Somewhere beyond the curtain, a phalanx of clerks, officials and the ten protection officers who in these post 9/11 days guard The Man day and night. Also, unseen in steerage, the hacks, mostly political correspondents with no interest whatever in Africa or the Commonwealth; 'Half of them are here to make trouble,' I remark to The Man as he goes backstage to talk to them.

'Only half?' he says with a sardonic smile.

Once we are airborne and the hacks have been attended to, the mood lightens. Everyone has changed into the lightweight grey pyjamas that are standard issue for denizens of the First Class cabin. Champagne is served. The Man mingles. Several times he comes over to where I am sitting. Hilary Benn's name is mentioned. Someone remarks on Hilary's uncanny resemblance to his old man. 'Yes,' I say, 'same mannerisms, drinks tea, keeps a diary …'

The Man's ears prick up. 'Does he?' He then launches into a diatribe about political diaries, how self-serving and subjective they are, citing by way of illustration those of Paddy Ashdown. Alastair's diaries are mentioned. 'They will never be published,' says The Man firmly. He speaks with great assurance. I assume he means 'while I am in office', but that's not what he said.

'Have you got that in blood?'

He smiles. I am sure Alastair will remain loyal to the end, but I am also confident that I will live long enough to see his diaries published.

The Man laments the wickedness of the media and interference by Murdoch. I mention that John Major once thought seriously about breaking up the empires – one daily, one Sunday everything else on the market – but dropped the idea because those queuing to buy whatever came on the market are at least as unsavoury as existing owners.

'Oh I don't know,' he says. 'There are Germans and other Europeans who would be much better.'

I press the point: 'You would have to strike with deadly force, a week after we win a third term.'

He is about to reply, but stops himself. He did remark firmly that the owners of the *Daily Mail* would never be allowed to get their hands on the *Telegraph*. 'Have you got a plan?' asked Liz Lloyd, but again he did not respond. I may be wrong, but I had the impression that he is toying with taking on the media – if he lasts long enough.

Tuesday, 9 December

To the House, where I sat beside The Man on the front bench as he reported back on the Commonwealth summit. He seemed tense and wound up and barely acknowledged my existence, except that several times, as the Tories were firing questions, he'd mutter, 'What's the answer to that?' The first time it happened I was struck dumb, not having heard the question and my later answers were inadequate. He can't have been impressed. Anyway he arrived without so much as a hello and departed without a goodbye, leaving me wondering whether I'd upset him.

Sunday, 14 December

With the children to South Shields, to buy a Christmas tree. On the way back I turned on the car radio and heard that Saddam Hussein has been captured. This evening the news bulletins were full of pictures of a dishevelled man with a long grey beard meekly submitting to a medical inspection. 'He looks very kind,' commented Emma.

Tuesday, 16 December

Jack was absent from Foreign Office Questions so we all had a greater share than usual – half a dozen in my case. I went in early and spent a couple of hours studying the fat briefing file, bristling with tags which cover every conceivable eventuality. The trouble is that, once the shooting starts, there is no way I can find my way into the file so I just have to busk. I get uncommonly nervous, my mouth goes dry and my mind empties. Fortunately, Nick Winterton was first up today huffing and puffing about Zimbabwe and I saw him off easily, after which everything went smoothly.

Wednesday, 17 December

A nasty little sketch by the malignant Simon Carr in today's *Independent* about yesterday's Question Time. He writes: 'The Foreign Office front bench is the worst in the government ...'

'Don't worry about it,' says Jack at the morning meeting, but I do. The truth is I am feeling a teeny bit vulnerable.

Michael Williams, who works for Jack, called in. Jack, he says, recently asked him a curious question: were there any countries which have abolished the death penalty and then reinstated it? What can Jack be thinking of? The Soham murderer, Ian Huntley, who was sentenced today?

Michael also said that the Hutton report is due out soon. 'Jack's worried,' he says. Not for himself, but for The Man.

Thursday, 18 December

A bad night. Eyes and nose streaming; shivering and shaking. Scarcely a wink of sleep. I got up at 5.45 a.m. and, barely able to talk, took a couple of paracetamol and fell back into bed before rising an hour later and staggering to the office. By lunchtime I was feeling better and went over to Portcullis House for a bowl of soup, where I ran into Jeff Rooker. 'The deal has been done,' he said.

'What deal?'

'Blair will stand down in March or April and Gordon will take over.'

Jeff says he heard the news from a colleague in the Lords who is close to the Brown camp. Plausible, but not necessarily true. It wouldn't be the first time that The Friends of Gordon have misread the tea leaves. All the same, there is a sort of fin de siècle mood about.

I returned a call from Gil Loescher. The first time we have spoken since he lost his legs in the bombing of the UN building in Baghdad. He sounded the same as ever. Cheerful, forward-looking, talking about getting back to work. No one would guess he has been through the fires of hell (he was unconscious for weeks). He can remember everything, even the moment the bomb went off. He and a colleague (who died in the explosion) had just come from a meeting with America's pro-consul, Paul Bremer. Bremer's last words as they parted were 'The security situation has greatly improved.'

Wednesday, 24 December
Sunderland

We played Cluedo in front of the fire, taking care before we went to bed to extinguish it so that Santa Claus could get down the chimney. Before they went to bed Emma and Sarah (who plays along with Emma) left a plate containing a chocolate biscuit, a satsuma and a carrot for the reindeer; also a glass of whisky. Once they were safely asleep, it was my job to consume them, taking care to leave crumbs and teeth marks (in the remains of the carrot) in the interests of authenticity.

Monday, 29 December

Visited Mum in hospital, yesterday and again today. A series of mini-strokes is suspected but I have my doubts. Yesterday she was up, dressed and quite chirpy, if a little forgetful. Today she was bedridden, trembling and not that keen to see us although she put on a brave face. So sad to think that it is barely three years since Mum was delivering meals on wheels to people younger than her. Afterwards we took Dad home. He is talking about selling up and moving to sheltered accommodation, but I'd be amazed if Mum agrees.

CHAPTER SIX

2004

Thursday, 1 January 2004

The year of The Fall? Of regime change? Hutton is due shortly, a top-up fees crisis looms and The Man is increasingly showing intimations of mortality – 2003 was the year in which the magic faded irrevocably. Whatever happens, from now on, nothing will ever be the same again. The war and the alliance with Bush were massive misjudgements. Odds on that he won't see out the year. A decent interval after Hutton and then a dignified withdrawal? We shall see.

The one bright spot on my own horizon is the walled garden at Chillingham, the glittering prize that eclipses all else. There is a chance, just a chance, that something may come of it, in which case my woes pale into insignificance.

Monday, 5 January

To London. A brilliant, luminous red sunrise, streaking across the eastern sky as the train crossed the river, light mist hovering over the Wear valley between Newcastle and Durham. On the tube between Green Park and Westminster, a not unattractive blond girl with a grey complexion and a hooded West Indian youth. Boyfriend? Pimp? To my horror she flashed a false smile at the woman with the Harrods bag sitting opposite and then, under cover of her anorak, began injecting herself in the forearm.

To the ministerial lunch in the India Office Council Chamber.

Jack did nearly all the talking, rambling on about Europe, à la JP. Much as I admire Jack, I notice it is getting harder to hold his attention beyond a soundbite. I guess that's what happens after seven years at the top. Liz Symons expressed concern about the lack of progress with the Americans re Guantanamo. She said, 'It will go badly wrong soon.'

Tuesday, 6 January

Lunch with Ann Clwyd, who told of a 73-year-old Iraqi woman of her acquaintance whose home was raided by American soldiers; the woman was taken away hooded, and later made to go down on all fours while one of her (American) interrogators sat on her back, calling her a donkey; also, she was made to lie flat on a concrete floor and told to 'swim'. She was held for six weeks and only released after Ann intervened with Paul Bremer. Later Ann took a statement from her and handed it to both Bremer and The Man. This was several months ago. Today it was announced in Baghdad that two male soldiers and a woman have been discharged in disgrace for mistreating prisoners; another (female) soldier had earlier resigned.

Wednesday, 7 January

Among today's paperwork a 'secret, personal, need to know' partial transcript of The Man's conversation with George Bush yesterday in which he raised Uganda and the Lord's Resistance Army. Evidence that I am not, after all, entirely without influence. Tom, at any rate, seemed impressed.

Thursday, 8 January

Jack put his head around my door and chatted briefly. I made a point of telling him how much I enjoy this job. He gave me a friendly touch on the elbow and said, 'You're doing fine. If you weren't, I'd tell you.'

Wednesday, 14 January
Inter-Continental Hotel, Asmara

Arrived late last night in ill-humour, having spent an unscheduled 24 hours in Frankfurt, courtesy of the Aeroflot-like inflexibility of Lufthansa. In the event we switched to Eritrean Airways (the 's' is misleading, they have only one plane), who delivered us without incident.

My mission: to persuade the Eritreans and Ethiopians to stop posturing and start talking in the hope of averting a new bout of fratricide. Eritrea, unfortunately, is an uptight little one-party state, led by a hubristic ex-Marxist brought up on Albanian-style self-reliance and disinclined to accept advice from anyone (he even refused a call from Colin Powell). Unfortunately, the UN-appointed Boundary Commission, which was supposed impartially to delineate the border on the basis of old colonial treaties, has come down almost entirely on Eritrea's side (without regard for the realities on the ground), which has only caused both sides to dig themselves in deeper. The Eritreans, despite having started and lost the war, now (thanks to a bunch of academic lawyers in The Hague) occupy the moral high ground and are unlikely to be shifted by a single centimetre. Their position is that the Boundary Commission report should be implemented in full, no ifs or buts. I am the first British minister to visit for ten years and must count myself lucky to be received by President Isaias.

Asmara

Clean, unpolluted, bicycles, bougainvillea, faded Italian villas; shades of Hanoi before the onslaught of market forces. It sits on the edge of a vast escarpment which plunges nearly 7,000 feet to the Red Sea. Because of the altitude the temperature remains at around a pleasant 25 degrees for much of the year. As with Hanoi, however, appearances are deceptive. Most Eritreans are clinging to life by their fingertips. The neighbours are mostly hostile; trade, since the war with Ethiopia, non-existent. For all the talk of self-reliance, the country produces only a quarter of its own food and, outside of the cities, most children are not even in primary school.

According to a young architect, who has lived here for months,

Eritrea is a society in deep despair. A huge level of mobilisation is necessary in order to maintain the confrontation with Ethiopia (with 20 times the population). Conscription, for boys and girls, is universal and indefinite. On leaving school every young Eritrean is required to report for military training at a camp called Sawa where, it is alleged, bad things happen, especially to the girls; as a result many middle-class parents are withholding their children from education in order to avoid Sawa, and several hundred a month are fleeing across the border to their supposed enemy, Ethiopia, in order to escape the draft.

Thursday, 15 January
Asmara

This evening I was taken to see Isaias, an imposing, handsome figure who bears a passing physical resemblance to Saddam Hussein. Isaias is not your typical African dictator. He lives modestly, travels with minimal security and is nobody's poodle. He is fluent, well-informed and, despite his revolutionary origins, by no means an ideologue. All the same, he is leading his country to ruin. He welcomed us through clenched teeth. His opening words were uncompromising: 'I do not blame the Ethiopians, I blame the international community ...' As our (two-hour) conversation progressed he loosened up a little. He talked indignantly of misgovernment in Africa and of his time in China, during the Cultural Revolution ('I watched with my own eyes as the Chinese destroyed their heritage'). Gingerly, I inquired what mechanism existed in his country for correcting mistakes before they became catastrophes (given that his parliament is unelected, the media neutered and his critics detained on an island in the Red Sea). He offered a learned discourse on the need for checks and balances; he even went so far as to say, unprompted, that the state of war in his country should not be an excuse for the absence of democracy, but clearly it is. We reached no satisfactory conclusion. So far as the border is concerned, thanks to that damn Boundary Commission, Isaias is on the moral high ground and he knows it. All he has to do is keep chanting that it is legal and binding and we have no choice but to agree. In the meantime his country is going to the dogs.

Friday, 16 January
The Residence, Addis Ababa

We arrived this evening from Djibouti, a two-hour flight in a nine-seater Cessna. Flying for the first hour over an empty, barren wilderness. Then, once past Lake Awash, across a sloping plateau surrounded by jagged mountains and dissected by empty, meandering riverbeds, occasional corrugated metal roofs glinting in the sunlight. Finally, over the highlands: brown, yellow, green; the mountains, precipitous valleys, isolated farms and settlements perched precariously, every available inch of soil cultivated.

I was taken straight to see Prime Minister Meles. 'A spectacular country,' I said, 'but difficult to govern.'

'Spectacularly difficult,' he replied.

The atmospherics (as the diplomatic cables say) were good, but the message I am required to deliver is a tough one: accept the report of the Boundary Commission. I felt a bit of a cad delivering it, considering that the Ethiopians are more sinned against than sinning. For two hours I pressed him. I put it to him that the war against poverty was more important than the war against Eritrea; he agreed. I tried flattery: 'What's needed is an act of statesmanship; we think you are big enough,' etc. He took it in good part but clearly isn't going to budge and why should he? Most of the disputed territory is in Ethiopian hands, the Ethiopians can get by without access to the port at Assab, they know that Eritrea is bankrupt and they can afford to wait.

Then to the Residence for dinner with a dozen ambassadors and assorted other bigwigs and finally, exhausted, to bed.

Saturday, 17 January
Adigrat (Tigray)

Up at the crack of dawn and back to the airport for the flight to Mekele. Much saluting from the uniformed guards as we swept out of the compound in His Excellency's Range Rover, Union Flag flying arrogantly from the bonnet.

From Mekele we raced for two hours through a biblical landscape (stupendous crags casting huge shadows; brown, arid, worn-out topsoil; boulder-strewn valleys; churches perched precariously on every hill) to Adigrat to attend the opening of new classrooms (courtesy of the Japanese) and a new library (courtesy of HMG) at the local secondary school. Two hours, seated with other excellencies under a canvas awning, showered with gifts and kind words and, embarrassingly, plied with soft drinks, while the masses were crammed together in the hot sunshine. The school, we were told, is swamped with refugees from towns along the border. It has 6,000 pupils, crammed 100 to a class in two shifts. We were shown some of the old classrooms, floors of bare earth, ragged green canvas stretched over wooden poles. What do we know of hardship?

In the afternoon, accompanied by Indian officers from the UN force, we were taken to Zalambessa on the border. The Eritreans, who initially took the Ethiopians by surprise, occupied the town without a fight and, when eventually forced to evacuate, dynamited every building in the town – schools, churches, everything. Today, four years later, the people are still living in the ruins. A sobering sight. No wonder the Ethiopians are not inclined to settle. If I run into Isaias again, or any of his henchmen, I shall ask who gave the order to destroy the town and why.

Sunday, 18 January
Adigrat

Breakfast with the Bishop, a pleasant, lean young man who had spent time in Liverpool and Dublin. He took us to the roof and showed us (oh wonder of wonders) his walled garden, full of vegetables and fruit trees. The sun shines ten months of the year and at this height (7,000 feet above sea-level) it never gets too hot. Given water, anything will grow. In Wukro, further south, we called on Father Kevin, an Irish priest who has been 37 years in Tigray and has made the desert bloom. It rains for only a month or two a year so he has constructed an underground reservoir into which all his gutters and drainpipes flow, preserving every available drop of water. He runs a little agricultural school, teaching the locals to grow fruit and vegetables to supplement their meagre diet of bread and, occasionally, meat. Cattle, a symbol of status, are rarely killed for meat and sold only when the rains fail and famine threatens. At which point, of course, the price collapses because everyone is trying to sell at once. In the meantime the cattle are laying waste to the land, gobbling up every available piece of vegetation. Goats are worse, they eat the roots as well. As a result animals fare better than the humans. Everywhere there are handsome, sleek, bow-horned cattle shepherded by emaciated children with stick-like limbs. Everything grows in Father Kevin's garden. Mangoes, coffee, bananas, oranges ... We departed laden with gifts of cheese and honey.

Mekele

Twenty years ago this was the epicentre of the famine; the place where tens of thousands of dying, skeletal peasants converged in search of help. Today it is a modern, sophisticated provincial town of wide avenues, watched over by a grotesque monument to the revolution, a reminder that Albania was once the model for the Tigray People's Liberation Front. We were treated to a whistlestop tour of the university followed by lunch with members of the provincial government. The discussion was all about the border. They were adamant that there could be no surrender. Ethiopia had been cheated. To concede would bring not peace, but another war and even the fall of the government. Better to await the fall of Isaias.

Monday, 19 January
The Residence, Addis, 11 p.m.

Can any British embassy enjoy a grander setting? An Edwardian villa, wreathed in purple bougainvillea, in an 87-acre walled compound, a gift from the Emperor in 1896. A hundred servants, horses, giant tortoises, a miniature golf course, woodland, a vegetable garden. The entire embassy is housed within the estate, in villas scattered discreetly around the compound. And yet, so I am assured (and I have no reason to disbelieve), this place is extremely cost-effective, due to the cheapness of the labour and the absence of rents.

I am sitting on the terrace wall in the fresh, cool, insect-free air. The climate here is so perfect that flowers bloom for ten months of the year. The herbaceous border is crammed with French marigolds and rich blue delphiniums (in January, for goodness' sake). The only sounds, chirping crickets, a distant barking dog and singing from a church beyond the compound wall. Tomorrow is the feast of the Epiphany, the holiest day in the Ethiopian calendar when the sacred tabots will be taken from their sanctuaries and paraded through the streets. Already, as we drove back this evening, small groups of the faithful, lighted candles in hand, were assembling at vantage points. Any moment now HE's Range Rover will appear to convey us to the airport and the spell will be broken.

Tuesday, 20 January
London

The papers are as depressing as ever: '1.6 million gypsies ready to flood in', rages the *Express*; 'Blair hit by student fury' (*Mail*); 'Hutton: 48 per cent think Blair lied' (*Guardian*). The only good news is that Conrad Black has been forced to sell the *Telegraph* to the Barclay brothers, one of whom is hinting that they may even back Labour come the election. A fat chance, but it would be enough if they'd just order their hacks to stop telling lies about us.

Wednesday, 21 January

To the parliamentary party, where there was discussion about the next Queen's Speech. Ann Cryer said we needed a managed immigration policy, based on ability to find jobs; not on finding a wife or husband with a British passport, which is putting enormous pressure on young Asians. Jon Owen Jones told a story about an Algerian who had brought three people into the country by marrying and divorcing three times on top of which one of his former wives had remarried, bringing in a fourth Algerian. It was all a scam, he said, and time we put a stop to it. Amen to that. Despite the hoo-ha over asylum, we've barely touched the rackets that surround arranged marriages. What mugs we are. The trouble is that we are terrified of the huge cry of 'racism' that would go up the moment anyone breathed a word on the subject. There is the added difficulty that at least 20 Labour seats, including Jack's, depend on Asian votes.

Friday, 23 January
Sunderland

Among the bumf, a string of demands from the party High Command demanding to know what I am proposing to contribute to The Big Conversation, New Labour's latest pointless wheeze. Big Conversation, my foot. The very name invites derision. I propose to do nothing, unless forced at gunpoint, in line with my policy of minimising pointless activity.

Sunday, 25 January

Dad is in hospital after a fall and in poor shape; he's also got problems with his remaining eye and can hardly see. Despite promises, social services have failed to come up with help for Mum to live at home and so she's been sent temporarily to a care home. Mum is losing her short-term memory, although for the most part still *compos mentis*. The children and I had a long talk with her by phone in the evening. 'I don't know what I'm doing here,' she kept saying. 'I was told it was only for one night.' She also seemed to think that Dad was at home when in fact he is in Broomfield Hospital. Poor Mum.

Monday, 26 January
The Foreign Office

A big pow-wow in my room to discuss what can be done about the Lord's Resistance Army in Uganda. Hilary Benn came over from DFID, Liz Lloyd from Number 10, Adam Wood, Our Man in Kampala and a host of officials from various departments, including the SIS. When I first raised the subject six months ago nobody wanted to know, but now (as a result of the conversation with The Man on the plane home from Abuja) he has raised his little finger and the entire machine has suddenly sprung to life. The consensus was that Museveni can't hope to defeat the LRA militarily and so a way has to be found to open a dialogue with a view to offering their leaders safe passage; all very distasteful, considering the horrible atrocities they have committed. Afterwards, however, Adam Wood and the man from SIS stayed behind and told me confidentially that there was a chance – just a chance – that the Sudanese could be persuaded to lift the LRA leadership and hand them over. Now that would be a great prize.

Tuesday, 27 January

At the morning meeting in Jack's office, our whip Jim Murphy brandished the front page of the *Independent*, helpfully taken up with mugshots of the top-up fees insurgents. 'It's worse than this,' said Jim. The whips have been putting it about that the government is 20 votes down. Nobody believes them, but it is on a knife edge. Jack urged us to stay around the House after Questions and do some 'gentle cuddling'. At 10.40 Tom put his head round my door and said that Nick Brown, one of the leaders of the uprising, had declared that he would be voting with the government, after all. By the time we had finished Foreign Office Questions virtually the entire Cabinet had squeezed onto the front bench to hear Charles Clarke open the debate. 'What caused Nick Brown to back down?' I whispered.

'Presumably he realised that he was going to lose,' said Charles.

By lunch the word was that the government would win narrowly and in the event that's what happened, but it was a cliffhanger. I was standing by the door of the Aye Lobby as the last loyalist trickled out. Jim Fitzpatrick, our teller, was looking grim. I noticed he had 305 written on his notepad while, through the closed door of the other lobby a Tory whip was saying he had 311. Then, miraculously, another ten or eleven Members, who had been loitering out of sight around the corner, dribbled out of the Aye Lobby. One of Tommy McAvoy's little tricks. No wonder he looked calm throughout.

Afterwards I had supper with Jean Corston in the Tea Room. She now thinks The Man will lead us into the election. A few months ago she was saying she thought he'd be gone by the end of (last) year.

Wednesday, 28 January

By early afternoon it became clear that Lord Hutton had all but entirely acquitted the government of wrongdoing over the death of Dr Kelly and instead placed a good deal of blame on the BBC. Suddenly a great cloud lifted, the earth changed places with the sky. Our tormentors (temporarily at least) have been vanquished. The Man, looking happier than he has done for months, delivered himself of a dignified, gracious little statement. In contrast Michael Howard found himself, for once, entirely wrongfooted. Instead of graciously accepting the outcome and moving back to higher ground his response was grudging and nitpicking. 'He's hit bedrock,' remarked a Lib Dem, but no, he was still drilling. On and on he drilled in the face of some undignified hissing from our side; the Tories looked miserable, only their leader was unembarrassed. By the end he had begun to resemble Iain Duncan Smith. A celebration was called for. I went immediately to the Tea Room and splashed out on a large piece of fruit cake.

Only one question remained: How was the Harmsworth Lie Machine going to cope with this unexpected outcome? We didn't have long to wait before an early edition of the *Standard* dropped onto our table: 'BETRAYAL OF KELLY'. 'Blair cleared ...' was on page 7.

Thursday, 29 January

To Number 10 to greet President Museveni. The Man emerged looking better than he has done for ages. Gone is that haunted, dehydrated look. He even quietly admitted to being relieved. But ... still tense. The trouble is that, as I am beginning to realise, he never reads his brief. 'What do you want me to say, Chris – in a word,' he whispered as we hovered in the hall, waiting for the President's car. 'In a word ...?' At once I am reduced to blubbering incoherence. It was the same when I sat next to him during the Abuja statement the other day. He cannot be impressed. Neither can Sheinwald, whose mind is laser-like. Sooner or later someone is going to say that we need an Africa minister whose mind is less fuzzy. ('Someone who can focus.') Oh dear. The President arrives. We repair to the den. Twenty minutes of not very satisfactory conversation in which Museveni again declares his belief that the war will be over by the end of the dry season (it has been going on for 17 years). The Man (diffident, hesitant, glancing in my direction for reassurance) expressing mild scepticism. I am permitted one intervention. Then everyone departs, leaving The Man and the President alone. This is to enable The Man to say gently to Museveni that we don't think a third term (in reality his fifth) is a very good idea. At least we hope that's what he'll say. The Man is not very good at telling allies (especially Americans) what they don't want to hear. Outside the Cabinet is assembling.

Then to Lancaster House for lunch. Hilary Benn presided. The huge, gross portrait of Charles II behind us prompted Museveni to reminisce about his school days in Kampala, where needless to say he learned more about Britain than he did about Africa; a surprising amount has stuck – 1066, 1649; that Charles I was the son of James I; that Ben Nevis is our highest mountain (though he was about 40 feet out on the height). 'Any minute now, he'll start talking about his cattle,' whispered one of the Ugandans further down the table and, sure enough, he did. It is hard not to like Museveni. He has never fallen for all the old liberationist, quasi socialist bullshit that has wrecked so many other African countries and there is always a twinkle in his eye. He was once Clare's favourite, having done so much to transform his country from the ruins of the Amin/Obote era. Alas, however, there are signs that (like Clare?) he is getting too big for his boots. If he were to go when his term expires, he would be remembered as a great hero. But the odds are that, like so many African (and some British?) leaders, he will outstay his welcome.

Friday, 30 January

The Hutton fallout continues unabated. Gavyn Davies, Greg Dyke and Andrew Gilligan have gone,* but so far as our free press – broad-

---

*The BBC reporter Andrew Gilligan had suggested that the Prime Minister had deliberately misled Parliament over a claim that Iraq could deploy weapons of mass destruction within 45 minutes. Lord Hutton's inquiry concluded that his claim was unfounded, following which Davies and Dyke, Chairman and Director-General of the BBC, resigned.

sheet and tabloid (with the notable exception of the *Sun*) – are concerned these are the wrong victims. This is not how it was meant to be. They spent months preparing for a huge blood-letting and they are not about to give up quietly.

Monday, 2 February
Broomfield Hospital, Chelmsford

Poor Dad is deeply demoralised. 'If I can't see again, I will give up,' he kept saying. 'I've had a good life. I've visited just about every country north of the Equator.' At one point he said, 'I'm nearly 100, you know.'

'Nonsense, Dad. You're 83.'

As ever, he exaggerates (although in truth his situation is dire). One to one, he can hear clearly when he has his hearing aids in and, although his eyesight is very limited, I did notice him glance surreptitiously at his watch now and then. He would clearly like to go home, but the practical difficulties may be insurmountable. What will become of him?

Tuesday, 3 February
The Ambassador's Residence, Washington DC

A splendid dinner in honour of Mary Soames (née Churchill, mother of Nicholas), a dear, sweet, formidable old lady with a sunny, Queen Motherly disposition. She is here to open, in the presence of the President, an exhibition honouring her father's relationship with the US. Other guests include two Churchill grandchildren, Young Winston (who I haven't come across since he was annihilated in the 1997 landslide), Celia Sandys (daughter of Duncan) and Carl Rove, *éminence grise* of the Bush Administration. Like so many of our demons Mr Rove turns out to be charming and jovial. The Democrat primaries are in full swing. Who would he prefer to run against? Naturally, Howard Dean is his first choice. After that? To my surprise Mr Rove opts for Senator Kerry, presumably on the grounds that he has a long and destructible track record. And who would he least like? John Edwards, the handsome, squeaky-clean, silver-tongued Senator from North Carolina. In truth, I suspect, it doesn't matter. None of them will be a match for the Republican meat-grinder.

Wednesday, 4 February

Awake since five, reading Joe Klein's account of the rise and fall of Bill Clinton, a copy of which I found on the dressing-table. A fascinating analysis of the deterioration of American politics into a cesspool of abuse and character assassination in which, to the disgust and bewilderment of the electorate, rival party machines focus on mutually assured destruction, at the expense of such little matters as the survival of the planet. British politics seems to be going the same way.

Daylight reveals a fine view of the snow-covered garden, a single set of footprints leading from the walled rose garden across the lawn to a seat and back to the terrace. I am installed in a grand suite (four-poster bed, marble bathroom, huge sitting room) in a wing of this Lutyens mansion.

11 p.m.

A day which started with a speech to Africa policy wonks at the Council for Foreign Relations and ended with another grand dinner at the Residence (principal guest, Chester Crocker, the Reagan Administration's Africa man). In between, visits to Africa hands at USAID, the National Security Council and the State Department. Our principal mission (difficult in the best of times, but nigh on impossible in an election year): to encourage the Administration to keep Africa high on the agenda during the current US presidency of the G8.

Thursday, 6 February

A cold, clear day. The Potomac still iced over.

Breakfast before dawn with Catherine Manning (Sir David having already departed for the annual 'Prayer Breakfast' with the President); then the short flight to New York. The security was overwhelming. We were required to remove coats, jackets, shoes and for some that was not all. 'You have been chosen for additional screening,' Tom, my Private Secretary, was told as though he had won a lottery prize. He was taken to one side, instructed to open his bags, the contents duly rifled, and subjected to a close body search. Our boarding passes were examined once, twice, three times with cold-eyed courtesy. At the end of each procedure we were enjoined to 'have a nice day' but there was a hint of steel. The subliminal text was clear: one false move, a single unwise joke and we would be dragged away in chains to Guantanamo Bay. Protests that one was a member of Her Majesty's Government would be met with, at best, icy indifference; at worst, a straitjacket.

Even on the plane, there was no respite. 'For the first 30 minutes of any flight passengers are required to remain in their seats. Should anyone get up, for any reason, we shall be forced to divert to an alternative airport,' intoned our American Airlines hostess (blond, plump, cheerless – seconded from Aeroflot?). This repeated at least three times. One half expected her to add, 'Make my day, punk.' She approached a harmless-looking couple two rows ahead: 'Do you both know that you are seated in the emergency exit row?'

They nodded sheepishly.

'Are you comfortable with your responsibility to command an emergency evacuation?'

They nodded again, non-committally.

Whatever next? Will I be asked to fly the plane in the event that the pilot is struck down by al-Qaida?

1 Beekman Place, New York City

Two blocks from the UN; eleven floors up, fine views across Coney Island and the fast-flowing East River, spoiled only by a vast, red-neon Coca-Cola advertisement on the far side, allegedly Joan Crawford's revenge (she married the Coca-Cola heir) for being refused an apartment in this elite condominium.

Our hosts, Sir Emyr Jones Parry and his wife, Lynn, as agreeable and down to earth a couple as one could hope to find in Her Majesty's diplomatic service. As I am beginning to discover, the day of the toff is all but over at the Foreign Office (or else they are under deep cover, awaiting a more favourable political climate). So far as I can tell the toffs have been superseded by bright grammar school boys (and the occasional girl). Jones Parry is a Methodist from the Welsh valleys; Lynn, who retains her accent, is from a mining village and devotes her spare time to counselling victims of domestic violence. True, one still comes across a Sebastian or two and there is an Honourable Alice attached to the UN mission (but she turned out to be a single mother with six children).

Friday, 6 February
1 Beekman Place

A cold, grey day. At breakfast Sir Emyr tells a joke about an American general seconded to Sandhurst who asks of a passing lieutenant, 'Officer, can you tell me where the lecture theatre is at?'

The lieutenant duly tells him, adding pedantically, 'In Britain, sir, we don't put the preposition at the end of the sentence.'

'I get you, lieutenant,' replies the general. 'You mean I should have asked, "Where is the lecture theatre at, arsehole?"'

Today I addressed the United Nations, delegates from 106 nations, no less. It's true that by the time my turn came the big movers and shakers (Colin Powell, Kofi Annan, Dominique de Villepin) had left the stage. Sir E J P had also departed for an engagement elsewhere. Even so, the chamber was fairly full and the applause a tad above desultory. As ever, I was presented with an undeliverable text which had to be hastily redrafted between engagements. Thus the deletion of passages such as 'I commend the Transitional Government and the international community for putting in place the Results-Focused Transition Framework.' My job: to pledge our modest contribution to the rescue of Liberia.

Wednesday, 18 February

For the time being, Mum is going to have to remain at Heybridge, where, by all accounts, she is well looked after. Ngoc and I would be happy to have her live with us, but our house has stairs everywhere which she will find difficult to manage; anyway, Mum wouldn't agree to move so far away while Dad is alive.

What a mess. Four children, scattered around the country, with homes, money, none of us uncaring and yet none of us, for one reason or another, in a position to accommodate our aged parents now that their time has come. What will happen when our turn comes, as it will, not so long from now – 20 or 25 years in my case. The moral of the story is clear: stay close to your children and be prepared to compromise.

Monday, 23 February
The Residence, Paris

This place is straight out of *Les Liaisons Dangereuses*, save only that the footmen lack powdered wigs (though those serving dinner were wearing white gloves). It was purchased from Napoleon's promiscuous sister by the Duke of Wellington, a year before Waterloo. The steps up to the front door were the scene of Thatcher's last stand ('We fight on. We fight to win'). To the rear, a large walled garden spoiled only by an art nouveau lead obelisk. My suite on the second floor – four-poster bed, the latest *Country Life* by the bedside, white roses on the mantelpiece – affords a fine view across the gardens and beyond to Le Tour Eiffel, illuminated against the night sky and crowned with a laser beam scanning the heavens, à la Sunderland's Stadium of Light.

Tuesday, 24 February
The Residence

Tom and I took a turn around the garden; no sooner had we passed along the pebble pathway than a gardener appeared and raked away our footprints. You couldn't make it up.

A speech to the French equivalent of the Council for Foreign Relations, followed by a tour of the visa section. Then to lunch, hosted by First Secretary Giles Paxman (brother of Jeremy) at his splendid fourth-floor apartment in the Rue de Varenne. The guests, an amiable collection of advisers – from the Quai, the Elysée and the Matignon.

From the window, a distant view across roof tops to the Sacré Coeur, on which the sunlight came and went, turning it alternately from grey to luminous white.

Home by train from the Gare du Nord in time for supper at the House.

Thursday, 26 February

On the way down King Charles Street this morning I ran into Jack's special adviser, Michael Williams. 'Did you hear Clare this morning?' he inquired.

I did indeed. Casually alleging that Kofi Annan's phone was bugged and that she had seen transcripts. 'This will reverberate,' said Michael, adding that just about every phone in the UN building was bugged. Presumably it's the Americans who do the bugging and we share the product, but of course we can't say that. Yet more fallout from this disastrous war. As Michael said, 'It sticks like shit to your shoes.'

Monday, 1 March

One of my officials reported a conversation he had last week with the FCO's chief legal adviser regarding the Attorney General's opinion on the legality of the war, which the government is coming under growing pressure to publish. 'Scarcely credible,' according to the adviser; he added, 'although I haven't put that in writing.'

Meanwhile it is becoming clear that Clare (who has spent the weekend stirring the pot) may not, after all, have seen a transcript of Kofi Annan's telephone conversation. Tom says he never saw any such thing in all the time he worked with Valerie and she would certainly have been in the loop.

The lunchtime ministerial meeting was taken up mainly with a discussion, led by Mike O'Brien, on the alienation of the Muslim community post-Iraq. Apparently, they are all flocking to the Lib Dems, who, true to form, are promising to give them anything they want, even though many of their demands are distinctly illiberal. Denis

MacShane countered that we shouldn't pander: 'In the name of multi-culturalism, we already turn a blind eye to unacceptable practices that we would not accept from any other community.'

'Such as?' inquired Jack.

'Such as forced marriages masquerading as arranged marriages.'

There followed a long anguished debate about what was to be done. A worry for Jack whose seat could be at risk. The truth, however (as Jack more or less acknowledged), is that no amount of appease-ment will make any difference. We went through all this with Salman Rushdie and it soon passed. In any case, the scope for rational dia-logue is limited. After all, a fair swathe of the Muslim world still believes that 9/11 was the work of the Israelis.

Tuesday, 2 March

'I long for Iraq to go away,' Jack whispered during Foreign Office Questions this morning. 'Every morning I get up and it is still there.' He added, 'You voted against it.' As if to say, 'It's alright for you, you're in the clear.' Jack has several times recalled, without any hint of malice, that I opposed the war. He once remarked that this gave me greater credibility in certain quarters. Does Jack still think the war was a good idea? Did he ever? I wonder.

Wednesday, 3 March

In the afternoon, to Oxford to see Gil and Ann Loescher. Despite having been unconscious for weeks, Gil can remember everything up to the moment of the explosion, including someone saying 'Oh, shit' as the bomb went off (undoubtedly that person's last words). I found them both cheerful, optimistic, outgoing and without a trace of self-pity. Astonishing and deeply humbling.

Monday, 8 March

To Carlton Gardens for a meeting of the FCO board. The entire top brass assembled around the table in the dining room, watched over by life-size portraits of George II and Queen Caroline. With one exception, every one a forty- or fifty-something male. Main item on the agenda, Michael Jay's plan to reorganise along functional rather than geographical lines. Although Jack is said to be signed up in principle, there is a suspicion that we are being railroaded. The paperwork, which only turned up on Friday – after ministers had departed for their constituencies – is suspiciously thin on detail. At Mike O'Brien's suggestion, I sent Jack a note saying that he and I were unconvinced and, in order not to alert officials, we sent it up via his political adviser.

The meeting started with a little slide show, the gist of which was that, as a result of cuts being demanded by the Treasury, we couldn't carry on as we are and there would have to be post closures. Someone asked what value we got from our various American consulates. Someone else remarked that, but for our consulate in Houston, we would never have got so close to George W. Bush ('That's the case for closing it down ten years ago,' I whispered to Mike O'Brien). Michael Jay gave a little summary of his masterplan, taking care to emphasise that ministerial portfolios would remain unchanged. 'The holy grail,' he concluded, 'is a structure we can afford, so we aren't under constant pressure to salami slice.'

Mike went first, pointing out that, under the proposed new structure, there didn't seem to be much role for junior ministers; indeed the organogram included with our papers made no mention of ministers. Denis MacShane, who is broadly in favour of the changes, made the same point.

'Where are the numbers?' I inquired, only to be told they had not yet been finalised.

'That's odd, I was under the impression that there was a bit of paper somewhere in the system?'

'Nothing has been agreed.'

'When will they be available?'

'Next week.'

'Tomorrow,' blurted Dickie Stagg, the official in charge of the shake-up.

'Tomorrow? Why, when we are meeting today?'

We were treated to some guff about Dickie having been away at the end of last week.

'And when might ministers be allowed sight of the numbers?'

'At the end of next week,' offered Dickie.

'When we are ready,' said Michael Jay.

'Which?' asked I.

And so on.

We turned to Prism, the FCO's much delayed IT programme. 'How much extra will that cost?' I inquired.

'At least a million,' said someone.

At which point Jack sprang to life. 'That's the first I've heard of this. Why wasn't I told?' No one quite met his eye.

'Well done,' Mike scribbled on his notepad.

From officials, an eerie silence.

Later, Dickie Stagg let slip that there was, after all, a paper with numbers. I pounced. 'Oh, is there indeed? How many people have seen it?'

'I think I'm the only one,' giggled Dickie.

'About ten,' someone else replied simultaneously.

By now it was obvious to everyone that we were being given the runaround. I overheard Jack say to Michael Jay during the tea break, 'He's like a terrier when he gets going.'

Tuesday, 9 March

To Number 10 to greet President Biya of Cameroon. His is not a regime of which we entirely approve, but he is being given the full treatment (an audience with the Queen, a meeting with The Man etc). Yet another of the bills for our Iraq adventure. Cameroon was on the UN Security Council and, in the run-up to the war, Valerie Amos was sent to butter up Biya, bearing handwritten missives from The Man ('Do call in and see me next time you're in London ...'). In the event, Cameroon's support was never tested, but now it's payback time and here is the much-loved President rolling up Downing Street in a stretch limo to be photographed shaking hands with The Man in good time for his re-election campaign. Another little nail in the coffin of ethical government, but what can we do?

The plan is that I should take the President up to the White

Drawing Room, keep him chatting for half an hour, after which we will be joined by The Main Person.

One small difficulty looms. The President speaks French as does The Man, but the Minister for Africa does not. We have an interpreter for the first part of the proceedings, but for the second part there is a danger that The Man will wander in and start chatting away in French, leaving his wretched Minister marooned.

In the event, this is exactly what happened, but fortunately I had taken the precaution of enlisting the aid of our bright young ambassador to Yaounde who, as soon as The Man appeared, moved to sit beside me and whisper a translation. Humiliation narrowly avoided.

Biya is one of Africa's longest-serving rulers. Although by no means the most venal he presides over a regime where corruption and torture are endemic and where the political process, to put it mildly, lacks transparency. To what extent he is responsible for the bad things that happen in his country is unclear since his style of government is so laidback ('absent yet omnipresent,' says the briefing note).

We, The Man and I, have been briefed to deliver tough messages. The Man, however, doesn't do tough messages (except to the Labour Party), so it is down to me. The difficulty is that, like so many of his kind, the old rogue oozes charm and goodwill and talks like a seasoned democrat; he is also very long-winded, which limits the opportunities for messages of any sort. By the time we see him off the premises, only the haziest messages have been delivered and Biya could be forgiven for thinking he enjoys the almost unqualified support of HMG.

'He talks the talk ...' I murmur to The Man as we stand on the doorstep, waving goodbye.

'They all do,' he sighs.

An interesting little postscript to yesterday's board meeting: apparently, as soon as ministers were off the premises, officials held another meeting at which the version of the organogram containing the numbers miraculously appeared. As it turned out, it was thought to be unsaleable and the relevant officials were sent away to rewrite it. In the meantime every copy of the original was carefully collected up ... Pure Sir Humphrey.

Thursday, 11 March

A brief chat in the Tea Room with Ann Clwyd, who has just returned from Iraq. She says the Americans have detained about 6,000 people and are either unable or unwilling to release the names of many of them. As a result there are long queues of anxious relatives seeking information about their 'disappeared'. Ann has been pursuing allegations of torture and mistreatment (and apparently The Man has, too), but Paul Bremer (of whom Ann speaks highly) protests that he is powerless because the prisoners are in the hands of some sort of special interrogation unit controlled from Florida. Presumably the chain of command goes back to Rumsfeld. So much for winning hearts and minds.

To Chelmsford to see Dad – parched, emaciated, his skin hanging loose. He is being fed through a tube in his stomach. He keeps asking for water and managed to sip from a teaspoon. A tiny spark of humour. When I asked if there was anything I could get him, he replied, 'You could sneak me a few gallons of booze.' I sat with him about an hour, holding his hand and came away with tears in my eyes. 'Why can't I die?' he said to Liz the other day. I fear he will live for some time yet although he is slowly starving.

Friday, 12 March

A series of bombs have exploded on trains in Madrid. Huge casualties. It is unclear whether the culprits are al-Qaida or ETA.

Monday, 15 March

To London on the 09.00. Everyone paranoid in the wake of Madrid; people nervously eyeing the luggage rack, constant loudspeaker injunctions to keep our luggage with us at all times. Then: 'Will the person who has left a bag in the first class toilet please go to the guard's van?'

Followed ten minutes later by: 'If there is a William Etherington' – my colleague from Sunderland North – 'on board, would he please go to the guard's van?'

Wednesday, 17 March

To the weekly meeting of the parliamentary party, where David Blunkett described Immigration and Nationality as 'the most dysfunctional department in the civil service'. He went on, 'When I was in local government I could intervene in a dysfunctional department, but if I intervene in a government department they immediately cry foul. I could sack the entire senior management, but if I did they would leak every single bit of paper in the building.'

Thursday, 25 March

Up at five and to Cheltenham to spend an hour trailing the Queen and the Duke around the brilliant new GCHQ building. As usual, when confronted with royalty, I put my foot in it. 'Morning Ma'am, you've brought the rain with you.'

She (huffily), 'It wasn't raining when we left London.'

Then a minor spat with Philip. 'Would Charles approve?' I inquired, referring to the ultra-modern design.

'Charles, Charles who?' He knew perfectly well, of course. You could see him thinking, 'Who is this upstart who affects to be on first name terms with the Prince of Wales?'

Then back to London for a meeting with Hilary Benn and Patricia Hewitt, the purpose of which was to try and encourage the Department of Trade and Industry to take more interest in pursuing British mining companies who have been up to no good in the Congo. In the event, the train was 30 minutes late and so I ended up participating, via Tom's mobile, sitting outside a Sushi bar on Paddington station.

Monday, 29 March

To Carlton Gardens for a 'political' lunch. The party pollster Greg Cook gave us the lowdown on the latest polls. The news is not good. Levels of dissatisfaction and cynicism are approaching those of the Major years. There was a discussion on Europe, Jack said that the EC had had ten years of 'seriously crud' leaders – Santerre and Prodi. Prodi, he said, would be lucky to hold down even the lowliest government post in this country and yet in Italy he was considered prime ministerial material. The argument over the proposed EU constitution he referred to as 'a fucking fandango'; we were being squeezed by both the Lib Dems and the Tories. Denis MacShane said that we needed to expose the Tories for the 'isolationists' and 'withdrawalists' that they are. Liz Symons said, 'Our refusal to hold a referendum is becoming an issue of trust. We should reconsider.' Mike O'Brien agreed.

'Let's have a straw poll,' said Jack. 'What do you think, Chris?' Oh dear, I hadn't given the subject a moment's thought one way or the other, but I couldn't admit that so I said, 'I agree with Mike and Liz,' and regretted the words as soon as they were out of my mouth. Denis said a referendum would split the party. Ed Owen, one of Jack Straw's special advisers, said we would look hopelessly weak if we reversed our position. Jim Murphy said backing down would get us nowhere; we must stand firm and take our medicine in the Euro elections. Jack then explained the practicalities and it became clear in a blinding flash that a referendum wasn't a serious option. By my reckoning Jack used the f-word at least half a dozen times during the course of our lunchtime discussion. I remarked on this to Mike O'Brien as we walked back across the park. He replied, 'Blair swears a lot in private, too. Or at least he did when I was in his Home Affairs team.'

Tuesday, 30 March

A terrible moment at this morning's briefing. HM Consul in Bucharest has been suspended following the discovery that he has been leaking official documents to David Davis and a huge feeding frenzy has broken out following the publication of extracts in the press. Out of the blue Jack asked, 'Would Chris like to take us through the sequence of events?' Once again I was caught completely off balance. I had been informed about the suspension on the train coming back from Cheltenham last Thursday and immediately asked Tom to inform Jack's office, which he did. I also asked for the leaked papers, but as of first thing this morning they hadn't arrived. Jack, seeing my discomfort, took up the story himself. He, needless to say, had obtained the papers. Or some of them. He produced a memorandum dated April 2002 in which the suspended consul had complained at length about the visa scams being worked by migrant Romanians. The consul has apparently been complaining for two years, to no effect. Fortunately it is a Home Office document. There is no sign that he complained to us. Nor is there (thus far) evidence that his complaint reached Home Office ministers. Certainly he never received a response to that or many other complaints that he claims to have registered. It is a shocking story. A big row is brewing and I have failed to rise to the occasion.

Wednesday, 7 April

To St Margaret's, Westminster, for the memorial service for Rwanda. I sat in the front row, next to Linda Chalker and the Ambassador; a sprinkling of bigwigs attended, including Betty Boothroyd and Geoffrey Howe. A moving service – poems, songs, a parade of Rwandan children with lighted candles; the number of dead were read out province by province. There was a lot of 'never again' talk, but (I thought to myself) it is happening again. In Darfur. Now. At this very moment. And what are we doing? What can we do? There is not a hope in hell of sending troops. They are tied up in Iraq, Afghanistan, Kosovo and in any case the Sudanese are never going to allow in foreigners, even aid agencies are being denied access. I keep trying to be optimistic about Africa, but even where progress has been made – Sierra Leone, Liberia, Burundi, the Congo – it is fragile. And even the good guys – Kagame, Meles, Museveni – have their down side.

Good Friday, 9 April
Sunderland

With the family to Mount Grace Priory. We picnicked among the daffodils and then walked up through the woods to Osmotherley.

In Iraq the Lords of Chaos reign. Every night our television screens are filled with images of hooded gunmen rampaging at will; dancing, screaming, hysterical, arm-waving youths celebrating some new atrocity, columns of thick black smoke rising from ambushed oil tankers. Can there be anybody left – up to and including The Man himself – who doesn't recognise the Iraqi enterprise for what it is: a catastrophic misjudgement.

Easter Sunday, 11 April

With Mum to see the children swimming. Gently, I am trying to persuade her that she needs to consider moving to sheltered accommodation. Thus far I have been firmly rebuffed. Today's exchanges included the following: 'Sooner or later you will have another accident.'

'Someone will find me.'

'They may not.'

'There comes a time when you have to make room for others.'

Monday, 19 April

At the ministerial lunch in the Map Room the talk was all of The Man's sudden U-turn over an EU referendum. According to the papers, Jack and Gordon were the main persuaders. Jack ran through the reasons: 'One, which we are not making in public, is the parliamentary timetable. If the constitution had been ratified we could have got it out of the way before the election but, given that we can't, discipline on our side would not hold, the Lords would amend the Bill and we would be in for months of attrition, á la the Tories and Maastricht.' He added, 'The killer argument is that we've made rather an art form over referenda and so we are hoist on our own petard.'

'Yes,' said Bill Rammell, 'but which reason are we to make public?'

'That we've listened and changed our mind,' replied Jack disarmingly. 'If you see a bloody great mallet coming down on your head, the best thing to do is get out of the way.'

I said, 'The other day you made a pretty plausible case for not holding a referendum. When did you change your mind?'

'I was keeping my cards close to my chest.'

Outside in the corridor he whispered, 'About 18 months ago. I had to argue it out with Tony, who thought we could get it through. We had hoped we could talk the Lib Dems round, but we couldn't.'

Later, to a crowded meeting of the parliamentary party addressed by The Man, who was on sparkling form – fluent, relaxed, amusing, not a piece of paper in sight. Afterwards, supper with Jean Corston. Had she ever heard The Man say anything that might imply regret over Iraq? 'Not a word.' She recounted that her hairdresser had this morning remarked that he thought Tony Blair was a very good bloke, but added ominously, 'His problem is that he is now a war criminal.'

Wednesday, 21 April

This morning's press is full of The Man's U-turn, which, it turns out, was not even discussed with the Cabinet. All those who were demanding a referendum are now castigating him for weakness in conceding to their demands. Actually, it's a masterstroke. It gets us off the hook until both the Euro elections and the general election are out of the way and may never even be necessary if other countries kibosh the constitution before we do. Well worth a couple of days of pain. No wonder the Tories and their friends are apoplectic.

Jack, who makes little effort to conceal his Euro-scepticism, was amusing on the subject regarding the proposed constitution at this morning's meeting. 'It's a fucking conceit. Full of all kinds of crap ... As ye sow, so shall ye reap ...' And so on.

Another huge atrocity in Iraq. This time in Basra, our territory. Three car bombs have exploded, outside two police stations and a police academy. Among the dead two bus loads of children on their way to school.

Friday, 23 April
Sunderland

Today I did something worthwhile. I rescued a young woman from southern Sudan, an asylum seeker, due to be deported with her one-year-old son to where she faced a life of destitution, not to mention the fact that the minimum penalty for single motherhood in Sudan is 100 lashes. Now in her early thirties, she had led a life of unspeakable misery. When she was ten Arab bandits had burned her village, killing her parents; to this day she has no idea if any of her four brothers and sister survived. She then spent years slaving for an Arab family from whom she eventually fled, ending up in a refugee camp in Kenya, where again she was brutally mistreated and raped. Somehow or other she found her way to Heathrow wearing only the clothes she stood up in, from where she was dispersed to Sunderland. Her claim for asylum was rejected, as was her appeal (even though the adjudicator accepted that she and her child faced destitution). Two weeks ago she received notice that removal was imminent. I rang, wrote and faxed the Home Office; I put a letter personally into Bev Hughes's hands; when Bev resigned at the beginning of April, I started again with Des Browne. Today, out of the blue, a fax arrived saying that Des had granted indefinite leave on compassionate grounds. This afternoon she came to the office and I put it into her hands. From this day on her life, and that of her child, will be changed irrevocably and I have the satisfaction of knowing that, for once, I have made a difference.

Monday, 26 April

Supper in the Tea Room with Alan Milburn, who says, 'Tony must reassert his authority.' How? Not by sacking Gordon, surely? 'No but he can have a cull of Gordon's friends. A noticeably Blairite manifesto would send the right signal, too.'

Tuesday, 27 April

The main subject of discussion at this morning's ministerial meeting was the news that 52 retired senior diplomats have signed an open letter denouncing the government's Middle East policy. Denis Mac-Shane was disparaging, insisting that he had never heard of most of them. Michael Williams muttered something about 'supporters of a Middle East policy which had achieved nothing in 40 years'. Only Liz

Symons conceded there was a problem: 'There is a lot of criticism in the Lords about our subservience to the Americans.' Jack came down firmly on Liz's side: 'We must address their arguments. There are some sacred totems around which we shall have to navigate.'

In the evening, to the Hilton in Park Lane for a huge Labour fund-raising do. It was at this event, ten years ago almost to the day, that John Smith made his final speech. Someone on my table who had been there remembered that John had kept glancing at Gordon for reassurance. Cherie and The Man were in attendance. Every mention of His name was greeted by warm applause. The star of the show was Alastair Campbell, who treated us to some hilarious extracts from his road show. On the way out I came across Charlie Falconer and Patricia Hewitt fulminating about The Man's EU referendum U-turn. Charlie said, 'I had assumed I was one of about one and a half people who didn't know, but it turned out that most of us didn't.'

Wednesday, 28 April

A huge thunderstorm last night washed most of the blossom from the trees. I went to see Dad, who is now in Gay Bowers nursing home. He looks better than he has done for months – calm, cheerful, slightly fuller in the face, generally *compos mentis*. He lies all day in a bare room, with very little stimulus. No meals, not even a cup of water – the sign behind his bed still says firmly 'Nil by Mouth' – to break the monotony.

Tea in the House of Lords with Daphne Park and her nephew, a dispossessed white Zimbabwean farmer who seemed remarkably lacking in bitterness considering the scale of his losses. Daphne, now in her eighties, spent years representing the SIS behind the lines in Hanoi, Ulan Bator, Kinshasa. She told a story about a visit from a member of the Vietnamese politburo who turned up out of the blue early one morning and spent six hours chatting frankly on her veran-dah. 'We have agents in every ministry and every village in the south,' he had boasted.

'In that case,' inquired Daphne, 'why do you find it necessary to hang village headmen?'

'Because we are Leninists and Lenin believed in revolutionary terror.'

One nice story from Peking in 1970. She was staying at our embassy on R & R from Mongolia. It was in the days, just after the Cultural Revolution, when tipping was absolutely forbidden, but she wanted to offer a token of appreciation to the staff for having looked after her so well so she asked the Ambassador, John Addis, if he thought they might each be persuaded to accept a gift of a miniature flowering tree that she had seen on sale in the market. Addis duly summoned his chief steward, who did not reject the suggestion out of hand, but said gravely that he would need to take soundings. In due course he reported back that the flowering trees would be acceptable, but on one condition. Which was? 'That the size of each tree reflects the status of the recipient.' So off she went to the market and bought 13 trees ranging in size from a tall one for the major domo down to one barely a foot high for the lowly garden boy.

Tuesday, 4 May

At the morning ministerial meeting someone remarked that there was a good chance that the *Mirror*'s photographs purporting to show British soldiers abusing Iraqi prisoners were forgeries, in which case Piers Morgan would be in trouble.

'Keep lighting candles,' said Jack.

Rang Mum. The experiment in independent living has failed. Liz was helping Mum to pack. 'I'm going back to Brewster House. For good,' she said. It was like one of those sad Alan Bennett stories, 'A Cream Cracker under the Settee' or 'Soldiering On', that she used to like so much. As always, Mum put on a brave face, but I could tell she is deeply upset. She has lived at Manor Drive for 49 years and today is the last day. For the umpteenth time I assured her that if Brewster House doesn't work out, she can come to live with us, but she keeps saying that she doesn't want to be a burden.

Monday, 10 May

Jack was absent from the ministerial lunch. Bill Rammell presided. 'I don't know what others think, but on the doorsteps I get the impression that it's alright,' he said. It rapidly became clear that Bill was the only person present who thought so. Phyllis Starkey said, 'The Iraq torture allegations are dragging us down. We are being blamed for the behaviour of American troops. We need to put some distance between them and us.'

Eric Joyce, a former army officer, said, 'It looks as though the American mistreatment was systematic. It seems to have been agreed at a high level, whereas ours wasn't.'

I mentioned a report by Richard Norton-Taylor in the *Guardian* last week about an SAS training centre at Ashford where soldiers were subject to a programme of abuse. It even had a name: R21.

'But that was teaching them to resist interrogation,' said Mike O'Brien.

'Is it possible that someone has got muddled up?' I inquired. 'I've never understood why it's necessary to put hoods on prisoners' heads.'

'Oh that's to disorientate,' said Eric matter-of-factly. 'It's within the Geneva Convention.' Later he added, 'We do noise, too.'

'That's torture,' I said. Eric just smiled.

'I wouldn't let Eric anywhere near my constituents,' Phyllis said afterwards.

Tuesday, 11 May

'We have to put some clear blue water between us and the Americans, even if it means embarrassing Himself,' remarked Liz Symons at this morning's meeting.

'Guantanamo is the way to do it,' said Mike O'Brien.

'I have written to Colin Powell,' said Jack, adding that he had taken care to agree the text of his letter with Powell in advance.

Later, at Foreign Office Questions, Jack stuck up for the Americans. 'I wouldn't have been quite so effusive,' whispered Mike O'Brien. 'It's going to get a great deal worse yet.'

I entertained the Sudanese Foreign Minister to lunch in the

Churchill Room. For some reason he is being given the full treatment – a big limo, police outriders. Richly undeserved, given the horrors in Darfur. If I'd had my way, he'd have been lucky to get a cup of tea. Inevitably, he turned out to be charming. Afterwards I took him on the terrace and, when we were out of earshot of his colleagues, asked about the amputations. He assured me that they were rare and that only one had been carried out under the present regime. In passing, the Sudanese Ambassador whispered that the case I raised with him recently – of a 16-year-old boy facing cross-amputation – was resolved; the boy has been released, his sentence quashed.

Wednesday, 12 May

Liz rang at 07.30. 'Dad died a few minutes ago.'

I reached Danbury at ten o'clock and there he was: emaciated, pale, cold; head back, eyes closed, mouth slightly ajar, a sore on his upper lip. He lay on his back in twilight, the bed sheet up to his middle, hands crossed. Someone had placed a large fragrant pink lily in his hands. I talked to him for a while as though he were still there. Poor old Dad. After all he has been through in the last four months I never had a chance to say goodbye and thank you; he never conceded that he was dying and I lacked the courage to raise the subject.

Later, Liz and Pat arrived with Mum. Although it was obvious to the rest of us, I am not sure that Mum ever realised that Dad was dying. Until recently she was talking about taking him home and then, when we pointed out that that was unlikely, about taking him around Danbury Park in a wheelchair. We took her to see Dad; she shed a tear, kissed him on the forehead (something I never saw her do in life) and we left her alone with him for ten minutes. They have been married for 59 years.

On the way Jack rang to say how sorry he was and that I must take off as much time as I needed.

Thursday, 13 May

Speculation is rife about the fate of The Man. Andrew Marr was on the radio this morning saying that his situation was 'as bad as it has ever been' and that he was 'entering a very dangerous period'. The papers are full of calls for The Man to distance himself from the Americans, but, of course, he can't. As Alan Milburn said at the time, he's bet the whole shop.

My guess is that he'll hang on at least until after the local and Euro elections and probably until September. If, by then, it has become clear that he's a liability, he'll go.

Monday, 17 May

Among the papers crossing my desk today one which reveals the astonishing fact that between June last year and April this year DFID paid a staggering £606,000 to a company calling itself Meteoric Tactical Solutions to provide protection for one senior official based in Iraq. Silly me. For months I have been proclaiming that nowadays our aid money is firmly targeted on the poorest people in the poorest countries and all the while we are spending increasing amounts on mercenaries.

Wednesday, 19 May
Soweto, South Africa

Curiously, no one in Soweto rides a bicycle. They either walk or, in the case of the few who can afford to, drive. There is nothing in between. Odd since the bicycle is the obvious form of transport for a poor man. It is by no means all gloom here. Luxury hacienda are going up on the periphery which would not look out of place in the better parts of Sunderland, evidence that at least some of South Africa's vast wealth is trickling down. We passed the grim-looking hostels for Zulu migrant workers, once the source of a good deal of Apartheid-era violence, but now living in harmony with their neighbours. Someone pointed out Winnie Mandela's fortified condominium and the street where Nelson Mandela once lived and where Archbishop Tutu still has a modest house. Where else can you find a street which houses two Nobel Prize winners?

Friday, 21 May
Hotel Tivoli, Beira, Mozambique

We drove 30 miles north of the city to a village where a bunch of local high-school kids were educating Aids orphans. Lovely little people, some in rags, some with swollen bellies; traumatised, hungry, sitting under trees being taught to read and write. Some had been living wild, stealing sugar cane until a local boy intervened and persuaded three South African women from the nearby sugar plant to get involved. The women looked for all the world like spoiled Afrikaner house-wives, which just goes to show that one should never judge by appear-ances. 'Within two weeks of coming here my values had totally changed,' remarked one of the women. 'I wish I could show this scene to my nieces. All they care about is what clothes they are wearing and when they can go to the beach house.'

Saturday, 22 May
Beira

After breakfast, a short walk around the city centre. The most striking thing about Beira is the almost complete absence of the state, local or national. Streets littered with rotting garbage, drains blocked with domestic waste and from dark recesses an odour of (human) excreta; grey, grim multi-storey flats, a legacy from the long-departed Portu-guese, dominating the city centre, the upper storeys no longer reached by electricity or water. Pondering all this, I suddenly found myself losing sympathy. Do they really need foreigners to pick up the litter for them? Surely there must be something they could do for them-selves? What about a few pence per rubbish bag to the all-too-ubiqui-tous street children to pick it up?

Maputo airport

While awaiting our flight to Johannesburg we found ourselves caught up in the arrival of no less a figure than the prime minister of São Tomé for tomorrow's summit of the New Partnership for African Development (NEPAD). He received the full treatment: 100 metres of red carpet, a military band, a guard of honour, a choir of singing schoolchildren and the inevitable fleet of top of the range limos to whisk him away to his, no doubt five-star, hotel. Helpfully the limos all bore NEPAD number plates. The highest I saw was NEPAD 137. This is the organisation which is supposed to be leading Africa away from government by corrupt, self-serving elites into the sunlit uplands of democracy, transparency, accountability. Let us pray that there is more to NEPAD than luxury limos.

Thursday, 27 May

This afternoon I took the Dalai Lama to see Jack. I received him at the Members' Entrance and escorted him through Westminster Hall and along the Library Corridor to Jack's room. They didn't really engage. HH talked too much and Jack, who was on unfamiliar ground, confined himself to a handful of anodyne questions. At one point he inquired about the current population of Lhasa and HH replied that it was around 200,000. I could see Jack thinking, 'Is that all?' HH's command of English has scarcely changed since we first met 30 years ago. He still lapses occasionally into Tibetan and waits for Tenzin Geyche to supply the missing words. There were a couple of nice moments. One, at the beginning, when HH on seeing Jack said, 'I know your face from TV – Iraq.' The other when HH remarked that the BJP in India was 'the party of the rich' to which Jack (to the bemusement of HH and the amusement of everyone else) interjected, 'Like New Labour.'

As usual HH exuded optimism and good humour. As I showed him to his car, he remarked that the new railway which the Chinese are building across the Qinghai plateau could bring 30 million Chinese to Tibet. 'Tibetans must have more children,' I said.

He replied with a chuckle, 'Yes – and less monks.'

Saturday, 29 May
The Holmes, St Boswells

Latest additions to Mrs Dale's menagerie include half a dozen donkeys (a sign at the end of the drive proclaims that The Holmes is now a donkey sanctuary), a llama and a female pig named Matilda, who is supposed to be mating with Jasper but who thus far has shown no interest. Mrs Dale asked me to keep an eye out for signs of activity.

Monday, 8 June

Awoke to hear Hilary Benn, in Sudan, being quizzed by John Humphrys, who was doing his best to link the catastrophe in Darfur to Iraq, implying it was all our fault; at one point he alleged that a million people had died (whereas in fact the death toll so far is a few thousand, although it may well rise sharply unless large-scale help arrives soon). Hilary dealt with him calmly, patiently addressing each point and resisting the temptation to go for the smug Humphrys' throat. I am not sure I could have displayed such restraint.

'Iraq looks more hopeful than at any time recently,' opined Jack at the ministerial lunch in the India Office Council Chamber. The basis for his optimism, which is not widely shared, seems to be the progress at the UN on a resolution legitimising the transfer of sovereignty. 'By the end of the year,' Jack continued, 'we should be in a position to turn round and say to the Lib Dems: "What would you do, if Saddam was still there?"' In the absence of any Lib Dems he looked at me when making this point. I kept my mouth firmly shut.

Wednesday, 10 June

Up early to prepare for a Westminster Hall debate on Darfur, a catastrophe entirely man-made. As so often, there is a tightrope to be walked. The only thing that stops us forthrightly condemning the evil, rotten regime which has perpetrated the slaughter is the fact that we need the co-operation of the Sudanese rulers to get aid to the afflicted; and also to preserve the painstakingly negotiated recent agreement between north and south; finally, we want their help delivering up Joseph Kony and his Lord's Resistance Army, which from the safety of bases in southern Sudan has laid waste to northern Uganda. Whatever we do in Darfur thousands, perhaps tens of thousands, are going to die.

Thursday, 11 June

Making good use of an unexpected gap in the diary I mowed the lawn at Brixton Road and then walked around to the polling station to cast my vote for The People's Ken, who (shades of Cultural Revolution China) has now been miraculously transformed, in the New Labour pantheon, from 'a renegade, traitor and scab' to 'a hero of the people' – our only hope of salvaging something from what are otherwise expected to be catastrophic local election results.

And then to the office only to find a great flap going on. Jack – at the behest of Ed Owen – had asked why no minister was available to respond to Michael Ancram on the *Today* programme this morning on an item about a visiting Zimbabwean. Apparently, there was a message from *Today* late last night, but Bharat had been unable to get hold of me. He did in fact leave a message on my answerphone at the flat which I received when I returned at about 1 a.m. I simply took the view that the *Today* programme bid did not merit a response (which, as it turned out, was also the view of the press office) and went to bed. So, once again, Minister Mullin is in the proverbial. I have quietly asked Bharat to get the office pager out of the cupboard where it has resided since I assumed office.

Monday, 14 June

To a packed meeting of the parliamentary party where one might have expected some sort of post-mortem following our disastrous showing in the local and Euro elections in which The People's Ken was re-elected in London but we lost control in seven or eight cities, including Newcastle, where the Lib Dems swept all before them. Two stout policemen were posted by the door to prevent eavesdropping. A throng of hacks lurked in the hope of spilled blood. Instead an unnatural calm prevailed. The Man rose to the usual loud acclaim. As ever he spoke brilliantly, apparently unshaken by the drubbing we have just received. His message: hold our nerve, 'park' Iraq in a different place, deal with other problems such as asylum, draw some clear dividing lines between ourselves and the Tories and then make the electorate 'a good forward offer' (another one for the New Labour lexicon; how long before it enters the vocabulary of every Blair Babe?). No nastiness from the floor. No mention (save for a gentle side-swipe from Paul Flynn) of regime change. Several people actually remarked how well we had done in their area. Even as the snow falls and the troops are deserting we march steadily on towards Moscow, whistling a happy tune.

'I was interested to hear how well we'd done,' remarked Robin Cook acidly, later. Bryan Davies said, 'They're in denial. They can't read the writing on the wall. No leader would have got away with that 20 years ago.'

Tuesday, 15 June

A sudden outburst from Jack at this morning's pre-Questions conference regarding the inadequacy of the draft replies. It was prompted by a long essay which he was expected to read out in response to a question about India. 'How many times have I made clear that answers should be no longer than 50 words and that they should address the questions? The Foreign Office has been answering questions for 220 years. We ought to be able to get it right by now.' He went on at some length. 'Crap' and the f-word featured repeatedly. 'If necessary, I'll make the directors draft the answers personally. Why should ministers have to spend time redrafting this f-ing crap?' Later, a minute was circulated repeating the point, minus the purple passages.

Wednesday, 16 June

Liz Symons reported in ill again, as she is prone to do, so I was asked to receive a delegation of Guantanamo Bay relatives in her place. Actually, it was a put-up job organised by Vanessa and Corin Redgrave who, of course, have their own agenda. They came accompanied by some good and serious people, including Frank Judd, the Bishop of Oxford, Jim McKeith, Rabbi David Goldberg; plus Sarah Ludford, a venomous Lib Dem peer who was so worked up that she could hardly bring herself to look at me. I was given a Line to Take. The one we have been chanting for months. With every day that passes it sounds less credible. It also demonstrates beyond peradventure our utter lack of influence with our supposed closest ally. Poor Mr Begg had got it into his head that Tony Blair had only to say the word and his son would be returned; nothing I said could persuade him otherwise. Guantanamo was a moral issue, said the bishop. Why couldn't we speak out? Why indeed? If ever there was an issue where we need – for the sake of our credibility – to put some clear blue water between us and the Americans, this is it. That is Liz Symons's view and for all I know it is Jack's, too. Vanessa, fizzing with Trotskyist outrage, provided the only light relief. 'I don't believe a word said by anyone from the British government.'

'But Vanessa,' I smiled sweetly, 'that's been your position for at least the last 30 years.'

When they were gone I penned a note to Jack saying that, if nothing happened soon, we should speak out. We won't, of course. The Man simply wouldn't allow it.

The Terrace, House of Commons

What better place to dine on a warm summer's evening, after a hard day's governing? A cool breeze from the river, a heron flying east briefly spotlighted by the dying sun; the three Victorian pavilions of St Thomas's Hospital and the water tower, aglow. Only one small, dark thought clouds my mind as I sit here. What is to prevent some agent of al-Qaida standing on Westminster Bridge or on the far (but not so far) side of the river and raking the terrace with automatic gunfire?

Thursday, 17 June

In the absence of Liz Symons I was dispatched at 15 minutes' notice to conference room A of the Cabinet Office for a meeting of the Ad Hoc Ministerial Group on the Rehabilitation of Iraq. Geoff Hoon in the chair. The cast included Patricia Hewitt, Hilary Benn, Attorney General Peter Goldsmith, the Chief of the Defence Staff and the Permanent Secretary at the Ministry of Defence, Sir Kevin Tebbit, just back from Baghdad. Pessimism was the prevailing sentiment. Someone said, 'It's going to get worse before it gets better.' The enemy are growing more sophisticated by the day. 'They have learned in a year what it took the IRA 30 years.'

Afterwards a brief exchange with Peter Goldsmith, who has been negotiating with the Americans about Guantanamo. 'Outrageous' was the word he used.

Monday, 21 June
The Residence, Kinshasa

The Congo: a vast, chaotic, misgoverned, dysfunctional morass; its rulers historically preoccupied with looting rather than governing. The armed forces: bloated, parasitic, disloyal and generally useless, except in so far as they threaten the lives and welfare of the much put-upon civilian population. Although rich in mineral wealth and blessed with some of the world's most fertile agricultural land, most Congolese are among the poorest people in Africa.

My mission, to persuade all parties (including the meddling Rwandans) to stop squabbling and concentrate on making a success of the peace process. The Americans have also sent an envoy.

Ambassador Jim Atkinson showed us to our rooms, indicating the windowless hallway outside. 'If there is any shooting, this is the best place to shelter.' His point was not entirely academic. The most recent outburst of gunfire was on Sunday. The wall of his living room is scarred by a large bullet hole and underneath a bronze plaque which reads, 'A present from Brazzaville, 21 December, 1998'.

Tuesday, 22 June

Called on Vice-President Bemba (large, bombastic, rich), who delivered a long tirade on the wickedness of the Rwandans, at one point he seemed to be threatening war (unwise: the Congolese would be soundly thrashed). Like every self-respecting warlord Bemba has his own bodyguards, a motley collection of lounging soldiers, including a handful of Uruguayans provided by the UN. And parked by the river, an M18 helicopter, ready to whisk him to safety in the event of an emergency. The abiding image: a pick-up truck, parked at an angle across the road, machine gun mounted on the back pointing vaguely in the direction of Brazzaville, the custodian flat out, asleep on the floor, his legs resting at 45 degrees on the base of the machine gun. He was still comatose when we emerged from Bemba's office an hour later. Bharat wanted to take a photograph, but I cautioned against. Soldiers in the Congo have a tendency to over-react.

Wednesday, 23 June

A wasted morning, loitering on His Excellency's verandah, awaiting the call that President Kabila is ready to receive us. HE, chain-smoking, remarkably laidback. 'Don't worry, this is how it is in the Congo; it always works out in the end.' But we do worry. Our time is short. We have other business to attend to, all on hold until we hear from the President. Meanwhile HE, on his mobile, has rung the President's office; something he should have done three hours ago. As I feared, we are now being invited to meet Kabila at 13.00, which we can't because we have ten people coming to lunch. After some hard bargaining, a time of 14.40 is agreed upon.

Joseph Kabila became president three years ago because someone shot his father. He was aged just 29. The learning curve has been steep.

In his pictures Kabila junior looks a little like Baby Doc Duvalier. In the flesh, however, he is a small, unassuming man in an olive green safari suit. He enters unannounced through a side door and takes his seat without fanfare. He is wearing an expensive watch which he takes off and balances on the arm of his chair. His opening words are 'You wanted to see me?' He does not seem overjoyed; a little weary even. Gradually he warms up, insisting that he is committed to making a success of the transitional government and that he is anxious to avoid war with Rwanda.

Unlike his father (who had a penchant for the firing squad) Kabila II does not inspire fear, or even respect (one of his officials slept throughout our meeting). One could easily feel sorry for him, rattling around in that great, ugly palace by the river, not knowing who to trust. Odds are it will end badly. You can't become president of a place like the Congo in your twenties and expect to die peacefully in bed.

Thursday, 24 June

Up early for our flight, in a small private jet, to Rwanda, via Mbuji Mayi and Bukavu (the scene of recent fighting).

'There are no altruistic Congolese,' opines HE as we are driven to the airport. 'You only have to look at what the rulers have done to their people in the last 40 years.' He goes on, 'A mandate. That's the only way. The international community is wasting its time on a half-hearted effort. They should either take over and do it properly or get out. The Congolese would sort it out among themselves. Another strong man would emerge, like Mobutu. He'd make himself very rich, but some of it would trickle down, order would be restored and people would be able to get on with their lives.'

'Are you going to put that in your valedictory telegram?'

'No.'

Kigali, Rwanda

Just time for a shower and a change of clothes before being taken to see President Kagame. Tall, thin, youthful, softly spoken, calm, he gives the impression that – unlike poor Kabila – he is firmly in charge. My mission, to dissuade him from any rash action in the Congo, whatever the provocations (and they are considerable). The problem is that the Rwandans, and who can blame them, have absolutely no confidence in the UN. Presently there are an estimated 12,000 unre-pentant *génocidaires* sitting over the border in Congo, making occasional raids. The Rwandans, very reasonably, want to know why the Congolese and MONUC (the largest UN mission) have so far proved incapable of dealing with them and, in the absence of effective international intervention, they are threatening to do the job themselves.

Friday, 25 June
The Residence, Kigali

HM Ambassador, a fifty-something, chain-smoking (what is it about ambassadors in this part of the world?) woman. Friendly, competent, but oh, so noisy. She appears to survive on a diet of caffeine and nicotine and keeps up a continuous, fatuous running commentary. Every phone call a great drama. Impossible to think straight while she's buzzing around. Eventually, one of my officials gently took her aside and said, 'I think the Minister would like a little peace.'

'Oh dear,' she said. 'That's why my husband divorced me.'

The Genocide Museum, Kigali

A picture of a shiny-faced little girl and underneath the following caption:

FRANCINE MURENGEZI INGABIRE, aged 12
Favourite sport: swimming
Favourite food: egg and chips
Favourite drink: milk and Fanta tropical
Best friend: her elder sister Claudette
Cause of death: hacked by machete.

Saturday, 26 June
Kigali

The Rwandans are the Vietnamese of Africa. Energetic, self-confident, resilient, able to fight wars in the teeth of impossible odds and with absolute confidence in the rightness of their cause. The countryside, too, reminds one of Vietnam. Every inch, even to the highest hilltops, cultivated; in contrast to the Congo, a vast, indolent, uncultivated wilderness. And unlike the Vietnamese, the Rwandans are not burdened by an impossible ideology. At first glance, Rwanda is a glimpse of what Africa might look like if it worked. And yet it cannot be so simple. One does not have to look back far into history to realise that beneath the tranquil surface lies a terrible darkness.

Monday, 28 June
Sunderland

A long queue of supplicants at the Pennywell surgery and then to London on an evening train, armed with my dictaphone, a file of letters and one of Ngoc's excellent sandwiches. Among the mail, a round robin from a couple in Dulwich who claim to represent exactly that section of the middle class so assiduously wooed by New Labour. The covering letter says, 'We are writing to other MPs because we have lost our own – Tessa Jowell. She is now just a rubber stamp with "Tony Blair" incised on the bottom.' They begin:

> We are writing to disabuse Labour supporters of any spin that the Labour Party is still viable if Blair stays ... The present spin from the Blairist camp is that, given time, people like us will forget the war and things can go on as before. Forget that – because WE will never forget: we are not the sort. And no spin-crafted apology is going to affect us.

They conclude:

> If you want to save the Labour Party (and it is as desperate as that) get rid of Blair and his cronies. In the last few days the electorate has given this very verdict. Do not evade it or go into denial. If you do not respond with the only rational action you can take, then the consequences are going to be obvious.

I am not sure about the analysis. The length and nature of the charge sheet enumerated elsewhere in the letter suggests that the authors may not be quite as typical of the middle classes as they would like us to believe, but I couldn't resist a chuckle at the image of Tessa Jowell as a rubber stamp with 'Tony Blair' incised on her bottom.

Wednesday, 30 June

The Man has now formally asked George Bush for the return of the remaining four British prisoners – I have seen the letter – but for some reason he doesn't want it publicised so we just have to sit tight and take the crap from people like Vanessa Redgrave.

Friday, 2 July

Bharat reports some complaining at the Permanent Secretary's meeting this morning that Hilary Benn is doing all the media on Sudan (he was on *Today* again this morning). Actually, *Today* were after me, but I quietly passed it over to Hilary on the grounds (a) that having been there recently he is better qualified than I and (b) having worked until after midnight and being short of sleep, I was darned if I was going to get up at the crack of dawn. Fingers crossed that no one finds out that I gave it away. Far from being jealous, I am grateful to Hilary for taking it on. I will never make a good Whitehall warrior.

Sunday, 4 July

Awoke to the news that Peter Mandelson will be supporting Gordon Brown when the time comes. Do we need to know this? Does it matter? And does this shameless bit of spinning by any chance have something to do with the current vacancy for a European commissioner? Given that his appointment will involve a by-election that we are unlikely to win, I wouldn't have thought his chances were high, but you never know. Stranger things have happened in the New Labour court. Anyway, Peter has apparently given an interview to Channel 5, to be broadcast later in the week, and 'a friend' (no prizes for guessing who) has helpfully tipped off the *Observer*. The man is a compulsive self-publicist.

Saturday, 10 July

Mum's 84th birthday and the first without Dad. What is to become of her? Liz and Pat are firmly of the view that she should remain at the nursing home. Mum would like to try living at home, with a carer calling in a couple of times a day. Alternatively, she could come to live with us, but she resists that, too, on the grounds that she doesn't want to be a burden and, however much I try to reassure her that it would be our pleasure, she won't back down.

Monday, 12 July

'I'LL BE PM 5 MORE YEARS – Blair's Shock Blow For Brown.' Yes, it's another *Sun* exclusive. Trevor Kavanagh, no less. Exactly what the punters in their present surly mood don't want to hear. Shades of Margaret Thatcher going on and on. Which New Labour master-strategist has dreamed up this latest piece of nonsense?

Tuesday, 13 July

Questions. Jack and Bill Rammell dominated. What a confident, competent fellow Bill is. A voracious appetite for work, always on the lookout for new territory to conquer, he can turn his hand to anything. As ever, the only question I was called upon to answer was about Zimbabwe. Zimbabwe, Zimbabwe, Zimbabwe, that's all I ever get asked about. Of the nine or ten Question Times I have done since I came to the Foreign Office, all but one has involved answering on Zimbabwe. So obsessed are the Tories that when someone referred in passing to the genocide in Rwanda, Michael Ancram and Gary Streeter immediately started chanting, 'What about Zimbabwe?' As if what has happened in Zimbabwe – dreadful though it is – bears any comparison to the slaughter in Rwanda.

Wednesday, 14 July

To the chamber to watch The Man's statement on the Butler Report.* Another flawless, effortless performance. None of the tension that

---

*Robin Butler, the former Cabinet Secretary, had been asked to review the intelligence evidence for the suggestion that Saddam Hussein possessed weapons of mass destruction – the principal justification for Britain's involvement in the

surrounded Hutton. Howard was seen off as easily as IDS used to be in the old days. The Tories just looked glum, hobbled by the fact that they were keener on the war than we were and so it's a bit late to pretend they were duped into supporting it. Charles Kennedy, who at least had the merit of having opposed the entire enterprise, was boring, worthy and easily disposed of. None of which gets us round the awkward fact that we were entirely, albeit inadvertently, hoodwinked.

The war was never about weapons of mass destruction. It was about keeping in with the Americans, stupid. It pains me to say this. I like The Man and he is in most respects an outstanding leader. But he has made a catastrophic error and, if there is any justice in this world, he would go.

Thursday, 15 July
Sunderland

A minor crisis. Edward Clay, our estimable High Commissioner in Nairobi, has made a speech slating the Kenyan government for its failure to deal with corruption. Nothing wrong in principle, but he has gone a wee bit over the top:

> ... the practitioners now in government have an arrogance, greed and perhaps a desperate sense of panic to lead them to eat like gluttons. They may expect that we shall not see, or notice, or will forgive them a bit of gluttony because they profess to like Oxfam lunches. But they can hardly expect us not to care when their gluttony causes them to vomit all over our shoes ...

And so on. Needless to say the Kenyans, or at least their government, are mightily upset (imagine the reaction here if an ambassador accredited to us sounded off in similar terms). Apparently Edward sent the office an advance copy of his speech, but no one thought to run it past the Minister. I did a conciliatory little interview on *The World at One*, taking care not to undermine him, but at the same time keeping

---

invasion of Iraq. This followed allegations that the evidence had been 'sexed-up' by the Prime Minister and his advisers.

the door open to the Kenyans. This evening there was a call from Number 10, asking for a note for The Man's box by noon tomorrow. Bharat thinks I should ring the Kenyan Foreign Minister in an attempt to calm things down. I don't. When in doubt, do nothing.

Friday, 16 July

A chat with Edward Clay, in Nairobi, who was duly grateful that I hadn't disowned him. Apparently he's getting lots of support from the Kenyan public. We agreed it wouldn't be necessary for me to ring the Foreign Minister, at least for a few days. Give the message time to sink in.

We lost the Leicester South by-election and narrowly won Hodge Hill (thanks to the intervention of George Galloway's party). The good news is that the Tories came nowhere.

Saturday, 17 July

When Dad died Ann Grant, our High Commissioner in South Africa, sent a note saying that she still thought of her late father every day 'usually with affection'. And it's true. I think of Dad every day too. Which is odd because we weren't particularly close and I rarely thought of him when he was alive and well. Yesterday, when I inspected the garden, I thought: this is what Dad used to do when he came home from work. Even as I type this I can see him smiling down at me from the picture on the bedroom wall, holding Sarah by the High Force Waterfall when she was three. At least he lived long enough for her to remember.

Tuesday, 20 July

The Iraq debate. The Man, shamelessly brilliant. Howard, lacklustre. Charles Kennedy, surprisingly chipper, but then he's on a roll at the moment. William Hague also made a brilliant speech. He's so good that the Tories could do worse than make him leader again when they have done with Howard. At the very least, he will be foreign secretary in the next Tory government, assuming that there is one (which there will be). Robin Cook hit the nail on the head: our involvement in the war was never about Iraq, it was about keeping in with George Bush. Jack was (unusually and unwisely) absent for most of the debate to which he had to reply. Mike O'Brien whispered that he was tied up with something that involved Mandelson. The rumour is that Peter is to be our next European Commissioner.

Wednesday, 21 July
Brixton Road

Ngoc reports that Emma said something very touching this morning: 'Mum, I haven't had a kiss from Dad for three days. When he comes home tonight, can you ask him to kiss me, even if I am sleeping?'

Friday, July 23
Sunderland

Suddenly the political landscape is transformed. The Man is again riding high. The polls (despite recent disasters) all say that, faced with a choice between us and the Tories, we would win hands down. Incredibly, there is even a discussion in the media about whether Howard, after his poor showing on Tuesday is up to the job. No more talk of The Man's imminent demise. 'Four more years' no longer seems bravado. Truly he walks on water. And in case anyone should doubt that, it was announced today that Peter Mandelson is, as expected, to be the new European Commissioner.

Sunday, 15 August

To Heybridge to see Mum. I arrived unannounced. She was sitting in the day-room, an elbow resting on the arm of the chair, a hand shading her eyes, an empty teacup at her feet. Absolutely nothing to do. This is her life now. And it all happened so quickly. This time last year life was as it had always been. She and Dad were at home, bumbling along together, endlessly squabbling but caring for each other in their way. A struggle, but they were getting by. Now Dad is gone and there is no one to look out for Mum. It would be alright if she was gaga, but she isn't.

We drove into Maldon and sat by the river; the tide was out as it always seems to be at Maldon. Astonishing how little it has changed since we were children – the wooden kiosks, the little park, the mud. Mum chatted away happily and we moved slowly between kiosks – an ice cream here, a cup of tea there – but she is visibly deteriorating, partly no doubt as a result of the lack of anything useful to do. As ever we talked about old times. The same old stories about Eileen, Terence, great aunt Gabrielle and so on, but I don't begrudge them. In fact, I rather enjoy Mum's company. It is clear that Dad's death has hit her harder than anyone expected (I had thought that in some respects it would be a liberation). She seems never to have realised how ill he was. She keeps asking, 'Did you realise he was dying?'

Monday, 16 August

M called in, incredulous that The Man has allied the UK so firmly to a president who, as he puts it, is 'by far the worst in my lifetime, surrounded by people who are, at best, mediocre (Condi Rice) and at worst nuts (Rumsfeld, Cheney). Colin Powell is the only decent one amongst them and he is giving up.'

Tuesday, 17 August

The news from the front is uniformly awful. In Sudan, catastrophe. In Burundi another huge massacre of Congolese refugees. In Zimbabwe, Mugabe on course for a great election victory. There is even talk (which I shall firmly resist) of 're-engaging' with him afterwards or at least with his rotten party. And Côte d'Ivoire, one of the few west African countries that have not yet imploded, is on course to do so. My job is to put a positive gloss on all this, but it is getting increasingly difficult. Even the good guys have their dark side. In Uganda Museveni is busy turning himself into a president for life; in Ethiopia we are turning a blind eye to some very bad things; and the new regime in Kenya, of which we once had such high hopes, is again becoming mired in corruption. Are we all wasting our time? Should we bother? Of course we must. The alternatives are too awful to contemplate.

Wednesday, 18 August

Word reaches me that Bill Rammell, wearing his UN hat, is contemplating a visit to Sierra Leone. Do I object? As it happens I do. Sierra Leone is very firmly my territory. In any case I am due to visit soon and it does not require two ministerial visits. There would be calls on the President and all the other top brass and, before we know it, he would be popping up on the *Today* programme opining knowledgeably (he's also talking of dropping in on Côte d'Ivoire) on matters which lie firmly within my sphere of influence. Bill is a capable, likeable colleague, but his problem is that he doesn't have enough to do so he's always having to invent activity. And the fact that he has the UN on his list of responsibility gives him, in theory at least, carte blanche to tour the world raiding other portfolios. I popped up to see him in his palatial suite above mine. Without actually saying no, I did my best to indicate that I wasn't keen. We left it at that. If he does visit Sierra Leone, he will go after me and allow a decent interval to elapse before doing so. At least, I thought that's what we had agreed. Even before I was back downstairs Bill's slippery Private Secretary had been on the phone to Bharat discussing the possibility of a trip in October. I instructed Bharat to reply in writing that we had agreed no such thing. I will also enlist the aid of our Africa director, James Bevan. The time has come for a little Whitehall warriorism.

Thursday, 19 August
The Foreign Office

'We'll try and get you away early,' said Bharat – as he often does on a Thursday. Fat chance. I've been here until ten or eleven at night all this week, trying to get the paperwork under control. It's five weeks since I last set foot in Sunderland and the work is piling up at that end, too. To say nothing of the snails and the bindweed that have had free run of the garden since mid-July. And on Monday I am off to Uganda …

Wednesday, 25 August
The Residence, Kampala

A day touring refugee camps around the northern town of Lira. I am in my element. One day in the field is worth ten meetings with men in suits. Three times I was asked to make impromptu speeches. Once from the back of a pick-up truck to a crowd of several hundred, once to a group of paramount chiefs and once to 200 traumatised children who had recently escaped the clutches of Joseph Kony's Lord's Resistance Army.

Scenes I will remember: (1) the early-morning view of the Nile from our little Cessna, a long ribbon of silver in a damp, grey-green savannah emerging from Lake Victoria; (2) the refugee camps as we came in to land at Lira, row after row of mud and thatch houses topped with blue or orange plastic sheeting; (3) Jacqueline, 11 years old with wide eyes and a shy smile, who has for more than two years been camped with her exhausted mother and four siblings in a dark, derelict starch factory on the outskirts of town, one of the lower tiers of Hell; (4) Evelyn, aged 13, whose lower jaw was shot away, unbearable to look at; (5) the sight of the High Commissioner's daughter, a little blond nugget called Persephone, dancing on the terrace as we arrived back from Lira, oblivious to the stark realities of the world beyond our compound.

By 7 p.m., just as Jacqueline and her little family are bedding down in the ruins of the dark, dank starch factory, we have washed away the dust of Lira and are downing pre-dinner drinks on the terrace. How easily we Lords of the Universe commute between her world and ours.

Thursday, 2 September
Sunderland

How can we bring up our children to be optimists? Every day brings news of another atrocity. Last week two Russian passenger planes brought down by Chechen suicide bombers. Yesterday a dozen Nepalese cleaners (cleaners for goodness' sake) decapitated by Jihadi barbarians in Iraq. Today comes news that a crowd of (apparently) Chechen gunmen have taken over a school in southern Russia; the hostages include several hundred children. Tonight's television news shows crowds of distraught parents gathered outside, being restrained by soldiers. Goodness knows how this will end. Sieges in Russia have a way of ending badly.

Friday, 3 September

Sarah sulked all afternoon because Ngoc refused to let her go to the cinema with her friends. I am deeply unsympathetic, thinking of little Jacqueline and her family in the starch factory in Lira. Then we turned on the television to find that the siege in southern Russia has ended in huge slaughter. I advised her to think of those children and their families every time she is feeling sorry for herself.

Tuesday, 7 September

Jack made a statement on Sudan. While it was being drafted a message came from Colin Powell saying that he's proposing to describe what is going on in Darfur as genocide when he appears before his Foreign Relations Committee on Thursday. Immediately alarm bells started ringing. A declaration of genocide will raise the stakes dramatically.

Thursday, 9 September

Colin Powell dropped his bombshell ('… if this is genocide, which in my opinion it is …'). Immediately, the calls started coming in: do we agree with the Americans and, if so, what are we going to do about it? Ancram issued a weaselly statement accusing us of hiding behind the

African Union, but stopping well short of calling for military intervention. It was decided that I should do Channel Four News, *Newsnight* and *Today*. Michael Williams, Ed Owen and I hastily agreed a Line to Take ('It may be') and off I went. The line can be held for now, but not for long. 'One way or another,' said Michael as we parted, 'British troops are going to end up in Darfur.'

Home on the 21.00, taxi from Durham, to bed, 1 a.m.

Monday, 13 September

Another hurricane bearing down on Florida. This, though it pains me to say so, is good news. The only hope of the Americans waking up to global warming is for them to be hit where it hurts – in a Republican swing state.

Tuesday, 14 September
The Residence, Khartoum, 6 a.m.

Arrived, exhausted, four hours ago, having flown all day. Not a wink of sleep. Tortured all night by some sort of generator or water pump in the ceiling above the guest room, turning on and off every couple of minutes – the same as in Maputo. Even a sleeping pill didn't work. Result: I am worn out and angry. Not a good way to start a trip like this. In half an hour we must be up and on our way to Darfur.

9 a.m., Nyala, South Darfur

A pair of helicopter gunships, evil, green hawks, sit on the tarmac a little way from the terminal. These are the weapons that have helped create the mayhem to which we have come to bear witness. According to the Swede, who is managing the aid operation at the airport, the gunships take off most evenings just before dusk and reappear several hours later. It is unclear where they have been or what they have been doing (the last reported use of gunships was 26 August). He tried to get close enough to take their registration numbers, but was chased away.

Also, two huge Ilyushins disgorging Sudanese policemen in blue uniforms, a band playing; the minister of Social Affairs, resplendent in a white jalaba and head-dress, greets us with an insincere hand-shake. The police are crowded into open-topped trucks and driven away, waving and singing. Oh, and a VIP lounge. 'The Sudanese are good at building VIP lounges,' says the Ambassador. 'If only they were so good at building schools.'

Within 15 minutes we are airborne again. This time in a white UN helicopter.

Airborne, between Nyala and Zalingi

The land below is surprisingly green, intersected by meandering, dried-up, sandy river beds. Two months from now, once the rains are over, this will be a barren wilderness, but for now it is fertile. Now and then evidence of cultivation and circles of bare earth where tulkels once stood; once or twice we saw a herd of sheep or cattle. By and large, however, the land is eerily empty.

11 a.m., Zalingi

We land on the edge of a huge encampment; shacks as far as the eye can see, white plastic sheets stretched over improvised wooden frames; plastic sheeting, the tell-tale sign of refugees everywhere. Except, as I am several times reminded, these are not refugees; they are IDPs, Internally Displaced People, homeless in their own country.

There is a large police presence in the camp. According to Max, the UN man, they weren't here yesterday so they must be for our benefit. There are also surly security men, one attached to our party, eavesdropping on every exchange. We must tread carefully, there have been reports of arrests as soon as foreigners leave. The head of security appears and the Ambassador, an Arabic speaker, leads him away from our party so that we may talk to the IDPs without interfer-ence. I engage a group of women collecting water. Mainly they are dead-eyed, most have lost someone in their family. The questions and the answers are always the same:

'Why are you here?'

'Because we were attacked.'

'Who by?'

'Arabs.'

'When will you go home?'

'When it is safe.'

Ragged, fly-harassed children follow us everywhere, stretching out grubby hands to be shaken; astonishing how cheerful and resilient they are. Many, of course, are not yet old enough to know what deep trouble they are in.

Evening, Government Guest House, Nyala

An unflushed toilet, a black cesspit; a sink, hanging at an angle of 30 degrees to the wall, uncleaned in living memory; the shower emits a spurt of water and then gives up the ghost, the bed sheets washed ... weekly? Monthly? Still, this is only for one night. Think of the people in the camps.

We are entertained to dinner by the provincial Minister of Physical Planning and Public Utilities, a soft-spoken, civilised, courteous man; a hydrologist by profession. 'We have to get the tribal chiefs together,' he says. 'That is the only way to resolve this.' Later, as we are drinking tea, he whispers, 'I want to go back to my profession. Politics is a dirty game.'

Wednesday, 15 September

Kass

Dusty, fly-blown, 50 miles north-west of Nyala along a potholed road. On the way we stopped at an abandoned village. Only one tulkel was burned, but that had been enough to cause everyone to flee. The rest were looted, a few earthenware pots the only evidence of habitation. According to a passing Arab this was one of six villages here and they are all empty. Over the road, a large herd of cattle. Whose cattle are/ were these? Men on camels glide through the bush, a little distance away. Every one an Arab, there are no Fur left.

In Kass the IDPs are camped out in the town centre, in schools, public buildings and in every available space, too terrified to move even to the designated campsite, a kilometre away. The compound of the girls' school is crammed with the destitute and yet, incredibly, the school is functioning. Through the classroom windows, girls in blue tunics and white headscarfs, sitting at their desks as though everything outside was normal. I talked to a crowd of men, one had lost four children. Same questions. Same answers: 'We were attacked ... by Arabs ... on camels and horses' (and in one case, police in Land Cruisers). While we were at the Médecins Sans Frontières clinic an injured couple were brought in. Their story was that they had recognised their stolen donkey in the custody of a passing Arab. They had naively reported the theft to the police and had been badly beaten for their pains. In a square near the town centre, huge queues for the monthly food ration and in the middle a ragged woman, lying motionless on the ground. How long can this go on? How long before the attention of the world drifts elsewhere (already the food pipeline shows signs of drying up)? How long before an epidemic sweeps the camps?

By nightfall we are back at the Residence in Khartoum. Clean water, good food, a flushing toilet. The misery of the camps but a fading memory. We have looked the damned in the eyes. Shaken their hands. Sympathised. But with the wave of a wand (or more precisely three hours in an ageing Antonov) we have returned to our world and they are still trapped, light years away, in theirs. We are but visitors to the inferno. Tourists in Hell.

Thursday, 16 September
Camp Tillo, Nuba Mountains

Off again at dawn in a windowless Antonov flown by ubiquitous Ukrainians. Every pilot in Africa is either Ukrainian or South African (I tell a lie, we did come across a Bulgarian helicopter pilot). How did anyone get around Africa before the break up of the Soviet Union and the end of apartheid?

At Kauda we are met by General Wilhemsen, the highly respected Norwegian in charge of the Nuba Mountains Monitoring Commission. Then by helicopter across a vast, verdant plain, fringed by low mountains (cf. the Plain of Jars, without the bomb craters), to the sector headquarters at Kauda. Here we are greeted by Nigel, a very English Englishman. Almost before our feet have touched the ground,

Nigel is bending our ear on the iniquity of banning hunting with hounds. Satellite television has reached even this remote place and Nigel seems to have watched every minute of yesterday's debate. Apparently there was a bust-up. Demonstrators broke into the chamber and crowds of baying hoorays (Nigel's wife and daughter among them) laid siege to Parliament. All much more exciting than a decade of civil war in the south of Sudan.

We set off by Land Cruiser along an almost unnavigable road to the headquarters of the Sudan People's Liberation Movement, a huddle of stone-walled, thatched tulkels in a picturesque little valley. Nigel is in the driving seat. The Ambassador next to him. Which is just as well because for most of the way there Nigel is going on about the hunting. I keep my mouth firmly shut. A meeting with the SPLM leaders. Speeches. Always the same theme. I have heard it all over Africa: 'We have nothing. We need everything. Please help us.' On the way back Nigel is talking public schools.

Saturday, 18 September
The Residence, Khartoum

Breakfast with Colonel Symonds, a British monitor in Western Darfur. Then a live interview with Edward Stourton on the *Today* programme, who wasn't up for the possibility that what has happened in Darfur was anything other than genocide or that the attacks by the rebels might have played a part in unleashing the catastrophe. How easy everything must seem from the comfort of a *Today* studio.

A day of appointments. We raced back and forth across town in the official Range Rover, flag flying from the bonnet, weaving our way through the traffic with the aid of an energetic police motorcyclist. No tantrums or fist-waving, just balletic arm movements (sometimes rising in the saddle and waving both arms simultaneously) and lo the traffic parted. A true artist, a pleasure to watch him at work. We called on the ministers of Justice, Humanitarian Affairs, Foreign Affairs and, finally, on Vice-President Taha in his mansion by the Blue Nile. How reasonable they appear. Charming, fluent, civilised. Apparently sincere in their desire for peace. And yet these are members of one of the world's worst governments. This, after all, is a land of the cross-amputation, where torture, random brutality and corruption are endemic; where the government is at war with a fair swathe of its own people and has unleashed unspeakable horrors in the name of restoring order.

Then back to the Residence for a meeting with the UN Secretary General's Special Representative, Jan Pronk. He was followed by the head of USAID, Andrew Natsios (who arrived, sirens blaring, in a convoy of Land Cruisers with blacked-out windows, a truckload of soldiers bringing up the rear). This was followed by a press conference, interviews with Reuters, Channel Four and a man from *Panorama*, and a visit to a human rights organisation.

And then this evening 40 people came to dinner: among them a man from the President's office, resplendent in white turban and jalaba, and surprisingly indiscreet. The catastrophe in Darfur, he said, was the work of four people – 'We call them "the Taha clique."' Besides Vice-President Taha himself ('very sneaky') this consisted of Nafie Ali Nafie, Minister of Federal Affairs (and a former head of the security service), Salah Gosh (current head of Security and Intelligence) and Awad Al Jaz (Minister of Petroleum). It was they, he said, who unleashed the Arab militias in response to a rebel attack on Al Fasher in April last year. When it got out of hand they sealed off the province and misled the rest of the government, including the President.

'How did the President find out?'

'When the foreigners told him.'

The Taha clique, he said, funded their activities by using off-budget oil revenues (he told the Ambassador that up to half Sudan's oil revenues are unaccounted for, some disappearing into bank accounts in Switzerland and Malaysia). All this was recounted with a broad smile. As though it was a great joke. At no point did he attempt to lower his voice. I later ran this past HE, who said it squared with everything he had been told although there were those who said that the Taha clique included President Bashir himself.

I did my last interview (with the BBC World Service) just before midnight, packed, wrote thank you letters and at 2 a.m. Bharat and I were delivered to the airport for the flight to London – so tired that I practically kissed the steps of the plane.

Monday, 20 September

Up at 05.30 and at my desk in the Commons by 06.45 tapping out a note for Jack on my Sudan trip. Then to the FCO for a day which included meetings with the president of Malawi and lunch with John Garang, the leader of the Sudanese People's Liberation Movement and a mountain of paperwork. I am writing this at 21.30, still at my desk, having just discovered in the press round-up an article in the *Mail on Sunday*, by a loathsome hack called Peter Dobbie saying what an idle, useless bunch we MPs are.

Tuesday, 21 September
The Foreign Office

A note from Des Browne confirming that he will, as promised, raise to 18 the age at which girls can be imported into the country for arranged marriages. A little victory in the teeth of official foot-dragging – both here and at the Home Office. Ann Cryer and Alice Mahon put me up to it. They are inundated with desperate young Asian women trying to escape violent husbands or rapacious in-laws. The whole thing is a giant racket. If I could get away with it, I'd recommend raising the age limit to 24, as the Danes have done.

Thursday, 23 September
Sunderland

To Hartlepool for a couple of hours' canvassing. A deeply depressing experience. Lib Dem posters everywhere, lots of 'outs', entire streets with only a handful of 'weak' Labour. Some too weak even to drag themselves away from their television sets to answer the door. An unpleasant blond, forty-something woman was overheard to say that she was 'sick of the lot of us'. ('I'm not that keen on you either, love,' I wanted to say.) No one mentioned Iraq. A general air of indifference, apathy, depression. We'll be lucky to hold on …

Monday, 27 September
The Labour Party Conference, Brighton

A brief encounter with Gordon Brown and entourage in an upper corridor of the Metropole: he inflicted what I took to be a friendly punch on my right shoulder and walked on without either slackening his pace or altering his facial expression. 'Behaving yourself?' I called after him. From behind, only an icy silence. That's my card marked. What I should have said was, 'Brilliant speech, Gordon.'

Tuesday, 28 September
Brighton

For the first time in several years I went in to listen to The Man. Outside there were several thousand baying huntsmen and their hounds. And inside, too, as it turned out. About 20 minutes into the speech half a dozen zealots rose in their seats and heckled The Man to a standstill. He handled them well, remaining calm throughout and quickly getting back on track. Ten pledges, some rather modest (among the promises flashed up on the screen behind him was a promise to build 10,000 new social houses by 2008). His tone throughout was non-confrontational; there was even an air of contrition, but no actual apology. At no point did he sound like a man contemplating retirement.

Wednesday, 29 September
Brighton

Out with the Ramblers Association for a five-mile hike across the Downs followed by a pleasant lunch in a village pub. A last-minute change of route in order to outwit the Countryside Alliance, who, we were told, had laid on a big ambush. In the event, they lost our scent. Very satisfying.

I walked most of the way with Clare Short, who seemed happy and relaxed, but still very down on The Man. 'He should have made his support for the Americans conditional on a Middle East peace settlement. That was his moment. The Americans didn't want to go it alone.' She had pressed him on this. 'He said, "If I get Bush to publish the Road Map, will that make a difference?"'

She had said it would.

'"I'll ring him and come back to you tomorrow."'

That, according to Clare, is how she was talked out of resigning first time around.

Thursday, 30 September
Brighton

On parade first thing this morning for Jack's big speech. I, inadequate as ever, in my crumpled number three suit, the one purchased at Heathrow, en route to Addis. Shoes unpolished since yesterday's walk on the Downs. Jack has a thing about shoes. His are always gleaming. I suspect he judges others by the state of theirs, in which case that's another little test that I fail miserably. Sure enough, he glanced down at my feet as soon as he entered the green room and, it may have been my imagination, visibly winced. Never mind, he was in great good humour. 'I shall tell conference what a fine fellow you are.'

'Don't put it to a vote.'

'I won't.'

Much laughter.

Jack has been in his element this week, spending hours in back rooms, sweet-talking the unions out of backing a resolution calling for withdrawal from Iraq. Needless to say he has triumphed. 'The Politburo has met. It's all sorted. Just like the early eighties, except that no one smokes anymore.'

In the event he was rewarded with a standing ovation.

Thirty-four children killed in Baghdad in a series of car bombs aimed at American soldiers.

Friday, 1 October
Brixton Road

Great excitement. The Man has gone into hospital for what is described as 'a minor procedure' to correct a heart flutter. At the same time he announced (in television interviews last night) that, if re-elected, he intends to serve a full third term. And to cap it all, it has also been disclosed that he and Cherie are paying an alleged £3.6 million (where on earth have they got that kind of money? Not from Geoffrey Robinson, I hope) for a house in Connaught Square. What kind of signal does that send to the millions of struggling punters whose votes we need? Clearly a fall-back position is being prepared in case it all goes wrong. My guess is that, if we win a third term, Gordon will be removed from the Treasury. That is certainly what Alan Milburn will be arguing for.

Oh, and by the way, we won Hartlepool – the Tories were in fourth place, behind UKIP. God bless UKIP.

Thursday, 7 October
Sunderland

At long last my Birmingham Six papers – 30 or 40 boxes – have gone to the university library at Hull. Two men in a van came and carted them away. Who knows if they will ever be any use to anyone, but I couldn't bring myself to pulp them.

Friday, 8 October

A call from Nigel Sheinwald, just back from a lightning visit to Sudan and Ethiopia with The Man. They spent two nights in the air and one on the ground – in a hotel in Addis. Less than a week after his heart op. Barmy. What's he trying to do? Kill himself? Nigel said it was for 'security reasons'. Anyway, it seems The Man has decided he wants to sort out the Ethiopia/Eritrea border dispute. He wants me to get together with the Canadian mediator, Lloyd Axworthy, to see if we can come up with some way of breaking the deadlock. A fat chance, but who am I to argue?

Monday, 20 October

Awoke at 4 a.m., unable to sleep for thinking about Mum. I just want to go to her and say, 'Come on, Mum. The nightmare's over. I am taking you home.'

It has been decided by some shadowy Whitehall committee that I require protection for my visit to east Africa later this week. Why, for goodness' sake? No one has ever suggested that I need protecting before. This afternoon two Special Branch officers came to explain. Kenya, apparently, is the problem. Nothing personal, but there are credible if vague reports that a local franchise of al-Qaida is planning to celebrate Ramadan with an attack on Western interests. I pointed out (a) that I shall scarcely be leaving the W1 area of Nairobi and (b) that I am hardly likely to be noticed until after I have left. If anyone in Kenya needs protecting, it is our highly visible High Commissioner, Edward Clay, and he apparently doesn't qualify. Anyway, it seems I have no choice. It has been decided and that is that.

'How many will there be?'

'Only two – and they'll be very discreet.'

No sooner were they out the door than my diary secretary reported that six visas had been applied for. Six, for heavens' sake? I rang Edward Clay who confirmed that an advance party of three had already arrived. Goodness knows how much all this will cost the public purse. If I'd known earlier, I would have called the whole thing off.

Tuesday, 21 October
The Cabinet Room, Number 10

The Prime Minister's 'asylum stock take'. My first such meeting, having only just been given FCO responsibility for asylum policy. I have prepared carefully only to discover on arrival that the document which is to form the basis for discussion has been omitted from my file, placing me at a disadvantage to everyone else around the table. I sit, quietly seething, hoping not to be noticed. Which is not easy since the main ministerial line-up is Des Browne (in the hot seat),

David Blunkett, Jack (who departed early) and I. Various other ministers with peripheral interests are scattered around the end of the table. Fortunately Des performs magnificently in that ponderous, considered Scots lawyerly way of his. As it turns out my services are scarcely required, but after an hour and a half in which I do no more than nod ostentatiously in the right places I decide to register my presence with a point about the various fiddles surrounding arranged marriages. Briefly, I had The Man's full attention, even though this is a wholly new front, and politically very risky. Blunkett chips in, to the effect that there was uproar when he dipped his toe in that particular water.

'Political dynamite,' says Paul Boateng, 'don't touch it with a barge pole.'

The Man says gently, 'I think, Chris, we'll have to park that for the time being, although I acknowledge that there are issues.' And on we go.

Incidentally, it emerged that the number of new migrants from the Accession countries so far amounts to 75,000, rather than the 13,000 predicted by a bunch of academic researchers from London University. It was decided to present the figures as good news, evidence of a thriving economy etc. A nice try, but I somehow doubt the tabloids will fall for it.

At 5 p.m. Bharat and I set off for Heathrow and Nairobi.

Wednesday, 22 October
Nairobi

Suddenly, I am The Man. Yesterday I travelled to work on a number 159 bus and now, as if in a dream, I am racing around in a convoy of Land Cruisers shadowed by two minders, Steve and Toby, and a wagonload of Kenyan police officers headed by a rotund, cheerful female superintendent. Sirens wail, lights flash, doors open and close without my so much as touching them and, much to my embarrassment, the traffic is held back at junctions by saluting policemen to allow our convoy to pass. 'This side, please, sir,' says Toby indicating the seat behind his. 'Then I can get to you quickly.' Meekly, I obey, all resistance abandoned. From now on I shall go with the flow.

Item One on today's long agenda: a call on Abdullahai Yusuf, the new 'President' of Somalia. At the moment, of course, he is nothing of the sort. Just a man in a hotel in Nairobi. Later, in another hotel, I addressed the new Somali 'parliament', which comprises some of the very people who have reduced Somalia to rubble. My message: reconciliation, dialogue etc ... From the backbenches ominous cries of 'And unity.'

Friday, 24 October
State House, Nairobi

An hour and a quarter with President Kibaki, the last half-hour tête à tête; our first encounter since Edward's vomit speech. Kibaki as ever, ponderous, not entirely with it, at one point confusing Somalia and Sudan. He perked up a bit when we were alone. V pissed off with Edward. Why hadn't Edward come to see him, excellent access etc. (Edward says he had been trying to see him for months, but the flunkies kept on blocking.) We talked corruption. I suggested a register of interests for MPs, tighter procurement rules, suspension of ministers under a cloud etc. Kibaki insisted he's on the case, but that a register of interests would never get through Parliament as presently composed. One wonders whether the old boy is going to make it to the end of his first term, let alone a second. He was a big man in his day but his day was some time ago. His bad luck – and Kenya's – that he should have come to power in his declining years.

On television this evening I was asked if the UK isn't meddling too much in Kenya. Maybe, but why should we pour our aid into a big hole?

Saturday, 25 October
Al Mansoor Hotel, Hargeisa (Somaliland)

We flew up to Addis, lunched at the Residence, and touched down at Hargeisa in the late afternoon. 'No need to go into the terminal. We will just slip out the back', advised Bob Dewar as we taxied to a halt. I looked out of the porthole through which I could see miles of red carpet, a guard of honour, little girls holding fading pictures of the Queen, a police band and the entire government, minus the President, lined up waiting to greet us. "I think you've misread the tea-leaves, Ambassador" I replied.

Accompanied by the Foreign and Interior Ministers, we set off into town in a long convoy of Land Cruisers, preceded by an escort of policemen on Chinese motorcycles with flashing red poles on the back. Along the way, people applauding, waving, ululating and holding up signs saying 'No Mogadishu'. To make quite sure I had got the message, we did a lap of honour.

The most striking thing about Hargeisa is the plastic bags. The very trees are sprouting them. They infest grass and scrub, clog drains and streams. No public space is free of them.

This evening, dinner with President Riyale, who occupies just about the only house in Hargeisa that survived Siad Barre's holocaust. Before we set out Edna Adan, the Foreign Minister, showed me a video of Hargeisa as it looked circa 1991. The destruction is awesome. Before dinner a private meeting with the President, which sometimes got quite heated. I, as advised, urging dialogue and reconciliation. He, demanding to know why Somaliland has been abandoned by the West having done everything we asked: rebuilding their country from ruins, establishing a fledgling democracy, co-operating over terrorism … In truth I am entirely sympathetic. On no account must we sell these people down the river.

As I am preparing for bed, a knock on the door. It is one of my Special Branch minders. 'Sorry to disturb you, sir, but if the lights go out break one of these.' A luminous yellow glow. 'So we can see where you are,' he explains, adding, 'Whatever you do, don't pick up a red one. The person with the red one gets shot.'

Sunday, 26 October
Berbera

A dry, dusty, tired place that has seen better days. A huge, strategic deepwater port on the Gulf of Aden, enclosed by a long, thin spit of sand. Apart from the occasional drizzle, there has been no rain in Berbera for four years.

We swept into town in a huge convoy of Land Cruisers (at one point I counted 26), preceded by a truckload of police at the front of which stood a man in a luminous orange jacket and a crash helmet, vigorously waving down oncoming traffic. I travelled with Edna Adan, a formidable woman who trained in London as a midwife (Somalia's first), doing her rounds by bicycle in Kennington, Camberwell and Brixton. By the age of 30 she was married to the Somali president, later also the first president of independent Somaliland. Somewhere along the line he and Edna separated, Somalia disintegrated and she went off to work for the World Health Organisation, from which she retired with a good pension only to return in 1991 and, seeing the state of her country, felt obliged to come home and help rebuild. She started by building a gleaming new maternity hospital, her pride and joy which, a tad immodestly perhaps, is named after her.

Edna pointed out the sights – the hollowed-out shell of what was once a Russian hospital, the modest house where she spent her early childhood, the broken building with ornate porches that was once the local grocery store. And here and there magnificent, crumbling, derelict (yet multi-occupied) villas enclosed by verandahs on which in years gone by the panjandrums of a bygone age breakfasted as the sun rose over the Gulf of Aden.

Monday, 27 October
Al Mansoor Hotel, Hargeisa

Bharat is the latest member of our party to be struck down with a stomach bug. I, happily, remain unscathed.

Breakfast with John Drysdale, a delightfully refined old Englishman who came to Somaliland with the army in 1943 and has lived here on and off ever since. He is in the process of mapping and registering land-ownership for the entire country. Then to the war cemetery, where I laid a wreath in memory of British soldiers who died here, seeing off the Italians. Then to one of the mass graves on the outskirts of the city, where in 1988 the southern warlords murdered unknown thousands. ('General' Morgan, one of the chief perpetrators, is still swaggering around Nairobi. No wonder the Somalilanders fear an outbreak of 'peace'.) Then a meeting with half a dozen ministers, each of whom presented a long wish list of requests for aid.

Then to the fledgling parliament, to address a joint session. My aim, to assure the Somalilanders that the international community is not going to push them into a forced marriage with the south. This attracts one of the few rounds of applause. Talk of dialogue and reconciliation is received with less enthusiasm. For light relief I chide them gently over the absence of women. This is a big event. My speech is to be broadcast across the country. I stand at the rostrum, swatting cameras and tape recorders thrust to within an inch of my nose, pausing after every paragraph to allow for translation, looking them firmly in the eye. The applause, when I sit down, is lukewarm. Suspicion runs deep. Half a dozen questions. All on the same theme: the wickedness of the southerners, the perfidy of the international community and the inevitable demand for recognition. Our exchanges become heated. Several times the Speaker has to call for order. Once I, too, came close to losing my cool. At the end the redoubtable Edna made a little speech. I've no idea what she said, but it seemed to mollify them. We parted on reasonable terms, shaking hands along the way.

Tuesday, 28 October
The Residence, Addis

Our plane (to Nairobi) is delayed. I am writing this in bright sunshine, by the pergola, next to the thatched summer house in HE's garden. A giant tortoise (neck extended) eyes me cautiously from the lawn. As do my Ethiopian minders, discreetly concealed in the shrubbery. Where I go they follow, even trailing around HE's vegetable garden, affecting an interest in carrots, onions and artichokes. There was none of this nonsense on previous visits.

Today in the centre of Addis Ababa I glimpsed a sad little tableau: a small, bewildered, blind person, no more than five or six years old, standing alone on a little square of cloth, a hand tentatively outstretched, turning this way and that, as pedestrians hurried by, oblivious. She wasn't badly dressed, a headscarf knotted under her chin, a little pair of jeans, a warm jacket; her large round, swollen face. Observing from the shadows, a woman (the child's mother?) propped against a wall, enveloped in a dirty shawl. A few seconds and the little person was lost from sight, but I can see her still and will do for months to come.

Out before dawn for a stroll up the hill behind the embassy with Bharat, my two remaining minders, Steve and Toby, and a couple of Ethiopian guides. In the twilight, outside the Residence, we glimpsed a pair of jackals making their way across HE's lawn and into the trees.

Then to see Prime Minister Meles, at his request. Seyoum, the Foreign Minister also present. To my amazement Meles announced that he is proposing to do exactly what I have been urging on him: accept in principle the report of the Boundary Commission, pay Ethiopia's arrears and appoint delegates to the demarcation commission. First, he has to convince his executive and then Parliament. It will not be popular, he says, but he is confident he can swing it. He expects to be in a position to go public by the middle of next month. Until then we are sworn to secrecy.

'Wonderful, but what persuaded you?'

'You did.'

Somehow I doubt that. Others have been making similar points, but what seems to have registered was my oft-repeated phrase about the need for Ethiopia to scramble back onto the moral high ground until now (however improbably) occupied by the Eritrean president, Isaias. Of course, he's under no illusions: Isaias will denounce the move as a trick, but the Eritrean people, who are desperate for peace, may take a different view.

I came away with a spring in my step. For once we are not just going through the motions. An achievement beckons. Who knows, we might just possibly avert another war.

In the late afternoon we flew down to Nairobi where Edward Clay had arranged a dinner at the Muthaiga Club (where the recent John le Carré was filmed) with half a dozen ambassadors, to discuss Somalia. I did an interview with the BBC. Then, police cars fore and aft, we were taken in convoy back to the airport, departing for London just around midnight. What a day.

Monday, 1 November
The Foreign Office

An extraordinary situation. I have been asked to respond to two adjournment debates this week – a half-hour one on a British journalist who was shot by the Israelis in Gaza and the other a three-hour general debate on terrorism in response to a select committee report – but no one is willing to produce a speech. The reaction of the Consular Department when asked for a draft on the journalist was, 'We are too busy. Why don't you ask the MP to withdraw?' As for the other, the Counter-Terrorism Department is flatly, brazenly refusing to co-operate saying that it's a matter for the Iraq desk. Officials on the Iraq desk reply with equal insolence that they are too busy because they are moving office. Result: stalemate. Apparently this tug-of-war has been going on for a week. Caron, my Assistant Private Secretary, has been too embarrassed to tell me, and is tearing her hair out. In four years in government, I have never come across anything like this. Suddenly it becomes clear that, for many people in this building, accounting to Parliament is a low priority.

This afternoon we finally managed to wring from Consular officials half a dozen pre-cooked pages consisting of a long screed of dates listing ministerial representations to the Israelis and a lot of irrelevant material about the Middle East peace process. To the end and the beginning, someone has attached two or three sentences of guff which must have taken all of five minutes to tap out. This borders on contempt.

In desperation Caron contacted Michael Jay's office for advice, but word came back that he was too busy, we should sort it out ourselves. The consular debate is tomorrow afternoon. It looks as if this is going to go to the wire.

Tuesday, 2 November

At my desk by 07.30. Michael Williams called in and I unburdened myself to him. Apparently there have been problems elsewhere, too. Mike agrees we cannot let this pass. For the moment, however, I must concentrate on sorting out this mess. The consular debate is at 3.30

this afternoon and so far no one has blinked. I would write the damn speech myself except that (a) there is no slot in my diary and (b) I don't have the information. What angers me is that somewhere in this building there are people who could tap out the necessary words in no time at all.

Later

Help is at hand. Caron and Bharat have managed to secure the services of a couple of professional speechwriters, one of whom is going to do the consular debate and the other is promising a terrorism speech by noon tomorrow.

Result

By 3.30 p.m. a halfway decent speech on the poor guy killed in Gaza had been put into my hand. Just as well, his sisters were in the gallery. We live dangerously.

Wednesday, 3 November

Everyone pleased with my little breakthrough in Addis. Jack has endorsed my minute on the subject with the words 'good work' in his distinctive red ink. This afternoon I entertained Lloyd Axworthy, the Canadian mediator, to lunch. Later I took him to Nigel Sheinwald at Number 10 – and The Man dropped in for 20 minutes. It has been agreed that I should go back to Asmara soonest to test the water with Isaias.

Thursday, 4 November

To Westminster Hall for the terrorism debate, armed at last with a competent though bland speech into which I had spent the morning trying to inject some life. A simple matter and yet I was uncommonly nervous. Iraq and terrorism are not my natural territory and, as the only member of the government to have voted against the Iraq adventure, it was necessary to keep a straight face and stick strictly to the script. Endless questions: 'What is the government doing about human rights in Pakistan/poppy-growing in Afghanistan/WMD in Russia?' You name it. A huge, platitudinous flow of paper from officials. I, lacklustre, stumbling, dry-mouthed. I should have just got up and answered their questions instead of ploughing through my script. I could see them thinking, 'That Chris Mullin is not all he's cracked up to be.'

Home on the 20.00. A ghastly week. Thank God it's nearly over.

Friday, 5 November

The masses have rejected, by a margin of four to one, the proposed north-east regional assembly. That it was defeated comes as no surprise (though no one anticipated the scale of the rout). What clearer evidence could there be of the growing gulf between leaders and led? In 17 years I cannot recall a single letter from a citizen demanding a regional assembly whereas the rulers of the north-east talked of little else. Nor did it help that the referendum was held when politicians are at an all-time low in public esteem.

Tuesday, 9 November

Our family home, in Manor Drive, Great Baddow, changes hands today after 50 years. The new people are moving in immediately. Most of Mum's goods and chattels have gone to auction or to the dump. A few things have been spared – photo albums, the Tibetan rug, Dad's paintings have been shared out. So that's it. There is nothing left.

Wednesday, 10 November

In the Foreign Office courtyard, I came across David Manning, on his way to brief The Man for his visit to Washington at the weekend. He thinks there is a chance of progress on the Middle East. 'I believe there is a will in the White House. The death of Arafat opens a window of opportunity.' He seemed to agree with my suggestion that the only way to make the Israelis co-operate is to threaten the loan guarantees, as George Bush (senior) had done.

Tuesday, 16 November

An awkward question from Eric Avebury: 'When did HMG first receive reports of a possible coup in Equatorial Guinea?' The truth is that there have been rumours of coup attempts for months, some of which have even been reported in the press. Our original answer referred to press reports, but Jack deleted the reference, making it look as though we had advance knowledge which we kept to ourselves. As a result, a number of people with no particular interest in Equatorial Guinea, but with nothing better to do, are busying themselves trying to organise a crisis where none exists. The mercenary Simon Mann, at present in a Zimbabwean jail, is to be flown to Equatorial Guinea to testify at the trial of those accused of being involved; whether he's done so voluntarily and is ratting on his erstwhile colleagues or whether he is being extradited against his wishes remains to be seen. As yet it is unclear whether or not this will turn into a fully blown crisis, but one can see the possibilities.

Thursday, 18 November

The latest on Equatorial Guinea: South Africa is being asked to extradite Mark Thatcher. He is obviously worried and has asked to see our High Commissioner, Ann Grant, presumably with a view to learning what we can do to help. The possibility that Thatcher junior will end up in one of Obiang's stinking jails would set the cat among the pigeons. It can only be a question of time until we start receiving inquiries from Number 10. As luck would have it South Africa's airhead High Commissioner called on me this afternoon (to press her country's case for a seat on the UN Security Council – which she did with extraordinary incompetence). I took the opportunity to say that we didn't think it would look very good for South Africa to send Mark Thatcher to Equatorial Guinea and she undertook to pass the word. It's probably a false alarm. South Africa and EG have no extradition treaty.

Today – at last – we used the Parliament Act to force through the Hunting Bill. A huge hullabaloo from the hoorays, who are threatening fire and brimstone. Our side, buoyant, but not yet convinced we have carried the day. We have taken on the mightiest vested interest in the land and one with infinite resources at its disposal. This is a dispute we must win, having long ago ceased to be about the fate of a few thousand deer and foxes. It's about who governs. Us or Them? And on that the jury is still out.

Saturday, 20 November

Rang Mum, who sounded deceptively bright. In passing she remarked, without any trace of self-pity, 'I think I have overstayed my welcome on this earth.'

Friday, 26 November
Mamba Point, Monrovia, US Ambassador's Residence

To see Monrovia is to glimpse Armageddon. A million people live here without running water or electricity. This is a place where, until the coming of the UN, the Lords of Chaos had free rein. Where youths armed to the teeth and drugged to the eyeballs rampaged at will, looting, raping, murdering. Much of the city is derelict, shop fronts peppered with bullet holes, houses (still inhabited) half demolished or half built; roofless, windowless, burned-out buildings in every street. And in every street a church. Can there be any place on earth that has as many churches as Liberia? So many Christians and so little Christianity. God is everywhere. 'The blood of Jesus prevails over his enemies,' says a slogan on a billboard outside the Church of the God of Prophecy. 'Oh God, please give us your choice of leader for Liberia,' says another (divine guidance may well be required: so far more than 40 presidential candidates have declared – the latest an international footballer who has every chance of winning). A sign on the road from the airport read: 'Time is running out for Liberia'. You can say that again.

Sunday, 27 November
Butao, Nimba province

By helicopter to the interior for a hard day's factfinding. A burly, surly young Ukrainian in dark glasses, with a gold chain around his neck and camouflage trousers, wishes us a nice flight in a deadpan Aeroflot voice. Our party has been gatecrashed by a couple of ministers from the interim government, accompanied by a plump, overprivileged woman dressed as if for a party rather than a visit to the dispossessed. The Liberians are each carrying natty little plastic lunch boxes and the health minister has an ostentatious gold ring. They are here to give the illusion of activity. The truth is, of course, that the Liberian Ministry of Health is an empty shell; the only medical services are provided by foreigners. The man from UNHCR is apologetic: 'We know they are not real ministers, but we have to pretend that they are.'

We fly for 90 minutes over forested hills and uninhabited valleys, coming down in a clearing near the border with Côte d'Ivoire. A convoy of white UN Land Cruisers (I counted 16) awaits, watched by a gaggle of bemused Liberians. We set off along a forest track. I quietly fuming. How are we to have any meaningful contact with the locals, if we go about like this? The UNHCR man devises a plan: we let the others go ahead and then detach ourselves from the convoy and head off to the river crossing that leads into Côte d'Ivoire. Côte d'Ivoire looks like becoming the next west African domino to fall to the Lords of Chaos. In recent weeks ten thousand refugees have poured across. The aid agencies are faced with a difficult dilemma. Do they hand out food and risk becoming a magnet or do they let the refugees and their host families go hungry in the hope that they will make their way home? There is not much to see by the river. Just a few youths in a dugout canoe that serves as a ferry. After we have been there ten minutes the rest of the convoy arrives and we hastily clamber back into our Land Cruisers and head off in the opposite direction; as we look back we can see them turning round to follow us; it is like a scene from a *Carry On* film.

We make our way to a village. I insist on getting out and walking. Someone points out a tree laden with grapefruit, another with oranges; there are coffee beans, cocoa and wild swamp rice and on the way to the river we pass two small boys carrying home half a dozen small fish apiece. Yet cultivation is minimal. Everything grows randomly. This is a land in which almost anything will grow. And yet most of the country's food is imported. In Monrovia tomatoes are said to cost two dollars apiece.

The natives are friendly, but the air of dissatisfaction palpable. This is the fourth convoy of UN factfinders in ten days and so far not a grain of rice has reached them. Back in the village there is an impromptu outbreak of singing and dancing. A row of chairs has been set out. We can't just run away. A speech is called for. 'We are trying to help,' I say. 'I know your lives are hard. Please be patient.' More applause, ululating, singing. Then back into our air-conditioned Land Cruisers and away we go. As we were leaving, I overheard a woman say, 'They think we don't understand, but we do.'

On the way back our helicopter collides with a large bird. There is an ominous judder and then a single feather drifts in through the open porthole.

Sunday, 28 November
Monrovia

Breakfast with my host, US Ambassador John Blaney, in his conservatory. Outside a storm rages. Waves pounding the beach, the palm trees swaying.

Ambassador Blaney is a lonely man. His wife and daughters are in southern California, forbidden even to visit him in this dangerous place. So he lives alone, save for three servants, in this fortified mansion overlooking the limitless ocean. When he goes to bed at night he seals off the bedroom corridor behind a reinforced steel door. If he retires before us, he leaves out a copy of the Oxford Pocket Russian dictionary to indicate that we should slide the bolts. If the dictionary is not there, we leave the door unbolted.

Everyone is afraid of upsetting the African Union, being accused of neo-colonialism or racism, Blaney tells us. 'The fact is that this is a failed state. There aren't any functioning institutions to plug into. We've got to abandon our domestic hang-ups. Stop thinking

20th century liberal thoughts. We got to do what helps people. What works. And by the way, this is only the beginning of the 21st century. We're going to see lots more failed states. So why don't we sit down and think about it?' My sentiments precisely.

Monday, 29 November

Charles Taylor's ghost is everywhere in Monrovia. It is 18 months since he was ushered off the premises by a trio of West African presidents to the applause of a relieved and (at the time) grateful international community, not to mention a certain amount of relief among the citizens of Liberia, or most of them. In an ideal world he would have been delivered to the Special Court in Sierra Leone, where a cell ('the presidential suite') awaits him, to account for his crimes in that country. But west Africa is not an ideal world. Far from it. So instead ex-President Taylor enjoys a comfortable exile in Calabar, Nigeria, courtesy of his reluctant host President Obasanjo, who, having given his word that Taylor would have safe passage out of the country, feels obliged to stick by it.

As long as there is a possibility that he may one day return, a lot of people are going to keep their options open. It is unlikely that he will take a chance while there are 14,500 UN soldiers in the country, but they won't be there for ever. And if by chance he did arrive one morning at J. J. Roberts International Airport there is absolutely nothing the UN could do. Its mandate does not include a power of arrest.

We have time on our hands so we drive to the Ducor Palace Hotel, maybe 20 storeys of steel and (once upon a time) glass, dominating the city. From the terrace, fine views along the coast to the port. Here, in another age, the elite of west Africa cavorted. Not any more. Today the Ducor Palace is a vision of hell. A glimpse of what the Park Lane Hilton would look like after the end of the world. Not that it is empty. On the contrary, every room is taken. The destitute are crowded into every nook and cranny. The windows have gone and so have every fixture and fitting that matters – tiles, toilets, taps; not that it matters because there is no water or electricity anyway. At one end of the terrace a ragged child is sifting through several hundred cubic feet of garbage; we pick our way gingerly around the dollops of human excreta.

Tuesday, 30 November

Home to a new crisis. David Blunkett is ensnared in a messy row over access to a child he fathered with someone else's wife; also, tricky questions about the use of travel warrants, official cars and indefinite leave to remain for a Philippino nanny. Touch and go whether he can survive.

To Number 10 for a reception. Cherie radiant; The Man tired, tense, dehydrated, eyes wandering. Blunkett was there, too, looking lonely.

Wednesday, 1 December

Humphry Wakefield has been leaving me frantic messages all week. The walled garden at Chillingham has finally come on the market. Guide price £500,000 for the Estate House and £145,000 for the garden, although he expects it to go for much more. I will start work immediately.

Sunday, 5 December

This morning's news is that Blunkett's ex has asked to testify against him at the official inquiry into the nanny's visa. Until now I thought he would survive, but this could prove fatal.

Tuesday, 7 December

Jack took me aside after the morning briefing and asked, 'Where is this Blunkett business going?' Like everyone else, he has been supportive of David, but was annoyed to discover (courtesy of the *Daily Mail*) that Blunkett has been slagging him off behind his back.

Yesterday David rang to offer an apology, which Jack graciously accepted while at the same time reminding him that this was not a first offence: three years ago JP had complained in Cabinet about David's bad-mouthing of colleagues. Jack quoted the so-called Rumsfeld Rules: 'Never criticise a successor or a predecessor. You do not walk in their shoes.'

Wednesday, 8 December

A call to the Heritage Lottery Fund to get its act together regarding Chillingham. Alas, it is all very complicated. Before HLF can lift a finger it needs access, education, conservation and sustainability plans etc, all of which will take months, which we don't have. Can't they just buy it and sort out the details later? Apparently not. There is a fund for emergencies, but it is only for Titians, medieval manuscripts and the like; not 18th-century walled gardens.

Monday, 13 December

An interesting valedictory from Our Man in Mauritius, who complains that 'a doctrinaire over-emphasis on strategic priorities, resource management and performance has paradoxically become a straitjacket that reduces flexibility, constrains our bilateral relations and thereby lowers our standing.' He goes on:

> Perpetual re-examination, renaming and reprioritisation take their toll. Too much of our effort has gone into managing and studying ourselves with the result that the tools of our trade have rusted and bilateral relations have been downgraded. Substance is giving way to process. Correctness has become the enemy of another vital ingredient of diplomacy – a sense of humour. It is difficult these days to raise a smile in London.

The last gasp of the old guard; or does he have a point?

Tuesday, 14 December

On the bus this morning, thinking: this time last year everything was still in its natural place. If I dialled Chelmsford 71509, a familiar voice would answer. Dad was still shuffling between the drinks cabinet and the sofa in the living room, reading the *Telegraph* from cover to cover, making daily visits to the King's Head. Mum still out and about, back and forth between the kitchen and her seat by the French windows. Only a few more days of normality left.

To Number 10 for a meeting about the detentions at Belmarsh. Dramatis personae, arrayed along one side of the Cabinet table, include the Attorney General, the Home Secretary, the Noble Lord Grocott, Eliza Manningham-Buller, Charlie Falconer. On the other side: The Man, Jonathan Powell, Sally Morgan and a functionary taking notes.

The Attorney General outlines the options. His starting point is that we should obey the forthcoming Lords' judgement, which is expected to go against the government. Alternatively, we could amend the law – 'the difficulty is we don't know what to put in its place.'

'It will be a big thing, if we don't accept the judgement,' the Attorney General said.

To which Charlie Falconer added, 'If they go against us on whether or not there is an emergency, we're fucked.'

A chandelier swayed gently. 'Fucked' is not a word often heard in the Cabinet Room – especially not from the Lord Chancellor. The Man's eyebrow tweaked. Someone said, 'Excise that from the record.'

The Man was tapping the table. 'We can't have a lot of people going on TV saying, "It's disgraceful; this is how they treat Muslims." We can't have that. We have to be clear: these people are held on suspicion of involvement in terrorism and we can't take the risk of releasing them.'

That, for now, is the line, though how long it can be held is any-one's guess. As we were leaving Ms Manningham-Buller said to me, 'The Americans would be very upset if we let them go; they want some of them.'

Wednesday, 15 December

The Blunkett crisis refuses to die. I ran into John Williams, who said, 'Jack is so angry that I'm afraid he'll say something publicly and lose the high ground.' Later, just after six, as I was making my way to the Foreign Office Christmas party in the Locarno Room, it was announced that Blunkett had resigned. Whereupon up popped Jack and paid a dignified little tribute. A professional to his fingertips.

Thursday, 16 December

A lift back to the office with Jack after seeing President Kagame in the Four Seasons Hotel at Park Lane.

'You don't have a car, do you Chris?'

I gave my usual line about the numbers 3 and 159 buses continuing to run past my door, even though I am a minister.

'So how do you manage with boxes?'

An alarm bell rang.

'I remain at the office until the paperwork is finished; until midnight if necessary.'

'And how do you manage at weekends?'

Oh, oh, dangerous territory. On no account mention that in nearly four years in government, no red box has ever reached my home. Or that life in the foothills of government isn't quite the same as life at the top.

'The office ring or fax; in recesses they send up boxes to my office in Sunderland.'

That seemed to satisfy him, but one can never be sure. Jack has very good antennae.

A call to the top person at the Landmark Trust to try and interest him in Chillingham. 'Very sorry, we only take on buildings in decay; the house doesn't need us.'

'No, but the walled garden does.'

'Yes, but we only take on buildings.'

Slam goes another door.

Saturday, 25 December
Christmas Day

We opened the presents by the tree, then drove up into the hills to see our friends Malcolm, Helen and family. Snow, brilliant sunshine. Malcolm, who teaches in the village primary school, recounted how he found himself teaching a class of six children watched over by three OFSTED inspectors who were, in turn, watched over, by three of Her Majesty's Inspectors. You couldn't make it up.

Monday, 27 December

There has been a huge, apocalyptic disaster around the shores of the Indian Ocean – an earthquake, followed by a vast tidal wave. Unknown thousands have been washed away, including many tourists.

Wednesday, 29 December

This afternoon we returned Mum to the nursing home. Desperately sad, leaving her there, but what can we do? You can't help someone who doesn't want to be helped and Mum stoically refuses to co-operate with allcomers, refusing help with bathing and insisting on cutting her own hair (of which she has made a mess) even though there is a hairdresser on the premises. Above all, she refuses to contemplate a move.

Thursday, 30 December

The death toll from the tsunami is now said to exceed 120,000, and is rising.

Friday, 31 December
Brixton Road

When we arrived last night, I parked in the 'Residents only' section on Groveway, intending to move before the 08.30 witching hour. Alas, however, I arrived ten minutes late to find that not only had I been issued with a £60 ticket but that the car was shackled and on the point of being hoisted onto the back of a 'parking enforcement' truck; had I arrived a minute later it would have cost a minimum of £250 to retrieve. This is at 08.40 on New Year's Eve in a half-deserted street, for goodness' sake. How can this be justified for an offence specified on the ticket as being illegally parked between 08.36 and 08.38? Surely, a decent interval is supposed to elapse between ticketing and removal, indeed that used to be the case. Now, it seems, the newly privatised traffic wardens and the driver of the tow-away truck operate in tandem. 'This is Lambeth,' remarked the truck driver as he cheerfully removed the shackles from the car; the traffic warden, on the other hand, was surly. We had the following exchange.

'Are you on a percentage?'

'No comment.'

'I am only making a polite inquiry, brother.'

'That's a harsh question.'

'What is the answer?'

By now the car had been released. Without another word the wretched warden climbed into the passenger seat, ignoring my New Year good wishes, and off they went in search of another kill.

In the evening we went for a drink with Richard and Patricia Moberly in Wincott Street. Frank Field was there. He said he had told The Man that he needed more bright, young, attractive people in his Cabinet. The last thing we need, in my view. What we need is people of depth and integrity, with rather more experience of the world than a year or two as a special adviser. Talking of bright, attractive people: Frank agreed with my view that Hilary Benn is a potential leader.

Later, we walked down to Lambeth Bridge and watched the midnight fireworks, returning to Brixton Road to find a man lying sound asleep in the front garden.

CHAPTER SEVEN

2005

Saturday, 1 January 2005
Brixton Road

Awoke around eight and suddenly remembered the man asleep in the front garden. Peered gingerly through a gap in the kitchen curtains, fearing that he might be dead. Happily, however, he had disappeared, an indent in the leaves where his body had been.

Sunday, 2 January
St Bede's Terrace, Sunderland

An answerphone message from Sir Humphry. The walled garden has gone. So that's it, then. The dream is over. A life that might have been extraordinary will now be ordinary.

Monday, 3 January

My New Year's resolution (the first for years) is to reduce my possessions. A step change, as they say in New Labour, is called for. Our house is choc-a-bloc. Cupboards bursting, chattels stuffed under every bed. The back staircase is so crammed that it is barely passable. And still unwanted, unneeded goods flow in. We all accumulate far too much in our lives and it all has to be thrown out when we die by relatives who have little or no feel for what is important and what is not. The clearing of Mum and Dad's house has brought that home forcefully.

Wednesday, 5 January
The Foreign Office

An envelope marked 'personal' – from the Permanent Secretary, Sir
Michael Jay (to whom, just before Christmas, I gave a copy of *A Very
British Coup*) – appeared in my in-tray. Inside a spoof letter addressed
to Harry Perkins, purportedly from Cedric Snow, FCO Permanent Secretary in the late eighties – expressing regret at (and denying knowledge of) the manner of Perkins's overthrow. It is elegantly written
(Michael has obviously gone to some trouble) and would make an
amusing appendix, were there to be another edition.

Friday, 7 January

Up at 4 a.m. to see Ngoc off to Vietnam in a howling gale.

Saturday, 8 January

Gale force winds for the third night running. Half of the chimney
stack on the house behind us has been brought crashing down the
roof; the other half hangs precariously. Our back gate has also been
blown open and twisted beyond repair.

Sunday, 9 January

A new Blair–Brown crisis is being organised. Briefers in both camps are
hard at work, egged on enthusiastically by hacks from the *Mail* and
the *Telegraph* who can hardly believe their luck. And, blow me down,
we have yet another interim biography; this one of Gordon, by a
Sunday Telegraph journalist who has obviously had high-level access.
According to the Friends of Gordon, in late '03 there was a dinner
hosted by JP in his apartment at Admiralty House at which The Man
again promised to stand down the following spring. Should we believe
this? My guess is that there were a few caveats which Gordon omitted
from his account of the conversation, but there is no doubt something happened around that time. I remember Jeff Rooker saying in
December '03 that the Friends of Gordon were putting it about that a

deal had been done and that The Man would go in the spring. Anyway, it's all deeply destabilising.

Monday, 10 January

To a crowded meeting of the parliamentary party, where Gordon and The Man were given a bollocking the like of which I have never previously witnessed over the damaging revelations in the weekend press about their rift. Clive Solely fired the first shot, talking of 'anger and frustration' at the apparent warfare between the two camps and warning of impending disaster if it wasn't stopped. Of the anonymous briefers, he said, 'They are not as anonymous as they seem to think. Journalists gossip, too. If they don't stop, I will name them.' He sat down to prolonged applause. Angela Eagle called for discipline at the top and said we could still lose. Dale Campbell Savours told Gordon to his face that he had either to deny or withdraw his widely quoted remark attributed to him about the integrity of The Man ('there is nothing you can say to me now that I could ever believe'). 'We can't go into the next election with that still on the record.' Barry Sheerman said, 'You two are brilliant when you work together, the party owes you so much, but you won't be forgiven if you make a mess of it.' Claire Ward, whose seat is marginal, said that the current infighting was disheartening for those in the front line. 'We expect better and demand better.'

Then, of all people, Tam Dalyell came to the rescue. 'Forgive me for changing the subject,' he said to general hilarity. It is not every day that Tam and Iraq offer light relief.

The Man was visibly shaken. 'I hear what you say,' he said. Then, no doubt hoping that he was speaking for Gordon, seated not three feet away, he added, 'We all have, and we will act on it.' Will they? It takes two to tango and the fact is that most of this is Gordon's doing. Bloody Gordon. He has no God-given right to inherit. The only reason he didn't run in 1994 was because he correctly calculated that he would have been smashed out of sight, if he had. It would have been better for everyone had he run, then the matter would be resolved once and for all.

Afterwards I dined at the Adjournment with Jean Corston. She agrees that Hilary Benn would be the most desirable successor and says she will look for an opportunity to raise the subject with The Man. She also said that she told him that he would have to stand down in two and a half years and not go on until the autumn of 2008, which seems to be his intention. How did he react? 'He was very cross with me.'

Tuesday, 11 January

Tommy McAvoy remarked regarding the impending vote on the change to sitting hours for which he wants me to do some canvassing, 'If you do a good job, I'll get you out of Limbo. You know where that is, Chris? I thought you would.'

How very odd. I hadn't realised I was in Limbo.

Wednesday, 12 January

Tea in the Pugin Room with Bruce Grocott. Bruce thinks it inevitable that Gordon will be the next leader whenever the moment comes, but he agrees that Hilary would make an attractive candidate, subject to the caveat that he hasn't yet been seriously tested ('DFID is the easiest job in the Cabinet'). He thinks, whatever The Man says publicly, that the changeover is likely to be around the ten-year mark – ie two years into the next term. 'The Americans got it about right, limiting their Presidents to two terms, any more than that and you begin to go mad. Look what happened to Thatcher.'

'Have you said that to The Man?'

'More or less.'

Bruce says that Gordon has never got over the fact that TB was his junior partner during the years in opposition and agrees that it might have been better if Gordon had stood and been beaten in 1994.

The Cabinet, says Bruce (who has been a fly on the wall at Cabinet meetings for eight years), is composed mainly of people who are average. I challenged this on the grounds (a) that he and I are average and (b) that the world is for ever being screwed up by brilliant people.

He immediately conceded. 'What I mean is that so many of them have no discernible politics.' Those Bruce rates include Margaret Beckett, David Blunkett, Alan Johnson, John Prescott, John Reid and Jack Straw. The rest he dismisses as 'managerial types – capable, efficient, but without an ideological anchor'.

We discussed Iraq. Bruce said, 'Tony's experience of the Labour Party was Hackney in the 1980s. He, therefore, tends to assume the party is out of touch with the real world, but on this occasion the dear old Labour Party was in the mainstream of public opinion – along with the Pope and the Archbishop of Canterbury.' The Man, says Bruce, has no understanding of the seriously bad people he is mixed up with in America because he wasn't politically active at the time of My Lai or the death squads in El Salvador. He is also blissfully – and perhaps wilfully – unaware that his friend George W. Bush and his brother came to power in Texas and Florida signing death warrants.

Sunday, 16 January

Not feeling too good lately. My knees have swollen up again, making it hard to kneel or bend; also a sharp pain at the back of my skull, on the inside.

Thursday, 20 January

A depressing little clip on the *Today* programme this morning: interviews with a group of mature women in Watford, a key marginal, who had all voted Labour in the last two elections. They all claimed to loathe The Man (one using almost exactly the sentence attributed to Gordon – 'I no longer believe a word he says'), none of them liked Howard either; they liked Charles Kennedy, but doubted his ability to govern. When asked what mattered to them, none mentioned the economy or the public services; no one was bothered about Iraq, except for the cost; immigration and asylum was the big issue. Reluctantly, I am coming to the conclusion that I don't like the electorate any more than they like us. Time to go?

This afternoon the Sudanese Ambassador came in and I had the pleasure of telling him that he could forget any talk of debt relief until there was progress in Darfur.

Monday, 24 January

A bad night, pains behind my eyes and at the back of my head. Set out for London stuffed with paracetamol. From the train I rang the Council's chief executive, Ged Fitzgerald, about the plastic bags in trees all over Sunderland.

At the House I ran into Tam Dalyell, who said, 'Chris, what are we going to do about Iraq?'

'I think we are stuck. What would you do?' I replied.

'Declare victory and end the occupation.'

'What do you think would happen if we did?'

'I think there would then be a period of calm.' He quoted one of his Iraqi contacts in support of the proposition.

'How many refugees do you think there would be?'

He cited his Iraqi contact again, 'No more than 1,000 of those who have collaborated with occupation.'

A very optimistic scenario but, who knows, it may come to that eventually.

Michael Howard has played the immigration card with a speech of outrageous cynicism: 'People will face a clear choice at the next election: unlimited immigration under Mr Blair or limited, controlled immigration under the Conservatives.' As he well knows, this is an outright lie. Immigration has never been so tightly controlled. The number of new asylum seekers has fallen by 70 per cent in the last two years, removals are up from 7,000 a year in 1997 to 17,000 last year and 80 per cent of new asylum applications are now processed in about two months, as opposed to an average of 22 months in the last days of the Tory regime. Nevertheless, as Howard well knows, the poison is impossible to counter. If he can keep it up, he will strike deep behind our lines.

In the evening, at the Protection Squad party at Scotland Yard, I had a friendly chat with John Major. He came out with his usual line:

'What are you doing supporting a reactionary government like this, clamping down on asylum seekers, abolishing jury trial ...?'

And I came out with mine: 'I am an establishment figure now, John.'

'I was always too left-wing for my party. I am getting more left-wing.'

Maybe, but he's still as cautious as ever. I bearded him about Howard's disgraceful asylum speech.

'I'm not going to comment on that.'

A pity. It needs a Tory of his stature to speak up.

We were interrupted by Cherie Blair, who waltzed in, ignoring me, and started conversation about the difficulties of life in the stratosphere: 'We've all been there ... scars on our back ...' etc. Amazing, she has a golden life and yet she thinks of herself as a victim.

Tuesday, 25 January

Still the pains in the back of my head, kept at bay with regular doses of ibuprofen.

Wednesday, 26 January

Up at 5.30 a.m. and off to Nigeria; still taking tablets for the pains in my head.

Thursday, 27 January
The Residence, Lagos

Breakfast with HE and deputy in the pavilion at the end of the garden; a blue kingfisher dipping in the pool. Afterwards we set off in the High Commission's little boat across the lagoon, through shoals of drifting rubbish, to inspect the visa section. When I last visited 18 months ago there were crowds laying siege day and night to the building. Since then the collection of applications has been outsourced to 30 different locations around the city and so the crowds have gone, but the pressure on staff remains enormous. Lagos is our biggest visa operation, attracting more applicants even than Islamabad. As in Pakistan the scale of the fraud is awesome: 'students' applying for courses that don't exist in colleges that don't exist, sponsored by sponsors who are either non-existent or unrelated, supported by documents that are forged; stolen passports that have been expertly 'washed' enabling new identities to be inserted; genuine passports that have had false visas and date stamps inserted to establish a false pattern of travel; British passports that have had two or three owners. So great is the fraud and perjury that about 80 per cent of applications from first-time visitors aged 30 and under are rejected. To make matters worse, in the six months since outsourcing made the system more efficient the number of applications has increased by a staggering 80 per cent. What are we going to do?

Saturday, 29 January

Abuja, Milton Keynes on the Equator as someone called it. Monstrous, soulless, unfinished; dissected by vast treeless, people-free avenues, empty save for convoys of excellencies racing back and forth, sirens wailing, between the Hilton and the conference centre.

My first engagement, a visit to the new headquarters of the anti-corruption commission, run by an energetic, determined, courageous former police officer – a ray of light in this sea of darkness. Early days yet, but there have been one or two modest triumphs: the chief inspector of police has recently been dismissed after an unexplained £20 million was found in his bank account; the governor of Plateau state is in disgrace after having been found in London with a suitcase full of money and a bank account containing an unexplained £920,000 – he cannot be prosecuted (governors being immune whatever their degree of venality), but his associates can – and are. Oh, but there is such a mountain to climb. Nothing works normally in Nigeria: the State electricity company produces little or no electricity; virtually no trains run on the railways; smouldering, stinking piles of domestic waste lie uncollected; the four oil refineries refine little or no oil and, to crown all, the Ajaokuta Kogi steel mill, built 20 years ago at a cost of $4–5 billion, has yet to produce a single ingot of steel. Any notion that the solution to Nigeria's problems is more aid or even debt relief (save under the most stringent conditions) is pure bunkum. Honest government is the issue.

Sunday, 30 January
The Residence, Abuja

Awoken at 7 a.m. by HE in dressing gown, fresh from his morning dip, bearing a mug of tea. Then to the Hilton for a prayer breakfast presided over by presidents Obasanjo, Njuoma, Kagame and Museveni, together with AU chairman Konare and Kofi Annan. They each took turns to read a lesson. All except Museveni (introduced by Obasanjo as 'that great son of Africa'), who was called upon to deliver the homily. He started with a line from Deuteronomy about borrowing. 'Africans specialise in borrowing. If they lend, they lend in ignorance. Uganda has been a donor many times, but we donate in ignorance. A kilo of raw cotton costs a dollar, yarn three dollars, finished cloth ten dollars. So Uganda has been donating at least nine dollars a kilo to the West …'

Then to Matthew 25: 14–29: the parable of the talents. The gist of Museveni's argument is that the Asians used wisely the talents that God had given them, but Africans had squandered theirs. By now the Great Son of Africa was in full flow, treating us to a lengthy historical analysis of African history replete with references to the Russian Revolution, the wars in Europe. There were dangerous moments ('I have not read the Koran. President Gaddafi gave me a copy, but I didn't have time to read it.'). Frozen expressions on the faces of President Mubarak and the Egyptian delegation, a few tables away. An outrageous piece of grandstanding and when the Great Son of Africa finally resumed his seat, glowing with self-satisfaction, the applause was thin.

Then to the conference hall for the opening of the summit. In the best Nigerian tradition the leaders show up two hours late and when they do, the headphones don't work so Chairman Konare's speech, in beautifully enunciated French, is wasted on most of us; likewise the address in Arabic by the secretary of the Arab League. Obasanjo spoke in English, but mumbled, apparently unfamiliar with the text. Only Kofi Annan was calm, clear and to the point.

Monday, 31 January
The Residence, Abuja

A bad night; partly spent duelling with mosquitos, one of which was full of blood, mine presumably.

Tuesday, 1 February

The Attorney General – youngish, bright, sharp-suited – came to breakfast which, at my request, took place in the garden under the rubber tree by the pool. My brief, (a) to explain the difficulty of taking action against stolen assets in UK banks when the Nigerians were not doing so at source and (b) to request his urgent assistance regarding the signing of a memorandum on the return of illegal immigrants.

The Residence, Kaduna

A sad, tense, dusty place, half Christian, half Muslim. Crowds of desperate youths at every junction selling phone cards, washing windscreens … Sectarian violence never far below the surface. Five years ago a thousand people were hacked to death in Muslim–Christian rioting which could erupt again at any time.

We called first on the governor, an anaemic young man with a reputation for integrity and competence and aspirations to higher office. As we were leaving, a convoy arrived out of which tumbled a collection of pantomime figures in bright robes and headdresses – from the midst of which emerged no less a figure than the Emir of Zaria, one of the traditional rulers of the north. What a photo opportunity, but alas it didn't occur to me until too late. We called at the offices of the regional newspaper, where I answered questions for an hour, taking care to emphasise that good governance rather than lots more foreign dosh was the key to resolving Nigeria's many problems. Later the Archbishop, an infectiously friendly man in a purple shirt and slip-on shoes, called round for tea. And this evening we entertained to dinner several local prominenti, including one of the lesser Foots, Ben (brother of the late Paul), who heads the Save the Children programme in the north.

The Sheraton, Abuja

The ballroom. Our hosts, the Commonwealth Business Forum. There are to be no less than eight speeches, mine included. Afterwards a banquet at which HE has arranged, or so he thinks, for me to be seated at the right hand of His Magnificence. Unprecedently, the President has arrived on time and is presently closeted with the executive of the said Commonwealth Business Forum. Should we be grateful for his timely arrival? I have my doubts and in due course they will be substantiated.

We are ushered into a partitioned section of the ballroom where 300 Commonwealth businesspersons are waiting. We, the speakers, are seated on a raised dais facing the audience. The seat next to mine is empty. A fanfare of trumpets. A loud voice commands that we be upstanding for the arrival of His Excellency the President. We duly rise. Today His Magnificence favours a lime green *agbada* with a matching cap. We remain upstanding for the national anthem. The President sits; we sit. He leans across and shakes my hand.

The speeches are entirely lacking in content. Mainly taken up with homage to the President and the lengthy list of other present excellencies. Nigerians love protocol. Everyone of any significance has to have his presence acknowledged. His Magnificence is visibly bored. Within minutes he is slumped in his chair, drumming his fingers on the armrests, coming to life only to blow his nose loudly and at length.

My speech, double-spaced, covers just one side of paper. 'You will be relieved to hear,' I begin, 'that I am a politician who believes in making short speeches.' This is greeted with a round of applause more heartfelt than any so far. 'I wish to make just four short points ...' And then I make them: one, two, three, four. Just like that. Again, loud applause. Even the President is sitting upright. Just one problem, smart arse. The next speaker is Himself and he has a rather lengthy speech. Thankfully, however, he is not offended. On the contrary, he begins with a self-deprecating little joke about my four short points to which he refers more than once. As ever, however, His Magnificence mumbles and stumbles his way through the text with which he seems entirely unfamiliar. I strongly suspect that he has never seen it until the moment a flunky placed it on the lectern in front of him.

Eventually, but not before some time, it is over. The President returns to his seat. The band strikes up the national anthem. Only now does it become apparent, as I have correctly anticipated, that he has no intention of attending the banquet; instead, to the dismay of the organisers, he is heading for the exit, pursued by a retinue of flunkies and supplicants; it must have been like this at the court of the Tudors. Emergency action is called for. I have a message to deliver. 'Mr President,' I whisper, 'can you spare five minutes?' Fortunately, I am in favour. He is taking me with him. Hand in hand we march out of the hall, across the lobby and into one of the conference rooms, where he guides me to a sofa at the far end while the flunkies hover just beyond earshot. This is the moment. For several minutes I bend his ear on our urgent need to make progress on the removal of 4,000 illegal Nigerian immigrants, a matter about which his officials have been dragging their feet. I point out that we have an election coming up and the opposition have made immigration an issue: 'If we are not careful it is going to damage relations between our countries.' (Or to put it another way, 'If you want our help with debt relief et al, then for goodness' sake instruct your Foreign Minister to get his finger out.') The point does not need to be laboured. His Magnificence, who is in many respects not unlike our own dear JP, has very sound political antennae. Assuring me that he will do the necessary he rises and disappears into the throng. A man in a suit approaches and introduces himself as the President's Private Secretary, all the while glancing anxiously at the door through which his master is about to disappear. I repeat to him the message I have just delivered to the President and he scurries away. Suddenly I am alone.

There is time only for the first two courses of the banquet, during which I am showered with congratulations on the brevity of my speech although one astute Nigerian noted that my words of praise were hedged with caveats. 'There may have been one or two,' I say archly. 'There were three,' he replies.

At 21.30 Caron and I are whisked away to the airport in the flag car. By 23.00 we are airborne for Amsterdam. As we take off it occurs to me that this could be the last time I set foot on the soil of Africa. There will be no more outings between now and the election and, after that, who knows?

Thursday, 3 February

Touched down at Heathrow just after eight and straight to the office.

My first visitor was Michael Williams, who is concerned that Jack may give too much away to the Americans on the International Criminal Court and Sudan. Condi Rice is coming tomorrow and Mike is afraid that we may sign up to the American position, which is wholly untenable and will make us look foolish. I immediately penned a minute which I placed personally in Jack's hands, after he had finished his statement on the EU White Paper. He was equivocal: 'I don't want to get into a head to head with Condi on this one. She's a very tricky woman, nervous too. If it was Colin Powell, it would be different. It's about tactics, not principle. We need to play it long.' Personally, I can't think of a better issue (Guantanamo apart) over which to take on the Americans. The rest of the world is on our side; and so is half the Administration; everybody except Rumsfeld and the President. We'd win, if we dug in our heels.

Thursday, 10 February

Ngoc reports an amusing, but ominous exchange with Emma:

'Mum, don't you think it would be nice if Sarah had a boyfriend?'

'No, Sarah is too young. She needs to concentrate on her studies.'

'But, Mum, there is a boy who fancies Sarah.'

'Oh?'

'Yes, ...'s cousin.'

The Small Person may be excited by the prospect. We, needless to say, are not. There are exams to be sat.

Monday, 14 February
Sunderland

Oh happiness. A week working out of the constituency office. To work at nine; home by six, just as normal people do. Apart from a visit to the Labour Club at York University, I have a week of local engagements; above all I shall be able to make a long-overdue start on the arrangements for my re-election.

Or so I thought. Late this afternoon the office called to say I have to fly to Beirut tomorrow. A former Lebanese prime minister has been assassinated and our embassy is advising that a minister be sent to express condolences. Liz Symons, whose bailiwick this is, is on holiday in California so who else but Yours Truly? Hang on a minute, say I, what precisely is the point of all this? First, I am told that no one in the Lebanese government will be available to receive me and then it turns out that the family have asked for a non-state funeral. That clinches it as far as I am concerned. I ask to speak with the bright spark who thought up this madness and I am referred to Kara Owen in the Foreign Secretary's office. Kara, who seems to share my scepticism, says it was Our Man's idea and the point is to show solidarity with the bereaved family. Surely the Ambassador can do that? After all, what is an ambassador for? And if a minister is required, wouldn't it make more sense to wait until someone in the Lebanese government is available and then for the appropriate minister – in this case Liz Symons – to go? On the face of it this looks an entirely pointless exercise, but then – as we all know – there is so much pointless activity in politics. I have asked to speak to the Ambassador and the head of the Middle East section in the hope of talking them round, but if they appeal to Jack (who is in Pakistan) I'm done for.

Tuesday, 15 February

The threatened trip to Beirut seems to have faded. Neither the Ambassador nor the head of the Middle East section has responded to my request for a telephone conversation. Nor have they submitted anything in writing. The idea seems to have disappeared as quickly as it arose. Which only goes to show that one should never cave in at the first whiff of grapeshot.

Wednesday, 16 February

A long, sad telephone conversation with Mum. She sounds very down. 'I wish I could die. It's useless living like this. It would be better if I went to join Dad, wherever he is.' I've never heard her talk like this before. Usually she is so stoic.

Monday, 21 February

This afternoon a visit from the South African defence minister, who is also chairman of the ANC. An engaging, impressive man with no visible chips on his shoulder (unlike Mbeki). He thought the reason Mugabe was reluctant to contemplate retirement was because he is afraid of being called to account for the slaughter in Matabeleland in the mid-eighties. 'He has seen what has happened to Milosevic and Saddam and he doesn't want it to happen to him.'

Tuesday, 22 February

This afternoon I 'summoned' the Zimbabwean Ambassador to upbraid him about the latest harassment of foreign journalists. A rotund, bearded fellow, he was jovial but shameless. 'This is all because you don't like our land reform,' he said with mock indignation.

'No,' said I, 'I was one of those who celebrated Mugabe's election victory. What turned me off him was the massacres in Matabeleland in the mid-eighties.'

That set him off. He responded with a long, heartfelt diatribe about the problems in Matabeleland being the result of interference by the apartheid regime in South Africa, 'which was supported by the British'.

I tried another tack. 'If Zimbabwe was such a well-run country, why are there more than a million refugees in South Africa?'

'Because of the drought. We have had three years of bad rainfall. In two or three years' time we will be prosperous again. You will see.'

He had an answer for everything. Usually, except when replying to my point about the massacres, with a smile on his face which suggested that he didn't quite believe what he was saying, although this was precisely what he alleged about me. 'You are a stooge of your government. You are just saying this because you have to.'

The only time he got under my wire was with a reference to Belmarsh. 'We have the rule of law in Zimbabwe. We don't lock up people for years without trial, as you do in Belmarsh.' Ouch.

To the gleaming new Home Office building in Marsham Street for a meeting with Des Browne about asylum. The big problem – to be discussed at our next meeting with The Man – is what to do about returns. Countries like Iran, India, Pakistan, China, Turkey, Nigeria – the main sources of failed asylum seekers – are just playing with us. As Des says, all we are asking them to do is take responsibility for their own citizens. I favour a much tougher line. So does Des. So indeed does The Man. The difficulty is persuading officials, who keep pointing out that we have other fish to fry with most of these countries (on terrorism with the Pakistanis, and the Chinese send us billions of quids' worth of students). The way forward in my view is to pick a couple which need more from us than we do from them. Turkey and Nigeria are obvious candidates.

Wednesday, 23 February

Another visit to the Home Office. This time to discuss the growing trade in young east European girls who are being tricked and blackmailed into prostitution. Harriet Harman, who is trying to push the issue up the agenda, produced a grid charting successful prosecutions of traffickers; in nearly every case the culprit was Albanian or Kosovan, some of whom had been allowed in as refugees. Peter Goldsmith, the Attorney General, was there and as he was leaving I took the opportunity to press him about what can be done for the handful of British residents – for whom we have no legal responsibility – still stranded in the Guantanamo gulag. These people have been living here for up to 20 years, several have young families and the evidence against them is to say the least slender. In my view our position (that nothing can be done) is morally indefensible. That seems to be Peter's, too. The trouble is, as he pointed out, the last time this subject came up Jack was adamant and The Man wasn't interested either.

On the way over to the House I discussed with Mike O'Brien the inevitability of Gordon inheriting the throne, whenever the time comes. In Opposition Mike used to be on Gordon's team and so knows him well. 'Gordon,' he says, 'demands absolute loyalty and, if you let him down, he never forgives you.'

Thursday, 24 February

To Lancaster House to celebrate the final draft of the Commission for Africa report. All the African high commissioners and ambassadors were there, including my new friend from Zimbabwe, who shook my hand warmly despite our exchange the other day. Also, at the insistence of Number 10, a sprinkling of celebs, including Prunella Scales who played the Queen (to whom she bears a striking resemblance) so brilliantly in the Alan Bennett play about Anthony Blunt. Had Her Maj seen it? 'No one actually told me she had, but some time later I attended a reception at the Palace where we all lined up to shake hands and, just as she was letting go of mine, she whispered, "I suppose you think you should be doing this?"'

Friday, 25 February

Caron rang to say that Jack has now pronounced on my submission about the British residents in Guantanamo. He doesn't want to take it up formally, but is happy for Liz Symons to pursue their welfare with the Americans, a softening of his previous line. I have asked to see Liz before she goes in to bat.

Tuesday, 1 March

This evening on Channel Four, a riveting documentary alleging that the Americans have outsourced the use of torture. It described the existence of an Orwellian American outfit calling itself the Special Removals Unit which ghosts prisoners across the world, handing them over to torturers in Egypt and even, in at least one case, Syria. A former FBI man was interviewed who described a turf war in which the CIA simply snatched an FBI prisoner – of Libyan origin – and handed him over to torturers in Egypt, where he was persuaded to agree that there had been a link between Saddam and al-Qaida (a statement he recanted as soon as he was out of the hands of his tormentors). This seems to have been the basis for one of the key planks of Colin Powell's notorious UN speech.

The brother (a British citizen of Iraqi origin) of one of the British residents held in Guantanamo described how they had been kidnapped in Gambia, apparently after the SIS had tipped off the Americans. He was released after several days, but his brother, who had retained his Iraqi citizenship was duly 'rendered'. Until they were rumbled the Special Removals Unit used a plane (Gulf Air N379P) which was registered by a company calling itself Premier Executive Transport which turned out to be a lawyer's office in Arlington, Virginia – just down the road from CIA headquarters at Langley. As Sy Hersh says, 'The boys are back.' It's as though they had never been away. No doubt the truth will out in ten years' time when the present generation of insiders get around to writing their memoirs. There will be a new round of congressional hearings, a *mea culpa* or two, perhaps a Special Prosecutor appointed – and then they will do it all over again.

Wednesday, 2 March

A meeting with Liz Symons to discuss the British residents detained at Guantanamo. Her line is that she is willing to talk to the families and make representations about the welfare of the prisoners, but no more. She is understandably (given the Consular Department's workload) reluctant to do anything which implies responsibility for the 2.6 million UK residents who are not our citizens. In any case, we had no locus; our American allies would tell us to get lost if we started taking up the cases of people who were not our citizens. When, eventually, I was allowed a word in edgeways, I said that I thought our position was morally indefensible. As regards the men picked up in Gambia, we appeared to have a locus when it came to putting them away, so why shouldn't we have one when it came to getting them out? I mentioned last night's programme, but the mention of Gilligan's name only set Liz off again.

'Never mind Gilligan,' I said. 'Look at the evidence. There were interviews with a Swedish policeman, a former FBI agent and one of the men picked up in Gambia ... Some sort of shadow gulag exists and we appear to be going along with it. We are mixed up with some very bad people.'

She did have the grace to concede that my approach (proceeding on the basis of evidence) was a better one: 'I'm behaving badly. Guantanamo is outrageous. It's outside the law and violates all the norms. But I'm not going to say that in public.' Adding *sotto voce,* 'At least not while I'm a minister.'

Saturday, 5 March
Sunderland

Flicking through a copy of Piers Morgan's diaries in Ottakar's this afternoon I came across the following entry for Thursday, 7 January 1995:

> Chris Mullin, one of the harder left Labour MPs, has had a go at Murdoch and tabloids generally in one of his regular attacks on the 'gutter press'. I've had enough of him and wrote to Blair: 'Dear Tony, idiots like Mullin shouting their mouths off about "loathsome tabloids" and my owner in such an offensive manner do nothing to help us forge the relationship between us and the Labour Party that you and I wish for. If he is like this before you get into power, what on earth can we expect afterwards?'

On Wednesday, 25 January, Morgan notes:

> Blair ... has replied to my complaint about the idiot Mullin: 'Chris is one of Labour's strongest campaigners and has unwavering tenacity in pursuing causes about which he feels strongly. I am as keen as you to forge good relations between the shadow cabinet and your newspaper, but it is the nature of politics that there will be some Labour backbenchers with different views on this issue to mine ...'

Nice to know one occasionally gets under the wire, even if one doesn't find out until ten years later. How very decent of The Man to stick up for me, too. He could so easily have quietly disowned me and no one would have been any the wiser. It wasn't long after that that Morgan was ringing me up asking for articles for the *Mirror* about miscarriages of justice. Perhaps this exchange also helps to explain why I was approached by Donald Dewar, our then Chief Whip, on the eve of Murdoch's endorsement of New Labour and asked to keep my head down.

Sunday, 6 March

What a mess we are in. Every day the news grows bleaker. On Friday Ruth Kelly was jeered by a conference of head teachers. A survey in the current issue of the GPs' magazine, *Pulse*, suggests that only a tiny percentage of doctors are going to vote for us, compared to 30 per cent for the Tories, 29 per cent for the Lib Dems and 18 per cent who are undecided. If we can't take the doctors and head teachers with us after all the public money we have lavished on their respective professions (much of which has found its way into their pockets) who can we count on?

Tuesday, 8 March

Michael Jay called in. He is our G8 'sherpa', in charge of preparations for the G8 summit. He said the Americans are dragging their feet on both the key issues – global warming and Africa. 'They keep saying, "Don't think we owe you for your support in Iraq," – although they clearly think they do.'

The debate on nuclear proliferation went off well enough. Just like old times, in fact. Good speeches from Jeremy Corbyn and Julian Lewis. I managed to get through the entire hour and a half without revealing that I remain a paid-up member of CND. Later I remarked on that to Peter Hain and he replied, 'That makes two of us.'

Thursday, 10 March

Geoffrey Adams, Jack's Private Secretary, was my first caller. 'How is Jack getting on with Condi?' I asked, assuming she is much harder to engage with than Colin Powell. On the contrary, replied Geoffrey, Condi is easier. 'We had an excellent relationship with Powell, but we were never sure whether he would be able to deliver because he always had to go away and square the NSC and the White House, whereas Condi is inside the tent.'

To the House for what is expected to be an epic battle with the Lords over the Terrorism Bill.

6.45 p.m., Members' Lobby

Karen Buck says that she has received a letter from a constituent which reads, approximately, as follows: 'I am dying of lung cancer, but I intend to survive until May 5 so that I can crawl to the ballot box to vote you out.' Not a rabid Tory, but a former Labour voter. The issue? Iraq, of course.

10 p.m., Tea Room

The last train to the north long gone. All tomorrow's engagements wiped out. It looks as though we are here for the night.

A gloomy exchange with John Denham and Mike O'Brien. Both agree we are in deep trouble and that defeat is possible. Such pessimism was unthinkable three months ago. 'The tectonic plates are shifting. We're losing the will to fight,' said Mike adding that he was having difficulty finding party members to distribute leaflets, let alone canvass. 'What's our strategy?' asked John. 'We're drifting. We've become too managerial, witness the foolish attempt to reform local government pensions two months before a general election. Now we are in a mess over the Terrorism Bill, which has wiped everything else off the front page. No one seems to have a grip.'

08.30, Strangers' Cafeteria

Breakfast with Tony Banks (I should have been attending the launch of the Africa Commission at the British Museum, but only The Man, Hilary Benn and Gordon have been allowed out).

I managed a few hours' sleep, dozing under an overcoat, in the armchair in my office. Kate, the cleaner, put her head around the door at around seven, but I drifted off again and didn't even hear Big Ben strike eight. Banksie and I, urgently in need of fresh air and exercise, have agreed to meet at the Members' Entrance after the next round of divisions and go out for a walk.

09.30

Banksie and I take a stroll, in biting wind, over Westminster Bridge. On the way we pass two policemen cradling machine pistols. 'Ten years ago,' says Tony, 'we'd have been amazed to see policemen wandering the streets with those kind of weapons. Now we hardly bat an eyelid.'

Along the South Bank to Lambeth Palace, scooping up stray plastic bags and stuffing them in litter bins; loitering in St Mary's churchyard to decipher inscriptions on the tombstones. Then back across Lambeth Bridge and through Victoria Tower gardens, pausing only to remove a beer can and a soft drink bottle impaled on spikes above the gate. 'The good news,' said Tony as we re-entered the Palace of Westminster through a gate at the peers' end of the building, 'is that, so far as Parliament is concerned, today is still Thursday so these bastards can't claim their allowances for today.'

Monday, 21 March

Michael Williams called in. We discussed the impending election. I remarked that The Man seems to be becoming a serious liability. 'Jack thinks that, too,' said Mike.

Later, at a surprisingly (considering we were addressed by Gordon) thinly attended meeting of the parliamentary party, a sobering contribution from Dennis Skinner, who said that in recent weeks he had been to around 20 marginal seats trying to get party members to focus on the election, but all they wanted to talk about was Iraq and disunity at the top. He went on, 'We are entering into a campaign in which there is not a single newspaper – not one – wholly on our side. There's been nothing like it for 60 years.' Dennis said that in 1970 we had started 12 per cent ahead in the polls, defending a majority of 97 seats, led by a man with a double first from Oxford and up against a party headed by a man who nobody rated – and we lost by 40 seats. He added that he was not in favour of a May election on the grounds that we needed to get further away from Iraq. 'I am not as confident as I want to be or as some people seem to be – by God we've got some selling to do.'

Tuesday, 22 March

This evening, a party for Tony Benn's 80th birthday. All his children, and numerous grandchildren, were there along with a clutch of glamorous young women, including the actress Saffron Burrows. As for the old man, he was, as ever, on sparkling form although he seems to be shrinking a little, as you do when you get old. Nothing much has changed, he's still chasing around all over the country, stirring. Joshua said to me, 'You ring at 7.30 a.m. to see how he is, only to find that he's already gone out. You call again at midnight only to discover that he's not yet home …'

Wednesday, 23 March

There is a big behind-the-scenes tussle going on over the International Criminal Court. The Americans, in another piece of shameless unilateralism, are refusing to settle for anything less than guarantees of immunity for their citizens and are threatening to veto any Security Council resolution referring the alleged perpetrators of the slaughter in Darfur to the ICC.

If they get their way they will wreck the ICC before it starts. Jack is being very robust, telling Condi Rice that on this issue America's natural allies are among her most ardent opponents. For once we are standing up to the bullies. Fingers crossed that Number 10 doesn't interfere.

Thursday, 24 March

I spent 45 minutes on the front bench listening to Jack responding to an urgent question from the Tories about the Attorney General's advice on the war. It has emerged that he underwent a last-minute change of mind about the legality of it all and this has resulted in renewed demands that his advice be published. Jack handled it all masterfully but, as John Hutton sitting next to me whispered, 'not our finest hour'.

M from Washington called in. He says that there were only ever nine or ten people in Washington who supported the war and that (with the exception of Dick Cheney) most of them are departing. John Bolton wanted to be Condi's deputy, but she refused to have him so he's been sent to the United Nations. The CIA chief, Porter Goss, M describes as 'scarily incompetent' and busy surrounding himself with other incompetents. Condi is 'a cypher' (I guess we all knew that). The various Washington agencies are all openly rowing with each other and becoming increasingly dysfunctional. The only senior apparatchik of whom M speaks well is, oddly enough, John Negroponte, who he describes as 'sane, rational and non-ideological. He knows the situation in Iraq is bad and won't go along with an attack on Iran.'

Later, a three-hour debate on Africa in Westminster Hall. As so often, I was presented with an undeliverable draft so I simply put it aside and spoke for 40 minutes from notes. It went surprisingly well. It does make such a difference when you know your subject.

Saturday, 25 March

To see Mum. She seemed remarkably bright and cheerful and we even went outside briefly in the sunshine.

Friday, 1 April
Sunderland

The Security Council has voted to refer Darfur to the International Criminal Court. At the last minute the Americans dropped their threat to veto and abstained, after Jack told them that, if it came to a vote, we would go with the French. Like all bullies, the Americans back down when confronted. A pity we don't do it more often.

A triumph for Jack. Arguably, he's saved the ICC.

Monday, 4 April
Ministerial lunch

Jack reported an assessment of our election prospects delivered to the Cabinet at the end of last week. In a nutshell, we are in trouble. Our private polling is showing that about 30 per cent of those who voted for us last time are unlikely to do so this time round. 'Iraq, Trust and Tony are the issues.' He added that Gordon was now in the driving seat and this was good news. One can see that Jack is already preparing for life after Tony. Indeed one suspects preparations have been underway for some time.

This evening, we ministers entertained the parliamentary private secretaries and our esteemed whip, Jim Murphy, to a farewell dinner in the Churchill Room. Douglas Alexander arrived late, hotfoot from a campaign meeting at Number 10, bearing the bad tidings that a poll in tomorrow's *FT* puts us, for the first time in years, behind the Tories among those most certain to vote. Jack said that people were just getting tired of us. Tony had dominated British politics for so long that most people were under the impression that he'd been in power for eleven years, not eight. With every day that passes Jack is detaching himself from the New Labour bandwagon. As the wine flowed, we reminisced about old times. Someone pulled my leg about my supposedly Old Labour origins in the Campaign for Labour Party Democracy (which I never have repented and never will). 'On the contrary,' I said, 'I was New Labour ahead of my time. Safe seats for life was Old Labour. A contract renewable every four or five years is New Labour. My only offence was to be prematurely New Labour.' Jack backed me up, saying he had been a supporter of CLPD, too.

Someone mentioned the deputy leadership election in '81. I remarked that I had fallen out with Neil Kinnock over his decision to abstain.

'I abstained, too,' said Jack.

'No you didn't. You voted for Benn.'

'Did I?'

'Yes. What's more you put £50 on him to win.'

'How do you know?'

'You rang me up and told me.'

'You have a good memory.'

Indeed I do.

Tuesday, 5 April

The Dissolution was announced this morning, a police helicopter hovering as The Man gave his press conference outside Number 10. Douglas Alexander and Jim Murphy, sitting just down from me on the front bench, spent Question Time drafting their election literature. 'Do you think that was my last appearance at the Dispatch Box?' whispered Denis MacShane as we gathered up our papers.

'It could be the last for all of us,' I replied.

This afternoon I treated myself to a tour of the revamped Treasury building, courtesy of Dawn Primarolo's Private Secretary. The transformation is amazing. No longer the tired, dowdy, gloomy monstrosity that it once was but a light, airy 21st-century working environment. There are courtyards with trees, flower beds, flowing water and red and scarlet camellia. The big surprise, however, was Gordon's office. He has forsaken the long oak-panelled boardroom overlooking King Charles Street, once home to successive Chancellors, for a pair of modest rooms on the far side of the building. His private secretary seemed reluctant when I asked for a peep and I soon realised why: it's a complete tip. Paper everywhere. Stacked on seats, tables, the floor, everywhere. And in the inner sanctum, against the wall, three huge piles – two about four feet high and the other five feet. Gordon's filing system. How does he ever find anything? How come his officials tolerate this chaos? Presumably he refuses to let them throw anything away. And in the midst of it all, evidence that Gordon is human after all: toys and a framed picture of his toddler son, John. Just wait until the youngster starts reorganising those piles of paper. Or perhaps he has already.

This evening in the Tea Room Lynne Jones, who had consumed a glass or two of wine, talked loudly of finding someone to run against Gordon when the time comes (and it may do sooner rather than later). 'What about you?' she asked, 'the only member of the government to vote against the war.' Ann Clwyd, who was rather keen on the war, but with whom I am in sympathy on just about every other issue, was sitting with us. Behind sat Jim Murphy, our much-loved FCO whip, and I could see that he was earwigging.

'Robin won't run,' said Lynne, 'because he won't want to be defeated. We need someone who's prepared to risk humiliation ...'

'Gee, thanks Lynne.'

Lynne may be a bit crass, and a headbanger to boot, but she has a serious point. Gordon ought not be given a free run. The trail for many of our difficulties – the rows over lone-parent benefit and the 75 pence pension increase, not to mention much of the ludicrous spinning that did so much to undermine our credibility in the early days – leads back to him. As for Iraq, he would have backed Bush. He is even more in love with America than The Man. At the very least there needs to be a contest and, if not Robin, Jack or Hilary – who?

Thursday, 7 April

My last night at Brixton Road, after 32 years. I looked around sadly before I closed the door for the last time. I've had some good times here.

My last official engagements in London before the election: I addressed a meeting in the Moses Room of the Lords to commemorate the anniversary of the Rwandan genocide. Then a cup of tea with Paul Boateng, who has given up his seat to become (assuming we win) our High Commissioner in South Africa. I had meant to clear my personal effects from my desk in the Foreign Office to spare the humiliation of having them handed over in a plastic bag, if I don't come back, but there wasn't time. Finally, to King's Cross for the 20.00 train to the north. On Westminster tube station I overtook David Drew (Stroud, majority 5,000), also on his way home. He was trying to sound optimistic, but the odds are he won't be coming back.* Thank goodness I'm in a safe seat. I couldn't bear to be out of work in my fifties with two young children to support.

Saturday, 9 April

To the Stadium of Light to see Sunderland beaten 2–1 by Reading. If we get back into the Premiership – and it looks as though we might – we will be smashed out of sight.

Charles married Camilla this afternoon. The Queen looked remarkably cheerful as they emerged from St George's Chapel. As one of the commentators remarked, no doubt she was thinking, 'Thank Gawd that's over.'

Sunday, 10 April
Belair Hotel, Luxembourg

My first – and perhaps last – Euro-outing. I am here for the meeting between the so-called EU-troika and representatives of the African Union. Bharat and I arrived this evening via Amsterdam. We were met at the steps of the aircraft by a young woman from Prótocol and whisked away in a top-of-the-range silver Audi, preceded by three police motorcyclists with flashing lights and sirens, racing through red lights, all very pointless since the streets are largely deserted. One expects this sort of nonsense in Africa, where a vast gulf exists between the rulers and the ruled, but not in one of the most sophisticated parts of Europe.

---

*He was in fact re-elected.

Monday, 11 April
Luxembourg

Our silver Audi, complete with its trio of police motorcyclists, reappeared after breakfast and we set off for the conference centre, barging through rush hour traffic. Our police escorts behaved with Third World arrogance, waving their arms, shouting and generally throwing their weight around. All this for a mere parliamentary under-secretary. Ridiculous, embarrassing and positively dangerous (there were several near misses). One detects a certain resistance from the sturdy motorists of Luxembourg. Not everyone gets out of the way quickly enough and some seem wilfully to misinterpret the signals from our escort.

The meeting itself went off surprisingly well. I had been briefed to expect a fiasco, but it was nothing of the sort. The plenary was skilfully chaired by the Deputy Prime Minister of Luxembourg, a charming, cheerful, charismatic former postman. Most of the talking on our side was done by the European commissioners for foreign affairs and international development, Xavier Solana and Louis Michel. I was allocated a walk-on part in the 'governance' section. On the African side most of the talking was done by the Nigerian Foreign Minister, Oluyemi Adeniji, and the African Union Peace and Security Commissioner (in charge of the Darfur mission), Said Djinnit.The communiqué was finalised over a lavish lunch. The Nigerians wanted to reopen just about everything previously agreed – especially the line on debt relief – but were firmly slapped down by the chairman. Sure enough, contrary to what had been agreed at the preliminary session, the draft contained no mention of Zimbabwe, but we managed to get this reinstated.

By 3 p.m. it was all over. I then had two long bilateral meetings with Djinnit and Adeniji and then we climbed into our silver Audi, raced back to our hotel, waved goodbye to our police escort and (as soon as they were out of sight) Bharat and I slipped out for a two-hour walk.

Tuesday, 12 April
Luxembourg

Lunch at the Residence, a magnificent 18th-century mansion precariously perched atop the deep gorge that runs through the centre of the city. We were supposed to be delivered back to the hotel in time to be collected by our police escort but, on my instructions, Bharat rang to cancel. 'But that means you won't be able to use the VIP lounge,' said a mildly shocked voice at the other end of the line. 'So?'

By evening I was back in Sunderland. The last couple of days have been spent, it seems, trying to prove that Gordon and The Man really love each other, which, as everyone knows, is nonsense. They were on the news this evening looking tense and exhausted; Howard, by contrast, looks as fresh as a daisy.

Wednesday, 13 April
Sunderland

I am reading Piers Morgan's diaries which, although it pains me to say so, are riveting. Most astonishing is the degree of access he enjoyed. Morgan records: 'Bored one evening, I counted up all the times I had met Tony Blair. And the result was astonishing really, or slightly shocking – according to your viewpoint. I had 22 lunches, six dinners, six interviews, 24 further one-to-one chats over tea and biscuits and numerous phone calls with him ...'

He is forever being wined, dined and stroked by Alastair Campbell, Peter Mandelson and The Man. All to no avail since he turned on us big-time over Iraq. If they expended this much effort on the *Mirror*, one can only speculate as to the contortions they must have gone to keep the *Sun* sweet. Was it worthwhile? At the outset maybe, but once we had won I would have kept the ratpack at arm's length, instead of continually trying to suck up to them. It got us nowhere in the end.

Friday, 15 April

The asylum poison is having an impact. Kevin and I called at the club in South Hylton last night in search of signatures for my nomination papers and I could hear an oaf at the other end of the bar, married to a Labour Party member, muttering, 'I'm not voting for multi-cultural-ism.' It wasn't until I saw Robert Kilroy-Silk on the news that I realised where he had acquired the phrase.

Saturday, 16 April

Shopping in Asda this morning I was accosted by a fiftyish male, hair tied back in a long blond-going-on-white ponytail. His tone was friendly: 'Is Labour going to get back in again?'

'I don't know. What do you think?'

'Why aye, you'll walk it, man.'

'I am not so sure.'

A minute later he was back. 'Why aren't you confident, like?'

'Because it depends how many people bother to vote.'

'Aye well, it's all these foreigners coming in. Labour has slipped up a bit there.'

I pointed out that when Michael Howard was Home Secretary it took an average of 20 months to process a new application for asylum. Today it takes two. He looked sceptical and then changed tack: 'And Blair, of course, is never here. He's always over with his friend in America, lining up a job for when Brown takes over.'

That apart, no one else so much as nodded in my direction. The silence is eerie.

Not the whole story, though. Roy the hairdresser, who employs half a dozen people, told me that a small business like his always did best under Labour and that he will be voting for us despite his disagree-ment over Iraq and despite having a son in the army who is likely to be sent there at any moment. And my solicitor said that he would be voting Labour (for the first time) because he had been impressed by Blair's effort to win over the middle ground.

Tuesday, 19 April

The master strategists in the Ministerial Campaigning Unit at HQ dispatched me to Tynemouth, where Alan Campbell is defending a majority of 8,000, the nearest we have to a Labour-held marginal in the north-east. As I anticipated, it soon became clear that he didn't have much use for me, but I hung around for a couple of hours. A photo was taken of Alan handing me a petition about Africa and away I went, having enabled someone somewhere to tick a box.

Alan was fairly upbeat. He said that the sheer nastiness of the Tory campaign has galvanised some of his otherwise inactive members to call in and offer their services.

Thursday, 21 April

A visit to the new community school at Valley Road. One of the proudest fruits of our education policy. It has everything a poor community needs to start rebuilding from the bottom – a thriving nursery, parenting classes, healthy eating, a child mental health team based at the school. And yet … There are grave doubts as to whether it is sustainable. School rolls are falling and a large chunk of the costs have been borne by New Deal money which runs out in three or four years' time. What then?

Friday, 22 April

A brief chat with Jack. 'I am spending more time in the constituency than at any time since 1987,' he said. As well he might since about a third of his voters are Muslims. 'The older Muslims are okay, but I have had some trouble with the younger ones.' The good news is that he has about half a dozen fringe candidates competing for the dissident vote so they should divide it up between them, leaving Jack relatively unscathed.

Monday, 25 April

The postal votes go out tomorrow, but still no sign of my election address in the mail. The bloody Post Office. We busted a gut to comply with their copious rules, including the ludicrous insistence that we deliver them, bagged and bundled, to Hexham – 40 miles away. They've had five days to deliver and not one has yet arrived. If they don't come in tomorrow's post it will be too late.

Tuesday, 26 April

Kevin has been in touch with the Post Office, who were uncharacteristically apologetic, and swore that all my 10,000 postal voters will receive their election address by the close of business today. I am sceptical, but by nightfall we are receiving calls on our election telephone, which indicates that some at least have been delivered.

Wednesday, 27 April

Awoke this morning to the news that the Tories are neck and neck with us in the marginals, so Michael Howard's campaign is paying off, which presumably means that he will keep up the bombardment until polling day. Meanwhile we are said to be on the point of responding with a campaign entitled 'Nightmare on Howard Street'. For goodness' sake. This is war, not some schoolboy jape.

Friday, 29 April

To York Terrace, Silksworth, where gangs of truanting, feral youths are making a misery of the lives of the law-abiding citizens who live along the old railway track (now a cycle path) that used to connect the pit villages to the port. They want my help to close the cut that enables raiding parties of youths to come and go at will. Personally, I doubt whether closing the cut will make much difference. The problem has many causes – not least that 15 years after The Fall of Thatcher we are still manufacturing semi-literate, unemployable, useless youths, many of them second- or third-generation yob culture. I promise to do what I can, however, even though the local authority has already produced a list of reasons why nothing can be done. After leaving the complainants, I took a stroll down the said cut to the railway track and, sure enough, there were a gang of seven or eight youths up to no good in the bushes behind the terrace, some lobbing stones at the houses. And this at noon on a Friday. Goodness knows what they get up to after dark. On the way back to the office I stop off at the local community police, who, in keeping with the spirit of the times, are now based in the local school. We have a friendly enough chat, but it is a bit worrying that all half-dozen of them are sitting desk-bound in a hermetically sealed room rather than out and about among their flock. What must we do to get these guys to engage with the public they are supposed to be serving?

The polls keep saying we will win, but where are all these Labour voters? The Man took another hammering last night, answering questions in front of a (deeply hostile) live television audience. All this 'Blair is a liar' nonsense is beginning to degrade the entire political process. Actually, the only outright lie told during the course of this campaign was Michael Howard's assertion at the outset that we have uncontrolled immigration. The only consolation is that the electorate appear to loathe Howard even more than they do The Man.

Tuesday, 3 May

Iraq haunts us to the end. Every day a new atrocity and (almost) every day a new defection. Greg Dyke at the weekend. Today the young widow of a soldier killed in Basra is all over the media blaming The Man personally for his death. Even so, if the polls are to be believed, our support is holding up and the Tories remain becalmed. There are even tentative signs of a backlash. I spent the afternoon canvassing the flats at Gilley Law and, later, at Silksworth and several people came to The Man's defence over the dead soldier, saying that it was the job of soldiers to put their lives at risk and that anyway our armed forces were all volunteers.

The Lib Dems have fought a very good campaign. They were right about Iraq. They may not be wrong about Council Tax either. Charles Kennedy has come across as decent and straightforward, in contrast to Michael Howard and Our Own Dear Leader. They deserve to be rewarded but, please God, not too much.

Wednesday, 4 May

Steve Byers rang to discuss what line I should take in my 'victory' speech. I have prepared two different versions. One upbeat, if we seem to be on course for a third term, and one for use in the event of impending catastrophe. Steve says that, whatever the outcome, he does not want to go back into government (The Man rang this morning and Steve said no). Alan Milburn has still to make up his mind, but according to Steve he is unlikely to. Alan's partner, Ruth, is strongly against. When Alan went back last time, to help run the election campaign, The Man actually rang Ruth to persuade her to let him go for a few months. Plus, I guess, The Friends of The Man know that the game is almost up. If they were to rejoin the regime, it would only be for a few months at most. Even so, I asked Steve to pass the message that I wish to stay exactly where I am.

I asked how The Man was bearing up. 'Not well. This morning he sounded distant. Not really where it's at.' Steve reckons, as I do, that Gordon and his playmates will start playing up, 'sooner rather than later'.

Thursday, 5 May
General Election Day

Our count was over in 42 minutes, shaving a minute off our previous record. So once again, for about 40 minutes, I was the only MP in the country. It was clear from the exit polls that we were going to win so I gave Version One of the speech, which was apparently broadcast live. It rang a bit hollow, though, because we were clearly in for a bad night. The little people were in bed by about one. Ngoc and I sat up until around three, when it became clear that Steve Twigg had lost at Enfield.* The wheel has come full circle.

---

*The defeat of Michael Portillo at Enfield was a seminal moment in the 1997 general election.

Friday, 6 May
Sunderland, 9 a.m.

We have lost 47 seats. In London the swing to the Tories was stronger than expected (the *Evening Standard* factor?). Some bright spots. Jack had an excellent result in Blackburn. Ann Cryer is safely back in Keighley, in the teeth of strong opposition from both medievalist Muslims and the BNP. Ann Campbell (Cambridge), Jon Owen Jones (Cardiff Central) and astonishingly Keith Bradley (Manchester Withington) have fallen to the students and we have had close shaves in other student strongholds like Durham and Newcastle. Elsewhere the odious Tim Collins fell to the Lib Dems and incredibly we held Dorset South, but in east London George Galloway triumphed over Oona King. At Blaenau Gwent a popular independent has triumphed over a woman imposed by Central Casting (yet another New Labour fix comes unstuck. Will they ever learn?). The Man looks exhausted and miserable. He knows, of course, that for him The End is Nigh.

As for me, I shall just sit tight in my northern stronghold and await The Call. Or not, as the case may be.

12 noon

A long talk to Jack, who was on his way back to London, buoyed up by his unexpectedly good result. 'I'll do my best for you,' he said. I'm sure he will. Jack always sticks by his friends.

5.30 p.m.

Bharat called to say that Jack's boxes are being moved back into his office; a sure sign that he has been reappointed. An announcement is expected later this evening.

8 p.m.

A message on the answerphone from Bharat to say that Denis MacShane is out. He is to be replaced by Douglas Alexander, a less colourful, but safer pair of hands. Poor Denis will be upset, although not surprised.

Sunday, 8 May

A growing chorus of calls for The Man to go. So far, in public at least, they are confined to the Usual Suspects (Frank Dobson the latest), but who knows where it will end. Of course, the insurgents are being cheered on by the *Telegraph* et al who are only too keen to see us behaving as if we lost the election. Whatever happens, we mustn't play into their hands.

Monday, 9 May

I'm out. Death comes swiftly in British politics. As the day wore on without contact from Number 10, I began to assume I was safe since most of the departures were already announced. At quarter to four I was on the phone to Connie Newman, my opposite number in the US State Department, discussing what to do about the Liberian warlord, Charles Taylor. Five minutes later I was no longer the Minister.

The Man sounded remarkably cheerful. No hint of what was to come. We exchanged chit-chat about the result and then came the fatal words: 'I'm sorry Chris, but I am going to have to let you go.'

'Tony, I'm devastated. Why?'

There followed some nonsense about how he had to make room for new faces and how this was no reflection on my performance, which is no doubt what he says to everyone. Then he was gone, leaving me to contemplate oblivion.

Index

'CM' indicates Chris Mullin.

A

Abbotsford House, Melrose,
  Scotland 290–91
Abbott, Diane 108, 183, 320, 351,
  355, 359, 377, 382
Abuja, Nigeria 429–32, 529–31
Abuja statement (2003) 447
Accra, Ghana 422
Ad Hoc Ministerial Group on the
  Rehabilitation of Iraq 477
Adams, DC 411
Adams, Geoffrey 542
Adams, Gerry 373
Adan, Edna 504, 505, 506
Addis, John 467
Addis Ababa, Ethiopia xi, 441,
  443–4, 500, 503, 506–7, 509
Additional Costs Allowance 214
Adeniji, Oluyemi 550
Adigrat, Tigray 441–3
Adjournment restaurant, Portcullis
  House, London 525
Admiralty House, London 56, 79,
  101, 104, 523
Adonis, Andrew 321, 322
adoption, by gays and unmarried
  people 323

Advertising Standards Agency
  349–50
Aelred, Sister 159, 306
Aeroflot 50
Afghanistan 64, 142, 167–8,
  220–25, 229–34, 238–9, 241,
  243, 245–9, 251, 254, 258, 265,
  274, 276, 278, 282–3, 296, 297,
  299, 302, 312, 313, 314, 316,
  317, 318, 326, 355, 365, 366,
  381, 389, 462, 510
Africa Commission 542
African National Congress (ANC)
  536
African Union (AU) 491, 514, 530,
  549
'Agenda for Change' 400
Aids xi, 418, 427, 471
Ainsworth, Bob 39, 76, 115, 161,
  181–2, 353, 418
air traffic control 9, 11, 12, 15–16,
  19, 21, 25, 28–9, 30, 33, 34, 35,
  39, 40, 41, 45, 47–50, 53, 54,
  75, 78, 84, 97–100, 139,
  150–53, 162, 167, 213, 246,
  370
Air Traffic Control Centre,
  Swanwick 51
air travel, cheap 303–4, 305

air weapons 284, 286, 311, 324
airport capacity 20, 304
Airport Operators' Association 132
Akaev, Askar 177, 178
    *The Transition Economy through
    the Eyes of a Physicist* 177
Al Fasher, north Darfur, Sudan 496
Albanians 62
Alexander, Douglas 546, 547, 557
Alexandra, Queen 322
Ali, Tariq 129, 393
Allen, Councillor Dave 166, 374,
    388
Allen, Graham 9, 145
Alma Aty, Kazakhstan 173–4
Ambassador's Residence,
    Washington DC 449–50
American Airlines 451
Amin, Idi 448
Amos, Valerie 190, 206, 403, 404,
    409, 423, 454, 457
anarchists' riot (London, 2000) 97
ANC (African National Congress)
    536
Ancram, Michael 398, 474, 483,
    490–91
Anderson, Donald 134, 224
Andre (Cherie Blair's hairdresser)
    432–3
Angola 418
Anguilla, Prime Minister of 37
animal rights 137, 185–6
Annan, Kofi 224, 378, 452, 454,
    530, 531
Anne, HRH The Princess Royal 417,
    422
annual reshuffles 3
Anti-Ballistic Missile Treaty 192
anti-social behaviour 324
Anti-Terrorism Act 235, 239–40,
    241, 244, 245
Arab League 530

Arafat, Yasir 225, 510
Archer, Jeffrey 157
arms sales 262–3
Armstrong, Hilary xvi, xvii, 14, 24,
    55, 59, 69, 104, 139, 203, 205,
    206, 207, 209, 226, 251, 262–5,
    267, 293, 295, 321, 333, 334,
    345, 362, 372, 382, 384,
    387–90, 396–9, 402, 405–6,
    409, 416, 418
arranged marriages 252, 444, 497,
    502
Article 36 committee 297
Ashbrooke, Sunderland 290
Ashdown, Paddy (Baron Ashdown
    of Norton-sub-Hamdon) 433
Ashley, Jackie 371
Asian bank meeting (Honolulu,
    2001) 171
Asmara, Eritrea 439–40, 509
Association of Chief Police Officers
    235
Association of Residential
    Management Agents 44
Aston, Pat (CM's assistant) xvii,
    120, 170, 416
asylum and immigration White
    Paper 255
asylum seekers 20, 41, 44, 47, 54,
    62, 86, 98, 159–60, 210,
    218–19, 222, 226, 255–7, 260,
    273, 279, 281, 284, 286, 287–8,
    292–3, 310, 314, 329, 342, 346,
    348–9, 352–7, 360, 363–6, 372,
    402, 403, 405, 464–5, 501–2,
    526, 527, 528, 537, 552
Asylums Bill 20, 292
Atkinson, Christine xvi
Atkinson, Ambassador Jim 477
Atrium restaurant, Millbank,
    London 105, 335
Attorney Generals 282

Avebury, Eric 511
Avebury, Wiltshire 399
aviation summit (2001) 141
aviation White Paper 140
Axworthy, Lloyd 500, 509
Aziz, Tariq 390

B
BAA *see* British Airports Authority
Ba'ath party 398
Backhouse Park, Sunderland 371
Baghdad, Iraq 172, 354, 363, 394,
    396, 398, 435, 438, 499
Bagram airport, Afghanistan 239,
    247, 361, 393
Baird, Vera 265, 266, 267
Baisya, Sanjib xvi, 163, 173, 174,
    179, 207
Baker, Kenneth 17
Baker-Cresswell, Charles and
    Barbara 411
Bali massacre (2002) 327
Balkan war 389
Balkans 64, 283
ballistic missiles 278
Balls, Ed 47, 198
Bangalore University 322
Banks, Tony xvii, 88, 183, 186, 210,
    289, 542, 543
Banqueting House, London 303
Barak, Ehud 225
Barclay brothers 444
Barclays Bank 90–92, 93
Barna, Denise 78, 141
Barnes, Harry 186
Barre, Siad 504
Barron, Kevin 377
al-Bashir, President Omar 496
Basra, Iraq 464, 555
Bate, Charles 197, 387
Battle, John 165–6, 205
Bayley, Hugh 383

BBC 128, 239, 259, 273, 289, 362,
    413, 507
    World Service 496
Beach Boys 291
'Beacon Councils' 104
Beckett, Margaret 162, 203, 337,
    338, 339, 416, 526
Begg, Azmat 476
Beira, Mozambique xi, 471
Beirut, Lebanon 535
Beith, Alan 224, 372
Bell, Steve 92, 94
Bell, Stuart 347
Belmarsh prison, Greenwich,
    London 518, 537
Bemba, Vice-President 478
Bemersyde House, Scottish Borders
    291–2
benefit culture 229–30
Benn, Hilary xvii, 207, 244, 407,
    433, 448, 460, 473, 477, 482,
    521, 525
Benn, Joshua 544
Benn, Stephen 354
Benn, Tony xvii, 7, 28, 53, 119, 183,
    184, 202, 205, 227, 243, 264,
    290, 300, 311, 336, 354, 544,
    547
Bennett, Alan 538
    'A Cream Cracker under the
    Settee' 467; 'Soldiering On' 467
Bennett, Andrew 315, 337
Berbera, Somalia 504–5
Bercow, John 198
Berlusconi, Silvio 375–6
Beslan school hostage crisis, Russia
    (2004) 490
Best, Harold 377
'Best Value' 69
Bevan, Aneurin (Nye) 210
Bevan, James 488
Bewick, Thomas 94

Bichard, Michael 22
bicycles 17, 26, 60
Big Conversation 445
Bigham, Violet and Andy 340
Billy Elliot (film) 133
bin Laden, Osama 220, 222, 223,
    225, 232, 236
biological warfare 215, 278, 360,
    425
Birmingham 57
pub bombings (1974) 44
Birmingham Six case 19, 93, 184,
    212, 328, 500
Birt, John 259
Bishkek, Kyrgyzstan 174–5, 177
Biya, President Paul 457–8
BJP (Bharatiya Janata Party), India
    472
Black, Conrad 143, 267–8, 300, 356,
    444
Blackburn 338, 557
Blaenau Gwent 557
Blair, Cherie 111, 209, 227, 294,
    303, 308, 334, 335, 365, 369,
    430, 431, 432, 466, 500, 528
Blair, Euan 295
Blair, Kathryn 301
Blair, Leo 206, 301
Blair, Tony xv, 10, 407–8, 458, 537
    junior partner to Gordon while
    in opposition 525; offers CM a
    job in Environment 1, 2–4;
    response to cabinet show of
    solidarity 6; prioritising of
    transport 7; government car
    service 15; hunting 28, 154,
    244, 271; air traffic control 41,
    240–41, 246; at Number 10 46,
    186–7, 209–10, 295; computer
    course 49; pep talks by 74, 134;
    London Mayor elections 81,
    84, 99; perma-smile 92, 227;
    impressed with cleverness 93;
    WI fiasco 107–8; series of
    meetings with junior ministers
    108–9; education 125;
    Brighton conference speech
    (2000) 131; and Mandelson
    157; September 11 attacks
    220–24; personality 221,
    222–3; asylum seekers 226,
    355–6, 363–4; best-ever speech
    227; Afghanistan 239, 243,
    245–6, 247, 302, 312; 'historic
    third term' reference 249; NHS
    252; 'wreckers' accusation 254;
    visit to Africa 258; arms sales
    262–3; post offices 268; Iraq
    268–9, 272, 301–2, 306, 307,
    311–13, 315, 316, 317, 324,
    344–8, 358, 363, 367–71, 373,
    378, 383–90, 395, 396, 397,
    401, 412, 414–15, 475, 486; on
    Saddam Hussein 278; housing
    benefit 283, 284, 286; Queen
    Mother's funeral 294*n;*
    relations with Gordon 308,
    370, 381, 551; and Miliband
    309–10; firefighters' dispute
    329, 330; US/British values
    350–51; recklessness 363, 371,
    374, 375; Short's personal
    attack 404; on top form 413;
    Bush's visit (2003) 427, 428;
    and the media 433–4; EU
    referendum U-turn 463, 464,
    466; heckled at Brighton
    (2004) 498; heart flutter
    corrective surgery 499;
    intention of serving a full third
    term 500; house in Connaught
    Square 500; Dissolution
    announced 547; tells CM he is
    no longer the Minister 558

Blaney, Ambassador John 514
Blix, Hans 327, 361, 373, 390–91
Blix report 353–4
Blond, Anthony 105
Blunkett, David xvii, 206, 207, 252, 311, 319, 402, 409, 526
government car service 15; and education 82, 83–4, 89, 168, 319; tipped to be Home Secretary 154, 195–6; hunting 154; and Chris Woodhead 179; becomes Home Secretary 203; meeting with CM 207–8; aims to abolish blasphemy 237; Anti-Terrorism Bill 241; on Parliament's priorities 244; on the Home Office 244, 252; asylum seekers 255, 329, 502; police lobby against reform plans 268; drugs 298–9, 300; Zimbabweans 314; Iraq 346; slow-hand-clapped 376; nanny's visa issue 516; bad-mouthing of colleagues 516–17; resignation (2004) 519
Blunt, Anthony 537
BNP see British National Party
Boateng, Paul 414, 502, 548
Bogarde, Dirk 46
Bognor Regis 134
Boldon multiplex, Sunderland 133, 252
Bolton, John 545
Bond, Kevin 44, 45
Boothroyd, Betty 53, 104, 191, 311, 462
Bosnia 296
Boundary Commission 439, 440, 441, 507
Bowman, Elizabeth 180
Boyd, Jim 201
Boyd, William 375

Bradley, Keith 72, 150, 385, 557
Brain, Chris xvi, 91, 95, 105, 122, 128, 133, 138, 191–2, 251
Branson, Richard 95
Bratt, Claes 293–4
Bremer, Paul 436, 438, 459
Bridge, Lord 328
Brighton 45
Brind, Don 74, 82
Bristol flats fiasco 334, 365
Bristol Zoo 85
British Airports Authority (BAA) 20, 101, 102, 138, 405
British Airways 46, 50, 148
British Council 429
British Gas 102
British Geological Society 43
British Midland 148
British National Party (BNP) 338, 360, 557
British Overseas Territories, governors of 196–7
British Rail 135
British Union of Fascists 169
Brixton Road, London 8, 55, 63, 195, 338, 342, 343, 401, 474, 521, 548
Broadcasting Bill 331
Broadcasting House (Radio 4) 128, 129
Brodie, Mildred 72, 94
Broomfield Hospital, Chelmsford, Essex 319, 445, 449
Brown, Gordon 283, 414, 546
air traffic control 25, 30, 34, 37, 153, 167, 213; Blair as his junior partner while in opposition 525; single-parent benefits 37; 'PM in all but name' 45; 'disappears for months at a time' 58; public spending 86, 117–18; fuel crisis

128; minimum income guarantee 130; Brighton conference speech (2000) 130; as prospective successor to Blair 166–7, 168, 272, 295, 402, 415, 417, 435, 524, 538; Clare Short on 196; personality 213; at his best 242; death of baby Jennifer 247, 295; anti-poverty strategy 264; hunting 269–70; efficiency savings 277; budget (April 2002) 279; the Euro 301; relations with Blair 308, 370, 381, 551; pre-Budget statement (2002) 329–30; tax credits 332, 399; Iraq 346, 362; Brighton 2004 498; 'demands absolute loyalty' 538; his office 547–8

Brown, Jennifer 247, 295
Brown, John 548
Brown, Nick 308, 370, 376, 381, 446
Brown, Sarah 247
Browne, Des 465, 497, 501, 502, 537
brownfield developments 59
Bruce (CM's cat) 270–71, 282, 285
Brussels 297–8
Buck, Karen 542
Buckingham Palace, London 105, 181, 282, 291, 322–3
Burnley 66, 338
Burrows, Saffron 243, 544
Burundi 462, 487
bus services, rural 17
Bush, George H. W. 510
Bush, George W. xi, 216, 221, 225, 237, 247, 251, 253, 265, 272, 301, 303, 306, 315–18, 324, 339, 347, 352, 355, 357, 373, 381, 384, 385, 410, 420, 422, 427, 428, 437, 438, 486, 487 signs death warrants as Governor of Texas 146, 526; Presidency 137, 146; and bombing of Iraq 172; popular speech to Congress 222–3; Heath's advice to Blair 227–8; 'a puppet' 231; and the Republican Party 249; Blair as possibly a moderating influence 269; Dennis Skinner's comment 276; and a Palestinian state 297; and compensation for bomb survivors in Afghanistan 299; address to the UN General Assembly 309; Blair's view of 312, 316; Hitchens on 315; British government 'not Bush's poodles' 327; Blair's 'influence' 335, 348; his attitude to the UN 358; relationship with Blair 368; alcoholic past 369; Palestine 386–7

Bush, Laura 257
Bush House, London 170
Bussell, Darcey 46
Butler, Robin 483–4n
Butler Report 483–4
Byatt, Ian 57
Byers, Steve 87, 229, 232, 237, 240, 252, 259, 261–2, 271, 272–3, 286–90, 293, 305, 306, 331, 368, 374, 380–81, 387, 556

C
Cabinet Office 11, 79, 128, 171, 188, 204, 477
Caine, Michael 337
Calabar, Nigeria 515
Caldwell, Jane 165
call centres 308

Cambridge 557

Cameron, David xvii, 215, 234, 240, 276, 287

Cameroon 457

Camilla, Duchess of Cornwall 549

Camp Tillo, Nubia Mountains, Sudan 494–5

Campaign for Labour Party Democracy (CLPD) 546

Campaign Group 289

Campaign for Nuclear Disarmament (CND) 541

Campbell, Alan 553

Campbell, Alastair x, xv, 4, 15, 56, 58, 90–91, 128, 139, 154, 223, 257, 294, 335, 355, 394, 432, 433, 466, 551

Campbell, Anne 137, 311, 347, 557

Campbell, Menzies 213, 294

Campbell, Ronnie 268

Campbell Savours, Dale 157, 250, 524

Camrex House, Sunderland 47, 54

Canavan, Dennis, MP 79–80n

Candler, Peter 401

Canterbury, Archbishop of 401, 526

Caplin, Carol 334, 365, 369

car ownership 60

car-clamping 520–21

Cardiff 254

Cardiff Central 557

Caribbean Bank 171

Carlton Gardens, London 455, 460

Caron (CM's Assistant Private Secretary) 508, 509, 534, 538

Carr, Simon 435

Carter, Denis 258

Castle, Barbara 130

Cawsey, Ian 73

Central African Republic 420

Central Intelligence Agency see CIA

Central Office of Information 27

Central Statistical Office 30

Chakrabarti, Suma 423, 424

Chalker, Linda (Baroness Chalker of Wallasey) 462

Channel Five 332, 349, 350, 374, 397, 412, 482

Channel Four 28, 107, 332, 349, 354, 358, 496, 538
    News 105, 491

Channon, Chips x

Charles, HRH Prince 214, 344, 460, 549

Charles II, King 423, 448

Chatsworth, Derbyshire 8

Chaytor, David 186

Chechen suicide bombers 490

Chechnya 64

Chelsea Arts Club 293

Cheltenham 21

chemical warfare 269n, 278, 315, 360, 425

Cheney, Dick 374, 487, 545

Chernobyl 61

child benefit 283

Chillingham Castle, Northumberland xi, 437, 516, 517, 519, 522

China, asylum seekers from 537

Chirac, Jacques 358

Chissano, Joaquim 431

Chomsky, Noam 334–5

Christina Noble Foundation 113

Christine (CM's Private Secretary) 161, 163, 171, 179, 196, 207

Churchill, Sir Winston 97, 210, 316, 449

Churchill, Winston (grandson) 449

CIA (Central Intelligence Agency) 307, 395, 539

Civil Aviation Authority 101, 109–10

civil service 263–4

Clapham, London 100
Clark, Alan x, 73
Clarke, Charles 14, 15, 216, 262, 266, 269, 289, 407, 446
Clarke, Kenneth 316, 323–4
Clay, Edward 484, 485, 501, 503, 507
Clinton, Bill 297, 315, 450
Clwyd, Ann xvi, 41, 216, 226, 233, 243, 253, 262, 301, 302, 318, 355, 367–8, 369, 381, 390, 396, 438, 459, 548
CND (Campaign for Nuclear Disarmament) 541
Cobbett, William 298
Cohen, Harry 393
Cold War x, 254, 425
Collins, Tim 557
Colman, Tony 108, 138
Colville, Jock x
Commission for Africa report 538
Commonwealth 430, 433, 532
Commonwealth Business Forum 532
Commonwealth conference (Australia, 2002) 265
Commonwealth Parliamentary Association 182
Communications Bill 332, 349, 372, 376, 397, 412
Competition Commission 102, 122
Concorde 10, 67, 237
congestion tax 7, 76, 84
Congo, Congolese 418, 420, 460, 462, 477–81, 487
Congress Club, Great Peter Street, London 56
Connarty, Mike 53, 277
Connery, Sean 368–9
Consular Department 508, 539
Cook, Greg 460
Cook, Captain James 9

Cook, Robin 19, 132, 161–2, 168, 190, 203, 213–16, 226, 239, 242, 248, 266, 269, 270, 278, 284–5, 313, 320, 321, 333, 344, 345, 348, 356, 362, 373–4, 376, 380–83, 390, 404, 414–15, 475, 486
Cookson, Jan 305
Cooper, Yvette 47, 108, 112, 185
Cooze, John 105
Cooze, Una 104–5, 185
Corbett, Robin 206
Corbyn, Jeremy 186, 236, 300, 541
Cormack, Sir Patrick 182, 391
Corston, Jean xvi, 34, 43, 81, 119, 209, 226, 232, 244, 245, 262, 263, 266, 267, 270, 271, 280, 301, 311, 312, 320, 321, 333, 352, 354, 365, 369, 379, 380, 383, 384–5, 387, 388, 389, 396, 404, 406, 407, 408, 410, 412, 418, 446, 464, 525
Côte d'Ivoire 487, 513
Council for Foreign Relations 450, 453
Council of Ministers 298
Council Tax 555
Counter-Terrorism Department 508
Countryside Alliance 154, 498
Countryside Bill/Act 70, 77, 87–8, 97, 161
County Hotel, Durham 281, 290, 300
Cousins, Jim 116, 118
Cowan, Rex 259
Cranston, Ross 52, 282, 352–3
Crawford, Joan 451
Crédit Suisse 48
crime 208, 324, 360, 365
Crime Bill 328
Crimewriters Association 281
Criminal Justice Bill 331, 396, 398, 409

Crocker, Chester 450
Cromwell, Oliver 144
Crook, Mike 89
Crown Prosecution Service 282
Cryer, Ann 252, 444, 497, 557
Cultural Revolution (China) 440, 467, 474
Cunningham, Jack 21, 30, 343–4
Curran, James and Margaret 259
Curry, David 328
Curzon, Lord 326
cycle lanes 17
cyclos 99

D
Dacre, Paul 300
Dáil 71
Daily Express 151, 349, 354, 431, 444
Daily Mail 33, 46, 92, 147, 158, 165, 193, 294, 334, 335, 338, 353, 434, 444, 516, 523
Daily Mirror 29, 126–7, 158, 334, 335, 394, 467, 541, 551
Daily Record 289
Daily Telegraph 19, 70, 90, 143, 179, 184, 216, 227, 241, 267, 295, 399, 434, 444, 518, 523, 558
Dalai Lama xi, 472
Dale, Mrs 290, 291, 411, 473
Dalyell, Tam 183, 231–2, 233, 262, 272, 354, 377, 397, 524, 527
Dam Sen water park, Vietnam 115
Darfur, Sudan 462, 469, 473–4, 490, 491–2, 496, 527, 544, 546, 550
Darling, Alistair 42, 144, 303, 304, 337, 374–5
David (diary secretary) 5, 13
Davies, Bryan 475
Davies, Gavyn 448
Davies, Nick 83–4, 208
Davis, David 216, 254, 317, 461

Deakin, Philip and Marjorie 143
Dean, Howard 449
Dean, Janet xvii, 215
Dearing, Ron 407, 425
Debenham's store, Sunderland 16
debt relief 67, 527, 530, 533
Deedes, Bill 19
Democratic Party (US) 297
Denham, John 542
Department for Environment, Food and Rural Affairs (Defra) 203
Department for International Development (DFID) 209, 244, 293, 402–3, 404, 406, 470, 525
  CM offered post 158–9; CM's new home 160–61; officials' lack of experience of legislating 182; CM leaves 204, 207
Department of Environment, Transport and the Regions (DETR) 293
  CM accepts a post 1–3; CM's induction 4–6; CM's responsibilities 6, 8–9, 11; first decisions 9–10; Countryside Division 10, 85; press office/ officers 15, 32, 49; research budget 77–8; Corporate Management Section 251; Mottram's comment 261
Department of Health 18, 30, 208, 279–80
Department of Trade and Industry (DTI) 45–6, 56, 72, 163–4, 205
departmental press offices 15
development banks 171–2
Dewar, Bob 505
Dewar, Donald 541
Dewhirst, Ian 67, 255, 283
Dewhirst factories 67, 255, 260
Diana, Princess 323
Disraeli, Benjamin 210

Djinnit, Said 550
Dobbie, Peter 497
Dobson, Frank 30–31, 77, 80, 87,
     88, 338, 360, 382, 558
Dobson, Sally 288
Dodds, Councillor Brian 166
Donnelly, John 387
Donohoe, Brian 4
Donoughue, Bernard 4, 397–8
Dorset South 557
Downing Street press office 15
Doxford International 201
Doxford Park, Sunderland 309
Draper, Derek 160
Drew, David 549
Drown, Julia 318
drugs 208, 209–10, 215, 233–4, 238,
     240, 241–2, 272, 274, 275–6,
     289, 298–9, 300, 333, 360, 366
Drysdale, John 505
Dublin Convention 256, 281, 286
Ducor Palace Hotel, Monrovia,
     Liberia 515–16
Duncan Smith, Iain (IDS) 216, 275,
     303, 311, 316, 323, 335, 361–2,
     365, 447, 484
Dunwoody, Gwyneth 9, 11, 21, 50,
     56, 98, 100, 153, 214, 265, 328,
     391
Durham 557
     miners' gala 300
Durham Cathedral 416
Durham County Cricket Club,
     Chester-le-Street 26–7
Durham jail 300
Duvalier, Baby Doc 478
Dyke, Greg 448, 555

E
Eads, Brian 293
Eagle, Angela 10, 79, 84, 120, 311,
     378, 524

Eagle, Maria 212, 386
Easington, County Durham 133
Eastbourne policy forum 59
Eden, Anthony (Earl of Avon) 348
Edmonds, John 254
education 82–6, 89, 109, 125, 165,
     179–80, 250, 319, 407, 440,
     520, 553
Edwards, Senator John 449–50
Efford, Clive 334
Egan, Sir John 140
Egypt 538, 539
Eland House, Westminster, London
     4, 12, 24, 29, 43, 119, 161, 163,
     250–51
Electoral Commission 356, 414
Elizabeth, Queen, the Queen
     Mother 273–5, 284, 294–5
Elizabeth II, Queen xi, 105, 144, 145,
     189, 291, 295–6, 322–3, 427,
     429, 430, 457, 460, 538, 549
Ellison, Dick and Gwen 393
Employment Service 229
Enfield, London Borough of 556
environmental emergencies 61–2
Equatorial Guinea 511
Eritrea, Eritreans 420, 439–40, 441,
     500, 507
Eritrean Airways 439
Eritrean demonstrators (London,
     2000) 103
Etherington, Bill 283, 388, 459
Ethiopia, Ethiopians 418, 439–44,
     487, 500, 503, 506–7
ethnic cleansing 132
EU White Paper 534
EU-troika 549
Euro, the 23, 301, 316, 407, 409
Euro elections (2004) 470, 474
Euro-Just 298
European Charter of Human Rights
     234

European Commission (EC) 263, 267, 460
    aid programme 169–70; Justice and Home Affairs council 241, 297, 298
European Parliament, Brussels 298
European Union (EU) 67, 461
Evening Standard 37, 78, 289, 294, 340, 347, 356, 361, 365, 369, 405, 447, 557
Excellence in Cities (EIC) programme 89
Extradition Bill 331

F
faith schools 246
Falconer, Charlie 124, 185, 250, 282, 328, 398, 403, 466, 518
Falkender, Marcia, Baroness 36
farm animal welfare 51
farmers' subsidies 73
Farringdon, Sunderland 309
Farringdon Community School, Sunderland 111
FBI (Federal Bureau of Investigation) 538–9, 540
Federal Mogul 253, 255, 283, 308
Fellowes, Sir Robert 323
Fenwick department store, Newcastle 14
Field, Frank 6, 263, 264, 265, 266, 267, 270, 521
Field, Sir Malcolm 101
firefighters' dispute 317, 318, 325, 329, 330, 336
Fitzgerald, Ged 527
Fitzpatrick, Jim 446
Fitzsimons, Lorna 377
Fitzwalter, Ray 372
Fletcher, Tom xvii, 430, 431, 432, 438, 451, 453, 454, 461

Flint, Caroline 211
Florida 137, 491
Flynn, Paul 327, 475
Foley, Brian 62, 193
Food Standards Agency 171
Foot, Michael 105, 300
Foot, Paul 532
foot and mouth outbreak (2001) 187–8, 191, 194
Football Disorder Bill 116, 117
Foreign Affairs Select Committee 224, 353, 413
Foreign and Commonwealth Office 30, 31, 37, 66, 142, 161, 162, 163, 166, 168, 182, 188, 190, 193, 196, 236, 240, 292, 313, 314, 326, 365, 403, 407, 409, 415, 548
    CM accepts Africa job 416; CM's office 417; toffs superceded by grammar school boys/girls 452; board meeting 455–7; responsibility for asylum policy 501; CM loses his post at 558
Foreign Relations Committee (US) 490
Forgan, Liz 87, 217, 259, 305, 306, 366
Forth, Eric 243
Foster, Derek 51, 240
Foster, Don 38
Foster, Peter 334
Foulkes, George 31, 158–9, 161, 207, 295
Foundation hospitals 401, 402, 407
Fountains Abbey, north Yorkshire 274
Four Seasons Hotel, Park Lane, London 519
Fox, Charles James 210
Frater, Charles 193

Freedom of Information Act 235, 284
Friends of the Earth 30, 46, 51
FT (*Financial Times*) 546
fuel crisis (2000) 125–7, 128, 139
fuel escalator 25
Fylingdales early-warning system 216

G
G8 450
summits 297, 412, 541
Gaddafi, Colonel Muammar 530
Galbraith, Gill 98
Gale, Roger 389
Galloway, George 397, 399, 485, 557
Galtieri, General Leopoldo 315
Gambari, Ibrahim 419
Gambia 420, 539, 540
Gamekeeper's Cottage, Northchapel, West Sussex 12, 121
Garang, John 497
Garvey, Kate xv, 1, 2, 158, 432, 433
Gatwick 66
Gavin (in charge of logistics) 432
Gay Hussar restaurant, Soho, London 267
Gaza 508, 509
GCHQ building, Cheltenham 460
general election (2001) 186–7, 188–9, 198–203
general election (2005) 542, 543, 544, 546, 552–7
Geneva Convention 355–6, 392, 468
George, Bruce 224
German chancellery 79
Gerrard, Neil 292–3
Ghana 412, 422
Gibbon, Gary 107

Gibson, Andrew 18
Gilbert, John xvii, 95, 257–8, 265, 363
Gillan, Cheryl 183, 184–5
Gilley Law, Sunderland 555
Gilligan, Andrew 448, 540
girl guides 124
Gladstone, William Ewart 76, 210, 411
Glatt, Sam 343, 380, 387
globalisation White Paper 164
GM foods 171, 185
GNER (Great North Eastern Railway) 136
Goldberg, Rabbi David 476
Goldsmith, Attorney General Peter 282, 376–7, 477, 537
Goodman, Elinor 105
Gorbachev, Mikhail 179
Gore, Al 137, 192
Gorman, Teresa 294
Goss, Porter 545
Gothenburg, Sweden 294
Gould, Philip 118, 119
government car service 5, 6, 8, 13–14, 15, 21, 23, 30, 43, 46, 51, 52, 75, 416
Government Hospitality 424
Gracey, General 386
Graham, David 18
Gramsci, Antonio 355
Grangetown Primary School, Sunderland 133
Grant, Ann 485
Great Baddow, Chelmsford, Essex 510
Great Minster House, Horseferry Road, London 51
Green, Sir Andrew 310
Green, Damian 156
Green, David 429
Grenada 307

Griffiths, Jane 147
Griffiths, Nigel 205
Grindon Hall Christian School,
    Sunderland 273
Grocott, Bruce, Baron xv, 3, 4, 35,
    78, 92, 93, 109, 139, 154, 209,
    221, 518, 525–6
Grogan, John 349
Grove Cranes 50, 308
Guantanamo Bay 393, 397, 419–20,
    438, 451, 468, 475–6, 477, 534,
    537, 539, 540
Guardian 29, 30, 37, 54, 57, 83, 87,
    90, 92, 95–6, 127, 150, 155,
    204, 205, 208, 219, 307, 316,
    326, 340, 345, 348, 351, 357,
    361, 371, 395, 444, 468
Guildford Four 19, 169, 328
Gulf of Tonkin incident (1964) 339
Gunn, Ben 235
gypsies 152

H
Hackland, Brian xv, 33, 36
Hackney, London 526
Hague, William 91, 107, 116, 131,
    138, 157, 198, 201, 213, 485–6
Haig, Lord 292
Haig family 291
Hain, Peter 132, 150, 358, 541
Haley, John 261
Hall Farm, Sunderland 197
Hallam, David 432
Hammond, Sir Anthony 253, 288
Hanoi, Vietnam 175, 439, 466
Hansard 118, 379
Hanson, David xv, 4, 232, 285, 293,
    316, 361, 376, 385, 390, 407,
    410
Hargeisa, Somaliland 503–4, 505–6
Hargrave, John 380, 387
Harman, Harriet 282, 537

Harmsworth press 348
Harris, Robert 295
Harrogate (Tory conference, 2002)
    272
Harrow School 154
Hartlepool 285
by-election (2004) 497, 500
Harvey, Nick 349
Haselhurst, Alan 68–9
Hastings, Max 294
Hatfield train crash (2000) 288
Hattersley, Roy 43
Hatton, Derek 33
Havelock Primary School,
    Sunderland 165, 416
Hawkins, Nick 333
Heal, Sylvia 83
Healey, Denis 130
Heath, David 97
Heath, Sir Edward 227–8
Heathcoat-Amory, David 10
Heathrow airport 20, 153, 240, 342
Heddon-on-the-Wall, Tyne and
    Wear 187
Heffer, Eric 382
Hellawell, Keith 233, 299
Hencke, David 87
Henderson, Doug 66
Hendon, Sunderland 98–9, 129,
    159, 260, 285, 393
Heppell, John 39
Herat, Afghanistan 167, 238
Heritage Lottery Fund 517
Herring, Mr (photographer) 193–4
Hersh, Sy 539
Heseltine, Michael 9, 84, 383
Hewitt, Patricia 272, 372, 460, 466,
    477
Heybridge, Essex (Brewster House
    care home) 452, 467, 486
High Hedges Bill 161, 250
Highcliff Hotel, Bournemouth 28

Hill, Gordon 256
Hill, Keith xvi, 52, 103, 155, 159, 251, 287, 325, 355, 359, 377, 388, 398–9
 government car service 5; air traffic control 7, 21, 39; transport 17, 38; walking document 26; New Labour lexicon 61; *Question Time* 66; Transport Bill 70–71, 76; night flights 140; Iraq 345
Hill, Robert xv, 223, 293, 316
Hilton hotel, Blackpool 132
Hilton hotel, Park Lane, London 466, 515
Hinduja inquiry (Gopichand and Srichand Hinduja) 155, 156, 158, 160, 162, 253
Hitchens, Christopher 315
Ho Chi Minh City, Vietnam 94, 112, 114
Hodge Hill, Birmingham by-election (2004) 485
Hodge, Margaret 331
Hodgkinson, Mike 101
Hoey, Kate 205, 299
Hogg, Douglas 419
Hoggart, Simon 29, 140
Home Affairs Select Committee x, 6n, 34, 37, 121, 156, 182, 206, 207, 208, 215, 233–4, 237–41, 297, 310, 328, 346, 366, 372, 402, 405, 461
Home Housing 18
Home Office 14, 22, 32, 35, 44, 98, 137, 206, 208, 224, 233–4, 244, 252, 264, 292, 311, 346, 368, 403, 462, 465, 537
Homes Bill 152
Hongkong and Shanghai Bank 113
Hoon, Geoff xvii, 30, 33, 66, 229, 232, 233, 241, 248, 249, 351–2, 359–60, 389, 394–5, 477
Horam, John 350, 351
Horse Guards 144
Hospital Trust 18
House Judiciary Committee 251
House of Lords reform 247–8, 343–4
House of Lords' Science Select Committee 112
housing 33–4, 45, 66, 84, 86, 132, 147
 Green Paper 59, 85
house prices 304, 308
housing estates 18
Housing Action Trusts 33, 34
housing benefit 85, 105, 144, 161, 283, 284, 286
Housing Corporation 10
Howard, Michael 210, 215, 420, 447, 484, 485, 526, 527, 528, 551, 552, 554, 555
Howarth, Alan (in House of Lords) xvii
Howarth, Alan, MP xvii, 355, 357
Howarth, George 185–6, 235, 265, 267
Howe, Geoffrey (Baron Howe of Aberavon) 182, 307, 382, 383, 462
Hoyle, Doug xvi, 226, 278, 302, 304, 312, 339, 344, 397
Hughes, Beverley, MP xvi, 3, 4, 8, 24, 237, 311, 363, 372
Hughes, Kevin 243, 330
Hull 285
 university library 500
Human Rights Act 138, 141, 235
Human Rights Committee 267
Human Rights Convention 355
Humphries, Barry 291
Humphrys, John 87, 93, 259–60, 413, 473

Hunt, Philip 383–4
Hunter, Anji xv, 36, 182, 223, 225, 237, 394, 432
hunting 28, 49–50, 111, 153–4, 186, 193, 244, 258–9, 269–70, 271, 337, 495, 498, 511–12
Hunting Bill 269, 271, 337, 511–12
Huntingdon Life Sciences 137, 152
Huntley, Ian 435
Hussein, Saddam 132, 188, 224, 257, 265, 274, 276, 278, 302, 307, 311, 312, 313, 315, 318, 324, 339, 344, 345, 347, 352, 353, 354, 357, 360, 363, 364, 367, 370, 371, 372, 378, 379, 396, 397, 425, 434, 440, 473, 483n, 536, 539
Hussey, Duke 349, 350
Hutton, John 103, 208, 545
Hutton, Lord (James) 447
Hutton report 435, 437, 444, 448n, 484

I
ICA (Institute of Contemporary Arts), The Mall, London 55–6, 58
ID cards 224, 226
IMF (International Monetary Fund) 130
immigration 165–6, 170, 252–3, 255, 294, 310, 444, 526, 527, 533
immigration detention centre, Harmondsworth, near Heathrow 346
Immigration and Nationality Department 264, 329, 460
Independent 187, 188, 403, 435, 446
India
    asylum seekers from 537; earthquake (2001) 160, 161, 164

India Office, London 437, 473
Ingabire, Francine Murengezi 480
Ingram, Adam 156, 223
Institute for Public Policy Research 106
Institute of Contemporary Arts see ICA
Institute of Directors 91
Institute of Waste Management 43–4
Institution of Electrical Engineers 23
Intelligence and Security Committee (ISC) 207, 210, 212, 372, 413
intelligence services 18
Inter-American bank meeting (Chile, 2001) 171
Internally Displaced People (IDPs) 492, 493
International Criminal Court 534, 544, 546
International Development Bill 180, 182–3, 192–3
International Monetary Fund (IMF) 130
International Water Exhibition (Birmingham, 1999) 36–7
Into Work programme 141
IRA (Irish Republican Army) 71
Iran 311, 335, 537, 545
Iraq 132, 172, 188, 220, 224, 243, 257–8, 265, 266, 268–9, 271, 302–3, 307, 311, 315, 316, 317, 324, 327, 335, 339, 343–8, 350–55, 358–62, 366, 367, 369–89, 462–3, 470, 486–7, 545
    protests against the war 364, 392, 393; big debate on 367–70; CM votes against the government over Iraq 389,

394, 405, 406, 409, 418, 455, 509; beginning of attack on 390; American prisoners shown on Iraqi television 392; Iraqi prisoners of war 393; deaths of women and children 394, 395; statue of Saddam toppled 396; mayhem in Baghdad 398; Prince Turki's comments 400–401; growing row over 412; killing of Nepalese cleaners 490; ending the occupation 527; and the 2005 general election 542, 544, 552, 555
Irranca-Davies, Huw 377
Irvin, Joe xv, 26, 28, 49, 126
Irvine, Derry, Baron Irvine of Lairg 111, 245, 247–8, 278
Isaias Afewerki, President 439, 440, 442, 443, 507, 509
Ishiguro, Kazuo 46
Islamabad, Pakistan 529
Isle of Wight 122
Israel, Israelis 225, 236, 277, 278, 294, 307, 354, 374, 510
ITN 375–6
ITV 331, 332, 372

J
Jackson, Glenda 347, 362
Jackson, Helen xvi, 160, 226, 245, 246, 330, 333, 339, 344, 362–3, 396
Jackson, Robert 392
Jalalabad, Afghanistan 230, 238
James, P. D. 46
Jamieson, David 38, 39
Jay, Sir Michael xvii, 456, 457, 508, 523, 541
Al Jaz, Awad 496
Jenkin, Bernard 282–3

Jenkins, Roy 411
Jiang Ximin 36
J. J. Roberts International Airport, Liberia 515
Jobseekers' Allowance 230
John Paul II, Pope 365, 401, 526
Johnson, Alan 526
Johnson, Boris 129
Joint Intelligence Committee 413
Jones, Barry 280
Jones, Emma 294
Jones, Jon Owen 444, 557
Jones, Kevan 323, 375, 376, 379
Jones, Lynne 250, 548
Jones, Nigel, MP 72
Jones Parry, Sir Emyr 451, 452
Jones Parry, Lady Lynn 451, 452
Jordan, PC Les 309
Joshi, Bharat xvii, 474, 478, 482, 485, 488, 496, 502, 505, 509, 549, 550, 551, 557
Jowell, Tessa 332, 481
Joyce, Eric 468
Judd, Frank 476
Judge, Igor 328
judges 329

K
Kabila, President Joseph 478–9
Kabul, Afghanistan 221, 230, 238, 239, 248, 251, 315, 381
Kaduna, Nigeria 531–2
Kagame, President Paul 462, 479, 519, 530
Kampala, Uganda 489
Kandahar, Afghanistan 302
Karzai, Hamid 247, 253–5, 299, 318, 355
Kass, Sudan 493–4
Kauda, Sudan 494
Kaufman, Gerald 170, 328, 350, 383
Kavanagh, Pat x

Kavanagh, Trevor 483
Kazakhstan 173
Keighley 557
Kelly, Dr David 447
Kelly, Ruth 541
Kelly, Tom 432
Kemp, Fraser 388
Kennedy, Charles 484, 485, 526, 555
Kennedy, Ludovic 399
Kennedy, Moira 399
Kennon, Andrew 234, 300
Kent, Bruce 129, 130, 132
Kenya 418, 465, 484–5, 488, 501, 502–3
Kerr, Sir John 22–3
Kerry (CM's assistant) 86, 251
Kerry, Senator 449
Kewvin, Father (in Tigray) 442, 443
Key Potential UK 16
Khanh (CM's brother-in-law) 113, 114
Khartoum, Sudan 491, 494, 495–6
Kibaki, President Mwai 503
Kiet, Vo Van 112
Kiet, Mrs Vo Van 112
Kieu (in Ho Chi Minh City) 113
Kigali, Rwanda 480–81
Kilfoyle, Peter 15, 73
Kilroy-Silk, Robert 552
King, Oona 352, 557
Kinnock, Glenys 284
Kinnock, Neil 28, 53, 58, 111, 150, 262, 284, 547
Kinshasa, Democratic Republic of the Congo 466
Kissinger, Henry 221
Kisuma, Kenya 426
Klein, Joe 450
KLM/UK Air 9
Konare, Alpha Oumar 530
Kony, Joseph 474, 489

Kosovars 62
Kosovo 19, 130, 231, 257, 302, 315, 462
Kozak, Dmitri 301
Krebs, John 171
Kulov, Felix 175, 176
Kumar, Afghanistan 232
Kumar, Ashok 253
Kunduz, Afghanistan 243
Kuofor, President John 426
Kurds 132, 188, 302, 367–8, 396
Kursk (Russian submarine) incident 122, 123
Kyoto 51
Kyrgyzstan 173, 174–9

L
Labour Party conferences
Blackpool (2002) 314;
    Bournemouth (1999) 27, 58;
    Brighton (2000) 130–31;
    Brighton (2001) 218, 227;
    Brighton (2004) 498, 499
Lagos, Nigeria 423, 528–9
Lake District 151–2, 225
Lake Windermere 68, 151
Lamb, Lennie 285
Lambeth Council 55, 63
Lammy, David 293
Lamont, Norman (Baron Lamont of Lerwick) 234
Lancaster House, St James's, London 21, 422, 448, 538
Lander, Stephen 234–5
Landmark Trust 519
Lane, Geoffrey 169
Lane, Sue 387
Lansbury, George 354
Laos 269n
Laurence, Mike 303
Lawton, Sir Frederick 169
Le Carré, John 507

Le Qua (in Ho Chi Minh City) 114–15, 132
Le Touquet 358
Leeds 44
Leicester South by-election (2004) 485
Leigh, Edward 350, 351, 391
Lenin, Vladimir 179, 467
Letts, Quentin 193–4
Letwin, Oliver 255, 299, 355
Lewington, Richard 173
Lewis, Julian 541
leylandii trees 10, 12, 32–3, 35, 36, 46, 105, 120, 150, 161, 251, 271, 342
Liaison Committee 303, 328, 350, 391
Liberia 418, 419, 422, 452, 462, 512–16
    Ministry of Health 513
Liddell, Helen 6, 9
Lilley, Peter 299
Linford, Paul 6
Linklett Bay, North Ronaldsay 218
Lira, northern Uganda xi, 489
'Listening to Old People' event (Queen Elizabeth Centre, 2000) 103
literacy 89, 105, 250
Liverpool 33–4, 37
    city council 34
Livingstone, Ken 51, 77, 78, 80–81, 83, 84, 87, 88, 99, 127, 130, 289, 474
Lloyd, Liz 432, 434
Lloyd, Tony xvi, 166, 211, 215, 258, 268, 304, 327, 330, 390
Llwyd, Elfyn 312
local elections
    2000 95–6, 98, 99; 2002 285; 2004 470, 474
local government bill 85

Loescher, Ann 455
Loescher, Gil xviii, 404, 435–6, 455
London Assembly 127
London Chamber of Commerce 106
London Mayor 31, 51, 77, 78, 79, 83, 84, 99, 127, 259, 289, 474
London Underground 167, 213, 289, 370
London University 502
Lord Chancellor 32
Lord Chancellor's Department 31
Lord's Resistance Army 438, 445, 446, 474, 489
Ludford, Sarah 476
Lufthansa 439
Luton air crash (1999) 24
Lutyens, Sir Edwin 450
Luxembourg 549–51
Lyell, Nicholas 91

M

Maastricht Treaty (1992) 383, 463
McAvoy, Tommy 71–2, 145, 205, 325, 333, 446, 525
McCarthy, Mac 393
McCartney, Ian 46, 51
McDonald, Dennis 343
Macdonald, Gus xvi, 14, 31, 45, 52, 55, 128
    air traffic control 15–16, 25, 40, 41, 48, 97; transport discussion 17; on lack of team working in government 26; role to take the heat off JP 26, 56, 57, 58; review of the press office 49; 'repositioning' on cars 60, 61; performance targets 70; aviation 'summit' 101, 102; CAA salaries 110; fuel crisis 126; night flights 141;

transport spending programme
146; on sparkling form 155
MacDonald, Ramsay 315
McDonald's 218
McDonnell, John 377
McFadden, Pat 406
McGuinness, Martin 373
Macintyre, Don 205
McKeith, Jim 476
Mackinlay, Andrew xvi, 215, 226,
232, 263, 266, 268, 269, 270,
280, 284, 313, 324
McLeish, Henry 237
McNally, Tom 349, 350, 376
MacShane, Denis xvii, 91, 359,
454–5, 456, 461, 465, 547, 557
McSmith, Andy 267–8, 316, 352,
393
Mactaggart, Fiona 147
McWalter, Tony 211
McWilliam, John 268
Madrid bombs (2004) 459
Mahon, Alice 252, 254, 266–7, 277,
327, 355, 377, 382, 497
Mail on Sunday 334, 349, 357, 497
Major, John 79, 82, 84, 137, 143,
173, 324, 433, 460, 527–8
Maldon, Essex 487
Malins, Humfrey xvii, 276, 287, 324
Mamba Point, Monrovia 512
Manchester 132, 237–8
Manchester airport 20, 304
Manchester Withington 557
Mandela, Nelson xi, 190, 427, 470
Mandela, Winnie 470
Mandelson, Peter 30, 31, 124,
155–8, 160, 162, 185, 196, 206,
253, 288, 314, 409–10, 482,
486, 551
Mann, Simon 511
Manning, Catherine 450
Manning, Sir David 450, 510

Manningham-Buller, Eliza 366, 401,
518
Maples, John 294
Maputo, Mozambique 491
airport 472
March, Graham (CM's assistant)
xvii, 44, 47, 170, 228, 399
Marchioness (ship) 59
Marks & Spencer 67, 255, 260
Marquand, David 95
Marquis, Kevin 96, 197, 200
Marr, Andrew 380, 470
Marshall, Lord 46
Marshall-Andrews, Bob 91, 117,
231
Martin, Michael 134
Martin, Tony 117
Matabeleland, Zimbabwe 536
Mates, Michael 224, 391
Matthew, Jessica
CM's private secretary xvi, 4;
and the government car service
5, 13, 14, 21, 23, 30, 52, 75;
CM's mobile phone/pager 5,
11–12, 48; and CM's first
decision-making 9; summarises
issues 10; and security 11;
complains about CM 39; rare
mistakes 43; and the Transport
Bill 69; and the Utilities Bill
78–9; and CM's unknown
detractor 82; leaves the
Department 86
May, Theresa 262, 290
Mayhew, Patrick 282
Maynard, Joan 110, 274
Mazar, Afghanistan 238
Mbeki, Thabo 431, 536
Meacher, Michael xvi, 57, 94, 133,
416
upbeat and cheerful 1–2; and
transport 7; government car

service 21, 23; leylandii 32, 33; World Trade talks 51; on JP's negotiating skills 51–2; pollution 61; Utilities Bill 72, 73; Countryside Bill 77; leylandii 120; not a team player 122; and Mandelson 157–8; property portfolio row 157; GM foods 171; foot and mouth outbreak 191; infuriating to work for 192; regarded as a more successful minister 192; nuclear power stations 337–8

Meale, Alan 1, 22

Meale, Diana 1

Medical Aid for Palestine 294

Mekele, Tigray 441, 443

Meles Zenawi, Prime Minister 441, 462, 507

Mellon, Mr (surgeon) 303

Melrose, Scottish Borders 106

Members' salaries 212, 214

Menwith Hill early-warning system 216

Mephan, David xvi, 189, 190, 196

Mertoun, Scottish Borders 411

Meteoric Tactical Solutions 470

Metropolitan Police 156

MI5 xi, 234, 366, 425

Michael, Alun 186, 269, 270, 271, 337

Michel, Louis 550

Migrationwatch 310

Milburn, Alan 30, 254, 263–4, 280, 327, 338, 370, 381, 386, 400, 402, 414, 465, 470, 500, 556

Miliband, David 193, 198, 221, 268, 293, 309–10, 317, 370

Miliband, Louise 309

Millennium Dome 74, 124, 131, 138, 156, 195

Milošević, Slobodan 231, 315, 536

minimum income guarantee 130

Ministerial Campaigning Unit 553

Ministerial Group on Biotechnology and Genetic Modification (Misc 6) 185–6

Ministry of Defence (MoD) 15, 73, 83, 97, 188

missile defence 216, 351

Missile Defence Shield 186, 192

Mitchell, Austin 349

Mitchinson, Naomi 46

Mitrovice, Kosovo 62

Moberly, Richard and Patricia 521

mobile phone masts 260

Mobutu Sese Seko 479

Mogae, Festus 430

Moldovans 62

Monrovia 512, 514–15

Montserrat 162

MONUC 480

Moore, Charles 268

Moore, Jo 232, 259, 261

Morgan, 'General' 505

Morgan, Piers 335, 467, 540, 541, 551

Morgan, Rhodri 80n

Morgan, Sally xv, 15, 204, 283, 284, 293, 358, 386–7, 406, 412, 518

Morley, Elliot 31, 49–50, 73, 159, 416

Morris, Estelle 83, 203, 313, 319, 331, 356

Mosley, Sir Oswald 169

Motorola 195

Mottram, Sir Richard xvi, 7–8, 30, 45, 58, 70, 105, 126, 261, 293

Mount Grace Priory, north Yorkshire 392, 462

Mowbray Park, Sunderland 16, 120

Mowlam, Mo 30, 171, 185, 272, 295, 307

Mozambique 83, 418, 471–2
Mozart, Wolfgang Amadeus 303
MPs' expenses 284–5
Mubarak, President Hosni 530
Mudie, George 347
Mugabe, Robert 426, 427, 431, 487, 536
Mullin, Christopher John (Chris)
    offered a job in Environment
    1, 2–4; mobile phone/pager 5,
    11–12, 23, 48, 91, 143, 163,
    168, 416, 421, 474;
    responsibilities 6, 8–9, 11;
    induction course 21–3; debut
    at the Dispatch Box 37–8, 90;
    Question Time 40, 52–3; Parris
    on 42; an unknown detractor
    74, 82; Barclays boycott affair
    90–92, 93; Iron Laws of Politics
    95; birthdays 145, 336; offered
    a job at International
    Development 158–9; returns to
    the backbenches (2001) 203–4,
    206; Home Affairs Committee
    2001–3 207, 215; talks with
    Blunkett and Blair 207–10;
    re-elected to the parliamentary
    committee 215; 'despicable'
    speech 320; accepts Africa job
    at the Foreign Office 416–17;
    votes against the government
    over Iraq 389, 394, 405, 406,
    409, 418, 455, 509; meets
    Mandela 427; death of his
    father 469; visits the Sudan
    491–7; New Year's resolution
    522; wins his seat at the
    general election (2005) 556;
    returns to the backbenches
    (May 2005) xii, 558; *A Very
    British Coup* 35, 106, 127, 207,
    523

Mullin, David (CM's brother) xviii
Mullin, Emma (CM's daughter)
    xviii, 8, 24, 41, 60, 90, 133,
    137, 143, 145, 149, 197, 217,
    218, 282, 291, 296, 305–6, 336,
    337, 340, 341, 392, 434, 436,
    486, 534
Mullin, Leslie (CM's father) xviii,
    111, 319, 341, 374, 395, 399,
    436, 445, 449, 453, 459, 466,
    469, 482, 485, 486–7, 510, 518,
    522, 536
Mullin, Liz (CM's sister) xviii, 395,
    459, 467, 469, 482–3
Mullin, Pat (CM's sister) xviii, 469,
    482–3
Mullin, Sarah (CM's daughter) xviii,
    24, 41, 42, 59–60, 111, 121,
    133, 137, 145, 180, 197, 217,
    218, 252, 285, 305–6, 336, 337,
    340, 392, 401, 436, 485, 490,
    534
Mullin, Teresa (CM's mother) xviii,
    111, 319–20, 340–41, 374, 395,
    399, 436, 445, 452–3, 463,
    467, 469, 482–3, 486–7, 501,
    510, 512, 518, 520, 522, 536,
    545
Muluzi, Bakili 430, 431–2
Murdoch, Rupert 300, 323, 332,
    349, 350, 372, 374, 397, 398,
    433, 540, 541
Murdoch press 117, 118, 129, 143,
    348
Murphy, Jim 446, 461, 546, 547
Museveni, President Yoweri 418,
    430, 431, 445–6, 447–8, 462,
    487, 530
Muslims 294, 454–5, 518, 553,
    557
    Shia 132, 302
Muthaiga Club, Nairobi 507

N

Nader, Ralph 192

Nafie, Nafie Ali 496

Naipaul, V. S. 115

Nairobi, Kenya 501, 502–3, 505, 507

Narey, Martin 277

National Farmers' Union 51, 73

National Health Service *see* NHS

National Insurance payments 332

National Security Council 450

National Trust 94

NATO 361

    summit (Prague, 2002) 329

Natsios, Andrew 496

Negroponte, John 545

Nether Stilton, north Yorkshire 66

Neven, North Ronaldsay 217, 218

New Deal 116, 229, 553

New Forest national park 28

New Labour 22, 31, 42, 74, 82, 83, 84, 89, 93, 111, 118, 145, 195, 272, 546

    lexicon 61; 'Best Value' 69, 104; new public spending 86; 'Listening to Old People' event 103; 'Beacon Councils' 104; obsession with spin and control freakery 105; Millennium Dome 124; and the economic cycle 139; obsession with targets 156; hyperactivity 172; Woodhead attacks 179, 180

New Partnership for African Development (NEPAD) 472

New York 450–51

Newcastle 135, 401, 557

Newcastle University Medical School 111

Newman, Connie 558

Newsnight programme 160, 260, 491

Nguyen Co Thach 386

Nguyen Thi Hanh (CM's sister-in-law) xviii

Nguyen Thi Ngoc (CM's wife) x, xviii, 2, 59, 94, 96–7, 113, 114, 115, 149, 155, 170–71, 173, 205, 214, 217, 218, 260, 271, 282, 290, 296, 306, 337, 341, 342, 392, 452, 481, 486, 490, 523, 534, 556

NHS (National Health Service) 84, 156, 200, 210, 211, 213, 216, 250, 252, 254, 263, 294, 303, 338

Nicola (assistant private secretary) 5, 86, 251

Nielsen, Poul 169, 170

Nigeria, Nigerians 110, 423, 424, 528–33, 537, 550

night flights 76–7, 105, 108, 138, 140, 141, 142, 146–7, 148, 152, 161, 181, 240

Nissan plant, Sunderland 158

Nixon, Richard 316

Njuoma, President Sam 530

Norman, Archie 75, 93

Norris, Steve 80, 99

North American Trade Association 267

North Korea 265, 348, 351, 355

North Ronaldsay 217, 306–7

north-east regional assembly (rejected proposal) 510

north–south divide 124

Northallerton 135

Northern Alliance 224, 238–9, 243, 246

Northern Group of MPs 257, 338

Northern Ireland Assembly 71

Northumberland xi

Norton-Taylor, Richard 468

Norwich 285

Nuba Mountains Monitoring
Commission 494
nuclear power stations 61–2, 337–8
nuclear proliferation 541
nuclear warfare 122
Number 10 Policy Unit 10
numeracy 250
Nunn, Senator Sam 257
nurses' pay 83, 147
Nuthill Priory Hotel & Spa, Redhill
154–5
Nyala, South Darfur, Sudan 491–2,
493
Nye, Sue 288

O
Oaks, The, Sunderland 340
Obasanjo, President 422–4, 432,
515, 530–31
Obote, Milton 448
O'Brien, Mike xvii, 49, 50, 109, 142,
158, 198, 205, 206, 253, 263,
287, 288, 292, 326, 328, 365,
366, 381, 384, 398, 408, 418,
454, 456, 461, 468, 486, 538,
542
Observer 121, 267, 482
Odinga, Oginga 426
Odinga, Raila 426
OFSTED 82, 85, 89, 520
OFWAT (Water Services Regulation
Authority) 57
oil companies 125–6
Old Labour 34, 546
Omar, Mullah 315
One2one 201
Organ, Diane 377
Orkneys 305
Osborne, Sandra 40
Overseas Dependent Territories 37
Owen, David, Baron Owen of
Plymouth 95

Owen, Ed 461, 474, 491
Owen, Kara 535
Oxford, Bishop of (Richard Harries
(Baron Harries of Pentregarth))
476

P
Paddick, Brian 240, 241–2
Paddington rail disaster (1999) 35,
36, 38
Pakistan 233, 510, 529, 537
Pakistan Airlines 20
Palestinian road map 386, 499
Palestinian state 297
Pallion, Sunderland 129
Palmer, Nick 157
Palmerston, Lord 411
Panorama (television programme)
496
Paris 453–4
Park Authority 151
Park, Daphne 466–7
Parliament Act 258, 259, 269, 271,
511
Parliamentary Committee 226, 239,
241, 243, 247, 262, 267, 277–8,
280, 284–5, 296–7, 301, 318,
321–2, 334, 344–5, 348, 373,
390, 407, 413
CM re-elected 215
parliamentary party meetings 211,
231–2, 236–7, 242, 245, 249,
252, 264, 269, 271, 301,
332–3, 376–7, 383, 464, 524,
543
Parliamentary Recording Unit 90
Parris, Matthew 42
Pashtuns 246
Paxman, Giles 453
Paxman, Jeremy 363, 453
Pennywell, Sunderland 78, 129,
260, 290

Pennywell Neighbourhood Centre 141, 159

Pennywell School, Sunderland 82, 256

pensions 83, 96, 98, 130, 131, 139, 145–6, 167

Pentagon 230, 420
    attack on (2001) 219

performance targets 70

Pergau Dam, Malaysia 180, 193

Perkins, Ann 352

Peterlee, County Durham 67

Philip, HRH Prince, Duke of Edinburgh 291, 322, 323, 429, 430, 460

Phuoc, Pham Huy 113

Picasso restaurant, Kings Road, London 18

Pickthall, Colin 403

Pilger, John 132

Pimlott, Ben 259

Pinochet, General 81

police 172, 208, 235, 268, 279, 403, 550, 555

Police Bill 208

Police Federation 199

Police Reform Bill 279

Portcullis House, Westminster, London 184, 249, 288, 310, 334, 350, 391, 404, 405, 435

Porthouse, Stuart 98

Portillo, Michael 70, 73, 118, 198, 216, 297, 316, 323, 324, 556n

Post Office 263, 268, 269, 272, 554

Potters Bar train crash (2002) 288

Powell, Colin 225, 249, 327, 360, 408, 420, 439, 452, 468, 487, 490, 534, 539, 542

Powell, Enoch xii, 93, 183, 403

Powell, Jonathan xv, 36, 79, 80, 518

power-boating 68, 151

Premier Executive Transport 539

Prentice, Bridget xvi, xvii, 324, 330

Prentice, Gordon xvi, 40, 215, 226, 242, 246, 253, 258, 261, 268, 313, 330, 339, 344, 348, 359, 362, 367, 377, 407

Prescott, John xv, 10, 229, 239, 252, 265, 266, 302, 526
    Meacher on 1–2; welcomes CM 3, 5; vast responsibilities 14; difficult to locate 14, 21, 24; image problem 14, 49, 145; intervenes over Pakistan Airlines issue 20–21; management style 25, 35, 48, 58; as a charismatic 26; short car ride incident 28, 29; Labour Party conference 28–9, 58; air traffic control 25, 30, 34, 37, 49, 53, 97–8, 100, 153, 240–41; leylandii issue 36; loyalty to colleagues 38–9, 41; meets delegation of backbenchers 45; government car service 46; 'Two Jags' 49; 'Save JP' offensive 55–6; *Sunday Times* episode 57, 58; small decisions rather than the big picture 65; at his best 76; rented flat in Clapham 100; bemused at middle-class women's aggression 100; aviation 'summit' 101, 102; CAA salaries 109, 110; visits Nigeria 110; success with the Treasury 119; fuel crisis 126; night flights 142, 161; proposed Railtrack renationalisation 186; north Wales egg incident 199; hunting 258, 259; firefighters' dispute 317, 318, 329, 330; Afghanistan 319; Iraq 362; and Philip Hunt 383–4; *tour de force*

speech 412–13; on Clare Short and Robin Cook 415
Prescott, Pauline 100, 101, 112
Press Association 4, 204
Press Complaints Commission 349, 356
Preston, Peter 155–6
Prestwick airport 40
Primarolo, Dawn 295, 320, 332, 333, 400, 547
Prime Minister's Questions 92, 138, 169, 212–13, 347, 358, 364, 379, 393
Prism IT programme 457
prison officers 403
Prison Service 277
Prodi, Romano 460–61
Pronk, Jan 496
proportional representation 139
Prosser, Gwyn xvii
prostitution 537
Protection Squad party, Scotland Yard 527
Prudential Insurance 421
PSBR (public sector borrowing requirement) 16, 49, 84
Public Accounts Committee 254, 263, 264, 267, 270
Public Finance Initiative 370
Public Lending Right 152
public service reform 324
Pulse magazine 541
Purchase, Ken 161, 213, 250, 321
Puttnam, David (Baron Puttnam of Queensgate) 331, 349–50, 372, 374, 397
al-Qaida 234–5, 239, 278, 400–401, 451, 476, 501, 539

Q
Qalaye Niazi, Afghanistan 247

Queen Elizabeth Centre, Belvedere Road, London 103
Queen's Speech 49, 50, 208, 324, 444
Question Time 40, 52–3, 61, 66, 81, 361–3, 435
Question Time (television programme) 294, 295
Questions 75, 81, 107, 167, 195, 316, 355, 363, 373, 413, 483
   Business 243; Foreign Office 234, 434, 446, 455, 468
Quiet American, The (film) 337
Quiet American, The (Greene) 115
Quin, Joyce 66, 205, 392
Quinn, Lawrie 403

R
Radice, Giles and Lisanne 281
Rafferty, Jim 18
Railtrack 135, 156, 186, 272, 273
Ramblers' Association 315, 498
Rambo (Congolese asylum seeker) 287–8
Rammell, Bill xvii, 463, 468, 483, 488
Rawnsley, Andrew 121
Raynsford, Nick xvi, 9, 13, 79, 152
   promotion 4–5; hand-me-downs 13, 45, 132; work rate 39; on JP 59; Transport Bill 69; air traffic control 75, 100; housing benefit 84–5, 129, 144; intelligence 95; asylum seekers 98; in Sunderland 129; firefighters 318
Reading 147
Reading Football Club 549
Reagan, Ronald 307
recycling 56, 145, 146
Red Cross 44, 287
Redgrave, Corin 475–6

Redgrave, Vanessa 475–6, 482
Redwood, John, MP 56, 66, 144
Reeves, Sue 433
Refugee Council 54
Regulation of Investigatory Powers
    Act 235
Reid, John 250, 321–2, 349, 356,
    359, 396–7, 405, 413, 526
Republican Party (US) 249, 267,
    297, 301, 318, 351, 491
Reuters 496
Rice, Condoleezza 327, 487, 534,
    542, 544, 545
Richards, Ed 375
Richards, Keith 101
Ridley, Yvonne 229
Rimington, Dame Stella 234
Ritter, Scott 301
Riyale Kahin, President Dahir 504
road pricing 17
Robertson, George 19
Robinson, Geoffrey 157, 196, 500
Robson, Sir Stephen 101–2
Rogers, Mrs (friend of the
    Savchenkos) 284, 286
Rohsler, Caron xvii
Rooker, Jeff 23, 91, 273, 279, 281,
    286, 315, 435, 523–4
Rooney, Terry 349
Roper, John 95
Rove, Carl 231, 449
Rover 87
Royal Commonwealth Institute,
    Kensington, London 164
Royal Garden Hotel, Kensington,
    London 110
Royal Institute of Civil Engineers
    164
Ruddock, Joan 276, 347
Rumsfeld, Donald 354, 374, 420,
    459, 487, 534
'Rumsfeld Rules' 517

rural development 21
Rushdie, Salman 455
Russell, Bob xvii, 215
Russia
    submarine incident (2000) 122,
    123; Beslan school hostage
    crisis (2004) 490
Rwanda, Rwandans 462, 477–81,
    483, 548
Ryanair 69

S
Saigon 115, 217, 218, 337
Saigon Children's Charity 113
Sainsbury, David 171, 185
Sainsbury, Lord 77–8
St Anthony's Catholic Girls' School,
    Sunderland 159, 306
St Bede's Terrace, Sunderland 1, 68,
    522
St Boswells, Roxburghshire (The
    Holmes) 290, 411, 473
St Helens 198
St James's Park, London 36, 66, 80,
    139, 322
St Margaret's, Westminster 462
Saleh, Dr Barham 381, 396
Salmond, Alex 234, 368–9
Salter, Martin 45, 50, 54, 147
Sanday 217, 218
Sandys, Celia 449
Sandys, Duncan 449
Santerre, Jacques 460
SAS training centre, Ashford, Kent
    468
Saudi Arabia 335, 400
Saudi group, all-party 400
Savchenko, Sasha 284, 346
Savchenko family 256–7, 273, 279,
    281, 284, 286, 287
Save the Children programme 532
'Save the Pound' 200, 201

Savidge, Malcolm 186, 267, 351, 401

Sawa camp, Eritrea 440

Sayeed, Jonathan 352

Scales, Prunella 538

school exclusions 277

Scotland Yard, London 241–2

Scott, Sir Walter 93, 290

Scottish Office 26, 159

Scottish Parliament 79n

SDP 95

Seaham, County Durham 133

Searchlight 338

Seaton, Jean 259

Secret Intelligence Service (SIS) 420–21, 425, 445, 466, 539

security service 244

Sedgemore, Brian 292

Selby train crash (2001) 182

Senior Salaries Review Body 212, 214

September 11 attacks (2001) 219–24, 231, 235, 239, 256, 257, 268–9, 312, 348, 357, 455

Serbia 132

Seyoum Mesfin 507

Shapinsay 218

Sharon, Ariel 225

Shaw, Jonathan 352

Shayne (assistant private secretary) 5, 86, 90, 142–3, 146, 151, 251

Sheehy, Sir Patrick 44

Sheerman, Barry 524

Sheinwald, Nigel 432, 447, 500, 509

Shelter 20

Shephard, Gillian 92

Shia Muslims 132, 302

Shienwald, Nigel 297

Short, Clare xvi, 150, 159, 181, 194–5, 376, 381, 388, 408, 414, 422, 448; government car pool 15; enjoyment of her job 67, 94, 168; Mozambique helicopters row 83; very hands-on 161; personality 162, 166; Montserrat 162; a formidable politician 163–4; good relationship with Gordon Brown 164, 184; in action 167; and Vereker's complaint 172; and Mandelson 185; Iraq 188, 346, 374, 375, 376, 379, 412; Palace Street office space dispute 189, 190; plan for a third minister 190, 191; praised 192, 197, 207; on Gordon as potential leader 196; and loss of CM as deputy 204; pager incident 295–6; opposes war in Iraq 313; asylum seekers 314; threatens to resign 374, 499; calls Blair reckless 374, 375; her future in doubt 380; resignation 403; personal attack on Blair 404; JP on 415; and Kofi Annan 454; walks on the Downs with CM 498

Sierra Leone 419, 462, 488

Sikhs, homeless 97, 101, 102–3

Silksworth, Sunderland 197, 374, 554–5

Silverglade 193

Simpson, Keith 183

Simpson, OJ 251

Singh, Marsha xvi, 215

single-parent benefits 37, 139, 167

Sinn Fein 71

Sinsenbrenner, Jim 251

Sixsmith, Martin 261, 286

Skinner, Dennis 3–4, 40, 74, 183, 188, 211, 212, 249–50, 275, 276, 363, 543–4

Smith, Andrew (*Sunderland Echo* editor) 261
Smith, Angela 193
Smith, Chris 205, 332, 369, 377, 382
Smith, Jacqui 24
Smith, John, QC ix, 111, 466
Smith, Pat 197
Soames, Mary 449
Soames, Nicholas 92, 97, 158, 275, 295, 449
Solana, Xavier 660
Soley, Clive xviii, 119, 166–7, 184, 277, 356, 409, 524
Somalia 243, 355, 503, 505
Somaliland 503–4, 505–6
South Africa/South Africans 426, 427, 513, 536, 548
South Downs national park 28
South Hylton, Sunderland 260
South Hylton Working Men's Club, Sunderland 551–2
South Shields 192, 309, 401, 434
Southmoor Community School, Sunderland 89, 180
Soviet Union, disintegration of 174
Soweto, South Africa 470–71
Speaker, election of 134
Special Branch 394, 501, 504
Special Removals Unit 538, 539
speed limits 25
Srebrenica 132
Stadium of Light, Sunderland 549
Stagg, Dickie 456–7
Stalin, Joseph 178
Stansted Airport 68–9
Star, the 29
Star Wars 213, 220, 254, 257, 339
Starkey, Phyllis 468
State Opening of Parliament 144, 325
Stevens, John 242

Stinchcombe, Paul 111
Stockport 66
Stourton, Edward 495
Strang, Gavin 50, 54, 75
STRAP 2 (Top Secret) information 11
Strategic Rail Authority 34, 76
Straw, Charlotte 35
Straw, Jack xvii, 206, 211–12, 229, 240, 313, 314, 393, 408–9, 422, 435, 468, 526, 537
asylum seekers 20, 54, 62; leylandii 35; on JP 35; air traffic control 35, 78; hunting issue 49–50; and Pinochet 81; and new public spending 86; London Mayor elections 88; Football Disorder Bill 116, 117; animal testing 137, 142; travellers 137–8; criminal youths 166; all-night courts 172; fast-tracking police officers 172; Police Federation 199; becomes Foreign Secretary 203, 213; Afghanistan 231, 236, 254; talks with Colin Powell 249; and British relationship with US 318; Iraq 327, 358, 362, 375, 382, 398, 403, 455, 473, 486, 499; weapons of mass destruction 353–4; confident and witty 377; and CM's appointment at the Foreign Office 416; attention span 438; and proposed FCO reorganisation 456; on EC leaders 460–61; leaked papers issue 461–2; EU referendum issue 463–4; Euro-scepticism 464; meets the Dalai Lama 472; and inadequacy of draft replies 475; Sudan 490;

Equatorial Guinea 511; and Blunkett 516–17, 519; and Condoleezza Rice 534, 542, 544; on Guantanamo 538; ICC 546; CLPD 546; his Muslim constituents 553; loyal to his friends 557

Streeter, Gary 192, 193, 197, 483

Stronsay 218

Stuart, Gisela 3, 4, 205

student fees 331, 339, 356, 370, 407–8, 431

Sudan 464–5, 482, 487, 490–97, 500, 503, 534

Sudan People's Liberation Movement (SPLM) 495, 497

Sun, the 29, 59, 92, 127, 150, 158, 189, 222, 236, 294, 300, 334, 349, 354–5, 449, 483, 551

Sunday Mirror 272

Sunday Telegraph 523

Sunday Times 57, 58, 160, 162, 325

Sunderland 60
CM's surgeries 41, 44, 47, 72, 78, 111, 159, 170, 256, 272, 278–9, 287, 380, 399–400, 481; asylum seekers 41, 44, 47, 54, 62; job losses in 50, 51, 253, 255, 260, 308; Dewhirst's clothes factories 67; local election apathy 95

Sunderland Echo 82, 93, 124, 125, 177, 206, 218, 222, 255–6, 261, 303, 305, 325, 360

Sunderland Football Club 549

Sunderland Patriot 360

Sunderland South Labour Party 331

Sunderland University 120, 331

sustainable drainage 135, 136

Sutherland, Duke of 411

Swallow Hotels 51

Swanwick 51

Swayne, Desmond 52

Swaziland, King of 265

Sweden, and immigration 293–4

Sylvester, Rachel 216

Symonds, Colonel 495

Symons, Liz xvii, 223, 304, 438, 461, 465–6, 468, 475, 476, 477, 535, 538, 539, 540

Syria 395, 397, 398, 538

T

Taha, Vice-President 495, 496

Taliban 167, 168, 223, 224, 226, 229, 231, 236, 239, 241, 249, 302, 317

Tan Son Nhut airport, Vietnam 115

Tanayev, Nikolai 176

Taverne, Dick 95

tax credits 55, 89, 141, 230, 264, 332–3, 399, 400

Taylor, Ann 34, 35, 77, 100, 171, 205, 240–41

Taylor, Charles 419, 515, 558

Taylor, Dari 351

Taylor, David 359

Taylor, Laurie 259

Taylor, Paul 19

Tebbit, Sir Kevin 477

Temple Morris, Peter 318

Tenzin Geyche Tethong 472

Terrorism Bill 542

terrorism debate 509–10

Thames House, Millbank, London 234, 235, 366

Thames Water 9, 44

Thanet 66

Thatcher, Denis 243

Thatcher, Margaret, Baroness xi, 22, 84, 147, 183, 210, 243, 307, 316, 331, 364, 382, 453, 483

Third World debt 184

Thomas, Sir Philip 423, 431, 432
Thornhill School 393–4
Tigray People's Liberation Front 443
Times, The 42, 70, 74, 82, 361, 413
Today programme (Radio 4) 31–2,
    83, 87, 90, 91, 128, 153, 187,
    188, 221, 260, 289, 299, 364,
    413, 474, 482, 488, 491, 495,
    526
Tonge, Jenny 185
Top Salaries Review Board 127
Torbay 66
Torquay 294
Touhig, Don 284
Toynbee, Polly 37, 87, 130, 357
Tracey, Michael 372
trade unions 7, 47, 48, 50, 75, 100,
    126, 339, 499
Transform 238
Transport 2000 107
Transport Bill 41, 53, 68, 69, 70–71,
    73, 76, 88, 241
transport safety 37–8
travellers 137–8
Travellers' Club, Pall Mall, London
    169
Treasury 48, 92, 101, 283
    air traffic control sale 16, 45,
    49; performance targets 70;
    social housing 84; JP's success
    119; British Rail 135; Indian
    earthquake 164; NHS 213;
    Gordon's efficiency savings
    277; demands cuts from FCO
    456
Treasury Select Committee 281
Trend, Michael 108
Tribune 169
Tribune rally, Blackpool conference
    (2002) 314–15
Triesman, Dave 325, 326, 356, 359
Trimble, David 373

Trinity Hospice, Clapham, London
    104
tsunami (2004) 520
TUC (Trades Union Congress) 219
Turkey 367, 537
Turki al-Faisdal, Prince 400–401
Turner, Dennis 388, 403
Turner, Des 327
Tutu, Archbishop Desmond 470–71
Twigg, Steve 556
Tyne Tees television 236

U
Uganda 418, 438, 445, 487, 489
Ukraine 256, 273, 281
Ulan Bator, Mongolia 175, 466
unemployment 183–4, 230, 308
UNESCO 166, 207
UNHCR 513
Unionists 71
United Nations (UN) 193, 195, 223,
    224, 231, 239, 258, 277, 312,
    313, 314, 316, 327, 344, 345,
    347–8, 351, 357, 358, 360, 368,
    374, 378–9, 387, 406, 408, 439,
    442, 451, 452, 454, 473, 479,
    512, 514, 545
    Conventions 349; General
    Assembly 309; Powell's
    notorious speech 539; Security
    Council 339, 343, 353, 386,
    457, 511, 544, 546
United States
    consumerism 64; White House
    79, 80, 219, 231, 257;
    September 11 attacks 219–23;
    tariff on textile imports from
    UK 261, 283; relationship with
    Britain 318;
'urban' White Paper 140
USAID 381, 450
Utilities Bill 72, 73, 76, 78–9, 88

V

Valley Road Community Primary
    School, Sunderland 553
Vaughan, A. J. 127
Vaux 51, 308
Vaz, Keith 31, 66, 158, 162, 165,
    170, 196
Vereker, Sir John ('Two Buzzes') xvi,
    172, 181, 184, 185, 189, 190,
    191, 244
Very Hungry Caterpillar, The (Eric
    Carle) 143
Vietnam 110, 112–15, 116, 132,
    265, 342, 466–7, 480, 523
Vietnam War 96–7
Villepin, Dominique de 452
Vine, Jeremy 260
Virgin 95, 148
Vitorino, Commissioner 298

W

Wade, Rebekah 349
Wakefield, Sir Humphry xi, 516,
    522
Wales, acid rain in 66
Wall Street Journal 228
Wallington, Northumberland 242
Walters, Simon 257
Ward, Claire 524
Ward, Judith 300
Warren House Conference &
    Training Centre, Kingston-
    upon-Thames 145
waste disposal 10–11, 56
water companies 44–5
water meters 10
Watford, Hertfordshire 526
Watkinson, Angela xvii, 276, 287
Watson, Paul 387
Watson, Tom xvii
weapons of mass destruction
    (WMD) 224, 265, 276, 302,
307, 344, 347, 353–4, 408, 412,
    414–15, 448n, 483–4n, 484,
    510
Webber, John 79
Wellingborough, Northamptonshire
    110–11
Welsh Assembly 80n
West Drayton air traffic control 153
West, Rose (Rosemary) 300
Westland 262
Westminster Abbey, London 275
Westminster Hall, London 274,
    275, 509
Whelan, Charlie 308, 387
Whitbread 51
White, Michael 6, 94, 204, 219, 348
Whitty, Larry xvi, 16, 25
Widdecombe, Ann 198, 366, 372,
    405
Wilberforce, William 210
Wilhemsen, General 494
Wilkes, John 210
Wilkinson, Dave 82
Wilkinson, Francis 240
Williams, Alan 391
Williams, Betty 186, 395
Williams, Gareth 245, 248, 301
Williams, John xvii, 416, 519
Williams, Michael 435, 454, 465,
    491, 508, 534, 543
Williams, Sheila 105
Willis, Phil 317
Wills, Michael 292, 293
Wilson, Brian 159
Wilson, Canon 66
Wilson, Des 20
Wilson, Richard 3, 21, 22, 80
Windsor Castle, Berkshire 105, 284
Winnick, David xvii, 74, 215, 234,
    236, 276, 359, 382
Winstone, Ruth x
winter fuel allowance 42, 148

Winterton, Ann 40
Winterton, Sir Nicholas 391, 434
Wintour, Patrick 92, 94
Wise, Audrey 27, 127
Witherow, John 325–6
Wolfensohn, Jim 423, 424
Women's Institute 107–8
Women's Room, The (Marilyn
    French) 100
Wood, Adam 445, 446
Woodhead, Chris 179–80
Woodward, Shaun 38, 40, 60, 198
Woolacott, Martin 222
Woolas, Phil 146, 377
Woollacott family 87
Works of Art Committee 183
World at One, The (Radio 4) 188,
    484–5
World Bank 423
World Food Programme 225
World Health Organisation 505
World Trade Center attacks, New
    York (2001) 219, 220, 229
World Trade Organisation talks
    (Seattle, 1999) 31, 51
Wortley, Pam 290
Wright, Tommy 388

Wright, Tony 350
Wukro, Tigray 442

Y
Yeltsin, Boris 25
Yes, Minister (television programme)
    32
York 135, 136, 194
York environmental community
    centre 99
York University: Labour Club 535
Yorkshire Water 44
You and Yours programme (Radio 4)
    65
Young, George 134, 161, 303, 417
Younger, Sam 414
youths 105, 166, 212, 554–5
Yusuf, Abdullahai 503

Z
Zahir Shah, ex-King of Afghanistan
    239
Zalingi, Sudan 492–3
Zaria, Emir of 531
Zimbabwe, Zimbabweans 314, 374,
    418, 426, 430, 431, 434, 466,
    483, 487, 536–7, 538, 550

p 126. Interventionist
p 283
p 377 Goldsmith Advice
p 376. Followup ur - ba goed
p 413 Iraq Lab nogicab.
p 304 Asian vores
p 454 Allenation g Muslims